OOIS'97

Springer
*London
Berlin
Heidelberg
New York
Barcelona
Budapest
Hong Kong
Milan
Paris
Santa Clara
Singapore
Tokyo*

Also Available:

OOIS'94
1994 International Conference on Object Oriented Information Systems
19-21 December 1994, London

Edited by D. Patel, Y. Sun and S. Patel

OOIS'95
1995 International Conference on Object Oriented Information Systems
18-20 December 1995, Dublin

Edited by John Murphy and Brian Stone

OOIS'96
1996 International Conference on Object Oriented Information Systems
16-18 December 1996, London

Edited by D. Patel, Y. Sun and S. Patel

OOIS'97

1997 International Conference on Object Oriented Information Systems 10-12 November 1997, Brisbane

Proceedings

Edited by

Maria E. Orlowska
The University of Queensland, Brisbane, Australia

Roberto Zicari
Johann Wolfgang Goethe-Universität, Frankfurt am Main, Germany

Supported by

Sponsored by

Maria E. Orlowska
School of Information Technology, University of Queensland,
Brisbane Q4072, Australia

Roberto Zicari
Johann Wolfgang Goethe-Universität, Frankfurt am Main, Germany

ISBN-13:978-3-540-76170-9   e-ISBN-13:978-1-4471-1525-0
DOI: 10.1007/978-1-4471-1525-0

British Library Cataloguing in Publication Data
International Conference on Object Oriented Information Systems (1997 : Brisbane)
   OOIS'97 : 1997 International Conference on Object Oriented Information Systems 10-12 November
   1997, Brisbane : proceedings
   1.Object-oriented methods (Computer science) - Congresses
   I.Title   II.Orlowska, Maria E.   III.Zicari, Roberto
   005.7'57
   ISBN-13:978-3-540-76170-9

Library of Congress Cataloging-in-Publication Data
International Conference on Object Oriented Information Systems (1997 : Brisbane, Qld.)
    OOIS '97 : 1997 International Conference on Object-Oriented Information Systems, 10-12 November
   1997, Brisbane : proceedings / edited by Maria E. Orlowska, Roberto Zicari.
      p.   cm.
   Includes bibliographical references.
   ISBN-13:978-3-540-76170-9 (paperback : alk. paper)
   1. Object-oriented databases- -Congresses.   I. Orlowska, M. E. (Maria E.)   II. Zicari, Roberto
   III. Title
   QA76.9.D3I55875   1997   97-35571
   005.1'17- -dc21   CIP

Typesetting: Camera ready by editors

34/3830-543210 Printed on acid-free paper

Preface

This publication contains the proceedings of the 4th International Conference on Object-Oriented Information Systems. The first three OOIS conferences were held in London UK (1994), Dublin Ireland (1995) and again in London in 1996.

In response to the Call for Papers we received 91 submissions which were reviewed by members of the Program Committee. Each paper was refereed by at least three reviewers, and following discussion with PC members, 40 of the papers were accepted for presentation at the conference, and for publication in this volume.

In addition to the contributions from authors, this volume includes an abstract of the Keynote Speaker's presentation. At OOIS'97 in Brisbane in November, Dr Dan Fishman, the Chief Architect for Informix Software Inc., traced some of the early developments in information systems through current day technology, and further explored possible future directions and potential for object-oriented information systems.

The papers included in the proceedings consist of various aspects of object-oriented concepts and they have been presented to the reader under the following thematic sections:

- Object Oriented Methodologies
- Query Processing
- Modelling Issues I
- Transaction Processing and Concurrency Control
- Applications
- Modelling Issues II
- Re-Usability I
- Modelling Issues III
- Re-usability II
- Architectural Issues
- Object Orientation in Spatial Structures
- Database Design and Views
- Software Engineering/Development
- Large Scale Environments

This conference has received tremendous support from the School of Information Technology at The University of Queensland. We would also like to thank the Australian Computer Society (ACS) for their support, and we are especially grateful to our sponsors: Distributed Systems Technology Centre (DSTC) and Iona Technologies.

In preparing for this conference, we would also like to thank the Queensland Tourist and Travel Corporation, and the Queensland Department of Environment for their advice and support. A number of individuals also deserve special thanks including Kathleen Williamson of The University of Queensland who has provided invaluable help in the preparations for this conference, and Rebecca Moore at Springer Verlag for her help and advice.

Finally, we would like to thank the Program Committee members and the external referees for their expertise and help in evaluating the submitted papers.

Maria E. Orlowska, Roberto Zicari
Program Co-Chairs, OOIS'97

Programme Committee

Alphabetical List of OOIS'97 Contributors

M.A. Bailey, MBS (1997) Massey University, New Zealand
Department of Information Systems, Massey University,
Palmerston North, New Zealand

P. Baumann, PhD (1993) Technische Hochschule Darmstadt, Germany
FORWISS, Bavarian Research Center for Knowledge-Based Systems,
Munich, Germany

M. Beheshti, PhD (1992) University of Southwestern Louisiana, USA
Department of Computer & Mathematical Sciences,
University of Houston-Downtown, 1 Main Street, Houston TX, 77002, USA

Z. Bellahsene, PhD (1982) The University of Paris VI, France
LIRMM UMR 55060 CNRS, Montpellier II, 161 Rue ADA
34392 Montpellier Cedex 5, France

M. Bellavia, student of Computer Science, University of Milan, Italy
Università Statale di Milano, Italy

H. Bentaleb, DEA (1994) Université Paul Sabatier, France
Institut de Recherche en Informatique de Toulouse,
Université Paul Sabatier, Toulouse, France

J. Biskup, Dr. rer. nat (1975), Habilitation (1981) RWTH Aachen
Fachbereich Informatik, Universität Dortmund, Dortmund, Germany

F. Buddrus, Dip-Inf (1992) University of Dortmund, Germany
Johann Wolfgang Goethe-Universität, DBIS FB20,
Robert-Mayer-Str 11-15, 60325 Frankfurt am Main, Germany

C.R. Carlson
Department of Computer Science & Applied Mathematics,
Illinois Institute of Technology, Chicago, USA

R Chafi, PhD (1996) Illinois Institute of Technology, Chicago, IL
Department of Computer Science & Applied Mathematics,
Illinois Institute of Technology, 10 West 31st Street, Chicago IL 60616, USA

J.W. Chang, Ph.D (1991) Korea Advanced Institute of Science & Tech
Department of Office Automation, Kijeon Women's Junior College,
Chonju, Chonbuk 560-701, Korea

I. Choudhury, PG-Dip (1991) University of Wales College of Cardiff, UK
School of Computing, Information Systems & Mathematics,
South Bank University, 103 Borough Road, London, SE1 0AA, UK

G. Cugola, MSc (1994) Politecnico di Milano, Italy
Dipartimento di Elettronica e Informazione, Politecnico di Milano,
P.za Leonardo da Vinci 32, 20133 Milano, Italy

T. Dillon, PhD (1974) Monash University, Melbourne, Australia
La Trobe University, Melbourne VIC 3083, Australia

E.E. Doroshenko, BAppComp(Hons) (1994) The University of Tasmania, Australia
Department of Information Systems, University of Tasmania,
PO Box 1214, Launceston TAS 7250, Australia

T. Elrad, PhD, Technicion Israel Institute of Technology, Israel
Department of Computer Science & Applied Mathematics,
Illinois Institute of Technology, Chicago, USA

W. Emmerich, Dr (1995) University of Paderborn, Germany
Interoperable Systems Research Centre, City University,
Northampton Square, London EC1V 0HB, UK

G. Fernandez, MSc (Mathematics), University of Buenos Aires, Argentina
Royal Melbourne Institute of Technology, Melbourne, Australia

D. Fishman, PhD (1973) University of Maryland, USA
Chief Architect, Informix Software Inc, USA)

J. Freitag, Dip.-Inf (1983) University of Dortmund, Germany
Fachbereich Informatik, Universität Dortmund, Dortmund, Germany

P. Furtado, MSc CS (1994) University of Coimbra, Portugal
FORWISS, Bavarian Research Center for Knowledge-Based Systems,
Orleansstr 34, 81667 Muenchen, Germany

C. Ghezzi, Full Professor (1980) Politecnico di Milano, Italy
Dipartimento di Elettronica e Informazione, Politecnico di Milano,
P.za Leonardo da Vinci 32, 20133 Milano, Italy

A.G. Grosse, Dip (1994) University of Karlsruhe, Germany
Institute of Telematics, University of Karlsruhe, PO Box 6980,
76128 Karlsruhe, Germany

J. Hartroth, Dip (1994) University of Karlsruhe, Germany
Institute of Telematics, University of Karlsruhe, 76128 Karlsruhe, Germany

B.H. Hong, DSc (1988) Seoul National University, Korea
Department of Computer Engineering, Pusan National University,
30 Changjeon-Dong, Kumjeong-Ku, Pusan, 609-735, Korea

E.H. Huang, PhD (1997) Illinois Institute of Technology, USA
Department of Computer Science & Applied Mathematics,
Illinois Institute of Technology, Chicago, USA

K. Hung, MSc (1995) South Bank University, UK
School of Computing, Information Systems & Mathematics,
South Bank University, 103 Borough Road, London, SE1 0AA, UK

J.L. Johnson, PhD (1973) University of Minnesota, USA
Computer Science Department, Western Washington University,
Bellingham WA 98225, USA

Y. Karabulut, Dip.-Inf (1983) University of Dortmund, Germany
Fachbereich Informatik, Universität Dortmund, Dortmund, Germany

J. Kennedy, MPhil (1985) Computing Paisley University, Scotland, UK
Department of Computer Studies, Napier University, Canal Court, 42
Craiglockhart Avenue, Edinburgh EH14 1LT, Scotland, UK

Y.H. Kim, Ph.D. Korea University (computer engineering major)
Department of Computer Science, Suwon Industrial College,
Botong-ri, Jungnam-myun, Whasung-gun, Kyungki-do, 445-960, Korea

M. Kolp, MSc (1994) University of Louvain, Belgium
Université Catholique de Louvain, IAG-QANT,
1 Place des Doyens, 1348 Louvain-La-Neuve, Belgium

D.A. Kottmann, Dip (1996) University of Karlsruhe, Germany
Institute of Telematics, University of Karlsruhe, 76128 Karlsruhe, Germany

B.B. Kristensen, MSc (1974) Aarhus University, Denmark
The Maersk Mc-Kinney Moller Institute for Production Technology,
Odense University, DK-5230 Odense M, Denmark

T. Kunishima, DEng (1997) Kyoto University, Japan
Graduate School of Information Science, Nara Institute of Science and Technology,
8916-5, Takayama, Ikoma, Nara 630-01, Japan

S.E. Lautemann, Dip. -Inf (1993) Technical University of Karlsruhe, Germany
Johann Wolfgang Goethe-Universität, Frankfurt am Main, Germany

H.J. Lee, Master (1997) Chonbuk National University, Korea
Department of Office Automation, Kijeon Women's Junior College,
Chonju, Chonbuk 560-701, Korea

S.H. Lee, PhD (1979) Universiy of Texas at Austin, USA
Department of Computer Engineering, Seoul National University, Korea

H. Li, MSc (1993) Southwest JiaoTong University, China
School of Information Technology, The University of Queensland,
Brisbane Q 4072, Australia

P.T.T. Li, DEA (1993) ORSAY University, Paris XI, France
Department of Computer Studies, Napier University, Canal Court,
42 Craiglockhart Avenue, Edinburgh EH14 1LT, Scotland, UK

X.D. Li, PhD (1994) Nanjing University, China
The National Laboratory of Computer Software New Technology,
Department of Computer Science & Technology, Nanjing University,
Nanjing, Jiangsu 210093, China

J. Liang
INRIA, Domaine de Voluceau, Rocquencourt, 78153 Le Chesnay, France

C.F. Liu, PhD (1988) Nanjing University, China
Distributed Systems Technology Centre, Level 7 Gehrmann Laboratories,
The University of Queensland, Brisbane Q 4072, Australia

D. McDermid
Curtin University of Technology, Perth, Australia

S.H. Moon, MSc (1994) Pusan National University, Korea
Department of Computer Engineering, Pusan National University,
30 Changjeon-Dong, Kumjeong-Ku, Pusan, 609-735, Korea

N. Mouaddib, DSc (1995) PhD (1989) The University of Nancy I, France
Institut de Recherche en Informatique de Nantes (IRIN), BP 92208,
 44322 Nantes, France

H. Naja, PhD (1997) The University of Nancy I, France
Centre de Recherche en Informatique de Nancy (CRIN), BP 239,
54506 Vandoeuvre-lès-Nancy, France

K. Nguyen, MSc (1973) Canterbury University, Christchurch, New Zealand
Victoria University of Technology, PO Box 14428 MCMC,
Melbourne VIC 3000, Australia

M.E. Orlowska, DSc (1980) Technical University of Warsaw, Poland
School of Information Technology, The University of Queensland,
Brisbane Q 4072, Australia

J. Owens, PhD (1995) Aberdeen University, Scotland, UK
Department of Computer Studies, Napier University, Canal Court,
42 Craiglockhart Avenue, Edinburgh EH14 1LT, Scotland, UK

F. Paradis, PhD (1996) Universite Joseph Fourier, France
CSIRO Mathematical & Information Sciences, 723 Swanston Street,
Carlton VIC 3053, Australia

J.S. Park, MS (1992) Seoul National University, Korea
Department of Computer Engineering, Seoul National University,
San.56-1, Shillim-Dong, Kwanak-Ku, Seoul 151-742, Korea

F. Pasinos, BIS(Honours) (1997) Australian Catholic University, Australia
Department of Computing and Technology, Australian Catholic University,
Sydney, Australia

D. Patel, PhD (1996) South Bank University, UK
School of Computing, Information Systems & Mathematics, South Bank
University, 103 Borough Road, London, SE1 0AA, UK

C.E. Perritt, BSc (Comp Sci) University of New South Wales (1986)
BHP Information Technology, Wollongong, Australia

G. Pervan
Curtin University of Technology, Perth, Australia

A. Pirotte, PhD (1976) University of Louvain, Belgium
Université Catholique de Louvain, IAG-QANT, 1 Place des Doyens,
1348 Louvain-La-Neuve, Belgium

A. Rasheed, MSc Asian Institute of Technology, Thailand
Department of Computer Technology, Monash University, Melbourne, Australia

W. Reimer, Dip-Inf (1995) University of Dortmund, Germany
Department of Mathematics & Computer Science, University of Paderborn,
D-33095 Paderborn, Germany

R. Ritsch, Dipl-Inf. (1995) Technische Hochschule Darmstadt, Germany
FORWISS, Bavarian Research Center for Knowledge-Based Systems,
Munich, Germany

T. Rose, MSc (1981) Kingston University, UK
CAD Consultants Ltd, 797 London Road, Thornton Heath, Surrey CR7 6XA, UK

P. Ryder
Curtin University of Technology, Perth, Australia

K.U. Sattler, Dip (1994) University of Magdeburg, Germany
Department of Computer Science, University of Magdeburg, PF 4120,
D-39016 Magdeburg, Germany

P. Schleifer, PhD (1997) South Bank University, UK
School of Computing, Information Systems & Mathematics, South Bank
University, 103 Borough Road, London, SE1 0AA, UK

S. Sédillot
INRIA, Domaine de Voluceau, Rocquencourt, 78153 Le Chesnay, France

J. Seruga, PhD (1991) Moscow State University, Russia
Department of Computing and Technology, Australian Catholic University,
Sydney, Australia

H. Shin, Ph.D candidate (1997) Chonbuk National University, Korea
Department of Office Automation, Kijeon Women's Junior College,
Chonju, Chonbuk 560-701, Korea

O. Smørdal, Cand. Scient (1992) University of Oslo, Norway
Department of Informatics, University of Oslo, PO Box 1080,
Blindern N-0316 Oslo, Norway

B. Sprick, Dip.-Inf (1996) University of Hildesheim, Germany
Fachbereich Informatik, Lehrstuhl 6, Universität Dortmund,
August-Schmidt-Str 12, 44227 Dortmund, Germany

Y. Sun, PhD (1993) Staffordshire University, UK
Compuware Ltd, 163 Bath road, Slough, Berkshire, SL1 4AA, UK

A.M. Vercoustre, PhD (1970) Universite de Paris (Jussieu), France
CSIRO Mathematical and Information Sciences, 723 Swanston Street,
Carlton VIC 3053, Australia

R.J. Whiddett, PhD (1982) University of Lancaster, UK
Department of Information Systems, Massey University,
Palmerston North, New Zealand

N. Widmann, Dipl-Inf. (1995) Technische Universitaet Muenchen, Germany
FORWISS, Bavarian Research Center for Knowledge-Based Systems,
Munich, Germany

X.Q. Wu, PhD (1989) University of Dortmund, Germany
Deutsche Telekom AG, Technologiezentrum, Postfach 10 00 03, Am
Kavalleriesand 3, D-64295 Darmstadt, Germany

H. Yao, PhD (1997) University of Tsukuba, Japan
NTT International Corporation, 16-3 Higashi-Ikebukuro 3-Chome,
Toshima-ku, Tokyo 170, Japan

K. Yokota, DEng (1995) Kyoto University, Japan
Faculty of Computer Science and System Engineering,
Okayama Prefectural University, Soja, Okayama 719-11, Japan

A. Zaslavsky, PhD (1987) Academy of Sciences, USSR
Department of Computer Technology, Monash University,
900 Dandenong Road, Caulfield East VIC 3145, Melbourne, Australia

G.L. Zheng, BA (1961) Nanjing University, China
The National Laboratory of Computer Software New Technology,
Department of Computer Science & Technology, Nanjing University,
Nanjing, Jiangsu, China 210093

P. Zoller, Dipl-Inf. (1996) Technische Universitaet Muenchen, Germany
FORWISS, Bavarian Research Center for Knowledge-Based Systems,
Munich, Germany

Additional Reviewers

Contents

TRANSACTION PROCESSING AND CONCURRENCY CONTROL

APPLICATIONS

MODELLING ISSUES II

ARCHITECTURAL ISSUES

OBJECT ORIENTATION IN SPATIAL STRUCTURES

DATABASE DESIGN AND VIEWS

SOFTWARE ENGINEERING/DEVELOPMENT

LARGE SCALE ENVIRONMENTS

KEYNOTE ADDRESS

Object-Oriented Information Systems in the 21st Century

Dan Fishman
Informix Software Inc., USA

Abstract

Object-oriented technology is increasingly being adopted as the basis for new information system implementations. Object and particularly, object-relational database systems will soon become the platforms of choice for new information systems, and the object/component technologies of CORBA, COM, and JavaBeans are becoming the basis for implementing large-scale distributed information systems. This talk will trace some of the early developments in information systems through current day technology, and based on current hardware, software, and business trends explore possible future directions and potential for object oriented information systems.

OBJECT ORIENTED METHODOLOGIES

Complexity and Maintenance:
A Comparative Study of
Object-Oriented and Structured Methodologies

Richard J. (Dick) Whiddett and Michael A. Bailey,
Department of Information Systems, Massey University
Palmerston North, New Zealand

Abstract

It has been suggested that using Object-Oriented methods instead of traditional Structured Methods may reduce the cost of maintenance of an information system. This study evaluates the relative increase in complexity of systems designs when they are subjected to a change in specifications. It was found that overall, the object-oriented system underwent a smaller increase in complexity, and it may therefore be easier to maintain than the structured system.

1. Introduction

A common idea among many authors in the object-oriented field is the claim that an object-oriented system should be more maintainable since object-oriented systems are generally less complex than similar systems developed using a structured methodology. For example, Meyer [1] says that "apart from its elegance, such modular object-oriented programming yields software products on which modifications and extensions are much easier to perform than with programs structured in a more conventional procedure-oriented fashion" (p.178). A further illustration is provided by Henry & Humphrey [2] who showed that "building applications with object-oriented languages (like C++ or Objective C) results in final systems that are much more maintainable than systems constructed with procedural languages (like Pascal or C)" (p.2).

However, to date there has been little empirical evidence to support the supposed benefits of object-oriented approaches, for example, Fichman & Kemerer [3] performed a comparison of a selection of Object-Oriented and conventional analysis and design methodologies. After extensive qualitative comparisons which tend to favour the OO approaches they note in their conclusion: *"little empirical evidence exists to support many of the specific claims made in favour of object-orientation"*

The most objective and convincing source of empirical evidence to support a particular methodology would come from some form of controlled experiment, such as the work by Whiddett et al. [4] which compared the time taken to implement changes to a system specification for structured and object-oriented approaches. This paper describes a similar experiment which attempted to determine *whether*

8

an object-oriented system does in fact undergo a relatively smaller increase in complexity when subjected to a change in specifications than a similar structured system, and is therefore easier to maintain.

The study concentrated on the results of the systems analysis phase of a case study, rather than the results obtained from systems design or a programming language. Thus, this study is more concerned with the models of the system that are developed as a result of the analysis using both an object-oriented methodology and a structured methodology. The reason that this study was limited to the systems analysis phase rather than including the design phase is because the analysis phase gives a view of the system that is unaffected by physical implementation issues. Had the design phase been included, then these physical problems with the implementation of the system could colour the results. Thus, by using only the analysis phase it was possible for this study to effectively show the effects of a change on the systems complexity.

The rest of this paper is composed of three main sections, the next section describes the experimental methodology that was used to investigate the maintainability of the systems models, the second section presents the results of the experiment and the final section discusses the results draws some conclusions.

2. Methodology

The hypothesis, that the object-oriented model will suffer a smaller increase in complexity when subjected to change, was tested by developing two analysis models for the same system using two different methodologies and evaluating their complexity. The two models were developed by the same analyst and they described the same set of requirements. The system that was modelled was of a fairly conventional order processing system for a furniture manufacturer. The models were based on a hypothetical case description that has previously been used in the department for teaching systems analysis courses. For each methodology and initial model of the system was created and then it was expanded to add a new feature, to allowed a customer to include payment with their order.

Booch's Object-Oriented methodology [5] was used to model the object-oriented system and Yourdon'sModern Structured methodology [6] was used to model the structured system. These methodologies were chosen because they are well established   and because the analyst had previous experience in both methodologies.

The complexity of each model was measured using an appropriate metric set. Different metrics had to be used for the object-oriented and the structured models since currently there are no appropriate metrics that can be applied to both structured and object-oriented systems. That is, the metrics are methodology specific, so a structured metric cannot be applied to an object-oriented system for example (see[5,7,8] for futher discussion).

Chidamber & Kemerer's MOOSE metric suite [9,10] was used to measure the complexity of the object-oriented models. The ability of the metric to be applied to a diagram rather than to program code was an important consideration in this study, since only the diagrams produced as a result of the analysis phase were studied. For the structured approach, McCabe's Cyclomatic Complexity metric [11] was used to evaluate the complexity of the dataflow diagrams and a modified version of Chidamber & Kemerer's Coupling Between Objects metric [9,10] were used to measure the complexity of the entity relationship diagrams.

Unfortunately, the results of the complexity measures can not be directly compared, but it is possible to compare the proportional change in complexity of the model which arises from the change in requirements.   The results were therefore converted into a value for the precentage change in complexity to facilitate comparisons between the different measures and the different analysis methodologies.   The percentage changed figures used throughout this article have been calculated by using the following formula:

$$y = \frac{(a - b)}{b} \times 100$$

where a is complexity of the modified model, b is the complexity of the initial model, and y is the size of the change as a percentage.

An attempt was made to control for analyst bias and to determine the reasonableness of the models that were developed in the study by comparing them with models developed elsewhere.   The structured model was compared to the analysis models developed a groups of students who were working from the same case description, and the Object-oriented model was compared with a model order processing system developed by Booch [5].

The results obtained by each of the metrics were also checked to determine whether or not the metrics are capable of giving consistent results for similar systems by applying them to the above models. While this process will not be discussed in this article, it was found that all of the metrics used do give reasonably consistent results when they are applied in a similar system, further details can be found in Bailey [12].

Finally, the results of the change in complexity from the structured system were compared with the object-oriented results on a percentage change basis. The results of this indicate that the object-oriented system underwent a relatively smaller increase in complexity than the structured system when subjected to modification, and therefore this approach delivered systems that are easier to maintain on a long term basis.

Since this project followed a case study approach there is of course the caveat that the results obtained here are specific to the particular case. However, it should be possible to draw some general conclusions which may be able to be applied to other systems.

3. Results

This section of the paper will briefly discuss each of the analysis models which were developed, and describe how their complexity was measured.

3.1 Object-Oriented Model

The object-oriented model was developed using the Rational-Rose CASE tool. The system is composed of 29 classes, of which 4 (*payment, cash, cheque, credit card*) were required to provide the extra functionality of paying with order. In addition to the class diagram, interaction diagrams were developed and methods were identified.

The complexity of both of the versions of the order processing system was measured using all six of the metrics outlined in Chidamber & Kemerer's MOOSE metrics set [9,10]. A summary of the results obtained using the MOOSE metrics set is shown below in Table 1, below.

	WMC	*DIT*	*NOC*	*CBO*	*RFC*	*LCOM*
Before	32	29	16	34	49	25
After	37	32	19	42	53	28
Percentage Change	15.6	10.3	18.75	23.5	8.2	12

Table 1: Summary of the results from the MOOSE metric set before and after changes were made to the object-oriented model.

As can be seen above, the addition of the payment facility to the model order processing system has lead to an increase in the values of all six of the MOOSE metrics. In order to be able to better understand these results it is necessary to discuss each of the six metrics in turn and to demonstrate how each of the metrics is related to the maintainability of the system.

3.1.1 Weighted Methods Per Class Results (WMC).

WMC attempts to estimate the complexity of each class by examining the methods it provides. The above results show that there was a 15.6% increase in the complexity of the classes in the object-oriented system after the change was made. The result of this increase is that the classes in the changed version of the system will need more maintenance as they are becoming more complex. This statement is supported by Chidamber & Kemerer [10] who say that "the number of methods and the complexity of methods involved is a predictor of how much time and effort is required to develop and maintain the class" (p.482).

3.1.2 Depth Of Inheritance Tree Results (DIT).

DIT measures the complexity of inheritance within an object-oriented system. The results for this study show an overall increase from 29 to 32, a 10.3% increase. While deeply nested classes can be considered to be more complex, it can also be argued that classes at a deeper level in the hierarchy are generally better than those classes that are not at such a deep level since there is a greater potential for the reuse of inherited methods [10]. Because the DIT metric is used to measure the depth of the inheritance hierarchy, Sharble & Cohen [13] state that "generally, it is better to have depth rather than breadth, since this promotes reuse and reduces redundancy in the system" (p.72).

3.1.3 Number Of Children Results (NOC).

Related to the DIT metric is the NOC metric which also measures complexity in the inheritance hierarchy. However, unlike the DIT metric which measures the depth of the inheritance in a system, the NOC metric measures "the breadth of the inheritance hierarchy" (Sharble & Cohen [13] p.72).

The results in table 1 show that the overall NOC increased from 16 to 19, an increase of 18.75%. According to Chidamber & Kemerer [10], "if a class has a large number of children, it may require more testing of the methods in that class" (p.485). Thus, the class *Order Document Set* will require a good deal of testing due to the fact that in both versions of the order processing system it has a value of 6 for the *Number Of Children*.

3.1.4 Coupling Between Objects Results (CBO).

CBO is used to measure the complexity of the interaction between classes [13]. This particular metric shows the greatest increase in the complexity of the system with an increase from a value of 34 to 42, which represents a 23.5% increase.

Such a significant increase in the overall CBO suggests that maintenance will become more difficult as changes to one object may have an effect on another object. This idea is supported by Chidamber & Kemerer [10] who state that "the larger the number of couples, the higher the sensitivity to changes in other parts of the design, and therefore maintenance is more difficult" (p.486). Thus, those individual classes which obtained a low value from the CBO metric are considered to be better for maintenance.

3.1.5Response For A Class Results (RFC).

RFC is designed to measure the complexity of the classes and the interactions in the system. The results show again an increase in from 49 to 53, an increase is equal to an 8.2%. Thus, the potential communication between classes has increased [10].

However, while the increase in the overall value of the RFC metric can mean increased communication, it can also mean that the complexity of the individual classes has increased because more methods can be invoked. This point of view is supported by Chidamber & Kemerer [10] who argue that "the larger the number of methods that can be invoked from a class, the greater the complexity of a class" (p.487).

Furthermore, an increased number of methods means that maintenance becomes a much more complicated task due to the fact that "if a large number of methods can be invoked in response to a message, the testing and debugging of the class becomes more complicated since it requires a greater level of understanding on the part of the tester" (Chidamber & Kemerer, [10] p.487).

3.1.6 Lack Of Cohesion In Methods Results (LCM).

LCM is used to measure the complexity of a class in terms of "the lack of cohesion among the methods of a class, or how many unrelated activities a class is performing" (Sharble & Cohen, [13] p.68). These results show an increase from a value of 25 to 28, a 12% increase.

The biggest increase in an individual class is seen in the *Customer* class which increased its complexity by 25%. The *Customer* class and the *Order Document Set* class both have some of the higher values for the LCM metric. Such high results suggest that these classes are performing more unrelated activities than the rest of the classes in the system. It can also be argued that a high value of LCM is an indicator of a class which is being controlled [13]. This is related to the idea that classes with a high CBO control other classes [13].

In summary, the modification of the object-oriented model only required the addition of four new classes (from 25 to 29) , a growth of 16% and many of the classes were unaffected. The complexity measures increased in the range 8.2% to 23.5% giving an average increase of 14.7%.

3.2 Structured Analysis Model

The Structured Anlalysis resulted in two major models, dataflow diagram (DFD) and the entity relationship diagram (ERD). It was necessary to use two different measures to evaluate the changes in the complexity of the two models.

3.2.1 Complexity Of The Dataflow Diagram.

The initial model was decomposed to produce 7 processes at the lowest level, and the modified system contained 8 processes. The complexity of the dataflow diagram was measured using McCabe's cyclomatic complexity metric using the method described in the paper by McCabe & Schulmeyer [14]. In order to be able to apply McCabe's complexity metric it was first necessary to convert the lower level of the dataflow diagrams into a flowgraph for both the original version and the revised version of the order processing system, the latter flowgraph is illustrated in figure 1 below. The flowgraph represents the way that the processes are invoked and the way that control can be passed from one process to the next. The complexity of the system is caused by 'decision nodes' which may pass control to more that one other node depending on the results of their processing. The results obtained by applying McCabe's complexity metric are shown below in table 2.

As can be seen, the structured version of the order processing system has had a slight increase in complexity after the changes to the system were made. The change in the level of complexity from 3 to 4 is a change of 33%. This change is the result of the extra decision involved in *process payment.*

	Complexity Before Changes	*Complexity After Changes*
Order Processing System	3	4

Table 2: Results of McCabe's complexity metric before and after changes were made to the structured model.

Because both levels of complexity are less than 10, the structured version of the system remains easy to maintain. Had the values obtained for the structured system been over 10 then this would be an indicator that the system needed to be redesigned and partitioned further. Thus, the results obtained with McCabe's Cyclomatic complexity metric suggest that while the complexity of the system has increased, the level of complexity within the order processing system is still at an acceptable level.

3.2.2 Complexity Of The Entity Relationship Diagram.

The second metric which was used to measure the complexity both before and after changes to the structured model was the *Coupling Between Objects* metric from the MOOSE metric set. The final ERD differed from the original ERD by the addition of the *Payment* entity. The results obtained using this metric are shown below in Table 3. As can be seen, the increases in the *Coupling Between Objects* figure tends to be isolated to only those entities which are directly affected by the changes which were made. In this case, the addition of a payment system has lead to increases in the *Order*, and *Payment* entities. The results obtained using the *Coupling Between Objects* metric show an increase in coupling and therefore an increase in complexity. The lower values are generally considered to be less complex and easier to maintain by authors such as Sharble & Cohen [13].

The flowgraph node numbers are prefixed by a letter to show which subsystem the process belongs to.

V = Validation subsystem

P = Process Customer Order subsystem

Node Number	Process
V1	Validate Order
V2	Determine Order Status
P1	Respond to Order Information
P2	Respond to Receipt of Order
P3	Process Orders
P4	Produce Order Summaries
P5	Produce Delivery Plan
P6	Process Payment

Working:

Number of Compares   = 3

McCabes Complexity

    = Number of compares + 1
    = 3 + 1
    = 4

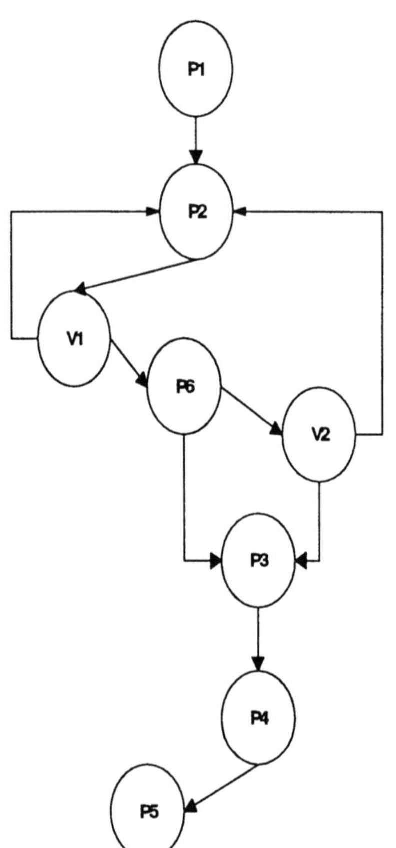

Figure 1: Flowgraph of Modified System

Entity Name	*CBO Before Changes*	*CBO After Changes*
Customer	1	1
Order	2	3
Payment	n/a	1
Product	2	2
Product Brochure	1	1
TOTAL:	6	8

Table 3: Results of the Coupling Between Objects metric applied to the Entity Relationship Diagram before and after changes were made to the structured system.

The total value of the *Coupling Between Objects* metric for the structured system has changed from 6 couplings in the original version to 8 couplings in the changed version. In percentage terms, such a change is equal to a 33% change in complexity.

The results show that the addition of new user needs will result in an increase in coupling between entities. Further, it does not matter what type of entity is added to the system, as there needs to be a relationship between the new entity and at least one of the existing entities.   Thus, as more entities are added during the system's life the complexity of the system will continue to grow as the system evolves. Such increases in complexity are inevitable in any system which has to be responsive to changes in user needs and an order processing system is a good example of such a system.

The results that were obtained for both parts of the structured analysis are consistent and indicate that the system is 33% more complex.   Note that the complexity of the system grew at a faster rate than that of the size of the system, the DFD only increased by 1 process from 7 to 8 lowest level processes (12%) and the ERD increased by 1 entity from 4 to 5 (25%).

4 Discussion

Although a number of different metrics were used in order to find the change in complexity within the object-oriented and the structured models of the order processing system, some comparisons can be made in terms of the percentage change in complexity rather than in terms of the actual figures obtained.

In general, it can be said that the changes to the structured model resulted in a greater increase in complexity than the changes to the object-oriented version. While the results for the structured model showed an increase of 33%, none of the metrics used to measure the object-oriented system showed as great an increase in complexity. In comparison, the metrics used to measure the object-oriented model measured increases ranging from 8.2% to 23.5%, with the highest value being for the *Coupling Between Objects* metric, and an overall average value of 14.7%.

One noticeable feature of the results of this study is that the different models appear to have been developed to different extents. However, it can be argued that this is due to the functions of the different diagrams. When the class diagram of the Object-oriented system is compared to the entity relationship diagram in the structured version of the same system, it appears as though the entity relationship diagram is not developed to the same level. However, the differences in the model are due to the fact that the functionality of the system is distributed across the diagrams in different ways. The result of this is that in the structured model each diagram only contains some aspects of the design, and therefore the structured diagrams appear to be less complex than the object-oriented diagram. So, while the class diagram apprears to be much simpler than the ERD, it also contains information relating to the implementation of several of the processes which are present in the dataflow diagram, such as the validation of an order. In order to compare the different systems it is necessary to compare both the dataflow diagram and the entity relationship diagram to the class diagram. When the two systems are examined in this context it is possible to see that the structured system has indeed been developed to a similar extent as the object-oriented system.

Because the *individual* models have been developed to different extents, there will obviously be an effect on the metrics when any changes are made to the models. The outcome of this problem is that a relatively small change to the model, such as adding a single entity, will result in a greater proportional change in complexity for the simpler models than for those models which are considerably more complex. A good example of this point is the entity relationship diagram which is relatively simple in comparison to the class diagram. In this particular case, the addition of the payment facility had a much greater effect on the complexity of the entity relationship diagram than was the case with the class diagram. This was because the entity relationship diagram had only a small number of entities and relationships present to begin with in comparison to the large number of objects and relationships that were present in the class diagram. If all the individual models had a similar level of complexity then it could be argued that the use of such a method of comparison is reliable. However, this is not the case due to the different functions that each individual diagram performs in the system as a whole. Consequently, the addition of the payment facility may have had a greater proportional effect on the entity relationship model as a result of the size of the model. Unfortunately, such a situation has the potential to distort the results.

5 Conclusions

The results of this study tend to suggest that overall, information systems that are developed using object-oriented methodologies, such as Booch [5], do not increase in relative complexity as much as similar systems which are developed using a structured methodology such as Yourdon [6], and therefore object-oriented systems should be easier to maintain.

The general trend in the results obtained using the MOOSE metric set shows that the range of increases in percentage terms (8.2% to 23.5%, average 14.7%) is much lower for the object-oriented model than the range obtained from the metrics used to measure the complexity of the structured model (33%). This difference in the range of increases is further evidence that the complexity of the object-oriented system was not affected by the changes as much as the structured system was.

The major problems encountered during this study arose from the unavailability of a suitable tool to measure the complexity of different systems and which could cope with the different constructs and formulations of the models. The most important need that is indicated from this research is to investigate ways of making complexity measurements that can be applied to a wide variety of systems. A appropriate metric needs to be able to take into account the unique differences of both the structured and object-oriented methodologies. An example of this point, is the fact that the class diagram in Booch's (1994) object-oriented methodology is performing many of the same functions and processes that are present in both a dataflow diagram and an entity relationship model in a structured methodology. Such a metric would need to combine the complexity results of both the dataflow diagram and the entity relationship model in order to make an equivalent, and therefore reliable comparison to the complexity of a class diagram in an object-oriented methodology. Such a tool would allow future studies to make meaningful and reliable comparisons between systems that were designed using either structured or object-oriented methodologies, and bring more objectivity to debates regarding the relative merits of the different methodologies.

References

1. Meyer, B. Towards a two dimensional programming environment. In *Readings in Artificial Intelligence* (p.178). Palo Alto: Tioga, 1981
2. Henry, S. & Humphrey, M. Comparison of an object oriented programming language to a procedural programming language for effectiveness in program maintenance. *Journal of Object_Oriented Programming.* **6,** (3). 1993 pp. 41-49.
3. Fichman, R.G., & Kemerer, C.F. Object-oriented and conventional analysis and design methodologies: Comparison and critique. *IEEE Computer.* October, 1992 pp. 22-39.
4. Whiddett, R.J., Dasari, S. & Woodfield, T. Comparisons of Development Methodologies: Study of Object-oriented and Structured Analysis Techniques. *N.Z J. of Computing,* **6.1,** 1995 pp. 107-114
5. Booch, G. *Object-oriented analysis and design with applications. (2nd ed.)* Redwood City: The Benjamin/Cummings Publishing Company, Inc. 1994
6. Yourdon, E. *Modern Structured Analysis,* Prentice Hall, Englewood Cliffs, N.J., 1989
7. Johnson, R.E. & Foote, B. Designing Reusable Classes, *J. Object-oriented Programming,* **1.2** 1988 pp.22-35
8. Wilfs-Brock, R.J., Wilkerson, B. & Wiener, L. *Designing Object-Oriented Software.* Prentice Hall, Englewood Cliffs, N.J., 1990
9. Chidamber, S.R., & Kemerer, C.F. Towards a metrics suite for object oriented design. In *Proceedings 6th ACM Conference of Object Oriented Programming, Systems, Language, and Applications (OOPSLA)* pp. 197-211. Phoenix: ACM. 1991
10. Chidamber, S.R., & Kemerer, C.F. A metrics suite for object oriented design. *IEEE Transactions on Software Engineering.* **20,** (6). June, 1994 pp. 476-493.
11. McCabe, T.J. A complexity measure. *IEEE Transactions On Software Engineering.* **SE-2,** (4). December, 1976 pp. 308-320.
12. Bailey, M.A. *Complexity And Maintenance: A Comparative Study Of Object-Oriented And Structured Methodologies* MBS Thesis, Massey University, Palmerston North, N.Z. 1997
13. Sharble, R.C. & Cohen, S.S. The object-oriented brewery: A comparison of two object-oriented development methods. *ACM SIGSOFT Software Engineering Notes.* **18,** (2). April, 1993 pp. 60-73.
14. McCabe, T.J., & Schulmeyer, G.G. System testing aided by structured analysis (A practical experience). In T.J. McCabe (ed.), *Structured Testing* (pp. 51-56). Silver Spring: IEEE Computer Society Press. 1983

Systems Oriented Analysis and Design Directions:
A Suggested Evolution from the Object Model

Craig E. Perritt
Senior Consultant
BHP Information Technology
Wollongong, Australia

Abstract:

BHP Information Technology has used Object Technology in industrial applications for four years. Object orientation borrows a subset of *systems'* characteristics. Systems Science[1] is the science of understanding complex systems. The increasing complexity of, and failures in the software industry[2], demonstrate the need for a better control model. The science of *systems* is the logical framework for the evolution of the object model. A *systems* object model is suggested.

1.1 Introduction

BHP IT has invested considerably in object technology over the last four years. In "pure" object orientation this investment includes 5 major process scheduling systems[3] based on a common framework[4], 5 Process Control systems[5] a quality control system[6] the development of two knowledge engineering products and a CAD system. The company followed the sensible path of moving from research to pilot to production and utilised experienced mentors. Common infrastructure libraries were and continue to be developed and it could be argued that the adoption of objects was according to best practise.

Yet best practise is a long way from ideal for BHP IT. Like others in the computing industry, the complexity of the needs of customers as a whole is increasing. Building solutions using objects spawns a whole new breed of complex challenges of its own. In adopting a distributed object model, for example, software engineers shift from a database manipulation model to a communication model. This is a model few companies are ready for or really understand. The technology itself is still only an approximation to what is needed. The pace of change in the technology itself presents a major challenge for those controlling software development. The evidence indicates that this challenge is still largely not being met.

1.2 Are Objects Making us Better at Producing Software?

Watts Humphrey at Object World Australia 1996[7], compared Software Engineering (SE) performance to that of the Architecture discipline. He contended that based on the incidents of project failure in SE world wide and the increasing tendency toward failure and project overruns, that if the same performance was exhibited in Architecture we would live in cities where nothing over three stories high was ever built! In promising so much with objects we should ask, "does object oriented address the fundamental issue of control and stability amid increasing complexity?"

1.3 Cause and Cure

A number of explanations have been given for the slow progress the industry is making in terms of fundamental control. Two major reasons stand out:
- The software discipline is only adolescent compared to others;
- Customer demands are increasing in complexity.

Unfortunately neither of these factors can be changed.

The energy exerted in the commercial market is an indicator of what solutions are thought to address the problem or to increase profit, whichever comes first. The energy is largely directed into:
- Tools and automation; and
- Methodology notations.

Automation assumes the process is worth automating, so the tools market should not necessarily be seen as the source of major advances, though that is their pitch, by and large. While debates on methodology notation generate considerable heat in confined circles, it is hard to argue that they shed much light on the fundamental control problem.

This paper argues that the very reason objects have increased leverage in software engineering is the reason the current object model itself should be challenged. Why are objects more powerful in concept than their predecessors? Because they borrow a few attributes of what is called in the *systems* sciences, "general systems structure". Inheritance, Polymorphism, encapsulation - these are all things that are exhibited by organic and other real world systems when they are functional.

This begs the question: given that real world systems have these characteristics and that *systems* are *ideal practice* in terms of control and dynamic stability, should we assume these are the only characteristics required to achieve that control and stability? Real world systems deal with the most complex set of constraints we know of and do a fine job when left to themselves - surely a more systemic model for software engineering is going to be more successful in gaining the control required?

BHP itself has shown considerable interest in and is applying the principles of the systems sciences in organisational engineering. These principles are gaining considerable respect in other disciplines world wide and are also used in specific domains such as stochastic mathematical and computing problems[8]. It is time to discuss what applicability they have to software engineering in general.

1.4 Systems Science - Paradigm and Dynamics

Systems Science can be defined as:
> The art and science of making reliable inferences about behavior by developing an increasingly deep understanding of underlying structure[9]

Another perspective states:

> It is a question of identifying nonvariants- that is, the general, structural, and functional principles- and being able to apply them to one system as well as another. With these principles it becomes possible to organize knowledge in models that are easily transferred and then to use some of these models in thought and action.[10]

Surely these aims are identical to those of the software engineering discipline? Having a brief definition then, what does systems science contribute?

Systems Dynamics is the foundation theory of feedback and flow in systems. It provides a method for modeling and simulating systems of considerable complexity. This leads to a capability of identifying dysfunction in systems as well as the design of functional systems. A range of simulation tools based on this theory are in use.[11]

General Systems Theory (Ludwig. von Bertalanffy, 1954), describes in mathematical language the totality of systems found in nature.

Cybernetics (Norbert. Wiener, 1948), is the study of control in living organisms and machines.

Systems Thinking is a paradigm or way of thinking about the world. It includes both first order and second order systems thinking. First order systems thinking is the study of the behaviour and structure of systems as already discussed. Second order systems thinking consciously includes the observer as part of the system under observation. That is, the act of observing affects the system being observed.

Having now a brief definition of the major contributions of systems science the potential contributions to software engineering and its various support systems can be defined. These contributions are considered at macro and micro levels. The first is organisational and the second is technical.

1.5 Systemic Macro Influence - Organisational Interaction

Software engineering shares with other commercial technical disciplines the need to work with supporting systems such as the customer, marketing, finance, project management and so on. It is certainly the case that these systems and their interaction are key influences on the effectiveness of the software engineering endeavour. Flaws in any of these or any combination of these have major ramifications and risks.

These interacting systems are of considerable complexity. The whole is not equal to the sum of the parts and the uniquely holistic approach of systems science stands out in capability terms within the organisational engineering domain. Second order systems science highlights that the interaction is not static, each interaction changes each system as does analysis of the system. While actors in each system tend to see other's systems as static, they are not. All systems can be considered to be in motion, and usually in acceleration or deceleration. The software engineering system and its supporting systems would benefit greatly from adopting systemic principles.

The systemic approach identifies how to account for both primary and secondary effects when making decisions that will allow strategic goals to be achieved with minimal injury to the organism.

The organisational benefits of the systemic approach have been well demonstrated elsewhere and are only included here for completeness. That is to say, any improvement in the actual engineering model itself can be quickly undermined by a dysfunctional organisational model. Alternative organisation models should be simulated and tested using the systems dynamics approach.

1.6 Systemic Micro Influence - Expanding the Object Model

The major contribution of this paper is to identify the gap between the object model and the systems model and to suggest a way ahead for evolving the object model to account for systemic principles.

The challenges of distributed objects have already been discussed. It is acknowledged here that considerable effort in the standards community is going into defining the rules and constraints that should apply to make distributed computing effective.[12] Others are working on adding intelligence to objects.[13] Agent technology and object middleware are two prongs of the strategy to expand the object model from the basic "Function/Data/Event Model" to encompass these other requirements. By way of empirical effort then, the object model is being expanded to cope with new demands. But what is the reference model for the reference model?

1.7 Gap between Object Orientation and the Systems Model

Expanding the object model begs the question - what is an object that we can expand it? This is the paradox of objects, an unsurprising one given their origin as an abstraction to support convenience in coding programs.

Object oriented defines what things can be objects, but avoids defining what objects themselves are. The danger is that in addressing new and complex demands, without a reference model, gains may be made at the expense of losses elsewhere in the model. With a systemic reference model, the object model can be expanded in a consistent fashion. Furthermore, these structures can be modeled and their behaviour simulated to identify potential dysfunction in the model as it develops.

The systemic model withstands the above criticism since it answers the question of what a system is. A system has values, it has knowledge and learning behaviour. It is the fundamental organ of control in the universe. You either get it right or it becomes non-systemic and decays to lower order systems. Systems reject dysfunctional behaviour and structure, either by repair or by decay. Objects have no such values. People may, but objects don't.

The remaining elements of the paper outline what a system object model looks like, both structurally and dynamically. It then suggests ways the object model could proceed to adopt the necessary characteristics to become truly systemic. It should be made clear that the objective in pursuing this path is to achieve what can be termed "organic information systems". This is where software engineering thinks in terms of cells, organs and systems and that these cells, organs and systems know not only what to do, but why they exist. They evolve with their customers and may even suggest to their customers how a further evolution might give that customer new leverage in its market or environment.

1.8 A Systems Object Model - Static and Dynamic Views

Given that there is not a significant body of work to draw upon directly in producing a systems model that aligns with the software world a first principles technique was adopted.[14] The approach was to[15]:

- brainstorm all the possible behavioural scenarios that general systems go through[16];
- Identify structural characteristics to support this behaviour;
- Identify the locus of the behaviour within the structure;
- Test the structure against the behaviour;
- Identify missing fundamental scenarios resulting from the testing;
- Repeat the process until the model stabilises.

The analysis follows. Firstly, the structural object model (Diagram following), identifies two major entities in the world. These are systems and resources. Resources are consumed and/or produced by systems. Systems are composed of systems and can be considered to be functional or dysfunctional. Systems and resources, as shown in diagram 1 share some characteristics and these are abstracted out into what are called *objects*. Objects, then, are really things that occupy space (either physical or otherwise) and time. That is all you can say about them. Objects may become resources in the context of an interested consumer system.

It becomes clear from this viewpoint that Object Oriented "objects" sit somewhere between these three types. They are more than conceptual *objects* as per the model, are sometimes *resources* and borrow some features of *systems*. The element of chaos has been added to show that other forces are involved in the intercourse between these entities. Chaos may well be highly complex systems, but that is another subject. This model then, covers not just the behaviour of systems when they are doing their job, but their entire life cycle - how they emerge, decay, are resourced, attract, combine and adapt . This has its parallel in computer systems. *Emergence* and *engagement* are design behaviours, Consumption is capitalisation behaviour(ie. software consumes money, people and computers).

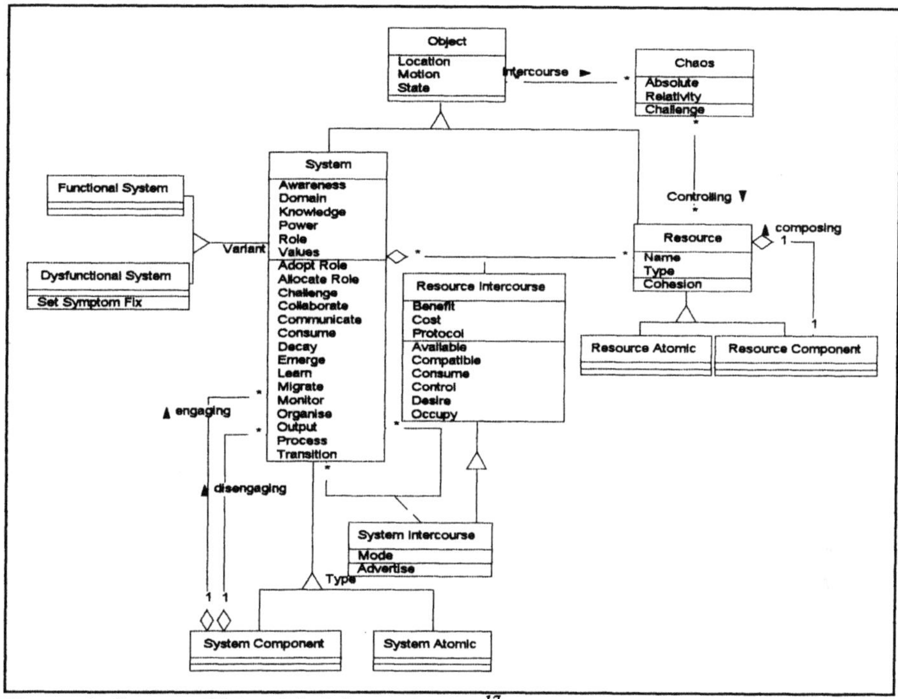

Figure 1: Systems Object Model - static view[17]

1.8.1 Dynamic systems view

The life cycle of a general system can be expressed as a state transition model (Figure 2). This state transition model has its counterpart in software development methodologies. Methodologies however are typically empirically derived. The dynamic model which follows attempts to understand the fundamental states a system *must* go through to be systemic.

The life cycle model can be explained thus: a system emerges, that is, it becomes self aware in some limited sense. Because of attraction to another system or to a resource for which there is competition, it seeks interest in collaboration to achieve the benefits of the attraction or the power to compete for the resource. Negotiation then follows to determine compatibility of goals and roles. Once compatibility is established, engagement follows. Alternatively the negotiation can fail or be deferred. Once engaged we now have a new system, a collaboration of compatible systems for a new purpose. This phase is called the "Evolutionary Phase". It includes two other states "Monitor Goal" and "Diagnostic". These are discussed below.

The next phase is the "Commerce Phase". Here the new system performs some processing and secures and consumes resources to be able to continue processing.

The processing state has two concurrent substates. One is to *Monitor Health* while the other is to *Monitor Goal.* That is, the system must constantly check its health relative to its user's expectations and its internal rules while at the same time monitoring its goal achievement. When the goal is achieved, new collaborations may result.

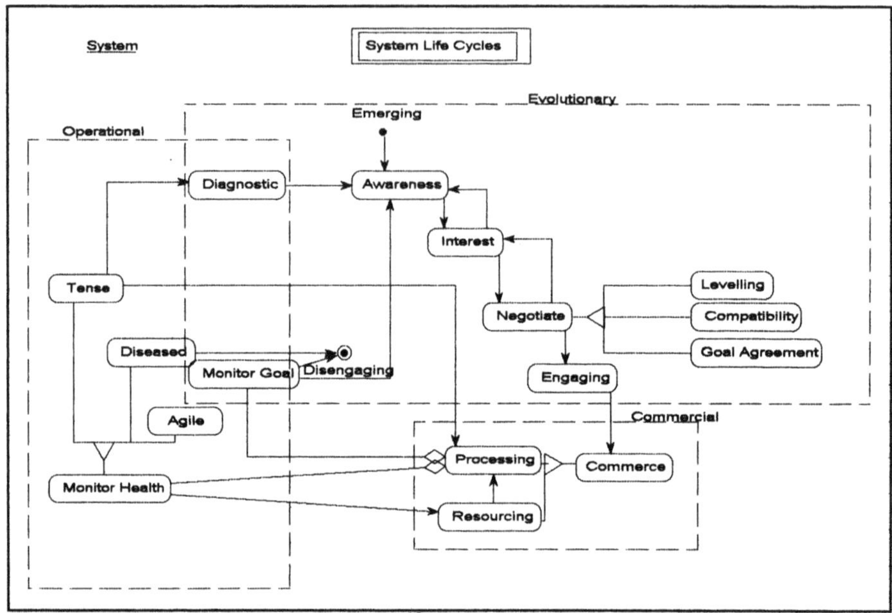

Figure 2: General Systems Life Cycle[18]

The next phase is called the *Operational Phase*. This is a concurrent phase with the commerce phase. Here the system is being monitored to check health, achievement of goals and to diagnose any problems. In software terms this is the debugging phase or the messages to the console for example. The system at this stage can decide whether the health is sufficient to continue commerce or whether reconfiguration or additional resourcing is required.

This is the test of a truly systemic entity. There are three types of diagnosis which can result.

1. Agile - the system is in good shape
2. Tense - there is disparity between the current reality and the system's role;
3. Diseased - Decay or radical reconfiguration must result.

A systemic approach is to always act on and in fact stimulate the tense state. This is sometimes called "creative tension", the gap between desire and reality.

The dynamic model then identifies the typical states of a system. It also demonstrates three orthogonal views of any system. Evolution - getting organised; Commerce - getting the job done; and Operation - monitoring the success of the enterprise.

One key recommendation is that each of these interfaces to a system be treated as distinct though collaborating views. Any object (system) should have an interface for each view.[19]These interfaces should be part of the implemented system, not just in external documentation. A typical dialogue with a system component would be: "What are you doing?", "How is it going?" and "Why do you do it?"[20], without leaving the system.

1.9 Summary

1.9.1 Macro level implications for BHP IT and like companies

Companies like BHP IT will benefit by specifically accounting for the trajectory of supplier and customer and the second order effect of the software engineering process on the relationship itself. As discussed, modeling and simulation are powerful tools for achieving this integration. The industry should specifically address the systems which support Software Engineering using systemic principles of organisational engineering. This would increase the holistic success of the organisation and reduce internal inconsistencies;

1.9.2 Micro level implications for software engineering

The recommendations of the paper follow. The recommendations are aimed at the methodologists and scientists in the industry as well as experienced developers who will refine, test and challenge the evolution.

1. Evolve the structure of the object model using the suggested or some better System Model as a starting point in combination with the resources offered by Systems Science.
2. Refine the object model to account explicitly for the 3 phases of the system life cycle required to build *organic information systems* - the Commercial, Operational and Evolutionary phases.
3. Approach the issue of finding a systemic organisational structure for developing component (cell/organ) based systems using modeling and simulation techniques.

1.10 The Vision: organic information systems

This paper arises from a vision of achieving Organic Information Systems as discussed. The object model itself while removing some barriers, doesn't actively help with this challenge. A useful software paradigm has to aim at the average developer[21]. It cannot only be useful to a small percentage of the market and be dangerous for everyone else. Object orientation can address a wider range of system types than previous methods, but this capability is conditioned upon increased maturity and experience in designers. BHP IT's experience with objects is that it is not at all like putting Lego blocks together. Lego blocks don't have state transitions unless you put them in the microwave oven. Therefore, more systemic intelligence needs to be in the engineering model itself, not just in optional external support mechanisms. Developers talk about *systems* until it gets to coding. Then talk turns to *objects*. The real world isn't like that, in the real world, all the good work is done by systems, some big, some small.

Appendix: System Object model Descriptions

The following table describes the major entities and their characteristics as shown in Figure 1.

Table 1: Descriptions of System Object Model

Object: *An entity that has location in space and time, physical or otherwise.*
Location: Where the system lives in space/time.
Motion: Accounts for motion of object along some dimension, physical or social.
State: Health of the system. Also the life cycle ie a state machine.
Resource : *An object which is useful for powering systems. May need refinement before use.*
Name: The identifier of a resource. Could cover class or instance.
Type: The type of a resource. Covers various classifications, such as physical state.
Cohesion: The energy required to refine a resource for consumption.
System: *A fundamental unit of organisation.*
Awareness: What other objects the system is cognoscente of.
Domain: The range of freedom or scope of the system.
Knowledge: The body of knowledge the system has. It is increased by Learning
Power: The power the system can exert. Priority in access to resources.
Role: The reason for the system's existence. Roles may be context sensitive.
Values: Rules through which the system deals with its environment.
Adopt Role: Role adoption can take place either by: Command and control from the designer, the body corporate or by Awareness of change in external or internal environment
Allocate Role: The system controller allocates roles when the collaboration between systems is organised.
Challenge: Challenge occurs when a component system has evidence that the composite system is out of kilter (rigid archetype). It communicates this back to the composite system. eg. nerves and pain communication.
Collaborate: Form contract for collective action or synchronisation.
Communicate: The system can communicate with all other systems it is aware of.
Consume: The system consumes resources to provide the energy to perform tasks.
Decay: The process of disengaging from higher order to lower order systems.
Emerge: This means to create itself, recreate itself or to be created.
Learn: The technique of explanation.
Migrate: Movement required to gain access to resources.
Monitor: Monitoring is how the system keeps track of its internal state or the apparent states of other systems and the alignment between its roles and values.
Organise: The process of moving from awareness of other systems, establishing contact, negotiating and engaging.
Output: An output can be either a resource or a tax for another system or a system.
Process: Processes are services which do transform, qualify, refine and so forth.
Transition: The system's movement between states.

References

1. Humphrey, Watts (Software Engineering Institute, Carnegie Mellon University): "What if your life depended on Software?, address at Object World Australia 1996. Volume 1, Object World Australia
2. Richmond, Barry: 1994 International Systems Dynamics Conference, Scotland
3. De Rosnay,Joel: "The Macroscope",(1979), New York : Harper & Row, 1979
4. Graham, Ian: Object-oriented methods, Reading, Mass. Addison-Wesley, 1991,
5. International Standards Organisation: "Reference Model for Open Distributed Computing". ISO/IEC 10746- 1 to 4. ISO, 1996.
6. Wirfs Brock, Sally: *Designing object-oriented software* N.J. Prentice Hall, 1990
7. Selic, Bran; address at Object World Australia 1996. Volume 1, Published by Object World Australia
8. Hamilton, Margaret: *"Automated Tinker Toys for Developers: The Paradigm of Development Before the Fact"* Technology Trendlines, Jessica Keyes ed. New York : Van Nostrand Reinhold, 1995.

---

[1] Systems Dynamics is one of the more well known disciplines in Systems Science. A term coined by MIT's Professor Jay Forrester in 1971.

[2] Humphrey, Watts, 1996 pp??.

[3] These cover one each of Maintenance, Steelmake, Construction and 2 Despatch scheduling systems.

[4] BHP Research developed AFUS, (A Framework for Unit Scheduling) which has been the basis for the scheduling work.

[5] This includes process and operations control for Steelmaking, Plate Rolling, and Steel Treatment stations.

[6] Steel grade management

[7] Humphrey, Watts :1996 (ibid)

[8] Systems Dynamics simulation techniques are usefully applied to logistics problems.

[9] Richmond, Barry; 1994 p4

[10] De Rosnay,Joel; 1979, Chapter 2.

[11] Dynamo, Stella, iThink, Vensim are examples. These tools and techniques have been used to model and simulate systems as diverse as drug addiction, supply chain management and the US Economy (with interesting and useful findings).

[12] See ISO's "Reference Model for Open Distributed Computing".

[13] Ian Graham; 1991 advocates the concept of "rulesets" to describe intelligence in objects.

[14] This is not to say that the problem has not been indirectly considered. Hamilton, 1995, identifies key structural and behavioural elements of systems, from a computing perspective.

[15] This *is* equivalent to the Class Responsibility Collaboration technique defined by Wirfs Brock, 1990

---

[16] Examples are: reproduce, challenge, consume, migrate, generate, decay and so on. Given that organic systems have the greatest complexity, these were used as a starting point

[17] Appendix provides full descriptions of the features named in the model. The modeling notation is Unified Modeling Language (UML). Diamonds represent a "collection" or "composition" and triangles represent generalisation.

[18] Diamonds represent "concurrent" states and triangles represent super and sub states.

[19] This concept is not totally new. Selic, 1996 recommended a "management" interface as a separate part of the notation in object modeling.

[20] It should be noted that the Microsoft COM model provides a metadata (descriptive) interface on COM objects. CORBA objects provide an interface repository for some metadata.

[21] Microsoft ActiveX middleware may excite technology buffs and gain wide market penetration, but it does not address this issue.

QUERY PROCESSING

Query Evaluation in an Object-Oriented Multimedia Mediator

Joachim Biskup, Jürgen Freitag, Yücel Karabulut, Barbara Sprick
Fachbereich Informatik, Universität Dortmund
{biskup | jf | karabulu | sprick}@ls6.informatik.uni-dortmund.de

Abstract. A multimedia mediator aims at providing a well-structured gateway to some application dependent part of a federated multimedia system. Our specific design employs proxy objects for external multimedia items and introduces a new concept of semi-structured and self-describing types for multimedia items. Query evaluation and optimization hide all details of communication with external sources and explore the external parallel computation capacities, the selectivity of local preprocessing, and the impact of materialization.

1 Introduction

A multimedia system can be considered as a distributed, federated, extensible information system that supports a wide range of object types and allows a high degree of autonomy of its components. A *multimedia mediator* aims at providing a well-structured and controlled gateway to some application dependent part of the whole system. Our design of such a mediator is based on multimedia schemas and on object-oriented concepts. In particular we employ proxy objects for external multimedia items and introduce types for semi-structured multimedia items. High level query processing hides all details of external communications, and query optimization takes advantage of parallel processing capacities of external sources and of materializations of previous query answers in the proxy state.

Presenting our design of query evaluation in the multimedia mediator, we
- discuss the role of proxy objects in representing external multimedia items,
- describe two basic approaches for querying proxy objects,
- show how communications with external sources can be hidden transparently,
- outline optimization methods for query processing dealing with the time tradeoff between local selectivity and external parallelism,
- explore the impact of persistent materialization of query results, and
- reconsider types for semi-structured multimedia items and introduce a new concept of semi-structured and self-describing types.

Our presentation is organized as follows. Section 2 summarizes the general architecture of our multimedia mediator. Section 3 presents basic approaches to query evaluation with external communication. Section 4 studies optimization of query evaluation. Section 5 deals with persistent materialization of attribute values. Section 6 deals with semi-structured multimedia items. Finally, Section 7 briefly compares our design with alternative approaches.

2 Architecture of the multimedia mediator

A multimedia system can be considered as a distributed, federated, extensible information system that supports a wide range of object types and allows a high degree of autonomy of its components. Seen as a *distributed* system, a multimedia system is based on a communication infrastructure that, at least potentially, allows worldwide communication. A mediator provides a transparent, application specific view on the whole system. Seen as a *federated* system, a multimedia system allows access to heterogenous information sources by providing appropriate translations between the various data models and protocols for interaction of its components. A mediator implements such translations and protocols in a transparent fashion. Seen as a *type system*, a multimedia system supports a broad spectrum of types. A mediator integrates the various types required for the specific application within a uniform type system, which includes appropriate types for semi-structured data. Seen as an *extensible* system, a multimedia system can be extended with respect to the federation structure and with respect to the type system. A mediator easily adapts any such extension.

Our general approach for a multimedia mediator is based on two established technologies for database systems: using *multimedia schemas* as a self-description of a specific application, in order to achieve well-structuredness and control on the one side, and employing *object-oriented concepts*, in order to federate heterogenous, distributed and evolving information sources on the other side. The resulting overall architecture is sketched in Figure 2-1, and the basic features are explained below.

A *multimedia schema* has three layers. The *view layer* offers interfaces for the local and external users. The *conceptual layer* constitutes the instantiation of the me-

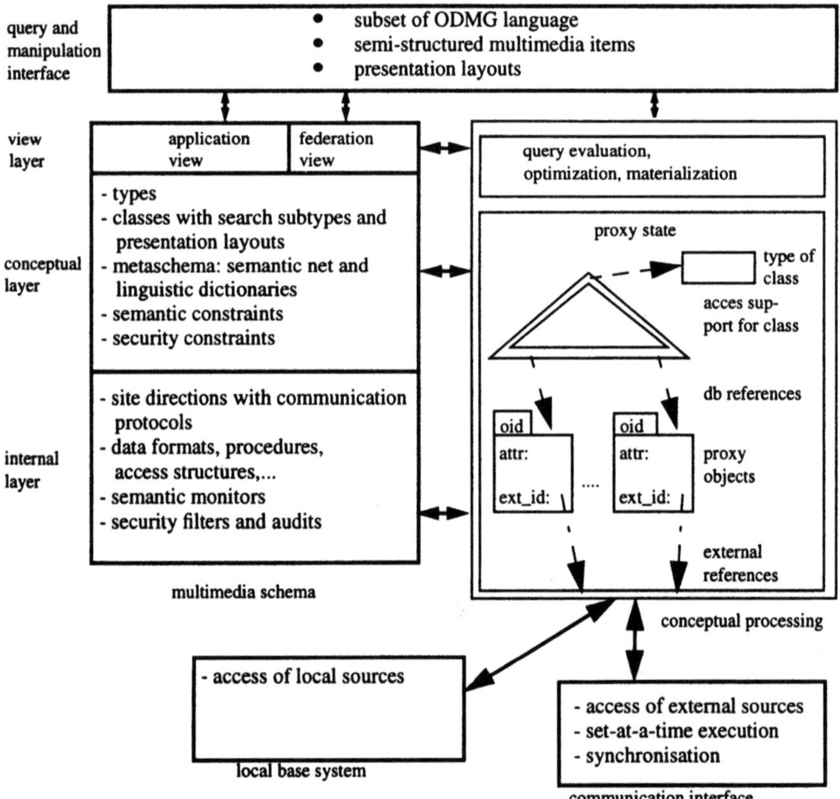

Figure 2–1 Architecture of the multimedia mediator

diator for the specific multimedia application. It contains a full structural and operational description, including multimedia *types*, *conceptual classes*, *semantic constraints*, *security constraints*, and a *metaschema* as abstract knowledge representation tool. The *internal layer* provides the details of how the conceptual items are implemented. Most importantly, it comprises *site directions*, for indicating whether a conceptual multimedia item is locally available and, if not, for providing communication protocols for accessing that item elsewhere in the multimedia system.

We employ *object-oriented concepts* as in any traditional object-oriented information system. Besides that, we take advantage of object-orientation for hiding the heterogeneity and distribution of the information sources within the whole multimedia system.

Firstly, any multimedia item visible in the mediator's view is represented by a uniquely identified object that is under the control of the mediator. If the represented item is locally stored, we call that object a *local object*; otherwise, if it is externally stored, that object is used as a *proxy object*. We also allow that a single object is used in a mixed way. Thus the mediator maintains a full *proxy state* of the application driven view of the whole multimedia system, which consists of all created objects of any kind. Accordingly, a user of the mediator gets the illusion of dealing with just this proxy state and he is not at all aware of the storage sites.

Secondly, the class specific procedures for types hide all the subtle details on how to actually access the items represented by the local and proxy objects.

Our multimedia mediator is designed to serve as an integration tool within an ambitious project for building a high performance multimedia query server, HPQS. The overall goal of the HPQS is to provide high-level, user-friendly, and interactive access to an application domain. This domain is represented by both classical knowledge representation techniques, in particular semantic nets and linguistic dictionaries, and various kinds of multimedia items, in particular texts and images.

In order to achieve high performance, the HPQS is based on a specialized parallel computing system which can be tailored to the most frequently required elementary search requests on texts and images of an application. In principle, there can be more than just one underlying specialized parallel system, and these systems can be remote from the user site. Therefore, given a semantically meaningfull query issued by some application oriented user, our multimedia mediator has to extract appropriate sets of elementary subtasks to be processed by the possibly external parallel systems. It is important to note that the mediator has to forward *sets* of elementary subtasks which are *as large as possible* in order to take advantage of the parallel processing capacities of the underlying parallel systems.

On the one hand, we assume mass of data, i. e. texts and images, processed by underlying parallel systems, and on the other hand, we recognize semantically elementary but computationally complex search requests on texts and images as a dominant cost factor for query evaluation. Thus, we designed our multimedia mediator to employ not only *parallelism* but also *materialization*, in order to avoid recomputations of elementary requests whenever possible and useful.

3 Query evaluation with external communication

From the user´s point of view the multimedia mediator should appear like an ODMG compliant database, which has been augmented by additional features, in particular with transparent access to external multimedia items and with types for semi-structured multimedia items.

Let us consider the type of a class. We assume that for any structural component of the type, i.e. an attribute, there is a class specific standard procedure for reading the attribute value for a given object. We distinguish three cases:
1) The attribute value is locally stored and thus can be simply fetched.
2) The attribute value must be determined from an external item by means of a communication.
3) The attribute value is redundantly available both by fetching from local storage and by querying an external source.

The last two cases only apply if the attribute belongs to a proxy object and represents a property of an external item. Basically, the procedure for reading an attribute value first tries to find the value locally and if this attempt fails, it generates an appropriate command to query the external source. The details of such procedures are discussed below.

When evaluating a query, we have to call the procedures for reading attribute values, typically while iterating over the population of some class. There are two simple brute force approaches to handle the calls of these procedures: the one-pass approach and the two-pass approach. These brute force approaches can be combined and refined to optimized approaches.

In the *one-pass approach*, the original query is processed nearly as usual. However, whenever a call of a reading procedure starts an external communication, the query process is suspended until the external value has been supplied. More precisely, we assume that for any attribute A there are two standard procedures *one_pass_read_A* and *write_A*, which serve for reading and writing, respectively, an attribute value. Moreover, the type of attribute A necessarily has to contain a special value *extern* that is different from any regular value. If for attribute A only the special value *extern* is locally stored, then the reading procedure calls a function *communicate* the purpose of which is to supply the (real) attribute value from an external source. Then the standard procedures can be sketched as follows:

- *procedure one_pass_read_A( ): attribute_type;*
  begin
  > *if A = extern*
  > *then write_A(communicate(external_source, A_op, oid, external_ident));*
  > *return A*
  end one_pass_read_A;
- *procedure write_A(new_value: attribute_type);*
  begin
  > *A := new_value*
  end write_A;

Here *communicate* is a globally known function that implements the communication with an external source, say by an RPC-like protocol. The function *communicate* needs appropriate parameters, say of type *communicate_input_type*, which are retrieved from the currently considered object:

- *external_source* uniquely identifies the external agent that must be queried for supplying the required attribute value;
- *A_op* is used as an operation symbol supposed to be known by the external agent;
- *oid* uniquely identifies the object under consideration within the mediator;
- *external_ident* uniquely identifies the multimedia item that is represented by the object under consideration, where now identification is within the external agent.

If the function *communicate* sends the last three parameters to the external agent identified by the first parameter, *external_source*, then this agent interpretes the second parameter, *A_op*, as an operation which is applied to the item denoted by the fourth parameter, *external_ident*. The result of this operation is sent back to the function *communicate*, which in turn delivers it as its return value. Of course, instead of just sending an operation symbol, *A_op*, we also could send an executable program, say written in Java, to the external agent. All such details are declared in the internal layer of the multimedia schema. As a side effect, after a call of the reading procedure the (real) value of attribute *A* is always locally materialized. Depending on a materialization strategy, such values can be made persistent.

In the *two-pass approach*, the original query is processed in four steps:

a) The original query *Q* is syntactically analysed to determine, which calls for reading procedures are required. Based on this analysis, a new transformed query *Q_external* is generated. As a query result, it just delivers the set of all parameters to be passed to the function *communicate* later on, and finally to be forwarded as commands to the external sources.

b) The transformed query *Q_external* is actually executed.

c) Its output is appropriately sent to the external sources. Afterwards, the returning answers, containing the attribute values, are interpreted as insert commands that materialize the attribute values locally. Thus, when all answers have been returned, then all attribute values required by the original query are locally available.

d) Finally the original query *Q* is executed. Since now all required attribute values can be locally fetched, query processing can be done as usual.

For the two-pass approach we need a slightly modified reading procedure for an attribute *A*. The modified procedure delivers either a parameter tuple for external communication, i.e. of type *communicate_input_type* or a (real) value of type *attribute_type*:

- *procedure two_pass_read_A ( ) : attribute_type union communicate_input_type;*
  begin
      if A = extern
      then return tuple_of(external_source, A_op, oid, external_ident)
      else return A
  end two_pass_read_A;

Whereas in the one-pass approach the global function *communicate* is immediately and directly called with appropriate parameters, now the reading procedure only has to supply the appropriate parameters, but the actual call of the function *communicate* is deferred to step c). Thereby, we can use a variant of the function *communicate* that accepts a whole set of parameters which is sent as a bulk to the external agent (or even to several external agents if the quadrupels in the set differ in the first component). The external agent then interpretes all commands that it has received, preferably in parallel, and after completion it returns the set of all results. Of course, now any single result value must be tagged with the pertinent object identifier and the pertinent attribute, i.e. instead of just any *value* we get a triple of the form *(value, oid, A_op)*. Once the returned result set is available at the mediator, the results can be materialized in the proxy state by executing appropriate writing procedures.

In order to illustrate the two-pass approach, we present a very simple example. Let the original query *Q* be as given in Figure 3–1. Then the evaluation of *Q* consists of the following four steps:

a) The original query *Q* is transformed into the query *Q_extern* that is intended to deliver the set of all parameters to be used by the global function *communicate*. *Q_extern* is determined as given in Figure 3–2.

b) Then the transformed query *Q_extern* is executed (as usual). The query result is denoted by some identifier, say *commands*.

<table>
<tr><td>

select *x.A*
from *x* in *population*
where *x.A* ≤ *"const"*

</td><td>

select *x.A*
from *x* in *population*
where *x.A* = *extern*

</td></tr>
<tr><td>

Figure 3–1 query *Q*

</td><td>

Figure 3–2 query *Q_extern*

</td></tr>
</table>

---

c)   Subsequently, the global function *communicate* is executed with the actual parameter set *commands*. The returned set of tagged values is denoted by some identifier, say *results*. By iterating over *results* we can materialize the (real) attribute values as sketched by the following fragment of pseudo code:

$$for\ all\ (value,\ oid,\ A\_op)\ of\ results\ do\ oid.write\_A(value)\ end$$

d)   Finally, executing the original query *Q* (as usual) we get the overall answer.

4 Optimization of query evaluation

The one-pass approach treats all external communications sequentially, and thus it is unlikely to be efficient. The two-pass approach treats all external communications simultaneously, but it has three other obvious drawbacks. Firstly, it does not allow parallelism between local processing and external communication. Secondly, it cannot take advantage of any optimization technique to reduce the number of attribute accesses or related features (for instance semi-joins or side-way information passing). Finally, it actually only works for a restricted kind of queries that allow to precompute the set of all objects for which an attribute value must be determined. Therefore, besides the brute force approaches there is room for a large variety of optimized evaluation strategies. The query optimizer of the mediator should be able to select an appropriate strategy for any given query.

As an example, we outline an optimized evaluation strategy for conjunctive (object) queries. Such queries have the following general syntactical form:

$$select\ xi.Ai,... \ from\ xi\ in\ Ci,... \ where\ xk.Ak = xl.Al\ and\ ...\ and\ xj.Aj = const\ and\ ...$$

Here, as above, *Ci* is a class (identifier), *xi* is an object variable, the clause "*xi* in *Ci*" binds the object variable *xi* to range over the population of class *Ci*, and *xi.Ai* denotes the value of attribute *Ai* of the object denoted by *xi*.

The optimized evaluation strategy is based on the classical heuristic to perform the selections, which are required by the where-clause, as early as possible in order to minimize the size of intermediate results. In particular, the selections required by conditions of the form *xj.Aj = const* are executed before any other operation, and selections required by conditions of the form *xk.Ak = xl.Al* are performed immediately after the set of all pairs of objects (*xk,xl*) that must be examined is actually available. In order to pursue this heuristic, the original flat query is syntactically transformed into a nested query in which intermediate results of subqueries are explicitly denoted by identifiers. The nested query in turn can also be expressed as a sequence of simple flat queries. Starting with innermost nested queries, any single flat subquery is treated as in the two-pass approach. As a result, we get something like a "multiple two-pass approach". This outline is illustrated by an example query.

---

select *y.D*
from *x* in *firstpop*, *y* in *secondpop*
where *x.A* = *"multimedia"* and *x.B* = *y.C*

Figure 4–1 conjunctive query *Q*

Consider the conjunctive query Q shown in Figure 4–1. Following the optimization heuristic, we can rephrase the flat query Q by an equivalent sequence of queries as follows. The outermost query $Q3$ is shown in Figure 4–2, the definition of *intermediate_2* is given by query $Q2$ shown in Figure 4–3, and finally the definition of *intermediate_1* is given by query $Q1$ shown in Figure 4–4.

select $y.D$ from y in *intermediate_2*	select y from x in *intermediate_1*, y in *secondpop* where $x.B = y.C$	select x from x in *firstpop* where $x.A = $ "*multimedia*"
Figure 4–2 query $Q3$	**Figure 4–3** query $Q2$	**Figure 4–4** query $Q1$

The original query Q is equivalent to the query sequence $Q1$, $Q2$, $Q3$, where each subquery Qi can be treated separately by the two-pass approach. In Figure 4–5 to Figure 4–7 we only present the transformed queries Qi_extern.

select $x.A$ from x in *firstpop* where $x.A = extern$	select $x.B$ from x in *intermediate_1* where $x.B = extern$ union select $y.C$ from y in *secondpop* where $y.C = extern$	select $y.D$ from y in *intermediate_2* where $y.D = extern$
Figure 4–5 query $Q1\_extern$	**Figure 4–6** query $Q2\_extern$	**Figure 4–7** query $Q3\_extern$

The outline for an optimized evaluation strategy for conjunctive (object) queries does not completely specify, how to precisely decompose a query into appropriate fragments. Obviously, as usual in query optimization, for each issued query we have to explore various possibilities for decomposition, thereby estimating the expected evaluation costs, and finally determining the expectedly best available option. Basically we are faced with a fundamental time tradeoff between

- *selectivity* of the *mediator´s* local operations on the proxy state on the one side,
- *parallelism* of the *external agents* operating on external multimedia items on the other side.

Here, the selectivity *sel* measures the impact of the mediator´s heuristic to perform selections early, where *sel* with $0 \le sel \le 1$ is the ratio of actually selected objects to inspected objects. And the parallelism, *par*, describes the impact of parallel computing capacities of external agents, where *par* with $1 \le par$ is the number of items that can be processed in parallel. If *card* denotes the number of objects, or equivalently of represented external items, in the search space of a subquery under consideration, then the evaluation time, *time*, of the subquery is roughly estimated as follows (where proportional constants are omitted for the sake of succintness):

$$time \approx \frac{sel}{par} \times card$$

Unfortunately, the essential parameters *sel* and *par* of a decomposition are not independent. Additionally, the actual selectivity *sel* does not only depend on the current instance, the characteristics of which could sometimes be determined from the schema, but also on the materializations stemming from preceding queries. And finally, the parallelism can also be affected by the decomposition, since any conjunctive query can be considered as containing some kind of m-ary (object) join operation, which has to be translated into a tree like structure of binary joins. For an issued query, some translations may result in a tree that allows parallel evaluation of subtrees whereas other translations do not.

When lacking detailed information for better estimates, we pragmatically propose to favour selectivity as a default, i.e. the optimizer should assume some small fixed default value for *par* and examine only selectivity in detail by using the usual query optimization techniques.

5 Persistent materialization of attribute values

Any evaluation strategy potentially supplies some attribute values that have not been locally available before. This offers the option to materialize these newly available values permanently in the local storage. If they are subsequently needed for further queries they can be simply fetched, and thereby their possibly time and resource consuming recomputation can be avoided.

Pursuing this option we have to deal with several problems, including:

- *Materialization* strategies: based on the knowledge of the application, in particular as it is represented by the linguistic dictionaries, we have to decide which attributes are both suitable and worthwhile to be materialized.
- Assumptions on *incomplete knowledge*: if an attribute is materialized we have to decide whether query evaluation should be done under the usual closed world assumption or a partial open world assumption is more appropriate.
- *Refreshment* strategies(out of the scope of this paper): if the external multimedia items, from which the materialized attribute values are computed, can be updated, then the materializations must eventually be updated also.

Materialization and assumptions on *incomplete knowledge* are decided on the basis of the type of an attribute. The full type system of our mediator is outlined in Section 6 below. Here we only need the distinctions between a scalar and a setvalued attribute, and between a structured and a semi-structured attribute. For a scalar attribute, we assume that the standard procedures are for reading and writing the scalar value, as already used in the previous discussions. For a setvalued attribute, instead we suppose that the standard procedures do not deal with the whole set but only with single members, i.e. they have the parametrised form *is_member_A(x)*, *insert_A(x)*, and *delete_A(x)*.

A *scalar and structured* attribute is always materialized. If there is a stored value, then any reference to such an attribute is evaluated solely on the basis of this materialization, i.e. we use the usual closed world assumption.

A *setvalued and structured* attribute is materialized if the cardinality of the set of possible member values is a small finite cardinal. This situation is recognized by inspecting all components of the structure whether their possible values are bound by a small, explicitly enumerated range. Typically, such an enumeration is given by a finite subrange of cardinals or by a finite collection of constants . In this case, any materialization of the set is interpreted under a partial open world assumption: the stored values are supposed to represent definitely true statements, while the truth of statements corresponding to values that are possible but not stored in the set is assumed to be unknown. As a consequence, any query explicitly or implicitly referring to values of the latter kind must be evaluated by reinspecting the original multimedia item.

A *scalar and semi-structured* attribute is always materialized. A reference to a subcomponent that is included in the actually stored self description (see Section 6 for more details) is evaluated solely on the basis of this materialization. A reference to a subcomponent that may occur according to the semi-structured type but is not included in the actually stored self description is again treated under a partial open world assumption. And thus the reference must be evaluated by reinspecting the original multimedia item.

For a *setvalued and semi-structured* attribute we don´t have a general rule as yet. We expect that such an attribute is typically used for feature extracting from images or other highly complex and semantically rich multimedia items. Presently, we suggest to decide on materializations of such attributes case by case on the basis of the application semantics, rather than on more syntactically oriented reasoning as for the other three types of attributes. If the attribute is materialized, it is again treated under the partial open world assumptions sketched above.

Obviously, the cases and our standard decisions for materializations possibly need to be refined and revised according to a specific application. Therefore, our treatment should be merely taken as a default. Furthermore, our approaches to query evaluation must be suitably adapted to deal with our decisions on incomplete knowledge.

Persistent materialization of attribute values offers the option that the multimedia mediator uses its proxy state to *cumulatively learn* more and more aspects of its application field. This option is particularly powerful in combination with semi-structured attributes: learning may enhance the knowledge about both the *structure* and the *content* of multimedia items. We can also speed-up the learning rate by running specially chosen queries in times where the mediator and the external agents would be idle otherwise. The only purpose of such queries is to result in new materializations.

6 Dealing with semi-structured multimedia items

Traditional database management systems deal with structured data only. Accordingly, for that kind of systems we can achieve a clear separation of raw data and the structural description of raw data. This distinction is accomplished by sharply distinguishing between the time-varying database instance, the raw data, and the time-independent database schema, the structural description of the raw data. If data is only semi-structured, then, at most, only a part of its structural description can be time-independently declared in the schema, while any single data unit has to individually carry the description of its particular structure on the instance level. Then, of course, the particular structures on the instance level have to conform to the partial structural description on the schema level. Thus the partial structural description on the schema level is taken as an invariant to be maintained under update operations, like for traditional semantic constraints.

In order to formalize this outline, we first reconsider an ODMG like type system. Such a system is built from some atomic types, say **boolean, integer** and **string**, by applying the type constructors **n_tuple_of**, for all cardinals n (omitting the attribute identifiers for the sake of succint presentation), **set_of, reference_to** (and possibly some further related ones which are not treated here). Any type σ is described by its syntax tree, where the leaf nodes denote the atomic types involved and the nonleaf nodes denote the use of type constructors. Thus a type σ can be considered as a pair $< temp, label >$, where *temp* describes the pure graph theoretical structure of the syntax tree and *label* describes the annotations at the nodes of the syntax tree. Of course, the annotation of a nonleaf node must be compatible with the tree structure at this node, i.e. a nonleaf node with n subtrees demands for an n-ary type constructor.

Next we discuss a (partial) embedding order on types, where type σ_1 is embedded in type σ_2 roughly means, that the values of type σ_1 can be understood as values of type σ_2, and that values of type σ_2 can be queried as if they were of type σ_1. There are three reasons for embeddings:

- The first reason results from containments of atomic types. Here, an atomic type t_1 is contained in an atomic type t_2, $t_1 \leq t_2$, iff the set of values of t_1 can be seen as a subset of the set of values of t_2. For instance we specify that **boolean** $\leq$ **integer** $\leq$ **string**, where, for instance, the boolean value *false* is identified with the integer *0*, which in turn is identified with the string "0".
- The second reason results from refinements of constructors. Here a constructor c_2 is a refinement of a constructor c_1, $c_1 \leq c_2$, iff all components of constructor c_1 are also components of constructor c_2. For instance we can specify that for $n \leq m$, **n_tuple_of** $\leq$ **m_tuple_of**. It should be noted, however, that the n components generated by the tuple constructor **n_tuple_of** can also be simulated by a cascade of tuple constructors each of which may have an arity less than n.
- The third reason, not present in an ODMG like type system, results from refinements of the trees which underly the types. Here a tree $temp_2$ is a refinement of tree $temp_1$, $temp_1 \leq temp_2$, iff there is a mapping i of the nodes of tree $temp_1$ on the nodes of tree $temp_2$ such that i is injective on the set of leaves of $temp_1$ and for each edge (n,m) of tree $temp_1$ there exists a corresponding nonempty path in $temp_2$ connecting the nodes $i(n)$ and $i(m)$. There are two implicit assumptions underlying this definition of refinement. First, omitting an explicit constructor like **scalar**, we implicitly assume that a scalar component is refined by prefixing it with the **set_of** constructor. Second, we assume that any type can be refined by prefixing it with the **reference_to** constructor.

Given the containments of atomic types and the refinements of constructors and of trees, we can define an *embedding order* on types:

$< temp_1, label_1> \leq < temp_2, label_2 >$:iff
$temp_1 \leq temp_2$ via a leaves-injective mapping i, and $label_1(n) \leq label_2(i(n))$, for all nodes n of $temp_1$ such that $label_1(n)$ is not a tuple constructor.

As an example, we consider the type $\sigma_1 = < temp_1, label_1>$ of Figure 6-1. Its tree structure $temp_1$ consists of a root node and three descendant leaves. And its annotation $label_1$ assigns the constructor **3_tuple_of** to the root and the atomic types **string, integer, integer** to the three leaves, respectively. This type can be embedded in the more elaborated type $\sigma_2 = <temp_2, label_2>$ of Figure 6-1. Here the tree structure has been refined by adding a fourth edge leaving the root and by substituting the second and the third edge by some nontrivial trees. And the annotation $label_2$ has been adapted as follows. It assigns the constructor **4_tuple_of** to the root which refines the original constructor **3_tuple_of**. The assignment **text** to the first child is understood as a refinement of the original type **string**. The right leaf of the new subtree for the second edge gets the type **integer** as its corresponding node in the original tree. Here we also use the convention that the original single component can be seen as part of a pair as described by the constructor **2_tuple_of** appearing in the new subtree. The assignment **string** to the leaf of the new subtree for the third edge is a refinement of the original type **integer**. Here we also use the assumption that the original scalar component can be embedded into a setvalued component as described by the constructor **set_of** appearing in the new subtree.

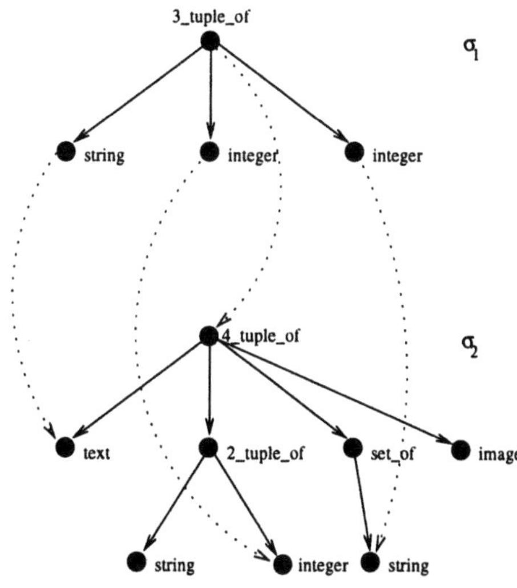

Figure 6-1 Sample embedding of types

For our multimedia mediator we designed an extensible augmentation of an ODMG like type system as follows. We add new atomic types that are relevant for multimedia applications, in particular the atomic types **text** and **image**. On the resulting set of atomic types we define the containments **string** $\leq$ **text** $\leq$ **image**. We could also add new type constructors that are relevant for multimedia applications. In particular, it appears that constructors involving some notion of sequential or parallel time, for instance for so-called "guided tours", are necessary for many applications. This topic, however, is out of the scope of this presentation. On the resulting set of type constructors we would have to define appropriate refinements. If a type constructor is based on time and some timeless types, then tuple constructors may be refined by a sequential time constructor, and a set constructor may be refined by a parallel time constructor.

Finally, we introduce the type constructor **self_describe** with two parameters which is used for multimedia items that are semi-structured as well as self-describing. The first parameter must be a usual type, as for the other type constructors, and it specifies the time-independent minimal constraints on the structure of allowed multimedia items. The second parameter must be a *meta-type* the values of which are types. It specifies which types are allowed as a time-varying self description for the multimedia items that are allowed by the first parameter. The first parameter, a type, and the second parameter, a meta-type, must be *compatible* in the sense that the first parameter can be embedded in all types given by the second parameter. For any type σ occuring as a first parameter, we can use the corresponding meta-type Σ, consisting of all types τ such that σ can be embedded into τ, as a default for the second parameter, meaning that all compatible types are allowed as self description. For each type σ and for each compatible meta-type Π, we define the embedding $\sigma \leq$ **self_describe**(σ, Π).

Considering the example types σ_1 and σ_2 of Figure 6-1 once again, we can specify $\sigma =$ **self_describe**(σ_1, Σ_1) for semi-structured items. Here, Σ_1 is the meta-type corresponding to σ_1, where the type σ_2 is an element of Σ_1. As an application, suppose that the three leaves of σ_1 denote the attributes identified by *name, year (of birth), and phone*, respectively. If we declare the type σ for some class, then we require that these three components are present for any item of this class. Accessing them, however, might demand to follow some paths, as for example in σ_2, and to convert the component types appropriately. For that purpose, any specific item of the self-describing type σ carries its particular type $\tau \in \Sigma_1$, together with the leaves-injective mapping i that maps the structure of σ to the structure of τ.

7 Comparison with other approaches and conclusion

The paradigm of a mediator has first been advocated by G. Wiederhold [20], and since then it has attracted many researchers, see for instance [18, 19].

Taking advantage of database technology for multimedia applications, in particular using and extending an ODMG like object oriented database management system has also been explored by several projects, see for instance [2,10,11,12,16,17]. The advanced work of [2] is focused on using so-called structuring schemas to neatly represent and efficiently query tree like SGML documents, featuring among others union types and paths. The experimental system of [16] highlights the combination of object management, a user-defined function library and massively parallel computations on very high data volumes. Our emphasis is on representing a partially materialized view on possibly heterogenous and external multimedia sources, featuring both transparent and optimized set oriented access to external sources. In particular, our optimization approach is directed to employ both parallelism, as provided by external multimedia sources, and materialization, as provided by the proxy state.

There are already many studies and proposal on dealing with semi-structure data, see[1] for a recent survey. Our particular proposal for embeddings of types, which includes the new type constructor **self_describe,** combines aspects of previously discussed multimedia types such as in [17], of structuring schemas and tagged union types [2,3], and of graph schemas [8]. Aspects of temporal constructors are treated for instance in [4,6,13,14].

There are also many studies on materialization of database views in general and some suggestions to employ materializations for multimedia systems, see for instance [5,15,16].

Since high efficiency is of great importance, also multimedia query optimization has been studied under various aspects, see for instance [2,5,7,9,19]. One special interest for our multimedia mediator has been to exploit the potentials of parallelism of external agents and its tradeoff with materialization.

Our design of the multimedia mediator is currently started to be implemented in a prototype fashion. The prototype is intended to be used within the HPQS project. The implementation tries to use generally available systems as far as possible. For the database functionality we base the mediator on the O_2 system. For the communication functionality we base the mediator on the CORBA proposal.

There are many avenues for future work. Most importantly, our design of a multimedia mediator has to be evaluated and tuned with respect to performance characteristics. The impact of maintaining a proxy state should be determined also experimentally, in particular the tradeoff between selectivity, which is effected by the materialization strategies, and parallelism of the external agents. Conceptually, query optimization should be studied in more detail, in particular taking into consideration the impact of the extended type system. A depth-in study of a our proposal of the type constructor for semi-structured data would also be worthwhile.

8 References

[1] S. Abiteboul, Querying semi-structured data, Proceedings *6th International Conference on Database Theory*, ICDT '97, Delphi, Greece, Lecture Notes in Computer Science 1186, Springer, Berlin etc., 1997, pp. 1 - 18.

[2] S. Abiteboul, S.Cluet, V. Christophides, T. Milo, G. Moerkotte, J. Siméon, Querying documents in object databases, Journal of Digital Libraries , to appear.

[3] S. Abiteboul, D. Quass, J.McHugh, J. Widom, J.L. Wiener, The Lorel query language for semistructured data, Journal of Digital Libraries , to appear.

[4] Y. Abiza, A. Leger, M. Crehange, Conceptual modelling for information filtering in broadcast interactive video applications, In: *Multimedia Modeling - Towards the Information Superhighway* (eds: J.P. Courtiat, M. Diaz, P. Sénac), World Scientific, Singapore etc., 1996, pp.35 - 50.

[5] S. Adali, K.S. Candan, Y. Papakonstantinou, V.S. Subramahnian, Query caching and optimization in distributed mediator systems, Proceeding *1996 ACM SIGMOD International Conference on Management of Data*, SIGMOD Record (1996) 25:2, pp. 137-148.

[6] M. Adiba, STORM: an object-oriented multimedia dbms, In: *Multimedia Database Systems* (eds: K.C. Nwosu, B. Thuraisingham, P.B. Berra), Kluwer, 1996, pp. 47 - 88.

[7] E. Bertino, F. Rabitti, S. Gibbs, Query processing in a multimedia document system, ACM Transactions on Office Information Systems (1988) 6:1, pp.1 - 41.

[8] P. Buneman, S. Davidson, M. Fernandez, D. Suciu, Adding structure to unstructured data, Proc. *6th International Conference on Database Theory*, ICDT '97, Delphi, Greece,Lecture Notes in Computer Science 1186, Springer, Berlin etc.,1997, pp. 336 - 350.

[9] S. Chaudhuri, L. Gravano, Optimizing queries over multimedia repositories, Proceeding *1996 ACM SIGMOD International Conference on Management of Data*, Montreal, Canada, SIGMOD Record (1996) 25:2, pp. 91 - 102.

[10] C.Y.R. Chen, D.S. Meliksetian, M. Cheng-Sheng Chang, L.J. Liu, Design of a multimedia object oriented dbms, Multimedia Systems (1995) 3, pp.217 - 227.

[11] N. Fuhr, Object-oriented and database concepts for the design of networked information retrieval systems, Proceedings *5th International Conference on Information and Knowledge Management*, 1996, pp. 164 - 172.

[12] K. Groenbaek, J.A. Hem, O.L. Madsen, L. Sloth, Cooperative hypermedia systems: a Dexter-based architecture, C. of the ACM (1994) 37:2, pp. 64 - 74.

[13] L. Hardman, D.C.A. Bulterman, G. van Rossum, The Amsterdam hypermedia model: adding time and content to the Dexter model, C. of the ACM (1994) 37:2, pp. 50 - 62.

[14] S. Hibino, E.A. Rundensteiner, A visual multimedia query for temporal analysis of video data, In: *Multimedia Database Systems* (eds: K.C. Nwosu, B. Thuraisingham, P.B. Berra), Kluwer, Boston etc., 1996, pp. 123 - 159.

[15] J.J. Lu, G. Moerkotte, J. Schue, V.S. Subrahmanian, Efficient maintenance of materialized mediated views, Proc. *1995 ACM SIGMOD International Conference on Management of Data*, San Jose, California, SIGMOD Record (1995) 24:2, pp. 340 - 351.

[16] W. O'Connell et al, A teradata content-based multimedia object manager for massively parallel architectures, Proceeding *1996 ACM SIGMOD International Conference on Management of Data*, Montreal, Canada, SIGMOD Record (1996) 25:2, pp. 68 - 78.

[17] M.T. Özsu, D. Szafron, G. El-Medani, C. Vittal, An object-oriented multimedia database system for a news-on-demand application, Multimedia Systems (1995) 3, pp. 183 - 203.

[18] V.S. Subrahmanian, HERMES: a heterogeneous reasoning and mediator system, submitted for publication (see http//www.cs.umd.edu/hermes).

[19] J.D. Ullman, Information integration using logical views, Proceedings *6th International Conference on Database Theory*, ICDT '97, Delphi, Greece, Lecture Notes in Computer Science 1186, Springer, Berlin etc., 1997, pp. 19 - 40.

[20] G. Wiederhold, Mediators in the architecture of future information systems, IEEE Computer (1992) 25:3, pp. 38 - 49.

A Concatenated Signature Scheme on Path Dictionary for Query Processing of Composite Objects

Hakgene Shin

Dept. of Office Automation, Kijeon Women's Junior College
Chonju, Chonbuk 560-701, Korea

Heeju Lee and Jaewoo Chang

Dept. of Computer Engineering, Chonbuk National University
Chonju, Chonbuk 560-756, Korea

Abstract

Because of the wide acceptance of object-oriented database systems, query processing and indexing have become an important factor in the success of object-oriented database systems, especially when we deal with composite objects. To tackle the issue, we propose a c-signature scheme, which is a combined approach with the path dictionary. In the c-signatures, the signatures are abstracted from objects in a path in concatenation and stored in class-oriented way, so as to reduce search space. we compare the c-signature scheme with other indexing schemes such as path index, path dictionary, class unit signatures and s-signatures. Finally, we conclude that the c-signature scheme shows significant improvements in the retrieval operation.

1 Introduction

OODBSs dealing with composite objects require expensive traversal costs to process queries. Therefore, there are many studies on indexing scheme to support efficient query processing against nested objects in OODBSs. Access Support Relations (ASR) proposed in [1] use a relation containing object identifiers (OIDs) on paths and key fields with the B-tree. Path index, nested index, and multiple index using an inverted file are proposed in [2,3,4]. The path index, which is recommended for an aggregation hierarchy with a long path and is virtually equivalent to the ASR, requires high storage overhead and costly index maintenance to support various key fields. The path dictionary scheme introduced in [5] has shown its lower storage overhead and its universality. In spite of the advantages, the path dictionary also lacks an access method not only for the databases but also for the path dictionary itself. The class unit signature scheme[6] combines object signatures with path information. However the class unit signature rarely considered the reference sharing in composite objects. To resolve the problems of the path dictionary, [7] has proposed the s-signature scheme on the path dictionary. The s-signature filters the s-expressions at the initial stage of query processing. However, the s-signature scheme suffers from multiple target OIDs in an s-expression filtered by the s-signatures. Therefore, it is necessary to design a new access method that fully utilizes the advantages of the path dictionary.

In this paper, we propose a new signature scheme, called the *c-signature,* on the path dictionary to efficiently support query processing of different types of queries. Our new c-signature scheme uses path information without any redundant OIDs and also provides an access method to the path information. For this, we generate a signature from each object in the s-expressions of the path dictionary, and concatenate those signatures to form c-signatures for the s-expressions. Each s-expression may contain several paths terminating at the same object. The c-signature provides an efficient filtering mechanism that will not access the database at the initial stage of query processing, which is required in the original path dictionary scheme. The c-signature also provides an efficient access method for the path dictionary instead of the sequential scanning method. Finally we compare our c-signature scheme with path index, class unit signature, path dictionary, and s-signature methods to show that the our scheme achieves significant improvements in the retrieval operation.

The organization of this paper is as follows. In section 2, we will review some concepts and definitions involved in the query processing of OODBS and describe some conventional indexing schemes. In section 3, we propose a new signature scheme for the path dictionary and describes a retrieval and an update algorithm using our c-signature scheme. In section 4, we compare the c-signature scheme with the conventional indexing schemes. In section 5, we draw our conclusion.

2 Related Work

2.1 Definitions and Concepts

Let us review some definitions and concepts, which follows the leads of [2,3,5]. Figure 1 shows a graphical representation of an *aggregation hierarchy*, and is used to illustrate some key concepts. The class **Person** has three *primitive attributes*, **SSN**, **age**, and **residence** along with two *composite attributes*, **owns** and **name**. The domain of the attribute **owns** is **Vehicle**. The class **Vehicle** has two primitive attributes, **model** and **color** along with two composite attributes, **manufacturer** and **drivetrain**. The manufacturer's domain is **Company** and consists of two primitive attributes and a composite attribute. Furthermore, the **drivetrain** object consists of combinations of primitive and composite attributes. Every object in the database is identified by a unique *object identifier* (OID). By storing the OID of an object O_{i+1} as an attribute value of another object O_i, an aggregation hierarchy is established between two objects. We call O_i the *parent* object of O_{i+1}. A predicate on a nonnested attribute will be called a *simple predicate*, while a predicate defined on a nested attribute will be called a *composite predicate* or a *nested predicate*.

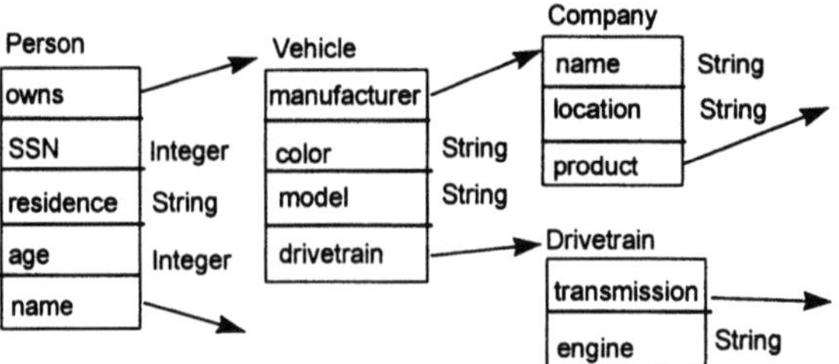

Figure 1: Aggregation hierarchy

An example query such as "retrieve all vehicles manufactured by Ford and owned by a 50 year old person" can be expressed as follows.

```
retrieve Person.Vehicle
where Person.Vehicle.Company.name="Ford"
and Person.age=50
```

The class from which objects are retrieved is called the *target class*, while the class involved in the predicate is called the *predicate class*. In the example, Vehicle is the target class and Company and Person classes are the predicate class.

To answer the above example query in the top-down approach, the system must retrieve all the objects in the class Person and screen out those with age 50. Then the system retrieves the Vehicle referenced by the 50 year old persons. The system then retrieves the Company objects referenced by the vehicles and checks if the company names are Ford. Finally, those vehicles satisfying both predicates are returned. In the bottom-up approach, the system retrieves the objects in the class Company and checks if their names are Ford. In this paper, we assume there is no backward reference, which means a child object does not carry the OID of its parent. So, without the backward reference, the screened OIDs are stored in a set S. Then the vehicle objects in the class Vehicle are examined to identify those vehicles made by the companies in S. The qualified vehicle objects are collected in a set S'. Finally the Person objects are retrieved to see if they are 50 years old and own a vehicle in S'. As we can see from the above query processing, the traversal between a predicate class and a target class requires a high processing cost. To overcome this cost, several indexing schemes have been proposed.

2.2 Indexing Schemes

Given a path, a path index on the path P is defined [2,4] as a set of pairs *(O,S)* where S is a nonredundent instantiation (either partial or complete) of the path and O is the ending object of a path. Here, O is also the indexed attribute. For instance, considering the objects in Figure 1, the path index will contain the following pairs:

(Ford, {Person[3].Vehicle[5], Person[7].Vehicle[5], Person[4].Vehicle[12] })
(GMC, { Person[1].Vehicle[6], Person[5].Vehicle[9]} ...) ...

The short coming of the path index is that it expects a primary or a secondary key field to be used. In other words, in the OODBSs with composite attributes, we can not always predict which key attribute will be used to access the database.

The path dictionary extracts the composite attributes from the database to represent the connections between objects[5]. To represent the connection information along the aggregation hierarchy, an s-expression scheme encodes all paths into a recursive expression terminating at the same object in a leaf class. The definition of s-expression is as follows:

$S_1 = O_1$, where O_1 is the OID of an object in class C_1 or null.

$S_i=O_i(S_{i-1}[,S_{i-1}])$ $1<i\leq n$, where O_i is an OID of an object in class C_i or null and S_{i-1} is an s-expression for the path $C_1,C_2,...,C_{i-1}$.

```
Company[1](Vehicle[5](Person[3],Person[7]),Vehicle[12](Person[4]))
Company[2](Vehicle[6],Vehicle[9](),Vehicle[11]())
Company[3](Vehicle[3]())
Company[4](Vehicle[4](),Vehicle[7](Person[1],Person[6]))
Company[5](Vehicle[1](Person[2]),Vehicle[2](Person[8]),Vehicle[8](Person[5]),Vehicle[10]())
((Person[9]))
...
```

Figure 2: S-expression scheme for a path dictionary

For instance, Figure 2 shows an example of the s-expression. The s-expression maintains all the connection information for the objects located on the path Person.Vehicle.Company. Since we assume each primitive attribute has only one value, the advantage of the s-expression scheme is that every object on the path appears only once in the path dictionary and that it provides an efficient traversal means along the aggregation hierarchy. However, the path dictionary scheme does not have an access method for the database and the path dictionary file itself. Thus, when a query has C_t as the target class and C_p as the predicate class, this scheme sequentially searches the database for OIDs satisfying C_p. When the qualified OIDs are available, the scheme again sequentially searches the path dictionary to locate the s-expressions that contain the qualified OIDs.

In the s-signature scheme[7], for every path terminating at the same object of the aggregation hierarchy, signatures for the paths represented by an s-expression are generated and superimposed. Since the s-signatures are extracted from the object values, any given query predicate can be compared with the s-signature. Every signature in an s-signature file has an entry $<s\text{-}sig(i), pointer\_s\_expression>$ in the file. The $s\text{-}sig(i)$ is the signature of objects found in an s-expression and the $pointer\_s\_expression$ is the pointer to the corresponding s-expression. In this way, the s-signature represents all the objects in one s-expression. Therefore, the s-signature provides a filtering mechanism of the s-expressions in the path dictionary. However, the s-signature loses the OIDs of objects in the s-expression while the s-signature is generated. Therefore, when the s-signature scheme filters out an s-expression, it does not know which OID is the target OID. To overcome this, it is necessary to do expensive post processing.

3 C-signature on s-expression

In this section, we propose a c-signature scheme and discuss how this new scheme is applied to the path dictionary. First, we describe the c-signature scheme and then describe a way to combine the c-signature with the path dictionary.

3.1 C-signature

In section 2-2, we discussed a main bottleneck in the path dictionary scheme, which is the sequential scanning of the database and the path dictionary. To resolve the problem, an efficient access method is needed for the path dictionary and the database. Since the path dictionary only contains the connection information for the objects, that is, OIDs, in the paths, we can not directly compare the predicate given in a query with the path dictionary. However, it provides fast traversal means and processes different types of queries, so we need to develop a new signature scheme on the path dictionary to gain the advantages of the path dictionary as well as provide a means of fast access. The access method must provide the following features:

1. support for scanning of the database and the path dictionary.
2. support for different types of queries.

Before describing the new signature, let us again look at the s-expression in the path dictionary. The s-expression encodes into a recursive expression all paths terminating at the same object in a leaf class. In other words, within an aggregation hierarchy, there may be many paths terminating at the same object. This is called reference sharing and has a major impact on the cost of query processing [4].

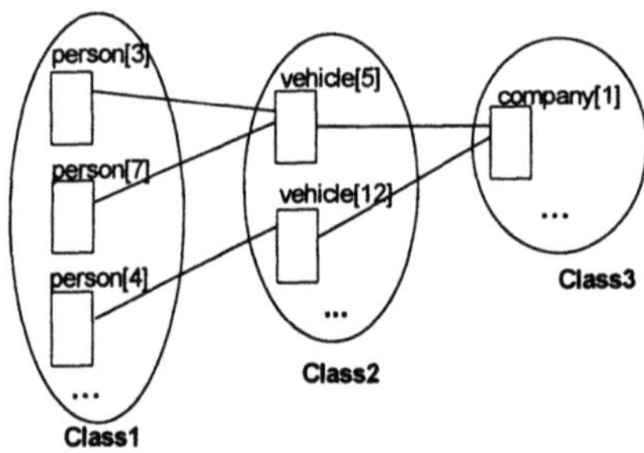

Figure 3: Paths with reference sharing

Figure 3 shows possible paths terminating at the same object, Company[1], which we can find at the first s-expression in Figure 2. For every path terminating at the same object of the aggregation hierarchy, we create signatures for the objects in an s-expression. Basically the signature is extracted from attribute values of the objects in the s-expression. We call this the c-signature because we put the object signatures in concatenation. The construction algorithm of the c-signature for an s-expression can be defined as follows:

Algorithm : const_c_sig
Input : s-expression
Output : c-signature

1. retrieve every object contained in the s-expression.
2. create the signature of each object by ORing the signatures made from primitive attribute values.
3. concatenate all the object signatures with OIDs to form an c-signature.
4. sort the object signatures by each class and put them in separate files

Algorithm, const_c_sig and Figure 4 show how the c-signatures from the example s-expression in Figure 2 and Figure 3 are generated. As Figure 4 shows, the signature is extracted from every primitive attribute value in an object, so that an object signature may represent the object in the database. Whenever a query predicate contains any attribute values from the object, the query can be processed without scanning the database. Since we concatenate all the object signatures from an s-expression to form a c-signature, the c-signature represents all the objects in one s-expression. Therefore, the c-signature provides the filtering mechanism of s-expressions in the path dictionary. In other words, once we find whether or not a c-signature matches the query signature generated from the query predicate, we do not have to scan the path dictionary. We just use the pointer from the c-signature in the c-signature file to point to the s-expression.

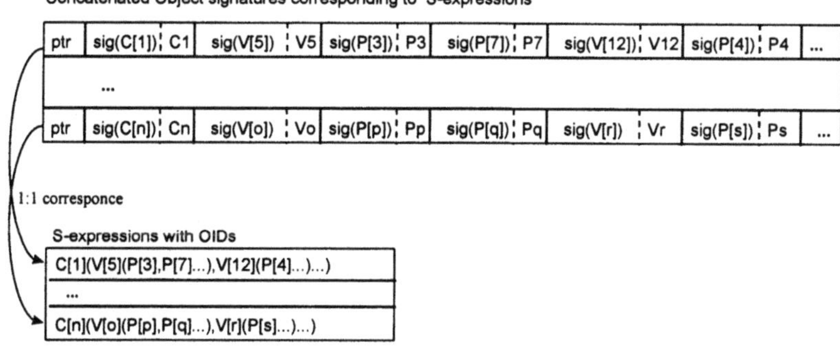

Figure 4: Generation of c-signature

The c-signatures generated based on the s-expressions can be stored in several c-signature files to reduce search space. If we put all c-signatures in a file, we have to scan all signatures to find the matching c-signature. But, by separately putting the c-signatures from each class, like in Figure 5, while keeping the pointers to its s-expression, we can only scan the c-signature file corresponding to a predicate class.

Figure 5 depicts that every signature has an entry *<c-sig(i),OID, pointer_s_expression>* in the file. The *c-sig(i)* is a signature of an object found in the s-expression pointed by the pointer, *pointer_s_expression*. *OID* is the object identifier of the object which is used to generate the c-signature. The *pointer_s_expression* is the pointer to the corresponding s-expression. This pointer implies the c-signature has been generated from objects in the s-expression.

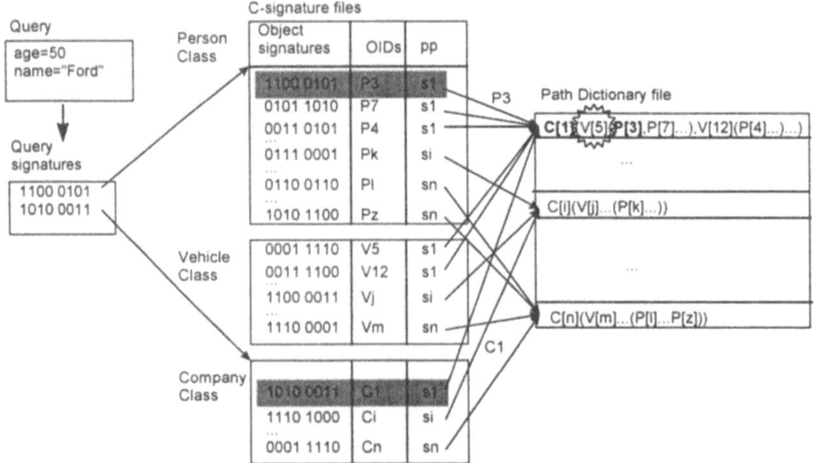

Figure 5: C-signature scheme on s-expression

The c-signature scheme on an s-expression file can filter out a candidate s-expression without a sequential search on the database and find an OID specified in a query out of the path dictionary. Those processes are considered as the most time consuming tasks in the conventional path dictionary approach. For the fast search of the c-signature file, a bit-sliced signature file scheme [8] instead of a bit-string scheme can be adopted for an implementation of the c-signature file.

3.2 Query Processing with C-signature

We now discuss how to use the c-signature scheme for retrievals and updates. We assume that the c-signatures for each s-expression are available.

Retrieval

Suppose there is a query Q that has C_t as the target class and C_p as the predicate class, where $1 \leq t, p \leq n$. Here, n is the number of classes on the path. The retrieval algorithm is defined as follows:

Algorithm : c_sig_retrieval
Input : query Q with C_t and C_p
Output : a set of objects

1. Generate the query signature using C_p .
2. Match the query signatures against the c-signatures to select candidate c-signatures, OID(s), and pointers to an s-expression.
3. Read the s-expression pointed by the selected pointers.
4. Based on the qualified OIDs in the s-expression and OID(s) from c-signatures, obtain the OID(s) of C_t.
5. Retrieve the object(s).

The c-signature scheme avoids searching the database sequentially. In addition, the s-expression avoids accessing any objects between C_t and C_p in the database.

Update

When there are changes in the database, the c-signature and the path dictionary should be updated. If there are changes in primitive values, it is not necessary to change the path dictionary because the changes of primitive values will not change the links among objects. However, the changes of the composite attributes should be reflected on the c-signature and the path dictionary files. Suppose an object O_i has a nested object O_{i+1} and an update operation changes O_{i+1} to O'_{i+1}. The update algorithm can be clarified as follows:

Algorithm : c_sig_update
Input : OIDs, that is, O_i ,O_{i+1} , and O'_{i+1}
Output : c-signature file and path dictionary after updating

1. find O_{i+1} and O'_{i+1} in c-signature file, C_{i+1}
2. retrieve s-expressions, S_1 and S_2, pointed by the c-signatures of O_{i+1} and O'_{i+1}
3. change the ancestor list of O_{i+1} to O'_{i+1} and rewriting new s-expressions
4. do backward traversal to O_i to change the pointer from S_1 to S_2
5. repeat step 4 up to O_1 in root class

At the stage 1 in each case, because the c-signature file has OIDs, the signature file can be used to avoid scanning of the entire database to find the objects, O_i, O_{i+1} and O'_{i+1} .

4 Performance Comparison

We compare the c-signature scheme with the path index, the path dictionary, the s-signature, and the class unit signature in terms of retrieval costs. Suppose a path of 4 classes with the cardinality of N_1 equals 200,000 and the average size of an object is 150 bytes. The size of the c-signature, F, depends upon the number of objects, D, in the path and upon the false drop probability, Fd. Fd is $1/N_n$ in the test, so that there is no false drop in theory. If $k_1=k_2=k_3=k_4=1$, the number of objects in the aggregation hierarchy is the same as the number of classes, that is, 4 in the test case. So the values of k_i representing the degree of reference sharing decide the number of objects in the path. The size of the path index also depends on the value of k_i, $1 \leq i \leq 4$ and let's assume $k_4=1$ for convenience. We vary k_1, k_2, k_3 to observe the change of the retrieval cost for the path index (PIR), the path dictionary (PDR), the class unit signature (CUR), the s-signature (SSR), and the c-signature (CSR) methods. Furthermore, we suppose the parameter k_2 only changes from 1 to 1000, while other k values are set to 1.

For the comparison of the retrieval cost, we adopt different kinds of queries used in [5] as follows:

1. Three queries in which the indexed attribute of C_4 is the only predicate attribute, and each with C_1, C_2 or C_3 as the target class.
2. Three queries in which a non-indexed attribute of C_4 is the predicate attribute, and each with C_1, C_2 or C_3 as the target class.
3. Two queries in which C_1 is the target class, and each with C_2 or C_3 as the predicate class.

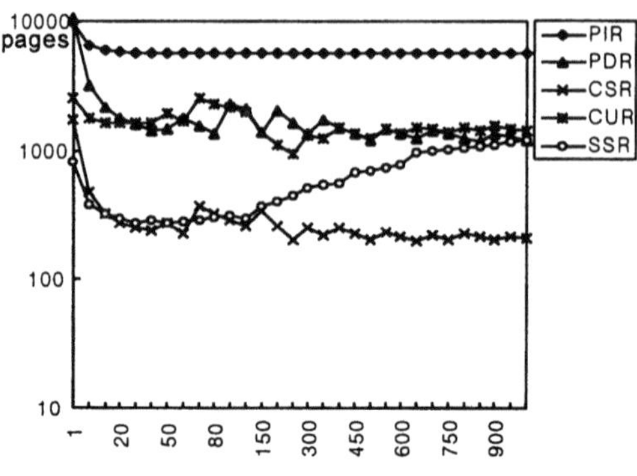

Figure 6: Retrieval cost

When the 8 different kinds of queries are given as above, Figure 6 shows the retrieval cost. It is shown from the result that the c-signature approach has a better overall performance than the path dictionary, the class unit signature, the s-signature and the path index. Only the s-signature has better performance at the range of low reference sharing. Besides, the c-signature scheme is a more general approach than the path index because the c-signature may be used to process queries with predicate classes against any attribute in any object on the path. This result has important implications, since queries in an OODBS can be very flexible and we can not predict which key attribute will be used in a query. In contrast, inverted indexes anticipate the primary or secondary indexed key used in a query. Furthermore, it is impractical to use as many inverted files as there are attributes to support various query patterns because the inverted files result in too much storage overhead. Therefore, we believe the c-signature method is appropriate to the query processing involved in composite objects in OODBSs.

In the comparison of the indexing schemes in terms of update costs, for simplicity of the comparison, we assume all update operations are applied to composite attributes. We also assume that the query used in the comparison of update cost has C_1, C_2, and C_3 as the target classes and C_4 as the predicate class, and the indexed attribute is the attribute in the predicate class. Figure 7 depicts the update cost. It is shown from the result that the update cost of the c-signature (CSU) is relatively higher than other schemes because it is optimized for retrieval operations. The path index (PIU) is superior to the path dictionary(PDU), the class unit signature(CUU), the s-signature(SSU), and CSU in this analysis. But the path index would show poor performance if the predicate applies to random attribute without the inverted file on the attribute.

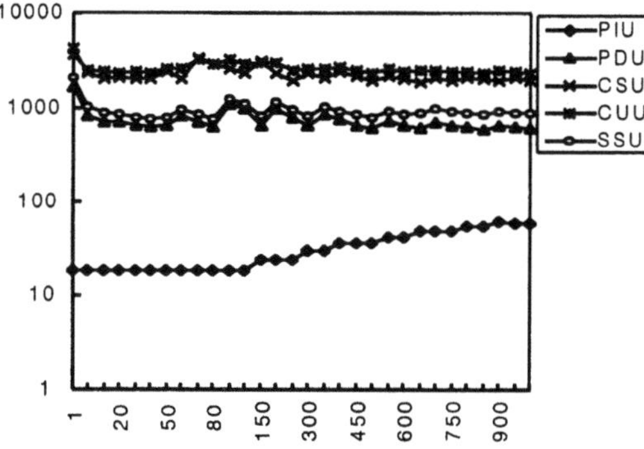

Figure 7: Update cost

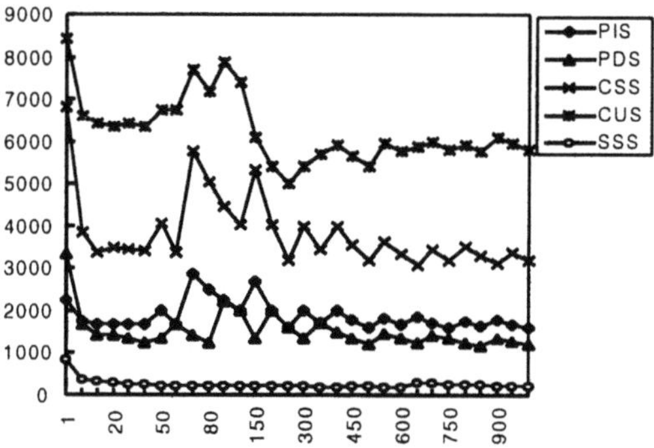

Figure 8: Storage overhead

Figure 8 shows a storage overhead for the c-signature (*CSS*) that is higher than the path index (*PIS*) the path dictionary (*PDS*) and the s-signature(*SSS*) but lower than the class unit signature(*CUS*). However, the path index scheme has lower storage overhead because we suppose there is only one indexed attribute, an attribute in class C_4, in the entire aggregation hierarchy. If there are indexed attributes as many as the number of classes, the storage of the path index scheme will be much higher than *PIS* in the Figure 8. The path dictionary (*PDS*) and the s-signature(*SSS*) have lower storage overhead than the c-signature because they are not put in class-oriented way. The class unit signature has the highest storage overhead because it has many redundant OIDs.

5 Conclusion

Since queries in an OODBS can be very flexible, it is difficult to predict which key attribute will be used in a query. However, the inverted file methods anticipate that a key field will be used in a query. The path dictionary encodes the connection information of class aggregation hierarchy and shows an effective way to process different kinds of queries. However it suffers from the lack of an efficient access method. In this paper, we proposed the c-signature scheme on the path dictionary and developed cost models for retrieval, update operations, and storage overhead. Using the cost model, we compared the c-signature with other schemes under different degrees of reference sharing and demonstrated its efficiency and universality for different kinds of queries. Based on the results, we showed the c-signature method is appropriate to the efficient retrieval and flexible query processing in OODBSs. We believe the c-signature scheme is applicable to the nested relation in extended relational database system and object relational database system. At present, we are studying the implementation issues of the c-signature and other schemes.

References

[1] A. Kemper and G. Moerkotte, "Advanced query processing in object bases using access support relations", In Proc. of the 16th VLDB Conference, Brisbane, Australia, 1990, pp.290-301

[2] E. Bertino and W. Kim, "Indexing technique for queries on nested objects", In IEEE Trans. Knowledge and Data Engineering, 1(2), 1989, pp.196-214

[3] W. Kim, K.C. Kim, and A. Dale, "Indexing techniques for object-oriented databases", In Object-Oriented, Concepts, Databases, and Applications, W. Kim and F.H. Lochovsky, eds., Addison-Wesley, Reading, MA, 1989, pp.371-394.

[4] E. Bertino and C. Guglielmina, "Path index: An approach to the efficient execution of object-oriented queries", In Data and Knowledge Engineering, North Holland, 10, 1993, pp.1-27

[5] D.L. Lee and W.C. Lee, "Using Path Information for Query Processing in Object-Oriented Database Systems", In Third International Conference on Information and Knowledge Management, Gaitherburg, MD, 1994, pp. 64-71

[6] H. Yong and S. Lee, "Signature File Generation Techniques for Query Processing in Object-Oriented Databases", In Journal of The Korea Information Science Society, Vol. 21, No 5, 1995, pp.922-930

[7] H. Shin and J. Chang, "Signatures of Complex Objects for Query Processing in OODB", In Seventh International Conference on Database and Expert Systems Applications", Zurich, Switzerland, 1996, pp.323-332

[8] C. Faloutsos, "Signature Files", In Information Retrieval: data structure and algorithms, W.B. Frakes, R. Baeza-Yates, eds., PTR Prentice-Hall, Englewood Cliffs, NJ, ,1992, pp. 44-65.

An Approach to Query Translation in a Federation of Distributed Heterogeneous Database Systems

Xuequn Wu

Deutsche Telekom AG, Technologiezentrum
Postfach 10 00 03, D-64276 Darmstadt, Germany
eMail: wu@tzd.telekom.de

Abstract

In this paper we present the approach to query translation in the federated database system VHDBS, which has been jointly developed by a research project at the Technology Center of Deutsche Telekom and at the Fraunhofer Institute ISST. We introduce the corresponding algorithms and describe how a query against the federated database is translated into subqueries for different local databases, and how the results of the subqueries are synthesized to form the final result for the federated database.

1. Introduction

Currently there is a growing need for an enterprise to manage distributed and heterogeneous data and to support cooperative use of these data. During a research project we have designed and developed the system VHDBS, which provides a way to integrate the pre-existing as well as legacy database systems in a distributed and heterogeneous environment, and fills the data modeling gap between applications and distributed heterogeneous database systems. An object-oriented data model is used as a common data model, that is more adequate to integrate heterogeneous data. A CORBA Object Request Broker [OMG96] is included in the system architecture and used to support the communication between client applications and database servers. Several mapping layers of the architecture allow for an open system, which provides a high degree of scalability.

In this paper we discuss the query translation for VHDBS. To support federated queries, the repository concept is introduced. A repository provides an object view to support the combining of information from different local databases, and serves as the basis for formulating federated queries. The common query language FQL is used as both the query language and the specification language for repositories. Rather than inventing yet another query language, FQL adopts SQL and OQL of ODMG-93 [CAD+94] as the base language, making adaptations and extensions. These extensions result from our particular effort for cooperative use of databases in a distributed and heterogeneous environment, while ODMG-93's focus is on the standardization of logically centralized object-oriented database systems, and is therefore different from ours.

1.1 Related work

Recently there have been various projects on the integration of heterogeneous database systems [Chu90] [LMR90] [Ahm91] [Kim93] [Su96]. Most of these projects focus on the schema translation technique and on resolving the syntactic and semantic heterogeneities that arise upon integration. These systems show weakness by system scalability. Only such database systems that are based on some given data models can be integrated into such systems. Adding or disconnecting a local database system is a very costly task. Unlike these systems, VHDBS relies on an object-oriented client/server architecture that can be easily extended and an object-oriented data model that can be easily mapped to different data models. Actually, there are no restrictions on the data models of the database systems that are to be integrated into VHDBS. Furthermore, it provides the repository concept for specifying the integrated view.

The approaches presented in [UA95] [KFA94] employ the object-oriented queries and an object-oriented data model for the federated level. However, the local databases are restricted to relational databases. The Garlic project [Car95] supports the integration of different databases similarly to VHDBS in many ways. Moreover, Garlic has focused on the integration of sources that are not necessarily structured databases. Unlike VHDBS, Garlic's database servers are "thin" modules that support the directly specified queries. While the extensions can be easily made on every level by VHDBS, all extensions have to be made on the federated level by Garlic.

2. Some Basic Concepts

Some basic concepts of the data model used by VHDBS and an overview of the system architecture are summarized in this section. We propose an object-oriented data model (ODM) [Wu96], and such a data model offers a high level of abstraction by the data modeling. This model provides the most necessary and needed concepts for modeling different data, so that it is easy to map data models of existing database systems and database applications to ODM and vice versa. By the design of the data model we take the ODMG-93 [CAD+94] object model as a basis and are closely related to the InORM project [Wu91a] [Wu91b], which uses an object-relational data model to model relational and multimedia databases. Some adaptations and extensions are made to the ODMG-93, which are necessary for cooperative use of distributed databases in a heterogeneous environment, as ODMG-93's focus is on the standardization of logical centralized object-oriented database systems, and is therefore different from ours. Such extensions are for example the repository concept and the metadata.

Objects in VHDBS are typed. There are two sorts of types: simple types and complex types. Simple types are such types as Integer, Float, Boolean, String, Date, Media etc., most of which are commonly given by existing programming languages. The complex types are based on different constructor types, which are often called parameterized types by many object models. The constructor types are Collection, Set, Bag, List and Tuple.

Repository is a basic concept introduced into VHDBS. Repositories are the first class constructs of the system VHDBS, and the objects are organized as well as stored into repositories. The queries are always formulated on the basis of the repositories, and the results of the queries are put into repositories. Thus, repositories are the storage of the objects (virtual or logical storage at the federated information level) and the entry points to reach the objects. The repositories are also the anchor to browse objects at the graphical interface of VHDBS. By means of the repositories, VHDBS provides users the views on the objects. These objects are actually stored in local databases.

The schema of the VHDBS system consists of two parts:
- The type system including all defined types and the graph of types according to inheritance. These types may be related to different local databases.
- The schemas of the repositories, each of which groups some types defined in the type system.

There are two kinds of repositories: mirror repositories and combi-repositories (combi-repository stands for combined repository). By means of mirror repositories the definitions (not the contents) of physical repositories of component databases will be mirrored to the federated level. Physical repositories are storage units of component databases, which are for instance relations in relational databases and database entries by some object-oriented databases. There is a one-to-one relationship between a mirror repository and a physical repository, i.e. a physical repository will be reflected to exactly one mirror repository.

Combi-repositories are defined through combining some existing repositories, which may be mirror repositories or themselves combi-repositories. Thus, a combi-repository can be used to define a rather complex relationship between the objects, which are stored as well as managed in some local databases. To specify such a relationship, restrictions and conditions should be given. Therefore, combi-repositories are defined and formulated through queries. The queries are formulated in the query langauge of VHDBS, which is based on OQL of ODMG with extensions.

VHDBS has a multi-layered architecture [Wu96], including the interfaces, the federated server, the database servers and the local database systems, the metadata server and its metadatabase, as well as the CORBA component (Orbix [Ion95]). VHDBS is accessible through interactive and programming interfaces. Currently, two interactive interfaces are supported. One interactive interface is a command-line interpreter for FQL. The other one is the graphical interface FGRAPH. It allows the user to retrieve the database with graphical displays. VHDBS supports a C++ programming interface (VHDBS API), by which FQL can be used as a embedded language within C++.

The federated server mainly consists of the global object management component, the query processing subsystem, the type system and the metadata management component (metadata server). Using the type system a type graph is defined and maintained. The type graph consists of the system types and the types imported or mapped from the local schemas of the local databases, and it defines the inheritance relationships between the types. The metadata server manages the metadata, which is used to provide the information about the definitions of the types and the repositories of the system, as well as the locations of the data. The metadata plays an important role for supporting cooperative use of distributed and heterogeneous local databases. With the aid of the metadata server, the query processing subsystem establishes an execution plan for a query. A uniform interface for database servers includes typical server operations that can be used commonly by different applications to access the data within any local database. CORBA, an industrial standard for distributed object computing, is included in the architecture, to support distribution of all components of the architecture. Our system is developed using IONA's Orbix.

3. Query Transforming

Queries are main requests submitted by client applications or end users to the federated database server. A query against the federated database will be decomposed and transformed to a set of subqueries, which are to be submitted to different local databases. A query against the federated database has the following form. For simplicity, the discussion is restricted to two databases that are indexed with numbers. However, by this restriction we do not lose generality. The discussion followed is based on the following form of federated queries:

FORM1: SELECT X1, [X2], ... FROM ... R1, ... R2, ... R12, ... WHERE C

The terms specified in the SELECT part may come from both databases, but may also come only from one of them. The result of the subquery submitted to DB1 is a set of X1 values that meet the part of the condition C, which is related to DB1. The same principle holds for the subquery submitted to DB2. The part of C, which is related to both databases, cannot be treated until the results of both subqueries are returned back to the federated level. Since this part has to be treated on the federated level, it is called remaining federated condition. The corresponding subquery based on the remaining federated condition is called remaining federated query. Thus, C will be decomposed into C1 and C2 for participating databases and CFED that is only treatable on the federated level. Both subqueries based on the subconditions produce results that have to be filtered through CFED.

3.1 Algorithm for Processing Federated Queries

Before describing the algorithm for processing of federated queries, we have to introduce the concept of query tree very briefly. The query language FQL is independent of any query languages used by local databases. If a federated query were transformed directly to a local query according to the syntax and semantics of the query language, the federated database would be dependent of that local database. Therefore, a federated query will be transformed to an intermediate structure called query tree.

A query tree is an attributed syntax tree [ASU86] and a binary tree at the same time. A node of the tree contains the following information: The concerned operation that may be any binary or unary operator such as AND, OR, NOT, and EQUAL TO, any global function such as CARD and AVG, or any method of a type; The kind of the node, which may be a FQL key word, an operation, or a content[1]; and the left and right son, and the father of the node. There is a type defined for query trees, which provide an interface containing the methods to trace and manipulate a query tree.

The queries taking the form FORM1 given before are processed as follows:
1. Parse the query. As result a query tree will be produced.
2. Classify and mark the query tree for different local databases and for the federated database.
3. Establish subqueries for local databases.
4. Hand over the subqueries to local databases. The subqueries will be mapped to the queries of the local databases and be executed on the local databases.
5. Treat the remaining federated query. Based on the results of step 4, the remaining federated query will be established, and then executed.

In the following we will discuss steps 2, 3, and 5 in detail. Step 4 will be discussed in section 3.2.

3.1.1 Classifying and Marking of Query Trees

For the sake of the limited space, we consider only the condition in the WHERE part, which is the most difficult part to decompose. The goal of this step is to decompose the condition C into terms C1, ..., Ci, ..., CFED. CFED is the remaining federated condition, and Ci is a subcondition that will be evaluated by a local database system. There may be more than one subcondition, which will be evaluated by one local database system.

A query tree is classified and marked in a bottom up way, following the post order tree tracing. A node will be marked with one of the following values:

Marks:= {FED, DB1, ..., DBn, CON}

FED is used to mark a subtree that will be treated on the federated level, while DBi-subtree will be treated in the database DBi. There is such a mark for every local database. A CON-subtree contains only constants, which can be evaluated in any local databases. A CON-mark in subtrees can be replaced (rewritten) with a FED or a DBi mark. A node will also be marked with FED, if its content only exists in the federated database.

The classifying and marking of a query tree is carried out as follows:
- In case of a leaf (the leaves are attributes or constants):
  - if the leaf contains a constant then it will be marked with CON.
  - if the leaf contains an attribute,

---

[1] Only a leaf has a content, and in that case the type of the content has to be indicated (e.g. string, integer and media).

- if the corresponding repository has a physical mirror in the database DBi, then the leaf will be marked with DBi.
- if the corresponding repository belongs to a temporary repository and does not have physical mirror in local databases, then the leaf will be marked with FED.
- In case of a node with one son (e.g. the negation operator, a global FQL function, or a method defined by users):
  - the same mark as that of the son will be used to mark the node.
- In case of a node with two sons (e.g. a logic connection or a comparison operator):
  - if both sons are marked with the same database DBi, or if one son with DBi and the other with CON, then the node will be marked with DBi.
  - if one of the sons is marked with FED, or if the two sons are marked with DBm and DBn ($m \neq n$), then the node will be marked with FED.

3.1.2 Establishing Subqueries for Local Databases

In order to establish a subquery for a local database DBi, a complete tree with SELECT, FROM, and WHERE part has to be produced:

- The SELECT part consists of the elements that are in the original SELECT part of the federated query and are related to the database DBi. In addition, the SELECT part will be extended to include all those variables in CFED, which are related to DBi. The values of these variables will be used on the federated level for the final evaluation of the original federated query.
- The FROM part consists only of those elements, which are related to DBi.
- The WHERE part is a synthesis of the DBi-subtrees of the original WHERE part.

An example is given as follows:

```
SELECT r1.x, r2.y, r1.z
FROM r1 in DB1, r2 in DB2, r12 in DB12
WHERE r1.k = r2.m AND r1.x > r1.z AND r2.y LIKE "S*" AND
r12.a1=20 AND r12.a2<10;


=>


DB1: DEFINE F1 AS
     SELECT r1.x, r1.z, r1.k, r12.a1
     FROM r1 in DB1, r12 in DB12
     WHERE r1.x > r1.z AND r12.a1=20;


DB2: DEFINE F2 AS
     SELECT r2.y, r2.m, r12.a2
     FROM r2 in DB2, r12 in DB12
     WHERE r2.y LIKE "S*" AND r2.a2<10;
```

In this example a federated query is transformed to a DB1 and a DB2 subquery according to the algorithm given above. r12 in the FROM part of the original federated query is an alias for a combi-repository, which is related to DB1 and DB2.

This is an example for the case given in the analysis of federated queries. The analysis is given at the beginning of section 4. In form of query trees, these subqueries will be handed over to the corresponding databases. They will be executed in the local databases, and the query results will be put into the intermediate repositories F1 and F2 respectively.

3.1.3 Processing of Federated Remaining Queries

After the subqueries returned the results to the federated level, the remaining federated query will be established, which will supply the final result for the original federated query. A federated remaining query is established as follows:
- The SELECT part is the same as that of the original federated query, however, it will be evaluated on the intermediate repositories (in our example, the intermediate repositories are F1 and F2).
- Correspondingly, the repositories in the FROM part of the original query will be replaced with these intermediate repositories.
- In the WHERE part, the condition CFED will be applied, which is produced according to the corresponding query tree similar to that shown in Fig. 3.

The federated remaining query for the example given in section 4.1.1.2 is produced according to the above algorithm and it is given as follows:

        FED: SELECT r1.x, r2.y, r1.z
             FROM   r1 in **F1**, r2 in **F2**
             WHERE **r1.k = r2.m**;

The AND operator of the original query is expressed now through the FROM part. The SELECT part produces the combination of the objects from F1 and F2, for which the additional condition r1.k = r2.m holds.

3.2 Mapping of Queries

In this section we discuss the mapping for the step 4 of the algorithm given in section 3.1. The established subqueries will be mapped and transformed to the queries of the corresponding local database systems. For this purpose the mapping and transforming of the federated concepts, data types, and the constructs of the VHDBS query language to those of the query languages of the local database systems have to be defined. In the following we show how the mappings are defined for three different databases Oracle, ObjectStore and O2. These database systems are used for our case study and are already integrated into VHDBS.

3.2.1 Mapping of Concepts

The database systems to be integrated employ very different concepts. The mapping of the concepts of VHDBS to these concepts builds the basis for the mapping of the data types and the language constructs. The mapping of the concepts is given in Table 1.

VHDBS	ObjectStore	O2	Oracle
repository	named root object	repository	table
type	class, persistent variable, collection type	class, type	data type
attribute	variable of a class	attribute	field, attribute
operation/method	member function	method	not supported
inheritance	supported	supported	not supported
object	object	object	tuple
OID	OID	OID	primary key
named object	named object	named object	not supported
object reference	foreign object reference	foreign object reference	foreign key

Table 1. Mapping of the federated concepts

3.2.2 Mapping of Data Types

The mapping of the federated types to those of the three given databases are illustrated in Table 2 and Table 3. While the first one shows the mapping of the simple types, the second one is for the constructor types.

VHDBS	ObjectStore	O2	Oracle
String	char*	string	string, char
Char	char	char	char
Integer	long, short, os_int32	integer	long, integer, number, unsigned
Float	float, double	real	float, decimal
Boolean	unsigned short	boolean	unsigned
Date	short	date	date
Media	unsigned*	bits, bitmap	raw, varraw, long raw

Table 2. Mapping of the Federated Simple Types

VHDBS	ObjectStore	O2	Oracle
Collection	os_collection	collection	table can be used some times
Bag	os_bag	set	table can be used sometimes
Set	os_set	unique set	table (DISTINCT) can be used sometimes
Tuple	object with os_members	tuple	tuple

Table 3. Mapping of the Federated Constructor Types

3.2.3 Mapping of Query Constructs

As mentioned, a federated query is decomposed into subqueries on the federated level. A subquery is transformed at first to a query tree, and then will be transformed as well as mapped to the query of the corresponding local database system. The mapping of the VHDBS query language constructs to those of the aforementioned databases is given in Table 4. "OK" in the table means that the construct of the query language of the local database system has the same or very similar form and semantics to that of the VHDBS query language, and "implemented" means that there is no direct support for the mapping of the concerned construct, but the mapping is implemented by us.

VHDBS	ObjectStore	O2	Oracle
attribute	OK	OK	OK
operation	function only in clients, not in server	OK	not supported
operation parameter	not supported (see above)	OK	not supported
constant	OK	OK	OK
NULL	nil	nil	NULL
dot notation (path expression) a.b.c	OK	OK	not supported

AND, OR, NOT	OK	OK	OK
comparison operations	OK	OK	OK
LIKE	implemented	implemented	OK
( )	OK	OK	OK
DISTINCT	implemented	OK	OK
COUNT, CARD, AVG, MIN, MAX, SUM	implemented	OK	OK
select-project	implemented	OK	OK
association of repositories	not efficient implementable	OK	OK

Table 4. Mapping of Query Constructs

6. Conclusion

In this paper we presented our approach to the query translation for VHDBS. The advantage of our approach is that the repositories employed by VHDBS can be used to describe the association as well as the combination of objects from distributed and heterogeneous databases, or to transparently retrieve data from the local databases using the object-oriented view. The algorithms for processing and transforming queries in such a federated database system were introduced. We discussed how a query against the federated database is decomposed into subqueries for different local databases, based on an intermediate structure called query tree, and the marking as well as classifying of the query tree. We discussed also how federated data model concepts, data types and query constructs are mapped to those of the local databases, and how the results of the subqueries are synthesized to form the final result for the federated database, using a sophisticated query transformation technique to produce the remaining federated query.

References

[Ahm91]   R. Ahmed et al. The Pegasus Heterogeneous Multidatabase System. IEEE Computer, Vol. 24, 1991.

[ASU86]   A.V. Aho, R. Sethi, and Ullman. Compilers - Principles, Techniques and Tools. Addison-Wesley Publishing Company, 1986.

[CAD+94] R. G. G. Cattell, T. Atwood, J. Duhl, G. Ferran, M. Loomis, and D. Wade. The Object Database Standard: ODMG-93. Morgan Kaufmann Publishing Inc., September 1994.

[Chu90] C.W. Chung. DATAPLEX: An access to heterogeneous distributed databases. Communications of the ACM, 33(1), 1990.

[Car95] M. Carey et al. Towards Heterogeneous Multimedia Information Systems: The Garlic Approach. In Proceedings of the IEEE Workshop on Research Issues in Data Engineering, March 1995.

[Ion95] IONA. Orbix Programming Guide. IONA Technologies Inc., Dublin, Ireland, 1995.

[KFA94] W. Klas, G. Fischer and K. Aberer. Integrating Relational and Object-Oriented Database System using a Metaclass Concept. Journal of Systems Integration, Vol. 4 No. 4, 1994.

[Kim93] W. Kim et al. On Resolving Schematic Heterogeneity in Multidatabase Systems. Journal of Distributed and Parallel Databases, Vol. 1, 1993.

[LMR90] W. Litwin, L. Mark, and N. Roussopoulos. Interoperability of Multiple Autonomous Databases. ACM Computing Surveys, Vol. 22, 1990.

[OMG96] OMG. The Common Object Request Broker: Architecture and specification. Object Management Group, Inc., Revision 2.0, Updated July 1996.

[Su96] S.Y.W. Su et al. NCL: A Common Language for Achieving Rule-Based Interoperability among Heterogeneous Systems. Journal of Intelligent Information SystemsVol. 6, 1996.

[UA95] S. Urban and T.B. Abdellatif. Object-oriented Query Language Access to Relational Databases: A Semantic Framework for Query Translation. Journal of Systems Integration, Vol. 5 No. 5, 1995

[Wu91a] X. Wu. A type system for an object-oriented database system. In Proceedings of the Fifteenth Annual International Computer Software & Applications Conference, pages 333-338, Tokio, Japan, September 11-13 1991. IEEE Computer Society Press.

[Wu91b] X. Wu. A query interface for an object management system. In Proceedings of the 2nd International Conference on Data Base and Expert Systems Applications, Berlin, Springer Verlag, 1991

[Wu96] X. Wu. An architecture for interoperation of distributed heterogeneous database systems. In Proceedings of the 7th International Conference on Data Base and Expert Systems Applications, Zürich, Springer Verlag, LNCS 1134, 1996.

MODELLING ISSUES I

A Practical Formally-Based Modelling Method for Object Oriented Information Systems

Kinh Nguyen

Victoria University of Technology, Melbourne, Australia 3000
kinh@matilda.vut.edu.au

Tharam Dillon

La Trobe University, Melbourne, Australia 3083
tharam@latcs1.cs.latrobe.edu.au

1   Introduction

Most of the popular modelling methods that have been used for object oriented information systems are *informal*, and their use seems to impose certain limits that are difficult to overcome. Firstly, informal methods tend to produce low-quality models. For example, Hayes and Coleman has shown in [5] that the OMT models of Rumbaugh method are ambiguous, incoherent and incomplete. Secondly, informal methods also tend to lead to ineffective modelling processes. The problem can often be traced ultimately to the informal characteristics of the model. Essentially, an imprecise model cannot effectively alert the analyst as to what kinds of information to look for and what kinds of problems to consider; nor does it provide a suitable framework to record all the relevant information obtained during the modelling process.

To address these problems, we propose a simple practical formally-based object oriented modelling method. The method makes use of a small number of formal concepts and techniques from the formal notation Object-Z [3] [6] and Petri nets. For ease of reference, the method is called EMS (Employing a little Mathematics for Specification).

In this paper, we describe the EMS method and highlight its desirable properties. We also illustrate how a fact-based data modelling technique, such as NIAM [4], can be effectively incorporated into the method.

2   Illustration of the EMS Method

Figure 1(a) gives an overview of the EMS method. The core of the method is the *main procedure* in which we construct the four models listed in the big box. The last one, the Object-Z* model, is a complete specification of the system. In addition, we can use suitably chosen *supporting techniques*. Their roles and interactions with the main procedure are discussed in section 3. We will illustrate the EMS method with a simple case study:

> An application is required to maintain information on students and units. Each student has a unique id, a name and a phone number. Each unit has a unique code and a title. A student can enrol in zero or more units and each unit may have zero or more students enrolled in.
>
> The following system operations are needed: (1) add/delete a student to/from the database, (2) add/delete a unit, (3) enrol a student for a unit, (4) withdraw a student from a unit, and (5) change a student's phone number.

2.1 Step 1–Object Relationship Model

The purpose of this model is to capture graphically the usual static properties of the system: the kinds of objects we have in our system; their *literal* attributes; the non-hierarchical relationships among the objects (associations); the hierarchical relationships among objects (aggregation); and the inheritance relationships between the classes.

The common notations for entity relationship modelling are sufficient for our purpose. The Object Relationship model for the Student-Unit system is given in Figure 1(b).

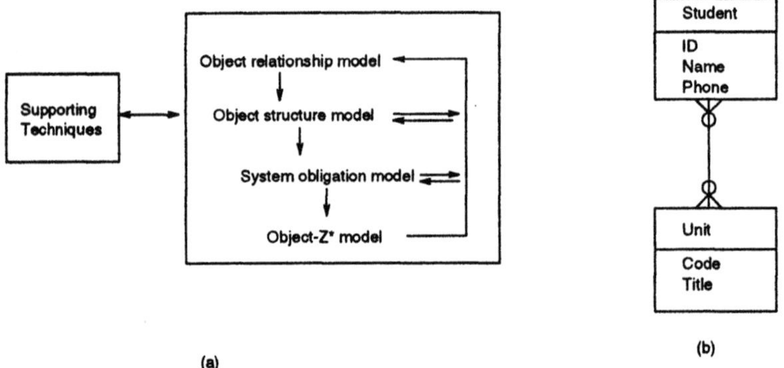

Figure 1: (a) Overall view of the EMS method, (b) Object relationship model for Student-Unit system

2.2 Step 2–Object Structure Model

The purpose of this model is to specify formally (in Object-Z) the *data structure* of objects involved in the system. To construct this model, though the previous model serves as the primary source of information, two kinds of decisions must be made.

First, we need to choose *how to represent the relationships*. In general, we have four choices (for binary relationships): (1) Embed the relationship as attributes in *both* objects; (2) Embed it as an attribute in *one* of the objects; (3) Create a *new* object type to represent the relationship; (4) Do *not* represent the relationship *statically*, but *calculate* it based on the values carried in the objects. For the case study, due to the "symmetry" of the "enrolment" relationship, we choose to represent it in *both* associated objects.

Second, we need to decide on *what attributes the system object should have*. The decision would determine the access entry points (i.e. what O2 calls "hooks") and access paths available to access objects in the system. In general, several choices may exist. For the case study, it is quite reasonable that the system object should have two attributes *students* and *units* of types *Set of Student* and *Set of Unit*, respectively.

With such choices, the following object structure model can be practically derived:

$$[ID, NAME, PHONE, CODE, TITLE]$$

```
┌─ Student ──────────────────────┐   ┌─ Unit ─────────────────────────┐
│ ┌────────────────────────────┐ │   │ ┌────────────────────────────┐ │
│ │ id : ID                    │ │   │ │ code : CODE                │ │
│ │ name : NAME                │ │   │ │ title : TITLE              │ │
│ │ phone : PHONE              │ │   │ │ takenBy : ℙ Student        │ │
│ │ taking : ℙ Unit            │ │   │ └────────────────────────────┘ │
│ └────────────────────────────┘ │   │ ...                            │
│ ...                            │   └────────────────────────────────┘
└────────────────────────────────┘
```

```
┌─ SUSystem ──────────────────────────────────────────────────────────┐
│ ┌──────────────────────────────────────────────────────────────────┐ │
│ │ students : ℙ Student                                             │ │
│ │ units : ℙ Unit                                                   │ │
│ ├──────────────────────────────────────────────────────────────────┤ │
│ │ ∀ s : students • s.taking ⊆ units            (a)                 │ │
│ │ ∀ u : units • u.takenBy ∈ students           (b)                 │ │
│ │ ∀ s : students; u : units •                                      │ │
│ │     s ∈ u.takenBy ⇔ u ∈ s.taking             (c)                 │ │
│ └──────────────────────────────────────────────────────────────────┘ │
│ ...                                                                   │
└───────────────────────────────────────────────────────────────────────┘
```

In above specification, constraints (a) and (b) are *reference integrity* constraints (in this case, they specify that *persons* and *cars* are the *extents* of the two classes). Constraint (c) is a *relationship integrity* constraint (in ODMG-93 Standard, this is enforced by declaring *taking* and *takenBy* to be *inverse attribute* of each other). Most of the constraints belong to these two kinds.

2.3 Step 3–System Obligation Model

The purpose of this model is to describe for each system operation (i.e. an operation that the user can perform against the system) exactly *what* the system has to fulfill. This is given by a special kind of Petri net, which we call "system obligation net", whose formal semantics is given in terms of coloured Petri net. This is based on and extends the idea of using Petri nets for object oriented modelling as explained by Dillon and Tan in [2].

As an example, Figure 2 shows the system obligation for the system operation "Enrol a student in a unit". The net specifies unambiguously: (1) What *input* the system receives from the environment (the student's id and the unit's code); (2) Under what *condition* the system will allow the operation to *go ahead* (the student and the unit exist, and the student has not yet been enrolled in the unit); (3) What *changes* the system may undergo (the student is enrolled in the unit); and (4) The *output* the system will send back to the environment (none in this example).

By constructing a system obligation net for each of the system operations, we obtain the complete system obligation model – complete with respect to all the *update* system operations and pre-defined queries.

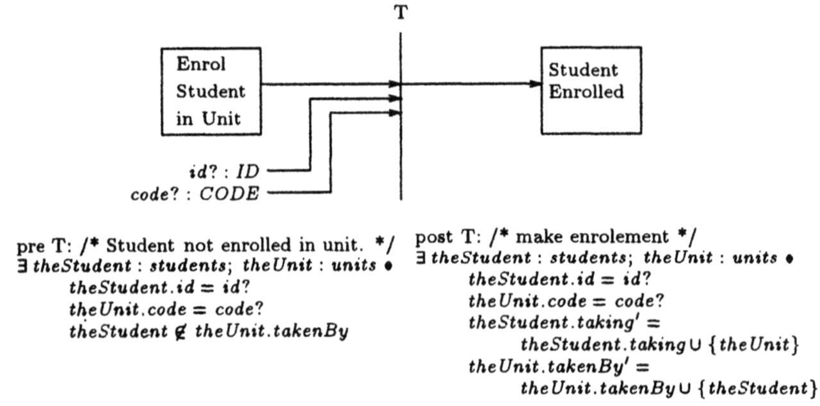

Figure 2: System's obligation diagram for *enrol* operation.

2.4   Step 4–Object-Z* Model

We can now derive a complete specification of the system from the system obligation model. The specification is written in Object-Z*, which is Object-Z with a few simple syntactic modifications. Two modifications used in this paper are concerned with *promotion* of object operation to a higher level: (1) the promotion is denoted inside the higher-level schema by a black right triangle; (2) substitutions of input, output variables are given explicitly, even when they are lexically identical.

To construct the model, we consider each system operation described in the previous model, and work out the services and communications required for all the objects involved.

Consider, for example, the system operation "Enrol a student in a unit". From the system obligation net (Figure 2), we can derive the methods required as follows. The system object (of class *SUSystem*) must provide an instance method: to get the student's id, the unit's code; to check the pre-condition that the student and unit exist and the student has not been enrolled in the unit; and to ensure that the enrolment relationship is updated by sending appropriate messages to the objects involved. Thus the instance method required of the *SUSystem* class is:

$$
\begin{array}{|l}
\hline
\text{\textit{PCSystem}} \\
\quad \begin{array}{|l}
\hline
\text{\textit{Enrol}} \\
\hline
\textit{id?} : \textit{ID} \\
\textit{code?} : \textit{CODE} \\
\hline
\exists\, \textit{theStd} : \textit{students};\ \textit{theUnit} : \textit{units}\ \bullet \\
\quad \textit{theStd.id} = \textit{id?} \\
\quad \textit{theUnit.code} = \textit{code?} \\
\quad \textit{theStd} \notin \textit{theUnit.takenBy} \\
\quad \blacktriangleright\ \textit{theStd.AddUnit(theUnit/unit?)} \\
\quad \blacktriangleright\ \textit{theUnit.AddStudent(theStd/student?)} \\
\hline
\end{array} \\
\quad \cdots \\
\hline
\end{array}
$$

In expression $\blacktriangleright$ *theStudent.addUnit(theUnit/unit?)*, *theUnit* is the "actual parameter" whereas *unit?* is the "formal parameter" defined in operation *AddUnit* given below. The semantics of such an expression is the promotion of operation *AddUnit* with the appropriate substitution of objects drawn from the environment of the system object. Promotions correspond to the sending of messages to other objects. It is then clear that class *Student* and class *Unit* must provide the instance methods specified below:

$$
\begin{array}{|l}
\hline
\text{\textit{Student}} \\
\quad \begin{array}{|l}
\hline
\text{\textit{AddUnit}} \\
\hline
\textit{unit?} \\
\hline
\textit{unit?} \notin \textit{taking} \\
\textit{taking}' = \textit{taking} \cup \{\textit{unit?}\} \\
\hline
\end{array} \\
\quad \text{In the above schema, we omit} \\
\quad \text{the delta list.} \\
\quad \cdots \\
\hline
\end{array}
\qquad
\begin{array}{|l}
\hline
\text{\textit{Unit}} \\
\quad \begin{array}{|l}
\hline
\text{\textit{AddStudent}} \\
\hline
\textit{student?} \\
\hline
\textit{student?} \notin \textit{takenBy} \\
\textit{takenBy}' = \textit{takenBy} \cup \{\textit{student?}\} \\
\hline
\end{array} \\
\quad \cdots \\
\hline
\end{array}
$$

Thus, we have identified and specified all the methods required to support the system operation "Enrol student in unit". By going through all system obligations and collecting all the methods together, *class by class*, we would end up with the complete specification of the system – the Object-Z* model.

2.5 Smalltalk prototyping and ODMG C++ Implementation

The Object-Z* model provides a complete and unambiguous blueprint for prototyping, design and implementation. It is quite straight forward, for example, to convert it into a Smalltalk prototype, for two main reasons. First, because we choose to represent relationships as attributes of objects, all the expressions in the formal specification, with very rare exceptions, are expressed in terms of mathematical *Set* (rather than *relations* or *functions*). Second, Smalltalk provides very good support for *Set* operations. The six methods: *add:, remove:, includes:, detect:, select:, collect:* have been found to be adequate for most applications.

As an illustration, we show below the instance method *Enrol* of *SUSystem* written in Smalltalk (except for the use of ? for input variables). It can be seen that the translation is largely a matter of *substituting* the mathematical expressions by the equivalent Smalltalk expressions.

```
enrolStudent id? inUnit: code?
  | pre theStudent theUnit |
  ''Calculate precondition. Retrieve the student and the unit ''
    theStudent := students detect: [ :s | s id ] ifNone: [ nil ].
    theUnit := units detect: [ :u | u code ] ifNone: [ nil ].
    pre := ( theStudent ~~ nil) & ( theUnit ~~ nil)
          & ( theStudent notIn: theUnit takenBy ).
  ''Effect postcondition.''
    pre ifTrue: [  theStudent addUnit: theUnit.
             theUnit addStudent: theStudent. ]
```

Because object databases typically provide similar facilities to deal with sets of objects, Object-Z* specifications can be easily translated into languages supported by such systems. The code below shows the previous operation in ODMG-93 C++. For more details about the relationship between the ODMG-93 standard and Object-Z, the reader can refer to [8].

```
void  enrol(){
  // get student id, unit code
     char * the_id, the_code;
     cout << ''Enter id and code'';
     cin >> the_id >> the_code;
  // attempt to retrieve student, unit
     database->lookup(Student::students,''students'');
     database->lookup(Unit::units,''units'');
     Ref<Student> the_student;
     Ref<Unit> the_unit;
     oql(the_student,''element(select s from s  \
        in students where s.id = $1s'',  the_id));
     oql(the_unit, ''element(select u from u  \
        in units where u.code = $1s'', the_code));
  // add enrolement if precondition met.
```

```
// Inverse relationship is handled by the DBMS.
  if(the_student && the_unit &&
    !(the_unit.takenBy contains_element(theStudent))
      the_student->enrol( the_unit);
}
```

2.6   Remarks on Multi-staged Obligation Nets

For simplicity, we have used only system obligation nets with a single "stage".
However, we can construct models with several stages as shown in Figure 3
for system operation "Change a student's phone number". Such models are
very close to the way the end user perceives the operation. Therefore, they are
very useful for validation purposes. We refer to them as "multi-staged system
obligation nets". Their formal semantics can also be given in terms of coloured
Petri nets.

We would like to note here, without going into detail, that the use of single-
staged system obligation nets is sufficient to build systems that are completely
functional (any identified system operation can be performed) and consistent
(the state of the system always satisfies the invariants specified in the object
structure model).

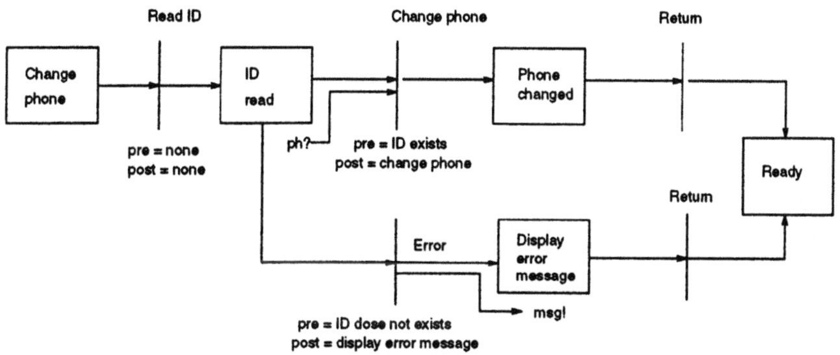

Figure 3: Multi-staged System Obligation Net.

3   The Gymnastics Case Study

In Section 2, we illustrate the basic features on EMS. In practice, depending
on the nature of the system involved, different aspects of the main procedure
may be emphasized and additional techniques may be used. In this section, we
report on a case study to illustrate this point. This case study was originally
published by Iseult White, of Rational Software Corporation [10]. It is sufficiently complicated that the whole book is devoted to it as an illustration of
how the Booch method can be applied to object oriented analysis and design.

3.1   Problem Statement

The purpose of the Gymnastics System is to keep information on the gymnasts, their clubs, the organization of the competitions and the competitions' results. This system is concerned with only one league, which consists of several clubs, and only for one season (this is a slight and immaterial simplification of the requirements given by I. White).

For each gymnast, we record an ID (unique), a name, a date of birth and a gender. Each gymnast belongs to one club. Each club has a name (unique), an address and a phone number.

Meets, Competitions and Events. The season's competition is organized in a series of meets. Each meet is held in the course of one day. Each meet consists of several competitions. Each competition consists of a series of events run on different equipment. Figure 4 shows a sample of the result of a competition in a meet. Each meet is identified by a name and has a date on which it is held. A competition within a meet is identified by its name. Thus, a competition within a meet is identified across the system by the combination of the meet name and the competition name.

```
Meet: Town Invitational
Date: 12/3/96
Competition: Women's Senior Team

              Event Scores

Club          Beam    Vault   Bar    Floor

Flippers      41.5    40.3    44.6   43.7
Acrobats      42.2    38.5    41.0   40.7
Tumblers      38.4    39.8    42.6   41.3
Jugglers      36.2    41.0    37.4   39.6
```

Figure 4: The Scoring of a Competition.

Teams in Competitions. When a club enters a meet, the club enters some subset of its members in a competition. This subset is a team. When a team is in a competition, it must enter all the events of that competition. A team must have the same set of members entered each event within a competition ([10] p.34). Thus a team is identified by the name of the club that it represents and the competition that it enters.

Scoring. Each event in a meet has a judging panel assigned to it. These people are qualified to give scores for this event. Each judge rates each gymnast on the event. The highest and lowest scores will be thrown out, and the rest is averaged to be the gymnast's score for the event. The team score is the sum of all its members' scores. Competition scores are the sum of the scores for each of the event. Meet scores are the sum of the competition scores.

System Operations. The purpose the the Gymnastics System is to help to prepare the schedule of meets for the season, to ensure that qualified judges are assigned, to register teams and gymnasts, to run the meets, and to publish the results in various forms. Some of the system operations are: (a) Register a club in a meet; (b) Register a team in a competition; (c) Assign a judge to an event; (d) Score trials, events and competitions; (e) Mail competition schedules to gymnasts and judges.

3.2   A Case for NIAM as a Supporting Technique

The system presents at least two problems: the problem of *mutating concepts* (described below), and the problem of *complex constraints*.

While "club" and "gymnast" concepts do not pose any problem, concepts such as "competitions", "events", "teams" have to be handled very carefully.

A careful reading of the problem statement reveals two concepts of "competition": (a) one refers to the "competition type" (such as "Women's Senior Team"); (b) the other refers to the "competition in a meet" (such as "Women's Senior Team" in the "Town Invitational" meet). Thus, the term "competition" can change its meaning – the meanings refer to related but quite different concepts. We use the term "mutating concept" to designate this kind of phenomena.

The concept of "team" requires even greater care. As explained by White:

> "When a club enters a meet must it enter all the competitions in the meet? The answer is no. Must a club has the same set of gymnasts entered in all competitions of a meet? Categorically no, or you could not have men's and women's competitions. In fact, the club enters some subset of its members for a competition. This subset is a team." ([10] page 34)

Here we enter two related concepts: (a) the kind of team (e.g. Women's Senior Team), and (b) the actual team that participates in a competition. White seems to get the two concepts totally mixed up:

- In the quote above, "team" takes on the second meaning. In this sense, a gymnast can belong to *many* teams (identified by meet name + competition type name + club name) and a team is for only *one* competition (identified by meet name + competition type name).

- But in Figures 4-9 (p.50) and 5-4 (p.60), the relationship cardinalities are incorrectly given, where it shows that each gymnast can belong to only *one* team and each team can participate in *many* competitions. Perhaps, the term "team" is thought of wrongly in the first sense;

- Then again, in Figure 6-6 (p.71), it is stated that a gymnast can belong to many teams (correct for "team" in the second sense), and a team can belong to many competitions (correct for "team" in the first sense).

In addition, there are numerous constraints that have to be identified and enforced. For example, a gymnast participates in a team must be of certain age and gender, and must belong to the club.

The data model developed by White is based on text analysis of the problem statement (examine nouns, verbs, etc.). Such a process is *labour-intensive* (every noun in principle has to be considered, even briefly, before it can be discarded, or accepted for inclusion or accepted for further consideration), *unsystematic* and *error-prone*.

It is well-known that a fact-based data analysis method such as NIAM [4] can handle the problems mentioned very effectively. In particular, the requirement of identifying the "reference mode" (how "objects" are identified) allows closely related concepts to be readily distinguished.

Thus, for this case study, we have decided to use NIAM as a supporting technique for the construction of the Object Relationship model. We give below a sketch of the extended procedure. A fuller report on the case study is available in [9].

3.3   The Extended Modelling Procedure

3.3.1   Constructing the NIAM Conceptual Schema Diagram

First, we perform fact type analysis and construct the NIAM conceptual schema diagram (NIAM CSD). Though in principle we can identify fact types in any order, we found it very useful to do that in the order of "data dependency". For example, we cannot enter a *competition* until we enter the *meet* that it belongs to. So as a way to facilitate fact type identification, we consider those about *meet* before those about *competition*.

The fact types are identified generally in the following order: (1) competition types, (2) event types, (3) clubs, (4) gymnasts, (5) judges, (6) meets, (7) competitions, (8) events, (9) teams, (10) scorings.

We then go through the fact types to check for errors and identify the dependencies (or constraints). For example, a judge can only judge the events that he/she is qualified for. The dependency also indicates some of the data (or objects) to be held in the database can be automatically generated. For example, as soon as a team and its members are entered, we can generate (incomplete) data related to scoring (to be completed when the scores are entered).

We also obtain the relational schema from the NIAM CSD purely for inspection purpose. The inspection gives us greater confidence in the NIAM model. We find this extra step simple to perform and quite worths the effort.

3.3.2   Constructing the Object Relationship Model

The NIAM CSD contains fact types that can be derived from other fact types. So we first mark all the fact types that we choose not to maintain as persistent data. We then convert the CSD with remaining fact types into the object relationship model (which is just an ER diagram). Generally, simple fact types which attach to a NIAM-entity can be grouped together and form an object (in the object oriented sense). The remaining fact types can be represented as relationships.

3.3.3 Constructing Object Structure Model and the Rest

We now have to decide how the relationships are to be represented. In general, we usually embed the relationships in both objects. However, there are other choices at our disposal.

For example, we may to maintain the direct navigation path from *Gymnast* object to *Club* object, but not vice versa. That is, each *Gymnast* object contains its *Club* object (so when we retrieve a *Gymnast* object we also have its related *Club* object as an *attributes*). In other words, we embed the relationship in the *Gymnast* object. Note that with this choice, given the name of a club, e.g. *clubName?*, we can "calculate" all the club's members by a simple set selection expression:

$$\{g : gymnasts \mid g.club.name = clubName?\}$$

As another example, we may choose not to maintain a static relationship between *Gymnast* and *CompetitionType*. That is, we choose instead to work out this relationship dynamically, when needed, based on *gender* and *age*.

Once the decisions regarding relationship representation have been made, it is straight forward to specify the object structure model. And once the object structure model has been constructed, it is essentially a routine matter to complete the last two models to arrive at the complete Object-Z* specification.

4 Discussion and Conclusion

In this paper, we have presented the EMS method. We have shown that the method produces specifications that are precise, and consists of expressions that can be readily translated into object database languages. Furthermore, for the reasons listed below, we believe the method provides an effective modelling procedure suitable for practical application.

(1) The modelling process is systematic and coherent. Each model of EMS in the main procedure has a clearly defined purpose. There is a natural flow from one step to the next.

(2) The formal contents of the models prompt us to ask the right questions at the right times. In addition, any oversight or omission in one stage can be easily discovered and corrected in the next. Thus, the models provide a very valuable internally generated validation check.

(3) The clearly defined purpose of the models allows us to be flexible while maintaining full control of the development process. For example, if we experience difficulties in the process of constructing the object relationship model, then we can bring in NIAM analysis, and we then know precisely where it fits in (step 1 of the main procedure) and where its results are used (to construct

the object relationship model). In other words, EMS has inherent properties to effectively integrate additional supporting techniques.

(4) EMS models are not difficult to read: the mathematics required is really "minimum" (predicates and sets), and the specification structure is based directly on the familiar object oriented concepts (class, attributes, methods, message sendings, etc.). Moreover, the Object-Z* specification can be readily prototyped or implemented.

(5) Finally, in comparison to the popular industry-strength methods such as Rumbaugh's and Booch's, EMS can get to the relevant information more quickly and record the findings more concisely. Therefore, it should scale up effectively. Moreover, we can always apply the use case approach to decompose a large information system, and apply EMS to small groups of use cases, and then combine them (a similar approach for informal method is proposed in [7]).

References

[1] Cattell R., Ed (1994) *The Object Database Standard: ODMG-93*, Morgan Kaufmann Publishers, San Mateo, California.

[2] Dillon T. S., Tan P. L. (1993) *Object Oriented Conceptual Modelling*, Prentice Hall, Australia.

[3] Duke R., Rose G., Smith G. (1995) Object-Z: a Specification Language Advocated for the Description of Standards, to appear in *Computer Systems and Interfaces*.

[4] Halpin T. (1995) *Conceptual Schema and Relational Database Design*, Addison-Wesley.

[5] Hayes F., Coleman D. (1991) Coherent Models for Object Oriented Analysis, *'91 Conference on Object Oriented Programming, Systems, Languages, and Applications*, ACM Press.

[6] Lano K., Haughton H., Ed (1994) *Object-Oriented Specification Case Studies*, Prentice Hall, Hemel Hempstead, UK.

[7] Lorenz M. (1993) *Object-Oriented Software Development: A Practical Guide*, Prentice Hall, New Jersey.

[8] Nguyen K. (1995) Formal Specification of Object Oriented Databases applications Using Object-Z, *Technology of Object-Oriented Languages and Systems TOOLS 18*, Prentice Hall, Sydney, Australia.

[9] Nguyen K. (1997) *Gymnastics System: A Comparative Case study*. In postscript form at http://matilda.vut.edu.au/ kinh.

[10] White I. (1995) *Using the Booch Method: A Rational Approach*, Adison-Wesley, USA.

Viewpoints in object-oriented databases

Hala NAJA

Centre de Recherche en Informatique de Nancy (CRIN)
B.P. 239, 54506 Vandœuvre-lès-Nancy, France.

Noureddine MOUADDIB

Institut de Recherche en Informatique de Nantes (IRIN)
B.P: 92208, 44322 Nantes, France.

Abstract

*Proposed object-oriented approaches are still in an initial stage of in-
vestigation and are not powerfull enough to modelling Computer-Aided-
Design (CAD) applications which manipulate ill-defined, evolving and
multifaceted objects. In this paper, we argue in favour of a model, called
CEDAR, which aims at easing the modelling process by endowing the
object-oriented approach with a viewpoint notion.*

keywords: object-oriented databases, computer-aided-design (CAD) applications, viewpoint.

1   Introduction

New techniques are needed to help the designer in the development of large
applications. Object-oriented techniques are particularly suited to deal with
such applications, and especially with applications which manipulate complex
objects. However, the object-oriented approach is not powerful enough to
model ill-defined, constantly evolving and multifaceted objects. In the literature, many approaches have been proposed to make up for the deficiencies of
the object-oriented approach: in the database field, some approaches propose
the definition of view mechanisms on top of object-oriented database manager
systems (OODBMS) [1, 5, 20]; in the knowledge representation field, others
propose classification mechanisms for evolving and incomplete objects [12], or
for multifaceted objects [7, 12].

In this paper, we propose a model for object-oriented databases [16, 15]
which addresses applications which need to have different representations of
the real world. It is based on the *viewpoint* notion. A viewpoint leads to a
representation of the world with emphasis on a specific set of concerns. The
resulting representation is an abstraction of the real world, that is, a description
which recognises some distinctions (those relevant to the concern) and ignores
others (those not relevant to the concern). Different viewpoints address distinct
concerns, but there is common ground between them.

In [3], the Ansi/X3/Sparc group distinguished between three levels of data
representations when designing a database: *the conceptual level* which defines

the database schema by using the DBMS data model, *the external level* which defines sub-schemas or views [20, 21] on top of the schema database and *the physical level* which implements data and takes into account constraints in relation with the machine.

The schema defined at the conceptual level contains the *totality* of information of the real world. Its elaboration, especially in the case of large applications such as CAD applications, is a fastidious task because it necessitates to collect into one hierarchy a bulk of knowledge coming from a great number of human experts.

To facilitate the elaboration of a database schema, we propose to consider a schema as a *multifaceted entity*, which can have many representations. A representation of a schema is a hierarchy describing the real world according to a viewpoint. So that, the totality of information about the real world is not, as used to, collected into one hierarchy, but is sliced into several hierarchies. Each hierarchy can be conceived by a different designer. No integration of the different hierarchies is needed.

The rest of this paper is organised as follows: section 2 briefly discusses the limitation of the object-oriented approach to capture viewpoints on entities and introduces the main features of a model with viewpoints. Section 3 presents the main characteristics of CEDAR. Section 4 discusses the modelling of a CAD application with the model. Section 5 briefly presents the CEDAR system. Finally, section 6 concludes and gives some directions for future work.

2 From mono-viewpoint to multi-viewpoints object models

According to the conventional object-oriented model, an object is a direct [1] member of a single class which is its instantiation class. Instantiation is fixed definitely at creation time and consequently an object can never be a direct member of more than one class at the same time. This constraint called in [6], the constraint of *unique and fixed representation*, turns out to be rigid for modelling real world situations. Indeed, real world objects often have to be described from different viewpoints (multi-expertise), and an object description should be able to evolve reflecting the changes of the real world object (especially for long-lived objects). Many approaches have pointed out this limitation. We can cite some: in [4, 19, 18, 2, 10, 11], the *role* concept is proposed. In [6] the *multiple inheritance* is used to express viewpoints on objects. In [9], the *subject* notion is proposed. It is defined by an hierarchy of classes describing the structure of the real world according to a viewpoint. A detailed study of these approaches and comparison between them can be found in [17].

Defining a multi-viewpoint model needs to extend conventionally object model, that we call mono-viewpoint model, by additional capabilities or features which are:

---

[1]an object is also a non direct member of all super-classes of its instantiation class.

1. **MR**–*Multiple Representation of an entity*:
   it consists in the capacity of supplying multiple descriptions or representations to the same entity; each one describing it according to a viewpoint.

2. **IR**–*Independence between Representations*:
   different designers can separately define their representation of an entity, without any one needing to know the details associated with this entity by others.

3. **CR**–*Communication between Representations*:
   when defining a partial representation of an entity, a designer can need to access to some information defined by another designer and associated to the same entity. Therefore, communication between representations is an interesting feature.

4. **RMR**–*Referential of the Multiple Representation*:
   Referential of the multiple representation is a « pre-representation » on which rely partial representations. It is a description of an entity independently of any viewpoint.

5. **CMR** – *Coherence of the Multiple Representation*:
   to ensure the coherence of the multiple representation, two kinds of constraints must be defined : constraints which ensure a local validity of partial representations, and (2) constraints which ensure compatibility betweeen partial representations.

6. **EMR**–*Evolution of the Multiple Representation*:
   during its life, an entity does not keep the same representations, but it can undertake or relinquish numerous partial representations. So, it is important to endow the multiple representation with evolution capabilities.

In the following section, we propose the CEDAR model which is an object model extended with the viewpoint notion and which is defined with the goal of endowing it by the six features defined above. In this paper, we detail how the four first features are managed. The fifth is out of the scope of this paper. It is studied in detail in [13]. The sixth one has not been studied yet.

3   The CEDAR Model

The CEDAR model is based on the conventional concepts of the object-oriented approaches. Thus, it relies on the objects and classes notions and on the inheritance and instantiation mechanisms. Objects do not have behaviour and multiple inheritance is not authorised.

In CEDAR, not only objects can be considered according to different viewpoints, but also classes, schemas and bases. Objects, classes, bases and schemas are considered the base entities of our model.

84

Contrary to standard models where each base entity has only one representation (a value or state for an object, a structure or type [2] for a class, a hierarchy for a schema, a set of objects for a base), in CEDAR, each base entity (object, class, schema or base) of the model, can have many representations. Thus, we call *multiview object*, an object which has many states, *multiview class*, a class which has many structures, *multiview base*, a base which is defined by many sets of objects and *multiview schema*, a schema which is defined by many hierarchies. More generally, we call *multiview entity*, an entity which has many representations.

In section 3.1, we detail these four notions.

3.1 The multiple representation in CEDAR

The multiple representation of a multiview entity consists in splitting its representations in many parts: (1) a part containing properties which form the referential of the multiple representation (*RMR* feature, see § 2), and (2) parts containing partial representations, which are entities, called *view-entities*; these parts ensure the independence in the multiple representation (*IMR* feature, see § 2). A view-entity is tied to the mutliview entity by a relation denoted $\Re_{view-of}$.

In the following paragraphs, we define the four types of multiview entities defined in CEDAR.

3.1.1 Multiview class

A multiview class has many types or structures:

- a structure describing a set of real entities independently of any viewpoint; it is the structure of the multiview class itself and constitutes the referential of the multiple representation (*RMR* feature, § 2).

- a set of structures, called *partial* structures, such that each one describes a set of real entities according to a viewpoint; these structures are split into classes called, *view-classes*. The type of a view-class is a sub-type of the *mvc* type.

3.1.2 Multiview object

A multiview object is an instance of a multiview class *mvc*. It has many states or values:

- a value which describes the multiview object independently of any viewpoint; its type is that of the instantiation class *mvc*; it constitutes the referential of the multiple representation (*IMR* feature, § 2).

---

[2] The type of a class is defined recursively from the following constructors : atomic types (real, integer,...), tuple type, list and set.

- a set of values, called *partial* states, such that each one describes the multiview object according to a viewpoint; these states are split into objects called *view-objects*. Each view-object is an instance of a view-class which is tied to the multiview class *mvc*.

3.1.3 Multiview schema

A multiview schema is a schema defined by many hierarchies:

- an hierarchy h, composed by multiview classes tied together by specialization/generalisation links; it constitutes the referential of the multiple representation (*IMR* feature, § 2); it models the structure real world independently of any viewpoint.

- a set of hierarchies, called *partial* hierarchies, such that each one describes the structure of the real world according to a viewpoint; these hierarchies are split into schemas called, *view-schemas*. A partial hierarchy is composed by view-classes, imported classes from h, and monoview classes which are classes added in the partial hierarchy and not linked to any class in h. In a partial hierarchy, the specialization/generalisation links between classes are submitted to some conditions which are not presented in this paper.

3.1.4 Multiview base

A multiview base owns many sets of objects:

- a set s of multiview objects such that each one describes a real entity independently of any viewpoint; this set is contained in the multiview base itself.

- sets of objects such that each one gathers objects which represent real entities according to a viewpoint; these sets are split into bases called *view-bases*. A view-base is composed by view-objects, and monoview objects which are added in the view-base and not linked to any object, and imported objects from the s.

As we have mentioned before, view entities have been defined to model partial representations of multiview entities. Each view-entity (*i.e* view-base, view-schema, view-object and view-class) is tied to its multiview base by a relation, denoted $\Re_{view-of}$. We call *similar* entities, view-entities that are tied to the same multiview entity by a $\Re_{view-of}$ relation.

3.2 Visibility between viewpoints

Different viewpoints address distinct representations. Some information defined in a viewpoint must be accessed by another viewpoint [3]. Therefore we have

---

[3] It is the *CMR* feature (see § 2).

defined a link called the **visibility link** which allows a view-class vc to access some attributes contained in the structure of another class vc'. vc and vc' must be *similar*.

A visibility link is defined from a view-class vc to another view-class vc'; it is based on the definition of a *filter* which makes visible some attributes of vc to vc'. A filter is defined by:

- an input: it contains the entire structure of view-class vc;

- an output: it contains the result of the filtering, which is a set of attributes selected from vc and made visible to vc'.

4   CAD applications–some characteristics

The design process in CAD applications can be considered as the transition from the object to conceive to the realized object over a number of intermediate steps. The design process is characterised by at least two important aspects which make the management of multiple representations necessary:

- the evolution aspect: the design of an object is not achieved during one operation but needs the succession of many operations such that each one refines and enriches the description of the object. Generally, three representation levels [8] are identified: the geometrical level, the qualitative level and the quantitative level.

- the multi-expert aspect: generally, an object is not elaborated by one person. Its realization often needs the intervention of many experts who work towards the elaboration of the object. Each expert has his own representation of the object. Interaction between representations must be possible.

4.1   How to model an architectural application with CEDAR

Our present study deals with the multi-expert aspect of the design process and it is based on a restricted application domain, that of architecture. The realizations of architectural objects (wall, floor, ceiling,...) need to realize several functionalities (acoustic, thermal, water-resistance, basic-structure, electrical installation,...). Each functionality defines a viewpoint on objects because it determines specific representations on them. To simplify the example, let us consider vertical faces only and focus on basic-structure, thermal, and water-resistance functionalities.

4.1.1   Multiview schema of the architectural application

In figure 1, a multiview schema containing only one multiview class is created. Also, three view-schemas are created: *S-Stb*, *S-Wr* and *S-The*; each one is defined in a viewpoint and contains view-classes and monoview classes.

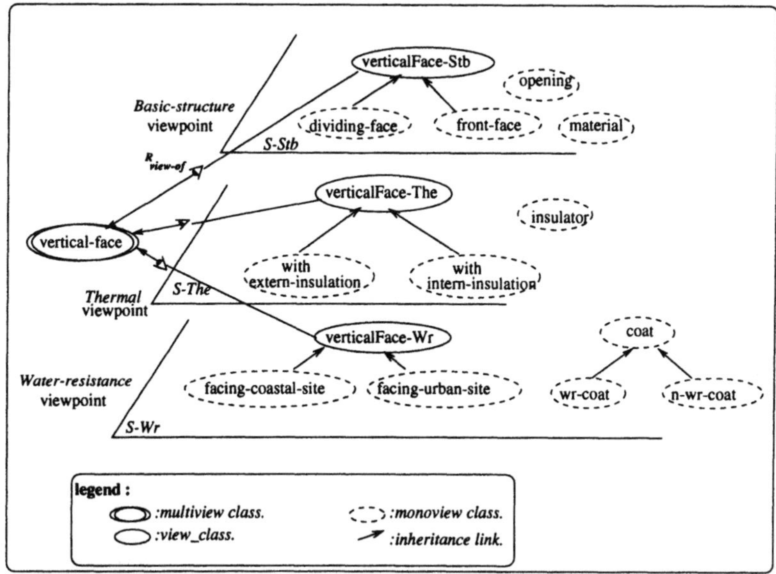

Figure 1: *Modelling vertical faces according to three viewpoints.*

View-classes *verticalFace-Stb*, *verticalFace-Wr* and *verticalFace-The* are linked by $\Re_{view-of}$ relations to multiview classes *vertical-face*. Each view-class can have specific attributes. For instance, *verticalFace-Stb* is described by **height**, **width**, **limits**, **openings**, **material-coat** and **same-kind-spaces** attributes.

In the *Thermal* viewpoint (see figure 2), the material coat (basic-structure data) and the coating coat (water-resistance data) used must be known in order to calculate the resistance of the vertical face. In the same way, in the *Water-resistance* viewpoint, the material coat (basic-structure data) must be known in order to choose the coating coat. Therefore, the definition of visibility links is necessary.

In figure 2, three visibility links are defined: the first two links, the filters of which are f and g, select attributes **material-coat** and **coating-coat**, defined respectively in the *verticalFace-Stb* and *verticalFace-Wr* classes, and make those attributes visible to view-class *verticalFace-The* .

As the visibility link, the filter of which is h, it selects the **material-coat** attribute defined in *verticalFace-Wr* and makes it visible to view-class *verticalFace-The*.

4.1.2 Multiview Base of the architectural application

The architectural application has B as multiview base, which is associated with the multiview schema S. It contains a set of multiview objects. View-bases *B-Stb*, *B-The* and *B-Wr* are view-bases associated with respectively *S-Stb*, *S-The* and *S-Wr*. Each view-base contains view-objects and monoview objects, and is linked to B by a $\Re_{view-of}$ relation.

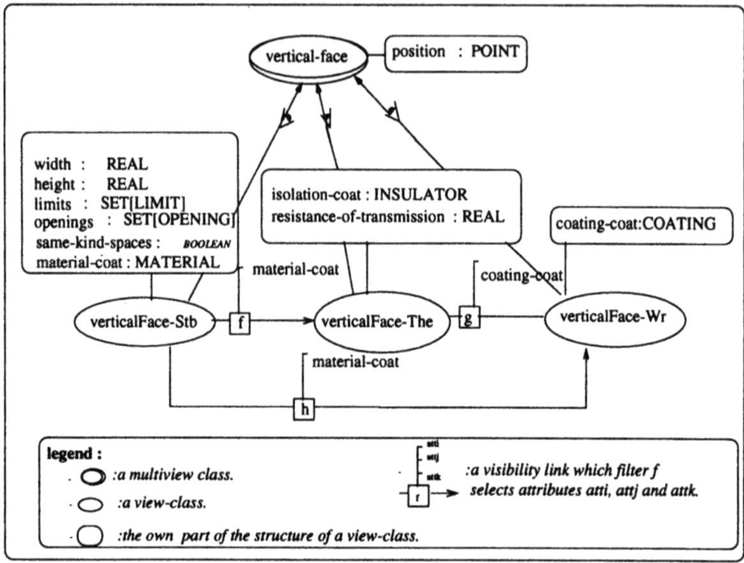

Figure 2: *Definition of visibility links between view-classes.*

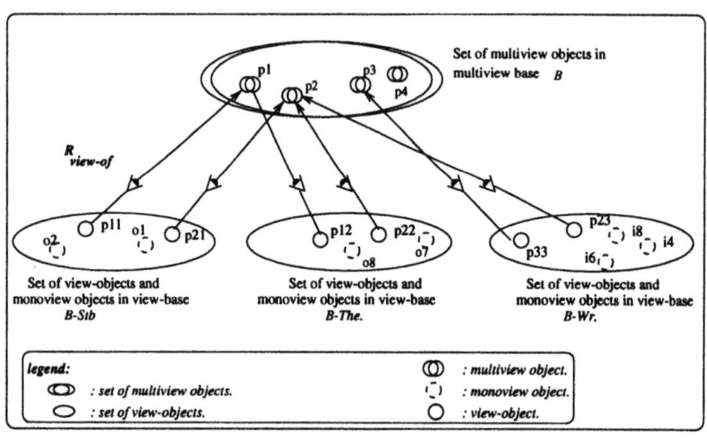

Figure 3: *The bases of the architectural application.*

Figure 3 shows portions of the four bases. Each multiview object in base B can have (none, one or more than one) partial representations. Each representation is modelled by a view-object.

5 The CEDAR system

This project is the subject of a prototype implemented in Smalltalk-80. The MVC (Model, View, Controller) architecture of the language makes easy the elaboration of user interfaces.

The CEDAR model is implemented by a Smalltalk schema, called *meta-schema* to differentiate it from schemas created by CEDAR application. The CEDAR meta-schema is composed of Smalltalk classes, called Cedar-meta-classes, which implement the concepts of the model (multiview class, view-class, multiview schema,...). Each time, a designer creates an entity (a schema, a base,...) the corresponding meta-class is instantiated. The meta-schema is not visible to users.

The created system is an environment for modelling applications according to different viewpoints; it provides tools allowing the elaboration of schemas and the creation of bases; it is composed of a set of browsers, which allow navigation and manipulation of schemas and bases of a CEDAR application. A browser is a window comprising views. Each view deals with a kind of entity (objects, classes,...) and can have a set of sub-views associated with it which provide a lower level of detail of entities. A view can have menus allowing the manipulation (creation, delete, update) of entities. The system allows the intervening of many : on the one hand the coordinator who supervises the modelling activity and elaborates the referential of the multiple representation. On the other hand the experts who model the different partial representations.

The tools provided by the CEDAR system are:

- the *multiview schema* Browser: it allows the coordinator to create or update the multiview schema of an application. Also, it permits other designers to navigate in the hierarchy of the multiview schema,

- the *multiview base* Browser: it allows the coordinator to create or update the multiview base of an application. Also, it permits other designers to browse through the multiview base objects,

- the *view schema* Browser: it allows an expert to design a viewpoint, or to create or update the view-schema of the viewpoint. Moreover, it permits the filtering of attributes from view-classes defined in other view-schemas.

- the *view base* Browser: it allows an expert to create or update its view-base.

Due to space limitation, we cannot give further details on implementation aspects (refer to [14]).

6 Conclusion

In this paper, we propose a model which extends the conventionally object-oriented approach with the viewpoint notion. This model relies on six features (see § 2) and has two main characteristics:

- multiple representation of *each* base entity of the model: the object, the class, the schema and the base;

- visibility between viewpoints: a *visibility* link based on the *filter* notion is defined; it allows a view-class to access attributes belonging to another view class.

The presented approach facilitates the elaboration of the conceptual level(*i.e.* the designing of the database schema): it proposes to split up a schema into individual sub-schemas which reduce its complexity. Another advantage of this approach is that it brings up the task of designing the database schema into sub-tasks which can be performed by different designers.

A system implemented in Smalltalk-80 is realized. It has been validated on an architectural application, which is a CAD application.

Although CEDAR has proved its efficiency, it is not completely satisfactory for, at least, the following reasons:

- as the model is intended to be used in a DBMS, it would be interesting to define a request language which can question objects according to a specific viewpoint. An outline of a request langage for CEDAR is presented in [13]. Also, it is important to study the implementation of our model in a DBMS,

- the model does not attach behaviour to objects. Our proposition of describing objects according to many viewpoints is limited to the static aspect (*i.e.* attributes). In the future, this proposition must be extended to capture the dynamic aspect (*i.e.* methods), and to express several behaviours of a same object according to different viewpoints.

References

[1] S. Abiteboul and A. Bonner. Objects and views. In *International Conference on Management of Data*, pages 238–247, Denver, Colorado, June 1991.

[2] A. Albano, R. Bergamini, G. Ghelli, and R. Orsini. An object data model with roles. In *Proceedings of 19th VLDB, VLDB'93*, pages 39–51, Dublin, Ireland, 1993.

[3] ANSI/SPARC. Study group on data management systems : interim report. *FDT, ACM*, 7(2), March 1975.

[4] C.W. Bachman. The role concept in data models. In *3rd International Conference on Very Large Databases, VLDB'77*, pages 464–476, Tokyo, China, October 1977.

[5] E. Bertino. A view mechanism for object-oriented databases. In *3rd international conference on Extending database technology, EDBT'92*, pages 136–151, Vienna, Austria, March 1992.

[6] B. Carré, L. Dekker, and J. Geib. Multiple and evolutive representation in the ROME language. In *Conference TOOLS*, Paris, France, June 90.

[7] J. Ferber and P. Volle. Using coreference in object oriented representations. In *ECAI 88*, pages 238–240, 1988.

[8] Y. Gardan. *La CFAO : Introduction, techniques, et mise en oeuvre.* Hermes edition, December 1991. *3ème édition entièrement revue et complétée.*

[9] W. Harrison and H. Ossher. Subject-oriented programming (a critique of pure objects). In *8th ACM Conference on Object-Oriented Prgramming Systems, Languages and Applications, OOPSLA'93*, pages 411–428, Washington, D.C., September 1993.

[10] B. Kristensen. Object-oriented modeling with roles. In *2nd international conference on Object-Oriented Information Systems, OOIS'95*, pages 57–71, Dublin, Irlande, December 1995.

[11] B. Kristensen and O. Østerbye. Roles: Conceptual abstraction theory and practical languages issues. *Theory and Practice of Object Systems*, 2(3):143, 1996.

[12] O. Mariño, F. Rechenmann, and P. Uvietta. Multiple perspectives and classification mechanism in object-oriented representation. In *ECAI*, pages 425–430, Stockholm, July 1990.

[13] H. Naja. Towards a model for multiple representation handling constraints. In *IVème Rencontres des Jeunes Chercheurs en Intelligence Artificielle, RJCIA'96*, pages 159–166, Nantes, France, August 1996.

[14] H. Naja. *CÈDRE : un modèle pour une représentation multi-points de vue dans les bases d'objets*. PhD thesis, Université Henri Poincaré – Nancy 1, July 1997.

[15] H. Naja, Y. Lahlou, and B. Comte. Une approche basée sur les points de vue pour la modélisation et l'interrogation de données dentaires. In *INFormatique des ORganisations et Systèmes d'Information et de Décision, INFORSID'96*, pages 119–137, Bordeaux, France, June 1996.

[16] H. Naja and N. Mouaddib. The multiple representation in an architectural application. In *6th International Conference on Database and Expert Systems Applications, DEXA'95,*, pages 237–246, London, United Kingdom, September 1995. in Lecture Notes in Computer Science, n: 978.

[17] H. Naja and N. Mouaddib. Un modèle pour la représentation multiple dans les bases de données orientées-objet. In *Langages et Modèles à Objets, LMO'95*, pages 173–189, Nancy, France, October 1995.

[18] M.P. Papazoglou. Roles: a methodology for representing multifaceted objects. In *2nd International Conference on Database and EXpert systems Applications, DEXA'91*, pages 7–12, Berlin, Germany, 21-23 August 1991.

[19] B. Pernici. Objects with roles. *ACM/IEEE office information systems in SIGOIS Bulletin*, 11(2-3):205–215, 1990.

[20] E. Rundensteiner. Multiview: a methodology for supporting multiple views in object-oriented databases. In *Proc. of the 18th VLDB Conference*, pages 187–198, Vancouver, Canada, 1992.

[21] C. Souza Dos Santos. Design and implementation of object-oriented views. In *6th International Conference on Database and EXpert systems Applications, DEXA95*, volume 978 of *Lecture Notes in Computer Science*, pages 91–102, 1995.

CONSTRUCTION OF A MODELLING FRAMEWORK FOR
HEALTH INFORMATION

Ryder Paul, Pervan Graham & McDermid Donald
Curtin University of Technology, Perth

Abstract:

Substantial national and international resources have been invested in the research and development of a number of health information models, eg. the National Health Information Model (NHIM), the NSW Health Community Health Information Model (CHIM), the American Joint Working Group for a Common Data Model (JWG-CDM) and the CEN (Comite Europeen de Normalisation) European Healthcare Record Architecture. Although these models have assisted in the development of a standard definition and structure, they only address the data requirements of an organisation and have been developed through the identification of agreed patterns of data. This paper discusses the benefits of developing an information framework that incorporates the business functions and behaviour as well as data, and argues that the framework be Object-Oriented (OO).

1. Introduction

Over the past several years substantial national and international resources have been invested in the research and development of a number of health information models, eg. the National Health Information Model (NHIM), the NSW Health Community Health Information Model (CHIM), the American Joint Working Group for a Common Data Model (JWG-CDM) and the CEN (Comite Europeen de Normalisation) European Healthcare Record Architecture. In Australia the NHIM has been proposed as a framework for all health information modelling to improve the overall information standards and support in the health industry, and the CHIM has obtained substantial endorsement as a representation of community health data. Both of these models have been developed using Entity-Relationship (ER) techniques, with the CHIM model consisting of over 200 entities and 500 relationships. An iterative approach across organisational boundaries has been taken in the development of these models focusing on the identification of common patterns of data. Although these models have assisted in the development of standard data definitions and structure, they do not provide a framework for the validation and consistent implementation of a health information model.

The production of a common model of data that can be applied consistently across organisational boundaries is contingent upon the belief that data remains constant across the different organisations. The Joint Working Group for a Common Data Model, stated: *"These approaches are based on the recognition that...the subject matter for health care is drawn from a data model of health care and health care processes. It follows that a common data model of the health care domain can be used as the starting point of any health care standard"*, (JWG-CDM, 1996, pp3-4). Representing this data in the form of a data model or Entity-Relationship (ER) model further assumes that there are consistent relationships that can be modelled. A common model of data does not provide a solution to discrete differences in function or behaviour between organisations. There are identified problems associated with separating models of function and data *"...Owing to the fact that they are designed around how a certain behaviour shall be carried out (this being a common area of modification), modifications often generate major consequences"* (Jacobsen, 1992).

This paper discusses the benefits of developing an information framework that incorporates the business functions and behaviour as well as data, and argues that the framework be Object-Oriented (OO). An object-oriented healthcare information framework would provide models that represent the business, and assist in the implementation and interpretation of any derived object-oriented business models more effectively, rather than developing a single generic data model based on agreed patterns of data. The development of the framework specifically addresses the requirements of the community based health industry, but the proposed framework should not be regarded as addressing the health industry's requirements exclusively. These requirements are primarily related to the analysis, representation, communication and management of organisational information, and they could equally be applied to any other industry or information collection environment, with problems and conditions similar to those observed in the healthcare industry.

2. Community Based Health Domain

It is beyond the scope of this paper to provide a detailed description of the healthcare industry. As community based health has been chosen as the initial testing ground, a general overview will assist in understanding certain issues and aspects of the proposed approach. In simplistic terms the community based health area is involved in the delivery of services, including health and welfare services to the wider community. It covers all aspects of health and welfare outside of institutional environments, eg. hospitals. The development of a common model of community based health is difficult due to the diverse range of organisations involved; the different types of clients, multi-disciplined service providers and autonomous management and service delivery. The identification of the recipients of services can be difficult due to the numerous types of clients and related issues requiring intervention. Add to this different sources of funding and management, and the business of providing community based services becomes extremely complex. Therefore, it is proposed that an information framework that is able to support community based health organisations would also provide the basis for a future generic health information framework that can be applied to all health related organisations. The following is a high-level overview of the key components of service delivery within community based health care:

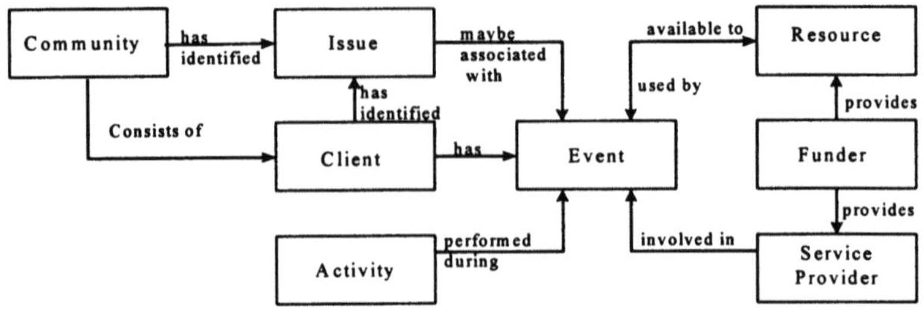

figure 1. Community Based Health Care Overview

2.1 Key Components of Community Based Health Care

There are a number of key components within a community based health care model, as shown in figure 1. These include:

Community: A community can broadly be described as a collection of individuals, organisations or groups brought together under a common interest: "group with shared origins or interests; the public society" (Collins, 1996).

Issue: An issue is a broad term related to the identification of a specific need by the community or client. This can include health or welfare issues. An issue may affect more than one client but have no relationship between the individual clients, eg. asthma, or it may be an issue that affects more than one client with a recognised common source, eg. earthquake.

Activity: An activity is the unit of work associated with an event. This can be in the form of a client intervention (service activity), non-client related activity, eg. administration, education and training, or a client activity not associated with a service delivery, eg. population activity.

Client: Clients are the recipients of community based health care(CBHC) activities. There has been much debate on what or who are the clients CBHC. In a hospital environment it is fairly well agreed that services are provided to "patients" and on the whole a patient is an individual. However, in the CBHC arena a client may be an individual, an organisation, a group of individuals or a group of organisations.

Event: An event is an identified period of time when a recognised activity is performed. An event can incorporate one or more clients, one or more service providers and one or more resources. An event in CBHC may not have a related client, eg. administrative or service provider education, and may not have a related service provider, eg. an earthquake in a community may be regarded as a community or population event.

Service Provider: A service provider is involved in the delivery of services to clients. A service provider can be identified as an individual or an internal or external organisation. The role of the service provider is to deliver services to a client or the community to satisfy identified issues. The services provided are dependent on the availability of service providers with the necessary level of skills and associated resources.

Resource: Resources can be classified as financial, facility, asset or consumable. Human resources have been extracted and classified as service providers.

Funder: Funding for community based health care services can be provided from a number of different sources. The complexity of financial funding requires the identification of the source of funding for each service delivered.

3. Developing a Community Based Health Care Information Model

In order to provide a common model which supports the business of community based health care as described above, it is necessary to represent the data, the business rules and the functions. Each community based health care organisation performs functionally similar tasks and the generic data captured is similar, however the rules and operations applied to the business are implemented differently throughout the community based health care environment. The different rules are not just between states bodies or organisations, they can be at different levels within a single community based service delivery unit. It is essential that any model is able to accommodate an individual organisation's requirements, whilst retaining a common approach to the documentation of data and functional processing.

3.1 Current Modelling Methods

The introduction and use of methodologies has provided an approach to the analysis, design and development of information systems. A number of analysis and design methods have been introduced over the years, which have basically provided approaches to the modelling of data and functions. However, they have been developed to model only one aspect of an organisation, eg. data in data models, activities and process models, activity decomposition or function models. It is quite often left to the ability of the analyst to demonstrate the link between the different components, eg. describe how the data and function models are related.

Interpreting many of the aspects of community based health care using an entity-relationship model can be difficult due to the inability to represent the business rules associated with the relationships between entities. The previous description of a client is one particular example as it requires the ability to define the type of client and differentiate the attributes associated with each entity. The operators and processing of a client may also differ between organisations, which cannot effectively be represented in a data model, eg. registration of clients in some organisations is only possible after ensuring that they are eligible for the services requested. However, in other situations, a client may be registered simply on notification of the request for service. Although the relationships between entities can be represented in a data model (as in figure 2 below), the business rules and selection criteria cannot.

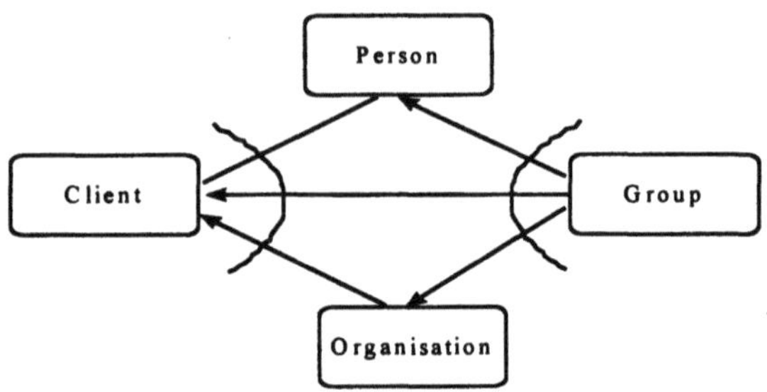

Figure 2. Client Related Entities Data Model Representation

A fundamental component of any community based health model is the incorporation of event related data. The event entity identifies some level of activity or intervention for a specific period. An event can take on numerous roles including: service activity, a community or population event, eg. a natural disaster effecting a community or the population, and a non-client related event, eg. education or training. The type of event is also dependent on the type of community based organisation, ie. indicates the types of services that can be provided, service provider and type of client. Each event may have different attributes dependent on the event type, but requires the collection of common data, eg. who was the event for (client)?, what activity was involved (service)?, where was it performed (location)? and when was it performed (date & time)?. The representation of the relationships between entities associated with events is complex, with numerous optional selection criteria.

The existing models of health data have been based on accepted data modelling principles, mainly entity-relationship modelling. *"...entity-relationship model adopts the more natural view that the real world consists of entities and relationships. It incorporates some of the important semantic information about the real world.."* (Chen, 1976). These models assume a level of abstraction in order to provide a generic model that can be more easily understood by users. The abstraction components include *"Aggregation: the relationship between objects is regarded as a higher level object, and Generalisation: a set of similar objects is regarded as a generic object"*, (Smith & Smith, 1977, pp. 105-133, Codd, 1971, pp.33-64). The concept of abstraction is an important aspect of all the models as it supports the development of hierarchical levels of the models providing a means of including relationships with possibly different interpretation across organisations, *"...With each new product, it was necessary to learn a new way to implement even simple actions"* (Khoshafian, 1990, pp. 274). Unfortunately, the introduction of aggregation and generalisation in complex data models can lead to difficulties in interpretation and communication to a wider audience *"a system may have too many details for a single abstraction to be intellectually manageable"* (Smith & Smith, 1977, pp. 105).

The JWG-CDM has used a common method of identifying patterns of data entities and is consistent with work conducted by many other groups. Peter Coad (1992) discussed the use of patterns based on the Websters Dictionary's definition of a pattern: *"a fully realised form, original or model accepted or proposed for imitation: something regarded as a normative example to be copied; archetype; exemplar"* (Coad, 1992, pp. 152). The identification of patterns in the definition of a standard model is the most widely used approach adopted by the JWG-CDM, NHIM and the CHIM. It supports the assumption that there is commonality of data that can be modelled and agreed by suitably qualified and informed groups. Although a legitimate approach, it lacks an overarching framework that explains how the data models were derived; why there is consistency in the data and relationships between organisations, and the ability to validate the models other than by consensus, *"..patterns have been an important aspect of much actual re-use. However, the emphasis is on documentation rather than specification, and certainly there is no concern for verification of correctness"* (Butler & Lan, 1995, pp.143).

ER models by definition include the relationships between the entities. In order to provide a generic data model it is often necessary to develop generic relationships, eg. the relationships tend to become optional with many-to-many cardinality. Without substantial explanation it becomes difficult to determine how aspects of the model support the specific business requirements of an organisation, and the models must be modified for specific implementation. The NHIM is one such example: it is a very high level entity-relationship model incorporating aspects of generalisation and aggregation. The inclusion of numerous relationships between the entities is difficult to follow, and possibly superfluous at the level of generalisation.

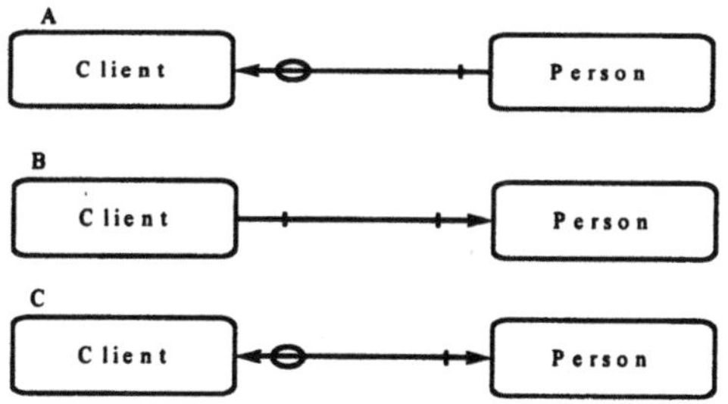

Figure 3. Different Implementation of Client Relationships

Figure 3 demonstrates how the interpretation of a model can differ with a change in the relationship between health organisations. A, B and C indicate organisations where a client must be a person, however the relationships represent differences in implementation and interpretation. "A" indicates that the client is optional, but a person must exist before creating a client and a person can have more than one client record; "B" tells us that the client and person records are mandatory, but a client can consist of many person records; whilst "C" could be an aggregation and generalisation of the relationships expressed in A and B. What is required is a technique which enables each of the different implementations of the relationship to be documented whilst retaining a consistent definition of the data. The examples in figure 3 are only some of the possible instances found in different community based organisations. Add to this the complexity described in figure 2, and a single data model can become extremely difficult to document.

3.2 Object-Oriented Information Modelling

Why propose that the framework use an object-oriented method? *"Object orientation provides a more direct and natural representation of real-world problems..... Object-oriented concepts are abstract data typing, inheritance and object identity"* (Khoshafian, 1992). The proposed framework would provide the structure to analyse, develop and validate health information models, and it could be argued that the models could equally be ER models or the existing health data models. However, an OO technique provides a more holistic approach to organisational modelling, *"Most of the methods used in the industry today, for both information and technical systems development, are based on a functional and/or data driven decomposition of the system. These approaches differ in many ways from the approach taken by object-oriented methods where data and functions are highly integrated"* (Jacobson, 1992, pp. 465). The incorporation of models using techniques that only model one aspect of the organisation, eg. the data, would lose the integration between the data and the function, which could possibly lead to confusion in the interpretation of the models.

The development of an approach incorporating function and data that can be applied across organisational boundaries would provide greater consistency in the interpretation and implementation of any models. Rather than attempting to provide an all-encompassing data model through the recognition of common patterns of data entities, it would be more appropriate to develop a framework that can be applied consistently to each implementation, whilst incorporating specific aspects of the organisation, eg. include an organisation's business rules, specification of relationships at implementation. This could clearly define the functions and their associated data.

The use of an OO approach would not necessarily invalidate previous research and ER models, as the identification of health objects will utilise previous research in the identification of patterns within health data. However, the objects will also include the functions and behaviour through the inclusion of object instances and operations. An OO model could adopt much of the data and attribute definition from existing ER models.

4. Object-Oriented Health Information Framework

The word "framework" is used widely. The *Collins Dictionary* (1996) defines a framework as: *"a structure made of parts joined to form a frame; one designed to enclose a frame"*, whilst the *Oxford Dictionary* (1992) defines it as: *"put together, construct; a supporting structure"*. The JWG-CDM's (1996) definition of a framework is: *"a structure of processes and specifications designed to support the accomplishment of a specific task."* The JWG's task is the development of the CDM, and the framework incorporates the processes associated with the development, review and validation of the data models. They claim that a *"..data model provides a structured method for detailing the data content including explicit specification of data definitions and statement of the semantic links"*(JWG, 1996). The JWG framework supports the organisational and project based tasks associated with the development of the data model, not the data model definition. This has inherent weaknesses associated with the development of the models recognised by the JWG-CDM statement that the development of consistent data models is only possible if *"....individuals who serve on the JWG-CDM are actively involved in the data modeling activities"*. The weakness of this approach is that in order to understand and develop the common models, an organisation must participate in the development process. The framework will support the consistent implementation across organisational boundaries and will not be reliant on other non-related variables associated with the development of health models.

4.1 Object-Oriented Framework

The structure and contents of the theoretical framework has yet to be defined. However, as a minimum, it must incorporate support for:

Identification of Common Organisational Components (*Classes, Complex Objects & Objects*): the existing data modelling work has provided evidence to support common data entities across organisational boundaries. Using an object-oriented framework will extend this work to introduce common objects and classes. The classes will define the structure and instances of the class identifying behaviour of interface operations of objects (Achuthan et. al., 1995, pp. 116). The objects will encapsulate common definition of attributes and operations.

Documentation of Function and Behaviour (*Operations & Instances*): one of the previously documented weaknesses of a data model is the inability to represent functional differences with implementation across organisational boundaries. The inclusion of operations or services (Graham, pp. 226) would enable an organisation to supply their own interpretation of the appropriate processing of an object, whilst retaining the common definition of the object.

Definition of Data Items (*Attributes & Inheritance*): any framework and model must incorporate the associated data items. An object-oriented model would also include attributes, although each attribute of an object could potentially be another object or class definition. This ability greatly improves the readability and flexibility of future models. An attribute or object class can derive the definition, including attributes of previously documented objects.

Communication (*Instance Connections, Message Passing, States*): in order to provide a flexible model, the existing data models have included relationships with high-level cardinality rules. As previously discussed, a modification to a relationship for a specific organisational implementation will require a change to data model. The common acceptance of the existing health data models is based on an agreed pattern, modifying the relationships may change the common pattern. The proposed framework must provide the ability to define the association between objects during implementation. HL7 have recently recognised this requirement, and have included an object model which incorporates Instance Connections (HL7, 1996, pp. 24), providing the semantic linking and cardinality between objects.

4.2 Framework Example

Consider the object client and the operation client registration. This function and the associated objects would be common to all organisations, but as previously mentioned, each implementation may be different. By incorporating the operations, eg. Client_Registration, within the appropriate objects we are immediately providing greater meaning to the model by supporting the business functions with the data and attributes. Allowing components of the operations, eg. instance or cardinality, to be defined in an implementation specific message, we are enabling modification to be made to the models whilst retaining the common object model. The commonality is maintained through the definition encapsulated in the object classes and objects. It may also be possible to identify common operations to be used within the model, eg. identify the relationships between objects, with the flexibility to modify cardinality.

The possible object structure should, as a minimum, include:

- the object name;
- attributes, including the ability to represent repeating groups and nested groups of objects, eg. Client Group made up of many person; and
- Operations.

Individual organisations business rules and associations can be encapsulated in an operation object, identifying all the related objects including a message indicating the cardinality.

The use of an object-oriented approach does not negate the research development of health data models and identified patterns of health information as these models will assist in the identification of objects and classes. However, unlike the data models the object-oriented model provides greater flexibility in documentation and implementation of specific organisation relationships and business rules, eg. all persons requesting a service will receive a client record => Object Client - Client_Registration: Intake Mandatory Multiple (a Client can have more than one Intake record), a person requesting a service may not be registered => Object Client - Client_Registration: Intake Optional Multiple.

5. Conclusion

It is not yet clear what would be included in a health information framework or even the overall structure; this is the basis of ongoing research. However, it may not be possible to incorporate all the requirements in a single object-oriented model, the framework may include a number of different types of object models similar to the HL7 Message Development Framework (HL7, 1996), with a description of the association between the models and guide to implementation of the framework.

Competition for the "health dollar", associated with increased demand for services are placing greater demands on the provision of timely accurate information across organisational boundaries, which can only be satisfied when we have a consistency in the implementation of models of health organisations. The development of an information framework addressing the requirements of the health industry will greatly assist in an associated organisation's ability to improve overall organisational management and improve the quality and quantity of services delivered to their clients.

References:

Achuthan R., Alagar V.S. & Radhakrishnan T., An Object-Oriented Framework For Specifying Reactive Systems, *Object-Oriented Technology for Database and Software Systems*, ed. Alagar V.S. & Missauoi, World Scientific, Singapore 1995, pp. 114-133.

Atkinson, M., De Witt D., Manier D., Bancilhon F., Dittrich K. & Zdonik S., The Object-Oriented database System Manifesto, *Deductive and Object-Oriented Databases*, ed. W. Kim, J.M. Nicolas & S. Nishio, Elsevier Science, Holland 1990.

Blaha Michael R., Premerlani William J. & Rumbaugh James E., Relational Database Design Using an Object-Oriented Methodology, *Communications of the ACM*, Vol 31, No. 4, April 1988.

Butler G. & Lam C., The Preliminary Design of an Object-Oriented Framework for Combinatorial Enumeration, *Object-Oriented Technology for Database and Software Systems*, ed. Alagar V.S. & Missauoi, World Scientific, Singapore 1995, pp. 134-144

Chen, P. P-S., The Entity-Relationship Model - Towards a Unified View of Data, *ACM Transactions on Database Systems*, Vol. 1 No. 1, pp. 9-36, March 1976

Coad P., Object-Oriented Patterns, *Communications of the ACM*, September 1992, Vol. 35 No. 9, pp. 152-159.

Codd, E.F., Further Normalisation of the data base relational model. *Courant Computer Science Symposium 6: Data Base Systems*, Prentice-Hall, Englewood Cliffs, N.J., May 1971, pp. 33-64.

Comite European de Normalisation (CEN), Technical Committee 251/Medical Informatics, Electronic Healthcare Record, Working Group 3 1994 N94-092..

De Champeaux D & Faure P., *A comparative Study of Object-Oriented Analysis Methods*, JOOP, March/April 1992, pp. 21-33.

De Champeaux D., Lea D. & Faure P., Object Oriented Systems Development, Addison-Wesley, hewlett-Packard Company, 1993.

Graham I., Object Oriented Methods: *Object Oriented Programming Methods*, Addison-Wesley,

Health Level Seven (HL7) Working Group, HL7 Modeling & Methodology Committee: Message development Framework, Health Level Seven, Inc, Ann Arbor, 1996.

Jacobson I., Object-Oriented Software Engineering : A Use Case Driven Approach, Addison Wesley 1992.

Khoshafian S. Insight into Object-Oriented Databases, Information and Software Technology, Volume 32 No. 4 pp. 274-288, Butterworth-Heinemann Ltd., May 1990.

Kristensen B. B., Transverse Classes and Objects in Object-Oriented Anlysis, *Design and Implementation*, JOOP February 1993, pp. 43-51.

Monarchi D.E. & Puhr G.I., A research Typology for Object-Oriented Analysis and design, *Communications of the ACM*, Volume 35 No. 9 pp. 35-47, September 1992.

National Health Information Model Version 1, Australian Institute of Health and Welfare, Commonwealth of Australia, 1995.

NSW Health Department, NSW Community Health Information Model version 2.1, NSW Health 1997.

Rumbaugh J., Blaha M., Premerlani W., Eddy F. & Lorenson W., Object-Oriented Modelling and Design, Prentice-Hall 1991.

Sowa J.F. & Zachman J.A., Extending and Formalising the Framework for Information Systems Architecture, *IBM Systems Journal*, Volume 31, No. 3, pp. 590-616 1992

Smith J.M. & Smith D.C.P., Database Abstractions: Aggregation and Generalisation, *ACM Transactions on Database Systems*, Vol. 2 No. 2, pp. 105-133, June 1977

Wang S., Toward Formalised Object-Oriented Management Information Systems Analysis, *Journal of Management Information Systems*, Volume 12 No. 4 pp117-141, 1996.

TRANSACTION PROCESSING AND CONCURRENCY CONTROL

A Performance Evaluation for a Concurrency Control Mechanism in an ODBMS

Mohsen Beheshti
Dept. of Computer & Mathematical Sciences
University of Houston-Downtown
Houston, Texas

Abstract

Object Oriented transactions often imply the use of a large number of resources that are inaccessible to other incoming transactions if traditional two-phase locking is used to support concurrency. The goal of this research is to present the performance evaluation for a new concurrency control technique, Group Protocol (GP) [9], which is a combination of Two-Phase Locking (2PL) and Serialization Graph Test (SGT) techniques. GP improves the concurrency control performance by exploiting the navigational nature of long-running, transactions. Navigational Transactions may consist of two or more subtransactions. Depending on the nature of each subtransaction they may be executed using parallel processing. The performance evaluation done in this research indicates the applicability of this work for long-running navigational transactions.

1 Introduction

Conventional database systems deal with simple data types such as, integers and short character strings; they don't directly support applications with complex objects (data types) [12, 15, 32]. The new generation of database systems, provide traditional data management services, as well as support for long-running transactions with richer object structures [2, 3, 11, 13, 14, 16, 17, 18, 19, 20, 21, 22, 24, 25, 29, 30, 31]. Here, a transaction often accesses and accumulates data by navigating through objects and classes. An *object* refers to a set of data definitions and their operations, and a *class* is a set of objects which have similar characteristics. For this reason there may be an opportunity to improve the concurrent performance for long-running transactions.

One of the major issues in introducing a new concurrency control mechanism is analyzing the trade-off between the overhead versus the advantages of allowing more concurrent access to the database. Because of the importance of concurrency control mechanisms, and their performance issues, research in this area is very active [26,27,33]. Basically the amount of overhead is dependent on several parameters of the application and the concurrency control mechanism. In general, these parameters are, the size of transaction in terms of the number of objects accessed, the size or granularity of locks, and how long the locks are held [28]. The goal here is to study the performance of the concurrency control mechanism *Group Protocol* by: (1) characterizing the input, including the specification of characteristics of individual transactions, and the interaction among them, and (2) choosing the performance metric(s), establishing the base lines in two extremes i.e., *Two-Phase Locking (TPL)* a pessimistic protocol, and *Serialization Graph Test (SGT)* an optimistic mechanism, and performing a series of tests.

To study the performance of the introduced system as shown in Figure1, the characteristic of individual transactions and the interaction among them must be taken into consideration. In other words, the input to the system must be characterized. The parameters affecting the performance for each individual .

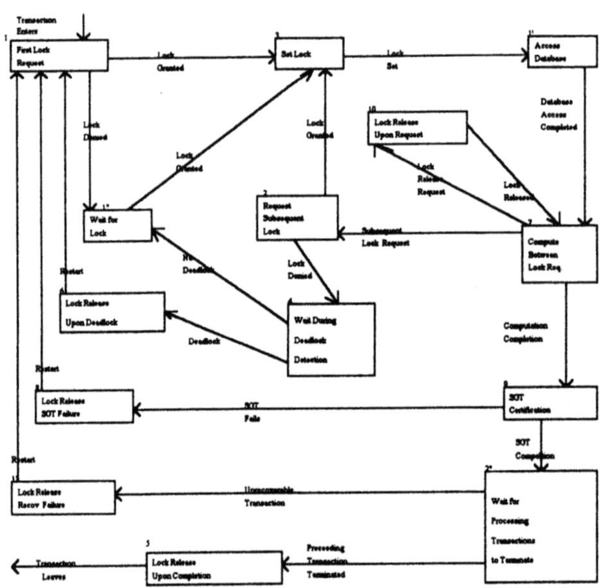

Figure1: state transition diagram

transaction are: 1)The number of nodes in each transaction, 2)The number of groups, 3)The average length of groups, 4)The location of update nodes, and 5)The number of update nodes. There are also some parameters which specify the relation among the active transactions and their interactions; these are: 1)Independent, 2)Follow the lead, 3)Single crossroad, AND 4)Deadlock. These parameters and the relations are explained in the next section with more details

In general, the concurrency control mechanism introduced in this research is expected to provide good performance when used for the first four cases, however it is expected to perform poorly in the cases where there are many collisions. These hypotheses will be tested through a series of experiments based on various settings for the above parameters. Lastly, they are compared against the established base lines (i.e., TPL, and regular SGT) to see how well this system performs.

The remaining of this paper discusses these issues in more detail. Section 2 gives an overview of the Group Protocol, Section 3 lists the parameters used to study the performance. Section 4 discusses the cost model used to evaluate the performance, Section 5 introduces the simulation model and sets up a series of tests to analyze and evaluate the performance of the concurrency control technique, and Section 6 gives the summary.

2 Group Protocol

In order to provide a high-level description of a transaction, the *Navigational Transaction Language (NTL)* [4,9,8] was used to indicate how a transaction navigates from one object (class) to another. Here an object is a single record and a class is a collection of related records (a file). NTL was introduced as a frame work to develop a logical optimization algorithm and a concurrency control mechanism [5,6,7]. A transaction represented by NTL is a collection of one or more subtransactions which can be processed in parallel. Given the navigational transaction, a new locking protocol, the *Group Protocol (GP)* was proposed to group the operations in the transaction. A group is a collection of Nodes (objects) and Edges (relationship between the nodes e.g., hierarchical). Each group may release their locks before the other objects in the transaction are locked (not a pure *two-phase locking* protocol). Thus, more objects may become available for incoming transactions. The proposed protocol does not guarantee serializability in all cases, therefore, a verification test (*Serialization Graph Test*) is conducted whenever a transaction completes its execution. The   *Group Protocol* is used to let the navigation path be traversed once. This is achieved by means of having at least two classes kept locked at any time to maintain the connection between them, and the effects of one class to the other. Navigating the path just once decreases the time needed for each transaction, and allows more parallelism thus, improves the performance

The *NTL* is a non-procedural language, because otherwise the reordering process won't be applicable. This high level language used by the user, specifies the objects, classes, and properties that the query requires. The reordering process is done in two steps: first an algorithm is used to generate the *Undirected Transaction Graph (UTG)* [4, 5] which is just the graphical representation of the query given by the user. The *UTG*, then is used in another algorithm to be reordered and produce the *Directed Transaction Graph (DTG)* or in short the *Transaction Graph (TG)* [4, 5]. The D*TG* is the graphical representation of the query after being ordered. The D*TG* can then be transformed to a textual representation using the *NTL*. This query now includes all the objects, classes, and properties, and the order in which they will be accessed. It also contains the type of locks (share, exclusive, or intent) that each class has, and the information about the time they will be requested, and the time that they will be released.

The *Group Protocol* [4,9], is based on multiple levels of granularity and various locks (regular and intention). Regular locks (shared and exclusive) [10] are used at the class level and object level; and intention locks (intention shared, intention exclusive, and shared intention exclusive) [9,12, 23] are used only at the class level. A *Transaction Graph (TG)* is the directed graphical representation of the transaction used to support the *Group Protocol*. Using *Group Protocol* involves the following steps: (1) construct the transaction graph (representing the read/write operations); (2) traverse the transaction graph to identify groups, group types, and nodes outside of groups; and (3) use the lock/release protocol associated with the groups during execution. The main idea of grouping the nodes is to have the capability of unlocking some of the nodes prior to the end of the transaction execution. The types of nodes which a group contains and also the order in which they appear in a group, determines if the group can release its locks immediately after reaching its last node or if it has to wait. There can also be nodes that appear ahead of the first group which they release their locks immediately (like a group of size one).

The nodes of a *Transaction Graph (TG)*, are traversed one by one starting from the first node (which is marked by the directed transaction graph) to provide the following static information about each transaction:

1. Identifying the *Loose Nodes (LN)*, the nodes which do not belong to any groups; not all the *TG's* have LN's however, if there are any, they appear starting at the beginning of the *TG* through out the end, or until the first group is identified. The *LN's* reflect navigational positioning (prior to the first update) and may be locked and unlocked individually.

2. Identifying the *Groups*, by marking the nodes which start the groups. A group is identified based on the type of nodes appearing in the group.

3. Based on the information given by the *TG* the type of locks and their granularity level may be established. A node may be used for update/display purposes on its local properties or just for navigational purposes.

Different granularity levels may be assigned to different properties. Here, all the simple properties and each navigational property of a node in the *TG's* are considered as a unit of locking granularity.

To guarantee the one time pass through the navigation path, the *Loose Nodes* have locks on two classes at a time, and *Groups* keep the locks on all the classes belonging to that group to prevent loosing the connections. This way the correctness of each transaction by itself is guaranteed. The definition of each node in the TG is identified as follows:

I. Information given with the transaction:
  A. Partition of nodes based on the transaction structure.
    1.   *Side Node (SN)*- A node connected to exactly one other node (i.e., a leaf node).
    2.   *Basic Node (BN)*- A node connected to exactly two other nodes (i.e., a node without branching).
    3.   *Compound Node (CoN)*- A node connected to more than two other nodes (i.e. a node with branching).
  B. Additional labels placed on two nodes.
    1.   *Transaction Start Node (TSN)*- The first node in TG to be traversed (usually a side node).
    2.   *Transaction End Node (TEN)*- The last node in TG to be traversed (usually a side node).
  C. Operations of nodes labeled by the user.
    1.   *Read Node (RN)*- A node where the data mentioned by the node will be fully or partially read.
    2.   *Update/Display Node (U/D)*- A node where the data mentioned by the node will be fully or partially updated or displayed.
II. Information established for the Group Protocol:
    1.   *Loose Node (LN)* - A node which does not belong to any groups.
    2.   *Group Start Node (GSN)*- The first node of a group (i.e. a SN, a CoN, or a U/D node).
    3.   *Group End Node (GEN)*- The last node of a group (i.e. a SN, a CoN, or a U/D node).

There are two types of groups, the *Update Group* and the *Read Group* [9], which are different because of the type of nodes they contain and the order in which they release their locks. A group is called an *Update Group (UG)* if its GEN is a U/D node. The nodes of a UG are marked to be locked as they are being traversed. However, once all the groups in a TG are locked (at execution time), and the transaction is completed then the groups can release their locks. A group is called a *Read Group (RG)* if its GEN is not a U/D node. There is no reason to keep an RG locked once its GEN is (a) traversed and, (b) is not locked by other groups in the

TG. This allows other incoming transactions to be able to access the nodes sooner. The following section presents the complete algorithm for the Group Protocol.

2.1 The Algorithm

Algorithm 1 gives the complete procedure to mark the *LN's*, generate the groups, establish the group type, and introduces the lock and unlock instructions, based on the groups. It takes a transaction graph as input, then statically specifies the groups. Then the order in which the locks are set and released for each group (update or read) is specified. In this algorithm, the *GroupIndex* is used to specify the order in which the groups are generated and locked. *CurrentNode* is the current node in the TG, which is being traversed. *NextNode()* is a function which returns the next node in the data access path to be traversed. The *GroupEndNode* and *GroupStartNode* specify the GEN and GSN of each group in the TG respectively. *GroupType* determines the type of the group which is set to either *RGroup* for RG's or *UGroup* for UG's.

2.1.1 Algorithm 1

This algorithm is divided into three parts [4, 9]:
  1. The first block of code *Main* traverses the path to identify and mark the *Loose Nodes*. If the node to be read is supposed to start a group then *GenerateGroup* (another block of code) is called.
  2. The *GenerateGroup* identifies the Group Start Node (GSN), Group End Node (GEN) and also the type of each group.
  3. The UnlockGroups is the last block of code which marks the release order of the locked Update Group's and Read Group's, once the TG is completely traversed. The Update Group's are marked to release their locks at execution time in reverse order. And finally the single remaining GSN is marked as the last node to be released.

3 Concurrent Execution

The behavior of a transaction (as illustrated in Figure1) and the data structures needed for the developed system were discussed earlier. To study the performance of the introduced system, the characteristic of individual transactions and the interaction among them must be taken into consideration. In other words, the input to the system must be characterized. The parameters affecting the performance for each individual transaction are as follows:

  1. *The number of nodes in each transaction*: as the number of nodes increases, the transaction length and the probability of conflict both tend to increase.
  2. *The number of groups*: as the number of groups increases, the number of update and compound nodes increases. This tends

to increase the lock time and decrease the degree of concurrency.

3. *The average length of groups*: the longer the groups the less probability of concurrency, because the nodes within the group stay locked for a longer period of time.
4. *The location of update nodes*: the closer they are to the end node of the transaction the smaller the update group(s), therefore the more concurrency.
5. *The number of update nodes*: as the number of update nodes increases, the number of update groups also increases and the degree of concurrency decreases.

There are also some parameters which specify the relation among the active transactions and their interactions; these are as follows:

1. *Independent*: this is the best case where no transaction at its execution time needs any node(s) used by other transactions. Therefore, the transaction experiences no delay and will not be aborted.
2. *Follow the leader*: this is when the order in which the objects are accessed by various transactions, makes the object available for the next transaction. In other words there are some nodes that are used by different transactions but the timing is in such a way that no delays are experienced.
3. *Single crossroad*: this is when there is a conflict between two transactions but it is just one single conflict. So, a transaction may delay but will not be aborted.
4. *Deadlock*: this is when two or more transactions can no longer proceed because there exist a circular wait. In this case based on the deadlock algorithm, one of the transactions needs to be aborted to let the execution proceed.
5. *Collision*: this is when a transaction has to be rejected because an aggressive approach is used and the transaction execution is not serializable. Collision leads to the abortion of one of the transactions, others may also be aborted to enforce the recoverability of the execution.

By just looking at the various types of interaction among the transactions, the following observations are made. In the first case (i.e., *independent*) this mechanism is as good as any others. In the second case (i.e., follow the leader) it seems that there may exist cases where the introduced technique would work better than the TPL protocol. This is because not all the objects have to stay locked till the transaction is finished. In other words, in some cases objects release their locks immediately after the next object in the path is locked. Therefore the next transaction can access the released object(s). The TPL protocol keeps the objects locked until the end of the transaction. Even though the SGT certifier is used at the end to check serializability, no transactions will be aborted. Therefore, the overhead is minimal.

In the third case (i.e., single crossroad), again like the previous case, the introduced technique seems to have better performance and provide more parallelism compared to TPL. This is basically because the lock on some objects is released before the transaction is finished. In the fourth case (i.e., deadlock) the overhead seems to be about the same compared to TPL protocol, and the SGT certifier can be thought of as a deadlock detection algorithm for the developed technique. The last case (i.e., collision) is the one which can be regarded as the worst case for the developed technique since the overhead will increase. This is basically because of the number of updates required in the introduced data structures, especially if recovery is also supported.

In general, the concurrency control mechanism introduced in this research is expected to provide good performance when used for the first four cases, however it is expected to perform poorly in the cases where there are collisions. These hypotheses will be tested through a series of experiments based on various settings for the above parameters. Lastly, they are compared against the established base lines (i.e., TPL, and regular SGT) to see how well this system performs. The next two sections discuss the performance metric (extra burden) and the results of the tests.

4 The Cost Model

To evaluate the performance of the developed concurrency control, the metric extra burden is used which represents the overhead on the transaction [1]. This performance metric recognizes finite resources and it considers both the impact that the concurrency control has on the probability that the transaction will run to completion without conflicting with another transaction and the overhead imposed by the concurrency control technique on the transaction. Here the overhead is considered as those instructions/operations, both CPU and I/O, that would not need to be executed if the transactions were run alone on a computer without any concurrency control mechanism. The possible outcomes for a transaction are: (1) the transaction runs to completion, commits and leaves the system (transaction succeeds), and (2) the transaction is aborted by the system and is restarted before it completes (transactions succeeds after rerun(s)). The overhead involved in the second case is actually in two parts: (a) the overhead from the time the transaction started until the time it is restarted by the system for the last time, and (b) the overhead during the final successful execution of the transaction from the beginning to the time it commits and leaves the system.

The overhead involved in case 1 and case 2(b) is the same. The overhead for case 2(a) includes the overhead incurred before the transaction abort plus the cost of the undo processing; and the execution cost of the transaction before it was restarted (i.e., CPU and I/O operations required to process the transaction). That is, if the transaction was run by itself this overhead would not have been imposed. The overhead or the *extra burden* imposed on a transaction by the concurrency control algorithm can be modeled as [1]:

$$extraburden = P_{succ} \times O_{succ} + P_{rerun} \times O_{rerun}$$

P_{succ} is the probability that the transaction ultimately succeeds; O_{succ} is the overhead incurred when the transaction succeeds and leaves the system; P_{rerun} is the probability that the transaction is rerun; and O_{rerun} is the overhead incurred when a transaction is restarted by the system (from start to restart).

A series of tests based on the cost model have been conducted through a simulation study which is discussed in the next section. The simulation program uses the assumptions and the various parameters to calculate the P_{succ}, P_{rerun}, O_{succ}, O_{rerun}, and finally the *extra burden*.

5 Simulation Study

The performance evaluation of the introduced concurrency control is done by simulation. Some of the parameters are: *Transaction Size, Multiprogramming Level, Number of Updates in a transaction*, and *the amount of CPU and I/O time* which are used for each of the states in Figure1. The simulation program is used to evaluate the overhead involved in concurrent transaction processing while one of the following techniques are used: (1) the *Group Protocol*, (2) the *Two-Phase Locking (TPL)*, or (3) the *Serialization Graph Test (SGT)*. The last two are used as base lines to compare the results and determine the cases in which the *Group Protocol* performs better.

The simulation program is run on a wide range of data sets. The graphical representation of the results of the simulation based on different runs are compared and discussed below. The following two subsections introduce the parameters and assumptions used in the simulation program and discuss the simulation process in more details.

5.1 Assumptions & Parameters

The assumptions made for the simulation program are as follows:

1   All transactions have the same size.
2   There is just one update group with a fixed size for each transaction.

3   The probability of conflicts and collisions are given as inputs.

4   No more than two transactions are involved in a conflict or collision.

Considering various sizes of transactions makes the model very complex to use (assumption 1). One update group or multiple update groups have about the same effect on performance as long as the total number of update group nodes in a transaction is the same (assumption 2). This is basically because all the update group nodes hold their locks during the entire transaction execution. The probability of conflicts and the probability of collisions (where Pcol <= Pconf), both have direct effects on performance. Thus they are provided separately by the user to investigate their effects (assumption 3). Probability of conflicts and collisions involving more than two transactions is very low and not noticeable in the overall performance (assumption 4).

The simulation program is run on a Vax machine which takes .001 milliseconds for a CPU operation (TCPU) and .020 milliseconds for an IO operation (TIO). Based on the above time units, the amount of time a transaction spends in each state in Figure1 is calculated. The other parameters used in the simulation program are as follows:

1   *Transaction Size (TS)*- Number of nodes in each transaction.

2   *Multiprogramming Level (MPL)*- The number of transactions that may be active at the same time.

3   *Number of Update Nodes (Upn)*- The number of nodes in a transaction that update the database.

4   *Probability of Conflicts (Pconf)*- The probability of read-write and/or write-write conflicts among transactions.

5   *Probability of Collisions (Pcol)*- The probability of restarting the transaction upon deadlock detection (in the case of TPL), or failing the validation test (in the case of SGT).

6   *Probability of the Update Group (Pupg)*- The probability that nodes in a transaction belong to the update group. Or the percentage of nodes in the transaction which belong to the update group.

5.2 Simulation Model

The behavior of a transaction is depicted in Figure1 and was discussed earlier. In the simulation model, a fixed number of transactions are generated and cycled continuously. After a transaction has completed and released all its locks, it is immediately sent back to the system and becomes a new transaction. The simulation model calculates the overhead involved for each transaction based on the assumptions and the parameters for each of the three techniques: *GP, TPL, SGT.* The simulation program was written in C.

5.2.1 Simulation Results and Discussions

The values of the parameters in the simulation model were chosen to include a wide range of values: small and large transactions, a low and a high level of multiprogramming, and various probabilities of conflicts, collisions, and update groups. The simulation program was run on data sets starting from:

$$TS = 5, MPL = 5, Upn = 1, Pconf = .1, Pcol = .01, and\ Pupg = .01$$

Up to:

$$TS = 10000, MPL = 10000, Upn = 5, Pconf = .9, Pcol = .5, and\ Pupg = 1$$

The purpose was to discover the parameters which have the most significant effect on the performance of the *Group Protocol* and the base lines. The time each transaction spends in each state in Figure1 was calculated based on *TCPU, TIO, MPL, TS, Upn, Pconf, Pcol,* and *Pupg.* The result of the simulation program for each data set is represented by a graph. An example of such a graph is shown in Figure2. Each graph contains information about the two base line concurrency control (cc) mechanisms (i.e., TPL and SGT), and the *Group Protocol.*

The graph compares the overhead involved for each concurrency control mechanism based on the number of transactions (*TS*), multiprogramming level (*MPL*), number of update nodes in a UGroup (*Upn*), probability of conflict (*Pconf*), probability of collision (*Pcol*), and various probabilities for the update groups (*Pupg*) ranging from .01 to 1. In each case, the two base line techniques exhibit a perfectly flat performance because both *TPL* and *SGT* are insensitive to the size of the update groups. Generally speaking the overhead of *TPL* exceeds the overhead of the *SGT* until the probability of conflict and collision go up significantly.

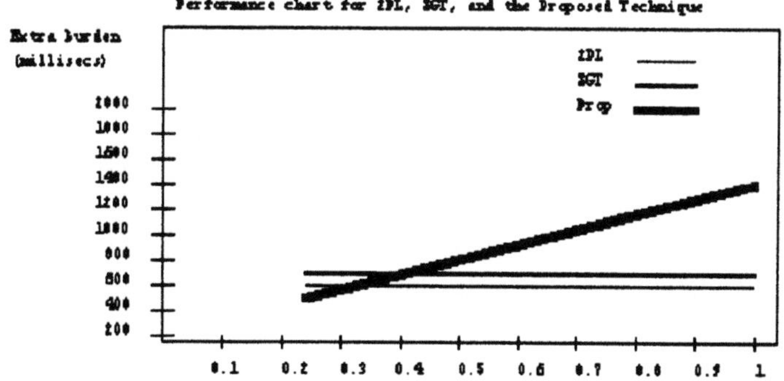

Prob. of Upg (ts=100, MPL=30, upn=1, Pconf=.3, Pcol=.25)

Figure2: Sample Graph

A series graphs where generated which were the result of changes in different parameters such as: Transaction Size, Multiprogramming level, Number of Updates, Probability of Conflicts and Probability of Collisions in the simulation program.

From the result of the simulation we observe that the three parameters Pconf, Pcol, and Pupg are the ones which affect the performance of the developed algorithm the most. To study these parameters and their effects on the developed algorithm the simulation program was run on additional data sets. These tests were basically performed to recognize cases where the developed algorithm has better performance than the base lines. The overall performance of the developed concurrency control mechanism and the type of transactions which benefit the most from this technique is illustrated by Figure3. It compares the performance of the developed algorithm to a pure *SGT*, and *TPL*. It basically shows under what percentage of update groups the *Group Protocol* performs better than the base lines. For example If Probability of Conflict is .3 (*Pconf=.3*), the Probability of Collision is .15 (*Pcol=.15*), and the Percentage of Update Groups is at most 35 percent (*Pupg<=.35*) then, *Group Protocol* performs better than the both base lines. Figure3 shows the type of transactions which perform better using GP compared to TPL. Here *GP* performs better than *TPL* for *.01<=Pconf<=.9, Pcol<=.25,* and *Pupg<=.55.* In regard to *SGT*, if *Pconf=.3* and *Pcol=.1*, then *GP* performs better than *SGT* for transactions which have *Pupg<=.3*, or simply the percentage of nodes in the update group is less than or equal to *30* percent. Basically the performance is better than *SGT* for *.1<=Pconf<=.5* and *.01<=Pupg<=.55.* For *Pconf>.5, SGT* dominates the performance specially when the *Pcol>.2.* The area below the *45* degree line in not feasible because we always have *Pcol<=Pconf.*

From Figure3 it can be observed that the *Group Protocol* has the opportunity to improve the perform up to *25%* compared to the base lines when the *Pupg, Pconf,* and *Pcol* of transactions are in a certain range. In general for *Pupg>.4* the performance is worse than the base lines (regardless of *Pconf* and *Pcol*). This is basically because the overhead involved in locking and releasing nodes and groups increases exponentially as *Pupg* increases. For the cases where *Pconf<=.5* and *Pcol<=.25* the developed algorithm performs better than the base lines given that *Pupg<=.30.*

In general the three parameters *Pupg, Pconf,* and *Pcol* have a direct effect on the performance of the developed algorithm. And the smaller these probabilities are, the better the performance of the developed technique compared to base lines is. Basically, the simulation study indicates that, the transactions of type follow the leader and single crossroad, perform better when the Group Protocol is used and the percentage of nodes in the update group is below *40%*. Even transactions of type deadlock or collision perform better when the *Group Protocol* is used and the percentage of nodes in the update group is below *20%*. However, if the probability of collisions or conflicts are above *.2* or *.5* respectively, then *TPL* is considered the favorite.

6 Summary

This performance study indicates that *GP* is more suitable for applications which deal with read operations more often than write operations. However, in cases where write operations exists, as long as the Probability of the Update Group is within a certain range (i.e., less than or equal to .4) the developed technique is expected to perform better than the two base lines. Notice that *Pupg* is always greater than or equal to the probability of the number of write operations in a transaction.

The performance evaluation here assumes that all the transaction are of the same type (i.e., *TS, Upn, Pconf,* and *Pcol* are the same). However, in reality that is not the case. In the introduced performance model the concept of multiple levels of granularity was not considered. This is basically because, multiple levels of granularity is independent of the developed concurrency control technique. Since navigational processing is considered to evaluate the performance of the introduced technique and the base lines, multiple levels of granularity are expected to improve the concurrency on all three techniques.

The number of update groups in the performance model is assumed to be one. In other words, the model assumes that all the update groups are located at the end of transactions, and all the read groups along with the loose nodes are located in front and treated as single read nodes. A transaction having three update groups each including 5 nodes, or having a single update group which contains *15* nodes have about the same effect on performance. Thus to make the performance model more manageable, the latter option is considered in this research.

References

1. Agrawal, Rakesh, and Dewitt, J. David, "Integrated Concurrency Control and Recovery Mechanism: Design ad Performance Evaluation", In ACM Transaction on Database systems, Vol., 10, o. 4, December 1985, Pages 529-564.

2. Bancilhon, Francois, "Object-Oriented Database Systems", Porc. of the 1988 SIGMOD Conf., Washington, DC, March 1988, P. 152-162.

3. Bancilhon, Francois, "The Design and Implementation of O2, and Object-Oriented Database System", Advances in Object-Oriented Database Systems: Second International Workshop on Object-Oriented Database Systems, Bad Munster am Sterin, West Germany. Also appears as Lecture Notes in Computer Science, No. 334, Springer Verlag, 1988.

4. Beheshti Mohsen, "Improving Performance in Object-Oriented Database Systems by Exploiting Navigational Properties", Ph.D. Dissertation, The Center for Advanced Studies, University of Southwestern Louisiana, Lafayette, LA, May 1992.

5. Beheshti Mohsen, and Delcambre Lois M. "A Logical Optimization Algorithm for an Object-Oriented DBMS", Arkansas Computer Conference - ACC'95, March 1995.

6. Beheshti Mohsen, and de Korvin Andre. "Logical Optimization When Uncertainty Is Present", 6th International Conference and Workshop on Database and Expert Systems Applications, DEXA'95, September 1995.

7. Beheshti Mohsen, and de Korvin Andre. "Applying Fuzzy Logic to an Object-Oriented Query Optimization Algorithm", 7th International Conference on Artificial Intelligence and Expert Systems Applications, EXPERSYS'95, November 1995.

8. Beheshti Mohsen, and Delcambre Lois M. "Query Optimization in an Object-Oriented Database Management System", The 1996 yearbook to the Handbook of Data Management, Auerbach Publications, 1996.

9. Beheshti, Mohsen and Delcambre, L. M. , "Concurrency Control in an Object-Oriented DBMS by Exploiting Navigation", 7th International Hong Kong Computer Society Database Workshop, May 1996.

10. Bernstein,P. A., Haszilacos, V., and Goodman, N., "Concurrency Control and Recovery in Database Systems", by Addison Wesley Inc., 1987.

11. Booch, Grady, "Object-Oriented Analysis and Design with Applications", 2nd Edition, The Benjamin/Cummings Publishing Company, Inc., 1994.

12. Date, C. J., "An Introductin to Database Systems" by Addison Wesley Inc., Vol. II, July 1984.

13. Deux O., et. al., "The Story of O2", IEEE Trans. on Knowledge and Data Eng., Vol. 2, No. 1, March 1990.

14. Dittrich, K. R., Dayal, U, and Buchmann, A., P., (eds.), "Topics in Information Systems: On Object-Oriented Database Systems", Springer-Verlay Berlin Heidelberg 1991, Printed in the United States of America.

15. Elmagarmid, Ahmed K., "Database Transaction Models for Advanced Applications", by Morgan Koufmann Publishers, Inc., 1992.

16. Fishman, D. H., et. al., "Iris: An Object-Oriented Database Management System", ACM Trans. on Office Inf. Sys., Vol. 5, No. 1, January 1987, p. 48-69.

17. Ford, Steven et. al., "ZEITGEIST: Database Support for Object-Oriented Programming", Texas Instruments Incorporated, P.O. Box 655474, M/S 238, Dallas, Texas 75265.

18. Garsa, Jorge F. and Kim, Won, "Transaction Management in an Object-Oriented Database System", Conf. Proc. on SIGMAD, Chicago Illinios, June 1988, P. 37-45.

19. Kim, Won, et. al., "Composite Object Support in an Object-Oriented Database System", OOPSLA '87 Conf. Proc., Oct 1987, P. 118-125.

20. Won, Kim et. al., "Features of the ORION Object-Oriented Database System", In KIM89.

21. Kim, Won and Lochovsky, F. H. "Object-Oriented Concepts, Databases, and Applications", By Addison-Wesley Publishing Company, ACM PRESS, New York, New York, 1989.

22. Kim, Won et. al., "Architecture of the ORION Next-Generation Database System", IEEE Trans. on Knowledge and Data Eng., Vol. 2, No. 1, March 1990.

23. Korth, H. F., and Silberschatz A., "Database System Concepts", by McGrow-Hill Inc., 1986.

24. Lecluse, Christopher et. al., "O2, an Object-Oriented Data Model", Proceedings of the ACM SIGMOS 1988 International Conference on Management of Data, Chicago, IL, 1988.

25. Maier, D., et. al., "Development of an Object-Oriented DBMS", OOPSLA '86 Proc., Sept. 1986, P. 472-482.

26. Rahm, Erhard, "Empirical Performance Evaluation of Concurrency and Coherency Control Protocols for Database Sharing Systems, ACM Tran. on Database Sys., Vol. 18, No. 2, Page 333, June 1993.

27. Park, Jong Soo, Chen Ming-Syan, and Yu Philip S., "An Effective Hash-Based Algorithm for Mining Association Rules", Sigmod Records, Vol. 24, No. 2, Page 175, June 1995.

28. Ray, Wayne Allen, "Concurrency Control Architecture in Distributed database Systems", Ph.D. Dissertation, Graduate School of Vanderbilt University, Nashville, Tennessee, December 1981.

29. Stonebraker, M. and Rowe, L. A., "The Design of POSTGRES", Proceedings of the 1986 SIGMOD Conference, Washington, DC, May 1986, P. 340-355.

30. Stonebraker, M., "Object Management in POSTGRES Using Procedures", Proceeding of the 1986 International Workshop on Object-Oriented Database System, Pacific Grove, California, Sept. 1986, P. 66-72.

31. Stonebraker, M., "The Implementation of POSTGRES", IEEE Trans. on Knowledge and Data Eng., Vol. 2, No. 1, March 1990.

32. Ullman, Jeffrey D., "Principles of Database and Knowledge-Base Systems", Volume I, By Computer Science Press, Inc., 1988.

33. White Seth J., DeWitt, David J., "Implementing Crash Recovery in QuickSotre: A Performance Study", Sigmod Records, Vol. 24, No. 2, Page 175, June 1995.

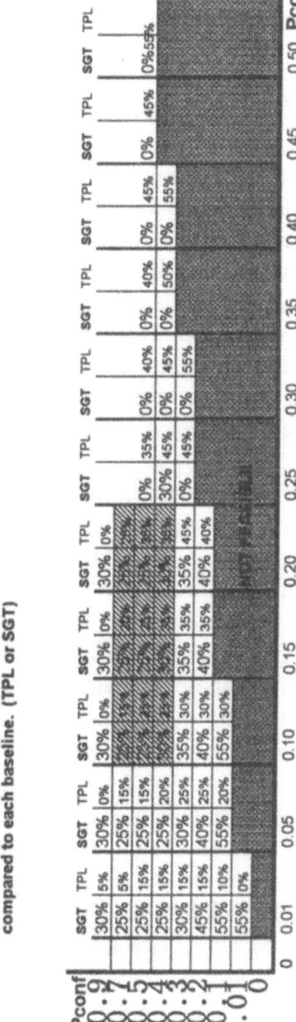

Figure3: Performance compared to SGI and TPL

A Transaction Model to Support Disconnected Operation in a Mobile Computing Environment

A. Rasheed, A. Zaslavsky
Department of Computer Technology, Monash University
Melbourne, Australia

Abstract

A mobile computing environment consists of stationary and mobile workstations (hosts). Its nature (frequent connections/disconnections, mobility and possible non-availability of mobile workstations) has forced the research community to revisit many areas of database management. In this paper we present a multi-layered approach to handle replicated data. The abstract model describes different layers for handling transactions and the layers at which the replication will be handled

1 Introduction

A mobile computing environment is a distributed computing environment, characterised by the fact that some of the hosts (workstations) are mobile while others are stationary (fixed) ones. Some of the fixed hosts, called *base nodes* are augmented with a wireless interface to communicate with mobile hosts. The area covered and controlled by a base node is called a *zone of influence* (or a *logical cell*). This area can either be a territorial division or a logical cluster of mobile and/or fixed workstations. At any moment, a mobile host can directly communicate with only one base node, regardless of whether it is a home base node, or a visitor base node [15].

In a distributed environment, a particular host might become unavailable due to network partitioning or the host might be mobile and will not be available at all times. Replication is considered as a more probable solution to handle non-availability of data due to non-availability of a host [1, 9, 10, 14].

Transactions and their ACID properties have traditionally been used to ensure consistent database management and atomic and isolated user actions. Recent research has shown that these properties are too strict and some of the traditional properties of transactions should be relaxed [8, 14].

In most of the research done on mobile computing environment, mobile computers are considered as clients who can connect to different servers and ask for certain services (client-server). To reduce the contention on the narrow bandwidth of the wireless channel, it is suggested to cache part of a database on mobile computers [3, 4, 7]. Some caching strategies for mobile computers have also been suggested [4].

In this paper we widen this view of mobile computing environment and present a model which can be used for disconnected/connected operation of a mobile workstation. Our goal is to ensure data availability and transaction processing even when a mobile host is not available. To achieve this goal some of the ACID properties of transactions are relaxed to ensure transaction processing under all situations.

In section 2 we discuss the replication and transactions in a replicated environment. Section 3 presents a multi-layered abstract model for handling replication and transactions. It also redefines the twin-transaction model and presents a simple synchronisation algorithm. The implementation of suggested model in an object-based distributed system is also presented and a reconciliation algorithm is discussed. Section 5 gives a brief discussion on some related work and finally section 6 provides conclusions and describes further work.

2   Replication and Transactions

Replication techniques were designed to handle failures by replicating portions of database at different sites in a distributed environment. Then if a site crashes or becomes separated from the network because of a partition, the portion of the database being maintained by that site can still be accessed, by contracting a different site that holds a replica. There are a few replica control protocols researched and developed [9]. The concurrency control subsystem is the portion of the system that is responsible for ensuring correct concurrent operation of transactions. Different concurrency control mechanisms are described in [2].

3   The Abstract Model

3.1   Multi-Layered Architecture

The proposed multi-layered architecture is depicted in figure 1. In the traditional way of handling replicated database replica control takes care of maintaining the consistency among replicas of a data item. The replica control also determines whether to let a transaction proceed or not using replica control protocol (quorum consensus, primary copy, etc.). The security, recovery and other aspects of a transaction management are omitted for the sake of simplicity.

The distributed concurrency control guarantees the correct execution of a transaction in a concurrent environment. While, in our model the operation of the two components is not changed much except that we present each data item as a distributed object. The concurrency control mechanism now operates on *logical replicated database*. Similarly, the replica control also sees the view presented by the logical replicated database. By having a one-to-one mapping for these layers any existing replication protocol will work without any modifications if the interface provided by the logical replicated database is consistent.

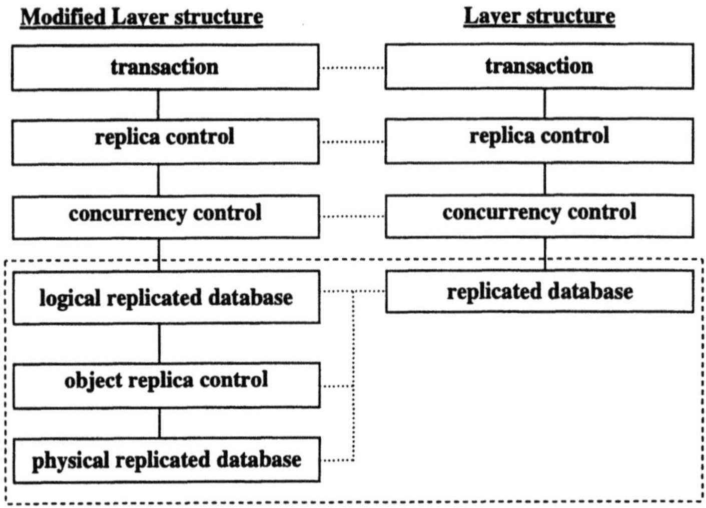

Fig. 1. Abstract model of the Multi-Layer Architecture

Logical replicated database (LDB) is a collection of objects, some (or all) of which can be replicated thus justifying the existence of replica control layer. Each **object** in the *logical replicated database* is a **collection** called meta-object, which provides one view for the replicas of a data item. We leave the granularity of data items unspecified. This collection of replicas is encapsulated within this meta-object. The **meta object** is responsible for the consistency control among different items in its collection. Thus **object replica control** layer is built within the **meta object** and is essentially a method of it. If the number of encapsulated replicas is one then there is a one-to-one mapping between logical replicated database and physical replicated database. **Logical replicated database (LDB)** is a collection of meta-objects, some (or all) of which can be replicated. The replica control layer handles the replication of these meta-objects.

3.2   Transaction Processing (Twin-Transactions)

For transaction processing on meta-objects (and maintaining mutual consistency among replicas encapsulated within meta-objects) we modify/adopt twin-transaction model presented in [14]. Twin-transactions replicate the process of transactions execution along with replicating a data item. We define a meta-object O_{meta} as a set X_{set} presenting a logical view for data item X which is defined as

- $\{X\}$, maintained by a single Data Manager (DM), or
- $\{X_a, X_b, \ldots, X_n\}$, maintained by **n** data managers (DMs).

In the twin-transactions model each replica will act as a virtual primary copy [10] and tries to propagate all the transactions via meta-object to other replicas. Meta-object acts as a control centre to authenticate transactions. The transactions are not propagated straight away but are kept in a log and are synchronised and then propagated to other replicas at a later stage. During this synchronisation some transactions will not be propagated and the replica originating that transaction will be informed of the result.

A replicated data item will receive transactions and each transaction T will be mirrored to generate twin-transactions $\{T_x, T_o\}$. One of the twin-transactions T_x will execute on the data item maintained by the host receiving the transaction T and the other twin-transaction T_o will be sent to the meta-object O_{meta}. If O_{meta} is not available (disconnected, some other reason) then the twin-transaction T_o will be kept in a history log H_o (transaction history) and will be transmitted to O_{meta} whenever it becomes available.

The meta-object O_{meta} will eventually receive transactions from different hosts maintaining replicas of data item X. O_{meta} is responsible to resynchronise all the replicas of data item X. Here we define a synchronisation relation $\Leftrightarrow$ to be applied whenever a meta-object becomes available. The histories H_o^1, H_o^2, ...H_o^n (transmitted to meta-object from hosts 1,2, ... n) are merged together to make a common history H. The following relation also holds.

$$H = H_o^1 \Leftrightarrow H_o^2 ...\Leftrightarrow H_o^n$$

This common history is then propagated to all the replicas, thus making all of them in sync with each other. This operation of resynchronisation will thus guarantee the consistency of a meta-object. If transactions only operate directly on meta-object, then other replicas will be out of sync with meta-object. Therefore the history of transactions on meta-object or the data item will need to be transmitted to other replicas from time to time (whichever is smaller).

A transaction T_o^k in set H_o^k is in conflict with a probability ρ with some transactions in set H_o^i where ρ is calculated as

$$\rho = F (HD_k, HD_i)$$

It is a function of patterns of previous conflicts arising while synchronising two sets H_k and H_i. HD_k is a set of data items to be updated by transaction T_o^k, and HD_i is a set of data items that have an update or read probability of more than a certain threshold on DM_i. This set is learned using the past history of transactions and is generated by transaction manager.

F is a function to determine the conflict based on the conflict set (data items in conflict). In case of X_{set} containing only one element, ρ will always be zero (no conflicts as conflict set will always be empty). Thus a transaction T can only be in conflict if any of its twin-transactions are in conflict. The transaction T will be strictly in conflict if its twin-transactions were generated on DM_i and T^i executing on DM_i is in conflict with another transaction on DM_i otherwise it will be in conflict with a probability ρ. When two histories are merged, there is a probability of two or more transactions in conflict with each other (executed on different copies of data items X_i, X_k). The calculation of cost of merging two histories is complex and is dependent on many factors

3.3 Synchronisation Algorithm

When a host is not available (mobile disconnected), then to determine whether to let a transaction proceed or not is purely heuristic. To make such heuristic decisions, the transaction manager needs to know about history of transactions (to learn the patterns of transactions). Also in real world these patterns change depending upon the time of day. Based on these patterns, the transaction manager can provide the requesting site the information about the probability of success of a transaction. A simplified algorithm in pseudo code, which supports twin-transactions, is presented in figure 2.

```
Steps to be taken when O_meta is X_set = {X_a, X_b, X_c, X_d } for transaction T on DM_a for replica X_a.
BEGIN
      Create twin-transactions T_a, and To.
      IF Conflict Probability ρ  < Allowed Conflict Probability
      THEN
            Send Twin-Transaction to meta-object O_meta.
      ENDIF
END

Steps for meta-object to synchronise H_a and H_b
BEGIN
      Execute synchronisation relation  H_a ⟺ H_b
      IF Transactions are compensated/aborted THEN
            Inform Originating Site (if abort required)
      END
      IF Transactions are committed in full THEN
            Inform Originating Site (if commit required)
      END
      Send result to other replicas
END
```

Fig. 2. Twin-Transaction Processing Algorithm with meta-objects

3.4 Object Model

Early works on transactions to object-based distributed systems leads to consider uniform mechanisms which view objects as simple data items on which read and write operations are performed. To guarantee atomicity, transactions are not allowed to perform interfering updates on shared objects. In this scenario the consistency restrictions and inter-dependency of different data items (objects) that is built into each data item (object) cannot be considered by the DM. This limit is not sensible for long transactions with localised concurrency bottlenecks (hot spots) [12]. When built-in inter-dependency is not known to DM, a potential problem exists in calculating the probability of success in twin-transactions.

To overcome this problem, the other approach is to build the concurrency control mechanism within an object. Thus the granularity of data items is not confined to an object. This approach is more feasible with twin-transactions as it enables each meta-object to maintain its own concurrency requirements with all the semantic knowledge and thus enabling maximum number of transactions to commit. In [11], authors have presented an optimistic concurrency control mechanisms which uses reconciliation to merge two versions of an object which are produced by conflicting method executions on a base version. Our model needs to be extended to cater for the object base systems. The paper [11] influenced the following discussion and formalism for the twin-transactions model.

In our model, an object base consists of a set of uniquely identified (OID) objects, each containing structural and behavioural component. The structural component is a set of uniquely identified data items referred to as attributes whose values define the object's state. The behavioural component is a set of procedures, usually called methods that are the only means of accessing the structural components and thereby modifying the object's state. The jth attribute of object O_i is denoted as a_{ij} [11]. Similarly, an object's method(s) are identified using the notation m_{ij}.

Object base users execute transactions on objects by invoking methods that manipulate their attributes. A transaction is a partial order of operations on objects in the object base. We denote an operation (ie. method invocation) of a transaction T^i on object O_j by m^i_{jk} and the set of all operations of transaction T^i by OS^i. All transactions terminate by either committing or aborting. $N^i \in \{commit, abort\}$ is the termination condition for T^i.

Definition 1 A transaction T^i is a partial order $(\Sigma^i, <^i)$ where:
1. $\Sigma^i = OS^i \cup \{ N^i \}$.
2. $<^i$ is the ordering relation.
3. For any two conflicting operations $m^i_{jm}, m^i_{jn} \in OS^I$, either $m^i_{jm} <^i m^i_{jn}$ or $m^i_{jn} <^i m^i_{jm}$.
4. $m^i_{jk} \in OS^i, m^i_{jk} <^i N^i$.

For a meta-object O_{meta} under twin transactions two (or more) versions of a single object O will exist (as different transactions might have executed on replicas of object O). It is necessary to understand how they coexist and interact. Transactions will be executed concurrently on both versions of the object O. This execution sequence must be captured by a history. Intuitively, a history is a partial order of the executions of transaction operations where the ordering relation must include those pairs of operations that conflict.

Definition 2 A history H, of a set of transactions $\mathbf{T} = \{T^1, T^2, ... T^n\}$, is a partial order $(\Sigma_T, <_T)$ where:
1. $\Sigma_T = \cup^n_{i=1} \Sigma^i$
2. $<_T \supseteq \cup^n_{i=1} <^i$

3. For any two conflicting operations m^i_{kr}, $m^j_{ks} \in \Sigma_T$, either $m^i_{kr} <_T m^j_{ks}$ or $m^j_{kr} <_T m^i_{ks}$

This definition enables us to reason about histories as transaction operation execution sequences are using the ordering relation $<_T$. For example, given that the initial state of an object O_k, prior to the execution of the transactions in T is S_k, then the three method invocations occurring in the order; $m^i_{kr} < m^j_{ks} < m^l_{kt}$ will move O_k into some state $S_{k'}$. This can be considered a sequence of state transition functions such that $S_{k'} = m^l_{kt}(m^j_{ks}(m^i_{kr}(S_k)))$.

Transaction models usually prove correctness using a serial ordering, where a single transaction executed alone on a consistent object base will produce a consistent object base. In case of twin-transactions, since possibly different set of transactions are operating on multiple copies of a consistent object (multiple sets of histories), this serial ordering cannot be guaranteed when the other sets are not available (possibly due to non-availability of the host). This makes the conflict detection a non-trivial task. When history becomes available, then using optimistic concurrency control any pair of concurrent method invocations on an object will result in a conflict requiring one method execution (and the corresponding transaction) to be aborted. One way to limit aborts, is through the use of a precise notion of conflict. The basis of conflict is still read/write and write/write conflicts but at a finer level of granularity than the entire object. A more serious serialisation problem exists if two (or more) transactions are operating on two (or more) objects. For example, suppose that initial states of objects O_x and O_y, prior to the execution of the transactions in T, are S_x and S_y. Then two method invocations occurring in the order; $m^i_{xr} < m^j_{xs}$ will move O_x into some state $S_{x'}$, and two method invocations occurring in the order $m^j_{yv} < m^i_{yw}$ will move O_y into some state $S_{y'}$. The two state transition functions are:

$$S_{x'} = m^j_{xs}(m^i_{xr}(S_x))$$
$$S_{y'} = m^i_{yw}(m^j_{yy}(S_y))$$

The two transactions T^i and T^j are interleaved. This situation can occur in twin-transactions. For example, if T^i originated from DM_a ($O_{x(meta)}$) and T^j originated from DM_b ($O_{y(meta)}$), and disconnected twin-transaction processing is carried out. In this particular case, both transactions need to be aborted if the method invocations are not associative.

As said earlier, in twin-transaction model the serial ordering cannot be guaranteed all the time. Thus, some conflicting operations on an object will be executed and one (or both) may be aborted later on when the set of transaction histories are merged together by meta-object O_{meta}. In twin-transactions, the emphasis is not on successfully executing all the transactions but to successfully execute the transactions for which the probability of success was determined to be more as compared to other transactions. Thus during reconciliation of conflicting operations, that operation (and corresponding transaction) will be aborted (redone) for which the probability of success was less, thus supporting learned transaction patterns (this abort will also be learned). This learning pattern can be tuned to suite for each meta-object.

Conflict may occur when two method invocations occur on the two versions of the object O_i (host might be mobile and disconnected). In this case, O_i is initially in some state S_i and two method executions (say $f^s = m^s_{ix}$ and $g^t = m^t_{iy}$) perform state transformations on the local copies of the object. Reconciliation is possible if we assume that f^s and g^s are unrelated and their execution order is irrelevant as long as it is serialisable. Thus to be correct, the new object state after the execution of f^s and g^s must either be $f(g(S_i))$ or $g(f(S_i))$. There is, however, no guarantee that an uncontrolled concurrent execution of f and g will produce a final object state equivalent to either. Transaction T^s which executes f will produce a version of O_i in state $f(S_i)$ while transaction T^t (executing g) will produce a version having state $g(S_i)$. These versions may not be compatible. Three "Reconciliation Cases" are possible depending on the kind of conflict which occurs (if any), each of which must be resolved to ensure object consistency. This reconciliation process is the synchronisation relation $\Leftrightarrow$ of twin-transactions.

Reconciliation Case 1:
> If f^s and g^t are both read-only transactions with respect to attribute of O_i, then no conflict occurred and no processing is required.

Reconciliation Case 2:
> If f^s is read-only at O_i but g^t is not then the new object state must be set to $g^t(S_i)$. Similarly, if g^t is read-only at O_i but f^s is not then the new object state must be set to $f^s(S_i)$. Additionally transaction T^s must be serialised before T^t in the first case and T^t must be serialised before T^s in the second.

Reconciliation Case 3:
> If f^s and g^t conflict and T^s has a higher probability of success then set the new object state to be $f^s(S_i)$ and re-execute g^t (which might involve aborting, restarting transaction T^t). Similarly, if T^t has a higher probability of success then set the new object state to be $g^t(S_i)$ and re-execute f^s.

If transactions are operating on multiple objects, then synchronisation relation $\Leftrightarrow$ (reconciliation) might be applied to a set of objects O_{set} that are involved in a set of transactions. In that case, the synchronisation process will involve selecting, one by one, each object from O_{set} and applying the synchronisation relation. The selection of objects mostly depends on the following parameters:
- Probabilities of success of transactions which operated on that object.
- What kind of reconciliation is required for that object? (Reconciliation Cases).
- Where O_{meta} is located (transmission costs)?
- Abortion cost of transactions (How many objects they have operated upon).

The synchronisation process (reconciliation) is heavily dependent on the probability of success, $1/\rho$, of transactions. Therefore, ρ must be calculated (predicted) in an accurate (or near accurate) manner. This calculation process is dependent on how much information regarding the transaction is available to DM. If the DM knows about other objects that are involved in a transaction then this calculation will be a bit easy, but that require from the transaction to inform DM about its intended access set (objects to be read/written). This is not desirable and not possible in most cases. The only information that is available to the DM is about the data items (objects) that are already accessed by a transaction. The DM must be able to make a decision to let the transaction proceed with a certain ρ value. To do that, the DM must categorise different types of transactions and keep record of all the transactions that are (usually) in conflict. Even when two transactions are in conflict, the DM must let them execute based on the learned patterns of transaction execution. The learned patterns must be constructed from the transaction histories and merging of histories and reconciliation of objects.

4 Related Research

Chrysanthis [5] provides an axiomatic definition for two transaction types, namely reporting transactions and co-transactions to model the interaction between a mobile host and its base node, but provides no support for operation during disconnection. In [13] the transaction concepts are revised for mobile computing and take into account of the vulnerability of the computation performed at mobile hosts, the concept of transaction proxies is introduced for supporting recovery. For each transaction executed at a mobile host a dual transaction, called proxy, will be executed at the base node of that mobile host. The proxy transaction only includes the updates of the original transaction. Thus, any time a transaction is submitted to a mobile host, its proxy is submitted to its base node. In that sense proxy transactions correspond to taking periodic backup of the computation, which is performed at a mobile host. The operation during disconnection is not discussed.

The proxy-transactions [13] and twin-transactions are different in their essence. The former is generated when the mobile is connected and a transaction is submitted to it, whereas the later is generated no matter whether the mobile host is connected or disconnected. Also proxy-transactions are used to take periodical backups of the computation done on mobile hosts whereas twin-transactions are more in the lines of emulating the transaction process running at a mobile host and stationary network and are used for synchronisation as well on reconnection.

In [6] the issue of data availability is discussed and data inference is used to reduce the degree of replication in the system.. Maintenance of a knowledge base for data inferencing is required when data is not available, possibly due to some site failures. In the model proposed to allocate data objects, rules based on application semantics are required to reduce the search space. An extension to traditional approach of data replication to increase reliability and availability without requiring a higher degree of replication is presented in [6].

5 Implementation, Conclusions and Future Work

Replication of data items maintained by a mobile host is one of the solutions to solve the problem of uncertain availability of a mobile host. In this paper we have described our multi-layered architecture for integrating replicas of a data item within a meta-object.. The meta-object encapsulates the location and replica management thus providing a logical view of the data item to transactions.

The twin-transactions concept is used to replicate the processing of a transaction and to guarantee successful completion of a transaction, even in case of disconnections of certain replicas, with a certain required probability of success. The probability of success of a transaction will be calculated using learned set of heuristics. These heuristics will be applied during the transaction initiation phase. The learning of heuristics is heavily dependent on keeping transaction histories and learning transaction patterns. Establishing the heuristics for the probability of success measures is an open problem. There might be a few ways to avoid it in a deterministic way. Much research is needed in this area.

The implementation of twin-transaction model and meta-object concepts in an object system (like Orbix), which provides services (methods as transactions) to clients, is currently in progress. For that purpose we are looking into few current object-oriented database products. We plan to build a logical object layer on top of a set of databases. This layer will present a logical view of the underlying databases in terms of meta-objects. The implementation of a meta-object will include the replication protocol, location information and twin-transaction execution (replication of transaction processing).

Concurrency control will be different for each meta-object and can be encapsulated within the object. This leaves open the question of the *'level'* of the object (in the inheritance hierarchy) and the relationship between the concurrency of objects in different classes at different *'levels'* - it is the usual tradeoff - locking at the highest level object ensures ACID properties but maximises potential concurrency conflict.

The synchronisation relation will be different in different meta-objects and will be dependent on the semantics of physical data items that are encapsulated within a meta-object. If the underlying data items are objects then the meta-object will try to reconcile the replicas using the presented method for reconciliation. For other types of data items, the semantics of the data items will be specified within the meta-objects. Based on these semantics the synchronisation process will check for any conflicts. Compensation of transactions is the only possible way when the effects of a transaction are to be removed.

We believe that object technology is rich enough to service the requirements of a mobile computing environment. Our suggested implementation of meta-objects will allow integration of a wide variety of data (object or non-object) systems. The performance of the resultant system will be dependent on many factors including the average number of replicas encapsulated within each meta-object, communication delays, size of learned heuristics, computation time for measure of probability of success and synchronisation time (when replicas within a meta-object become unavailable).

Acknowledgement

Support from the Australian Research Council and Monash University grant is thankfully acknowledged.

References

1. M. Ahamad, M.H. Ammar and S.Y. Cheung. Replicated Data Management In Distributed Systems. In Readings in Distributed Computing Systems, pages 572-591, 1992.
2. P.A. Bernstein and N. Goodman. Concurrency Control in Distributed Database Systems. In ACM Computing Surveys, 13(2): 185-221, 1981.
3. B.R. Badrinath and T. Imeilinski. Replication and Mobility. Proceedings of the Second Workshop on the Management of Replicated Data, pp.9-12, November 1992.
4. B.R. Badrinath and T. Imielinski. Sleepers and Workaholics: Caching Strategies in Mobile Environment. Proceedings of the 1994 ACM SIGMOD International Conference on Management of Data, pages 1-24, 1994.
5. P.K. Chrysanthis. Transaction Processing in Mobile Computing Environment. *In Proceedings of the IEEE Workshop on Advances in Parallel and Distributed Systems*, pages 77-83, October 1993.
6. W.W. Chu, B. A. N. Ribeiro and P.H. Ngai. Object Allocation in Distributed Systems with Virtual Replication. In Proceedings of Eighth International Conference on Data Engineering, pages 238-245, February 1992.
7. D. Duchamp. Issues in Wireless Mobile Computing. In Proceedings of the Third Workshop on Workstation Operating Systems, pages 2-10, 1992.
8. A. Elmagarmid, Y. Leu, J.Mullen, O.Bukhres "Introduction to Advanced Transaction Models", In: Database Transaction Models, Ed.A.Elmagarmid, Morgan Kaufmann, 1992
9. G.H. Forman and J. Zahorjan. The challenges of Mobile Computing, IEEE Computer, Vol 17(4), pages 38-47, Apr. 1994.
10. M. Faiz and A. Zaslavsky. Database Replica Management Strategies in Multidatabase Systems with Mobile Hosts. In *Proceedings of 6th International Hong Kong Computer Society Database Workshop: Database Reengineering and Interoperability*, Hong Kong, March 1995.
11. P. Graham and K. Barker. Effective Optimistic Concurrency Control in Multiversion Object Bases. Proceedings International Symposium, ISOOMS '94, pages 311-328, 1994.
12. R. Guerraoui. Toward Modular Concurrency Control for Object-Oriented Distributed System. Proceedings of the Fourth Workshop on Future Trends of Distributed Computing Systems, IEEE Computer Society Press, pages 240-246, 1993.
13. E. Pitoura and B. Bhargava. *Revising Transaction Concepts for Mobile Computing*, Proceedings of the 1st IEEE Workshop on Mobile Computing Systems and Applications, pages 164-168, Dec 1994.
14. A. Rasheed and A. Zaslavsky. Ensuring Database Availability in Dynamically Changing Mobile Computing Environment. *In Proceedings of the 7th Australian Database Conference*, Australia, pages 100-108, January 1996.
15. L.H. Yeo and A. Zaslavsky. A. Submission of Transactions from Mobile Workstations in a Cooperative Multidatabase Processing Environment. *In Proceedings of the 14th IEEE CS International Conference on Distributed Computing Systems*, Poland, pages 372-379, June 1994.

Legacy Transactional Systems Integration Framework

Simone Sédillot   Jian Liang

INRIA
Domaine de Voluceau - Rocquencourt
78153 Le Chesnay, France

{Simone.Sedillot/Jian.Liang}@inria.fr

Abstract

This paper focus on how to use a transaction bridge to make an Object Management Group's Object Transaction Service (OMG OTS) interoperate with X/Open oriented legacy transaction systems, so that an on-line transaction may span two heterogeneous domains. The transactional bridging framework is applied to a CORBA client accessing to a transactional DCE platform, and to a proprietary transaction system which, in terms of standards, supports only X/Open XA interface to database. A two-phase-commit protocol machine with network access which can be adapted to different interfaces is the necessary condition to achieve a flexible transaction bridge at low cost.

1. Introduction

Today, business critical applications become more and more complex and public. Sharing information (resource) is therefore a good way rather than redevelopment. Since these information originate from various enterprises throughout the world, development technologies and adopted technical supports are unavoidably different.

In distributed transaction processing community, some standards such as X/Open Distributed Transaction Processing (DTP) model [1] and Object Management Group's Object Transaction Service (OMG OTS) [2] have been defined to make compliant transaction systems interoperate. Very recently, the inter-model interoperability between the X/Open DTP model and the OMG OTS model has become a hot focus.

X/Open DTP and OMG OTS are specified by different organizations for standardization. The differences on the interest, on the strategy and on the communication paradigm lead to enormous heterogeneity on transaction services and communication protocol. This heterogeneity produces serious difficulties for making

OMG OTS system interoperate with legacy X/Open transaction systems. Moreover, most of legacy transaction systems are only partly conforming to the standards, for example, Transarc's Encina and BEA's Tuxedo. This reality rises additional problems.

In this paper, we discuss these problems and propose an integration framework for making OMG OTS transaction systems interoperate with open legacy transaction systems and with non open proprietary transaction systems. An open legacy transaction system offers a standard interface whereby it can be controlled by another transaction system. A proprietary transaction system does not offer such an interface. However, we assume that both support the standard interface to database.

Section 2 briefly presents the OMG Object Transaction Service and X/Open DTP model. Section 3 details the features of the integration framework from an engineering point of view. Section 4 applies the framework to the integration of an open transactional OSF Distributed Computing Environment (DCE [3]) system (conforming to X/Open TxRPC [4][5]) with an OTS transaction system. Section 5 applies the framework to a non open proprietary legacy system.

2. Distributed Transaction Processing Models

2.1 OMG Object Transaction Service

Object Transaction Service is one of the Common Object Service defined by OMG. It allows users to build transactional applications based on Common Object Request Broker Architecture (CORBA) [6]. The architecture of the Object Transaction Service is defined in terms of CORBA architecture (Figure 1). All interactions among components are defined by CORBA IDL interfaces and realized across Object Request Broker (ORB).

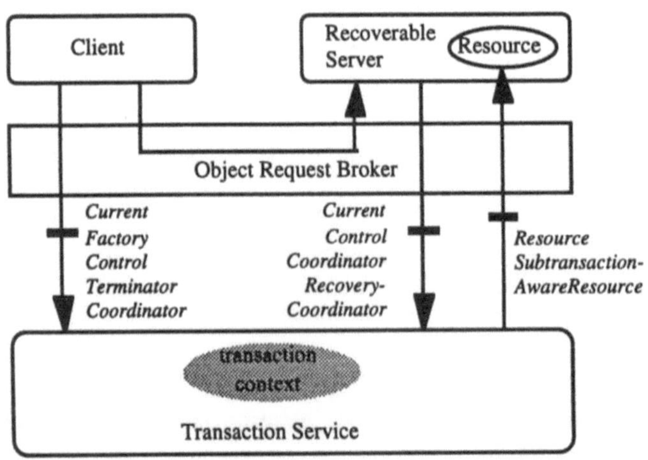

Figure 1: OMG Object Transaction Service

A transaction may involve multiple objects. The transaction scope is defined by a transaction context which is shared by participating objects. The Transaction Service provides transaction management services and transaction propagation protocol through a set of well-defined interfaces. The client is the transaction originator: it creates a transaction, invokes application operations and orders the transaction termination. A Recoverable Server, normally, consists of at least one application object and one Resource object.

The major interest for our concern is that two Transaction Services coordinate for the purpose of a consistent termination of a transaction. With regards to the transaction completion flows, the server Transaction Service is subordinated to the client Transaction Service. The subordinate (server) Transaction Service registers with the superior (client) Transaction Service as a Resource object. The superior Transaction Service propagates the transaction semantics to its subordinate without knowing whether it is real Resource or subordinate Transaction Service. This is one of the remarkable distribution transparency features of the OTS.

2.2 X/Open DTP Model

X/Open Distributed Transaction Processing model (DTP) is a software architecture which allows multiple application programs to share data provided by multiple resource managers, and allows their work to be coordinated into global transactions.

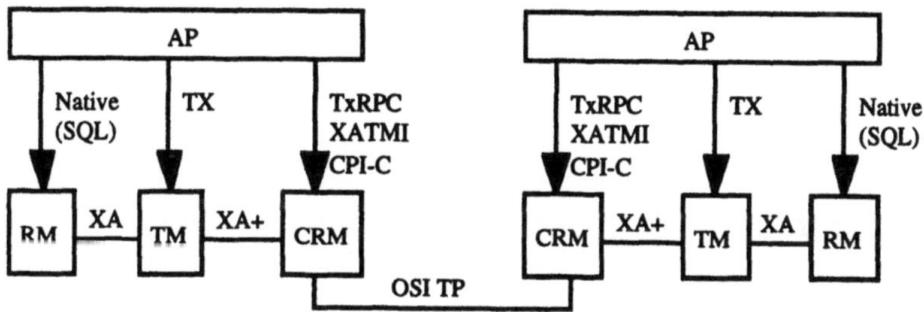

Figure 2 : X/Open Distributed Transaction Processing Model

The X/Open DTP model (Figure 2) identifies the basic functional components and their interfaces: Resource Managers (RMs) such as database or file access systems, control access to resource data. A transaction Manager (TM), assigns identifiers to transactions, monitors their progress, and takes responsibility for transaction completion and failure recovery. A communication Resource Manager (CRM) controls communications between distributed applications within or across transaction domains. A transaction communication protocol, provides underlying communications. ISO OSI TP [7] is officially part of the X/Open CRM.

We define an X/Open system as "open", if it offers the XA+ interface between CRM and TM, and as "non open" if it does not.

2.3 Open Legacy Transaction System - ACTranS TxRPC prototype

X/Open TxRPC allows DCE RPCs to be executed in the scope of a transaction. It is an integration of ISO OSI TP and OSF DCE. The European project ACTranS has prototyped a CRM based on OSI TP with XA+ interface. It adopts separated flows communication model for transmitting transactional RPCs, thus it uses the native DCE runtime to transmit RPCs and uses the OSI TP dialogue for the communication between the TMs. [8] [9].

2.4 Non Open Legacy Transaction Systems

Today, almost all X/Open compliant systems support TX and XA interfaces. However, not every transaction system implements the XA+ interface. Another type of implemented is that the TM and the CRM are integrated as a single component which provides the TX, XA interfaces and a proprietary communication paradigm interface. As such transaction systems are only partly conforming to the X/Open DTP specification, they are not open for directly interoperating with other transaction systems. We call them non open legacy transaction systems. The systems such as BEA Tuxedo, Transarc Encina, IBM CICS can be considered as the proprietary transaction systems.

3. Integration Engineering Framework

We are persuaded that there is a generic engineering which enables heterogeneous transaction systems to interwork. The reason for this is that there are three properties which are common in any interworking design, and they determine the framework design, namely, transparency, superior-subordinate relationship between the interworking systems, and modularity within the interworking with regards to applications and pure transactional operations.

3.1 Transparency

The constraints of making distributed transaction processing system interworking are to : (1) maintain existing transaction systems unchanged, (2) provide   maximum transparency to each of the existing systems.

Respecting above constraints, the framework created to achieve interoperability should be outside existing transaction domains. For this reason, the transaction bridge concept is adopted. This decision is in line with CORBA-DCE bridges already largely investigated [10][11].

In our case, a transaction bridge is inserted between two transaction domains. The transaction domains are maintained unchanged because the bridge offers to each domain one of its native interfaces. This is what we define as a transparent interworking. A transaction system shall completely ignore the features of another transaction domain. It may even ignore the existence of the transaction bridge but just consider it as a homogeneous participant. With this transparency, existing applications are reusable. This is very meaningful for users having already their own transaction systems and their relevant product-dependent applications. Moreover, as the bridge is developed outside existing transaction domains, the development cost is therefore reduced.

3.2 Abstract Superior-subordinate Relationships

According to the two-phase-commit algorithm which is used for the transaction termination, nodes in a transaction tree respect a hierarchy rule in the way they coordinate each other:

- Each OTS or TM is the superior of, respectively, Recoverable Objects and Resource Managers located within its domain. The latter are subordinates.
- When a request is sent from domain A to domain B, the OTS or the TM in the domain B becomes a subordinate of the OTS, or the TM in the domain A.

Our purpose in this paper is restricted to identify its invariance in terms of functionality. However, the implementation technologies are different: In OTS, these functions are implemented as operations in Resource interface; In X/Open, they are implemented as XA and XA+ functions; In ISO OSI TP, they are implemented as protocol element procedures. The result of these observations is that the role of the bridge, during the transaction termination, is to map one domain functions onto another domain functions.

3.2.1 Transaction bridge for Open systems

Figure 3 shows these functions in the case where an OTS system interoperates with an open transaction system: The bridge offers the OTS Resource Interface to the superior Transaction Service. The Resource interface methods map the transaction termination requests onto the OSI TP protocol data units.

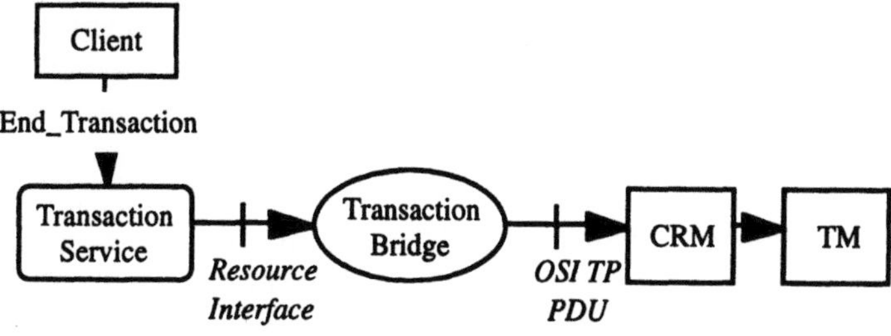

Figure 3: Transaction Bridge Mapping role for Open DTP domain

The transaction bridge encapsulates a transactional legacy domain in order to make it appear as an OTS Resource object, thus including transparently the legacy domain in the OTS domain.

3.2.2 Transaction bridge for non open systems

When the legacy domain is not open, (Figure 4), only the TX and XA interfaces are offered. The way to enforce such a domain to act as a subordinate in a transaction tree is that the bridge uses the TX interface in a coordinated fashion with the invocation on its Resource interface. Typically, the *prepare* operation will enforce the application to invoke the commitment of transaction (*tx_commit*). However, this is not sufficient, because the proprietary transaction system will decide to locally commit, as soon as all its local Resource Managers have responded with a *ready*. The way to enslave the proprietary transaction system decision to commit is to declare the bridge as one of its Resource Managers and synchronize its *ready* response to the time when the bridge *commit* operation is invoked by OTS. These mappings are more sophisticated than in the case of an open legacy system, but the transaction bridge still encapsulates the legacy domain transparently to the OTS domain.

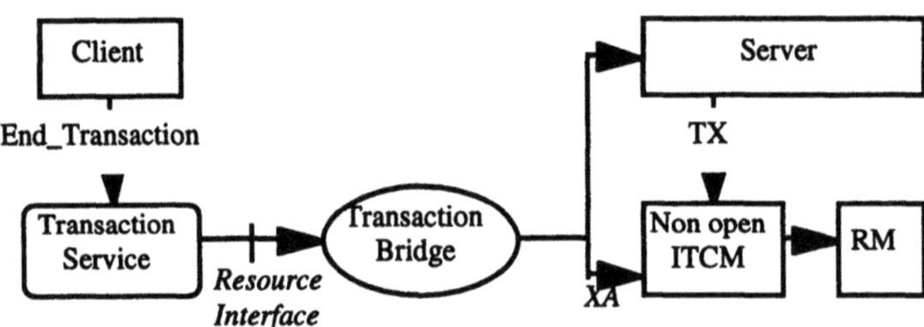

Figure 4: Transaction Bridge Mapping role for Non Open DTP domain

3.4 Bridge Engineering Framework

The complete interworking framework is supported by an application bridge and a transaction bridge. The application bridge has the responsibility of the CORBA requests translation into the appropriate legacy call. The transaction bridge has the responsibility to control the transaction behavior of the legacy system in a fashion which is consistent with the OTS execution. This implies a transactional node state machine, with logging and recovery functions, that is a two-phase-commit machine.

Based on the comparison between OSI TP and OMG OTS, we found that OSI TP services are richer than those of OMG OTS. In order to satisfy the requirement for X/Open model which uses OSI TP as communication protocol, the transaction bridge is built on an OSI TP protocol machine. The prototype which we use has facilities to adapt the network access points to different interfaces which may not necessarily be ISO stacks. Typically, the OSI TP network access to the superior is changed into an OTS Resource interface, whereas its network access to the subordinate is changed into the appropriate legacy interface.

4. Bridging DCE TxRPC to OTS-ORB

4.1 The CORBA-DCE Application Bridge

Today, many works have been concerned with the application interoperability between DCE and CORBA. A cost-effective solution is to develop application interoperability by means of an application bridge. The use of application bridge may avoid the modification to existing DCE and CORBA platforms. The Application Bridge is indicated by AB in Figure 5.

4.2 The OTS-CRM Transaction Bridge

When the transaction bridge communicates with the TxRPC transaction domain using OSI TP communication mechanism, it acts as a TxRPC CRM. When it interoperates with the OMG Transaction Service, it acts as a subordinate Transaction Service. The transaction bridge is indicated by TB in Figure 5.

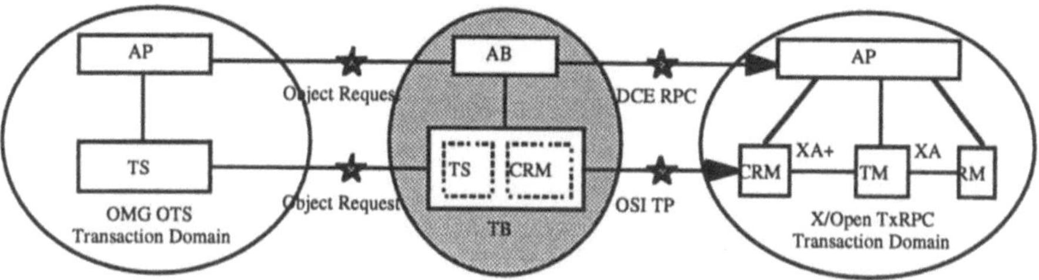

Figure 5: Transaction Bridge for Open Transaction Systems

Because of the difference in the domains communication mechanisms (one is based on OSI TP messages while the other is based on ORB requests), messages transformation is needed.

4.2.1 Relationship Establishment

In order to ensure the transaction semantics to be reliably propagated between distributed participants, a superior/subordinate relationship has been identified in the two protocols.

In OSI TP, the establishment of superior/subordinate relationship is always requested by the superior. In OTS, there is no superior/subordinate relationship until dynamic registration made by the Recoverable Server, thus, the establishment of the superior/subordinate relationship is requested by the subordinate.

Observing these behaviors, the Transaction bridge establishes the relationship with the superior OTS by registering itself as a Resource Object and requests the subordinate CRM to establish the relationship using OSI TP mechanism.

4.2.2 Execution Flows

The execution flows of the OTS-TxRPC framework are shown in Figure 6.

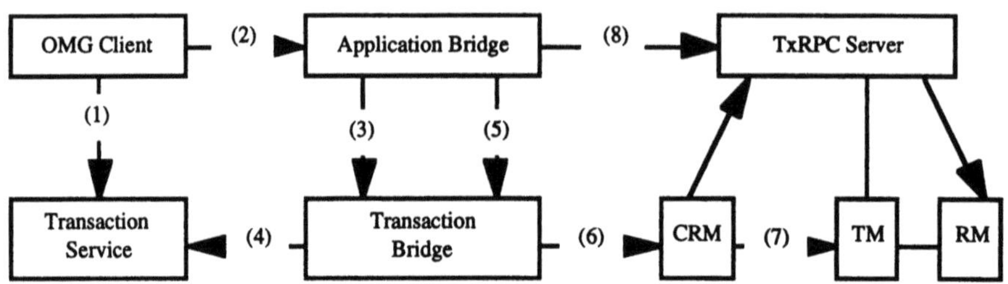

Figure 6: Transaction Bridge Execution Flows

(1) An OMG client invokes Transaction Service to begin a transaction.
(2) The OMG client invokes a transactional operation to the application bridge.
(3) The application bridge creates and invokes transaction bridge to perform registration.
(4) The transaction bridge registers with the superior Transaction Service as a Resource object.
(5) The application bridge translates the object request in the TxRPC call form and invokes the transaction bridge to establish an OSI TP dialogue with the server CRM.
(6) The transaction bridge establishes a dialogue with the server CRM, and transmits the transaction semantic messages.
(7) The server CRM notifies the TM of the reception of the transaction semantic messages so that the TM may associate its RMs in the scope of the transaction.
(8) The DCE call is transmitted on the DCE RPC flow. The TxRPC server executes the clients request and returns the result to the client.

5. Bridging a Non Open Legacy Transaction System to OTS

In the case of making OTS interoperate with an non open proprietary transaction system, the same approach that in the OTS-TxRPC bridge is taken (Figure 7). However, there is no open Communication Resource Manager (CRM) in the legacy system. In this case, the transaction bridge contains three parts: one part acting as a subordinate Transaction Service (TS); one part acting as a superior communication manager (RMcl) and one part representing Transaction Bridge (RMsv) located on the same host than the proprietary transaction system. The entry point of the X/Open transaction domain is the RMsv which contains a two-phase-commit OSI TP protocol machine. An unstructured user data transfer [12] is offered by RMcl and RMsv.

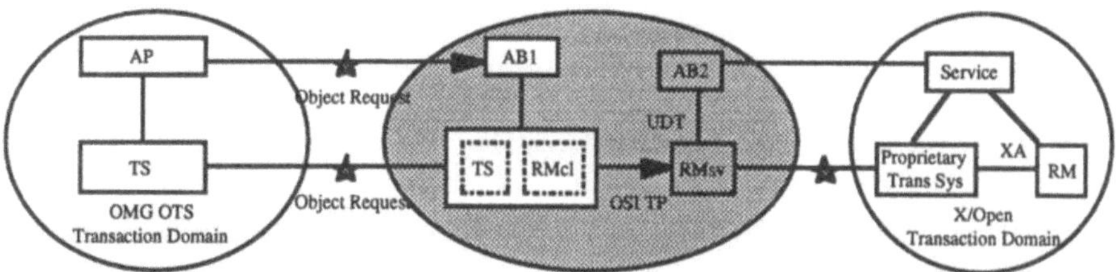

Figure 7: Transaction Bridge for Non Open Legacy Transaction Systems

5.1 Application Bridge

The application bridge contains two parts: AB1 and AB2. Once the AB1 receives the requests from the client, it maps them onto an unstructured transfer syntax and transmits them to the transaction bridge RMcl component. The RMcl transmits the user data to the AB2 application. The AB2 application acts as a client and transforms the call into the appropriate request to the service. This transformation is proprietary dependent, but is part of the AB2 code, thus it is transparent to the service.

5.2 Execution Flows

The execution flows of the OTS to proprietary transaction system are shown on Figure 8:

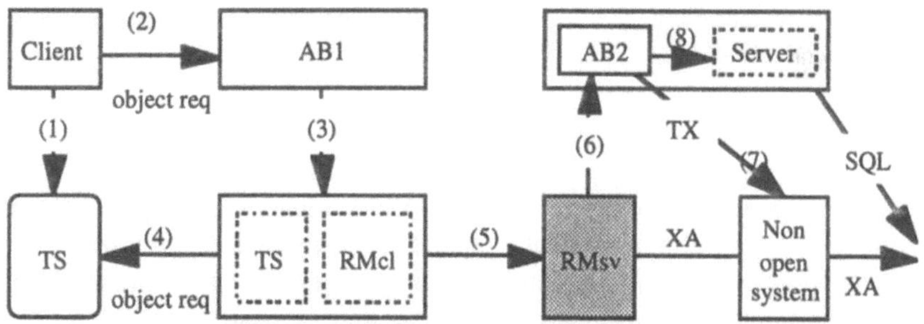

Figure 8: Bridge Execution Flows

(1) An OMG client invokes its Transaction Service to begin a transaction.
(2) The OMG client invokes a transactional operation on the application bridge (AB1).
(3) The AB1 translates the object request and invokes the transaction bridge.
(4) The transaction bridge registers with the superior Transaction Service as a Resource object.

(5) The RMcl establishes a dialogue with RMsv, transmits the transaction Identifier, then the call.

(6) The RMsv notifies AB2 the reception of the transaction Identifier and the call.

(7) The AB2 starts a transaction, using *tx-begin* on the TX interface. So that the TM may associate its RMs in the scope of the transaction

5.3 Technology and Commitment

Technology is driven by the RMsv role during commitment. The execution sequence during commitment is shown as follows:

(1) The RMsv receives from the bridge a *prepare* and provides it to AB2.

(2) The AB2 invokes *tx_commit* on proprietary transaction system.

(3) The proprietary transaction system invokes *prepare* on its local RMs XA interface, including the RMsv.

(4) The RMsv spies the other RM responses. When all have responded with *ready*, it returns a *ready* to the RMcl.

(5) When the RMsv receives from the bridge a *commit*, it responds a *ready* to the proprietary transaction system.

(6) The proprietary transaction system invokes *commit* on all its RMs through XA interface, including the RMsv.

It is beyond the scope of this presentation to go in the details of recovery and rollback, but this RMsv has been prototyped with success between a Tuxedo and an Encina system. It shows that using the full superior-subordinate relationship in a transaction tree and the appropriate standard interfaces, interworking can be achieved. Although the bridging is not as clean as with an open legacy system, AB2 and RMsv can be installed on the legacy system as normal client application and database respectively.

6. Conclusion

The target of transactional bridging is to incorporate a legacy transactional domain (implying its servers and transactional monitors) in a new transactional domain, so that a client in the new domain may span a transaction in the legacy domain. For the purpose of simplicity, we have considered a new transactional domain as an OTS compliant domain, with an OTS, and two kinds of transactional legacy domains: open DCE domain, and non open domains. We have proved that interoperability is always achievable because of the transaction termination invariant sequences of information exchanges. We have shown that integration transparency can be achieved, both in the integrating system (OTS) and in the integrated system (Open DCE and non open systems) by means of a bridging framework.

For the sake of transparency, the bridge needs to be a transaction node with a full two-phase-commit machine implying recovery and logging capabilities. In addition this machine must have two standard communication interfaces, one to the integrating system (OTS) and the other to the integrated system, through which the transaction semantic propagation takes place. We have selected two possible standard interfaces to legacy system: the widely used XA interface for non open legacy systems and the X/Open Communication Resource Manager (XA+ interface) for open legacy systems.

We have separated the application communication paradigm transformation (application bridge) from the transaction semantics exchanges (transaction bridge), in order to isolate the developments requiring different skill, and addressing different components of the systems.

All these features make our bridging technology adaptive and generic. The property of distributed computing platform independence is very meaningful, because it enables the transaction bridge to be easily migrated onto arbitrary distributed platforms.

Reference

1. X/Open guide, Distributed Transaction Processing Reference model Version 2, 1993
2. Object Transaction Service, OMG document 96-12-6.
3. OSF DCE Application Development Guide - Introduction and Style Guide.
4. Open CAE Specification (Sanity Check), Distributed Transaction Processing: TxRPC Specification. Draft August 3, 1995.
5. S. Diztzen, R Fleming, Requirement For Transaction Processing with DCE (Report of the DCE SIG Transaction Processing Working Group), http://www.transarc.com, January 1994.
6. Common Object Request Broker Architecture: Specification and Architecture, Revision-2 0, July 1995
7. ISO/IEC 10026, Part 1: Model, Part 2: Service Definition, Part 3: Protocol Specification
8. Simone Sedillot, Jian Liang, Joseph La Chimia, Integrating DCE RPC with OSI TP to offer a transactional RPC. First Workshop on High Speed Network and Open Distributed Platforms, St Petersburg, Russia, June 1995.
9. Joseph La Chimia, Per Igel, Jian Liang, Simone Sédillot, Susan Thomas, ACTranS Toolkit TxRPC Architecture, Project deliverable, February 1996.
10. Zhonghua Yang and Andreas Vogel, Archieving Interoperability between CORBA and DCE Applications Using Bridges. International Conference on Distributed Platforms. Chepman & Hall, London, 1996.
11. Tim Redhead, Zhonghua Yang and Andreas Vogel, On-demand bridging between CORBA and DCE applications. 1996.
12. ISO/IEC DIS 10026-6, Information Technology - Open System Interconnection - Distributed Transaction Processing - Part 6, Unstructured Data Transfer.

APPLICATIONS

A Dynamic Business Object Architecture for an Insurance Industrial Project

[1]**Kitty Hung**, [2]**Yuan Sun**, [3]**Tony Rose**

[1]*School of Computing, Information Systems & Mathematics, South Bank University*
103 Borough Road, London, SE1 0AA, U.K.
E-mail: hungks@sbu.ac.uk
[2]*Compuware Ltd., 163 Bath Road, Slough, Berkshire, SL1 4AA, U.K.*
E-mail: yuan_sun@compuware.com
[3]*CAD Consultants Ltd., 797 London Road, Thornton Heath, Surrey, CR7 6XA, U.K.*
E-mail:tony.rose@btrinc.com

ABSTRACT: We propose a Business Object Architecture (BOA) developed under the Dynamic Systems Development Method (DSDM) life-cycle environment to form a Dynamic Business Object Architecture (DBOA) aiming to narrow the semantic gap between software developments and business applications. The structure and process of DBOA are explained through the development work documented in this paper. An insurance industrial project was used as a case study to demonstrate the initial result of this approach.
KEY WORDS: Business Object Architecture, Dynamic Systems Development Method, Semantic Gap, Dynamic Business Object Architecture

1 INTRODUCTION

The rift between Information Technology (IT) developers and the end-users in the business world is still of concern [Hung97(b)] [Reenskaug96]. IT developers and researchers have attempted to bridge this gap by developing techniques such as Business Architecture [Bennett92], Requirement Engineering [Rowland96], System Engineering [Thome93], Use Case Engineering [Jacobson94] [Jacobson96] and Business Objects [Sutherland95]. These approaches provide different mechanisms to enable the IT practitioners to obtain better understanding of the business domain. However, they share the same weakness in the lack of 'Users' Involvement'. [Rolland96] recommends the use of Requirement Engineering (RE) to see the business world and to capture the business knowledge/requirements from different angles and dimensions. However, the strategies proposed only see the business from the IT developers' pair of "tinted glasses" with the developers see the business from their own perspective. The end-users are denied of having the access to this pair of "tinted glasses" to be informed of or to participate in the development. Business people are most fitted as the knowledge providers and system responders in the system development project. The Use Case Engineering (UCE) initiated by Ivor Jacobson [Jacobson94] also offers 'Requirement Gathering Techniques' such as the interaction between the Actors and the Use Cases. This is another "IT tinted glasses" to acquire the business knowledge. There is limited facility to collect users' feedback or to include users in the project development activities. Although the 'Usage-Centred Approach' suggested by [Constantine96] has addressed the importance of users as this approach produces a 'user-oriented' user interface to narrow the communication gap between human and machine, [Constantine96] only raises the issue of how to use the Object-Oriented frame work or any other techniques to deliver a system which can address the needs of user and the issue of utility and usability. It does not address the significance of users' participation in the development processes. [Hsia96] engages in similar research. His approach to three kinds of techniques namely the Object-Oriented Analysis, Usage Scenario and Incremental Delivery all encourages 'user involvement' but not in the complete sense as proposed in this paper. This paper focuses not only on semantic gap but also other inherent problems in software development. We describe how the Business Object Architecture (BOA) technology [Casanave95] and the Dynamic Systems Development Method (DSDM)

[DSDM95 (a)] [DSDM95(b)] life-cycle environment can be integrated to form a Dynamic Business Object Architecture (DBOA). The paper is organised as follows. Section 2 describes the background and structure of the proposed DBOA. Section 3 presents a detailed case study report describing the DBOA technique. Section 4 evaluates the case study result. Finally, Section 5 summarises this approach and Section 6 specifies future work.

2 FROM BOA TO DBOA

2.1 Business Object And Business Object Architecture

In recent years, Object-Oriented (OO) approaches have been favourably adopted by many organisations as their preferred method in developing their information system management and planning [Arrow95]. It is generally accepted by the software community that the distinct features of OO such as reusability, portability, maintainability, encapsulation, inheritance and polymorphism can assist the developers in modelling a better framework for complex systems [Partridge96]. However, the leverage of objects referred to above is primarily a technology oriented perspective [Ramackers96]. The real shape and structure of Business Objects are yet to be defined [OMG95]. Different people use the term 'Business Object' to describe different things. There is no standard criteria to determine how to either define the Object to reflect the business or to assist the business people to run their business. Our interpretation of Business Object in this paper is firstly to identify the functionalities and processes of any business activities. Secondly, we identify the related entity objects with attributes, operations and behaviour declared. The Business Objects should reflect the organisation's business activities. Business Object Architecture (BOA), defined by Cory Casanave, Chair of OMGBODTF, is an architecture to represent the components that are used to 'model' the business problems and build the system [Casanave95]. BOA is aimed at providing a conceptual understanding of the business and this architectural framework should contain a model of the business structures, processes, functions, behaviour, objects and the like within the organisation [Arrow95]. The importance of architecture is to transform the always fuzzy, illusive and hard to follow business abstractions to a more structured, more visible and easier to follow business map. We have adopted BOA as the framework model in this paper.

2.2 Dynamic Systems Development Method (DSDM) Life-cycle Environment

Life-cycle methodologies are used by software developers and project managers in facilitating controllability for their project management. There are different types of life-cycles such as Waterfall [Hargrave96], Spiral [Bohem86], Fountain, Pinball [Henderson-Sellers96], Rapid Application Development [Martin91], Dynamic Systems Development Method [DSDM95(a)]. DSDM provides an ideal environment to enable developers to produce quality software while deliver on time and within budget through the techniques of: joint requirement planning (JRP), joint application development (JAD), function points, time-boxing, clean room technique, feasibility studies, business studies, functional model iteration, system design and build iteration, implementation. Such holistic approach of DSDM is to form a vehicle to drive the developer and end-users together. Traditionally, developers tend to put a subjective view on their work presuming this is what the real world needs. A fundamental assumption of DSDM is that nothing is built perfectly first time. As a result all steps can be revisited as part of its iterative approach. Therefore the current step need be completed only enough to move to the next step. DSDM not only provides a life-cycle but also the necessary controls to ensure its success [Hung97(a)].

2.3 Dynamic Business Object Architecture

DBOA is a technique to develop a BOA using DSDM's holistic approach by means of substantial user involvement, frequent reviewing, testing, identification of problems at the early stages of development. The iterative life-cycle also enables developers to review and modify the model even on a conceptual level. Details of our proposal is illustrated through the case study report in Section 3 where the BOA is incorporated with DSDM.

3 CASE STUDY: A DYNAMIC BUSINESS OBJECT ARCHITECTURE (DBOA) FOR A DEBTOR PROFILE SYSTEM

3.1 Background of the Debtor Profile System Project

The case study was carried out at CAD Consultants Ltd. which involved in the Credit insurance industry. When there is a transaction of products between seller and buyer, the buyer is given a certain length of credit period of time after receipt of the goods. The seller then insures the value of the products. Credit Insurance is to protect the sellers (i.e. the Insurance Policy Holders) from insolvency if their buyers fail to pay after the credit period . It is a commercial coverage by a contract binding a party to indemnify another against specified trading loss in return for premiums paid.

CAD not only manages insurance policies on behalf of its customers but also has to determine Credit Risks of each individual buyer as well as the global risk exposure of the buyer's country. This case study is to develop a Debtor Profile System to monitor the debt exposure. Under the Credit Insurance terms and conditions, any buyers who have credit are referred to as debtors. The purpose of this Debtor Profile System is to provide decision support to the business end-users on the approval/rejection of any future Credit Insurance Applications.

3.2 Business Object Architecture for CAD's Systems

As a starting point to understand the organisation, Figure 1 shows the BOA framework outlining the business functions within the organisation. Both Top-Down and Bottom-Up approaches are adopted. After defining the Business Processes from a high level abstraction, Entity Objects are identified Bottom-Up. Finally, Business Objects are formed which integrate the Business Processes, functionalities and operations together. Business Objects do not encapsulate the Entity Objects (as opposed to the conventional way of Object-oriented encapsulation). Rather they call the Entity Objects when they want to use them. The Entity Objects stay in the same position at the bottom of the framework. Benefit of which is that a single Entity Object is shared by different Business Objects. Therefore, if we want to change the attributes of the Entity Object, we only have to change once. Another advantage is that not only we can reuse the Entity Objects but also we can reuse the Business Processes. Business Objects can also be reused as a package as well.

3.3 Dynamic Business Object Architecture for CAD's Systems

Figure 2 shows the DBOA model. The BOA is situated in the centre of the DSDM life-cycle model. Among each life-cycle, there is an incremental prototyping approach through these phases moving anti-clockwise from the top with feasibility studies, 1st phase functional prototype, 2nd phase functional prototype, design prototype and implementation. Black arrows show the transfer points from one phase to another and the grey ones show where the development can easily return to an earlier phase. The white arrow indicates that the BOA model can always be re-architectured at any stage of the life-cycle.

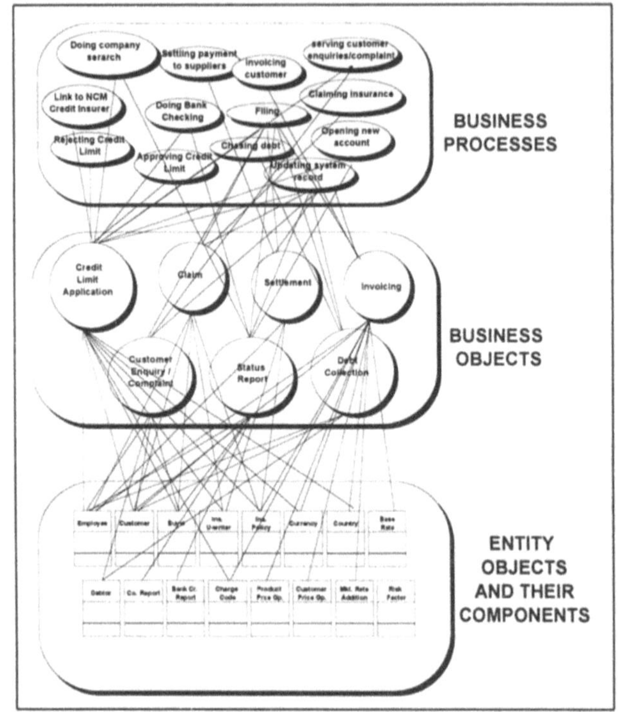

Figure 1 : Business Object Architecture for CAD's Systems

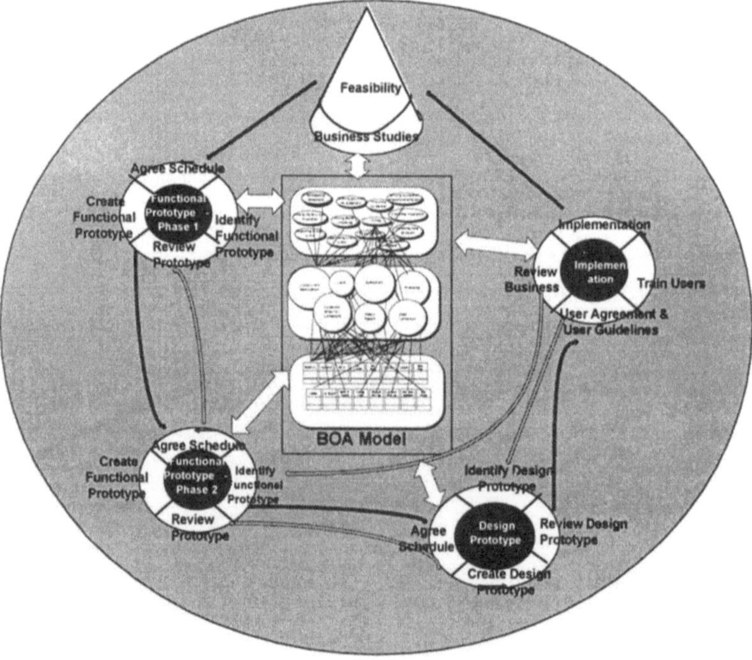

Figure 2: Dynamic Business Object Architecture for CAD's System

3.4 Credit Insurance Application Business Processes

Figure 3 is the breakdown of Figure 1 specifying one single aspect of the Credit Insurance Application Business Process. Jacobson's Use Case Engineering (UCE) was adopted as UCE provides a mechanism to enable the developer to understand the business. The Business Process model starts with Event Diagram followed by Interaction Diagram, Use Cases and Actors, Use Cases and Objects, Complete Use Cases Model and Business Use Cases and Business Objects Diagram.

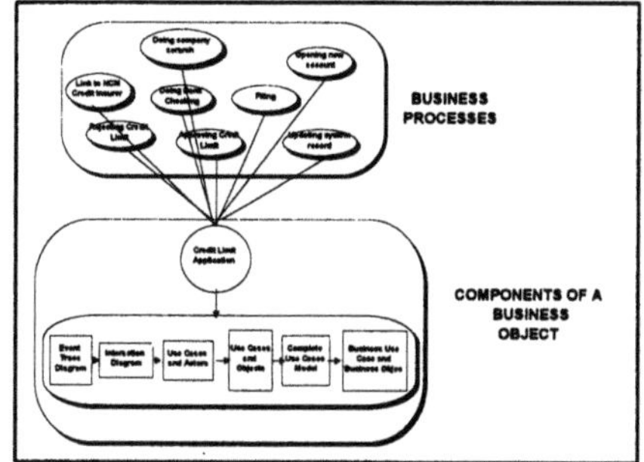

Figure 3: Business Processes for Credit Insurance Application

3.5 Credit Insurance Application Business Object

Figure 4 identifies the Entity Objects need to be used for a Credit Insurance Application business object.

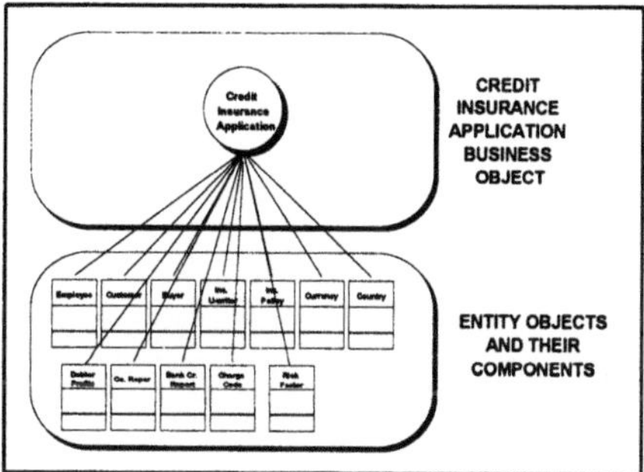

Figure 4: Credit Insurance Application Business Object

3.6 Project Estimation by using Function Points

The development of Debtor Profile system started with an estimation of the project size by using Function Points which are a method of estimating the "amount of functionality" required from an application and is also used to estimate project completion time. The basic idea involves counting screen inputs, outputs and other features of a description of functionality [IFPUG97]. Figure 5 shows the essentials of this estimation. The estimation strategy is by identifying each function as easy, medium or difficult in terms of expected development 'complexity'. Function points were set after the Joint Requirements Planning (JRP) meeting with the end-users where requirements were obtained from them. Three members in the project team from IT department were responsible for analysis, design, implementation and testing. Four members from the Business Department were responsible for providing the business information expertise, giving comments on the Business Object Model, and testing the prototype. The project spanned a five week period. As function points are the units used to measure the project, should there be changes in the user requirements during the project phases, the function points table will need to be re-scheduled accordingly.

It is important to note that within a tight timescale, it would be impossible to accommodate extra functionality without changes to the function point estimation. Therefore there are significant implications for the cost and/or duration of the project if such changes are required.

Functions	Points Allocated (1=easy; 2=medium; 3=difficult)	Estimated developer-hours (easy=6 hours; medium=12hours; difficult=18hours
Declared Month / Year (user entry)	1	6
Customer No. (user entry)	1	6
Customer Name *(auto display)*	1	6
Policy No. *(auto display)*	1	6
Policy Name *(auto display)*	1	6
Client Reference No (user entry)	1	6
CAD Buyer No. *(auto display)*	1	6
Buyer Name *(auto display)*	1	6
Country Code *(auto display)*	1	6
Amount (user entry)	1	6
Currency Code *(auto display)*	1	6
GBP Equivalent *(auto display)*	1	6
Insured Limit *(auto display)*	1	6
Total amount of debt (in GBP equivalent) for a particular debtor should be added up and shown at the bottom of the screen (auto display)	3	18
The entry of Major Debtor Profile record is done monthly. Transfer previous month to history	2	12
The new screen for entry of current month's record will be cloned from previous month and the end-users overwrite it.	1	6
Report by Debtors	1	6
Report by Currencies	1	6
Report by Countries	1	6
Report by Customers	1	6
Report by Period (i.e. monthly record)	1	6
Report by Amount (in GBP)	1	6
Report by Teams	1	6
Update Main Menu	1	6
Total :	27 points	162 hours

Figure 5: Function Point Table for Major Debtors Profile System

3.7 Time-Boxing

In the DSDM model for the Debtor Profile System project, heavy emphasis was placed on the importance of Time-boxing (Figure 6). As suggested by DSDM Manual [DSDM95(a)]: "Requirements can change, time can never slip." DSDM defines Time-boxing as 'setting a deadline by which a business objective must be met', and suggests that the Time-box set for the clearly defined delivery objective, such as a prototype demonstrating particular functionality, should be of the order of three to six weeks. The project comprised five such Time-boxes.

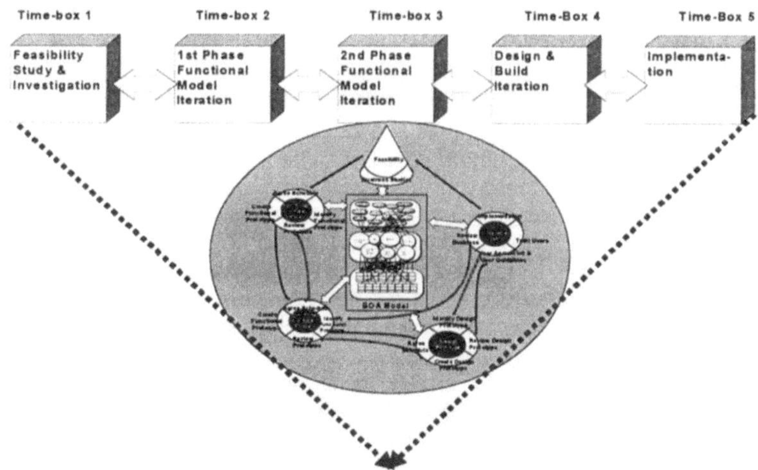

Figure 6: Time-boxing for Debtor Profile System

Imposing Time-boxes as short as one week may seem surprising, even for a project of this size. However, we found in practice that this very tightly controlled schedule was not only feasible, but kept the project team strongly focused on the work in hand. It is of course critical that the user community is as committed as the developers, and that events such as user acceptance testing are set quite definitively in terms of diary commitment. It has to be said that on occasions the schedule did seem severe, and there is an argument that such a strong emphasis on 'deadline' did detract from further useful discussion and debate. On balance however, both the developers and end-users would not have been so committed had any less rigorous approach to time management being adopted.

3.8 Prototyping Strategy

As Time-boxing controls the pace of design and development that is so essential to the project, computer based techniques make this feasible. It would indeed be quite impossible to entertain the idea of one week Time-boxes without a means of maintaining both design documentation and implementation in a flexible and responsive way. The implication for the quality of the delivered product is quite clear. Therefore, the criteria of both the Business Object design model and interface prototype must clearly reflect the business, be flexible to change, quick to build / assemble and support reuse.

3.9 Joint Requirements Planning (JRP) and Joint Application Development (JAD)

It is absolutely essential for such a project with heavy user involvement, that the right people assemble at the right time, and are given the right facilities to enable them to make the required design decisions. Design recommendations are not good enough. Empowered decision makers are essential.

JRP and JAD have provided an ideal environment to enable the business users and software developers to work together. A 'Project Development Team' was formed comprising three IT department staff and four from the Business Department (two Business Managers and two Account Executives). After the initial meeting of feasibility and business studies, meetings took place as a general rule, at the end of each of the one week Time-boxes. These took the form of a review of that Time-box phase, and identifications of requirements for the next phase. During these 'End-Of-Project-Phase' meetings, end-users were invited to test the prototype on-screen. The IT Department staff would collect the end-users' comments and feedback to modify the prototype.

3.10 Time-box 1 : Feasibility Studies and Investigation (5 days)

The initial JRP meeting with the users was to get to know the user requirements for this particular project; how they wanted to develop the Debtor Profile system. The project provided quite clear-cut requirements, in the technical context of a general need to provide information on all the current debtors for a particular customer.

The Debtor Profile Interface is in fact a consolidation of different database files such as Customer, Buyer, Credit Insurance Policy, Country, Currency and Exchange Rates. The Debtor Profile system correlates relevant data fields from different database files to the debtor Profile Interface. When the users enter the customer reference number, this customer reference number data field will trigger other correlative data fields to display all the existing debtors' details for that customer as well as the insured limit where CAD's customer is allocated to each buyer. Over and above these features, the end-user can also view a profile by currencies, countries and period etc. This Debtor Profile system is to assist the end-user in making decision making whether to approve or reject any future credit insurance application for a particular buyer. During this feasibility studies, object and class diagrams were generated based on our BOA framework model. The objective of the first phase functional model iteration was to produce a version of the working system, designed using Unified Modelling Language (UML) methodology [Rumbaugh96] and the interface was constructed using System Builder Plus [SB+] 4GL GUI Tools that could demonstrate to the user the essential features required to enable a Debtor Profile to be constructed.

3.11 Time-box 2: 1st Phase Functional Model Iteration (5 days)

The objective of the first phase functional model iteration was to produce a version of the working system, from analysis and design model, notation to implementation, that could demonstrate to the user the essential features required to enable a user view the debtor profile. The first day was spent developing aspects of the model using UML to created object, class, event trace and state transition diagrams. Data dictionary documentation was also produced. The second day was used for discussion and modification of the model, within the IT Department (i.e. without the involvement of any users). By the third day we could begin to map the UML design to SB+. The emphasis at this stage was on the development of data fields and the associated screen handling. This was no more than a 'rough' prototype, but it was able to demonstrate the essential features of the interface and some of the functionality of the new system. The fourth day comprised another 'IT internal' review; this time to test the prototype. A range of modifications and improvements were made, with suitable care to ensure that the UML model was maintained consistent with the SB+ implementation. It was necessary to involve users engaging in both management (the ambassador users) and clerical positions (the day-to-day users) as the prototype is in fact a work model to pave the way for future project development. Even at such an early stage, decisions were required from the users in determining whether the prototype was suitable to meet the business requirements. The objective of this JAD session was to give a feel to the end-users for what the Debtor Profile interface looked like. As the correlation was not set up yet, the end-users could not test the linkage. At this stage we had not attempted to transfer the data from different data files to the Debtor Profile file. We just wanted to show to the end-users the layout of the interface and whether there were any data fields missing. This session produced a substantial list of new or modified requirements such as:-

- produce a report grouping the Debtors together if they are parent company and subsidiaries
- change Client Buyer No. to Client Reference

- change Buyer No. to CAD No.
- add selection function to the Customer Reference No. data field so that the end-user can choose from the list without having to type out the Customer No.
- add name of Insurance Underwriter data field
- delete decimal points for all currency figures

Requirements were recorded as the tasks for the next time-box. As the new requirements were within the time scale, no developer hour was added to the Function Point Table. However, The IT Department staff would determine whether the change of requirements could be achieved within the Time-boxes or not. If so, IT staff would change the design and update the 'Function Points Table' accordingly. If not, the Project Development Team would negotiate an extension to the project deliverable deadline.

3.12 Time-box 3: 2nd Phase Functional Model Iteration (5 days)

The main objective of this second phase of the development of the functional model was to provide the bulk of the essential functionality to the model. The first phase had been mainly concerned with user interface design, with little in the way of 'business functionality'. An important issue of this early work in phase 2 was to revisit the BOA framework and its break down to find out whether the conceptual model framework was the right shape to drive through to deliver business systems/applications. We used the BOA conceptual model to pave the way for the system analysis, design and implementation. On the other hand we brought back changes made by the business end-users to re-architecture the BOA model. Such cycle goes iteratively so that we could check our model almost instantly. The first day was spent in creating a first cut design for the second phase functional prototype A meeting within the IT Department was held on the second day to discuss progress and modification. Much care had to be taken to keep adequate records of what could become a quite frantic rate of change unless careful controlled the project leader. Version control was a very real issue. The third day was spent in modifying the first phase functional prototype based on the feedback from the end-users and the conclusion reached in the previous day's meeting. On the fourth day, a session was held within the IT Department to review and test the second phase functional prototype. On the fifth and final day of Time-box 3 a project team meeting was held and the end-users tested the refined prototype. By this stage in the Time-box the changes were less significant, and to a large extent the session was more involved with user familiarity, identifying only minor points to take back to the next phase.

3.13 Time-box 4: Design and Build Iteration (5 days)

The schedule in Time-box 4 was similar to Time-box 3. However the essence of this phase is that we must design and actually build the system. Hence by the end of this phase the system must contain absolutely all functionality, in a form which is suitable for testing in the final JAD session. There should be no components of functionality left un-implemented if the schedule is to be met. This time the link between all relevant data fields from different data files was connected. The end-users could select a customer no. from the selection and when the end-user clicked the icon, the rest of the data fields were now being filled with details. The end-users could also choose the different styles of report from the menu arranged by the order of customers, countries, buyers, currencies or period. The JAD session revealed several further minor changes such as tidying up the positions of the data fields and the marginal setting of the report format. The IT Department facilitator was able to make these amendments during the JAD session. After the meeting, the prototype was transferred to a release version for implementation in Time-box 5.

3.14 Time-box 5: Implementation (5 days)

The first day was spent in testing the system with the end-users which was purely to test the reliability and to debug the system. No extra requirements from the users were accepted within this Time-box. If the user had wanted to make further changes, we would have had to reschedule the project development life-cycle. The second day was to obtain end-users' approval and the third was to prepare and issue User Guidelines. The third and fourth days were spent in organising training programmes to show the end-users how to use the new system properly. On the fifth day which was also the final day of the project phase, file conversion and data take-on were done before 9:00am. The new Debtor Profile system interface went live.

4. PROJECT EVALUATION

The 'Debtor Profile System' project had been delivered on time and was operational. BOA model was considered to be satisfactory as a vehicle to communicate with the end-users and interpret the business requirements for the new system and how it linked with other business objects. At the end of the project, the user community was satisfied, and had clearly felt very much involved in the whole process. The final success of the project was felt by the complete 'team'; not only the developers, but also the equally essential end-users who had been so actively involved in the JRP and JAD sessions and the user acceptance testing. The result of this case study has highlighted a few areas in which we feel that our adaptation of DBOA showed particular strength. None of them is particularly novel, but together they paint a picture of a successful interpretation of the method for a DBOA development in that:

- The gap between the conceptual model and software implementation had obviously been narrowed. Had it not been the DSDM approach, we would not be able to check whether our conceptual BOA model is the right model for the business. Communication between developers and end-users was much better. The users were very much involved, to the point where 'the team' was quite definitely a description applicable to the mix of people, developer and user, involved in the project. There was an integration of the two roles; a change of relationship from supplier/consumer to partnership. The final system was our system, not their system. Equally significantly, if not more so, the users enjoyed the experience of taking responsibility for their own system. It is also worth mentioning that the experience was (most of the time!) enjoyable for the developers.

- The holistic approach, as a result of the this partnership, has enabled the developers to obtain a better understanding of the business and its requirements. The intensity and effectiveness of the JRP and JAD sessions was beyond any doubt. The concept of getting the right people to concentrate exclusively on the problem, and of empowering them to make the right decisions, paid off. And because of the heavy involvement of the business end-users, an IT project has become more of a business project. This is consistent with the prototyping that the function of IT support is to solve business problems.

- The iterative approach to design worked. It enabled us to revisit the BOA conceptual model and modify it in response to the circumstances changes and business changes. It is not practical to obtain a correct design from a conventional requirement. We did not even try. The first functional prototype was very much imperfect. But at least it was something for the user to work with. The process of refinement which went on through Time-boxes 2, 3 and 4 resulted in numerous opportunities to fix the imperfections.

- We met, with comparative ease, what would have been an impossible deadline using the conventional life-cycle.

The whole rationale of this paper is "End-user involvement/contribution" in the DBOA development. With this two-way echo between the developers and the end-users, we consider we have successfully brought these acronyms together through our experience obtained from the above case study. Such synergy is to quickly and effectively react to the business changes. The holistic approach of DSDM has enabled the developer to build the right system, rather than build the system right even on the high level abstraction conceptual model development. The critical success factor is to provide an ideal environment for the developer to ensure that s/he knows what the right system is, but not to become endlessly involved in the often fruitless process of building the system right.

4.1 "S.M.A.R.T." Evaluation Criteria

An evaluation criteria framework called "S.M.A.R.T.", based on the characteristics of both the BOA and DSDM technique, has been developed to evaluate the DBOA schema in terms of:

'S'calable: As each business object component is individual, we can always increase the-e number of the business object without affecting the integrity of the existing one.

'M'easurable: Function Points are to measure the size and complexity of the system. Other metric techniques can also be used to measure the DBOA schema.

'A'chiveable: The holistic approach of DSDM life-cycle environment has increased the interactions between the end-users and the developers. Communication between them has thus been improved to enable the IT developers to deliver a software more achievable to the business requirements.

'R'euable The sharing of entity objects and process objects amongst those business objects is the classic way of object reuse. Business objects themselves can also be reused as a package as well.

'T'ime-manageable: Time-boxing technique has provided a good control of time management to run project in order to deliver the system on time and within budget.

5 CONCLUSION

Although the result of the above case study is considered to be successful, DSDM is still not a mature technology. There are several 'challenging' areas where we would have to warn the developers when using the DBOA approach:-

- *Friction between developers and end-users* : there is always a situation where the developers and the end-users do not get along well.

- *How to select the "right" people and to empower them to make "right" decision?*: this is more to do with business issue and it can only be improved through experience.

- *Time-boxing Syndrome*: everything is set inside a time-scale agreed with the business end-users. If planning is insufficient, developers would juggle between time-boxes. They will be forced to omit some unfinished tasks if they overrun the time-boxes or get panic to catch up at later time-boxes or they might have to abandon project if under pressure.

- *Work Pattern / Paradigm shift for developers* : the boundary between IT and business world is taken away. Developers have to cross the border to communicate with the business end-users and to experience business environment rather than developing the system in their own environment.

6 FUTURE WORK

- *Tackle the challenges*: Continue to research on the strategies to tackle the challenges as listed above.

- *Object Repository/Reuse Library:* Object Repository and Reuse Library for managing reuse is to be developed through CASE tools. As the DBOA is developed under a rapid and iterative life-cycle, appropriate CASE environment is critical. High level development tools and 4GL implementation will continue to be used in the future projects using DBOA as a foundation. The combination of both of these technologies means that design/implementation iterations which a few years ago may have taken a matter of weeks, could now be achieved in hours.

7 REFERENCES

1. [Angoss96]		*Angoss RAD Developer Manual.* Angoss Software Int'l Ltd., Toronto.
2. [Arrow95]		Arrow, L., Barnwell, R., Burt, C. and Anderson, M. "OMG Business Object Survey" in the *OMG Document 95-6-4*, 25th May 1995.
3. [Bennett92]		Bennett, M., Buson, S., Hicks, G., et al. "Characterising the Need for Enterprise Integration" in the *Proceedings of The First International Conference on Enterprise Integration 1992* (ed. Petrie, C.J.), PP 67-71.
4. [Bijron94]		Bijron, C. "Fillers To Fight The Software Crisis" in *the UT Mediair, Magazine, Jaargang, The Netherlands.* Source: http://www-trese.cs.utwente.nl/Docs/Ricot/UT-mediair-interview-engl.html.
5. [Boehm86]		Boehm, B. "A Spiral Model of Software Development and Enhancement" in *the ACM SIGSOFT Software Engineering Notes,* August 1986.
6. [Casanave95]		Casanave, C. "Business Object Architectures and Standards" in the *OOPSLA '95 Conference Business Object Design & Implementation Workshop II*, San Jose, CA, October 1996. Source:http://www.tiac.net/users/jsuth/oopsla/oo95summary.html.
7. [Constantine96]	Constantine, L. "Objects As If People Mattered" in the *OOPSLA '96 Conference, San Jose, CA, October 1996.* Source:http://www.acm.org/sigplan/oopsla/oopsla96/oopsla96.html.
8. [DSDM95(a)]		DSDM Consortium. *Dynamic Systems Development Method Version 2.0.* Tresseract Publishing, Surrey, UK, 1995.
9. [DSDM96]		DSDM Consortium. *The Underlying Principles of DSDM.* Source:http://www.dsdm.org/method.html.
10. [Freburger87]	Freburger, K. *"Rapid Prototyping Control Panel Interfaces"* in the OOPSLA'87 Conference, Orlando, FL., 1987. OOPSLA Proceeding Compendium ACM SIGPLAN CD-ROM.
11. [Hargrave96]	Hargrave, D. *SSADM4+ For Rapid Systems Development.* McGraw-Hill, 1996.
12. [Henderson-Sellers96]	Henderson-Sellers, B., et al. "Using Object-Oriented Techniques to Model the Life-cycle for OO Software Development" in the *1996 International Conference on Object Oriented Information Systems (OOIS'96),* London, Springer, London, 1996., pp211-220.
13. [Hsia96]		Hsia, P., Hsu, C., Kung, D., Hepner, M. and Wang, J. "An Object-Oriented Approach to Incremental Delivery of Software Systems" in the *OOIS'96 Conference, London, 1996,* Springer, London, 1996, pp 431-446.
14. [Hung97(a)]	Hung, K. and Linecar, P. "Experiences In Developing a Small Application Using a DSDM Approach" in the *British Computer Society Software Quality Management '97 Conference Proceedings.* Mechanical Engineering Publications, London, 1997, pp 165-178.
15. [Hung97(b)]	Hung, K. "Mind The Gap Please: The Semantic Gap Between Business and Software" in the *British Computer Society Object-Oriented Programming and Systems Specialist Group Journal,* Issue 29, March 1997, pp 8-10.
16. [IFPUG96]		International Function Point Users Group. Ohio, USA. Source: http://cuiwww.unige.ch/OSG/FAQ/SE/se-faq-s-2.html#S-2.
17. [Jacobson94]	Jacobson, I. et al. *The Object Advantages: Business Process Reengineering with Object Technology.* Addison Wesley, NY, 1994.
18. [Jacobson96]	Jacobson, I. "Use Case Engineering Tutorial" in the *OOPSLA '96 Conference, San Jose, CA,* October 1996.
19. [Martin91]		Martin, J. *Rapid Application Development.* Macmillan, NY, 1991.
20. [OMG95]		Object Management Group. *Object Management Architecture Guide.* John Wiley & Sons, Inc., N.Y. 1995.
21. [Partridge96]	Partridge, C. *Business Objects Reengineering for Reuse.* Butterworth-Heinmann, Oxford, 1996.
22. [Ramackers95]	Ramackers, G. and Clegg, D. "Object Business Modelling Request & Approach" in the *OOPSLA '95 Conference Business Object Design & Implementation Workshop, Austin, TX,* October 1995. Source:http://www.tiac.net/users/jsuth/oopsla/oo95summary.html.
23. [Reenskaug96]	Reenskaug, T. *Working With Objects.* Manning Publishing, Connecticut, 1996.
24. [Rolland96]	Rolland, C. "Challenges in Object Oriented Modelling: From Conceptual Modelling to Requirements Engineering" in *the OOIS'96 Conference, London, December 1996,* Springer, London 1996, pp3-17.
25. [SB+] System Builder Technology UK Ltd. *SB+ Version 2.3 Developer and Administrator Guide.* System Builder Technology UK Ltd., Prestbury, UK, 1995.
26. [Sutherland95]	Sutherland, J. "The Object Technology Architecture: Business Objects for Corporate Information Systems" in *the 1995 Symposium for VMARK Users, Albuquerque, USA,* 1995. Source:http://www.tiac.net/users/jsuth/
27. [Thome93]		Thome, B. *Systems Engineering.* Wiley, NY., 1993.

Automatic Drawing of Structured Digraphs

Hui Yao[1]
NTT International Corporation
E-mail: yao@ ntti.co.jp

Abstract

Our problem arose from the automatic drawing of large schema diagrams (LSD) in database field. Each LSD concerned here is represented by a directed graph (digraph) with a structure defined on it, i.e., the digraph is horizontally layered and each layer is vertically partitioned. This paper describes necessary techniques for drawing structured digraphs based on algorithms for unstructured digraphs.

1. Introduction

A *schema diagram* is the graphical representation of the conceptual schema of an information system and is used as the vehicle of communication in the database field. To improve the readability of a large schema diagram (LSD), in some advanced approaches (e.g., [PLAN93, OOMD91, ISP87]), an LSD is horizontally layered and each layer is vertically partitioned according to given criteria. Such an LSD is called structured in this paper.

From the view point of graph theory, a structured LSD can be represented by a digraph whose nodes are separated by a structure that is isomorphic with the structure defined on the LSD. This kind of digraphs are called *structured digraph*.

In a hierarchic drawing of an acyclic digraph, nodes are assigned to parallel lines, called *rank*s or *level*s, so that all the edges can be drawn in the same direction. An acyclic digraph, where the assignment of nodes to the k ranks is fixed, is called a k-ranked digraph. The length of an edge is measured by the ranks it spans. If an edge has a length of 1, then it is short, otherwise, it is long. If every edge in a graph has a length of 1, then this graph is proper, otherwise it is improper. An improper graph can always be replaced with a proper graph by adding virtual nodes to make the length of each edge be equal to 1.

Generally, there are four problems for graph drawing: 1) Assign nodes to ranks, 2) Reduce edge-crossing, 3) Set node-positions, and 4) Set arc-routes (optional). Problems for drawing unstructured digraphs have been widely studied (e.g., in [BETT94], about 300 graph-drawing algorithms are mentioned.) In the following sections, extensions to existing techniques are discussed for drawing structured digraphs.

A *structured digraph* is denoted by $G^s = (V, A, L, P)$, where V and A are the node set and arc set of G^s, $L = \{L_i : i = 1, \dots, I\}$, $L_i \cap L_{i'} = \varnothing$ for $i \neq i'$, each L_i represents a horizontal layering on the nodes of G^s and is itself vertically partitioned

---

1 The majority of this paper is written when the author was a doctoral student in Hotaka Database Lab. University of Tsukuba, Tsukuba, Ibaraki, 305 Japan.

into J_i cells, i.e., $L_i = \{P_j^i : j = 1, \ldots, J_i\}$, $P_j^i \cap P_{j'}^i = \varnothing$ for $j \neq j'$. To simplify the expression, we will use L_i to represent the ith layer of G' and the set of nodes belonging to L_i. Similarly, P_j^i is used to represent the jth cell of L_i of G' and the set of nodes belonging to P_j^i. By this convention, $G' = (V, A, L, P)$ is simply denoted by $G' = (L, P, A)$.

2. Rank assignment problem

Assume that our digraphs are acyclic ([Eades94].) Let $G = (V, A)$ denote an acyclic digraph, where V and A are the node set and arc set of G, a *rank assignment* on G is a partition of V into subsets R_1, R_2, ..., R_k, such that if $u \rightarrow v \in A$ where $u \in R_i$ and $v \in R_j$ then $i > j$. *"Longest path"* is the most commonly used approach for rank assignment problem. The drawback of this approach is that the lower part of a drawing may be very wide. [Eades90] In many circumstances, it will be desirable for a drawing to be neither too high nor too wide. This problem is *NP-hard*. For heuristic approaches, see [Eades90, Coffman72, Garey79].

For rank assignment problem, E.R. Gansner et al. [Gansner93] proposed an optimal algorithm. Their rank-assignment problem is defined to compute integer ranks for the nodes so that the total weighted length of the arcs is minimized. Given an acyclic digraph $G = (V, A)$, let $\lambda(v)$ be a rank assignment function, $l(v, w) = \lambda(w) - \lambda(v)$ be the length of arc $v \rightarrow w$, $\delta(v, w)$ be the minimum length of $v \rightarrow w$, usually 1, and $\omega(v, w)$ be the weight of arc $v \rightarrow w$, usually 1, which signifies the arc's importance (therefore, translates to keeping the arc short and vertically aligned), then the rank-assignment problem is captured in the following integer program:

$$\min \sum_{v \rightarrow w \in A} \omega(v, w)(\lambda(w) - \lambda(v))$$

$$\textit{subject to: } \lambda(w) - \lambda(v) \geq \delta(v, w) \quad \forall(v \rightarrow w) \in A$$

Rank-assignment problem on structured digraphs

Each of the previously mentioned methods has an implicit requirement, i.e., nodes must be freely moveable to any rank as the method suggests. However, in a structured digraph $G' = (L, P, A)$, nodes are bound by their layers, so it is not possible to apply these methods directly. Note that the vertical partition on each layer does not affect the rank-assignment, thus partitions defined on each layer are ignored, i.e., G' can be reduce to a layered digraph $G^l = (L_1, \ldots, L_i, \ldots, L_I, A)$.

The rank-assignment problem on layered digraph G^l ($RAP\,G^l$) is defined to compute integer ranks for the nodes under the constraint of the given layers so that the total weighted length of the arcs is minimized. Formally, the $RAP\,G^l$ is defined as followings:

$$\min \sum_{v \to w \in A} \omega(v, \ w)(\lambda(w) - \lambda(v))$$

subject to: $\lambda(w) > \lambda(v), \ \forall (v \to w) \in A$

$$\lambda(w) > \lambda(v), \ \forall v \in L_i, \ \forall w \in L_j, \ \forall i, j \left(i < j\right)$$

To remove the last constraint from the above formula, we need a *rank-assignment equivalent* digraph G_{rae}^l of the given G^l. There are three kinds of arcs in a layered digraph:

1) an arc $w \to v \in G$ is called an *inner-arc* if w and $v \in L_i$, for every i;

2) an arc $w \to v \in G$ is called an *inter-arc* if $w \in L_i$, $v \in L_{i+1}$, for every i;

3) an arc $w \to v \in G$ is called a *trans-arc* if $w \in L_i$, $v \in L_j$, for every $i, j, j\text{-}i{>}1$.

E.g., in *Figure 2* (a), $a \to b$, $b \to f$, and $c \to g$ are *inner-*, *inter-*, and *trans-*arc, respectively.

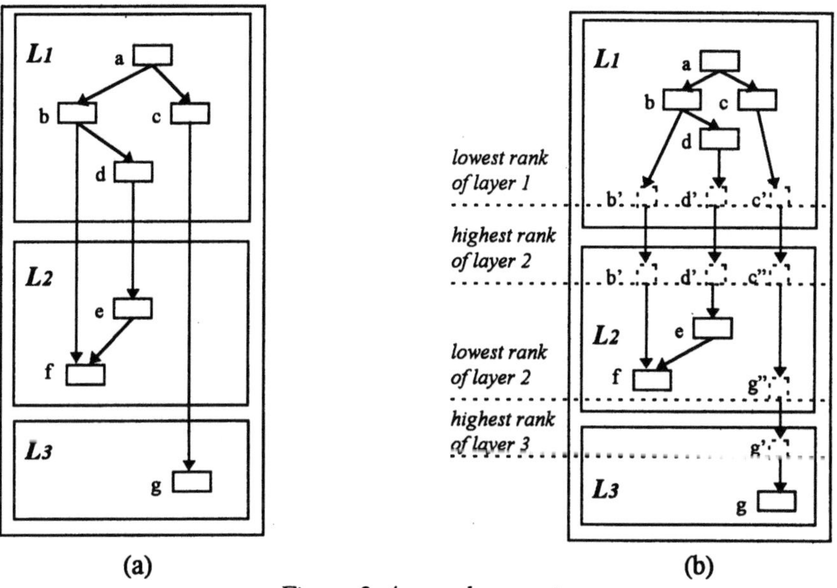

Figure 2 Arc replacement

An *inter-arc* $w \to v \in A$, $w \in L_i$, $v \in L_{i+1}$ can be replaced by three shorter arcs $w \to w'$, w and $w' \in L_i$, $\delta(w, \ w') \geq 0$, $v' \to v$, v and $v' \in L_{i+1}$, $\delta(v', \ v) \geq 0$ and $w' \to v'$, $l(w', \ v') = interval(L_i, \ L_{i+1})$, where w' and v' are the virtual nodes inserted to the lowest rank of L_i and the highest rank of L_{i+1}, respectively. The arc $w' \to v'$ is called a *between-arc*. Such a replacement leads to no change in the cost of the objective function if $\omega(w, w') = \omega(w', v') = \omega(v', v) = \omega(w, v)$ and $l(v, w) = l(v, v') + l(v', w') + l(w', w)$.

In the same way, without any change in the cost of the object function, an *trans-arc* can be replaced by a series of *inner-arc*s and *between-arc*s with the beginning and the end of the series being *inner-arc*s.

Theorem 1 *An optimal rank-assignment for the nodes of G^l_{rae} gives an optimal rank-assignment for the nodes of G^l .*

Let A_{inner} , A_{inter} , and A_{trans} denote the sets of all the *inner-arc*s, all the *inter-arc*s, and all the *trans-arc*s of G^1 respectively, i.e., $A_{inner} \cup A_{inter} \cup A_{trans} = A(G^l)$. And let A'_{inner} and $A_{between}$ denote the sets of all the *inner-arc*s and all the *between-arc*s of G^l_{rae} , respectively, i.e., $A'_{inner} \cup A_{trans} = A(G^l_{rae})$. Suppose, every *inter-arc* and *trans-arc* in G^l has been replaced by *inner-arc*s and *between-arc*s in G^l_{rae} , then:

$$\min \sum_{v \to w \in A(G^l)} \omega(v, w)(\lambda(w) - \lambda(v)) = \min \sum_{v \to w \in A(G^l)} \omega(v, w)l(v, w)$$

$$= \min\left(\sum_{v \to w \in A_{inner}} \omega(v, w)l(v, w) + \sum_{x \to u \in A_{inter}} \omega(x, u)l(x, u) + \sum_{y \to z \in A_{trans}} \omega(y, z)l(y, z)\right)$$

$$= \min\left(\sum_{v \to w \in A'_{inner}} \omega(v, w)l(v, w) + \sum_{r \to s \in A_{between}} \omega(r, s)l(r, s)\right)$$

Since each $r \to s \in A_{between}$ has a length equal to the interval between two adjacent layers and each interval has a fixed length for any given G^l (and G^l_{rae} as well), it follows that:

$$\min\left(\sum_{v \to w \in A'_{inner}} \omega(v, w)l(v, w) + \sum_{r \to s \in A_{between}} \omega(r, s)l(r, s)\right) = k + \min \sum_{v \to w \in A'_{inner}} \omega(v, w)l(v, w)$$

Since there is no $w \to v \in A'_{inner}$ that belongs to two layers simultaneously, we get

$$\min \sum_{v \to w \in A'_{inner}} \omega(v, w)l(v, w) = \min \sum_{i=1}^{I} \sum_{v \to w \ inside \ L_i} \omega(v, w)l(v, w)$$

$$= \sum_{i=1}^{I} \min \sum_{v \to w \ inside \ L_i} \omega(v, w)l(v, w)$$

Therefore, if we can find an optimal rank-assignment for each of the I layers on G^l_{rae} , then we get an optimal rank-assignment for the nodes of G^l . $\square$

3. Ordering nodes within ranks

An instance of the *node-ordering problem* (*NOP*) consists of a *bipartite graph* in which the node order in one part is fixed. The problem is to order the rest of the nodes so that the number of edge-crossings is minimized. A *node-ordering problem* is also called an *edge-crossing problem*. Since the direction of an arc does not affect the crossing of arcs, here, each arc is concerned as an edge. A widely used technique for the *NOP* of a k-ranked digraph is to transform it into a *proper k-ranked digraph*.

Crossing reduction is a fundamental aesthetic for hierarchical drawings [BETT94, Dresbach94]. Given a graph, how can we embed it in a planar surface so as to minimize the number of edge-crossing? This problem is *NP-Complete*, and thus there is not likely to be any efficient way to design an optimal embedding. [Garey83].

Among the heuristics developed for the *NOP*, the most widely used two are the "*barycentre*" and the "*median*" heuristics. The number of crossings, in the worst case, in the output of a *median* heuristic is always within a factor of three of optimal, while, in the output of a *barycentre* heuristic, it is $O(\sqrt{|R_0|})$ times optimal. [Eades94] Other heuristics are available, e.g., the assignment heuristic [Catarci88, 95] and the stochastic heuristic [Dresbach94]. But the barycentre and median heuristics are the only methods known to have provable performance. [Eades90]

Node-ordering problem on structured digraphs

A node-partitioned, two-ranked graph is defined as $G^p = (R_0, \ R_1, \ E, \ P)$, where R_0 and R_1 are disjoint node sets of G^p, $P = \{P_j : j = 1, \ ..., \ J\}$ represents a partition on the nodes of G^p, $P_j = \{R_0^j, \ R_1^j\}$. *Figure 4* shows an example G^p.

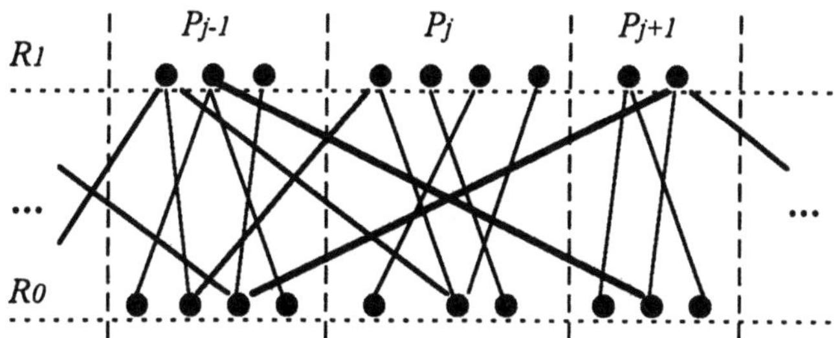

Figure 4 An example node-partitioned, two-ranked graph G^p

Without loss of generality, we can assume that nodes of R_0 and R_1 of G^p are aligned along two horizontal lines $y = 0$ and $y = 1$ respectively. Let $O_n = (O_n^1, \ ..., \ O_n^j, \ ..., \ O_n^J)$, $n = 0$ or 1, where O_n^j is the current order of the nodes $\{v : v \in R_n^j\}$. Further, let $cross(G^p, O_0, O_1)$ denote the number of crossings of G^p under the current O_0 and O_1.

Node-ordering Problem on G^p (NOP G^p): Given an node-partitioned, two-ranked hierarchy $G^p = (R_0, \ R_1, \ E, \ P, \ O_0)$ with fixed order O_0, find an order O_1 such that $cross(G^p, O_0, O_1)$ is as small as possible.

Existing heuristic approaches can not be applied directly to G^p because the nodes of G^p are partitioned so that not every node can be moved to the position as the method suggested. If we try to reduce edge-crossings for each of the subgraph $G^{pj} = (R_0, \ R_1^j, \ E^j, \ O_0)$, $E^j \subseteq R_0 \times R_1^j$, $j=1, \ ..., \ J$, individually, can we guarantee that the reduction of edge-crossing in one subgraph dose not lead to a increase in edge-crossing in other subgraphs? Theorem 2 gives an answer to this problem.

Theorem 2. *Solving NOP G^p, $G^p = (R_0, \ R_1, \ E, \ P, \ O_0)$, is equivalent to solve NOP on each subgraph $G^{pj} = (R_0, \ R_1^j, \ E^j, \ O_0)$, $E^j \subseteq R_0 \times R_1^j$, of G^p individually.*

In G^P, the adjustment of the position of any node $v \in R_1^j$ is limited by the left- and right- boundaries of cell P_j, for every j, therefore, the order of any node pair u and v, where $v \in R_1^j$, $u \notin R_1^j$ will not be changed by any re-ordering under the constraint P of G^P. In other words, the number of crossings formed by edges incident to nodes of different cells of R_1 is an invariable for a given G^P. $\qquad\square$

4. Node-positioning problem

Node positioning problem (*NPP*) is the problem of assigning absolute coordinate to each node, respecting current node-orders. Usually, X- and Y- coordinates are computed separately. The Y-coordinate assignment is to keep minimum sufficient separation between two adjacent ranks and is quite straightforward. On the other hand, the X-coordinate assignment problem is interesting, especially for structured digraphs. [Gansner93]

K. Sugiyama, et al [Sugiyama81] give a theoretical method and a heuristic method for *NPP*, called *Quadratic Programming Layout Method (QP Method)* and *Priority Layout Method (PR Method)*, respectively. "... the theoretical methods are useful in recognizing the nature of the problem, and the heuristic methods make it possible to enlarge the size of hierarchies with which we can deal." [Sugiyama81] The computing cost of the *PR* method is significantly less than the *QP* method.

E.R. Gansner et al. [Gansner93] proposed an optimal approach by applying a network simplex method and a heuristic approach that is, in fact, a refined version of the *PR* method. Their node positioning problem is defined as:

For a *n*-ranked digraph $G = (R, E, O)$,

$$\min \sum_{e=(v,\,w)} \Omega(e)\omega(e)\left|x_w - x_v\right|$$

$$\textit{subject to: } x_b - x_a \geq \rho(a,\,b)$$

where node a is the left neighbor of node b in the same rank, and $\rho(a,\,b) = \dfrac{xsize(a) + xsiz(b)}{2} + nodesep(G)$ is the required minimum separation between center points of a and b. $\Omega(e)$, an internal value distinct from the input edge weight $\omega(e)$, is defined to favor straightening long arcs. Suppose, e, f, and g are edges connecting (1) two real nodes, (2) one real node and one virtual node, or (3) two virtual nodes respectively, then $\Omega(e) \leq \Omega(f) \leq \Omega(g)$.

Node positioning problem on structured digraphs (*NPPSD*)

In a structured digraph, the left-boundaries of some cells of different layers are required to be aligned. These cells are said to belongs to a *Left-aligned cell set* S_m^L. Similarly, we define a *right-aligned cell set* S_n^R. The problem of node positioning for a structured digraph G' is to keep edges short and straight w.r.t. the given digraph structure. Given a proper structured digraph $G' = (L, P, A, O)$,

$L = \{L_i : i = 1, \ldots, I\}$, each layer L_i is horizontally divided into K_i ranks and is vertically divided into J_i cells. In addition, there are M left-aligned cell sets, and N right-aligned cell sets respectively. *NPPSD* is formally defined as:

$$\min \sum_{e=(v,w)} \Omega(e)\omega(e)\left|x_w - x_v\right|$$

subject to:
$$x_v - x_u \geq \rho(u,v),\ u,v \in R_k^i,\ O_{R_k^i}(u) = O_{R_k^i}(v) - 1,\ \text{for every } i,k$$
$$x_l\left(P_j^i\right) \leq x_v \leq x_r\left(P_j^i\right),\ v \in P_j^i,\ \text{for every } i,j$$
$$x_l\left(P_j^i\right) = x_l\left(S_m^L\right),\ P_j^i \in S_m^L,\ \text{for every } m$$
$$x_r\left(P_j^i\right) = x_r\left(S_n^R\right),\ P_j^i \in S_n^R,\ \text{for every } n$$

where $x_l(\cdot)$ and $x_r(\cdot)$ represent the X-coordinates of the left- and right- boundaries of the · respectively.

Optimal approach for *NPPSD*

The fundamental idea here is to remove the last three constraints from the above formula by adding auxiliary nodes as boundaries.

First, we need a *node-positioning equivalent* graph G_{npe} of G^s. The G_{npe} is obtained by, for every pair of horizontal cell neighbors P_j^i and P_{j+1}^i, inserting a boundary node v_{align}^k to every rank R_k^i of L_i between the two cells. Each of the boundary nodes $\{v_{align}^k\}$ belongs to an *aligned-node family* F_{align}^t and $x_{v_{align}^k} = X\left(F_{align}^t\right)$, for every k.

Further, if there is another cell $P_{j'}^{i'}$, P_j^i and $P_{j'}^{i'}$ are *left-aligned*, the boundary nodes inserted to every rank of $L_{i'}$ between $P_{j'}^{i'}$ and $P_{j'+1}^{i'}$ also belong to F_{align}^t. The same thing is required for every cell pair $(P_j^i, P_{j'}^{i'})$, where P_j^i and $P_{j'}^{i'}$ are *right-aligned*. *Figure 4/1* shows an example of obtaining G_{npe} from G^s.

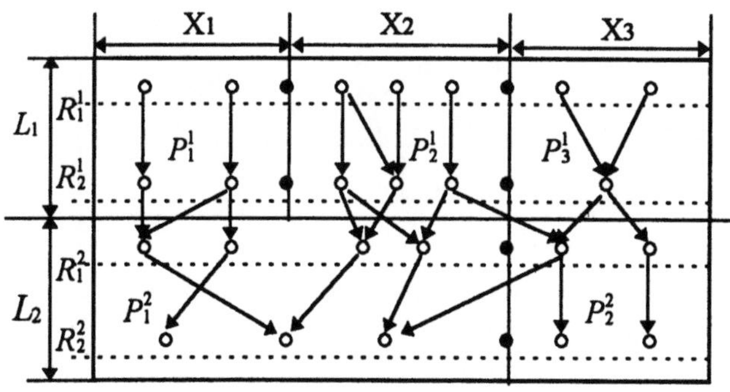

• : a boundary node

Figure 4/1 Inserting boundary nodes to a structured digraph G^s

Given a G_{npe} with τ aligned-node families, the optimal node-positioning problem on G_{npe} ($NPP\,G_{npe}$) is defined as the following integer program:

$$\min \ \sum_{e=(v,w)} \Omega(e)\omega(e)\left|x_w - x_v\right|$$

subject to: $x_v - x_u \geq \rho(u,v),\ u,v \in R_k^i,\ O_{R_k^i}(u) = O_{R_k^i}(v) - 1,\ \textit{for every } k,\, i$

$$x_{v_{align}^k} = x\!\left(F_{align}^t\right),\ v_{align}^k \in F_{align}^t,\ \textit{for every } k,\, t$$

Lemma 1 G_{npe} *and* G^s *are equivalent w. r. t. node positioning.*

Note that the boundary nodes in G_{npe} established boundaries between node sets of G_{npe} that are exactly required by the last three constraints of *NPPSD*. Therefore, any solution of the positioning problem on G_{npe} is also a solution of the positioning problem on G^s, and *vice versa.* $\square$

Next, we need to remove the last constraint from the formula for $NNP\,G_{npe}$. Recall that, in [Gansner93], an optimal solution of node positioning problem for an k-ranked digraph $G = (R,\,E,\,O)$ is found by applying a network simplex method to the equivalent auxiliary graph of G. The starting point is to construct a "good" initial feasible tree and the kernel of this simplex method is to lengthen each tree edge that has a negative *cut vale* until no such tree edge is available. However, in the G_{aux} of G_{npe}, each boundary node $v_{align}^k \in F_{align}^t$ must be assigned to the same "rank". This requirement makes the selection of a target tree edge difficult. Because, if the selected tree edge is incident to a boundary node $v_{align}^k \in F_{align}^t$, then it is lengthened if and only if the movement of every node in the set F_{align}^t results in a reduction of the total weighted edge length in G_{aux} (see *Figure 4/3*).

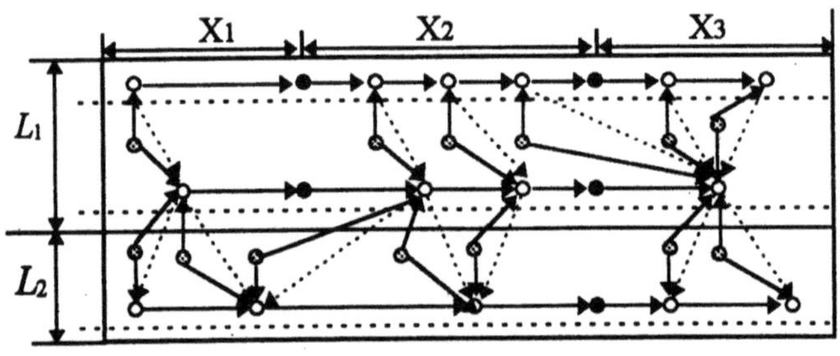

o··▸   : an original node and an original edge of G_{npe}

●   : a boundary node

: a node and two edges inserted to G_{npe} to replace an original edge

: an edges inserted to connect two node neighbors in the same rank of G_{npe}

Figure 4/2 The auxiliary graph G_{aux} of an example G_{npe}

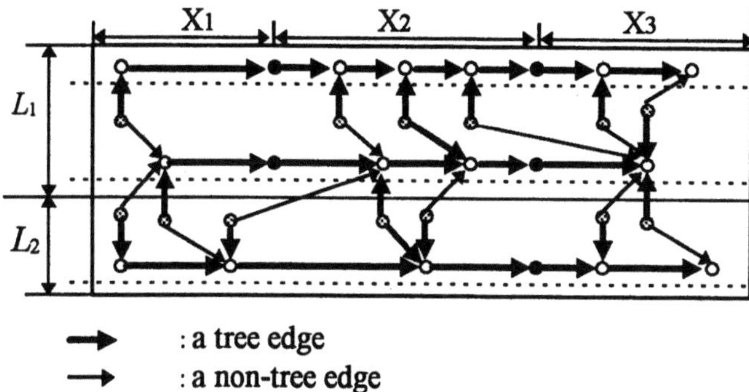

Figure 4/3 A feasible tree for auxiliary graph G_{aux} of G_{npe}

This problem can be overcome by constructing a *boundary-node reduction* G_{bnr} of G_{npe}. The G_{bnr} is obtained from G_{aux} by, for each F^t_{align}, arbitrarily selecting one v^k_{align} from F^t_{align} and redirecting each edge connected with other member of F^t_{align} to v^k_{align}. This selected node is called the *super-node* of the family F^t_{align} (see *Figure 4/4*.)

Lemma 2 *G_{bnr} and G_{aux} are equivalent w.r.t. rank assignment.*

Note that the only difference between G_{bnr} and G_{aux} is that each F^t_{align} in G_{aux} is replaced by its super-node in G_{bnr}. For any such super-node, since it is connected with exactly the same set of nodes as the members of its aligned-node family are, its movement has the same affect as its aligned-node family has, and vice versa.   □

Theorem 3 *Solving the optimal node-positioning problem for structured digraph G is equivalent to find an optimal rank-assignment solution for G_{bnr}.*

Theorem 3 is obtained as a straightforward application of Lemma 1 and 2.   □

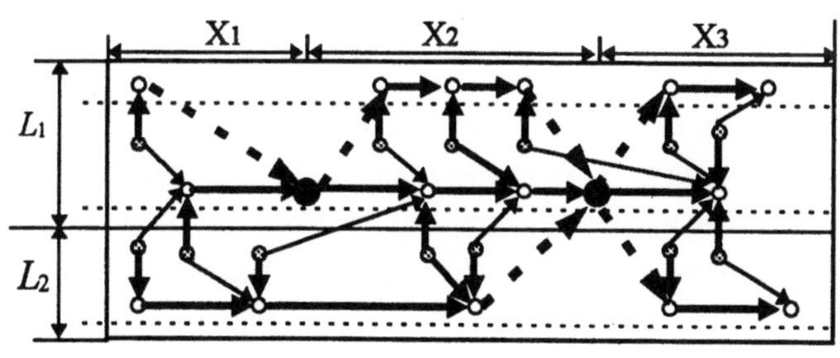

Figure 4/4 A boundary-node reduction G_{bnr} of a G_{aux}

166

Theorem 3 guarantees that an optimal node-positioning solution for structured digraph G can be found by finding an optimal rank-assignment solution from G_{bnr}. The size of G_{bnr} is computed as follow. If a structured digraph G has V nodes, E edges, L layers, and each layer L_l is horizontally divided into R^l ranks and vertically partitioned into P^l partitions, then the proper graph G_v obtained by adding virtual nodes to G has $V + D$ nodes, $E + D$ edges, where the D is the number of virtual nodes. Further, the *boundary-node reduction* G_{bnr} of G_v has

$$\left(V + E + 2D + \sum_{l=1}^{L}\left(P^l - 1\right)\right) \text{ nodes and } \left(V + 2E + 3D + \sum_{l=1}^{L} R^l\left(P^l - 2\right)\right) \text{ edges. Note}$$

that $\sum_{l=1}^{L}\left(P^l - 1\right)$ and $\sum_{l=1}^{L} R^l\left(P^l - 2\right)$ are relatively smaller than V and E, the graph

G_{bnr} has approximately $\left(V + E + 2D\right)$ nodes and $\left(V + 2E + 3D\right)$ edges.

Note: For a heuristic approach for node-positioning on structured digraph, refers to [Yao96].

5. Summary:

In this paper, we identified problems related to drawing structured digraphs and discussed extensions to existing graph drawing techniques for drawing structured digraphs.

Acknowledgment

Special thanks to Prof. Ryosuke Hotaka of University of Tsukuba, my sister and my family. This paper is dedicated to my beloved parents.

References

[BETT94] G.D. Battista, P. Eadess, R. Tamassia, and I.G. Tollis, "Algorithms for Drawing Graphs: an Annotated Bibliography," available via anonymous ftp from wilma.cs.brown.edu (128.148.33.66), files /pub/papers/compgeo/gdbiblio.ps.Z.

[Catarci88] T. Catarci, "The Assignment Heuristic for Crossing Reduction in Bipartite Graphs," Proc. of the 26th Allerton Conference, 1988.

[Catarci95] T. Catarci, "The Assignment Heuristic for Crossing Reduction," IEEE Trans. on Systems, Man, and Cybernetics, Vol. 25, No. 3, pp. 515~521, March 1995.

[Coffman72] E.G. Coffman, Jr and R. L. Graham, "Optimal Scheduling for Two-processor Systems," Acto Informatica 1, pp. 200-213, 1972

[Dresbach94] S. Dresbach, "A New Heuristic Layout Algorithm for Directed Acyclic Graphs," to appear in U. Derigs, A. Bachem, and A Drexl (Eds): "Operatons Research Proceedings 1994," Berlin, Springer 1995, 121-126.

[Eades90] P. Eades and K. Sugiyama, "How to Draw a Directed Graph," Invited survey paper, Journal of Information Processing, Vol. 13, No. 4, pp. 424~437, 1990

[Eades94] P. Eades and N.C. Wormald, "Edge Crossings in Drawings of Bipartite Graphs," Algorithmica, (1994) 11: pp. 379~403.

[Gansner93] E. R. Gansner, E. Koustsofios, S. C. North and K. P. VO, "A Technique for Drawing Directed Graphs," IEEE Trans. on Software engineering, Vol. 19, No. 3, pp. 214-230, 1993.

[Garey79] M.R. Garey and D.S. Johnson, "Computers and Intractability-A Guide to the Theory of NP-Completeness," Freeman, 1979.

[Garey83] M.R. Garey and D.S. Johnson, "Crossing Number is NP-Complete," SIAM J. of Algebraic and Discrete Methods, Vol. 4, No. 3, pp.312-316, 1983.

[ISP87] James Martin Associates PLC., "INFORMATION STRATEGY PLANNING HANDBOOK," Ireland, 1987.

[Mehlhorn84] K. Mehlhorn, "Graph algorithms and NP-Completeness," Springer Verlag, 1984.

[OOMD] J. Rumbaugh, M. Blaha, W. Premerlani, F. Eddy, W. Lorensen, "Object-Oriented Modeling and Design," PRENTICE HALL, Englewood Cliffs, New Jersey 07632, pp. 198-201, 1991.

[Papazoglou95] M. P. Papazoglou, "Unraveling the semantics of conceptual schemas" Trans. of ACM, Vol. 38, No. 9, Sept. 1995.

[PLAN93] Data research institute. (Japanese), "DOA seminar," 1993.

[Sugiyama81] K. SUGIYAMA, S. TAMAGAWA, and M. TODA, "Methods for Visual Understanding of Hierarchical System Structures," IEEE Trans. On Systems, Man, and Cybernetics, Vol. SMC-11, No. 2, pp.109~125, Feb. 1981.

[Yao96] Hui Yao, , "Schema Diagram with Engineering Precision," doctoral dissertation, Doctoral Program in Socio-Economic Planning, University of Tsukuba, Tsukuba city, 305 Japan, Oct, 1996.

[Yao] Hui Yao, et al, "An approach for the generation of standardized structured large schema diagram," to appear in Chinese Journal of Automation.

Making O_2 become a WWW Server

Frank Buddrus, Sven-Eric Lautemann

JWG-Universität, Frankfurt/Main, Germany

Marco Bellavia

Università Statale di Milano, Italy

Abstract

This paper deals with the idea of an ODBMS working as an Internet server for hypermedia documents. The approach introduced offers fine grained storage and retrieval of HTML documents, providing sophisticated document maintenance, supporting referential integrity, document integration, integration with application objects, access control, and versioning. In contrast to comparable systems it acts transparently to the WWW users, i.e. without using proprietary query languages or protocols. While achieving the full benefits of a modern document repository it keeps the ease of the traditional file system it replaces.

1 Introduction

The World Wide Web (WWW) became the most popular service of the Internet and its use is rapidly growing. Millions of documents, handled as normal files, build up the WWW. With just a few exceptions, WWW servers are run from standard file systems and therefore can provide almost no support for maintenance of these documents, consistency, real access control, document versioning, or document integration.

This paper introduces an approach called WOW (**W**WW and **O**DBMS as a **W**hole); a system that enhances the ODBMS O_2 [2] to a WWW server. This is done in three steps:

1. Providing a mechanism for O_2 objects to produce HTML [13] code (adopted from O_2Web [11]).

2. Implementing a system with the facility to store and maintain (HTML) documents at variable granularity within O_2.

3. Implementing an HTTP [3] daemon to handle HTML requests by returning O_2 objects.

WOW's main features include consistent documents, referential integrity (e.g. no unresolved links), document integration (documents sharing common parts without copying, integration with (application) objects managed by O_2, access control, different views of the same document, versioning of documents, and variable grained storage.

The remainder of this paper is organized as follows. Section 2 briefly describes the WOW approach. (For a more detailed description please refer to [7].) Section 3 gives an overview of the mechanisms for document maintenance focused on the sharing of document parts. After a short summary of related work in Section 4 we conclude the paper and give an outlook on future work.

2 WOW

We distinguish two types of WWW documents: *bitstream* and *HTML documents*. A bitstream document contains a single piece of information (image, animation, sound, etc.). HTML documents can contain bitstream documents and text and can furthermore refer to other WWW documents.

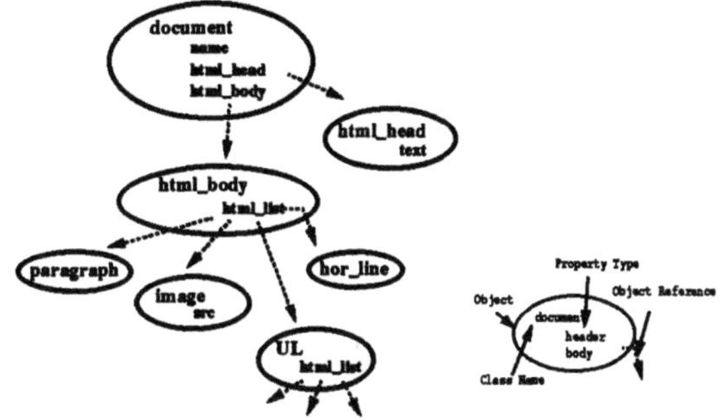

Figure 1: Structure of a WOW HTML document.

In contrast to O_2Web and similar approaches for database access via Internet, WOW supplements O_2 with the facility for integrating existing or creating new HTML documents and their embedded files (images, etc.). This is done by parsing HTML documents, transforming them into O_2 objects, and storing them in an O_2 database. A given HTML document will be decomposed according to its syntactic structure (HEAD, BODY, lists, tables, etc.) and stored in appropriate objects connected to each other (Figure 1 shows the increments of an HTML document maintained under WOW). These objects can then be accessed via a WWW server without the knowledge of complex queries or protocols. As in O_2Web, *o2report* methods and the possibility to query objects are provided to allow integration with application objects stored in O_2.

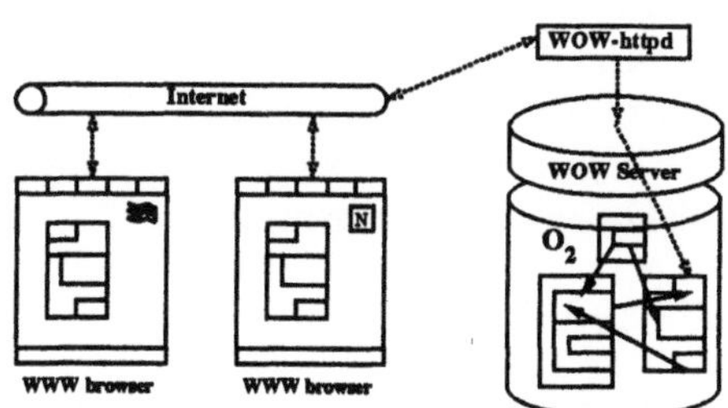

Figure 2: The WOW architecture.

The WOW HTTP daemon redirects HTTP requests to the WOW Server (see Figure 2). A request can either include the name of a WWW document or a query (as in O_2Web). The WOW Server identifies the corresponding object to the requested document, calls its unparse method (*o2report*), which recursively constructs the HTML code, and returns the result in order to serve the request. This is done in the same way for HTML and bitstream documents. The unparse method of bitstream documents simply returns the image, animation, etc. associated.

2.1 WOW Characteristics

This paper focuses on document maintenance and integration which will be presented in Section 3. We now describe briefly how other WOW features are realized.

Transparency: There are several types of links within a typical HTML document. Links can either be local or global hypertext references specified by the HREF tag or animations, sounds, etc. specified by special tags like IMG SRC. While populating and running the WOW document repository it has to be kept track of all these links in order to provide high level consistency. WOW combines the ease of traditional HTML coding with the advantages of automatically gained consistency. Importing an existing document from the file system into the WOW repository does not require any link update. WOW will remember file system type links and resolve them whenever necessary.

Access Control and different views of the same document are supported by adapting an access control mechanism for the ODBMS O_2 called SecOO [5], which uses Prolog-like statements to describe authorization and implication rules. Please refer to [6] for details of the WOW-SecOO authorization model.

Document Versioning [15] so far is roughly implemented in WOW using O_2's object versioning approach. Access to older versions of objects is provided by specifying the version number when requesting a document (static binding). By default the most recent version is served on any request (dynamic binding). Whenever a document is versioned, all (embedded and hypertext) links included in this document will be supplemented by their version number as long as they are not already (explicitly) given. However, changes of referred documents will be allowed as long as they do not result in new versions. Freezing a complete document therefore requires freezing of all documents referred to.

Integration with application objects stored in O_2 is done by supporting the *o2report* method and query facility as introduced by O_2Web. In this way any object can be mapped to a textual/graphical (HTTP compliant) description. This makes it possible both to retrieve an arbitrary number of objects and to refer to them from within any HTML document.

2.2 The WOW Architecture

The WOW system is highly flexible. The HTML parser, as well as the semantic machine (link maintenance etc.), which together build main parts of the current WOW Server, have been generated. Like the HTML documents discussed in this paper, any other type of document, e.g. Modula-2 source code, can be integrated into WOW. The WOW generator input mainly consists of two files, one containing the syntax of the documents concerned and one the semantics for integrating documents into the WOW system.

WOW is able to store any (textual) document whose concrete syntax can be described by a special Backus Naur Form (BNF [9]). The level of granularity of the documents maintained by WOW is up to the granularity of the document's BNF description. WOW generates an O_2 schema describing all increments of the language given by the BNF. Each increment gets a method *parse* to instantiate this increment from a given string (populating the database by providing already existing documents or document parts). Analogously for each increment an *o2report* method will be generated responsible for retrieving documents/increments from the database.

After having defined the BNF of documents to be stored in O_2 some semantics have to be given in order to allow an integration with the WOW infrastructure. This is done by providing a set of control structures and methods that allow keeping track of any action concerning a document of this type. The detailed description of WOW's semantic programming goes beyond the scope of this paper. However, the WOW Shell as part of the WOW Server has been constructed within this framework.

3 The WOW Shell

The profits deriving from storing HTML documents and related information in the form of objects instead of relying on the traditional file system approach are numerous: Consistency of documents can be guaranteed and maintained automatically, i.e. documents contain no references that cannot be resolved because the WWW documents or document sections referred to have been deleted, renamed, or moved. The second important advantage is the possibility to enable the sharing of parts of documents without creation of physical copies, which in addition avoids duplicated and incoherent information.

In the following subsections we will describe a set of implemented shell commands which simplify the task of inserting, maintaining, and manipulating the information content in a WOW Server. All this is accomplished keeping in mind the important goal of referential integrity.

3.1 Initializing the WOW Server

In order to initialize the WOW Server the following command has to be issued:

    initialize <DocumentRoot>

The parameter DocumentRoot specifies a directory path. This command is used if we already have a file system based WWW server and we want to move all its information to an O_2 based WOW Server. It specifies the directory in the file system from which the traditional HTTP daemon serves WWW documents.

As a result of the initialization of the WOW Server a *General Catalogue* (see Figure 3) implemented as an indexed set will be created: for each single HTML or bitstream document added to the O_2 database a new entry will be inserted into the catalogue. Each catalogue entry contains the relative path and the name of the document followed by the pointer to the associated object.

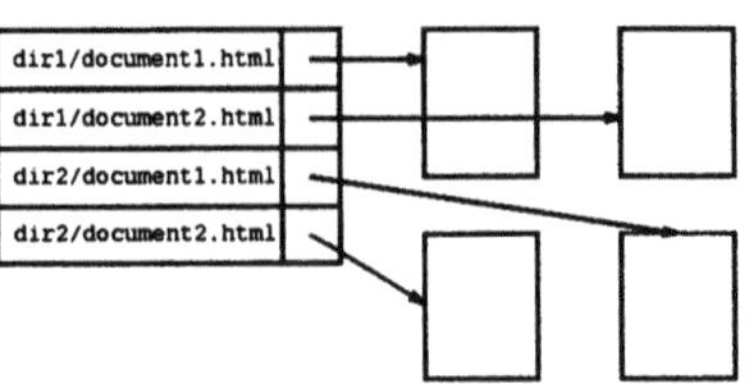

Figure 3: The General Catalogue.

3.2 Adding Documents

The add command can be used to insert a new HTML or bitstream document in the WOW Server:

add <DocumentPath&Name> [-DocType]

The first parameter contains the path and name (specified as the relative path from the DocumentRoot directory) of the file that we want to store in the O_2 based document repository. The type of WWW document we are importing (HTML or bitstream document) is automatically detected by the system according to the suffix of the file specified, but we can force the system to assume that we are importing an HTML or bitstream document using the optional switch DocType that can have one of the two values html or bits.

When executing the add command, the system first checks if any WWW document with the name and path specified is already stored in the WOW Server. Otherwise the document file is retrieved using the relative path and name specified DocumentPath&Name prefixed by the absolute path DocumentRoot specified as parameter in the initialize command. If no errors occur a new object is created. According to the suffix of the document being imported or to the switch DocType it belongs to class Document or BitStream. The message parse is then passed to the new object. This method receives as a parameter a stream like object containing either an HTML document or a bitstream document that we want to insert in the repository. It parses the information passed with the parameter and, if the operation is successful, the link to the new object is created and its relative path and name are stored in the *General Catalogue* making the object persistent.

When inserting a new HTML document in the WOW Server the parse method decomposes it according to its syntactic structure and stores it in appropriate objects connected to each other.

During the parse operation two types of hypertext links can be encountered: remote links using complete URLs [4] and links to local files:

<A HREF="http://www.example.edu/dir1/document.html">Hyperlink</A>

<IMG SRC="dir3/dir4/image.gif">

Documents containing remote links are put into the WOW base unaltered when parsing. On the other hand, if links to local WWW (HTML or bitstream) documents are found, WOW tries to store these documents into its database as well. Documents stored in the local file system are linked by a relative path from the DocumentRoot directory. If a local file has not already been parsed and stored in the WOW base earlier, it is loaded from the local file system and automatically included in the WOW base. If the document referred to by the hyperlink is not present in the O_2 repository and not available from the file system, a warning is shown to inform the user of an unresolved link:

> Warning: unresolved link dir3/dir4/image.gif

The unresolved link is added to a special *Link Table* (see Figure 4) associated to each object of class Document, containing a list of all resolved and unresolved links found during the parsing process.

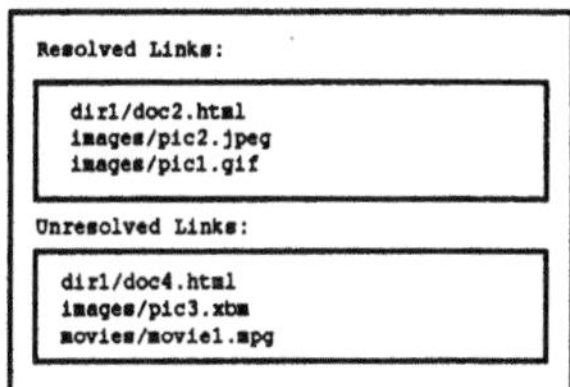

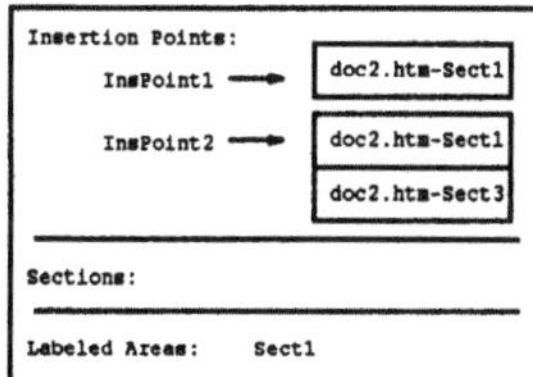

Figure 4: Link and Reference Table.

3.3 Sharing Document Sections

In this subsection we introduce a mechanism which lets HTML documents stored as objects in the O_2 based repository share sections of each other without making a physical copy of the data but using references between objects. This can be accomplished by taking advantage of the fine grained object structure approach used to keep documents in the repository. In order to refer from a section of a document to a specific position in the same or in another document we need a means to identify and name *sections* and *insertion points* within a document. This can be done using a standard HTML tag in association with a shell command enabling the dynamic reference between the section of a document and a specific insertion point in the same or in another document. It is important to distinguish between what we call a *link* and what we call a *reference*. The first is a normal HTML link to a HTML or bitstream document. The second is a specific concept of WOW and it is the means to establish a relation between an insertion point and a section.

As part of the standard HTML definition there is a tag normally used to create a named anchor (a sort of label) within an HTML document. The form of the tag is the following:

> <A NAME="label"> any HTML code ... </A>

3.3.1 Identifying and Naming an Insertion Point

Assume we want to identify an insertion point named `InsertionPoint1` in a document named `doc1.html`. The insertion point should be used to refer to a document section taken from another document named `doc2.html`. We use the regular <A> tag in `doc1.html` as shown:

> <A NAME="InsertionPoint1"></A>

Usually we do not put any extra text or HTML tag between the opening and closing tag. This is allowed though with the closing tag </A> identifying the insertion point concerned.

3.3.2 Identifying and Naming a Section

To identify a section within a document we use the <A> tag as well. The name and the beginning of a section is specified by <A NAME="SectionName"> and the end of the section is identified by the closing tag </A>. It is possible to nest sections into one another as shown in Figure 5 and to define insertion points inside of a section but it is not possible to intersect different sections. Note, that a single <A NAME> tag can be used both as section and insertion point at the same time.

Coming back to the example, in order to identify a section named Section1 in doc2.html we will use the following tag in doc2.html:

<A NAME="Section1"> ... Here is the section ... </A>

3.3.3 Refering from an Insertion Point to a Section

Once an insertion point and a section are defined, we can establish a link between them using the following shell command:

ref <DocNameI> <InsPoint> <DocNameS> <SectName>

The first two parameters tell the system the name of the document and the name of the insertion point it contains (by name we mean relative pathname) and the last two parameters specify the coordinates of the section. Considering the previous example, to refer from the insertion point named InsertionPoint1 in doc1.html to the section named Section1 in doc2.html the following command has to be used:

ref doc1.html InsertionPoint1 doc2.html Section1

From this moment on there will be a dynamic reference established between the given section and the insertion point. Whenever retrieving doc1.html from the WOW Server all the information contained in section Section1 of document doc2.html will be dynamically added to the document at the insertion point InsertionPoint1. Figure 5 shows an example of WOW documents.

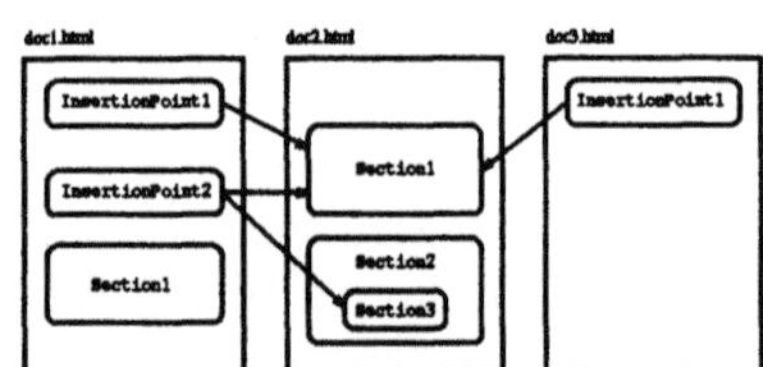

Figure 5: References among insertion points and sections.

For each object of class Document we maintain a special *Reference Table* containing information about the insertion points, the sections, and the labeled areas. For each insertion point we keep track of the coordinates of the sections to which it refers. For each section we have a list of insertion points refering to it. Figure 4 shows an example of a Reference Table.

It is allowed to refer from several insertion points in the same or in different documents to the same section. An example is shown in Figure 5. It is also possible to have two or more sections referred to by the same insertion point. They will follow one the other according to the order in which the WOW shell commands to establish the references have been applied.

It must be pointed out that there are some limitations in the use of the **reference** shell command. Circular references, as shown in Figure 6 are not allowed.

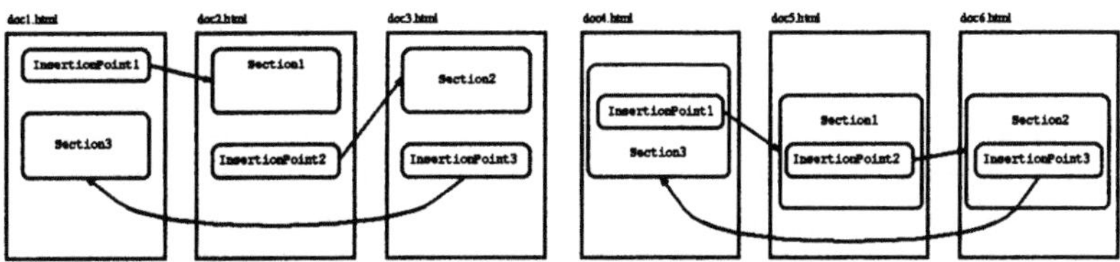

Figure 6: Circles: prohibited.

In theory, problems with circular references arise only if we nest insertion points into sections, like doc[4-6].html in Figure 6, but a stricter limitation in the definition of references simplifies the routines protecting the system from vicious circles (loops). The choice taken is supported by the analysis of the typical needs of a WWW administrator.

3.3.4 Information on Sections and Insertion Points

There is a shell command which returns information regarding sections and insertion points of a document:

> eval <DocumentName> [<Name_of_labeled_area>]

It lists for a specified document all (or a single if specified) labeled areas together with all insertion points referred by resp. sections refering to.

3.3.5 Erasing References

The **delref** command can be used to delete a reference established between an insertion point and a section:

> delref <DocNameI> <InsPoint> [<DocNameS> <SectName>]

The first two parameters specify the coordinates of the insertion point and the last two parameters specify the coordinates of the section. After breaking the reference between the insertion point and the section the Reference Tables of the documents involved in the operation have to be updated.

3.4 Renaming and Copying

Two commands are available to rename or copy of an object.

> rename <OldDocumentPath&Name> <NewDocumentPath&Name>

changes the name of an object of either class **Document** or class **BitStream**. Any link to the object and any information regarding insertion points and sections belonging to the object are automatically updated so that no unresolved links or references are created (automatic link and reference maintenance). The command is aborted and an error message returned if an object with the specified relative path and name already exists in the WOW base.

To copy an object the following command can be used:

> copy <OldDocumentPath&Name> <NewDocumentPath&Name>

The command is aborted if an object with the new relative path and name is already present in the WOW base.

3.5   Deleting Documents

The deletion of HTML or bitstream documents from the WOW repository is supported by the following shell command:

> delete <DocumentPath&Name> [-Policy]

The first parameter specifies the object to be deleted from the WOW Server and the optional switch indicates the policy to apply regarding links and references among documents. The switch Policy can have four different values. If Policy equals restricted (default) the object can be deleted only if no unresolved link is created and if it contains no section referred to by some insertion point of another document (this second consideration applies only if we are trying to delete an object belonging to class Document). If Policy equals consistent the object can be deleted only if no unresolved link is created, not considering the presence of references to its sections. Any reference to a section of the deleted document is automatically broken. If Policy equals inconsistent the object can be deleted only if it contains no section referred to by some insertion point (this second consideration applies only if we are trying to delete an object belonging to the class Document) but no attention is paid to the aspect of unresolved links. Finally, if Policy equals unrestricted the object is always deleted: references to sections belonging to the object are broken and unresolved links might be created.

Whenever unresolved links or broken references are created, the user is alerted with a corresponding message followed by a list of documents pointing to the deleted object. Whenever we delete a document the General Catalogue, the Link Table, and the Reference Table are automatically updated. Note that WOW disables unresolved links when serving requests by skipping the printing of the tags <A HREF>.

3.6   Updating Documents

It is possible to update the information stored in the O_2 based document repository whenever necessary. This can be accomplished by means of a shell command which overwrites an existing object belonging to the class Document or BitStream with a new object generated by parsing a newer HTML or bitstream document:

> update <DocumentPath&Name> [-DocType] [-Policy]

The first parameter specifies the relative path and name of the file that we want to parse in order to update the corresponding document in the base. The switch DocType has the same meaning as in command add. In order to explain the switch Policy we have to consider the problem of dealing with references established among possibly disappearing sections and insertion points defined in the document that we are going to update.

Assume the WOW repository contains an HTML document including sections being referred to by other documents. If we replace this document by a new version of it, the tags identifying sections might be no longer present: problems arise if tags identifying a section in the old document are no longer present in the new document. If Policy equals restricted (default) the system verifies that the new version of the document still contains all the tags identifying the sections present in the old document and referred to by other documents. Otherwise the update command is aborted. If Policy equals unrestricted the behavior of the system is different: for each *disappeared* section a warning is prompted and every reference to that section is automatically broken.

3.7 Miscellaneous Commands

In addition to the shell commands introduced in the previous sections there are two extra commands for copying the complete repository or a specified document to the file system (to the specified direcory fspath) and for changing the directory path in the file system (which had been previously set by the initialize command):

```
export [<DocumentPath&name>] <fspath>
newroot <DocumentRoot>
```

4 Related Work

Several approaches have been proposed to connect (relational) databases to the Internet. Most of them use CGI scripts [12] working as gateways between an HTTP daemon and the database's API (DB2WWW, KE Texpress, Oracle WebServe, R:WEB, Sapphire/Web, Sibylla, Software Engine, Spider (cf. [14])). Similar systems come up in the area of ODBMS (O_2Web, GemStone WWW Gateway). However, all of these systems use proprietary protocols or complex query languages to maintain information and handle links. WOW demands little from WWW authors and administrators. Documents and links are created in the usual manner.

In the area of document repositories there are some approaches that are comparable to WOW. STREAT/HyperStorM [1] provides sophisticated management for SGML documents based on the VODAK ODBMS. However, integration of application objects and non SGML document types is not supported. The same applies for LINCKS [10] and several commercial products like Hyper-G/HyperWave [8]. Most of the commercial products moreover simply handle documents as flat files attached to hyperlink information or vice versa.

5 Conclusion and Future Work

With standard file systems more and more WWW developers are getting problems to maintain and update the big number of WWW documents as well as the connections among them.

WOW solves this problem in an easy and powerful way. The O_2 based WOW system allows a flexible and efficient handling of a large set of WWW documents, providing facilities for consistent updates of the repository. The WOW generator and WOW Server provide the facility to process any type of document, to store and maintain them with O_2, and to let them being retrieved via Internet by WWW clients. Document integration is supported by adapting O_2Web's idea of generic unparse methods.

Advanced features like support for HTML forms and the complex field of distributed authoring have to be discussed in more detail. Moreover, an HTML editor based on WOW and transparently using the shell commands discussed is under development.

References

[1] K. Aberer, K. Böhm, and C. Hüser. The prospects of publishing using advanced database concepts. *Electronic Publishing Origination, Dissemination, and Design*, 6(4):469–480, Dec. 1993.

[2] F. Bancilhon, C. Delobel, and P. Kanellakis, editors. *Building an object-oriented database system, the story of O_2*. Morgan Kaufmann, 1992.

[3] T. Berners-Lee, R. T. Fielding, and H. F. Nielsen. *Hypertext Transfer Protocol – HTTP/1.1*, Jan. 1996. Internet Draft.

[4] T. Berners-Lee, L. Masinter, and M. McCahill. RFC 1738: Uniform Resource Locators (URL), Dec. 1994.

[5] F. Buddrus. Enacting authorization models for object-oriented databases. In *Proc. of the 7th Int. Conf. on Database and Expert System Applicati ons (DEXA)*, Zurich, Switzerland, Sept. 1996. IEEE Computer Society. Workshop Proc.

[6] F. Buddrus. Access control in an object-oriented document repository. In *Proc. of the 1st East-European Symposium on Advances in Databases and Information Systems (ADBIS '97)*, Sept. 1997.

[7] F. Buddrus and M. Bellavia. Surfing an ODBMS (maintaining WWW documents with O_2). In *Proc. of the 4th Int. Conf. on Document Analysis and Recognition (ICDAR)*, Aug. 1997.

[8] U. Flohr. Hyper-G organizes the Web — this could be the next big thing on the Web: a new hypermedia architecture that makes it easier to find what you're looking for. *Byte Magazine*, 20(11), Nov. 1995.

[9] D. E. Knuth. Backus Normal form vs. Backus Naur form. *Communications of the ACM*, 7(12):735–736, Dec. 1964.

[10] P. Lambrix, M. Sjölin, and L. Pagdham. LINCKS - a platform for cooperative information systems. Technical report, Department of Computer and Information Science, LiTH, Sweden, 1993.

[11] O2 Technology, 7 rue du Parc de Clagny, 78035 Versailles Cedex, France. *O_2 Web User Manual*, 4.6 edition, May 1996.

[12] C. Patchett. *CGI Cookbook; Perl and JavaScript*. Wiley, New York, NY, USA, Nov. 1996.

[13] D. Raggett, J. Lam, and I. Alexander. *The Definitive Guide to HTML 3.0*. Addison-Wesley, Reading, MA, USA, 1996.

[14] J. Rowe. Accessing a Database Server via the World Wide Web. Technical report, COMSO, Inc., 1995.

[15] S. Sachweh and W. Schäfer. Version Management for tightly integrated Software Engineering Environments. Technical Report 22, GOODSTEP ESPRIT-III project, July 1994.

MODELLING ISSUES II

Subject Composition by Roles [*]

Bent Bruun Kristensen

The Maersk Mc-Kinney Moller Institute for Production Technology
Odense University, DK-5230 Odense M, Denmark

Abstract

Subjects model different perspectives on a problem domain by collections
of related class hierarchies. Subjects can be seen as the result of separate
and possibly independent development processes for partial models. The
subjects can be efficiently composed by a technique that builds on the
notion of roles. The composition allows already combined subjects to be
further combined or to be dissolved and combined anew.

1 Introduction

In conceptual programming we model concepts and phenomena by classes and
objects, but extended with additional abstraction mechanisms [5]. The objective is to support concept formation explicitly and efficiently by extending the
powerful but limited existing abstraction facilities in object-oriented programming and modeling [1] and [11]. The *subjects* [3] model different perspectives
on a problem domain by collections of related class hierarchies. Subjects can
be seen as the result of separate and possibly independent development processes for partial models. Subjects can also be seen as the building blocks for
the support of the evolution of domain models as part of software evolution
process. The notion of roles (for example [6] and [10]) supports the need for
different perspectives on classes and objects. The subjects can be efficiently
composed by a technique that builds on the notion of roles. In the composition
the original structure of the subjects is preserved.

Paper Organization. In section 2 we motivate the composition of subjects
by the separate developments of partial domain models — and we introduce
the notion of roles [1]. In section 3 we describe the approach to the composition
of subjects by means of roles. In section 3.1 we describe the basic step that
includes the construction of a common new class hierarchy. In section 3.2
we describe a general step that allows the composition to be continued either
by redoing the previous composition or by simply repeating the process. In
section 3.3 we describe a technique for turning usual classes into role classes
for a new common class. In section 4 we briefly summarize the approach to
subject composition and discuss related work.

---

[*]This research was supported in part by the Danish Natural Science Research Council,
No. 9400911

[1]We discuss neither the use of roles in conceptual modeling nor class hierarchy composition
in general.

2 Perspectives and Models

Subjects. The subjects [3] model that different agents might view the same object from different perspectives. The agents do not only have a filtered view of an object, but some of the methods of the object may be there only because of the given perspectives of an agent. Usually, the criteria for deciding which properties of real-world phenomena to include in a model are based on a single perspective only.

Subjects can be seen as a logical organization of a model according to various relevant perspectives on the entire model of a problem domain. Alternatively, subjects can be seen as preliminary results of separate development processes of partial models. This development process can be intentionally separated into independent subprocesses, or subsequently independent models can be identified as partially overlapping sub-models. In any case there is a need for composition of the subjects. In the evolution process in general, new subjects may appear in order to support new additional requirements, and existing subjects may be replaced by revised subjects. In this software evolution perspective, efficient and flexible support of the composition of subjects is necessary.

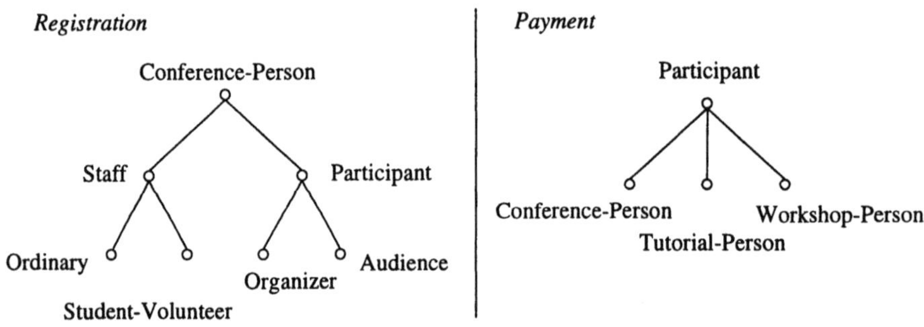

Figure 1: Perspectives: *Registration* and *Payment*

We use the "Conference Organizing Problem" [7] as a well-known context to illustrate our ideas. Several perspectives can be applied to the planning and holding of a conference. In Figure 1, we illustrate two perspectives, a *Registration* and a *Payment* perspective. In the *Registration* perspective we focus on identification aspects: Each person involved in the holding of the conference must be identifiable — must have a badge of one out of several categories. In the example we model this by the class `Conference-Person` with subclasses `Staff` (with `Ordinary` and `Student-Volunteer` as subclasses) and `Participant` (with `Organizer` and `Audience` as subclasses). In the *Payment* perspective we focus on payment aspects: Each person that participates in the conference, must register — must sign up and pay for some selected activities such as the conference, workshops, tutorials, etc. In the example we model this by the class `Participant` with subclasses `Conference-Person`, `Workshop-Person` and `Tutorial-Person`. The class `Participant` includes relevant individual information about social activities and possible reductions in fee.

Roles. The overall motivation for roles is to allow special perspectives on a phenomenon that is modeled by an object. A perspective is used by other objects in the model as a restricted, selective way of knowing — and accessing — the object. The perspective is a set of selected properties of the phenomenon — modeled by a set of methods. Other objects can access the selected set of methods. An important property of such perspectives is that they can change dynamically. The perspective is modeled by a language construct — the role abstraction mechanism. A role will include a set of methods, but can also include state (in the form of for example instance variables) when it is instantiated as a perspective on an object. The characteristics of roles [4] include visibility, dependency, identity, dynamicity, multiplicity and abstractivity.

The power of roles is to give restricted, possibly complementary perspectives on a complex and compound object, and to do this dynamically in order to support dynamicity in the composition. This is important because it corresponds to an essential understanding of how we conceive — and conceptually model — the world around us. We organize our understanding in terms of different perspectives on phenomena (and the concepts formed mentally to cover these) and the dynamicity of such perspectives. We use the following slightly modified combination of the terminology from [6] and [3]: The object, to which a role is allocated, will be referred to as the *intrinsic* object. The methods of an intrinsic object are referred to as *intrinsic methods*. A *subject* is a collection of class hierarchies that together models a certain perspective on a problem domain. In Figure 2 we illustrate the notation used in schematic diagrams. A role may be drawn glued onto a class (or another role).

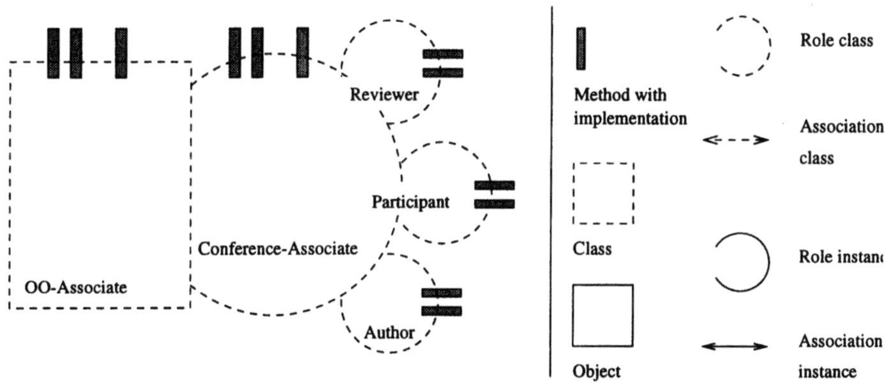

Figure 2: Example: Roles

In Figure 2 we also include an example from [4] to illustrate the use of roles to model various perspectives on a person (OO-Associate) who is related to some "OO" organization. Class OO-associate is not related to any particular conference, but models only the general information, such as for example Member-Id. The role Conference-Associate of OO-Associate will be associated to class Conference. A given Conference is related to a specific role of an OO-Associate only and not the entire OO-Associate. An OO-Associate object may have any number of `Conference-Associate` roles, because it may be involved in a number of conferences at the same time. We model `Participant`, `Author`, and `Reviewer` to be roles of `Conference-Associate` because the various relations to a given conference are related to these specific roles only (and not to `Conference-Associate` as a whole): A `Participant` is related to the `Conference`; an `Author` is related to the `Paper`, and a `Reviewer` is related to a `Paper`.

3   Subject Composition

We assume that a number of subjects have been developed. Each subject models the problem domain in its own subjective way. A subject consists of a number of class hierarchies. The composition of subject is based on the role concept — the class hierarchies are combined by letting the hierarchies become role hierarchies of a new *intrinsic class hierarchy*. The composition of subjects is described in three subsections. We described a basic step where the new intrinsic class hierarchy is constructed, then a general step that allows the composition to be redone or simply repeated, and finally the technique for turning usual classes into role classes for a new intrinsic class.

Subjects and Hierarchies. Given subjects S1 and S2, and some class hierarchies, CH1 from S1 and CH2 from S2, assume that we want to compose S1 and S2, specifically to compose the hierarchies CH1 and CH2. In Figure 3, we illustrate the subjects S1 and S2 with the hierarchies CH1 and CH2, respectively.

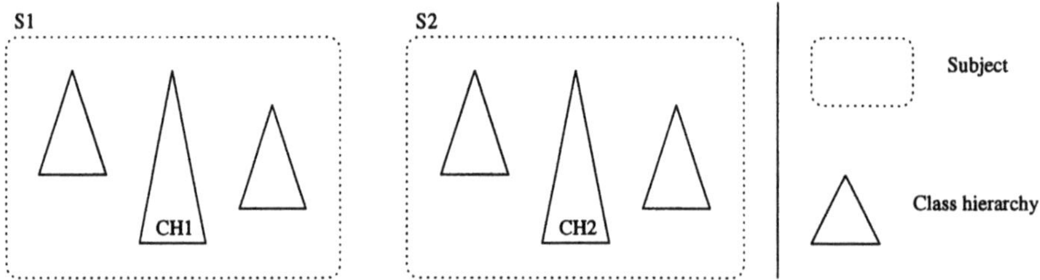

Figure 3: Subjects and Hierarchies

Assume that the class names in CH1 are different from the class names in CH2, except from exactly the class names in CH1 and CH2 that we want to match [2], i.e. to be identical by the composition. We denote the set of class names to be identified by the composition M. We require, for all pairs of class names to be matched by the composition, that any super class of the one element in the pair is to be matched by a super[3] class of the other element in the pair.

In Figure 4, we illustrate the classes A', B', ... and A'', B'', ... to be matched from the hierarchies CH1 and CH2. R' and R'' are the roots of the hierarchies

---

[2]If this is not the case we can always obtain this situation by renaming, or by explicitly identifying the classes to be matched by some kind of additional description.

[3]We use the super class relation to state this requirement. We could as well have used the sub class relation to obtain exactly the same requirement.

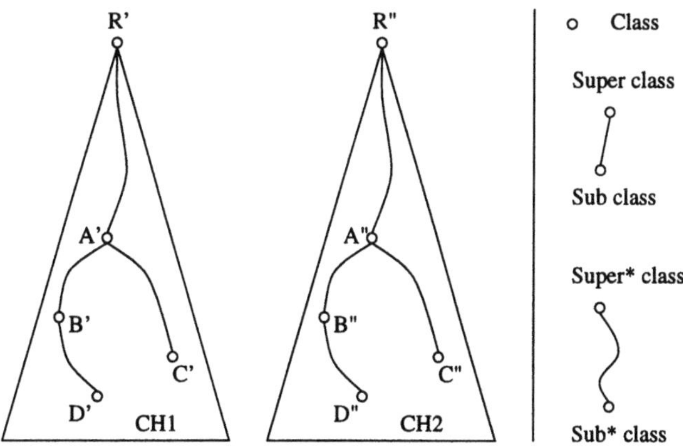

Figure 4: Hierarchies with Classes to be Composed

CH1 and CH2, respectively. If A is in M we indicate the classes to be matched from the hierarchies CH1 and CH2 as respective A' and A''. For any pair of class names A' and A'' in M to be matched, we require that for any other pair of class names B' and B'' in M also to be matched [4]:

(i) A' *super*∗ B' is equivalent to A'' *super*∗ B''

as a necessary condition in order to compose CH1 and CH2.

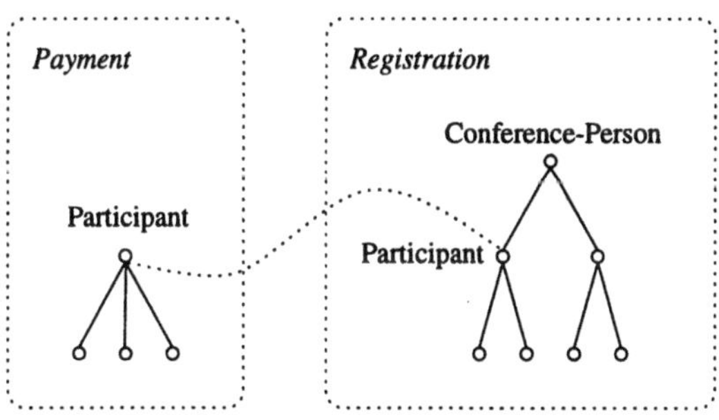

Figure 5: Subjects: *Registration* and *Payment*

"Conference Organizing Problem". In Figure 5, we illustrate the *Registration* and *Payment* perspectives as subjects (and in schematic versions). Each perspective represents a subject — as a special case with only one hierarchy in each for reasons of simplicity. We also illustrate how the two subjects are

---

[4]The relation *super* is defined as: A *super* B is true if the class A is a super class of the class B (and B is a sub class of A). The relation *super*∗ means the transitive closure of the relation *super* (the transitive closure can be defined inductively as (1) A *super*∗ A and (2) if A *super*∗ C and C *super* B then A *super*∗ B).

related: The class `Participant` from *Payment* matches the subclass `Participant` of `Conference-Person` from *Registration*.

3.1 Basic Composition

Basic Composition Step. To compose `CH1` and `CH2` we create an intrinsic class hierarchy, `CH`, with exactly the classes from M. The hierarchy `CH` has the structure induced form the relations in (i). In Figure 6, we illustrate the hierarchy `CH` that results from the composition of `CH1` and `CH2` from Figure 4 with $M = \{$`R`, `A`, `B`, `C`, `D`$\}$. Any class in Figure 6 has a matching class in both `CH1` and `CH2`. The hierarchy `CH` can be found in both `CH1` and `CH2` (possibly with with some additional classes mixed in between) because of the requirement (i).

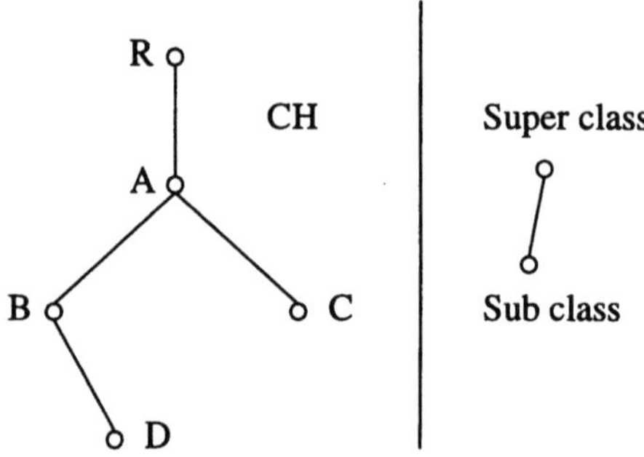

Figure 6: Hierarchy Resulting from Composition

If `R'` and `R''` are to be matched in the composition we are done. The root `R` of `CH` illustrates this situation. Else we create new artificial roots `R0'` for `CH1` and `R0''` for `CH2` and we match these new roots into the root `R` for `CH`. In the following, the roots of `CH1` and `CH2` are denoted `R0'` and `R0''` in any of these cases. For any class `A` in `CH` we make the classes `A'` and `A''` roles of `A` (and as a special case `R0'` and `R0''` roles of `R`). This composition of classes by roles is discussed below. In Figure 7, we illustrate the resulting intrinsic hierarchy `CH` with the role hierarchies of `CH1` and `CH2`. The role relations between the classes are illustrated.

Basic Step: Several Hierarchies. The generalization from two to several subjects and hierarchies is straightforward. To combine several hierarchies, `CH1`, `CH2`, ... , `CHn` the sets of classes in these hierarchies to be matched in the combination need not to be identical in order to form the hierarchy `CH` from M and (i). Again we denote the set of class names to be identified by the composition M. We assume that the class names in `CH1`, `CH2`, ... , `CHn` are distinct, except from exactly the class names in `CH1`, `CH2`, ... , `CHn` that we identify by the composition. We require that the resulting class hierarchy `CH` with the classes from M is can be deduced from M and `CH1`, `CH2`, ... , `CHn` and is well-defined (the graph must be coherent and contain no circularity). The

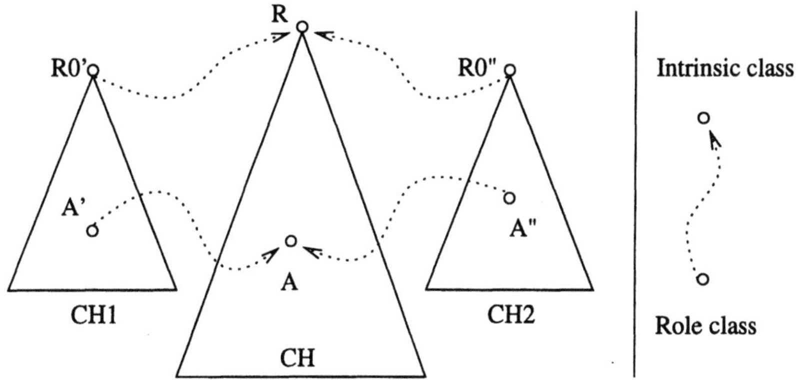

Figure 7: Intrinsic Hierarchy with Role Hierarchies

hierarchy CH is defined as follows [5]: For any hierarchy, CHi, for any pair of class names X and Y in both CHi and M

(ii) X *super*∗ Y in CHi implies X *super*∗ Y in CH

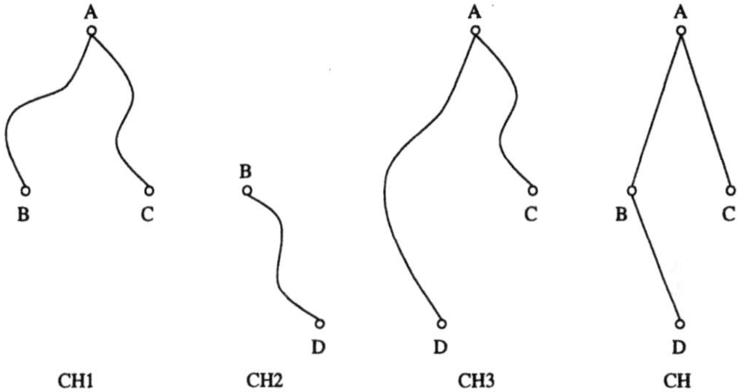

Figure 8: Example: Several Hierarchies

In Figure 8 we illustrate a general example for composition of several hierarchies: $M = \{$A, B, C, D$\}$, CH1 includes A, B and C from M, CH2 includes B and D only from M, whereas CH3 includes A, B and D from M. The resulting hierarchy CH includes exactly M and its inheritance structure is induced from CH1, CH2 and CH3.

"Conference Organizing Problem". In Figure 9, we illustrate another example from the model of the planning of the conference, namely a *Writing*

---

[5](i) is only defined for the special case with only two hierarchies and is slightly more restrictive than (ii), but (ii) implies (i).

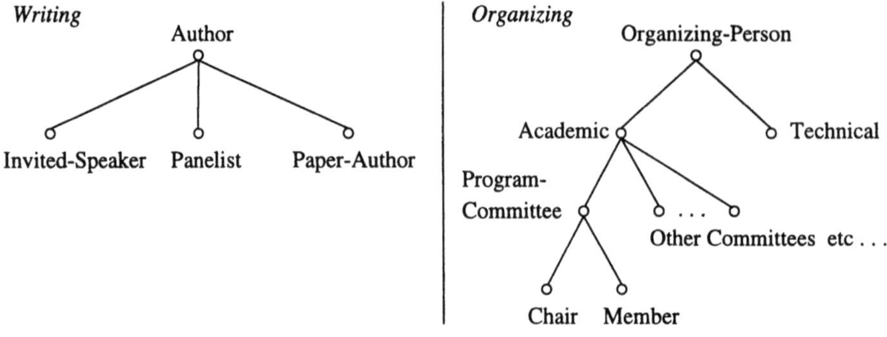

Figure 9: *Writing* and *Organizing*

perspective and an *Organizing* perspective. In the *Organizing* perspective we focus on the responsibilities during the preparation of the conference such as technical stuff and the various committees: Each person who organizes an aspect of the conference is included. In the example we model this by the class **Organizing-Person** with subclasses **Academic** and **Technical**. The **Academic**'s take care of the various committees and **Academic** has **Program-Committee** and other similar committees as subclasses. In the *Writing* perspective we focus on the categories of persons who are writing various documents (research, tutorial, etc) in relation to the conference: In the example we model this by the class **Author** with subclasses **Invited-Speaker**, **Panelist** and **Paper-Author** (several other categories exist, but we only include these). The class **Author** includes relevant individual information about the writing activity such as the title of the paper **Paper-Title**. The two subjects are related as follows: The class **Author** matches the class **Academic**.

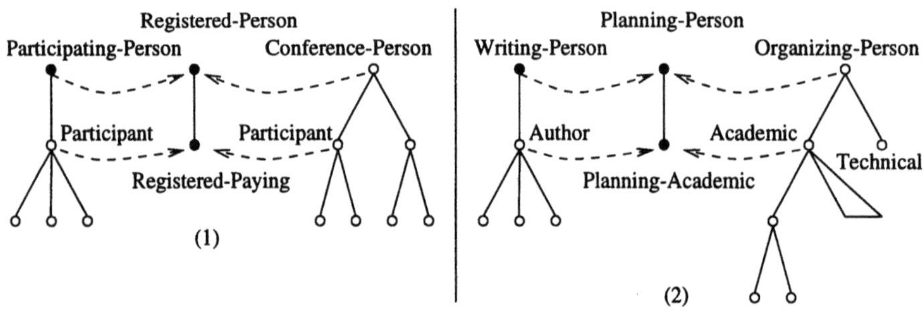

Figure 10: Schematic Compositions

In Figure 10, we illustrate (in schematic versions) the compositions of (1) the *Registration* and *Payment* subjects (with additional superclass **Participating-Person** and with resulting classes **Registered-Person** and **Registered-Paying**), and

(2) the *Writing* (with additional superclass `Writing-Person`) and *Organizing* subjects (with resulting classes `Planning-Person` and `Planning-Academic`).

3.2   General Composition

General Composition Step.   Given two (or more) results of composition of the form in Figure 7 we want to be able to compose these further, i.e. to compose for example R and S of Figure 11. It is assumed that R and S have the form of an intrinsic class hierarchy with role hierarchies as indicated by R' and R'' for R and S' and S'' for S. Note that each of the (role) class hierarchies R', R'', S' and S'' itself may have the same structure as for example R and S, i.e. that each of these may be an intrinsic (role) class hierarchy with role hierarchies associated. However, the focus here is to composed the hierarchies R and S.

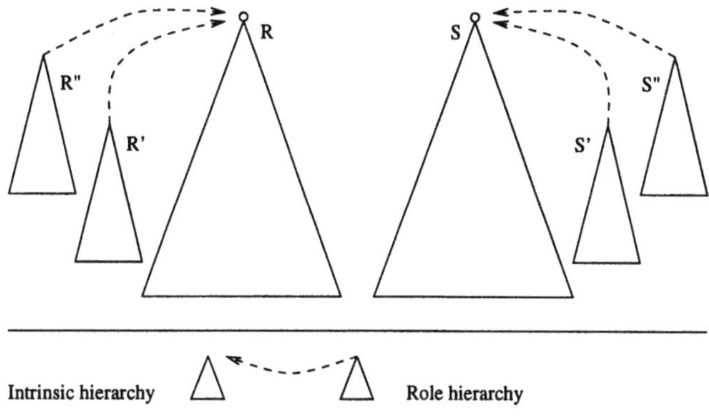

Figure 11: Intrinsic Hierarchies with Role Hierarchies

We assume that M is given for R and S and that the requirement (i) is satisfied. We propose two solutions to the composition of R and S. The actual choice between the solutions depends on our perspective of the evolution process in which these subjects are created and on our interpretation of their relationship.

Redo Solution.   First dissolve each of the compositions R and S into the hierarchies R', R'', S' and S''. Next use the basic composition technique described above to form a composition of R', R'', S' and S''. The set M is unchanged and (i) is satisfied for R', R'', S' and S''. The result is a hierarchy T with R', R'', S' and S'' as associated role hierarchies for T, as illustrated in Figure 12.

An interpretation of this solution is that the compositions R and S are some kind of preliminary compositions. These are created separately for some purpose at some given point in time. We choose this solution in order to redo these compositions. Because we consider R and S to be preliminary compositions we dissolve these and form a new composition with all the basic hierarchies. The preliminary compositions R and S are rejected.

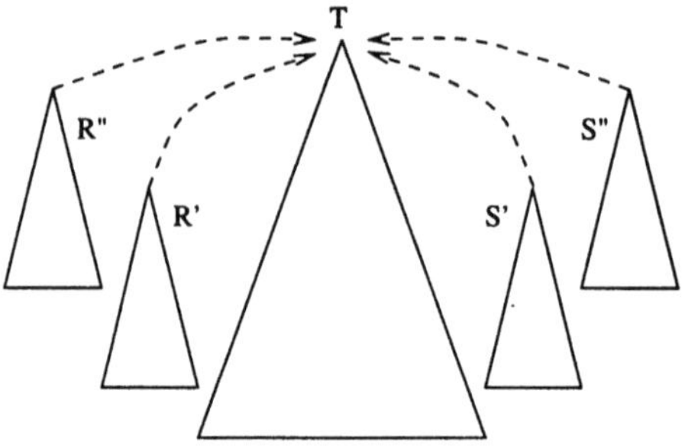

Figure 12: Redo Solution

Preserve Solution. Consider the hierarchies R and S in isolation, i.e. without taking R', R'', S' and S'' into consideration. Use the basic composition technique as described above on R and S to form an intrinsic hierarchy T (from M) with R and S as associated role hierarchies. The role hierarchies R', R'' and S', S'' of respectively R and S are preserved unchanged as illustrated in Figure 13.

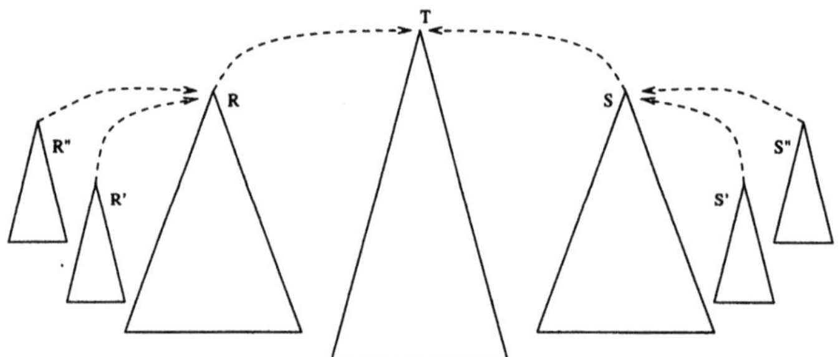

Figure 13: Preserve Solution

An interpretation of this solution is that the compositions R and S are partial, but permanent compositions. These are created separately for some purpose at some given point in time. We choose this solution in order to preserve these compositions. Because we consider R and S to be permanent compositions we preserve these and form a new composition from these hierarchies. The permanent compositions R and S are kept unchanged.

"Conference Organizing Problem". In Figure 14, we illustrate a *In-Charge* perspective from the holding of the conference. In this perspective we focus on who is responsible of what during the holding of the conference: Each person involved in the holding of the conference is responsible of one or several activities that are scheduled throughout the conference. In the example we model this by the class **Person-In-Charge** with subclasses **Technical**

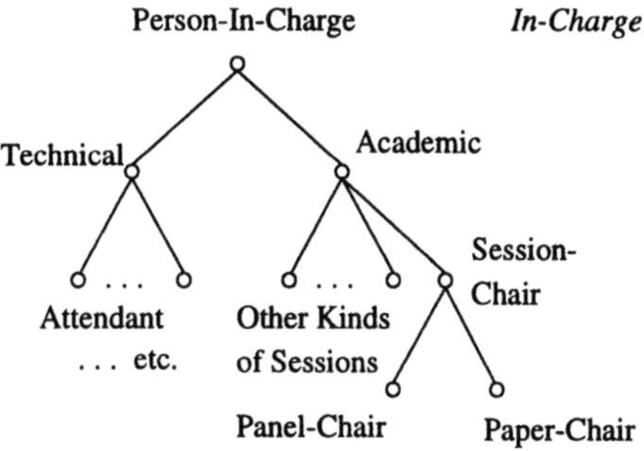

Figure 14: *In-Charge* Perspective

and `Academic`. The subclasses of `Technical` include for example `Attendant`, `Camera-Person`, `Light-Person`, etc. The subclasses of `Academic` include for example `Session-Chair` (with subclasses `Panel-Chair` and `Paper-Chair`) and responsibility for other kinds of sessions.

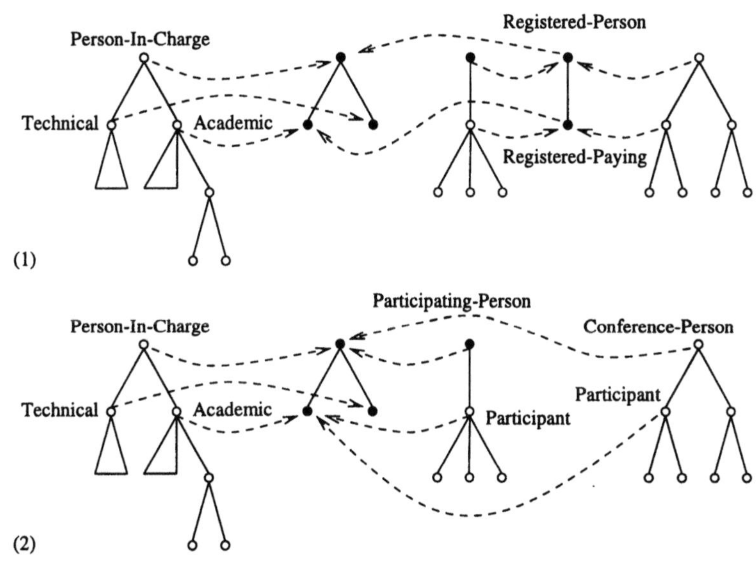

Figure 15: Preserve (1) & Redo (2) Example

In Figure 15, we illustrate the composition of the *In-Charge* perspective with *Registration* and *Payment* perspectives:

(1) In the preserve case we match `Person-In-Charge` and `Registered-Person`, `Academic` and `Registered-Paying`, etc.

(2) In the redo case we match `Person-In-Charge` and `Conference-Person` and `Participating-Person`, etc.

192

3.3 Hierarchy Composition

Class Roles. For any class in the resulting class hierarchy of the basic composition step, a number of classes are made role classes of the class. For example in Figure 7 the classes A' and A" are made role classes of class A in the resulting class hierarchy CH. The set of subclasses of for example A' forms a subclass hierarchy for A'. By the composition this hierarchy becomes a hierarchy of role classes. In general, the rule is that any class X' in this hierarchy (A' *super*∗ X') also becomes a role class of A ([6]). This rule implies that if class X' from CH1 and class X" from CH2 are role classes for class A then an object of A can have any pair of objects of such classes X' and X" as role instances.

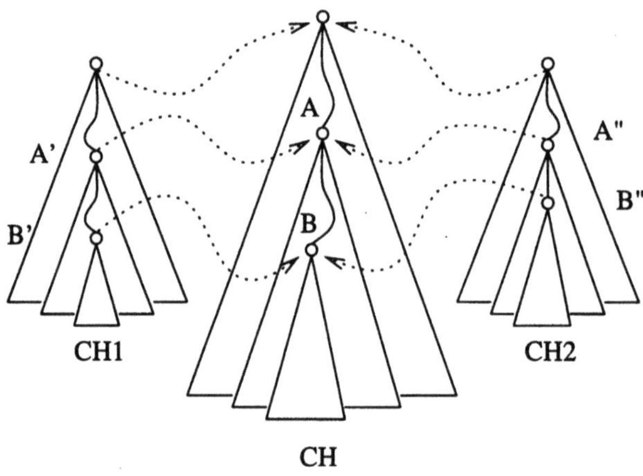

Figure 16: Composition of Role Hierarchies

The exception from this rule is illustrated in Figure 16. Assume that A' and A" from respectively CH1 and CH2 are role classes for the class A in CH. Assume also that A *super* B for some other class B in CH and that the role classes for B are the classes B', B" from CH1 and CH2, respectively. The rule in [6] states that for any class X' in CH1 such that A' *super*∗ X', the class X' is also a role class for A, except if B' *super*∗ X' (in which case X' is a role class for the class B in CH).

In Figure 17 a schematic example illustrates the rule and its restriction. Assume that the A's and B's are related as above. Any Xi' class is a subclass of A' and a role class for A. Any Yi' class is a subclass of A' but is also a subclass of B': Therefore, any Yi' class is a role class for B but not a role class for A. Any combination of instances of Xi' and Xj" can be role instances for an A object, whereas any combination of instances of Yi' and Yj" can be role instances for a B object, but can not be role instances for an A object.

Class Composition. When classes are related to another class as role classes we have to specify how the methods and instance variables of these classes are related. Several approaches to the general case are discussed in [4] and [6] — the problems and possible solutions are out of the scope of this article.

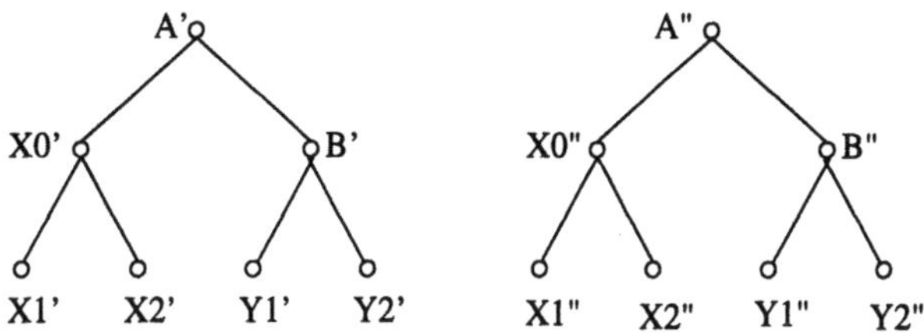

Figure 17: Example: Role Hierarchies

Assume as in Figure 7 that the classes A' and A" are made role classes of class A in the resulting class hierarchy CH. In the general case A is a usual class with its own methods and instance variables. Furthermore, because A' and A" in the general case would be defined explicitly as role classes for A the definition of the methods of A' and A" could utilize the methods of A (and possibly also its instance variables). The role classes A' and A" could be explicitly dependent on the intrinsic class A. We define the composition of classes for the special situation in this article only: We consider the classes A' and A" to be role classes, but these are not defined as such and there is no dependency on the class A. There may be more than two role classes, but this implies no essential complications to the composition strategy that we outline below. Actually, the class A has not be defined — it has to be defined through the composition.

The composition of the role classes A' and A" proceeds as follows: To obtain simplicity in our description we assume that the names are distinct in A' and A" unless two names are intended to represent the same method or instance variable, in which case the name (name) is indicated as name' in A' and name" in A" (else renaming for the purpose of composition is necessary). A distinct name, for example of a method n' from A' or of an instance variable j' from A', causes no changes. For identical names in A' and A" (or in any super classes of these) the composition involves:

- **Methods,** m' and m" from respectively A' and A": We specify m as a *subject* method of A ([6]) with the meaning that whenever any of the methods m', m" and m is invoked the bodies of both m' and m" are executed [6].

- **Instance variables,** i' and i" from respectively A' and A": We override i' and i" by private access methods with identical names in subclasses of A' and A" [7]. These access methods will access the instance variable i added to A.

In Figure 18 we illustrate class composition. The method m is a *subject* method for the methods m' and m" from A' and A". The instance variables i' and i" are replaced by access methods with identical names in subclasses of A' and A" and the instance variable i in A.

---

[6] The options include: The order of execution, input parameters to both method invocations, output parameters only from one method.

[7] If overriding of instance variables by methods is not legal, we may assume that all instance variables are accessed by access methods and then override these methods instead.

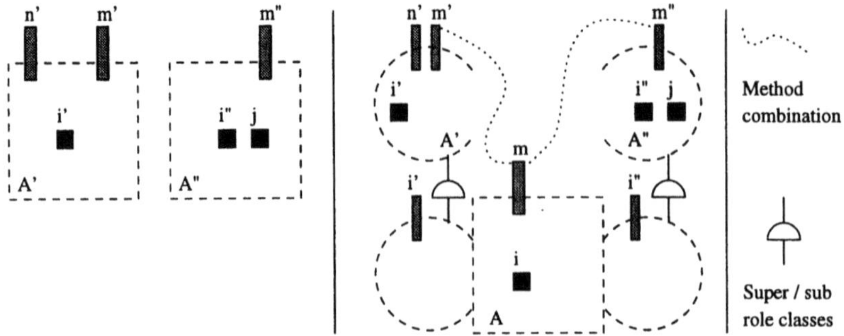

Figure 18: Class Composition

"Conference Organizing Problem". In Figure 19, we illustrate the composition of the `Writing-Person` and the `Organizing-Person` as an example. The illustration shows that

(1) the method `Schedule` exists in `Writing-Person` and `Organizing-Person` and has been added to `Planning-Person` as a *subject* method,

(2) the instance variable `Name` in `Writing-Person` and the `Organizing-Person`, has been overridden by access methods for the instance variable `name` that has been added to `Planning-Person`.

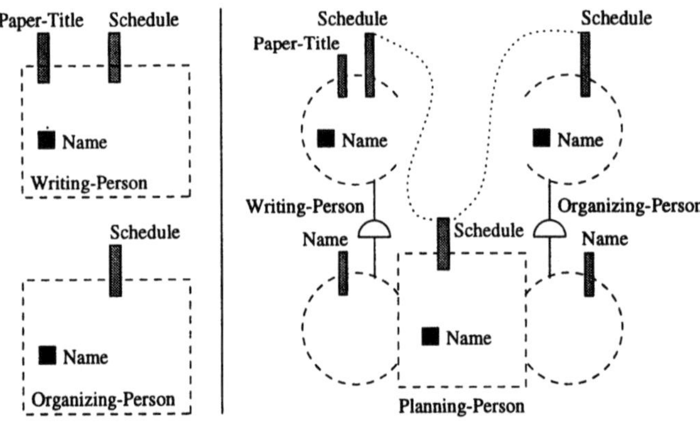

Figure 19: Class `Planning-Person`

4 Summary

Results. By the notion of subjects we can model the results of separate and possibly independent development processes of domain models. Subjects with different, possibly overlapping perspectives can be composed to form more complete models. A domain model can evolve over time — additional subjects can be added or existing (parts) subjects can be replaced by new versions.

Our approach to subject composition is characterized as:

- It builds on the notion of roles (a simplified case), that itself supports perspectives in models of phenomena.

- A subject already composed by the approach can be dissolved and re-composed differently.

- Subjects already composed by the approach can be further composed.

- In the composition the original structure (of the hierarchies) of a subject is preserved and the descriptions of classes are not modified.

- The composition is defined only in terms of classes — existing objects are not included.

Related Work. In [8] the combination of inheritance hierarchies is discussed. The objective is to make extensions to existing object-oriented systems. In the approach extensions are separated from a base hierarchy — the extensions, including extensions to existing classes, are kept in separate extension hierarchies. Extension hierarchies are combined with the base hierarchy by either an extension operator or a merge operator — conflicts may be identified during the combination. The approach addresses the addition of extended behavior to both classes and existing objects.

In [9] the composition of subjects is addressed. A number of composition rules are used to specify how the various details of classes should be combined. The rules are generic and exceptions to the general rules can be specified. A number of useful rules are described, including merge and override, as a first step towards a composition rule library. The approach addresses unanticipated extension and composition (without changing or recompiling existing source code) and decentralized software (class) development.

In [12] protocols are discussed as a means of defining interface compatibility for classes. Software adaptors are introduced to bridge the difference between object-oriented applications that have functionally compatible but type incompatible interfaces.

[2] introduces and solves the problem of composing different Before/After Metaclasses in the context of SOM. The metaclasses are used to define the implementation of classes that, by suitable construction of their instance instance method tables, arrange for each invocation of a method to be preceded by execution of a before method and followed by execution of an after method.

Acknowledgments. We thank Kasper Østerbye for our inspiring joint work on the theory of conceptual abstraction — in general ([5]) and in the case of roles ([6]).

References

[1] G. Booch: Object Oriented Analysis and Design with Applications. Benjamin/Cummings, 1994.

[2] I. R. Forman, S. Danforth, H. Madduri: Composition of Before/After Metaclasses in SOM. Proceedings of the Conference on Object-Oriented Programming Systems, Languages and Applications, 1994.

[3] W. Harrison, H. Ossher: Subject-Oriented Programming (A Critique of Pure Objects). Proceedings of the Conference on Object-Oriented Programming Systems, Languages and Applications, 1993.

[4] B. B. Kristensen. Object-Oriented Modeling with Roles. Proceedings of the 2nd International Conference on Object-Oriented Information Systems, Dublin, Ireland, 1995

[5] B. B. Kristensen, K. Østerbye: Conceptual Modeling and Programming Languages. Sigplan Notices, 29 (9), 1994.

[6] B. B. Kristensen, K. Østerbye. Roles: Conceptual Abstraction Theory & Practical Language Issues. Accepted for publication in: Special Issue of Theory and Practice of Object Systems on Subjectivity in Object-Oriented Systems, 1996.

[7] T. W. Olle, A. A. Verrijn-Stuart, H. G. Sol, Eds.: Information System Design Methodologies: A Comparative Review. North-Holland, 1982.

[8] H. Ossher, W. Harrison: Combination of Inheritance Hierarchies. Proceedings of the Conference on Object-Oriented Programming Systems, Languages and Applications, 1992.

[9] H. Ossher, M. Kaplan, W. Harrison, A. Katz, V. Kruskal: Subject-Oriented Composition Rules. Proceedings of the Conference on Object-Oriented Programming Systems, Languages and Applications, 1995.

[10] B. Pernici: Objects with Roles. Proceedings ACM-IEEE Conference of Office Information Systems (COIS), 1990.

[11] J. Rumbaugh, M. Blaha, W. Premerlani, F. Eddy, W. Lorensen: Object-Oriented Modeling and Design. Prentice Hall 1991.

[12] D. M. Yellin, R. E. Strom: Interfaces, Protocols, and the Semi-Automatic Construction of Software Adaptors. Proceedings of International Conference on Technology of Object-Oriented Languages and Systems, 1994.

Assessing Inheritance for the Multiple Descendant Redefinition Problem in OO Systems

Philippe Li-Thiao-Té, Jessie Kennedy and John Owens
Department of Computer Studies, Napier University, Canal Court,
42 Craiglockhart Avenue, Edinburgh EH14 1LT, Scotland, UK
e-mail: {p.li, j.kennedy, j.owens}@dcs.napier.ac.uk
http://www.dcs.napier.ac.uk/osg
Tel: +44 (0)131-455 5340 Fax: +44 (0)131-455 5394

Abstract

Current use of inheritance has illustrated that the introduction of conceptual inconsistencies is possible in a class hierarchy. This paper discusses the reasons why complete method redefinition infringes the essence of inheritance. A redefinition metric set is proposed and practical experiments demonstrate that the results obtained permit the detection of inheritance design problems. Appropriate design decisions are suggested.

Keywords: inheritance, object-oriented metrics, object-oriented design, method redefinition, class hierarchy, Smalltalk

1. Introduction

"Systems are not born into an empty world" stated Meyer [26]. The inheritance mechanism is one of the key points for the extendibility and reusability aspects of object-oriented (OO) systems [3, 8, 12, 13, 17, 26, 27, 28, 31]. Due to the inherent incremental development of a class hierarchy, it is important to consider the future additions of new classes [18, 29, 30] as they will influence the shape and structure of the hierarchy. Recently, a variety of models of inheritance have been well described by Taivalsaari [31]. Although they offer a vast extent of expressiveness, each of these mechanisms are still subject to conceptual design inconsistencies [2, 8, 12, 29]. In order to reuse the potential of classes, designers face the problem of property (attribute and method) reuse and method redefinition. The latter is a powerful mechanism which permits behavioural flexibility in a class hierarchy but can also affect the correctness of a class if wrongly used [18, 26, 28, 29]. This paper shows how the complete method redefinition mechanism in a superclass-subclass relationship pinpoints potential design problems in ancestors classes.

The increased interest in metrics for OO systems has been significant in the last five years [1, 9, 10, 15, 16, 20, 22, 23, 24, 25] following the pioneering work of Chidamder and Kemerer [9] with their OO metrics suite. We show how the use of measurement techniques for assessing the mechanism of method redefinition provides insights into the overall behaviour of a class hierarchy. Pragmatic experiments using our redefinition metric set were carried out on both commercial

198

libraries and on small, medium-size information systems. Specifically, the contributions of this paper are:

➢ an identification of design inconsistencies resulting from the multiple method redefinition problem in a class hierarchy,

➢ the proposition of a method redefinition metric set for assessing inheritance from a behavioural viewpoint,

➢ empirical validation of the metric set, results obtained from the Smalltalk class library are presented.

In section 2, we will explore the formal definition of inheritance from a property inheritance viewpoint. A description of the method redefinition variants and associated problems is given in section 3 followed by our proposed redefinition metric set in section 4. Derivation of the metrics, results and analysis are explained in section 5. Finally, we discuss related work on metrics for assessing inheritance in OO sytems and consider further work.

2. Properties Inheritance Scheme

Inheritance is the main mechanism which supports the realisation of criteria such as reusability and flexibility [17, 26]. An addition of a class to an existing class hierarchy specialises a branch of the tree, thereby extending it. By inheriting features from ancestor classes, reusability is also achieved. However, there exists many models of inheritance and the correct application of any model is debatable [2, 26]. The formal definition of inheritance is characterised as follows [4, 31]:

$$(1) \quad \boxed{C = P \oplus \Delta C}$$

where a new class C is shown as a combination ($\oplus$) of a set of properties inherited from an existing class P and the new properties (Δ) which make C a specialised version of P. In this equation, the relation superclass/subclass is assumed to be transitive, therefore P includes all cumulated properties from its own parents (C is also transitive). However, the inheritance scheme of properties from parent class to child class is open to many interpretations. Taivalsaari [31] explained that P represents the properties inherited from an existing object or class where, in fact, C is able to inherit from many classes either in the same descendant branch or multiple branches if in a multiple-inheritance situation. It is generally accepted that the deeper a class is in a hierarchy, the more difficult the control of inheritance becomes. Therefore, leaf classes are more subject to bad design than their parents.

If a subclass is to inherit its parents' properties, then the set of properties of a subclass SubCls of a class Cls becomes :

$$(2) \quad \boxed{SubCls = Properties\ (Cls) \oplus Properties\ (SubCls)}$$

where

SubCls < Cls i.e. SubCls *is_a* subclass of Cls,

Properties (class) = { inst I inst $\in$ <Attributes>, mth I mth $\in$ <Methods>}

Properties (class) is the set of attributes and methods of a class i.e. <Attributes>

and <Methods> respectively refers to the set of possible instance variables and the list of methods in the class.

Introducing the origin of properties in (2) gives:

(3) $$\boxed{\text{SubCls} = \text{Properties}_{\text{inherited}}\,(\text{SubCls}) \oplus \text{Properties}\,(\text{SubCls})}$$

where $\text{Properties}_{\text{inherited}}\,(\text{SubCls}) = \{\, x \mid x \in \text{Properties}\,(\text{Cls}),\ x \text{ is publicly available to SubCls}\}$,

From (2) and (3), a subclass SubCls is a combination of its inherited properties and its currently defined ones. (3) introduces properties overlapping in the definition when reuse of properties are achieved.

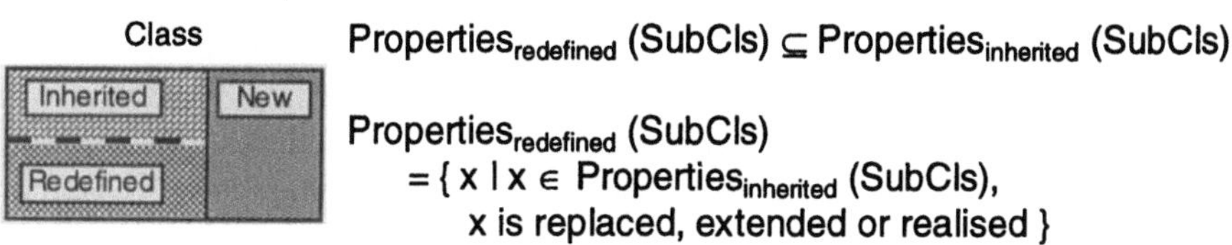

$$\text{Properties}_{\text{redefined}}\,(\text{SubCls}) \subseteq \text{Properties}_{\text{inherited}}\,(\text{SubCls})$$

$$\text{Properties}_{\text{redefined}}\,(\text{SubCls})$$
$$= \{\, x \mid x \in \text{Properties}_{\text{inherited}}\,(\text{SubCls}),$$
$$x \text{ is replaced, extended or realised}\,\}$$

Fig. 1: Class properties

$\text{Properties}_{\text{redefined}}(\text{SubCls})$ are the (inherited) redefined properties as opposed to $\text{Properties}_{\text{inherited}}\,(\text{SubCls})$ which is a superset including the ones accessible and used without modification. Because of the variety of possible modifications to a property, for instance, complete redefinition, extension or realisation, this is a possible source of incompatibility between a class and its subclass. As stated by Taivalsaari, inheritance use does not guarantee a conceptual specialisation intention. The mechanism of redefinition has been criticised [2, 12, 18, 26, 29] for not bearing any kind of semantic relationship with its initial implementation, especially when the method is completely overridden. Unfortunately, the *inheritance "scoping" control*[1] facility does not prevent this conceptually inconsistent situation. Indeed, a non-strict *is_a* policy is more likely to introduce unsubstitutable classes and is used either for convenience reasons or because it *uses_a* parent class property. The next section describes the different types of method redefinition and their associated characteristics.

3. Method Redefinition: Uses and Abuses

"Redefinition is an important semantic mechanism for providing the object-oriented brand of polymorphism" -- Meyer [26]. The basic principle of method redefinition is simple: it is a syntactic programming language facility which allows a class C to replace inherited implementations by keeping the same signatures for the new methods. Conceptually, one of the main reasons for using redefinition is to provide the flexibility of defining a different algorithm when the semantics of the method remain the same. Thereby the ability for a method to hold many forms in many subclasses, i.e. achieving polymorphism. At run-time, the correct behaviour will

---

[1] The process of declaring appropriate modifiers to a class, an attribute or a method will be referred to as the *inheritance scoping control* facility.

then be dynamically bound to the object which receives the message. In the following sections, a description of how incremental development leads to side-effects with the method redefinition problem is given.

3.1. The Method Redefinition Variants

Despite its very important role in a class hierarchy design process, the term redefinition, also known as overriding, is actually used in a confused way. Sometimes, it is referred to in the sense of method extension and other times in the sense of method replacement. Although, in both cases, the method is effectively redefined, their aims diverge completely. Method extension permits the reuse of the inherited property whereas method replacement stops the heritage of a parent property by not using it and replacing completely the inherited implementation with a new one. Method replacement seems intuitively unnatural unless in the case of a polymorphic method. For example, consider the following Smalltalk Collection branch:

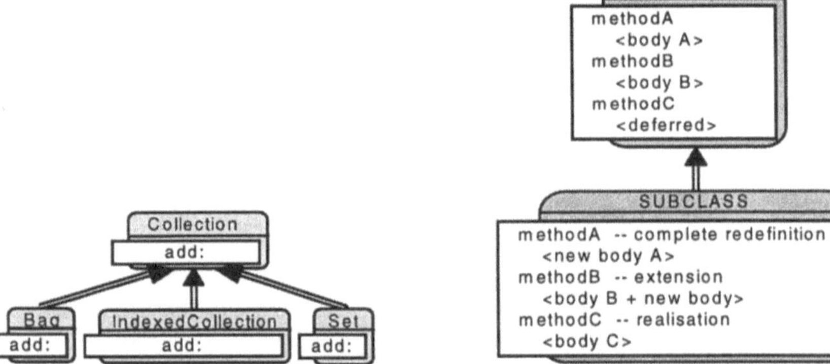

Fig. 2: Part of the Smalltalk Collection branch   Fig. 3: Method redefinition variants

The add: method of the class Collection is considered abstract (virtual in C++, deferred in Eiffel) indicating that any subclasses must provide the implementation of the method, therefore polymorphic. Firesmith described a set of inheritance guidelines which gives practical advice concerning a class hierarchy design [12]. However, in practice there are no guarantees that a given case of method redefinition is correct. A system can actually work without satisfying the guidelines or essence of inheritance.

In order to assess the "goodness" of a class hierarchy in terms of criteria such as coupling, cohesion, reuse or inheritance, it is important to understand and define what characteristics are to be measured. Our hypothesis is that a high level of redefinition or its variants suggest a possible conceptual design problem in the hierarchy e.g. a class which was wrongly-subclassed. The redefinition of a method will be assessed regarding its main variants [21] described in Fig. 3. The SUPERCLASS's methods are assumed to be publicly inherited. In SUBCLASS, the first case of the redefinition variants depicts an arguable case of inheritance where a complete redefinition of a method is done. Whereas the last two cases: extension and realisation, represent the recommended use of property inheritance. Cancellation of methods is an example of complete redefinition which restricts or stops the inheritance scheme. An extension to the implementation of methodB permits the reuse of inherited code and the addition of extra code which makes the subclass a specialised version. When a method is declared deferred in a parent class, the subclass must provide its implementation, i.e. the method is realised. It should be noted that all cases of inheritance fall under one of the different types of method redefinition mentioned. A method m of class C is redefined if and only if:

- m is an inherited method,
- m(C) signature is the same as in its original definition,
- m(C) implementation is either, replaced, extended or provided.

3.2. The Method Redefinition Problem

Why redefine if inherited? A major criticism of redefinition lies in the essence of inheritance itself. The two notions of property redefinition and property heritage are paradoxical. Surprisingly enough, method redefinition, including correct and incorrect use, happens more often than expected in a class hierarchy. For example, the redefinition metric results for the Smalltalk class library (Fig. 4) show that the amount of redefinition reaches 57.07% at DIT=4 (depth of inheritance metric [9]) in the hierarchy. On the first three levels of the hierarchy, the results obtained more than double from one level to another, denoting high "redefinition activity". One possible reason for such a redefinition profile is due to the incremental development of software. A closer look at the implementation of the same method redefined many times along a branch of the hierarchy revealed that common code had not been factorised. This phenomenon seems typical of the case of many developers working on the same part of a system without modifying the others' code (class dependency problem). Chidamber and Kemerer's *coupling between objects* (CBO) metric [10] permits the detection of weak and strong coupling. The CBO is recommended to be as low as possible. However, with new design techniques such as design patterns [13], the dependency between classes present in a pattern is high as they are strongly dependent (the purpose of a pattern).

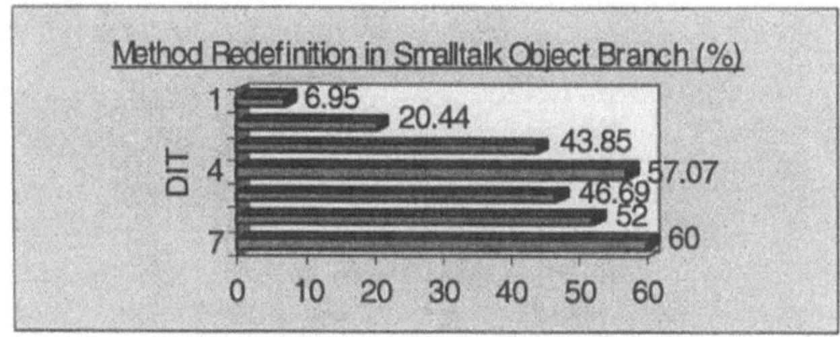

Fig. 4: Smalltalk hierarchy redefinition profile

3.2.1. Multiple Descendant Redefinition (MDR) Problem

The principle of inheritance involves an ownership transfer of features from the parent class to its subclasses. When a class inherits a method which has been publicly defined, the subclass has the right to change the property inheritance scheme for future heirs.

Fig. 5: Life history of the includes: redefined method in the Smalltalk Collection branch

In Fig. 5, the includes: method is used to test if an element is present in a collection. At first sight, a representation of the life history of the completely redefined includes: method casts doubt on the correctness of the design. Although, all IndexedCollection are Collection, they do not test the inclusion of elements in the same manner as IndexedCollection introduces a key for access. The solution is thus to redefine the includes: method to cancel the inherited implementation from the class Collection. Similarly, for OrderedCollection, the same method is completely redefined again. Clearly, the property inheritance scheme is broken and nothing is inherited from the parent class. Furthermore, the includes: method has not been originally declared as deferred and all its subclasses hold completely different forms, an incorrect case of polymorphism by definition. This situation will be referred to as the *multiple descendant redefinition* problem. It should be noted that such classification, although conceptually incorrect can be implemented in any programming language. Further complex method redefinition situations may also arise when a combination of many super calls exists in the same method. However, it is always possible to find an alternative construction to avoid complete method redefinition. For instance, mixin classes [4] are now well established and are a good candidate for solving the problem of redefinition.

3.2.2. Descendant Heritage Extent with and without MDR anomaly

Suppose that a branch of a hierarchy collapses. Instead of having many classes in the branch, an equivalent behavioural construction would be to regroup all the methods from all classes in the branch into a single larger class. This process is known as *flattening* [16]. In the flat class, all methods are unique and for the ones redefined within the branch, only the latest version appears. This method is sometimes convenient for assessing behavioural characteristics of the hierarchy. In Fig. 6 the extent of the expected descendant heritage is modelled for the Child class. When a class inherits properties from its parents, all of them are virtually present in the class plus the delta parts: x and y. In an *is_a* relationship, part of the inherited properties is reused without modification and another part is redefined. The right-hand side of Fig. 6 shows how a subclass' properties may recover the ones from its parents. The recovery part includes all the methods which are redefined in the Child class.

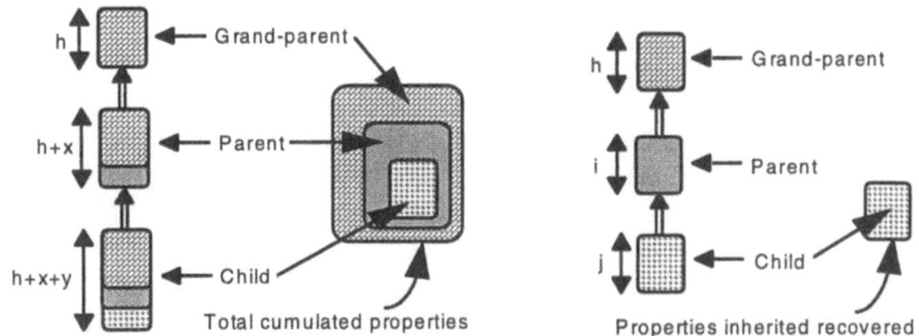

Fig. 6: Expected descendant heritage extent   Fig. 7: as Fig. 6 with MDR anomaly

In an extreme situation, suppose that the Parent class completely redefines all the Grand-parent's methods, and the Child class redefines all the Parent's methods, the extent of inherited properties is now completely recovered by the Child class (Fig. 7), therefore no features come from its ancestors although it is a subclass.

An MDR guideline can be formulated as:

> Providing the hypothesis that the multiple descendant redefinition problem breaks the properties inheritance scheme in a class hierarchy, a method m from a class C should not be completely redefined more than twice down a given branch.

In order to detect and thus assess such potential design problems in a class hierarchy, a set of method redefinition metrics is proposed and tested in the following section.

4. A Candidate Method Redefinition Metric Set

The approach taken to define our product metrics was based on the GQM/MEDEA (Goal Question Metric/MEtricDEfinition Approach [5]) approach which provide practical guidelines for building metric sets. Here, we will summarise the steps involved in applying the method.

Step 1: Experimental goal(s)
> *Object of study:* method redefinition mechanism in a class hierarchy
> *Purpose:* detection of MDR anomaly
> *Quality focus:* conceptual design consistency for property heritage
> *Viewpoint:* designer

Step 2: Assumptions
> *Assumption 1:* the deeper a class is in a hierarchy, the more complex it is.
> *Assumption 2:* the deeper a class is in a hierarchy, the more likely the MDR problem arises
> *Assumption 3:* see the MDR guideline formulated in section 3.2.2.

Step 3 and 4: Relevant measurement concept and product abstraction (see section 6 on "Abstract properties of metrics"). Further work is required for these two steps to formalise the redefinition metric set. However, since the rationale behind our redefinition metrics set is fairly straightforward, emphasis was placed on the fundamental steps 1 and 6.

Step 5: Define metrics (see section 4.1)

Step 6: Experimental validation of the metrics (see section 5)

The proposed set of redefinition metrics are :

- Percentage of redefined methods in a class (PRMC and PRMC').
- Percentage of redefined methods per level within a hierarchy (PRMH) which is decomposed into:
    * Percentage of completely redefined methods in a class (PCRM).
    * Percentage of extended methods in a class (PEM).

4.1. Percentage of Redefined Methods per Level Within a Hierarchy (PRMH)

Current metrics assessing inheritance are system or class-level metrics whereas our approach evaluates the amount of redefinition level by level. Providing that a class hierarchy is ideally designed, abstract classes should appear closer to the root of the hierarchy and specialised (or concrete) classes should be situated nearer to the bottom. Our redefinition metric is aimed at depicting such a profile. For instance, $PRMH_1$ metric (Fig. 8: branch A at level 1) measures the shaded classes. The PRMH metric can also be applied at the system level as classes are not necessarily organised in a class hierarchy. For simplicity, we will keep the numbering level absolute in comparison with the root (class Object) level 0. The notation $C_{m,n}$ gives the location of a class C, at rank n, for a given level m in the branch, e.g. class B at level 2 of branch A, is named $B_{2,1}$. The rank is arbitrarily numbered from 0 to n, n $\in$ N, from left to right at the considered level.

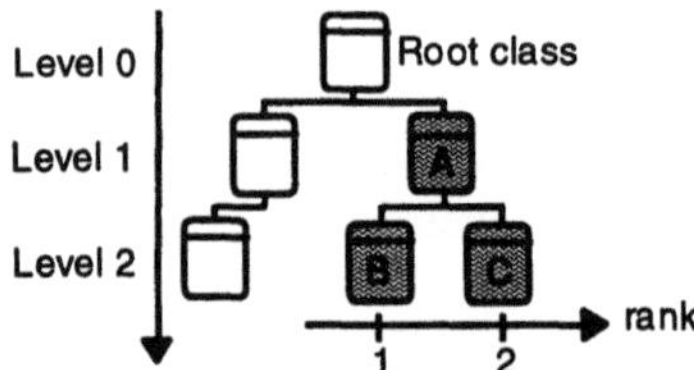

Fig. 8. Complexity metrics at hierarchy level

The redefinition metric for a class and for a given level m are defined as:

$$PRMC = \frac{NRM}{NIM} * 100 \qquad PRMC' = \frac{NRM}{NPIM} * 100 \qquad PRMH_m = \frac{\sum_{n=1}^{NC} PRMC_{m,n}}{NC} \qquad (a)$$

where NRM is the number of redefined methods, NIM is the number of instance methods, NIM > 0, NC is the number of classes for a given level m, NC > 0,

PRMC$_{m,n}$ is the percentage of redefined methods for all classes C$_{m,n}$. In the current calculation of **PRMC** (first approach), the equation is a function of the **NIM** defined locally. However, any class **C** inherits methods from all its parents, making them potentially available for use (via themethod lookup mechanism). For this reason, the *cumulative redefinition approach* to the same calculation is given by the **PRMC'** equation (second approach) where **NPIM** is the number of potential instance methods, NPIM > 0. Indeed, NPIM is expected to increase from top to bottom of a hierarchy, thus, **PRMH** decreases when **DIT** increases. Experiments with this metric are detailed in [22].

The **PRMH** in (a) is general. A refined version includes the redefinition variants:

$$PCRM = \frac{NCRM}{NIM} * 100 \qquad PEM = \frac{NEM}{NIM} * 100 \qquad PRMH_m = \frac{\sum\limits_{n=1}^{NC}(PCRM + PEM)}{NC} \qquad (b)$$

where NIM > 0, NC > 0, NCRM is the number of completely redefined methods and NEM is the number of extended methods.

Due to the inclusion of the **DIT** metric within our redefinition metric set, the depiction of *redefinition profiles* of hierarchies is possible.

5. Experiments on the **Collection** and **Stream** Branch

Our experiments were done on the Smalltalk Express[2] class library. An "OO system metric browser" tool was implemented in Smalltalk in order to test the proposed metrics. Additional facilities include a repository of metrics results stored as persistent objects and a method profiler for help in the localisation of potential suspect methods. Specification of the prototype metrics tool is described in [22].

The **Collection** classes in Smalltalk have been well-studied by many researchers [7, 14, 31], particularly those due to conceptual design problems occurring in leaf classes. Cook [7] proposed a complete new re-design of the **Collection** branch. A major problem concerns the amount of cancellation of property inheritance in leaf classes. Smalltalk's inheritance scoping control permits a class to stop the visibility and accessibility of a method to its subclasses in redefining the method with a body containing the code **self shouldNotImplement**. This situation is often recognised as source of bad design.

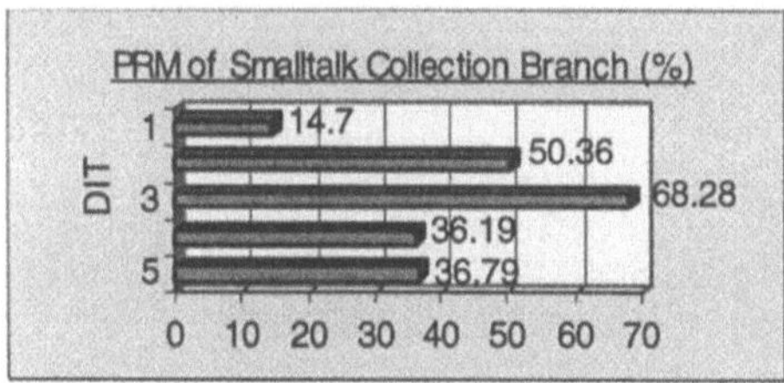

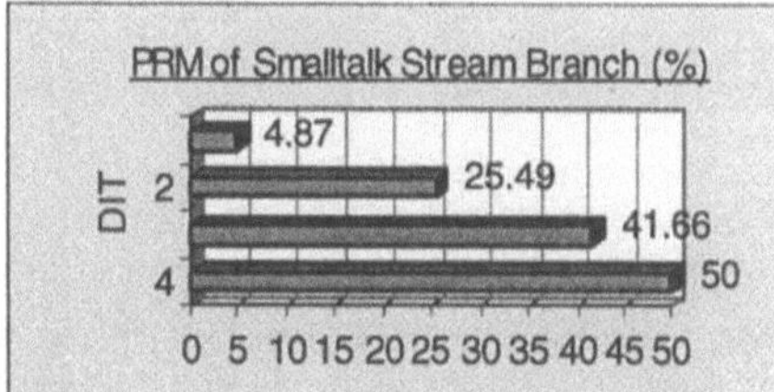

Fig. 9: **Collection** redefinition profile   Fig. 10: **Stream** redefinition profile

[2]In this paper, Smalltalk Express™ designates the version based on Smalltalk/V® Win16 and WindowBuilder® Pro/V provided by ObjectShare®, a Division of ParcPlace, http://www.objectshare.com

Fig. 9 and 10 represent the **PRMH** for the **Collection** and **Stream** branch. At DIT=2, the rate of redefinition is already high with 50.36% (Fig. 9). A simple explanation is that all classes at level 2 have realised the abstract methods which is normal. Supposing that a threshold of 50% of method redefinition should raise an alarm to potential design defects, we would take a closer look at the peak happening at DIT=3 (Fig. 9). A simple way would be to derive the **PCRM** metric for each class of the concerned level. Clearly, on Fig. 13 the **FixedSizeCollection** class holds 100% of methods completely redefined, an unusual result in such a hierarchy. Although the percentage of deferred methods is not shown on the figure, the above-mentioned class seems to be wrongly-subclassed. With the help of a method profiler tool [22], it has been possible to study and locate precisely, particular problems in methods of the concerned class.

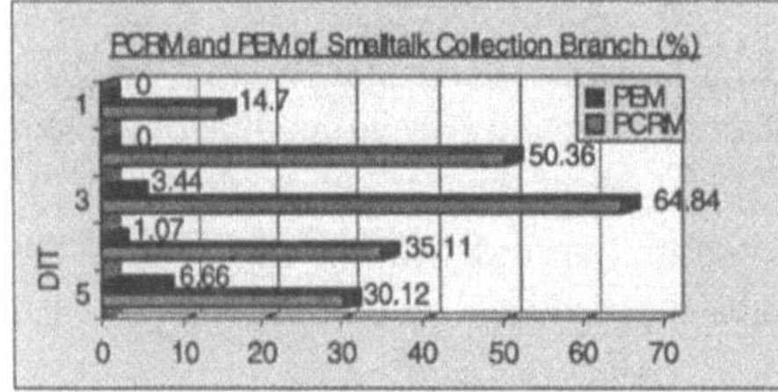

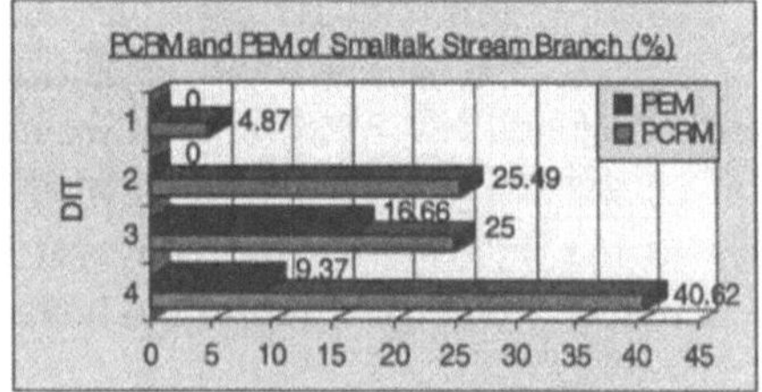

<table>
<tr><td>Fig. 11: Detailed **Collection** profiles</td><td>Fig. 12: Detailed **Stream** profiles</td></tr>
</table>

The **PCRM** for the **Stream** branch (Fig. 12, 14) is high with 40.62% at DIT=4, which represents a factor increase of 60% from the previous level. This confirms the Smalltalk **Stream** branch's generally recognised design defect. Due to the single inheritance scheme, the **ReadWriteStream** class inherits only from the **WriteStream** class. There is a duplication and redefinition of methods from the **ReadStream** to **WriteStream**.

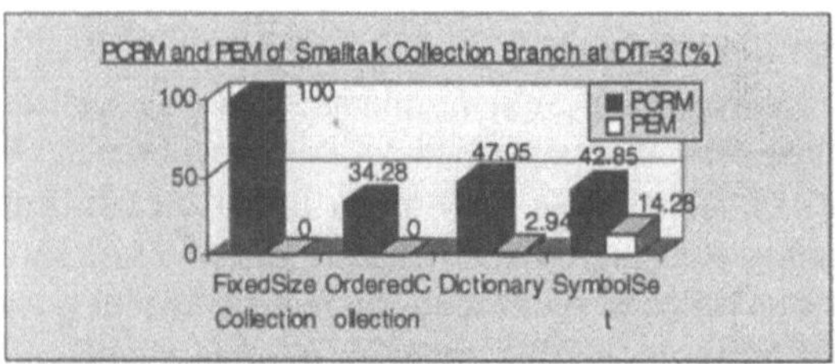

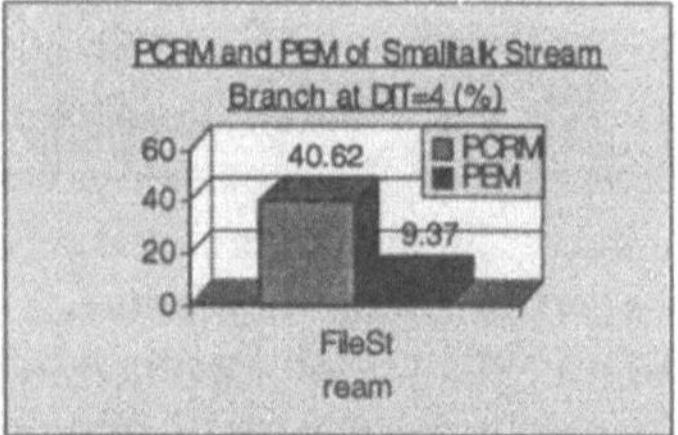

<table>
<tr><td>Fig. 13: **Collection** branch at DIT = 3</td><td>Fig. 14: **FileStream** redefinition profile</td></tr>
</table>

6. Discussion

Chidamber and Kemerer [9, 10] proposed a suite of six metrics for assessing the complexity of an OO model, 2 of which are related to the metrics described earlier. The **DIT** metric is based on the following assumptions:

- a class which is located deep in a hierarchy is more likely to inherit a great number of methods, hence increasing its complexity,
- a deep tree involves greater overall design complexity since the number of classes and methods are important,

- a class which is located deep in a hierarchy benefits from the potential reuse of inherited methods.

Our metrics set adopts these assumptions, however, rather than use DIT as a stand alone metric we have incorporated it into our PRMH metric to give a more meaningful metric. The WMC metric is the weighted method per class which takes into account the static complexity of methods in a class. If the complexity is equal to one, WMC becomes simply the number of methods metric. Churcher and Shepperd [11] showed that the metric was open to many interpretations when considering its use with constructors and destructors in C++. In addition, unlike our PRMH metric it makes no observations as to which methods are inherited and of those inherited, which are redefined and which are not.

Lorenz and Kidd [25] included in their metrics set, the number of methods overridden by a subclass and produced an average extracted from tests on project results. However, unlike our metrics it was done at class level only, no metrics were proposed at hierarchy level and system level. In addition, their metrics are not represented as percentages which clouds interpretation. For example, if number of overriden methods = 5, the class complexity is not the same if the class contains a total of 10 methods (50%) or if the class contains a total of 100 (5%).

The MOOD (Metrics for Object-Oriented Design) set [6] addresses the evaluation of the main keypoints of mechanisms of the OO paradigm. The six metrics are: the method hiding factor (MHF), the attribute hiding factor (AHF), the method inheritance factor (MIF), the attribute inheritance factor (AIF), the polymorphism factor (PF) and the coupling factor (CF). MHF and AHF refer to encapsulation as they detect the amount of hidden attributes and methods. Again, no differentiation is made in the nature of the methods when deriving their metrics for inheritance. Thus, because of the possible existence of completely redefined methods within a class hierarchy, their measure of MIF and PF are affected and does not assess inheritance in such cases.

Lewis [20] proposed a set of fine-grained metrics for assessing overloading, overriding and polymorphism issues. Related metrics are the overridden method references (ORMR), the degree of method overriding (DMOR), the degree of polymorphism (DP) and the degree of obscured polymorphism (DOP). ORMR is applied at method or class level and is taken in the general sense of overriding. ORMR is aimed to be used with DMOR which counts the number of existing forms of a method in the whole application. DP relates to the justified use of method overriding but DOP seems to be language-dependent as it is directed at measuring unspecified polymorphic methods. None of their proposed metrics are considered as ratios and no case studies were presented.

Current research on OO metrics has not yet addressed the multiple descendant redefinition problem. Our proposed metric set was aimed at the assessment of a class hierarchy from a behavioural viewpoint and the detection of abuses of the method redefinition mechanism. The results shown in the experiments revealed that such abuses exist in the current Smalltalk Express hierarchy, however they are theoretically possible in any language. As suggested earlier this may be simply due to the inherent incremental development of a class hierarchy, especially when different people are involved in the development. It should be emphasised that a system can be in a perfect working state even when containing MDR anomalies. The MDR problem increases the code re-engineering difficulty and affects the natural extension of the inheritance tree which becomes degenerated in presence of MDR.

A limitation of our metrics was that it required support from additional tools in order to precisely pinpoint defects in methods. Our method profiler realised that task by providing a life history of each redefined method of each class along a particular branch of the hierarchy. The analysis of suspect classes were facilitated.

An important area of measurement theory is the interpretation and analysis of metrics results. Most of the current metrics propose thresholds or averages as alarmers for raising potential design flaws in a system. Design decisions can only be suggested in this paper but the data interpretation technique from [23] was used. The MDR problem happens for at least two reasons:

➢ a class is wrongly-subclassing its parent class i.e. the class does not satisfy the *is_a* relationship,

➢ a bad design of interfaces of parent classes for example, lack of abstraction.

A possible solution for the first reason is to move the suspected class higher in the hierarchy so the class would inherit from early implementation of the method, thereby minimising the chance for the MDR problem. In return, the concerned class will have to resolve all **super** calls to the original parent. This can be handled by the introduction of the original parent class as an aggregate which is instantiated in a constructor method. The great benefit of this solution is that it can be executed automatically. As opposed to the first solution, the second reason will probably require manual intervention of the designer.

The experimental validation of the metrics confirmed that the metrics measured the desired characteristics. However, concerning some abstract properties of good metrics mentioned by Kolewe [19], further work is ongoing into the development of the necessary theoretical foundations needed. However, we shall briefly comment on the cited characteristics for our redefinition metric set:

✓ *noncoarseness*: we considered many different programs and were able to find different metrics results.

✓ *nonuniqueness*: if we consider two classes A and B derived from the same parent class where the same modifications on inherited methods are done and no added operations are made, we could be in the case where the PRMC is the same for both classes.

✓ *importance of implementation*: we assess a class's internal complexity by looking at its methods redefinition. The metric depends on the implementation.

✗ *monotonicity*: not applicable for our metric as its purpose is not to have a general value for the whole system. However, we could compute for two classes A and B their respective PRMC. Assuming that a class C contains all the methods from A and B with no name space conflicts, $PRMH^C = PRMH^A + PRMH^B$. For this characteristic, our redefinition metric can be extended in order to calculate a mean value of redefined methods for a whole system.

✗ *nonequivalence of interaction*: same comment as previous characteristic.

✓ *interaction increases complexity*: as inheritance is a strong form of coupling and interaction is implemented via methods in a class, inheriting or adding new methods to a class increases its complexity, therefore the PRMH vary accordingly. Further verification requires to be done.

✗ *nonequivalence of permutation*: not applicable.

Inheritance in current OO systems is still hazardous. A conceptual gap exists between OO modelling constructs and their mapping onto a language. The implementation of an inheritance relationship between classes using any OO programming language is actually a real source of design problems. In particular, this paper described the problem of multiple descendant redefinition with a refinement of the definition of inheritance. The MDR problem is recognised as a conceptual design inconsistency happening early in the design of the hierarchy. The derivation of our proposed redefinition metric set demonstrated that the knowledge of redefinition profiles of an OO class hierarchy gave us insights into the behavioural aspect. Precise detection of such anomalies have been possible. Similarly, the redefnition metrics can be derived on an OO system not necessarily organised as a hierarchy. We believe that the redefinition metrics and its variants are a strong and simple candidate for detecting complex design problems occurring within a class hierarchy. Further tests and development of its foundations is still necessary together with appropriate guidance for design decisions. Work is continuing in the areas of design transformation rules, (semi) automatic re-organisation of the class hierarchy and the design-evaluation cycle.

Acknowledgment: We would like to thank Mike Jackson (Wolverhampton University) for his comments on early versions of the paper.

References

1. D H. Abbot, T D. Korson and J D. McGregor. A Proposed Design Complexity Metric for Object-Oriented Development. Department of Computer Science, Clemson University, Clemson, SC29634-1906, 1994.

2. J M. Armstrong and R J. Mitchell. Uses and abuses of inheritance. Software Engineering Journal, Jan. 1994.

3. G Booch. Object-oriented analysis and design with applications. Benjamin/Cummings, 1994.

4. G Bracha and W Cook. Mixin-Based Inheritance. OOPSLA/ECOOP '90 Conference proceedings, Canada, 1990.

5. L Briand, S Morasca and V R. Basili. Goal-Driven Definition of Product Metrics Based on Properties. Institute for Advanced Computer Studies, Dpmt. of Computer Science, Univ. of Maryland, Technical Report CS-TR-3346, Sep. 1994.

6. F Brito e Abreu, M Goulão and R Esteves. Towards the Design Quality Evaluation of Object-Oriented Software Systems. Proceedings of the 5th International Conference on Software Quality, Austin, Texas, USA, Oct. 1995.

7. W R. Cook. Interfaces and Specifications for the Smalltalk-80 Collection Classes. OOPSLA '92 Conference proceedings, Vancouver, Canada, Oct. 18-22, ACM SIGPLAN 1992; Not. 27, 10:1-15.

8. L. F. Capretz and P. A. Lee. Object-Oriented Design: Guidelines and Techniques. Information and Software Technology, Apr. 1993; 35(4):195-206.

9. S R. Chidamber and C F. Kemerer. Towards a Metric Suite for Object-Oriented Design. OOPSLA'91 Conference proceedings, Oct. 1991; pp. 197-211.

10. S R. Chidamber and C F. Kemerer. A Metric Suite for Object Oriented Design. IEEE Transactions on Software Engineering, Jun. 1994; 20(6).

11. N I. Churcher and M J. Shepperd. Comments on A metrics Suite for Object Oriented Design. IEEE Transactions on Software Engineering, March 1995; 21(3).

12. D Firesmith. Inheritance guidelines. Journal of Object-Oriented Programming, May 1995; pp. 67-72.

13. E Gamma, R Helm, R Johnson J Vlissides. Design Patterns - Elements of Reusable Object-Oriented Software. Addison-Wesley, ISBN 0-201-63361-2, 1995.

14. A Goldberg and D Robson. Smalltalk-80, The Language and its Implementation. Addison-Wesley, ISBN 0-201-11371-6, 1985.

15. R Harrison and R. Nithi. An Empirical Evaluation Of Object-Oriented Design Metrics. OOPSLA '96 Conference proceedings, Workshop on "OO Product Metrics", 1996.

16. B Henderson-Sellers. Object-Oriented Metrics, Measures of Complexity. Prentice Hall Object-Oriented Series, ISBN 0-13-239872-9, 1996.

17. B Henderson-Sellers and Julian Edwards. BookTwo of Object-Oriented Knowledge - The Working Object. Prentice Hall, ISBN 0-13-093980-3, 1994.

18. K Koskimies and J Vihavainen. The problem of Unexpected Subclasses. Journal of Object-Oriented Programming, Oct. 1992; pp. 53-59.

19. R Kolewe. Metrics in Object-Oriented Design and Programming. Software Development, Oct. 1993; 1:53-62.

20. J A. Lewis. Quantified Object-Oriented Development: Conflict and Resolution. 4th Software Quality Conference, University of Abertay, Dundee, Jul. 1995; 1:220-229.

21. S Lewis. The Art and Science of Smalltalk. Prentice Hall/Hewlett-Packard Professional Books, ISBN 0-13-371345-8, 1995.

22. P Li-Thiao-Té. Integrating Measurement Techniques in An Object-Oriented Design Process. Tech. Report, Object Systems Group, Napier University, Edinburgh, 1996.

23. P Li-Thiao-Té, J Kennedy and J Owens. Mechanisms for Data Interpretation of Metrics for OO Systems. To appear in TOOLS Asia '97 Conference proceedings, 1997.

24. W Li and S Henry. Object-Oriented Metrics Which Predict Maintainability. Journal of Software Systems, 1993; 23(2):117-122.

25. M Lorenz and J Kidd. Object-Oriented Software Metrics. Prentice Hall Object Oriented Series, Englewood Cliffs (N.J.), 1994.

26. B Meyer. Object-oriented Software Construction. Prentice Hall International, C.A.R. Hoare, Series Editor, ISBN 0-13-629049-3, 1988. http://www.eiffel.com

27. A Newman and al. Special Edition, Using Java. Que Corp., ISBN 0-7897-0604-0, 1996.

28. J Rumbaugh, M Blaha, W Premerlani, F Eddy, and W Lorensen. Object-Oriented Modeling and Design. Prentice-Hall, 1991.

29. J Rumbaugh. A Matter of Intent: How to Define Subclasses. Journal of Object-Oriented Programming, Sept. 1996; pp. 5-9, 18.

30. E Seidewitz, Controlling Inheritance. Journal of Object-Oriented Programming, Jan. 1996; pp. 36-42.

31. A Taivalsaari. On the Notion of Inheritance. ACM Computing Surveys, Sept. 1996; 28(3):439-479.

An Aggregation Model and its C++ Implementation *

Manuel Kolp   Alain Pirotte

Université catholique de Louvain, IAG-QANT

1 Place des Doyens, 1348 Louvain-La-Neuve, Belgium,

e-mail: kolp@qant.ucl.ac.be, pirotte@info.ucl.ac.be

Abstract

Object-oriented conceptual models strive to capture more semantics in order to better represent requirements of real-world applications. Aggregation is a powerful construct for semantic modeling. Intuitively, it relates a composite object to its component objects. This paper presents a new version of aggregation, with a generalized version of cardinality constraints and a new subcategorization of part relationships, with an associated transitivity rule. An implementation in C++ is also presented.

Keywords: Object-Oriented Conceptual Modeling, Aggregation, Part-Whole Relationship, C++

1   Introduction

There is general agreement on the need for better modeling tools to handle the complexity of realistic applications. In recent years, the object-oriented paradigm has gained popularity in various modeling domains including database systems, World Wide Web and network applications, hypertext, multimedia and CAD/CAM systems, distributed computing, and sophisticated man-machine interfaces. Object-oriented application development methods (e.g., [16]) have led to new ways of thinking about problems with models organized around real-world concepts.

The nesting of objects is a powerful construct of object orientation; however, it does not necessarily imply an explicit relationship between aggregated objects. Making aggregation, the semantic notion that an object is a part (component) of another object (composite), explicitly available as a first-class construct enhances the expressiveness of object models. Surprisingly, only a few object-oriented systems and languages (e.g., SHOOD [3], VODAK [5], ORION [7]) provide it as first-class primitive.

This paper presents a new simple and powerful version of aggregation and implements it as a hierarchy of C++ classes. The paper is structured as follows. Our aggregation model is described in Section 2. We explain the key aspects of our C++ implementation in Section 3. Finally, conclusions can be found in Section 4.

---

*This work is part of the YEROOS (Yet another project on Evaluation and Research on Object-Oriented Strategies) project, principally based at the University of Louvain. See http://yeroos.qant.ucl.ac.be.

2 Our Aggregation Model

Conceptual object modeling consists in precisely describing application domains for purposes of understanding and communication. Recent research has made possible more adequate conceptual models by precisely defining classical abstractions, like aggregation, and by identifying new abstractions, like materialization [15].

Aggregation is generally defined as an abstraction mechanism by which a relationship between objects is considered a higher-level (aggregate) object [13]. In fact, two versions of abstraction coexist in the literature:

- the general version, through which an entity is analyzed in terms of its constituent parts.
  For example, a relation schema in the relational model is an aggregate of (attribute-domain) pairs.
- a relationship with additional specific semantics to characterize various kinds of dependencies between parts, or *component objects*, and aggregates, or *composite objects* [7]. This richer version is sometimes called part-whole [17] or simply part relationship [4].

This paper is concerned with the second version, that we will call *Part Relationship* (PR). It is defined as a binary relationship and noted (see Figure 1(a)) as a straight line with a diamond on the side of the composite. For example, Figure 1(b) shows three PRs, between components Editorial, Article, and Picture, and composite Newspaper. The rest of Section 2 presents the main ideas of our aggregation model. A more thorough discussion can be found in [9].

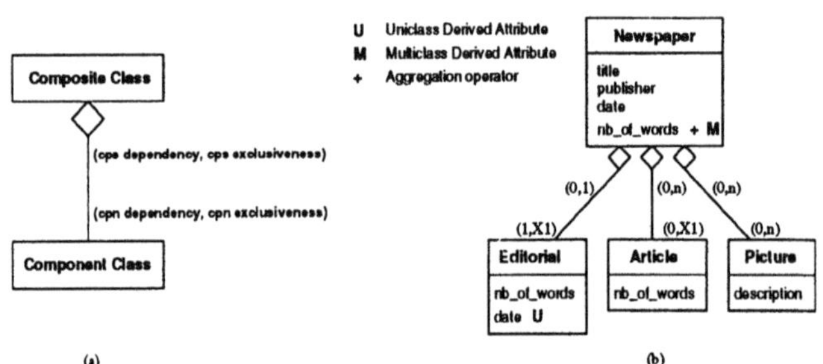

Figure 1: The Part Relationship

2.1 Exclusiveness and Dependence

Relationships in semantic models are usually annotated with cardinalities (two pairs of numbers) that express minimality and maximality constraints for related objects. We generalize usual cardinalities to model two dimensions of PRs: *exclusiveness/sharing* and *dependence/independence*. Variants of these constraints can bear on several PRs involving the same composite or component.

Thus each PR will be annotated with two pairs (cps dependence, cps exclusiveness) and (cpn dependence, cpn exclusiveness), that can be more general than plain numbers (see below), to model the dimensions of dependence and exclusiveness, for the composite class and the component class, respectively (see Figure 1(a)).

2.1.1 Exclusiveness/sharing noted on a single PR

A first group of constraints is defined on the component class Cpn of a single PR Pr: either they strictly concern Cpn and Pr only (in the case of global sharing) or they concern Cpn, Pr, and the set of all other PRs where Cpn participates as a component, without referring explicitly to individual PRs in this set (in the case of global exclusiveness).

- *Component local exclusiveness / global sharing* : any component cpn is related through Pr to at most one composite cps. The constraint is noted as "*cpn exclusiveness* $= 1$" (see Figure 1(a)).
  For example, in Figure 2(a), each article is part of at most one journal. The constraint does not preclude cpn to be be related to another composite via another PR. Thus, the same article, that is part of a journal, could also be part of a compilation, provided of course that all other constraints are satisfied.
- *Component local sharing / global sharing* : a component cpn can be related to more than one composite through Pr, while allowing, as in the previous constraint, cpn to be related to other composites via other PRs. Thus, this is the unconstrained case noted as "*cpn exclusiveness* $= n$".
  For example, in Figure 2(b), an article can belong to any number of compilations and this does not constrain the participation of the article as component in other PRs.
- *Component local exclusiveness / global exclusiveness* : every component cpn can be related to at most one composite via Pr, and cpn cannot participate as a component in any other PR. This is noted as "*cpn exclusiveness* $= X1$".
  For example, in Figure 2(b), if an article appears in some proceedings, then the article cannot appear in any journal or compilation.
- *Component local sharing / global exclusiveness* : a component cpn can be related to several composites via Pr, but that relationship excludes participation of cpn as a component in any other PR. This is noted as "*cpn exclusiveness* $= Xn$".
  For example, in Figure 2(c), a given instance of Binary (i.e., a program) can belong to any number of instances of Dos Software but that excludes its belonging to any instance of Unix Software, and conversely.

Similar constraints can be defined for composite classes. They are not indicated in Figure 2, nor in subsequent examples, to keep them simpler.

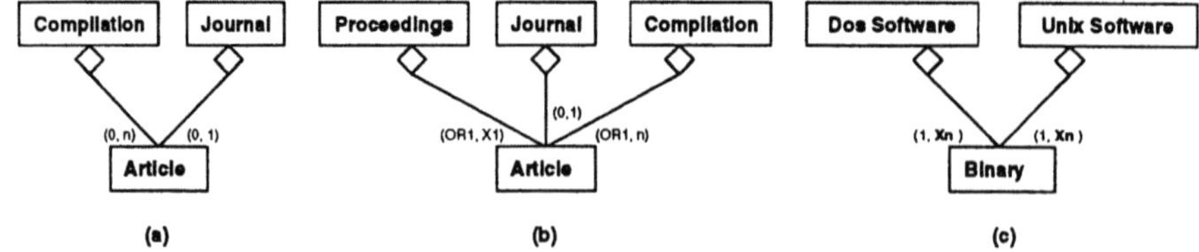

Figure 2: Exclusiveness and sharing

2.1.2 Exclusiveness/sharing constraints on several PRs

A second group of constraints bear on two PRs Pr_1 and Pr_2 with the same component class Cpn and with composite classes Cps_1 and Cps_2, respectively.

- *Component XOR local exclusiveness / global sharing* : any component cpn of Cpn is related to at most one instance of Cps_1 or Cps_2 via Pr_1 or Pr_2. There is no constraint on other PRs with Cpn as component. This constraint is noted as *"cpn exclusiveness = XOR"* for both Pr_1 and Pr_2. For example, in Figure 3(a), an article can appear in one newspaper or in one weekly, and in any number of compilations.
- *Component XOR local exclusiveness / global exclusiveness* : any component cpn is related to at most one instance of Cps_1 or Cps_2 via Pr_1 or Pr_2, and cpn does not appear in any other PR as a component. This is noted as *"cpn exclusiveness = XORX"* for both Pr_1 and Pr_2.

  For example, in Figure 3(b), an article can appear in one newspaper or in one weekly, and, if it does, it is not linked to any instance of Unpublished.

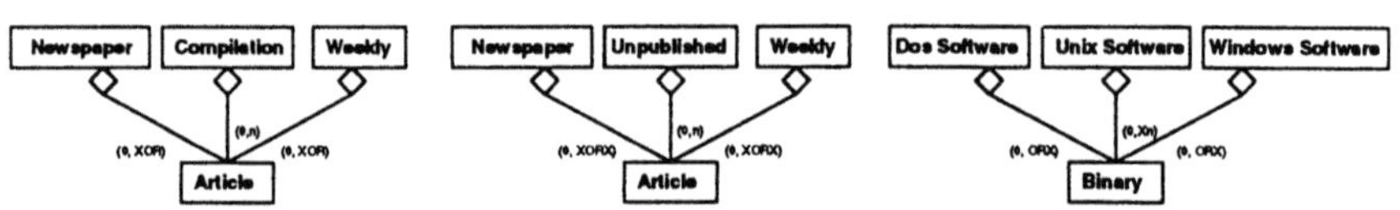

Figure 3: XOR, XORX exclusiveness and OR local sharing

- *Component XOR local sharing / global exclusiveness* : cpn instances are not constrained in their participation as components in Pr_1 or Pr_2, but they do not participate as component in any other PR. This is noted as *"cpn exclusiveness = ORX"* for both Pr_1 and Pr_2.

  For example, in Figure 3 (c), a given instance of Binary (i.e., a program) can belong to any number of instances of Dos Software or of Windows Software, but that excludes its belonging to any instance of Unix Software, and conversely (because *cpn exclusiveness = Xn* for the PR between Binary and Unix Software).
- *Component XOR local sharing / global sharing* is the same as *component local sharing / global sharing* (the unconstrained case) of Section 2.1.1.

Similar constraints can be defined for composite classes.

2.1.3 (In)dependence on a single PR

- *Component independence* : this is equivalent to a null minimal cardinality (optional participation) and is noted *"cpn dependence = 0"*.
  For example, in Figure 2(a), an article can or cannot be part of a compilation
- *Component dependence* : this is equivalent to a minimal cardinality $= 1$ (mandatory participation) and is noted *"cpn dependence = 1"*.
  For example, in Figure 2(a), each article belongs to at least one journal.

Composite independence and *composite dependence* are similarly defined for composite classes.

2.1.4 (In)dependence on two PRs

- *Component OR dependence* : for two PRs Pr_1 and Pr_2, any component *cpn* participates in at least one instance of Pr_1 or of Pr_2. This is noted as *"cpn dependence = OR1"* for both Pr_1 and Pr_2.
  For example, in Figure 2(b), every article belongs to at least one journal and/or at least one instance of Proceedings.

Composite OR dependence is similarly defined for composite classes.

2.2 Subcategorization of PR

Winston et al. [17] analyzed PRs, that they call *meronymic relationships*, into seven subcategories: 1) component – object; 2) feature – event; 3) member – collection; 4) portion – mass; 5) phase – activity; 6) place – area; 7) stuff - object.

Although such a subclassification appears useful in cognitive sciences or linguistics, it relies on pragmatic and cultural dimensions that are not easily formalizable with current object models.

In our model of PR, we distinguish three semantic types, called part relationship, part association, and part recursion; they are organized in a specialization hierarchy as shown in Figure 4. In other words, all part recursions are also part associations, which in turn are all part relationships. The right part of Figure 4 shows examples of structures of the semantic types at the left.

Part relationship is the relationship studied in Section 2.1. The same composite can be related to several components. For instance, a newspaper can be composed of editorials, articles, and pictures (see Figure 1(b)).

Part association, thus named after [1], specializes part relationship by relating a composite to a collection of components of the same class. In other words, a part association models the case where a class participates as a composite in a single binary part relationship. Part association has also been called *member-collection* [17] or *member-bunch* [14]. For example, in Figure 2(a), a compilation is composed of articles.

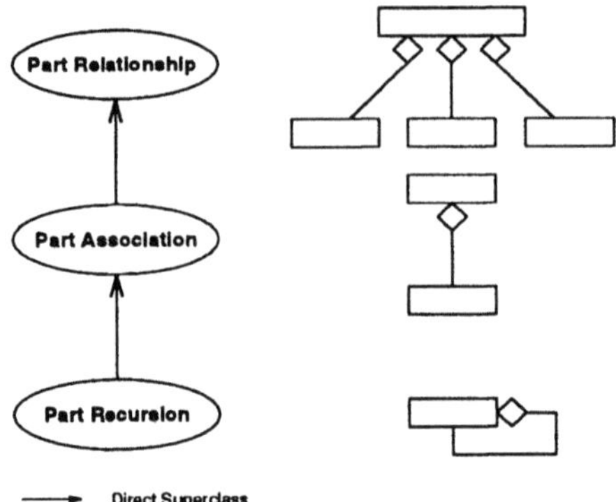

Figure 4: A simple hierarchy for PRs

Part recursion specializes part association: not only component objects but also composite objects belong to the same class. For example, a **program** could be described as composed of (sub)programs.

2.3 Reflexivity, Symmetry, Transitivity

The part relationship can also be characterized as to whether it possesses the classical properties of *reflexivity*, *symmetry*, and *transitivity*.

The part relationship is *instance-irreflexive*, as an object cannot be composed of itself nor belong to itself.

Part recursion is *class-reflexive*, as an object obj_1 of a class C can be composed of – or be part of – objects obj_2, ..., obj_i also belonging to C.

Part relationship is *antisymmetric for instances and classes*.

Transitivity of the part relationship is defined in the obvious manner: *if (A is part of B) and (B is part of C), then (A is part of C)*.

Few systems support any kind of transitivity. In Winston's subclassification (Section 2.2), a meronymic relationship is transitive when "A is part of B" and "B is part of C" belong to the same subcategory of meronymic relationship. This idea has inspired two object-oriented systems: SHOOD [3] and TELOS [12].

Our version of PR (Figure 4) enjoys a stronger support of transitivity:

- *"upwards" transitivity* is valid:
  if *(a is part of b)* $\in PCat_1$ and *(b is part of c)* $\in PCat_2$ and $PCat_1 < PCat_2$,
  then *(a is part of c)* $\in PCat_2$
  where $PCat_1 < PCat_2$ means that $PCat_1$ is a subclass of $PCat_2$ in the specialization hierarchy of Figure 4;
- transitivity within part relationship is also valid.

Thus, for example:

- if a ray is part of a wheel (part relationship) and the wheel is part of a bicycle (part relationship), then the ray is part of the bicycle (part relationship);
- if a (sub)program is part of a program (part recursion) and the program is part of a package (part association), then the (sub)program is part of the package (part association);
- if a sentence is part of an article (part association) and the article is part of a newspaper (part relationship), then the sentence is part of the newspaper (part relationship).

However:

- if a hand is part of a musician (part relationship) and the musician is part of an orchestra (part association), it does not hold that the hand is part of the orchestra [12];
- if a person is part of a sport_club (part association) and the sport_club is part of a recreational_institution (part association), it does not hold that the person is part of the recreational_institution [11].

2.4   Attribute Derivation

We define a mechanism for the derivation of attribute values in PRs that is bidirectional, specific, transitive dependent, and computable, as follows:

- *bidirectional*: attributes and their values can be derived and computed both *upwards* (from components to composites) and *downwards* (from composites to components);
- *specific* (or optional): whether or not an attribute must be propagated is application specific, and a generic mandatory mechanism is therefore inappropriate;
- *transitive dependent*: the validity of attribute derivation is bound by the transitivity rules of the PR (see Section 2.3);
- *computable*: an attribute value of a composite (or a component) can be modeled in terms an attribute value of several of its components (composites). Aggregate operators (e.g., +,-, *, min, max, avg, list) can be applied for computing the derived value from source values.

Derived attributes can thus be characterized as *uniclass* or *multiclass*:

- an attribute of a class C is said to be *uniclass derived (UD)* if its values are computed from attribute values of objects belonging to a single class C_1 related to C by a PR;
- an attribute of a class C is said to be *multiclass derived (MD)* if its values are computed from attribute values of objects belonging to classes $C_1, ..., C_n$, and C and $C_1, ..., C_n$ are related by n PRs with C as composite (resp., component) and $C_1, ..., C_n$ as components (resp., composites).

Graphical notations for attribute derivation are illustrated in Figure 1(b). Derived attributes are qualified as U (uniclass derived) or M (multiclass derived). Aggregate operators can qualify a derived attribute to indicate how values are computed from source attribute values.

Thus, nb_of_words is an upwards multiclass-derived attribute of Newspaper. The value of nb_of_words for a Newspaper instance is computed as the sum of values of nb_of_words for related instances of Editorial and Article. Attribute date is a downwards uniclass-derived attribute in Editorial: its values are propagated downwards from Newspaper.

3   A C++ Implementation

This section describes the general structure of our C++ implementation. A more complete description can be found in [2]. The implementation provides the following functions:

- instantiation of part links between instances of related classes;
- exclusiveness and dependence checking when instantiating a part link;
- attribute and value derivation compatible with transitivity rules;
- destruction of part links;
- destruction of objects and related part links, with dependence checking.

An application class participates in a PR by being declared as subclass of a special class that channels the necessary functionality to it. Thus, the following classes are defined for the example of Figure 1(b):

```
class Newspaper:                          class Picture:
    public Cpn_Set_Newspaper {                public Cps_Set_Picture {
        char * title;                             char * description;};
        char * date;
        char * publisher;                 class Article:
    public:                                   public Cps_Set_Article {
        char * publ_date() {return date;};};      int nb_of_words;
                                              public:
class Editorial:                                  Article(int i){nb_of_words=i;};
    public Cps_Set_Editorial {                    int Nbr_words() {return nb_of_words;};};
        int nb_of_words;
    public:
        Editorial(int i){nb_of_words=i;};
        int Nbr_words() {return nb_of_words;};};
```

For example, class Newspaper, which is a composite in three PRs, is declared as a subclass of a class Cpn_Set_Newspaper. The latter is a subclass of three classes (Cpn_e_n, Cpn_a_n, and Cpn_p_n), each corresponding to one of the PRs. Each of these three classes is an instantiation of the Cps_Cpn template class, which is the central class of our implementation.

The Cps_Cpn template - Template class Cps_Cpn provides instantiation, deletion, and constraint checking services to components and composites. Cps_Cpn is instantiated for each application class that participates in a PR, by instantiating its three class parameters:

- c_1, the application (resp., composite or component) class;

- c_2, another application class (resp., component or composite) related to c_1 by a PR Pr;
- part_rel, a class describing the specific characteristics of Pr.

Instances of the Cps_Cpn template are called Cps_Pr (resp., Cpn_Pr) when c_1 is instantiated as a composite (resp., a component) of part relationship Pr (see below).

Class part_rel serves to define an object Rel as data member of Cps_Cpn. Member functions of Cps_Cpn access the characteristics of part relationship Pr through Rel.

Through CreateLink and DeleteLink, Cps_Cpn calls functions Local_Const() for checking the constraints of local exclusiveness and dependence, and Global_Const() for global constraint checking. These functions set Boolean flags allowing or preventing CreateLink and DeleteLink to instantiate or delete a part link, depending on the current set of part links.

Consider two application classes A and B (subclasses, respectively, of class Cps_Set_A and class Cpn_Set_B) related by a part relationship P_A_B. Two objects a $\in$ A and b $\in$ B dialog via their functions CreateLink to instanciate P_A_B. Constraints are checked, a and b exchange their adresses if there is no constraint violation; otherwise the instantiation process is aborted. Both objects dialog via their functions DeleteLink when destruction of the part link is requested. As for creation, constraints are checked and the deletion process is aborted if necessary to avoid constraint violation. Destructor ~Cps_Cpn() applies deletion services for part links when objects are destroyed.

```
template<class c_1, class c_2, class part_rel>
    class Cps_Cpn:
        public set<c_1>{
            int NbrCpsOrCpn;                    // Set is a template providing set and list manipulation utilities
            boolean XORConst;                   // Number of composites (components) of an objet
            boolean XConst;                     //
            boolean ORConst;                    //
            boolean Sharing;                    // Boolean flags for constraints
            boolean Dep;                        //
                                                //

            void NbrCpsOrCpn+1();               // Keeps track of the number of composites or
            void NbrCpsOrCpn-1();               //    components of a c_1 object
            boolean Glob_Const();               // Global constraint checking
            boolean Local_Const();              // Local constraint checking
        protected: ~Cps_Cpn();
        public:
            part_rel Rel;                       // Characteristics of the (c_1-c_2) part relationship
            boolean CreateLink(c_1 * ptr);      // Create a part link
            boolean DeleteLink(c_1 * ptr);};    // Delete a part link
```

Classes Cps and Cpn - Template Cps_Cpn provides its template instances Cps_Pr and Cpn_Pr with generic functions for part relationships.

Each Cps_Pr (resp., Cpn_Pr) class manages one part relationship Pr from the standpoint of a composite (resp., component). Uniclass-derived attributes are handled in Cps_Pr and Cpn_Pr. Computing values for a multiclass-derived attribute on all relevant part links requires accessing objects of several application classes, while each Cps_Pr (resp., Cpn_Pr) can only deal with a single composite (resp., component) class. Values of multiclass-derived attributes are computed by derived classes Cps_Set_A or Cpn_Set_A that can access all composites (resp., components) objects related to a component (resp., composite) object of an application class A.

```
class Cpn_e_n:
    public Cps_Cpn<Editorial, Newspaper, part_newsp_edit>
      { public: int Nbr_words()     // derive an MDA
       ~Cpn_e_n() {};};                 // on part relationship

class Cpn_a_n:
    public Cps_Cpn<Article, Newspaper, part_newsp_art>
      { public: int Nbr_words() // derive an MDA on
       ~Cpn_a_n() {};};             // one a part relationship

class Cpn_p_n:
    public Cps_Cpn<Picture, Newspaper, part_newsp_pic>
      { public: ~Cpn_p_n() {};};
```

```
class Cps_n_e:
    public Cps_Cpn<Newspaper, Editorial,
                                part_newsp_edit>
      { public: char * date();   // derive an UDA
                     ~Cps_n_e() {}; };

class Cps_n_a:
    public Cps_Cpn<Newspaper, Article,
                                part_newsp_art>
      { public: ~Cps_n_a() {}; };

class Cps_n_p:
    public Cps_Cpn<Newspaper, Picture,
                                part_newsp_pic>
      { public: ~Cps_n_p() {}; };
```

The Cps_Set and Cpn_Set classes - Class Cps_Set_A (resp., Cpn_Set_A) of an object belonging to an application class A is derived by multiple inheritance from all Cps (resp., Cpn) classes implementing binary PRs in which A participates as composite (resp., component) class. They can thus manage all PRs in which A participates as composite (resp., component) class, e.g., for MD attribute derivation or for global constraint checking.

Thus class Cpn_Set_Newspaper is defined for the example of Figure 1(b):

```
class Cpn_Set_Newspaper:
    public Cpn_e_n, public Cpn_a_n, public Cpn_p_n {
      public:
        int Nbr_words()                        // Derives a multiclass attribute
          {return Cpn_e_n::Nbr_words() +       // from relevant part relationships
              Cpn_a_n::Nbr_words();};
       ~Cpn_Set_Newspaper() {};};
```

Classes Cps_Set_Editorial, Cps_Set_Article, and Cps_Set_Picture are defined in a similar fashion.

The part_relationship template - Each part_rel class is derived from the part_relationship template; part_rel defines a specific PR and supplies template Cps_Cpn with the characteristics of that relationship through object Rel.

```
template<char * cps_exclus, char * cps_depend,
    char * cpn_exclus,char * cpn_depend,
    char * transitiv_type>
      class part_relationship {
        public:
          char * Cps_Depend() {return cps_depend;}      // (In)dependence for composites
          char * Cps_Exclus() {return cps_exclus;}      // Exclusiveness/Sharing for composites
          char * Cpn_Depend() {return cpn_depend;}      // (In)dependence for components
          char * Cpn_Exclus() {return cpn_exclus;}      // Exclusiveness/Sharing for components
          char * Transitiv_Type() {return transitiv_type;}};    // Transitivity type
```

For the example of Figure 1(b), classes part_rel are as follows:

```
class part_newsp_edit: public part_relationship<"0", "1", "1", "X1", "rel"> { short dummy;};
class part_newsp_art: public part_relationship<"0", "n", "0", "X1", "rel"> { short dummy;};
class part_newsp_pic: public part_relationship<"0", "n", "0", "n", "rel"> { short dummy;};
```

4   Conclusion

This paper first proposes an original model for part relationships and presents class interfaces for a complete support of this model in C++.

The present work suggests many continuations. First, we are studying the formalization of other semantic links for object models. They include binary and *n*-ary relationships, aggregated relationships and conceptual cycles [10], generalization, and materialization [15].

Second, we are studying metaclass and metaobject mechanisms in systems such as CLOS [6]. This will help us define common metalevel specifications for semantic link support and enhancements to object-oriented models.

This will finally lead us to construct an integrated metamodel in order to propose a complete metalevel approach and implementation to enhance object models and systems with semantic relationships [8].

References

[1] M. Brodie and E. Silva. Active and passive component modeling: ACM/PCM. In T. Olle, H. Sol, and A. Verrijn-Stuart, editors, *Information systems design methodologies: a comparative review*, pages 41–91. North-Holland, 1982.

[2] F. Cornet and M. Kolp. Etude et implémentation de l'agrégation en C++. Technical Report YEROOS TR-96/10, IAG-QANT, Université de Louvain, Belgium, Dec. 1996.

[3] C. Djeraba and H. Briand. A design object concept. In *Proc. Int. Symp. on Advanced DB Technologies and their Integration, Nara, Japan, Oct. 1994*, pages 97–104, 1994.

[4] M. Halper, J. Geller, and Y. Perl. An OODB part relationship model. In *Proc. of the 1st Int. Conf. on Information and Knowledge Management, CIKM'92*, Baltimore, USA, Nov. 1992.

[5] M. Halper, J. Geller, Y. Perl, and W. Klas. Integrating a part relationship into an open OODB system using metaclasses. In *Proc. CIKM'94*, Gaithersburg, Maryland, 1994.

[6] G. Kiczales, J. des Rivières, and D. Bobrow. *The Art of the Metaobject Protocol*. MIT Press, 1991.

[7] W. Kim and F. H. Lochovsky, editors. *Object-Oriented Concepts, Databases and Applications*. ACM Press, 1989.

[8] M. Kolp. A metaobject protocol for reifying semantic relationship into open systems. In *Proc. of the 4th Doctoral Consortium of the 9th Int. Conf. on Advanced Information Systems Engineering, CAiSE'97 pages 89–100*, Barcelona, June 1997

[9] M. Kolp and A. Pirotte. An aggregation object model. Technical Report YEROOS TR-96/09, IAG-QANT, Université catholique de Louvain, Belgium, Mar. 1997.

[10] M. Kolp and E. Zimányi. Relational database design using an ER approach and Prolog. In *Proc. of the 6th Int. Conf. on Information Systems and Management of Data, CISMOD'95*, LNCS 1006, pages 214–231, Bombay, India, Nov. 1995. Springer-Verlag.

[11] R. Motschnig and J. Kaasboll. Part-whole relationship categories and their application in object-oriented analysis. In *Proc. of the 5th International Conference on Information System Development, ISD'96*, Sept. 1996.

[12] R. Motschnig-Pitrik. The semantics of parts versus aggregates in data/knowledge modelling. In *Proc. of the 5th Int. Conf. on Advanced Information Systems Engineering, CAiSE'93*, LNCS 685, pages 352–373, Paris, France, June 1993. Springer-Verlag.

[13] R. Motschnig-Pitrik and J. Mylopoulos. Classes and instances. *International Journal of Intelligent and Cooperative Information Systems*, 1(1):61–92, 1992.

[14] J. Odell. Six differents kinds of composition *Journal of Object Oriented Programming*, 6(8):10–16, 1994.

[15] A. Pirotte, E. Zimányi, D. Massart, and T. Yakusheva. Materialization: a powerful and ubiquitous abstraction pattern. In *Proc. of the 20th Int. Conf. on Very Large Databases, VLDB'94*, pages 630–641, Santiago, Chile, 1994.

[16] J. Rumbaugh, M. Blaha, W. Premerlani, F. Eddy, and W. Lorensen. *Object-Oriented Modeling and Design*. Prentice Hall, 1991.

[17] M. Winston, R. Chaffin, and D. Herrmann. A taxonomy of part-whole relations. *Cognitive Science*, 11:417–444, 1987.

RE-USABILITY I

Behavioral Pattern Analysis Approach

R. Chafi and C. R. Carlson
Department of Computer Science and Applied Math, IIT
Chicago, U.S.A.

1 Introduction

Behavioral patterns provide a template of reusable system behavior common across diverse applications. One of the biggest challenges that designers face today is the identification of these patterns. This problem is compounded by the lack of a behavioral model that provides a framework for developing behavioral patterns. This paper presents an analysis technique to assist designers in the identification of behavioral patterns based on a comprehensive behavioral model.

2 Background

Behavioral patterns have been identified in the pattern research of Coad [8], Gamma [11] and Coplien [9]. However, their patterns lack the support of a comprehensive behavioral model framework. This research, based on a comprehensive behavioral model, proposes a linguistic tool [3] to aid designers in the identification of behavioral patterns. The name of each pattern identifies the role of that pattern, and is synonymous with the type of behavior of that pattern. Coad [8] has used a similar approach that identified class objects and their roles in constructing structural design patterns. This paper takes this approach a step further by identifying the behavior required to support a behavioral framework that is supported by a behavioral model.

3 ERCDT Behavioral Model.

The behavioral patterns identified in this paper are based on the ERCDT behavioral model illustrated in Figure 1. The behavioral model proposes a behavioral lifecycle that provides a framework under which system behavior is applied. It is based on a phased approach to behavior modeling. The behavior lifecycle starts from the point when behavior is initiated with the occurrence of the triggering event, and ends at the point when system reaction to the event has completed. The lifecycle is composed of the following phases: Event / Recognition / Communication / Decision / Transaction (ERCDT). The diagrams in this paper follow the same notation used in [12].

The Event phase is the period when the behavior triggering event occurs. The Recognition phase focuses on the services needed to recognize that relevant events have occurred. During the Communication phase, the occurrence of the event is announced to interested objects of the system. The Decision phase describes how objects in the system evaluate an event and decide on a course of action. The Transaction phase describes how selected services can interface to provide the required actions in response to an event. To illustrate how objects interface within the behavioral model, the interface is represented graphically using an Object Behavior Diagram (OBD).

Each phase in the lifecycle is independent in function, yet relies on input from the other phases to determine its own behavior. Also, each phase provides output that can be used as input into other phases in order to further extend the behavior lifecycle. This scenario requires cooperation and interface amongst behavioral objects across different phases. The collective behavior across multiple objects within each phase represent a behavioral pattern that we will outline and discuss in the following sections of this paper.

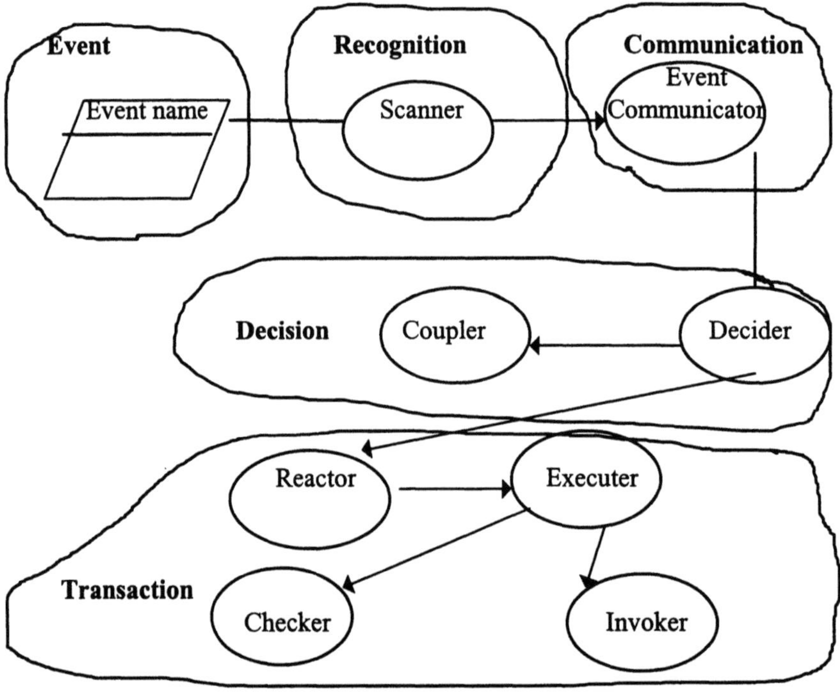

Figure 1, Generic Behavior Lifecycle Model (ERCDT)

4 Behavioral Analysis Technique

The behavioral analysis technique presented in this section is based on the Event / Recognition / Communication / Decision / Transaction (ERCDT) behavioral model [4]. It provides the tool to identify objects and their roles in a behavioral pattern. Further, it presents an approach that will help the designer to easily identify each pattern along with relevant information needed to construct the behavioral patterns. The role that each object plays may vary from one pattern to another. Some objects may play multiple roles within a pattern. The behavior and role that each object plays within a pattern is determined by the specific business rule to whom the pattern applies. In order to apply a pattern, the designer is expected to identify the objects and their roles. A scenario template is presented for each pattern to help identify these roles. The scenario template is constructed of a series of questions that will easily identify objects that make up the pattern, along with vital information for constructing a pattern.

Five patterns were identified based on the ERCDT behavioral model; Scanner Pattern, Communicator Pattern, Decider Pattern, Coupler Pattern, and Transaction Pattern. A Scanner pattern identifies objects that captures the occurrence of an event. A Communicator pattern identifies objects that allow the occurrence of an event to be broadcasted to the entire system. A Decider pattern identifies objects and information needed to evaluate an event and determine its relevance. A Coupler pattern identifies players and their roles in a composite event. A transaction pattern identifies behavioral objects that are capable of carrying out the details of a transaction in reaction to a given event. Each pattern is supported by a service method that provides the required behavior for that pattern. A Detailed discussion of service methods and their behavior is described in [4]. To illustrate the application of each behavioral pattern, an example is presented along with a template and an OBD that shows behavioral objects interface.

4.1 Scanner Pattern

This pattern identifies the roles that behavioral objects play in order to recognize the occurrence of an event. The behavioral services required by this pattern are provided by the scanner service method. The type of event dictates the type of scanner method used for this pattern. Below, a discussion of the role that each object plays in making up that pattern is presented.

- "What event?": This scenario will prompt the user to identify an EVENT. This object is identified by the name of the event. The ROLE of an event is to initiate the triggering behavior that starts the integrated behavioral framework.

"What type of event"?: Identifies the reason for which an event has occurred. An event can occur due to the change in the state of an object, execution of one of its methods or operations. If the event occurred due to a change in the state of an object, the state of the object is identified. When a method or an operation is the reason for an event occurrence, the name of that method or operation is identified. The ROLE of this information is to help identify the type of behavior that triggers the occurrence of an event.

- "Who recognized it?": Refers to the name of the SCANNER object that recognized the occurrence of an event. Different types of scanners may be used to provide the behavioral role of this object; State Scanner, Method Scanner or Operation Scanner. The ROLE that a scanner plays will depend on the behavior required by different types of scanners. It includes: MonitorEvent, VerifyEvent etc.

-"Who is the event applicable to?": Identifies the name of the class OBJECT with whom an event is associated. The ROLE of this object is to execute actions that will cause the event to occur. i.e. ChangeSelfState.

To illustrate how the scenario template is used to construct a scanner pattern, consider the following example:

A COLLECTION business rule requires that a SCANNER monitors a COLLECT event which occurs when the state of an object ACCOUNT changes to "OVERDUE". Figure 2, illustrates how the scenario template for the business rule is constructed.

The scenario template identifies that the event COLLECT is triggered by a change in the state of the object ACCOUNT to OVERDUE which is monitored by the state monitor. Figure 3, illustrates the OBD for the collection rule as constructed by the scenario template above. The diagram shows the scanner object monitoring the occurrence of the COLLECT event for the ACCOUNT object when it changes its state to OVERDUE.

Scenario	Pattern objects
What event?	EVENT: COLLECT EVENT ROLE: CreateCollectEvent.
What type of event?	EVENT TYPE: State event. ROLE: Identifies the need for state scanner.
Who recognized event?	SCANNER: State Scanner ROLE: MonitorCollectEvent.
Who is event applicable to?	OBJECT: ACCOUNT. ROLE: Change its state to "OVERDUE".

Figure 2, Collection Rule Scanner Scenario Template

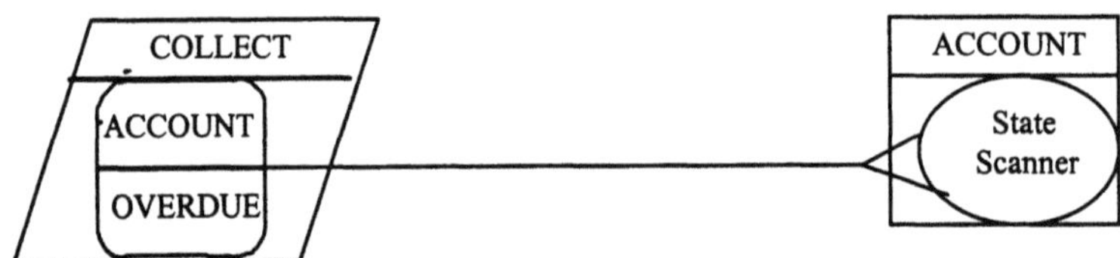

Figure 3, Collection Rule Scanner OBD

4.2 Communicator Pattern

This pattern identifies the class objects required to provide the behavior needed to communicate the occurrence of an event. Communication pattern provide a variety of services, however event communication are being presented at this point. Event communication behavior can be provided in the form of a broadcast service, or by delivering a message hat is intended for a given object. It is used by the scanner pattern to broadcast to interested objects that an event has occurred. A detailed discussion follows.

- "Who needs to communicate?: This scenario will prompt the user to identify the SCANNER service method that is interested to broadcast a message about an event. The ROLE that the scanner plays in this pattern includes: invoking the communicator.

"Who provides communication?": This question will help identify the communicator object. As stated earlier, EVENT-COMMUNICATOR is the only communication service addressed here, it provides the communication services needed to support the communicator pattern within the behavioral framework. The ROLE of this object is to either broadcast a message, or contact a decider to deliver a message sent by the scanner object.

- "What service is needed?": Helps the user identify the SERVICE TYPE. As stated earlier, the service type required will determine the communicator's behavior. The ROLE of this object is to identify the name of the service: i.e. Broadcast or Delivery services.

- "What is the message?": Identifies the structure of the MESSAGE to be communicated. The message is generated by the SCANNER object. The ROLE of this object is to identify the name of the event, and the object to whom the event is addressed as needed.

- "Who receives the message?": Will identify the DECIDER object that is interested in knowing about the occurrence of an event. The ROLE of the decider is to monitor for a broadcast regarding an event that has occurred.

To illustrate how the scenario template is used to construct a communicator pattern, consider the following example:

The COLLECTION business rule states that a STATE SCANNER needs to send a BROADCAST to announce that a COLLECT event that is associated with the object ACCOUNT has occurred and was recognized. The UNCONDITIONAL DECIDER monitors for that broadcast. Figure 4, shows how the communicator scenario template for the collection rule is constructed.

Scenario	Pattern objects
Who needs to communicate?	SCANNER: STATE SCANNER ROLE: Invoke Event Communicator.
Who provides communication?	COMMUNICATOR: EVENT COM-MUNICATOR ROLE: BroadcastMessage.
What service is needed?	SERVICE TYPE: Broadcast. ROLE: Identified the need for a broadcast service.
What is message?	MESSAGE: (ACCOUNT, COLLECT). ROLE: Identifies the event COLLECT is applicable to the ACCOUNT object.
Who receives the message?	DECIDER:UNCONDITIONAL DEC- IDER. ROLE: MonitorBroadcast.

Figure 4, Collection Rule Communicator Scenario Template.

The OBD for the above example is shown in Figure 5. It illustrates that the service method State-Scanner invokes the Event-Communicator service method which broadcasts a message that the COLLECT event associated with the object

230

ACCOUNT has occurred. Also, the diagram shows the Unconditional-Decider object associated with the object ACCOUNT is monitoring for the message so it can decide what to do about it.

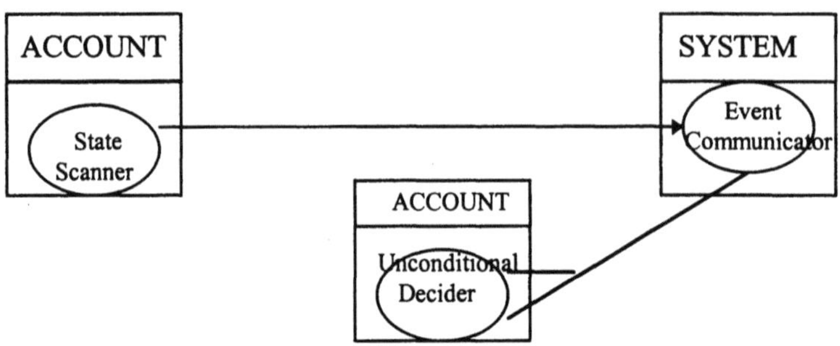

Figure 5, Communicator Rule OBD

4.3 Decider Pattern

This pattern identifies the behavior objects and information needed to determine the relevance of an event to the system, as well as decide what to do about it. Further, it identifies the roles that each behavioral object plays in providing the behavior of a decider pattern. This pattern evaluates an event based on its own predetermined decision rules. Decision rules are discussed in details in [4].

A detailed discussion of the objects that make up a decider pattern and their roles follow:

- "Who makes decision?": Prompts the designer to identify the name of the DECIDER object that evaluates an event then decide what to do about it. The ROLE of the decider may includes: Evaluating an event, then deciding which transaction to invoke in response to that event.

"What invokes the decision?": This question will identify the name of the EVENT that the decider is trying to evaluate. The ROLE of an event is to initiate the triggering behavior that starts the integrated behavioral framework.

- "What is the decision criteria?": Identifies the condition for the decision; DECISION EXPRESSION. If the decision is based on temporal rule, the temporal expression is identified. If the decision rule is based on the state of a Boolean expression, that expression is identified. Decision expressions and decision rules are discussed in details in [4]. The ROLE of this object is to identify the conditions that must exist before a decision can be made.

- "How to react to a decision?": Identifies the name of the REACTOR object. The ROLE of the reactor is to manage the transaction that is implemented as part of the reaction to the occurrence of an event and based on a decision that the decider makes.

To illustrate how the scenario template is used to construct a decider pattern, consider the following example:

A COLLECT event occurs one week after the ACCOUNT becomes OVERDUE. The decider scenario template is shown in Figure 6.

Scenario	Pattern objects
Who makes decision?	DECIDER: Conditional-Decider. ROLE: Evaluate the COLLECT event.
What invokes the decision?	EVENT: COLLECT. ROLE: VerifyEvent.
What is the decision criteria?	DECISION EXPRESSION: Delay(COLLECT Date, OneWeek) ROLE: Identifies decision rule.
How to react to a decision?	REACTOR: Collection Reactor ROLE: Manage the collection transaction.

Figure 6, Collection Rule Decider Scenario Template

The scenario template specifies that the conditional decider service object evaluates the COLLECT event associated with the object ACCOUNT against the decision rule specified in the DECISION EXPRESSION, "Delay(COLLECT Date, One Week)". The expression outlines that the COLLECT event becomes relevant one week after it has occurred has occurred. Further, it specifies that the decider made a decision to invoke a COLLECTION transaction in response to that event. Figure 7, shows the OBD for the collection business rule. The diagram shows the Conditional Decider associated with the object ACCOUNT monitors the occurrence of the COLLECT event and decides to invoke the COLLECTION reactor who manages the collection transaction.

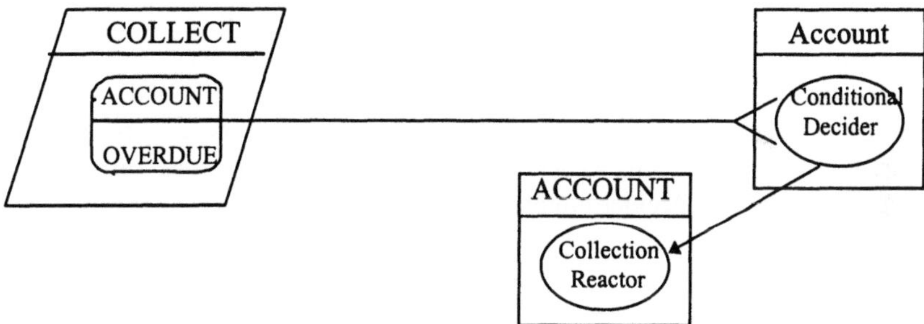

Figure 7, Collection Rule Decider OBD

The above example shows how the behavior of a simple event is implemented using the using our analysis technique. The Coupler pattern identified in the next section presents a scenario that helps the user identify the behavior associated with composite events.

4.4 Coupler Pattern

This pattern includes behavioral objects and information needed to identify a composite event. This pattern will define the behavior needed in compositioning multiple events into one. Simple events do not need this pattern. Following is a detailed discussion of the coupler objects and its roles.

"To Whom is the composition?": This question will help identify the name of the composite event. The ROLE of this information is help outline the name of the composite event that is used in the parameter by the Coupler methods.

- "What type of composition?": Will identify the coupling mode for the composition. The ROLE of this question is to help identify the type of coupler needed to handle the composition of the event.

- "Who makes the composition?": This question will identify the name of the COUPLER service method that handles the composition details of the event. i.e. Sequential Coupler, Concurrent Coupler. The ROLE that this service method plays is to apply the coupling mode behavior. i.e. Sequential Coupler verify that events have occurred in a sequential order.

- "Who is composed?": Identified by the names of event components that make up the composite event. The ROLE of this object is to participate in the composition of an event. When multiple events are involved, event names are separated by a ",".

- "Who needs to know about composition?": Prompts the designer to identify the name of the DECIDER object that evaluates an event then decide what to do about it. The ROLE of the decider may includes: Evaluating an event, then deciding which transaction to invoke in response to that event.

To illustrate how the scenario template is used to construct a coupler pattern, we will modify the above example to create a composite event: A COLLECT event occurs provided that customer REFUSED TO PAY and DID NOT RESPOND TO NOTICE. The coupler scenario template is shown in Figure 8. This scenario prompted the user to identify that COLLECT event is a composite event that occurs provided that REFUSED TO PAY event and DID NOT RESPOND event have both occurred. The Combine Coupler object monitors for the occurrence of both events. Further, once both events are recognized, it generates the COLLECT composite event. The Decider monitors for the occurrence of the COLLECT event.

Scenario	Pattern objects
To whom is the composition?	COMPOSITE EVENT: COLLECT. ROLE: COLLECT COMPOSITE EVENT.
What type of composition?	COUPLING MODE: Combine. ROLE: Identifies the need for a combine coupler.
Who makes the composition?	COUPLER: Combine Coupler ROLE: Verify all component events have occurred.
Who is composed?	COMPONENT EVENTS: REFUSED TO PAY and DID NOT RESPOND TO NOTICE. ROLE: Identifies all the events that make up the composite event.
Who needs to know about composition?	DECIDER: Conditional-Decider. ROLE: Evaluate the COLLECT event.

Figure 8, Collection Rule Coupler Scenario Template

The OBD for this example is shown in Figure 9.. It illustrates that a REFUSED TO PAY and DID NOT RESPOND events have to occur before the COLLECT event takes place. The REFUSE TO PAY event occurred when the method "Hangs up" associated with the object Customer has executed. The DID NOT RESPOND event occurred when the method "Denied Debt" method associated with the object Customer has executed. The Combine Coupler service method monitors for the occurrence of both events. Once recognized, the coupler invokes the composite event COLLECT. That event is monitored by the Conditional Decider who decide on a course of action.

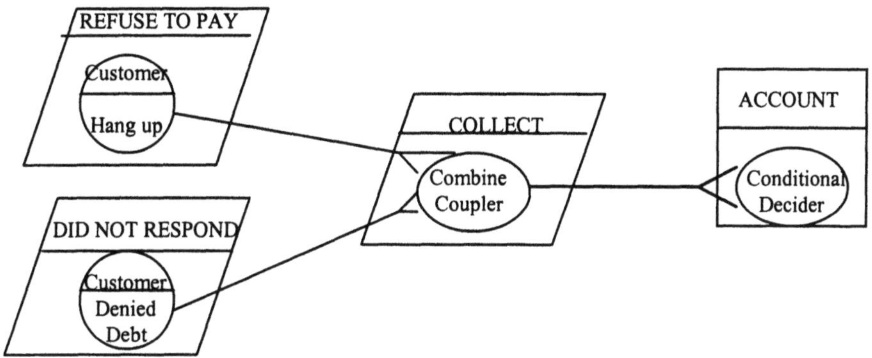

Figure 9, OBD For Collect Composite Event

4.5 Transaction Pattern

This pattern identifies the behavior objects and the information needed to implement the details of a transaction. Transactions are implemented as part of a reaction to an event. The behavior of this pattern requires interface between the reactor, executer, checker, and invoker method services. Behavior for individual class objects that make up this pattern are provided by behavioral service methods. When the transaction does not require a role for one of the behavioral objects, the service method that provides the behavior of that object is also omitted. The roles for each class object along with each perspective service method are discussed in the next section.

"Who is responsible for transaction?": Identifies the name of the REACTOR object that manages implementation of transactions. The responsibilities for applying a transaction can be delegated. The reactor delegates transactions to executor objects. The ROLE of the reactor includes: InvokeExecutor, MonitorExecutor., etc.

- "Who is responsible for Sub-Transaction?": Will help the designer identify the EXECUTOR object that will manage implementation of the details of a Sub-Transaction. The executor manages conditional tasks and actions as part of the details of rule for applying a transaction. Verifications of task conditions are delegated to the Checker object, while individual actions are delegated to Invoker object. The ROLE of the executor includes: InvokeChecker, MonitorChecker, InvokeActionInvoker, MonitorActionInvoker etc.

- "Who handles conditions?": The behavior for this object is identified by the name of the CHECKER object. It verifies that conditions that are part of the details for applying a transaction rule are satisfied. The ROLE that this object plays in a transaction includes; CheckCondition, etc.

- "What action?": The behavior for this object is identified by the name of the INVOKER object. Individual actions that are part of the transaction rule are the responsibilities of this object. The ROLE that this object plays include: InvokeAction, MonitorAction etc.

To illustrate how the scenario template is used to construct a transaction pattern, consider the following:

Example: COLLECTION transaction requires SALARY CONFISCATION which CHECK EMPLOYMENT, then CONFISCATE SALARY. Figure 10, illustrates how the transaction scenario template is constructed, while Figure 11, shows the OBD for this example.

Scenario	Pattern objects
Who is responsible for transaction?	REACTOR: COLLECTION REACTOR ROLE: InvokeCollectionExecutor
Who is responsible for Sub-Transaction?	EXECUTOR: CONFISCATION EXECUTOR ROLE: InvokeExclusiveChecker, InvokeMethodInvoker
Who handles conditions?	CHECKER: EXCLUSIVE CHECKER ROLE: CheckEmployment
What action?	INVOKER: METHOD INVOKER ROLE: ConfiscateSalary.

Figure 10, Collection Rule Scenario Template

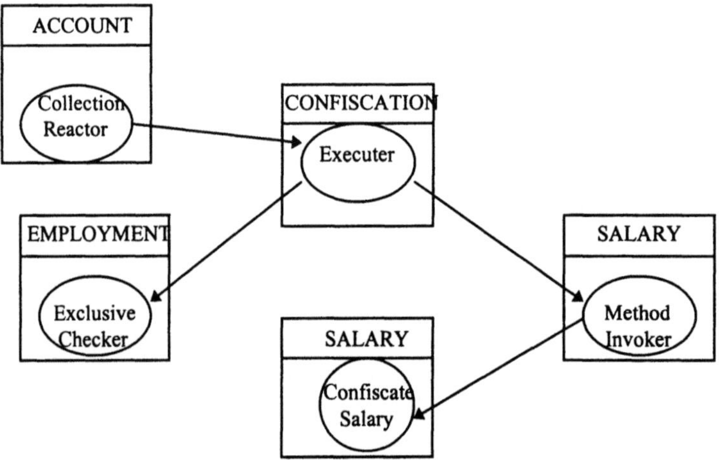

Figure 11, Collection Rule Transaction OBD

In the above example, the scenario template identifies the COLLECTION REACTOR associated with the object ACCOUNT who invokes the

CONFISCATION EXECUTOR to perform the details of the transaction. The scenario template identifies that the EXCLUSIVE CHECKER verifies employment, while the METHOD INVOKER Confiscates salary. The OBD in Figure 11, illustrates that the reactor invokes the executor who asks the checker to CheckEmployment, then call the invoker which executes the user defined method ConfiscateSalary which is associated with the SALARY object.

5 Conclusions

The pattern based analysis approach developed allows system designers to easily identify system behavioral patterns. It is an opportunity to identify system behavior in earlier stages of their development methodology. The patterns identified are based on the ERCDT behavioral model, and make use of the behavioral services identified in applying their behavioral rules. These characteristics make these patterns superior to patterns presented by other researchers where the context of where and how each pattern can be applied relative to the overall behavior of the system.

References

1. Carlson C.R., and Arora, A, K., "A Formal Tool for Expressing Database Update Semantics", Proceedings of the Third International Conference on Entity-Relationship, North Holland, NY, pp. 517-526, 1983.
2. Carlson C.R., Object Oriented Information System Architecture Strategies, Vicking Techinologies INC. 1993.
3. Carlson C.R., Object Oriented Modeling and design, Vicking Technologies INC. 1993.
4. Chafi R., Generic Object Oriented Implementation Design, Ph.D. Dissertation, Illinois Institute Of Technology, 1996.
5. Chakravarthy, S., "Rule Management and Evaluation: An Active DBMS Perspective", SIGMOD RECORD, Vol. 18, No. 3, September 1989.
6. Coad P., and Yourdon, E. Object-Oriented Analysis, Prentice-Hall, 1991.
7. Coad P., "Object Oriented Patterns", Communication of the ACM, Vol 35, No 9, pp. 152-159, Sept. 1992.
8. Coad P., Strategies, Patterns, and Applications, Prentice-Hall, 1995.
9. Coplien J., and Schmidt D., Pattern Languages Of Program Design, Addison-Wesley 1995.
10. Gamma E., Helm. R., Johnson R., and Vlissides J., Design Patterns; Abstraction and Reuse of Object Oriented Design, Technical Report, University of Illinois,   1992.
11.Gamma E., Helm R., Johnson R., and Vlissides J., Design Patterns, Addison Westley 1995.
12. Silva M., Active Object Oriented Database Modeling Technique, Ph.D. Dissertation, Illinois Institute Of Technology, 1995.

Enhancing Reusability and Maintainability in NDOOM *

Li Xuandong and Zheng Guoliang

The National Laboratory of Computer Software New Technology

Department of Computer Science and Technology

Nanjing University, Nanjing

Jiangsu, P.R.China 210093

E-mail: {lxd, zhenggl}@nju.edu.cn

Abstract

In NDOOM, an object-oriented extension of Modula-2 we are developing, for improving reusability and maintainability, we introduce a new encapsulation mechanism called *objectpattern*. It is used as a template for object creation instead of class so as to make it easy to change the representation and behavior of objects. It also can be used as a mechanism to relate a type with its implementation class so as to increase the chance to reuse a class.

1   Introduction

Most of existing object-oriented languages are class-based. In these languages, objects carry their own operations, and these operations are only visible part of an object. Each object is an instance of one class and is represented by a collection of instance variables, as defined by the class. Each class also defines a set of named operations (methods) that can be performed on the instances of that class.

In object-oriented languages, encapsulation and inheritance play important parts for software reusability and maintainability. Encapsulation is a technique for minimizing interdependencies among separately-written modules by defining strict external interfaces. It defines a data structure and a group of operations (or methods) for accessing this data structure. The data structure is accessed only through a well defined, carefully documented, controlled and standardized interface, and the interface to the data structure are defined in such a way as to reveal as little as possible about its inner workings. In object-oriented languages, encapsulation, also as known as information hiding, is the process of binding all of the details of an object that do not contribute to its essential characteristics [1]. Inheritance is a very important mechanism to support reusing code in object-oriented languages, which is for expressing similarity among classes, simplifying the definitions of classes similar to one(s) previously defined. By inheritance, each class may either implement a needed

---

*This work is partly supported by the National Natural Science Foundation of China.

method itself, or else rely on an implementation from one of its superiors in the inheritance hierarchy.

The practical benefit of a good encapsulation mechanism in programming languages is that certain changes can be made in the knowledge that no existing programs will break [2]. The sorts of changes in class-based object-oriented languages that we would wish to include in this category are adding, removing, renaming, or reinterpreting an instance variable in a class, and changing the specification or implementation of a method in a class. Because inheritance is introduced, no existing class-based object-oriented language enables a programmer to make all of these kinds of changes without potentially compromising existing code so that the encapsulation is severely compromised, and the reusability and maintainability are likewise compromised [3].

In existing object-oriented languages that are class-based, the function of a class in a program has two aspects. On one hand, a class is a syntactic mechanism which is used to define object's internal structure, that is, instance variables and methods. On the other hand, a class describes how its instances are built, is a template for object creation, and has an instance creation semantics. Because inheritance is introduced, a class has to export two distinct interfaces: a client interface to users of objects of the class, and a inheriting interface to designers of its subclasses. It results in the following two problems on reuse and maintenance:

- On one hand, since the only thing one can do with an object is to send a message for a operation to that object, the client interface of a class consists of only the specifications of the methods in that class. However, if the instance variables can be accessible to inheriting users of a class, the inheriting interface of that class has to consist of the instance variables and the specifications of the methods in that class. It results in the encapsulation issue that changing the representation of the objects, which is implemented by adding, removing, renaming, and reinterpreting the instance variables in a class, could potentially compromise existing code.

- On the other hand, by inheritance, each class may either implement a needed method itself, or else rely on an implementation from one of its superiors in the inheritance hierarchy. So, changing the objects' behavior, which is implemented by changing the methods in a class, could affect the objects' behavior of the other classes.

Some attempts [2, 4, 7, 10, 11] have been made at resolving these encapsulation issues. But we think that for solving the problems completely, a class should export only one interface and give up another. A class should give up the client interface so that changing the representation of the objects need not result in the requirement changing the instance variables in a class and that changing the objects' behavior need not result in the requirement changing the methods in a class. Once a class gives up the client interface, it is not a template for object creation and has not an instance creation semantics. So, a new encapsulation mechanism, which exports the client interface instead of class, has to be introduced. It is used as a template for object creation and has an instance creation semantics. A class is only a syntactic mechanism which is used to define object's internal structure, that is, instance variables and methods, and is encapsulated within this new encapsulation mechanism. In addition, the separation of types and classes in object-oriented languages has been attended. However, in the works on this field [5, 6, 8], there is not a mechanism which relates a type with its implementation class. The new encapsulation mechanism we present here just can plays this part.

This new encapsulation mechanism has been introduced in NDOOM, an object-oriented extension of Modula-2 we are developing. We call it *objectpattern*. We introduce NDOOM summarily in the following section. Section 3 gives an example. The advantages of this new encapsulation mechanism are illustrated in section 4, 5 and 6. Finally, section 7 draws some conclusions from our work.

2   Objectpatterns in NDOOM

In NDOOM, there are three mechanisms related with an object that are used respectively to specify, implement, and create the object. They are *objecttype*, *class*, and *objectpattern*.

An objecttype is a collection of objects that share the same externally observable behavior. It means that in deciding whether an object belongs to an objecttype, the only important aspects are which messages the object answers, in which order, and which relationship exits between the arguments and results of those messages. An objecttype describes how its elements can be used and is a specification of the behavior of its elements. An objecttype definition has the following syntax:

```
OBJECTTYPE objecttype-name;
    [SUPERTYPE {supertype-name
                RENAME methodname INTO methodname
                        {, methodname INTO methodname};}]
    [SUBTYPE {subtype-name
                RENAME methodname INTO methodname
                        {, methodname INTO methodname};}]
    METHOD methodname(...) {; methodname(...)}
    END objecttype-name.
```

An objecttype defines the interface of its instance objects, i.e. the operations (methods) they must export, and lists its supertypes and subtypes.

In NDOOM, a class is only a syntax mechanism which is used to defined object's internal structure, that is, instance variables and methods. A class is not a template for object creation, and has not an instance creation semantics. One can say that a class definition is a module with its own external interface which consists of the instance variables and the specifications of methods in that class. In NDOOM, multiple inheritance is supported, i.e., a class can inherit from more one other class. The name clashes in multiple inheritance are resolved by explicit rename, as in Eiffel [9]. A class definition has following syntax:

```
CLASS classname;
    INTERFACE (...);
    [INHERIT {classname [WITH (EXCEPT) methodname {, methodname};]
                    RENAME methodname INTO methodname
                            {, methodname INTO methodname};}]
    [REDEFINE methodname(...) INTO methodname(...)...
                    {; methodname(...) INTO methodname(...)...};]
    VAR ...;
    METHOD ...;
END classname.
```

In NDOOM, a new encapsulation mechanism called *objectpattern* is introduced. An objectpattern is a collection of objects that have exactly the same internal structure and externally observable behavior, that is, the same instance variables, the same methods, and the same objecttype. Each object is an instance of one objectpattern. Instead of class, an objectpattern describes how its instances are built, and has an instance creation semantics. An objectpattern definition has the following syntax:

```
OBJECTPATTERN objectpattern-name;
    OBJECTTYPE objecttype-name;
    CLASS classname [RENAME methodname INTO methodname;
                            {; method INTO methodname}];
    END objectpattern-name.
```

An objectpattern definition includes an objecttype specifying its instances and a class implementing its instances. One can say that an objectpattern definition is a module whose interface (specification) is an objecttype and whose implementation is a class.

In a program, after declaring an objecttype T, a class C which is used to implement the instance objects of objecttype T, we can declare an objectpattern P which is used to create the objects specified by objecttype T and implemented by class C as following:

```
OBJECTPATTERN P;
    OBJECTTYPE T;
    CLASS C
END P.
```

Then, we can declare a variable i which references the objects of objecttype T, and create an object of objectpattern P and assign it to variable i as:

```
VAR i: T;
    ...
    i := CREATE(P);
    ...
```

3 An Example

Now, let us look at an example. Suppose we want to use an object in a program, which represents a point in plane. First, an objecttype point, which is used to specify the object, would be declared as following:

```
        OBJECTTYPE point;
          METHOD vx():REAL; vy():REAL;
                    distance():REAL;
                    scale(factor:REAL);
                    translate(m,n:REAL);

          END point;
```

Each instance object of objecttype point represents a movable point in plane. Its externally observable behavior consists of five methods: vx, vy, distance, scale, and translate. vx and vy are functions that are corresponding to the cartesian coordinates of a point. distance is a function which is for the distance from the point to the origin. scale(factor:REAL) is a procedure which is used to scale the point by a ratio of factor. translate(m,n:REAL) is a procedure which is used to move the point by m horizontally, n vertically.

Then, a class cart-point, which is used to implement the instance objects of objecttype point, would be declared as:

```
CLASS cart-point;
  INTERFACE (x,y:REAL; vx():REAL; vy():REAL; distance():REAL; scale(factor:REAL);
              translate(m,n:REAL));
  VAR x,y:REAL;
  METHOD
   vx():REAL is DO
                 return := x
               END;
   vy():REAL is DO
                 return := y
               END;
   distance():REAL is DO
                 return := SQRT(SQUARE(self.vx) + SQUARE(self.vy))
               END;
   scale(factor:REAL) is DO
                 x := x * factor;
                 y := y * factor
               END;
   translate(m,n:REAL) is DO
                 x := x + m;
                 y := y + n
               END;
END cart-point.
```

It has two instance variables: x and y, that represent the cartesain coordinates of the points.

Last, an objectpattern plane-point, which is used to create the objects that

are specified by objecttype point and are implemented by class cart-point, would
be declared as following:

        OBJECTPATTERN plane-point;
            OBTECTTYPE point;
            CLASS cart-point
        END plane-point.

It is clear that the representation of objects of objectpattern plane-point is
specified in cartesian coordinates.

After declaring objecttype point, class cart-point, and objectpattern plane-
point, we can declare a variable i which references the objects of objecttype
point, and create an object of objectpattern plane-point and assign it to variable
i as:

        VAR i: point;

        ...

        i := CREATE(plane-point);

        ....

Then we can use this object representing a point in plane in the program.

It is clear that for using an object in a program, we have to give more declarations in the program with NDOOM than with existing class-based object-
oriented languages. For example, if we want use an object, which represents a
point in plane, we only need to declare a class $POINT$ in a program with Eiffel
[9] as:

class $POINT$ **export** $vx,\ vy,\ distance,\ scale,\ translate$
  feature
   $x,\ y{:}REAL$
   $vx(){:}REAL$ **is do**
          $Result := x$
        end;
   $vy(){:}REAL$ **is do**
          $Result := y$
        end;
   $distance(){:}REAL$ **is do**
          $Result := sqrt((vx)\,\hat{}\,2\ +\ (vy)\,\hat{}\,2\ )$
        end;
   $scale(factor{:}REAL)$ **is do**
          $x := factor * x;$
          $y := factor * y$
        end;
   $translate(m,n{:}REAL)$ **is do**
          $x := x + m;$
          $y := y + n$
        end;
 end – class $POINT$.

Then, we can declare a variable i which references the objects of class $POINT$,
and create an object of class $POINT$ and associate it with variable i as:

        $i{:}\ POINT;$

        ...

        $i.Create;$

We use Eiffel here in the spirit of ecumenicalism just to make the presentation more clear.

However, because of introducing the new encapsulation mechanism *object-pattern*, NDOOM can increase the chance to use a class and make it easy to change the representation and behavior of objects in a program. These advantages are illustrated in following sections.

4   Changing the Representation of Objects

Suppose we write a program with Eiffel. A class *POINT* such as the one given in last section is declared and a lot of its objects are used in the program. If we want to change the representation of a certain object i, we can declare a new class *POINT1* which defines a new representation and change the declaration i:*POINT* into i:*POINT1* in the program. If we want to change the representation of all the objects of class *POINT* in the program, we can finish it by two ways. One way is to change the instance variables in class *POINT*. But doing so will affect the descendant classes of class *POINT* in the program so as to compromise existing code because of permitting direct access to inherited instance variables. The other way is to declare a new class *POINT1* which defines a new representation and change the declaration of every object of class *POINT* in the program. It is a burden to the programmers. So it is hard to change the representation of objects without compromising existing code in a program with existing class-based object-oriented languages.

It is easy to change the representation of objects in a program with NDOOM. If we want to change the representation of the objects of objectpattern plane-point given in last section in the program so that it is specified in polar coordinates, instead of reinterpreting the instance variables in class cart-point we declare a new class polar-point as:

```
CLASS polar-point;
  INTERFACE (ρ,θ:REAL; vx():REAL; vy():REAL; distance():REAL; scale(factor:REAL);
             translate(m,n:REAL));
  VAR ρ,θ:REAL;
  METHOD
   vx():REAL is DO
               return := ρ * COS(θ)
               END;
   vy():REAL is DO
               return := ρ * SIN(θ)
               END;
   distance():REAL is DO
                return := ρ
                END;
  scale(factor:REAL) is DO
     ρ := SQRT(SQUARE(ρ * COS(θ) * factor) + SQUARE(ρ * SIN(θ) * factor))
```

$$\theta := ARCTG((\rho * SIN(\theta) * factor) / (\rho * COS(\theta) * factor))$$
```
    END;
  translate(m,n:REAL) is DO
```
$$\rho := SQRT(SQUARE(\rho * COS(\theta) + m) + SQUARE(\rho * SIN(\theta) + n))$$
$$\theta := ARCTG((\rho * SIN(\theta) + n) / (\rho * COS(\theta) + m))$$
```
    END;
END polar-point.
```

Then we modify objectpattern plane-point by replacing class cart-point with class polar-point as:

```
        OBJECTPATTERN plane-point;
          OBJECTTYPE point;
          CLASS polar-point
        END plane-point.
```

So, we change the representation of the objects of objectpattern plane-point, which is specified in cartesain coordinates, into the one specified in polar coordinates without compromising existing code. If you want change the representation of a certain object, e.g., the object referenced by variable i, you also need to declare a new objectpattern i-point as:

```
        OBJECTPATTERN i-point;
          OBJECTTYPE point;
          CLASS polar-point
        END i-point,
```

and change statement i := CREATE(plane-point) into i := CREATE(i-point) in the program.

5 Changing the Behavior of Objects

Intuitively, changing the behavior of objects can be implemented by changing the methods in a class, which includes changing the specifications and implementations of the methods, and renaming and removing the methods. Suppose we write a program with Eiffel. A class *POINT* such as the one given in section 3 is declared and a lot of its objects are used in the program. If we want to change the objects' behavior of class *POINT* without affecting the other objects' behavior, we can not finish it by changing some methods in class *POINT* because doing so will affect the objects' behavior of the descendant classes of class *POINT*. We have to declare a new class *POINT1* which modifies some methods on the basis of class *POINT*, and change the declaration of every object of class *POINT* in the program. So it is hard to change the objects' behavior without affecting the the other objects' behavior in a program with existing class-based object-oriented languages.

It is easy to change the objects' behavior without affecting the the other objects' behavior in a program with NDOOM. Suppose we want to change the implementation of the objects' behavior of objectpattern plane-point given in section 3 in a program so as to improve the execution efficiency of method distance without affecting the implementation of the other objects' behavior. First, we declare a new class cart-point1 as:

```
CLASS cart-point1;
  INTERFACE (x,y:REAL; vx():REAL; vy():REAL; distance():REAL; scale(factor:REAL);
             translate(m,n:REAL));
  VAR x,y:REAL;
  METHOD
   vx():REAL is DO
                 return := x
               END;
   vy():REAL is DO
                 return := y
               END;
   distance():REAL is DO
                 return := SQRT(SQUARE(x) + SQUARE(y))
               END;
   scale(factor:REAL) is DO
                 x := x * factor;
                 y := y * factor
               END;
   translate(m,n:REAL) is DO
                 x := x + m;
                 y := y + n
               END;
END cart-point1.
```

It is clear that the execution efficiency of method distance in class cart-point1 is better than the one in class cart-point given in section 3. The reason is that the instance variable x and y are accessed directly in the implementation of method distance in class cart-point1 instead of calling for method vx and vy. Then, we modify objectpattern plane-point by replacing class cart-point with class cart-point1 as:

```
        OBJECTPATTERN plane-point;
          OBJECTTYPE point;
          CLASS cart-point1
        END plane-point.
```

So, we change the implementation of the objects' behavior of objectpattern plane-point without affecting the implementation of the other objects' behavior in the program.

6 Increasing the Chance to Reuse a Class

The separation of subtyping and inheritance results in that the separation of types and classes is attended. The main idea underlying this concept is the understanding of types as specifications and classes as implementations. In the works on this field [5, 6, 8], the type of an object is its external appearance, that is, its interface to the outside world, while the class of an object dictates its internal shape, that is, its structure and the code to handle it. Since there is not a mechanism which relates a type and its implementation class, a class is not only a syntax mechanism which is used to define object's internal shape, but also a template for object creation and has an instance creation semantics. Thus, a certain type can be implemented by many classes, but a certain class can not be used directly as implementations of many types.

In NDOOM, the objecttype of an object is its external appearance, that is, its interface to the outside world, and the *class* of an object dictates its internal shape, that is, its structure and the code to handle it. Differentially, a class is only a syntax mechanism which is used to define object's internal shape, and has not an instance creation semantics. Instead of class, any object is created by its *objectpattern*. An objectpattern is a template for object creation and relates an objecttype and its implementation class. So, not only a certain objecttype can be implemented by many classes, but also a certain class can be used directly as implementations of many objecttypes so as to increase the chance to reuse a class.

For example, suppose objecttype point, class cart-point, and objectpattern plane-point given in section 3 have been declared in a program, and we want to use the objects representing a special kind of points in plane different from the points represented by the objects of objecttype point. The difference is that the points represented by these objects can not be scaled. First, we need to declare a new objecttype speciPoint as:

```
OBJECTTYPE speciPoint;
    METHOD vx():REAL;
            vy():REAL;
            distance():REAL;
            translate(m,n:REAL);
    END speciPoint;
```

Instead of declaring a new class, we can use class cart-point to implement objecttype speciPoint directly. So then we only need to declare a new objectpattern plane-speciPoint, which is used to create the objects that are specified by objecttype speciPoint and implemented by class cart-point as:

```
OBJECTPATTERN plane-speciPoint;
    OBTECTTYPE speciPoint;
    CLASS cart-point
END plane-speciPoint.
```

7 Conclusions

In existing object-oriented languages that are class-based, a class not only is a syntactic mechanism which is used to define object's internal structure, that is, instance variables and methods, but also is a template for object creation, and has an instance creation semantics. Because inheritance is introduced, a class has to export two distinct interfaces: a client interface to users of objects of the class, and a inheriting interface to designers of its subclasses. It results in the problems on reuse and maintenance. It is hard to change the representation and behavior of objects without potentially compromising existing code.

For improving reusability and maintainability in object-oriented languages, in NDOOM, we introduce a new encapsulation mechanism called *objectpattern*. It is used as a template for object creation instead of class so as to make it easy to change the representation of objects and the implementations of object' behavior. It also can be used as a mechanism to relate a type with its implementation class so as to increase the chance to reuse a class.

We have implemented a prototype of NDOOM by transforming NDOOM code into Modula-2 code, and are developing a programming environment based on NDOOM.

References

[1] Charles W. Krueger. Software Reuse. In *ACM Computing Surveys*, Vol.24, No.2, June 1992, pp.131-181.

[2] Mario Wolczko. Encapsulation, delegation and inheritance in object-oriented languages. In *Software Engineering Journal*, March 1992, pp.95-101.

[3] Booch, G. *Object-Oriented Design with Applications*. The Benjamin/Cummings Publishing Company, Inc. 1991.

[4] A. Snyder. Encapsulation and Inheritance in Object-Oriented Programming Languages. In *SINGPLAN Notices*, **28**, (8), 38-45 (1986).

[5] P. America. A behavioral Approach to Subtyping in Object-Oriented Programming Languages. In M. Lenzerini, D. Nardi, and M. Simi (eds): *Inheritance Hierarchies in Knowledge Representation and Programming Languages*. John Wiley & Sons Ltd. 1991, pp.173-190.

[6] Noemi de la Rocque Rodriguez. Types in School. In *SIGPLAN Notices*, **28**, (8), 81-89 (1993).

[7] M. Armstrong, Richard J. Mitchell. Uses and Abuses of Inheritance. In *Software Engineering Journal*. January 1994, pp.19-26.

[8] Roberto Ierusalimschy. A Denotational Approach for Type-checking in Object-Oriented Programming Languages. In *Computer Language*, Vol.19, No.1, pp.19-40, 1993.

[9] B. Meyer. *Eiffel, The Language*. Prentice Hall, 1992.

[10] Li Xuandong, ZhengGuoliang. Introducing Virtual Instance Variables in Classes to Provide Sufficient Support for Encapsulation. In *SIGPLAN Notices*, **30**, (7), 52-56, 1995.

[11] Li Xuandong, ZhengGuoliang. A Modified Inheritance Mechanism Enhancing Reusability and Maintainability in Object-Oriented Languages. In *Proc. Asia Pacific Software Engineering Conference (APSEC'96)*. IEEE Computer Society Press, 1996, pp.93-102.

Temporal Business Objects: A Waste of Time?

Paul Schleifer[1], Yuan Sun[2], Dilip Patel[1]
[1]School of Computing, South Bank University, London SE1 0AA, UK.
[2]Compuware Ltd., 163 Bath Road, Slough, Berks. SL1 4AA, UK.

ABSTRACT

It has been widely observed that temporal semantics and functionality are often developed on an *ad hoc* basis, and the benefits of temporal database research are rarely realised. The object-oriented paradigm offers many in terms of performance, semantic richness, and re-use; these advantages can be realised as conceptual and software components known as business objects. However, fundamental barriers to the use of temporal database research in real business software remain. These barriers, namely the absence of a consensus temporal object model and the lack of suitable temporal modelling tools, are addressed in this paper. Unless these issues are addressed, the development of re-usable temporal business objects will not yield tangible benefits in commercial environments.

1.   Introduction

It is a challenge to identify applications that do not have some requirement to store and manipulate data whose values are subject to changes with time[1]. Information about the past can be used to identify trends, optimal strategies, and causal and incidental links between certain kinds of events. Information about the future is used in planning and decision-making and may be used to automate aspects of an information. Information about facts pertaining to a certain time that have been corrected can be used to explain decisions and perhaps to establish degrees of liability.

These issues are addressed by a growing body of research into the field of temporal databases [2]. However, in spite of this body of research, temporal databases have had relatively little impact on commercial database applications. Most database developments are *snapshot* databases because they model the state of an enterprise at an instant in time [3], and temporal semantics are developed on an *ad hoc* basis rather than drawing on temporal database research [4].

The absence of temporal databases in the commercial arena may be explained by technical considerations. Firstly, temporal databases tend to be large repositories of information, which are expensive to maintain in terms of storage and processing. This factor is of decreasing importance due to improvements in computer hardware, and the growth of commercial interest in *data warehouses* [5] lends support to this notion.

Secondly, most temporal database research has been concerned with extending the *relational* database model to support the semantics of temporal data. The relational model impedes the development of temporal databases in several ways: data normalisation precludes the direct representation of multi-valued attributes [6]; the identity of a tuple may be destroyed over time because primary keys are sets of attributes whose values can change [7]; interpretative errors may occur because the encoding of the semantics of the data is delegated to client applications; and temporal objects tend to be complex objects whose manipulation incurs unacceptable processing overheads.

Adopting object-oriented database technology may reduce the overheads of extended relational database models. The direct representation of complex and multi-valued objects, the encapsulation of behaviour within data objects, and the potential executive efficiency offered by the navigational query of complex entities by object identity addresses many of the problems posed by relational technology. Furthermore, there is also a much greater potential for re-use of specifications, database structures and executable code in an object-oriented environment because of core object-oriented modelling features like class and class inheritance. With further abstraction, whole object schemata, specifications, and libraries can be built into re-usable enterprise-modelling components known *business objects* [8].

However, there are two unresolved barriers to the widespread adoption of temporal database research by the commercial world: the absence of a consensus temporal object model, and the lack of temporal modelling tools and techniques. These barriers are described in **Section 0**, and possible solutions to these are presented in **Section** Temporal Object Model Principles and **Section 0**. The conclusions of this paper and some indication of future areas of research are provided in **Section 0**.

2.   Object-Oriented Temporal Databases Issues

Computer hardware technology has evolved such that manipulating large data sets is no longer problematic. Furthermore, the remaining problems introduced by the use of relational databases can be ameliorated by the adoption of an object-oriented technology, which also facilitates re-use. There are two reasons why temporal database research might not feature in business applications that require temporal semantics.

Firstly, no consensus temporal database model has been accepted by the research community [9]. The only point of commonality is that most temporal database models are *bitemporal*, time-stamping data values with both a *valid time* (when the value holds in the modelled reality) and a *transaction time* (when the value is stored in the database) [10]. **Figure 0—1** shows the evolution of an object in these two dimensions of time, with different shapes indicating different object values.

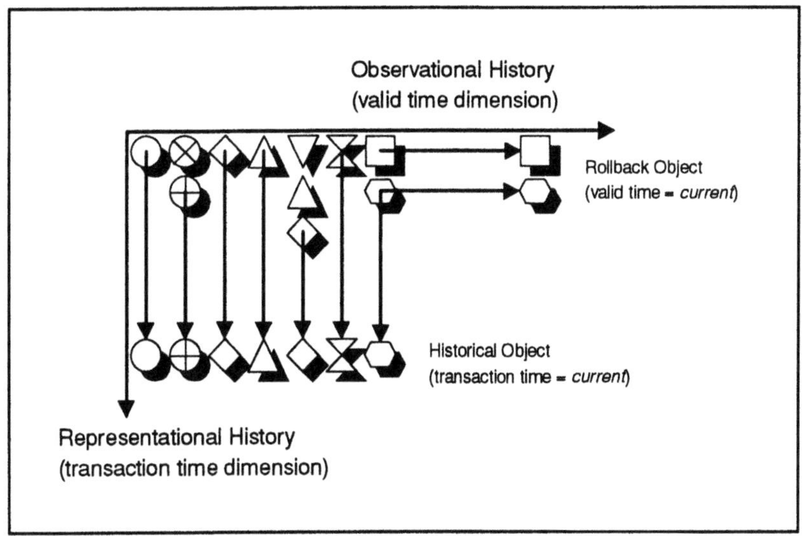

Figure 0—1: Bitemporal Data Model

A temporal object represented in this way can be mapped onto an *historical* object that can be used to generate an *observational history* [11]. A temporal object can also be mapped onto a *rollback* object, which gives a *representational history* of how the object evolves in its representation in the database.

Valid-time and transaction-time are readily modelled in an object-oriented database [12,13], but these concepts are insufficient in themselves to form a comprehensive temporal object model. Issues such as how temporal objects should be manipulated, how missing data are accommodated, and whether object schema should be similarly time-stamped need to be addressed. Without these considerations, a temporal object model is incomplete and therefore cannot form a core model for wide-scale commercial use.

The second barrier is the absence of modelling tools and notations. Object-oriented methodologies provide a rich set of modelling, but the ubiquitous dimension of time is ignored, despite the concept of a *variable* as a tacit recognition of an ever-changing Universe.

3.   Temporal Object Model Principles

In an attempt to answer the question, "What constitutes a temporal object model?", [14] propose eight loosely defined principles based on intuitive notions of a temporal object model. These principles provide a high-level ontology for the design of temporal object classes.

3.1   Temporal Extension Principle

Any temporal object model should be a consistent extension of a non-temporal object model. This principle is perhaps more practical than intuitive. Very few application domains do not have a temporal aspect. It would be intuitive, therefore, to regard a temporal object model as a step towards a complete representation of the Universe, with a non-temporal model being an extension to the more general model. However, in practical terms, application domains treat only a subset of its objects as temporal. Temporal models are therefore usually considered to be extensions to underlying data models (exceptions include financial instruments and real-time monitoring systems). This principle is therefore intuitive in terms of implementation, rather than as a characteristic of an ideal solution. It implies that temporal and non-temporal objects should be manipulated in the same way and that the underlying non-temporal model should not be redefined to accommodate temporal semantics.

It should be noted that most temporal database models are extensions of a non-temporal model, typically developed from the relational model. Temporal extensions to non-temporal models are usually applied to the data model [15,16], or to the query language [17], or both [18]. Extensions to the data model and to the query language can therefore both be regarded as facets of the Extension Principle.

In an object-oriented modelling environment, it is assumed that the Temporal Extension Principle is adhered to if the normal object-oriented techniques for extending the semantics of an existing object class are used. The semantics of a temporal object, if considered to be an ordered sequence of snapshot objects, is essentially the semantics of an ordered collection such as an Array. The Temporal Extension Principle is therefore observed by deriving a new class from this superclass by inheritance, with the addition and overriding of attributes and methods where appropriate.

3.2   Temporal Evolution Principle

A temporal object model should capture the specifications and relationships of the properties of an object over time (valid and transaction), preserving both its history and its identity despite changes in the object's roles and behaviours, and [19,20,21] stress the importance of capturing these features. The concept of identity is a key issue in temporal objects: real world entities can undergo many changes and still be regarded as the same entity. For example, a car can have many components replaced during repairs and maintenance, or be remodelled to change its appearance and performance, but it remains the same car. Identity must therefore be captured in a temporal object model, and is as important as the preservation of historical states.

[14] omit the issue of *schema evolution* in their set of temporal database principles [22,23,24,25]. Schema evolution provides the capacity to accommodate structural changes to a database schema, such as the addition and removal of attributes and

alterations to the attribute domains. These changes arise from decisions made during the analysis stage of modelling and from changes in the modelled reality. Changes to a database schema should be recorded in a temporal database in order to interpret the semantics of recorded instances.

3.3 Temporal Consistency Principle

For a given valid time, a condition cannot be both true and false. This principle can be considered a basic and important temporal integrity constraint. For example, an cannot be both "dead" and "alive" at a given valid time. However, the strict application of this principle to all temporal object models is undesirable. Decision support systems may require the storage of alternative and possibly temporally inconsistent data in "What if?" modelling, and temporal inconsistencies may also arise if support for branching time is required. Temporal consistency should be treated as an integrity rule rather than a principle of temporal object models, and the Consistency Principle is therefore.

3.4 Temporal Representation Principle

Events should be represented in a temporal object model in the same order that they occur in the modelled reality, or at least that a view of the data can be created that respects this order. This is a strongly intuitive principle since humans naturally perceive events in chronological order, record them as sequential narratives, and usually process information in a sequential manner [26]. In a bitemporal object model, events should be represented in chronological order with respect to both valid time and transaction time. The valid time order may be modified, since events may be retrospectively inserted, removed, or given a new time-stamp; transaction time order is not subject to this kind of modification, though superfluous transaction histories might be abridged. A branching structural model for valid time is essential for some types of applications. This principle may be considered as related to the dichotomy of *temporally grouped* and *temporally ungrouped* historical data models [27].

3.5 Temporal Incompleteness Principle

A temporal object model should support incomplete information for periods of time. Temporal databases may lack information describing an object over its entire life history [28], so a temporal object model should provide the semantics to record these gaps appropriately. This principle can be extended further. Where complete data exist for the entire life span of an object, time-stamp granularity and comparing data with different time granularities may both introduce uncertainty. The Incompleteness Principle applied to a temporal object model should therefore capture both data where the valid times are known and the values are not, and data where the values are known and the absolute valid times are not. [9] identify the need for relative valid times, in which the order of the states of an object is known, but suggest that the *interpretation* should be an application issue.

3.6   Temporal Abstraction Principle

This principle requires that a temporal object model should represent abstract temporal concepts like "when" and "before". However, a complete list of abstract temporal concepts does not exist despite [29] and there is no clear partition between the temporal abstractions that should constitute part of a general temporal object model and those which should remain application-specific [30].

The most basic requirement for this principle is that temporal objects should support manipulation by transaction time, valid time, and by object value. To refine this principle, [31] propose requirements for a good temporal query language. These can be used as a core set of abstractions for a temporal object model. These requirements are:

(R1) Well-known temporal algebraic operators: when, project, select, join, pack/unpack, slice and shift.

(R2) Time-based joins.

(R3) Manipulation of complex temporal objects in the same way as non-temporal objects.

(R4) Set aggregation over both the object and the time dimensions in a uniform way.

(R5) Modal operators, such as always and since.

(R6) Manipulation of non-linearly versioned objects in the same way as linear temporal objects.

Requirement **R6** is redundant by the inclusion of schema evolution as a facet of the Evolution Principle. The remaining five temporal operations must be facilitated by a temporal object model to satisfy the Abstraction Principle.

A further aspect to this principle is the issue of time *granularity*. Database applications deal with units of time that are relevant to the modelled reality. For example, a database of athletic performance might record events in terms of *milliseconds*, while a typical business application will concentrate on *working days*. A temporal object should therefore include an attribute to identify the unit of time granularity of the application.

3.7   Temporal Inference Principle

This principle states that a temporal object model requires a set of operations that can be used to infer certain properties of the data at time points for which there are no explicit records. These operations are interpolation methods, and the requirement for them is recognised by [9]. There are few general-purpose interpolation methods that can be applied to non-numerical data. This principle should be extended to state that inference operations could be added to the model as required by an application. This implies that a temporal object model should provide an extensible library of inference operations. Temporal objects must identify which interpolation function is used.

3.8   Temporal Derived Data Principle

This principle infers that the unknown state of an object is the same as the value recorded for the nearest preceding state. This assumption holds for certain kinds of data, such as an employee's address, but does not hold for continuously variable data. For example, a database of daily rainfall measurements might lack data for a given date, but data from the previous day might rarely hold for the next. However, this operation can be applied to many non-numerical and business data, and should therefore be provided in the library of inference operations described by the Inference Principle. It is functionally equivalent to the *stepwise* type [32].

Principle	Aspect	Temporal OODAPLEX	TOODM	Chronicle
Extension	data model	Satisfied	Satisfied	Satisfied
	query language	Satisfied	N/S	Satisfied
Evolution	valid time	Satisfied	Satisfied	Satisfied
	transaction time	Satisfied	Satisfied	Satisfied
	schema evolution	Satisfied	Satisfied	Satisfied
Representation	chronological order	Satisfied	Satisfied	Satisfied
	branching v-time	Satisfied	N/S	Satisfied
	temporally grouped	Satisfied	Satisfied	Satisfied
Incompleteness	sequential gaps	Satisfied	Satisfied	Satisfied
	relative valid time	Satisfied	N/A	Satisfied
Abstraction	temporal operators	Satisfied	N/A	Satisfied
	time-based joins	Satisfied	N/A	Satisfied
	complex temporal	Satisfied	Satisfied	Satisfied
	temporal aggreg^n	Satisfied	Satisfied	Satisfied
	modal operators	Satisfied	N/A	Satisfied
Inference	stepwise interpol^n	N/S	Satisfied	Satisfied
	extendible interpol^n	N/S	Satisfied	Satisfied

Table 0—1: Comparison of Object-Oriented Temporal Database Models
[Key: N/S - Not Satisfied by model; N/A - Not Addressed in literature]

3.9   Evaluation of Temporal Object Database Models

Three published temporal object models are compared in **Table 0—1** using the Temporal Database Principles. In all cases, most of the principles are adhered to, and those that are not could be addressed by further modification. Temporal OODAPLEX [31] adheres to all of the principles except the Temporal Inference Principle, which could be addressed by a simple extension of the model. TOODM [12] adheres to most of the principles, and its deficiencies could also be addressed by simple extensions to the model; a possible exclusion to this is that TOODM supports a declarative temporal query language that is not a consistent extension of the underlying query language. The Chronicle model [13] adheres to all of the principles because it was designed using the principles as a framework.

This comparison shows the need for some kind of ontology such as the Temporal Database Principles. Many features that could be supported are excluded simply because the authors did not consider them.

4. Modelling Temporal Business Objects

Using standard OMT notation [33], it is possible to represent an object schema which associates an instance of an Employee object class with an ordered history of snapshot Address objects, as shown in **Figure 0—1**. However, there are no specifications for temporal semantics like valid time, transaction time, or interpolation functions.

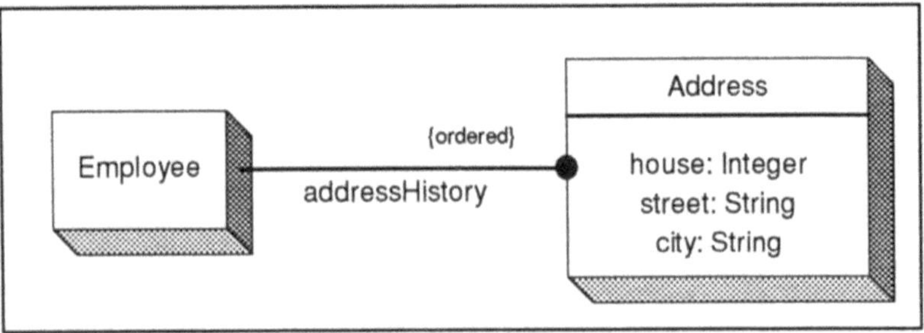

Figure 0—1: Employee Class with `address-history` Attribute

A notational solution to this problem is to use a specialised *temporal link class* to define link attributes, as shown in **Figure 0—2**. By specifying the Address class as a *snapshot*, this approach shows that Address instances are snapshot objects stored in a temporal object, the semantics of which are specified by explicitly valued link attributes.

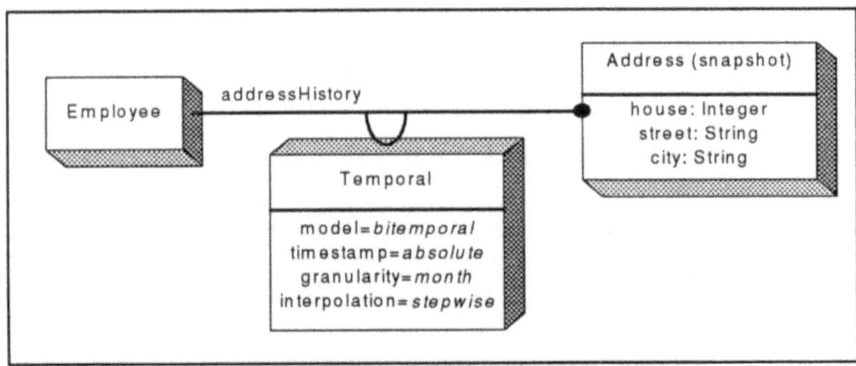

Figure 0—2: Employee Class with Temporal Link Attributes

The domains of the temporal link attributes are shown in **Table 0—1**. The *model* used for the temporal object depends on the functionality required by the application; some data may be temporally static, but it may be necessary to preserve a history of update errors. In other applications, only a record of how the data vary in the modelled reality may be required. The domain of the *model* attribute has a cardinality of three to accommodate these notions.

Temporal Attribute	Domain
model	{rollback, historic, temporal}
timestamp	{absolute, relative}
granularity	{second, day, month, ...}
interpolation	{stepwise, ...}

Table 0—1: Temporal Link Attribute Domains

The *timestamp* attribute reflects whether the application requires valid times to be stored as absolute time-stamps or if only the relative order of changes in the modelled reality is required. The *granularity* and *interpolation* attribute domains are not explicitly defined because these are extensible.

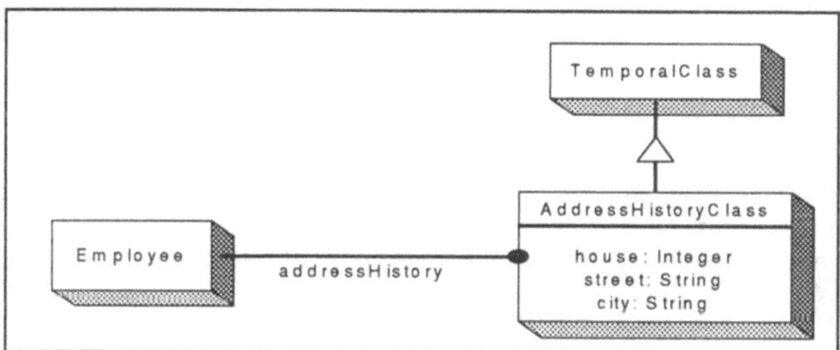

Figure 0—3: Temporal Class Modelling Using Inheritance

An alternative way to model temporal object schemata is to include the temporal class as a superclass, as shown in **Figure 0—3**. This solution is less satisfactory because it implies that an application must use class inheritance to confer temporal semantics. This may not be possible for some object schemata implemented in an object-oriented database that does not support multiple inheritance, and in some applications a compositional approach to creating complex objects might prove more effective.

5.   Conclusions and Future Research

Object-orientation offers great potential for the re-use of temporal semantics as object classes, as exemplified by the specialised data types designed to model time series data and calendars in the commercial object-relational database, Illustra [34]. However, without a consensus between class implementations, designers will still be forced to "reinvent" unnecessarily. The Temporal Database Principles examined in this paper provide a basis for the development and evaluation of re-usable object classes, but case studies are needed to identify the requirements of business applications.

The modelling technique described in this paper addresses the need for temporal modelling tools and techniques. Probably every *thing* in the Universe is subject to change over time, but not all objects in a database application need to reflect this fact. An application designer must decide which objects should adhere to the bitemporal model, and which objects are rollback, historical, and snapshot objects.

The representational and operative nature of temporal databases is well understood. An ontology is needed to provide a re-usable foundation of understanding and modelling business processes and facilities. For example, an employee's address has a temporal dimension, and it might be useful for a company to keep a record of all such home addresses. But when this information generally useful? Ontologies at this level help to identify temporal business semantics and facilitate the wide-scale re-use of lower level abstractions, such as temporal object classes.

References

1. Snodgrass, R.T., and Jensen, C.S. (1995). Temporal databases. *Twenty-first International Conference on Very Large Data Bases*, Tutorial Handout D.
2. Tsotras, V.J., and Kumar, A. (1996). Temporal database bibliography update. *ACM SIGMOD Record* 25(1).
3. McKenzie, E., and Snodgrass, R.T. (1991). Evaluation of relational algebras incorporating the time dimension in databases. *ACM Computing Surveys* 23(4):501-543.
4. Davies, C., and Lazell, B. (1995). How helpful is current theory for the representation of time in real databases? *Proc. 3rd European Conference on Information Systems*, Athens, Greece, pp.1207-1218.
5. Inmon, W.H. (1992). *Building the Data Warehouse*. John Wiley & Sons, Inc.
6. Hurson, A.R., Pakzad, S.H., Cheng, J.-B. (1993). Object-oriented database management systems: Evolution and Performance Issues. *IEEE Computer* 26(2):48-60.
7. Date, C.J. (1995). *An Introduction to Database Systems, Volume I*. Sixth Edition, Addison-Wesley Publishing Company.
8. Partridge, C. (1996). *Business Objects: Re-engineering for Re-use*. Butterworth-Heinemann, Oxford.
9. Pissinou, N., Snodgrass, R.T., Elmasri, R., Mumick, I.S., Özsu, M.T., Pernici, B., Segev, A., Theodoulis, B., and Dayal, U. (1994). Towards an infrastructure for temporal databases. *ACM SIGMOD Record* 23(1):35-51.
10. Jensen, C.S., Clifford, J., Gadia, S.K., Segev, A., and Snodgrass, R.T. (1992) A glossary of temporal database concepts. *ACM SIGMOD Record* 21(3):35-43.
11. Klopprogge, M.R. (1981). TERM: An approach to include the time dimension in the entity-relationship model. *Proc. 2nd International Conf. E-R Approach*, pp.473-508.

12. Rose, E., and Segev, A. (1991). TOODM - a temporal object-oriented data model with temporal constraints. *Proc. 10th International Conference on the Entity-Relationship Approach*, Texas, USA, pp.205-229.

13. Schleifer, P., Sun, Y., and Patel, D (1996). The implementation of a chronicle collection class in Smalltalk/DB. *Proc. 11tb Annual ACM Symposium on Applied Computing (Special Track on Database Technology)*, Philadelphia, PA. pp.209-216.

14. Pissinou, N., and Makki, K. (1993). Separating semantics from representation in a temporal object database domain. *Proc. 2nd International Conference on Information and Knowledge Management*, Washington, USA, pp.295-304.

15. Clifford, J., and Croker, A. (1987). The historical relational data model (HRDM) and algebra based on lifespans. *Proc. International Conference on Data Engineering*, Los Angeles, California., pp.528-537.

16. Gadia, S., (1988). A homogeneous relational model and query languages for temporal data. *ACM Transactions on Database Systems* 13(4):418-448.

17. Snodgrass, R.T., (1987). The temporal query language, TQuel. *ACM Transactions on Database Systems* 12(2):247-298.

18. Sarda, N.L. (1990). Extensions to SQL for historical databases. *IEEE Transactions on Knowledge and Data Engineering* 2(2):220-230.

19. Falkenberg, E.D., Oei, J.L.H., and Proper, H.A. (1992). A conceptual framework for evolving information systems. In *Dynamic Modelling of Information Systems II*. Sol, H.G., and Crosslin, R.L. (editors). Elsevier Science Publishers B.V.

20. Falkenberg, E.D., Oei, J.L.H., and Proper, H.A. (1993). Evolving information systems: Beyond temporal information systems. *Proc. 3rd International Conference on Database and Expert Systems Applications* 3:282-287.

21. Proper, H.A., and van der Weide, T.P. (1995). A general theory for evolving application models. *IEEE Transactions on Knowledge and Data Engineering* 7(6):984-996.

22. Andalay, J., Leonard, M., and Palisser, C. (1991). Management of schema evolution in databases. *Proc. 17th International Conference VLDB*, Barcelona, Spain, pp.161-170.

23. Banerjee, J., and Kim, W. (1987). Semantics and implementation of schema evolution in object-oriented databases. *Proc. ACM SIGMOD Conf.*, San Francisco, pp.311-322.

24. Lerner, B., and Habermann, A. (1990). Beyond schema evolution to database reorganisation. *ACM SIGPLAN Notices* 25(10):67-76.

25. Skarra, A.H., and Zdonik, S.B. (1986). The management of changing types in an object-oriented database. *ACM SIGPLAN Notices* 21(11):483-495.

26. Simon, H. (1972). The theory of problem solving. *Information Processing* 71:261-277.

27. Clifford, J., Croker, A., Grandi, F., and Tuzhilin, A. (1995). On temporal grouping. *Proc. International Workshop on Temporal Databases*, Zurich, , pp.194-213.

28. Gadia, S.K., Nair, S.S., and Poon, Y.-C. (1992). Incomplete information in relational temporal databases. *Proc. 18th Conference on Very Large Data Bases,* Vancouver, Canada, pp.395-406.

29. Jensen, C.S., Clifford, J., Elmasri, R., Gadia, S.K., Hayes, P., and Jajodia, S. [editors] (1994). A consensus glossary of temporal database concepts. *ACM SIGMOD Record* 23(1):52-64.

30. Kim, W. (1995). Introduction to part 1: Next-generation database technology. In *Modern Database Systems: The Object Model, Interoperability, and Beyond*, Kim, W. (editor), ACM Press, New York, pp.5-17.

31. Wuu, G.T.J, and Dayal, U. (1993). A uniform model for temporal and versioned object-oriented databases. In *Temporal Databases*. Tansel, A.U.T., *et al.* (editors), Benjamin/Cummings, pp.230-247.

32. Segev, A., and Shoshani, A. (1987). Logical modelling of temporal data. *Proc. ACM SIGMOD International Conf. on Management of Data*, San Francisco, pp.454-466.

33. Rumbaugh, J., Blaha, M., Premerlani, W., Eddy, F., and Lorensen, W. (1991). *Object-Oriented Modeling and Design*. Prentice-Hall.

34. Illustra (1994). *Illustra TimeSeries DataBlade*, technical information, Illustra Information Technologies, Inc.

MODELLING ISSUES III

Classifying Approaches to Object Oriented Analysis of Work with Activity Theory

Ole Smørdal
Department of Informatics, University of Oslo
e-mail: Ole.Smordal@ifi.uio.no

Abstract: There is a need to use object orientation to analyse work practices. This should be done based on a social theory on how computers mediate the work arrangement. This paper presents a conceptual framework based on activity theory in which two main schools of object oriented modelling are explained. Thus, several object oriented analysis approaches may be combined and contribute to more powerful representational forms.
Keywords: Collective work, Physical modelling, Role Modelling

1 Introduction

Various object oriented (OO) approaches have been used to analyse the real-world domain that the computer system is intended to maintain information about. Lately, object oriented approaches have also been used to capture aspects beyond this domain, and address the usage world, e.g., aspects relating to actors, communication, articulation of work, collective work, task flow, and work procedures (see e.g., Høydalsvik and Sindre 1993; Jacobson, et al. 1994; Bürkle, et al. 1995; Carstensen, et al. 1995; Krogh 1996). This is due to a shift of perspectives regarding the role of the computer in work settings; from a focus on the computer as means of control and administration of a real-world domain, to a focus that also include the computer as a mediator in the usage world, e.g., as in groupware or workflow applications.

Kaasbøll and Smørdal (1996) argue that this shift of perspectives has not been accompanied with extensions of the theoretical foundation for object oriented modelling. This is a problem for 'pure' object oriented approaches, because OO is a universal approach, and not particularly targeted toward analysis of the usage world. Therefore, many approaches combine OO with some other perspective, like a metaphor, a framework, or a theory that address work.

An important lesson from the Scandinavian systems development research tradition is that no single perspective is sufficient when relating to a complex situation. Rather, a multi perspective approach is necessary (see e.g. Nygaard 1986; Nygaard and Sørgaard 1987). Various OO methods and techniques address different aspects of work, hence a multi perspective approach seems easy to accomplish. However, selection and combination of the approaches may be difficult, due to differences in scope, concepts and inherent perspectives.

My contribution is thus not another technique or method, but a theoretical framework addressing object oriented analysis (OOA) of computers mediating collective activity. This framework is used to classify OOA approaches, in terms of what aspects of work they address. The framework is based on activity theory (Leontjev 1983; Engeström 1987; Fjuk, et al. forthcoming), and is here used as a bridging link between the social concerns and the technical concerns as it addresses human work in a social context and has a strong emphasis on how artefacts (like computer systems) mediate human activity.

The framework integrates activity theory and two schools of object oriented modelling, here denoted the physical modelling school and the role modelling school. Six selected object oriented approaches are explained using the framework, thus enabling comparing and contrasting the approaches.

The paper is structured as follows: The rest of the introduction presents the research approach for this work. Representations related to work arrangements are presented in Section 2. Section 3 presents an activity theoretical perspective on work. Section 4 presents the explanation of object oriented analysis in terms of activity theory. Six approaches to OOA are classified in terms of the framework in Section 5. Section 6 concludes the paper.

1.1 Research Approach

The method used in this work is presented and discussed by Kaasbøll and Smørdal (1996), who argues that object oriented modelling techniques should be developed according to knowledge about human work within organisations. In order to point to how to bring such knowledge into the process of developing techniques, a learning cycle consisting of practice, evaluation, theoretical contribution, and suggestion of improved techniques is outlined.

In order to develop the techniques such that they can model issues related to work, knowledge of work has to be included in the ways modelling problems are explained and new modelling mechanisms are suggested. Therefore, the theoretical scope of development of techniques should be widened from the focus on formal and implementation considerations to a system development research learning cycle that is open for any contribution to understanding the domain that is to be modelled. It is argued that the perspective on work is fundamental to the selection and development of theoretical foundations for modelling. (ibid.).

According to the learning cycle, the problems addressed in this paper are on a theoretical level. The work reported is a reflection upon problems a group of information systems researchers faced doing a needs assessment for a municipal agency in Norway dealing with town planning, building permits, and geodata (see Smørdal 1996 for details on this study).

2 Representations of Work

To be precise in the further discussion, I first define areas that can be modelled during system development, based on similar concepts in Mathiassen et al. (1993).

- The *problem domain* of a computer system is what the computer system is about; the part of the world that the computer system is supposed to handle, control or monitor. Examples (with basic components): a flight booking system (flights, seats, reservations, customers), a banking system (customers, transactions, accounts, loans, interests).

- The *application domain* of a computer system consists of the users, the organisational context, and the work in which the computer system is used, e.g., a travel agency, a bank. Elements of the application domain are employees, the coordination of work, communication, power structures, ad-hoc organised work, interruptions in work, etc.

- The *computer system* including its application program, data/object base, user interface module, and communication modules.

When analysing functionality requirements of a system, one could make a model of the application domain. Since it is assumed that the problem domain is more stable than the functional requirement, making an object-oriented model of the application domain is often not considered worthwhile.

A model of the future computer system will often be an extension of a model of the problem domain in order to include software modules and objects needed for implementation.

As mentioned in the introduction, a shift in the perspective in respect to the roles the computer systems may play in human work within organisations have been noticed. Earlier, a common view of the computer was that it was used for handling or controlling a problem domain, hence the models did not address elements in the application domain explicitly. Lately there has been an increasing attention in both system development practice and in the research community toward using the computer as a medium in the work organisation, thus enabling the use of computers as means of coordinating work and communication in and about work. (e.g. in the field of CSCW, see Simone and Schmidt 1993; Carstensen, et al. 1995). This implies that issues of the application domain need to be included in the models.

OO has an universal application, hence few clues on what aspects or phenomena that should be modelled are given. Therefore, many approaches combine OO with some other perspective, e.g.:

- A *metaphor*, like regarding workers as skilled craftsmen in a workshop. Models are then made of their tools and materials (Bürkle, et al. 1995).

- An *ortogonal modelling technique* that explains an object oriented model (e.g. Jacobson, et al. 1994).

- An *existing non OO framework*, seen in an object oriented perspective (e.g. Wang 1995).

- *Implications from a social theory*, (like articulation work (Strauss 1993)) (e.g. Carstensen, et al. 1995).

There is a potential problem when only one, or a few, perspectives are used when analysing a current work practice and how the computer systems mediate this practice. Due to differences in scope, concepts, and inherent perspectives combination of various OOA approaches may be difficult. The research question of this paper is therefore: How could some social theory on artefacts and work be used to classify OOA approaches, in terms of what aspects of work they address.

Generally, new approaches to modelling work are balancing between two pitfalls, on the one hand they contribute to more powerful representational forms in respect to work arrangements, but on the other hand they should recognise that abstraction and formalisation of work practices inevitably left something out of the representation. As Bannon (1995) claims:

> Models are thus seen [...] as interpretations, as constructions, which for some purposes, under certain conditions, used by certain people, in certain situations may be found useful, not true or false. (ibid, p. 67)

3   Computers Incorporated into Work Arrangements

This section presents a perspective on computers incorporated in work arrangements, based on activity theory, developed in Fjuk, et al. (forthcoming).

Activity theory originated as a psychological theory giving a notion of context to human actions in the world, in the sense that an activity orients a subject in an objective world. Central to this interaction is a motive, which is fulfilled by means of the activity and thus explains why an activity exists (Leontjev 1983).

The subject does not relate to the objective world directly, but through artefacts like concepts, heuristics, and tools. One of the claims of activity theory is that the nature of any artefact can be understood only within the context of human activity – by identifying the ways people use this artefact, the needs it serves, and the history of its development (Kaptelinin 1996).

An activity constitutes a hierarchical structure with inner dynamics, transformations and its own development. (Leontjev 1983). The driving force behind activity, action and operation is different, as can be seen in Figure 1:

Figure 1.The internal side of an activity, along with corresponding driving forces (ibid.).

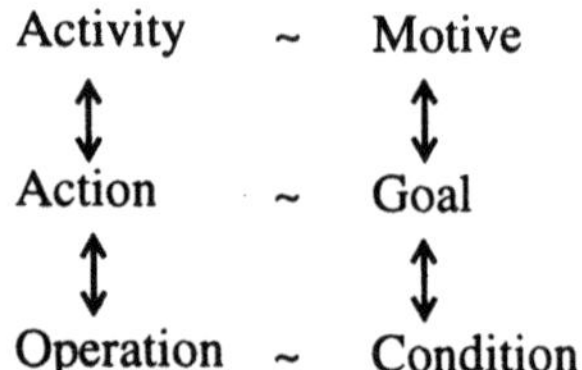

An activity is realised through goal-oriented processes, termed actions. An action can realise different activities as the given action may fulfil different motives. Before an action is performed, it is planned by a conscious subject. Actions are realised through operations, that face conditions in the objective world. Operations are typically initiated unconsciously—often even the collection of operations that accomplish the action is selected without explicit decision. The 'automatic' choice and routinesed performance are possible only for a knowledgeable and experienced subject. The development may be described in terms of habitualisation and institutionalisation (Berger and Luckmann 1966). But once acquired, this ability appears as a competence for situated action. Development of cognition is thus a process moving actions to operations, and operations into actions (e.g. instances of breakdowns). As the degree of routinisation increases, the action is moving towards operation.

Engeström (1987) presents an extension to Leontjev's model of activity, with three interacting entities (the individual, the object and the community) in order to analyse the social phenomenon of human activity. The objective of the model is to take the social context of human activity, by including rules of communication and division of labour. The model is illustrated in Figure 2. The upper triangle of the model illustrates Leontjev's basic interpretation of human activity. The two others represent the collective aspects of human activity.

Figure 2. The four aspects of collective activity

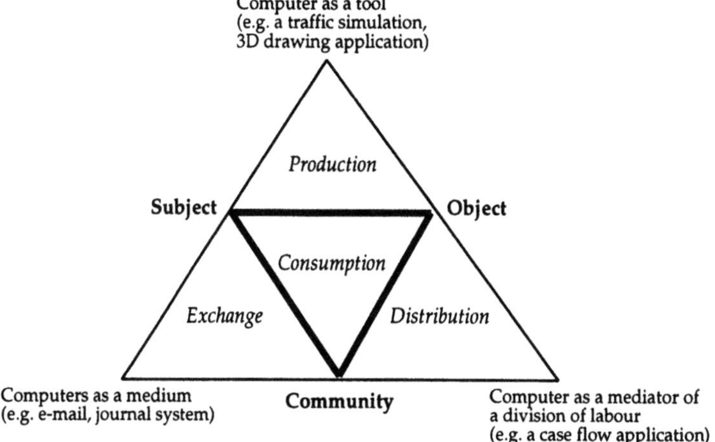

- *Production* denotes the relationship between subject (a human) and object. The relationship is mediated through (computer) tools.

- *Distribution* denotes the relationship between community (e.g. the workgroup or the employees in the organisation) and an object. This relation is mediated through the division of labour. The computer may be regarded a mediator of this division of labour, e.g. that coordination of work, or distribution of tasks, may be done by means of the computer.

- *Exchange* denotes the relationship between the a subject and the community. This relation is mediated through rules of social behaviour and communication. The computer may be regarded as a communication channel in this relation. E-mail and conferencing software are examples of this role in the work context.

- *Consumption* is covers the use of products and/or services of the activity. This implies an outside view on the activity, e.g. how customers or citizens use the services of an enterprise.

In the model, human activity is interpreted as a dynamic interrelation between the four aspects. The extended model of human activity shows that an individual is not isolated but is a part of a community, and the activity is affected by the individual's participation within this community.

4 Object Oriented Analysis of Work in an Activity Theoretical Perspective

4.1 Two Schools of OOA

Aristotle, in the classical Poetics, has a useful distinction between the *formal cause* and *material cause* of a thing. The formal cause of a thing is the form of shape of what it is trying to be. The material cause of a thing is what it is made of (Aristotle sited in Laurel 1993). (There are also two other causes, the end cause and the efficient cause, but they are not used here.) This distinction can be used to explain the difference between what in this paper is referred to as the *physical modelling* and the *role modelling* school of object oriented analysis. A similar distinction is made for object oriented programming by Madsen (1995), termed the modelling and the reuse school.

The Physical Modelling School
The modelling school (also known as the Scandinavian school) of object oriented programming is developed with real-world modelling in mind, were objects and classes in the models represent phenomena and concepts in the real world (Nygaard and Dahl 1981; Madsen, et al. 1993). Thus, the executing program is regarded a *physical model*, simulating the behaviour of the real world (Madsen and Møller-Pedersen 1988).

This idea, originated in a programming context, was later applied in many object oriented analysis approaches (e.g., Coad and Yourdon 1991; Mathiassen, et al. 1993). Due to the focus on modelling the real world, the approaches have poor support for representing how's, i.e. the collaboration among objects to do some job, or the organisation of objects in a large system.

The Role Modelling School
The reuse school of object oriented programming is developed with organisation of software systems in mind, were collaboration between objects and their responsibility in respect to the operations of the system are focused (see e.g. Goldberg and Robson 1983). Some object oriented analysis approaches are based on this view, and hence focus on collaboration and responsibilities of objects (Rubin and Goldberg 1992; Høydalsvik and Sindre 1993; Reenskaug, et al. 1996). Due to this focus, these approaches are suited for modeling aspects of the application domain, like the work organisation, but they are weak on conceptual modelling of the problem domain.

4.2 Mediating Action and the Aspects of Work

An activity orients a human in an objective world (c.f. Section 3). In a collective activity there are four aspects, each mediated by instruments like tools, media and the division of labour. These artefacts should be physically modeled, since they are phenomenta and concepts in the real world.

The realisation of production, by means of exchange and distribution is more focused toward the organisation of workers and their roles in respect to the work, and the communication needed to coordinate, inform and learn. Thus mediating this organisation by means of the computer, the communication and responsibilities of the objects must be represented. This is the material cause of the activity, and should be represented using role modelling.

Production

This aspect expresses the individual workers relation to their work. The computer mediates the problem domain, giving the worker clues on the structures and state of the object of work, thus enabling planning, selection of tools and procedures and giving context of the work in the total work arrangement. Thus, it is appropriate to make physical models that mediate the real world.

At the same time the worker is a part of a work organisation, and must interpret his/her responsibilities in relation to the collective activity. This interpretation results in individual actions that realises part of the activity. Role modelling is appropriate to represent the relationships between the worker as an actor, and the role (s)he has.

Distribution

The division of labour is necessary to organise and coordinate the different actions of the individual. Distribution is usually operationalised using a role concept, in the sense that the work is divided among roles, and that each role has some responsibility for a part of the whole job to be done. This perspective is also found in the role modelling school.

However, various artefacts mediate the distribution of labour, like organisations, projects, units, and groups. Also artefacts like schedules, plans, and routines may mediate this aspect. Hence also physical models have a role in this aspect.

Exchange

This aspect expresses communication among workers in order to get the job done. Representing the communication patterns is an important part of the role modelling school. Techniques like IDEF0 (IDEF0 1993) are used to capture the interaction among objects. In an object oriented context, the interaction consist of messages sent from one object that trigger some action in another object.

Also in this aspect we find artefacts that mediate the communication, like shared objects and communication channels. It is appropriate to make physical models of such artefacts.

Consumption

This aspect expresses the use of products or services made in production. Although the author have not identified any object oriented approaches that explicitly address consumption, it is believed that this area will become more important to model as customers use computers to access the outcome of production (e.g. through a www or edi interface). It seems appropriate to use physical modelling, because the computers should mediate the outcome of production to the customers, not the internal organisation of work.

5   Explaining Selected OO Approaches

This section uses the theoretical framework and the operationalisation that was developed in the previous sections, to explain some approaches that have been reported used to analyse the application world. General object oriented approaches with no reports on how work arrangements should be modelled are not included.

5.1 The Tools and Materials Approach

Bürkle et al. (1995) use general object oriented languages, but have applied a tools and materials metaphor as a pragmatic guideline for analysis and design of interactive systems to support office work. This metaphor is motivated by an intuitive conceptual division between objects into those that are worked on and those that are means of work. This view corresponds to the production aspect, with the tools and materials as mediators between the worker and the work. The approach belongs to the physical modelling school. This approach does not address work arrangements.

5.2 OOA (Aalborg)

This is a general object oriented analysis approach (Mathiassen, et al. 1993) in the physical modelling school, it is included here because Carstensen et al. (1995) and Krogh (1996) have used it to model cooperative work arrangements. The technique was useful for specifying the structural properties of coordination mechanisms as classes and objects. However, the dynamic properties of coordination mechanisms reflecting interaction between actors are not easily expressed (Carstensen, et al. 1995, p. 115). Krogh (1996) reports: "The strengths of the object oriented analysis approach lies in the structural powerful techniques, but the means for capturing dynamics are weak; mainly the support for modelling the application domains needs strengthening" (ibid. p. 337). These studies indicate that conceptual modelling alone is not sufficient when modelling work arrangements.

5.3 OO Task Analysis

Wang (1995) applies an object oriented perspective on task analysis, which is a non OO framework. The author distinguishes between computer tasks and human tasks. A task can be aggregated by subtasks. Detailed accounts of how a human uses a computer system can be made, and the approach is suitable for modelling production. Cooperation or responsibilities are not addressed.

5.4 Use-Cases

A use case (Jacobson, et al. 1994) is developed orthogonal to object models, as external views of the system. A use case defines a systems behaviour for a user for a given task. A use case model will not express concurrency, as use-case transactions are atomic and serialized (Jacobson 1995, p. 319). Thus it is difficult to express interdependency among workers in a use-case, which is necessary to address cooperation, but it is suitable for modelling one workers actions in order to realise part of the production.

5.5 Object Behaviour Analysis (OBA)

This approach (1992) emphasises what takes place in the system, called the system behaviours. Who initiates and who participates in these behaviours should be identified, and these objects are used as a basis for understanding the roles of different aspects of the system, and which parts of the system must take responsibility for providing services and managing system information (ibid, p. 48). This approach focuses on the work arrangement itself, and does not address physical modelling of some part of the application domain. Thus it supports representing the actions of exchange and distribution.

5.6   Object Oriented Role Analysis and Modelling (OORAM)

According to Reenskaug et al. (1996) objects can be thought of as clerks with in and out baskets, a private data file and book of rules. They cooperate through messages (ibid. p. 6). Høydalsvik and Sindre (1993) use OORAM to model organisational information systems. Focus is put on what roles people and phenomena in the application domain play in different contexts. Thus, OORAM supports representing exchange and distribution.

6   Conclusions and Future Research

A theoretical framework for object oriented analysis of work with computers, based on activity theory, is proposed.This paper suggests that a combination of two schools of OOA is necessary to address both the problem domain and the application domain. Physical modelling is suited for modelling how the computer mediates a work arrangement, in terms of tools, communication channels, shared materials etc. Role modelling is suited for modelling the responsibilities the workers have in respect to the work arrangement, this include the cooperation between workers in order to get the job done.

It is fair to conclude that none of the selected OOA approaches takes all the aspects of work into full account. However, there seem to be a rich potential for combining the best ideas of the various approaches.

Future work will explore the possibility to develop an OOA approach based on activity theory, that will explicitly combine physical modelling and role modelling.

Acknowledgements

Joan Greenbaum, Jens Kaasbøll and Leikny Øgrim joined me as members of the system development team doing the needs assessment that inspired this theoretical work. Kristen Nygaard, Haakon Bryhni, Dag Sjøberg, Birger Møller-Pedersen, Gisle Hannemyr, Else Nordhagen and Jan Erik Ressem gave useful comments to the ideas presented here.

References

Bannon LJ (1995) The Politics of Design: Representing Work. *Communications of the ACM* **38** (9), pp. 66-8.

Berger PL and Luckmann T (1966) *The Social Construction of Reality - A Treatise in the Sociology of Knowledge*. Penguin Books.

Bürkle U, Gryczan G and Züllighoven H (1995) Object-Oriented System Development in a Banking Project: Methodology, Experiences and Conclusions. *Human-Computer Interaction* **10** , pp. 293-336.

Carstensen PH, Krogh B and Sørensen C (1995) Object oriented Modelling of Coordination Mechanisms. In Dahlbom B, Kämmerer F, Ljungberg F, Stage J and Sørensen C (eds.)

Proceedings of The 18th Information Systems Research Seminar in Scandinavia (IRIS'18) (Gjern, Denmark), Gothenburg Studies in Informatics, Report 7.

Coad P and Yourdon E (1991) *Object Oriented Analysis.* Yourdon Press, NJ.

Engeström Y (1987) *Learning by Expanding. An Activity-theoretical approach to developmental research.* Orienta-Konsultit Oy, Helsinki.

Fjuk A, Smørdal O and Nurminen M (forthcoming) *Computer-Mediated Collective Action.*

Goldberg A and Robson D (1983) *Smalltalk-80, The language and its implementation.* Addison-Wesley, New York.

Høydalsvik GM and Sindre G (1993) Object-Oriented Role Modelling for the Analysis and Design of Organisational Information Systems. In *Proceedings of 26'th HICSS* , **3**, pp. 159-68.

IDEF0 (1993) *Software Standard Integration Definition for Function Modelling (IDEF0).* Federal Information Processing Standards Publication 183.

Jacobson I (1995) The use-case Construct in Object-Oriented Software Engineering. In Carroll JM (ed.) *Scenario-based design: envisioning work and technology in systems development.* Wiley, New York.

Jacobson I, Ericsson M and Jacobson A (1994) *The Object Advantage - Business process reengineering with object technology.* Addison-Wesley.

Kaptelinin V (1996) B Activity Theory: Implications for Human-Computer Interaction. In Nardi BA (ed.) *Context and Consciousness. Activity Theory and Human-Computer Interaction.* The MIT Press, Cambridge, pp. 103-16.

Krogh B (1996) Object Oriented Analysis of Groupware Applications. In Wrycza S and Zupancic J (eds.) *Proceedings of The Fifth International Conference Information SYstems Development - ISD'96* (Gda´nsk, Poland).

Kaasbøll JJ and Smørdal O (1996) Human Work as Context for Development of OO-Modeling Techniques. In Brinkkemper S (ed.) *IFIP WG 8.1/8.2 working conference on principles of method construction and tool support (Method Engineering' 96)* (Atlanta, USA), Chapman & Hall, pp. 111-25.

Laurel B (1993) *Computers as theatre.* Addison-Wesley Publishing Company, Reading, Mass.

Leontjev AN (1983) *Virksomhed, bevidsthed, personlighed (In Danish).* Forlaget Progress, Denmark.

Madsen OL (1995) Open Issues in Object-Oriented Programming. *Software Practice and Experience* **25** (S4).

Madsen OL and Møller-Pedersen B (1988) What Object-Oriented Programming may be — and what it does not have to be. In *European Conference of Object-Oriented programming (ECOOP'88)* (Oslo, Norway), pp. 1-20.

Madsen OL, Møller-Pedersen B and Nygaard K (1993) *Object Oriented Programming in the BETA Programming Language.* Addison Wesley.

Mathiassen L, Munk-Madsen A, Nielsen PA and Stage J (1993) *Objektorienteret analyse (in Danish).* Marko, Aalborg.

Nygaard K (1986) Program Development as a Social Activity. In Kugler H-J (ed.) *Information Processing 86* (Amsterdam), North-Holland, pp. 189-98.

Nygaard K and Dahl O-J (1981) The development of the SIMULA languages. In *History of Programming Languages.* Association for Computing Machinery, pp. 439-94.

Nygaard K and Sørgaard P (1987) The Perspective Concept in Informatics. In Bjerknes G, Ehn P and Kyng M (eds.) *Computers and Democracy: A Scandinavian Challenge.* Avebury Gower Publ. Comp. Ltd, Aldershot, pp. 371-93.

Reenskaug T, Wold P and Lehne OA (1996) *Working With Objects: the OOram Software Engineering Method.* Manning, Greenwich.

Rubin KS and Goldberg A (1992) Object Behavior Analysis. *Communications of the ACM* **35** (9), pp. 48-62.

Simone C and Schmidt K (1993) *Computational Mechanisms of Interaction for CSCW.* COMIC, Esprit Basic Research Project 6225, Lancaster University.

Smørdal O (1996) Soft Objects Analysis, A modelling approach for analysis of interdependent work practices. In Patel D and Sun Y (eds.) *3rd International Conference on Object-Oriented Information Systems (OOIS'96)* (London, UK), Springer-Verlag, pp. 195-208.

Strauss A (1993) *Continual Permutations of Actions.* Aldine de Gruyter, New York.

Wang S (1995) Object-oriented task analysis. *Information & Mangement* **29** , pp. 331-41.

Race Scheduling Controls for Object Systems

En-Hsin Huang and **Tzilla Elrad**

Department of Computer Science and Applied Mathematics
Illinois Institute of Technology, Chicago, USA
huanenh@charlie.acc.iit.edu, cselrad@minna.acc.iit.edu

1 Introduction

Concurrent object-oriented computing, a relatively new and rapid growing field, is the inevitable integration of object-oriented programming and concurrent computing technology. *Concurrent Object-Oriented Programming* is a programming methodology in which the system to be constructed is modeled as a collection of concurrently executable objects interacting by means of message passing. It is a powerful design methodology for modeling and implementing complex, concurrent systems [2,16,17,22]. Concurrency usually introduces non-deterministic behavior to concurrent computation within object systems. A synchronization mechanism is often required to ensure the proper coordination of communicating software components and to determine what operations can be done at a given time. It permits the specification of conditions by which all the concerned parties can perform their designated tasks in a synchronized fashion.

One critical issue arises when a host entity is presented with multiple requests competing for selection [8,18,22]. For instance, a database server must be properly equipped to process various real-time transactions originating from terminals situated distantly apart. An intelligent host entity must be equipped to resolve request conflicts and facilitate concurrent access to the shared resources within certain acceptable time period. An adaptive scheduling mechanism, when properly integrated to the host, can make such an object more responsive to changes/demands in a robust environment. It can also aid objects in managing stimuli and feedback for supporting reflective computation that requires a flexible means for controlling the course of computation, resource allocation and scheduling [9,17,21]. An adaptive request scheduling mechanism is crucial to the successful implementation of object-oriented software that supports real-time applications (e.g., manufacturing, robotics, control, transportation, aerospace and military systems). In many cases, these systems must be designed to monitor and control complex systems in dynamic, sometimes hazardous, settings. These applications must be reactive enough in processing input signals, even when facing lack of information and uncertainty in the operating environment.

Over the years, extensive studies [1,4,10,11,12,14,16,19] have been done in the area of providing linguistics supports for system designers/implementers to specify synchronization requirements for concurrent object-oriented system. Issue such as the difficulty in achieving reuse of synchronization constraint also has been extensively scrutinized [12,15,19,21]. Yet only a few works [7,9,18] consider the importance of endowing software implementers with the capability to formulate and fine-tune strategies for managing client request race. This paper will focus more on race management issue that is critical to the successful development of today's complex and intelligent object systems.

In Section 2, we present a classification scheme i) for identifying two major classes of message race conflicts that might occur within a server object; and ii) for examining the dynamics of the concurrency aspects of object systems as well as the existing concurrent object-oriented languages/systems. Section 3 presents an architectural design for modeling complex object entities. It serves as a framework for understanding how concurrency controls are to be integrated to object-oriented language and how message race is to be properly handled by reactive/adaptive object systems. Section 4 illustrates how to formulate and employ adaptive/reactive scheduling strategies for managing inter- and intra-method race conflicts. Section 5 illustrates how to support programming by extension through the incremental introduction of race management capability to newly defined objects. It also considers how to reuse existing scheduling controls in implementing object systems. Section 6 compares our proposed approaches to some related works regarding how explicit race control mechanisms are to be effectively introduced to object languages/systems.

2 Message Race

Message race occurs when multiple conflicting requests are competing to be scheduled within a server entity. These requests may be competing for different services (open method alternatives race to be selected) or the same service (method entry calls race to be accepted). We refer to the above scenarios as *inter-method race* and the *intra-method race*. Language capabilities to govern these conflicts and to impose a definite choice are termed *Race Controls* [8]. *Race Controls* are scheduling controls intended for resolving the message race problem and are further categorized as *Preference Control* and *Forerunner Control* respectively. These scheduling controls serve to prioritize the choices of request selection. Language supports for *Race Controls* are crucial to real-time and adaptive systems, as they heavily rely on the enforcement of specific response patterns. This classification scheme provides a framework for understanding the dynamics of the concurrency aspects of concurrent object systems.

2.1 Inter-Method Race Scheduling Mechanism

The *inter-method* race scheduling mechanism is concerned with resolving conflicts among executable method entries inside an object. Because requests may arrive for possibly different services, an intelligent scheduling scheme must determine the best choice to meet system requirements (e.g., mission statements). *Preference Control* can serve to formulate a scheduling policy that supports description of indeterminate object behaviors, and provides a preferential ordering to method entry alternatives. Three options are currently available to a language designer: 1) *Random Selection* scheme. All method alternatives are treated with equal preference and message race is resolved arbitrarily. It simplifies the scheduling job, but fails to express the relative preference relationships among alternatives. One extreme case is to permit complete freedom of choice by not controlling what is to be done next among the qualified alternatives. 2) *Context-Oriented* scheme. The relative preference relationships are described in terms of the textual layout of method alternatives in the program context. The one that is located closer to the top of a *select* statement or similar construct receives higher preference. This approach makes objects non-responsive, and requires extensive modifications whenever the overall preference relationships change. Languages adopting such a scheduling scheme include Eiffel // [4] and POOL-I [1]. 3) *Preference Specific* scheme. It offers explicit language constructs for expressing relative preference relationships among execution paths. It provides expressive power to programmers for the better control of non-determinism, and contributes to the responsiveness of the resulting software.

A *non-adaptive preference specific* scheme resolves all preference issues at compile-time. This approach is relatively easy to implement, but cannot reflect the volatile environment where priorities may vary with time. In Ada 83[5], the *count* attribute when used with a low-level system queue, though unsatisfactorily, can simulate the *non-adaptive Preference Control*. On the other hand, the *adaptive preference specific* scheme allows preferences to be updated and modified at run-time. [7,18] attempt to provide some extended language constructs for concurrent language Ada to support such a scheduling scheme. However, these solutions are limited to concurrent programming and are not fully compatible with object-oriented computing.

2.2 Intra-Method Race Scheduling Mechanism

The *intra-method* race scheduling mechanism is concerned with requests racing for the same object service. It aims to manage request selection over the waiting calls in an entry queue. *Forerunner Control* can serve to formulate a scheduling policy that deals with the method-entry level race.

There are three scheduling schemes commonly adopted by language designers: 1) *Arbitrary Selection* scheme. The underlying run-time system provides the default scheduling mechanism for managing *intra-method* race. Programmers are not in control of how requests are to be processed. This approach makes the object-oriented software unpredictable. 2) *Order Preserving* scheme. Client requests are selected based on the order of message arrival. The resulting scheduling mechanism is often hidden underneath the language semantics, and thus cannot support user-defined selection requirements. Ada 83 adopts such an implicit scheme, which is over simplified and fails to handle situations where calls must be aborted or be given immediate attention. 3) *Criteria Specific* scheme. The message selection condition is stated in terms of the message contents, possibly also including information passed from client objects. This method permits formulation of a more responsive and intelligent scheduling mechanism. The simulated support can be found in the *answer* statement of Eiffel // [4] and the *requeue* construct of Ada 95 [6]. Concurrent programming languages such as Concurrent C/C++ and SR allow user-defined specification of selection criteria for searching a queue of pending requests. Nevertheless, these approaches fail to promote the formulation of reusable *Forerunner Control* scheduling policy.

2.3 Explicit and Implicit Scheduling Controls

Race Controls can be implicitly or explicitly integrated into a programming language. Under the implicit scheme, race controls are often embedded in the language semantics. The underlying system automatically assumes sole responsibility in managing message race. Programmers have no control over a server object in specifying how client requests are to be received and processed. This approach requires no explicit programming of control threads [4,8,9]. It fails to resolve the situation wherein a low-priority task can interrupt a high-priority task. It also provides fewer options in dealing with the non-determinant behaviors of concurrent object entities.

On the other hand, the explicit approach enables users to specify how client requests are to be handled at the target site. It permits the explicit programming of control threads, and supports the implementation of a more efficient message reception mechanism. Programmers can thus fine-tune the existing scheduling policies, and assume full control over behavior of objects [1,3,7]. An explicit scheme increases the flexibility of the applications and makes the reuse of the existing system features feasible. A properly abstracted explicit control can aid in formulating solutions that effectively promote programming by extension and reusability. Some languages, such as Eiffel //[4], POOL[1], Ada[5,6] and Concurrent C/C++[10,11], adopt a mixed approach to manage message conflicts. For example, Concurrent C/C++ employs explicit control for intra-method race and implicit control for inter-method race. This can lead to serious consistency issues as noted in [8,9].

3 Architectural Design for Adaptive Concurrent Objects

A well-defined concurrent object must provide encapsulation support for shared resources and, at the same time, offer a consistent public interface to its clients. In this way, object interaction will be restricted to making and receiving message calls. All the internal operations, local resources and state information of an object must be properly encapsulated. In our study, an adaptive concurrent object is modeled as an event-driven encapsulating entity which schedules requests and maintains the integrity of the shared resources. It processes events (request messages) according to pre-defined scheduling policies and manages the appropriate state transitions.

We present an architectural design for concurrent object-oriented entities with the following objectives: 1) to prevent the exposure of private data and implementation details; 2) to ensure state-consistency of an object; 3) to facilitate building of modular software; and 4) to promote reuse and extension of the existing scheduling controls. In our model, a concurrent object entity is composed of six components (See Fig. 1). The *public-event interface* component constitutes the interface to the outside world and forms a protective fence for the object. The *encapsulated resource* component includes both *instance attributes* for denoting shared data and *state attributes* for modeling object states. The *internal activities* component covers *local operations, state evaluators* (for synchronization purposes) and *state transformers* (for managing object state). The *class housekeeping* component provides a means for supporting the initialization and finalization of the encapsulated data and object state. The *policy depository* component contains request scheduling policies (e.g., preference controls and forerunner controls).

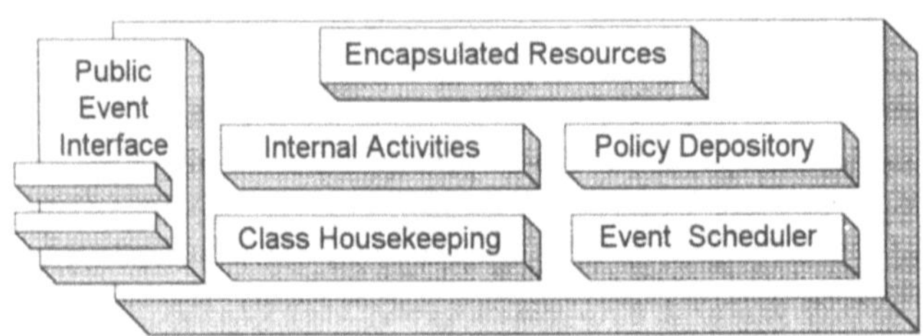

Figure 1. The Proposed Architectural Design for Concurrent Objects

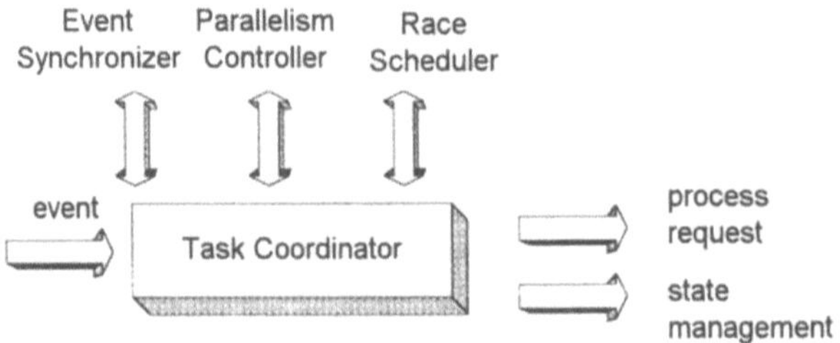

Figure 2. The Event Scheduler for Managing Client Requests

The *event scheduler* component takes control over how client requests are to be received and processed. It consists of four functional sub-components interacting for managing object-wise synchronization and scheduling of requests (See Fig. 2). The *task coordinator* is the center piece of the *event scheduler*. It acts as a resource manager controlling concurrent access to the encapsulated shared resources. At the same time, it also serves to enforce the user-defined synchronization scheme and to resolve possible scheduling conflicts. By default, messages are accepted unconditionally and executed in mutual exclusion. Calls to the same method are processed in First-In-First-Out (FIFO) order. When a more efficient and intelligent scheduling capability is required, the *task coordinator* will communicate with other functional components. The *event synchronizer* is first called upon to manage conditional acceptance of client messages based on some pre-determined synchronization requirements. Next, the *parallelism controller* interacts with the *task coordinator* in deciding which open methods can proceed in parallel. The *race scheduler* will then resolve possible *inter-* and *intra-method* race conflicts. Finally, the *task coordinator* schedules the selected method(s) for execution and triggers some post-action codes (if any) for reflecting changes in object state.

In a concurrent environment, it is highly possible to have the occurrence of either or both forms of request race. The *race scheduler* must resolve race issues as follows: 1) Only *inter-method* race occurs: race is resolved based on the arrival order of calls or on the relative preference relationship specified by the pre-defined *preference policy*, if there is one. 2) Only *intra-method* race occurs: race is resolved according to the arrival sequence of pending calls or the criteria specified in the pre-defined *forerunner policy*, if there is one. 3) Both *inter-* and *intra-method* race occur: *inter-method* race is handled first, then the *intra-method* race by following directions stated in rules 1 and 2.

3.1 Adaptive Class Mechanism

We present a class construct with a collection of concurrency constructs for defining concurrent objects. This set of constructs aims to enforce the encapsulation principle and provides protection for shared resources. It also supports the devising of adaptive and dynamic scheduling mechanisms for managing *inter-* and *intra-method* race conflicts. Besides code reuse, these constructs permit formulation of reusable race scheduling controls. A concurrent class definition consists of a specification part and an implementation body. Class inheritance is adopted as the inheritance mechanism for defining classes in terms of the existing classes with some localized modification or extensions. The keyword *CLASS* states a new class name with the optional parent class name. By adopting the terminology introduced in C++, we use the term *base class* to denote the class that is inherited and the term *derived class* to denote the inheriting class.

By default, all operations are executed in mutual exclusion. An operation is executed only if its associated synchronization conditions and the associated race control policies (if any) are satisfied. The *constructor section* and the *destructor section* permit the formulation of object initialization and finalization routine respectively. The *event-public section* states the public interface of an object. The *instance section* allows declaration of instance attributes and local methods in the same manner as variables and member functions in C++ [20]. The *state section* covers the declaration of *state attribute*, *state evaluator* and *state transformer*. *State attributes* are used in expressing state predicates (e.g., Boolean expressions) for representing and validating object status. A *state evaluator* encapsulates its assigned state predicates and is invoked for obtaining synchronization and for state validation purposes. A *state transformer* implements operations related to state transition and is often included as part of post-action codes. Both *state evaluator* and *state transformer* methods are specified with the equivalent syntax as C++ member functions except that no return type is needed.

As an example, the class *buffer* encapsulates a set of shared data denoted by the instance attribute *buf* of type character (See Fig. 3). The three state attributes *in*, *out* and *max* are employed in composing state predicates and expressing state related information. The state evaluators *Empty* and *Full* serve to validate current object state by evaluating their respective encapsulated state predicates. In the *task-coordinator section*, users can associate the selected synchronization scheme, forerunner control and state transition mechanism with each member method (e.g., as done with methods *put* and *get* in Fig. 3). The *when* clause is employed for the purpose of describing how the object-wise synchronization can be achieved (e.g., in terms of logical operator and *state evaluator* calls). For instance, the synchronization conditions for method *put* and *get* are stated as *not(Full( ))* and *not(Empty( ))* respectively. The optional construct *post-action* will trigger state transition at the end of code execution of the associated method (e.g., invoking the respective *state transformer* method). For example, after code execution of method *get*, the state transformer *updateMark* is invoked to update the status of the buffer object represented by state attributes *in* and *out*.

This study will focus more on providing message race scheduling capabilities, not object-wise synchronization mechanisms, to adaptive objects. In the following sections, we will discuss how the other components (e.g., *policy section* and *preference control section*) can be employed to formulate adaptive and extensible scheduling strategies.

4 Formulating Message Race Scheduling Strategies

4.1 Intra-Method Race Conflict

Passed arguments (e.g., message content) from client objects can be used to arbitrate the order by which requests are to be admitted for service. This capability is specially helpful in devising the *intra-method* scheduling policy for sorting and selecting requests from the message waiting queue. The *Forerunner Control* enables the specification of selection criteria that include input arguments. It thus allows prioritization of calls by performing a screening process based on the client information. In the *forerunner policy section*, programmers can specify the *intra-method* race scheduling policy.

As an example, we can program a disk server object to process requests according to some ordering of disk track numbers (e.g., serving the one nearest to the current position of the disk head). The object *nearestFirst* gives higher priority to I/O requests that are located closest to current position of the disk head (See Fig. 4). The *governed-by* clause specifies which forerunner control strategy is to be employed for selecting pending requests. The forerunner policy *queueSelection(long blkNo)* incorporates values of the parameter variable *blkNo* (bound at run-time) and, thus supports a dynamic scheduling scheme. This feature permits a server entity to take into account both user's requirements (e.g., level of urgency) and current system information (e.g., the overall performance) before reaching any decision. It permits the formulation of a more responsive and intelligent scheduling mechanism.

4.2 Inter-Method Race Conflict

A *non-reactive/non-adaptive* scheduling mechanism tends to resolve race issues at compile time. It provides no support for the concurrent components of objects to interact meaningfully with their environment. Approaches for resolving *inter-method race*, such as the *context-oriented* scheme and the *non-adaptive preference specific* scheme, impose severe restrictions on how an object manages the relative preference relationships among the executable methods. One major drawback is the inability of the software to interact timely with the outside world during execution. It also fails to reflect the operating environment where priorities may vary with time. The *reactive/adaptive* scheduling mechanism provides a better alternative by considering external factors in managing requests.

For managing *inter-method* race, the adaptive version of the *preference specific* scheduling scheme permits modification of preference values of method entry alternatives during program execution. The three functional components (the *class constructor*, *preference control* section, and *preference policy*) interact cooperatively to form the nucleus of an *inter-method* race scheduling mechanism which may be *adaptive* or *non-adaptive*. In the *preference policy* section, users can formulate the *inter-method* race scheduling policy. A preference policy always returns a discrete value denoting the preference level of its associated member method. The *preference control section* allows the specification of the relative preference relationships among object member methods. Users (with the keyword *prefer* and the clause *of_level*) can explicitly associate preference policies (defined in the *policy section*) with the appropriate member methods. The role of *state attributes*, besides representing object state, also denotes the relative preference ordering of public member methods. For the *non-adaptive* scheduling scheme, the class *constructor* method serves to initialize state attributes for representing the relative preference relationships among alternatives. These variables are bound automatically, specified by users, upon object creation. A *preference variable* can be associated with more than one member method. Once the value is assigned, no further changes are allowed.

In an *adaptive* scheduling scheme, preference variables can be modified at run-time to reflect changes of system/mission priority. This feature makes concurrent software components more configurable in terms of their ability to respond intelligently to feedback. For instance, the *Food Sever* object takes turns in serving requests for the preparation of sandwich and soup (See Fig. 5). The initial set-up (after executing class constructor method) ensures that calls for service *prepare_sandwich* are given higher priority. After processing a request for sandwich, the server will prioritize requests for service *cook_soup*. The *prefer-of_level* construct permits association of member methods and their respective preference policies. To reflect changes in the relative preference relationships, the *state transformer* method *updatTurn* is invoked after the execution of a method body. Precaution must be taken to ensure that the reordering of preference relationships will not lead to the starvation of other pending requests. Note that it is permissible to have member methods share the same preference level; all the executable methods are scheduled in the FIFO (First-In-First-Out) order.

5 Formulating Reusable Scheduling Controls

One major benefit of applying object-oriented programming in designing complex systems is the ability to achieve reuse of method codes. This enables programmers to save time and minimize errors in constructing new software. We advocate the further expansion of the notion *code reuse*, not only limited to the reuse of a method body, but to include reuse of race scheduling management functionality (e.g., forerunner control and preference control). The concept of formulating object functional components as reusable and stackable modules, and using them as basic building blocks, can be applied to the construction of *intra-method* race scheduling in the newly derived subclass. All previously formulated race policies, inherited from the upward reachable path of the newly defined subclass, are implicitly available to programmers. In addition, new scheduling controls can be introduced locally as part of the new policy.

As an example, the class *prefBuffer2* (See Fig. 6), derived from class *prefBuffer*, introduces a new preference policy *getPrefLevelHigh* to be associated with the inherited method *get*. This policy allows all *get* requests to proceed when the current buffer is at least one fourth full. The locally defined method *get2*, designed to remove two consecutive elements from the buffer, is associated with the inherited policy *getPrefLevelNormal*. This example demonstrates how the previously designed plug-compatible components (e.g., preference control policies) can be reused by new classes in formulating more appropriate local scheduling schemes. Note that no part of the implementation codes from the inherited methods (e.g., get and put) is ever modified.

The same reuse principle can be applied to the formulation of forerunner control strategy. The object *elevatorDisk* processes I/O requests based on the elevator scheduling algorithm for minimizing changes in the disk head movement (See Fig. 7). Before the occurrence of changes in the disk head direction, client requests in the current direction will be served first. The class *priorityElevatorDisk* is a specialized version of the base class *elevatorDisk*. Both classes differ in how I/O requests are received and scheduled. The inherited forerunner policy, *elevatorPolicy*, employs the elevator scheduling algorithm for serving disk requests. The new stackable forerunner policy, *priorityQueue*, assumes a priority-based scheduling. These two policies are combined to enable the new disk server to process requests more responsively. Note that state transition component for method *request* is implicitly inherited from its parent class and is thus left unspecified here.

6 Comparison with Other Related Works

Elrad and Maymir-Ducharme [7] was the first to attempt to introduce the adaptive scheduling capability to Ada 83 tasks [5]. Olsson and McNamee [18] presents an alternate solution by incorporating the dynamic scheduling facility to the concurrent language Ada 83. Both approaches only address scheduling conflicts that occur when clients make entry calls for different services at the server site. These solutions adopt the similar concurrent programming model in which concurrently executable entities are represented as Ada tasks communicating through the *rendezvous* form of interaction. Under this concurrency model, a process body (such as the Ada task body) usually serves as the central depository for implementing extended linguistic supports for resolving *inter-method race* conflicts. The tight coupling of race resolution codes and program codes often leads to difficulty in obtaining code reuse. The same problem is manifested in object-oriented languages like uC++[3], Eiffel // [4] and POOL[1]. These implementations adopt the similar tasking concurrency model where message preference is based on textual ordering of entry alternatives in the program context. These languages impose rigid rules on how inter-method race can be resolved and thus are not suitable for real-time applications. In addition, the control flow codes are explicitly stated within the object bodies, and making it difficult to reuse and extend the existing scheduling strategies.

Actor model-based language/system such as the Enabled-Set mechanism [21] and ABCL/1[23] provide only limited support for formulating static preference scheduling strategies. The exiting facility does not permit expression of equal preference levels among alternatives. In this case, once the overall relative preference relations for method entries are determined at compile time (decided based on textual appearance of method entry names), such relations cannot be changed further.

All the above approaches provide no explicit language support for handling intra-method level message race. The scheduling strategy is implicitly embedded within the language semantics. In most case, client requests racing to be scheduled for the same service are processed based on their order of arrival. This type of scheduling policy ensures fairness by guaranteeing that all eligible requests will not be postponed indefinitely. However, it imposes deterministic selection strategy and limits its usefulness for adaptive object systems.

Our approach addresses the issue of supporting adaptive and reusable scheduling controls (inter- and intra-method race controls) for concurrent objects from object-oriented programming perspectives. We provide language constructs (handlers) for the explicit specification and manipulation of message race decision making strategies. Users can formulate appropriate scheduling strategies to address message race at the respective level of concern (as discussed in Section 2). This increases the control programmers have over the responses and behaviors of concurrent adaptive objects. All scheduling controls and strategies are visible to programmers, and nothing is hidden within the language semantics. In addition, by associating the handlers with various programmer-specified race control strategies, users can fine-tune the scheduling strategy until an acceptable system response is attained. In order to promote the principle on separation of concerns, the proposed architectural design permits the specification of system functionality and scheduling policies as separate building blocks. It aims not just to provide a means for textual reuse, but also to allow users to design modular and extensible software components that can be integrated into a large-scale system.

To ensure that a user-specified race management scheme will not suffer from the problems with reuse and extension, we have race scheduling mechanisms (policies) isolated from any control flow (e.g., within a body) with respect to decision making. All race control strategies are confined in the separate specification part which in turns permitting association of various software functional sub-components and their respective synchronization and race control strategies. It thus supports declarative programming of race controls at inter-method and intra-method level.

7 Conclusions

This work examines some of the essential issues related to the design of today's complex object systems. These systems (e.g., soft-real time and adaptive systems) requires request scheduling mechanisms that are intelligent, responsive and dynamic as to obtain a more responsive and timely interaction with their surrounding environments. We present a framework for addressing issues specifically related to the occurrence of message race within concurrent object entities. It also covers an architectural design required for managing these scheduling conflicts. We further present the proposed object design and scheduling control constructs for illustrating how to achieve proper integration of these race controls and object-oriented features,. This approach differs from most previous attempts in 1) enforcing the notions of separation of concerns: race scheduling specification can be stated in a declarative manner and isolated from its implementation codes; 2) promoting the reuse and extension of existing scheduling strategies in designing new software system; and 3) the localization of scheduling policies as modular and reusable encapsulated entities.

To promote software reuse, our architectural design permits the specification of system functionality and scheduling policies as separate building blocks. The ability to formulate reusable scheduling policies can further promote code reuse in designing new object systems and can also facilitate the systematic and incremental development of object-oriented systems. It aims not just to provide a means for textual reuse, but also to allow users to design modular and extensible software components that can be integrated into large-scale systems. The proposed concurrency constructs serve to illustrate how to formulate scheduling policies that are both adaptive and reusable. We demonstrate how to effectively formulate scheduling policies that are intelligent in responding to feedback from the operating environment. This work also illustrates how to promote the structured reuse of scheduling controls in supporting programming by extension.

Currently, a graphic based concurrent object-oriented software environment has been implemented to enable software designers/implementers to employ the proposed framework in developing adaptive object systems. Programs written with the proposed race scheduling controls may execute in the DPC-Capsule (operating in a shared memory multiple-processor environment).

```
CLASS buffer {
    Instance:                    char *buf;        /* shared data */
    State:                       int in, out, max;   /* state attributes */
        Evaluator:               Full( )  {return (in+1)%max == out;};
                                 Empty( )      {return in == out;};
        Transformer:             updateMark(int *ptr) {*ptr = (*ptr+1) % max;};
    Constructor:            buffer(int size) {max = size;  buf = new char[max]; in = out = 0;};
    Task-Coordinator:
                when not(Full( )) => accept put(char c) post-action: updateMark(&in);
                when not(Empty( )) => accept get(void) post-action: updateMark(&out);
    Event-Public           /* public member method declarations */
                void put(char c);   char get(void);                         }
}
```

Figure 3. Class Specification for Object *Buffer*

```
CLASS nearestFirst {
Instance:       int ABS(int pos) {if pos >= 0  return pos,; else return -pos;};
                int CYL(int pos) {return pos/(19*32);};
State:          int curPos;
    Transformer: /* state transition */
    updatePos(long blkNo) {if (CYL(blkNo) == Max) curPos = 0; else curPos =CYL(blkNo);};
Policy:
    Forerunner:  /* determine how requests  for the same service are to be scheduled */
                queueSelection(long blkNo) {return ABS( curPos - CYL(blkNo));};
Task-Coordinator:
                accept request(opCode op, long blkNo, char *buf)
                        governed-by: queueSelection(blkNo) post-action: updatePos(blkNo);
Event-Public
                        void request(opCode op, long blkNo, char *buf);            }
```

Figure 4. Disk Scheduler Object with Intra-Method Race Management Strategy

```
CLASS  Food_Server {
State:          int  soupPref, sandwichPref;  /* preference variables */
                Transformer:  /* update preference variables */
                    updateTurn(int soupTurn, int sandwichTurn) {
                        soupPref = soupTurn; sandwichPref = sandwichTurn;};
Constructor:        Food_Server(void) { soupPref = 0; sandwichPref = 1;};
Policy:         Preference: /* return the values of preference variables */
                    sandwichPrefLevel(void) {return sandwichPref;};
                    soupPrefLevel(void) {return soupPref;};
Preference Control:
                prefer  prepare_sandwich(void) of_level: sandwichPrefLevel(void);
                prefer  cook_soup(void) of_level: soupPrefLevel(void);
Task-Coordinator:   /* specify new preference relations in post-action section */
                accept  prepare_sandwich(void) post-action: updateTurn(1, 0);
                accept  cook_soup(void) post-action: updateTurn (0,1);
Event-Public:
                void  prepare_sandwich(void);  void  cook_soup(void);            }
```

Figure 5. A Server Processing Requests without Causing Clients to Wait Indefinitely.

```
CLASS  prefBuffer2 : prefBuffer { /* prefBuffer (inherited from buffer) -- when the buffer is more
than half full, calls for get is given higher preference. Otherwise, calls for put are prioritized */
State:
                Evaluator:  moreThanTwoElementsLeft(void) {return ABS(in - out) >= 2;};
Policy:     Preference:  /* new plug-compatible preference policy */
                getPrefLevelHigh(void) {int count; count = ABS(in - out);
                    if count >= max/4 { /* at least 1/4 full */
                    ... /* compute the new relative preference relations */}; return getPref;};
Preference Control:   /* prefers objects returning the highest value */
                prefer get(void) of_level: getPrefLevelHigh(void);
                prefer get2(void) of_level: getPrefLevelNormal(void);
Task-Coordinator:
                when not(full(void)) and moreThanTwoElementsLeft(void)
                => accept get2(void) post-action: {updateMark(out); updateMark(out);};
Event-Public:
                char get2(void);                      }
```

Figure 6. Designing New Object Entity with the Reusable Preference Control Policies

```
CLASS  elevatorDisk : nearest First {
State:   int dir;     /* denoting current disk head direction */
         Transformer:
                       updateHeadDir(long blkNo) {
                             if (CYL(blkNo) != curPos) dir = CYL(blkNo) > curPos;};
Policy:  Forerunner:
                       elevatorPolicy(long blkNo) { long cylNo;  maxCyl = 1000;
                          cylNo = CYL(blkNo);
                          if (dir == 1) {
                            return (cylNo >= curPos ? cylNo : maxCyl +curPos- cylNo);
                            else return (cylNo <= curPos ? - cylNo : cylNo);};
Task-Coordinator:
                       accept request(opCode op, long blkNo, char *buf)
                          governed-by: elevatorPolicy(blkNo)
                          post-action: {updateHeadDir(blkNo); updatePos(blkNo);};   }


CLASS   priorityElevatorDisk : elevatorDisk {
/* inheriting  all attributes, forerunner policy and state management handlers */
Policy:
      Forerunner:  /* newly defined forerunner policy */
                       priorityQueue(long blkNo) {
                       /* giving higher priority to requests that lie in the current disk head
                             direction and the requested cylinder belongs to the first 100 cylinders,
                             giving higher priority to objects returning the lowest value */};
Task-Coordinator:
                       accept request(opCode op, long blkNo, char *buf)
                          governed-by: elevatorPolicy(blkNo) and priorityQueue(blkNo);   }
```

Figure 7. Designing New Object Entity with the Reusable Forerunner Control Policies

References

[1]   America, P., and Linden, F., "A Parallel Object-Oriented Language with Inheritance and Subtyping," *ECOOP/OOPSLA '90 Proceedings*, pp. 161-168, 1990.

[2]   Booch, G., *Object-Oriented Design with Applications*, Addison-Wesley Publishing Company, MA, 1989.

[3]   Buhr, P. A., Dichfield, G., Stroobosscher, R.A., and Younger, B.M., "uC++: Concurrency in the Object-Oriented Language C++," *Software-Practice and Experience*, Vol. 22, No. 2, pp. 137-172, 1992.

[4]   Caromel, D., "Toward a Method of Object-Oriented Concurrent Programming," *Communications of the ACM*, Vol. 36, No. 9, pp. 90-102, 1993.

[5]   DoD 83., *Reference Manual for the Ada Programming Language*, Silicon Press, ANSI Standard Ada, 1983.

[6]   DoD 95. ,*Ada 95 Reference Manual*, ANSI/IS/IEC-8652:1995, U.S. Government, 1995.

[7]   Elrad, T., and Maymir-Ducharme, F., "Distributed Language Design: Constructs for Controlling Preferences," *Proceedings of the 1986 International Conference on Parallel Processing*, Illinois, 1986.

[8]   Elrad, T., "Comprehensive Race Controls: A Versatile Scheduling Mechanism for Real-Time Applications," *Proceedings of the Ada Europe Conference*, Madrid, Spain, June 1989.

[9]   Elrad, T., and Verun, U., "A Hierarchical and Reflective Framework for Synchronization and Scheduling Controls," *Future Generation Computer Systems* (457), pp. 1-14, 1996.

[10] Gehani, N., and Roome, W. D., *The Concurrent C Programming Language*, Silicon Press, NJ, 1989.

[11] Gehani, N., *Capsules: A Shared Memory Access Mechanism for Concurrent C/C++*, AT&T Bell Laboratories, NJ, 1992.

[12] Kafura, D.G., and Lee, K.H., "Inheritance in Actor-Based Concurrent Object-Oriented Languages," *The Computer Journal*, Vol. 32, No. 4, pp. 297-304, 1989.

[13] Karaorman, M., and Bruno, J., "Introducing Concurrency to a Sequential Language," *Communications of the ACM*, Vol. 36, No. 9, pp. 103-116, 1993.

[14] Lohr, K., "Concurrency Annotations for Reusable Software," *Communications of the ACM*, Vol. 36, No. 9, pp. 81-89,1993.

[15] Matsuoka, S., and Yonezawa, A., "Analysis of Inheritance Anomaly in Object-Oriented Languages," *Research_Directions in Object-Based Concurrency* ed. G. Agha, P. Wegner, A. Yonezawa, The MIT Press, Cambridge, MA, pp.107-150, 1993.

[16] Meyer, B., "Systematic Concurrent Object-Oriented Programming," *Communications of the ACM*, Vol. 36, No. 9, pp. 56-80, 1993.

[17] Nierstrasz, O., "Composing Active Objects: The Next 700 Concurrent Object-Oriented Languages," *Research_Directions in Object-Based Concurrency* ed. G. Agha, P. Wegner, A. Yonezawa, MIT Press, MA, pp.151-174, 1993.

[18] Olsson, R.A., and McNamee, C. M., "Inter-Entry Selection: Non-Determinism and Explicit Control Mechanisms," *Computer Languages*, Vol. 17,No. 4, pp. 269-282,1992.

[19] Ryu, K., and Maeng, S., "Specifying and Inheriting Concurrent Objects," *Microprocessing and_Microprogramming*, Vol. 3, No. 4, pp. 160-170, 1992.

[20] Stroustrup, B. , *The C++ Programming Language*, Addison-Wesley, Reading, MA, 1986.

[21] Tomlinson, C., and Singh, V., "Inheritance and Synchronization with Enabled-Sets," Proceedings of OOPSLA '89, *ACM SIGPLAN Notices*, Vol. 24, pp. 103-112, Oct. 1989.

[22] Wyatt, B. , Kavi, K., and Hufnagel, S., "Parallelism in Object-Oriented Language: A Survey," *IEEE Software*, November, pp. 56-86, 1992.

[23] Yonezawa, A., Shibayama, E., Takada, T., and Honda, Y., "Modeling and Programming in an Object-Oriented Language ABCL/1," *Object-Oriented Concurrent Programming* ed. A. Yonezawa and M. Tokoro, The MIT Press, MA, pp. 55-90, 1993.

Quality of Service Object-Oriented Modeling at the Operating System Level

Hanan BENTALEB

Institut de Recherche en Informatique de Toulouse, Université Paul Sabatier
Toulouse, France

Abstract

The development of new technologies for high-performance networks includes that of multimedia applications. The performance required as regards time and space imply the definition of new computing platforms better suited for these applications. This paper aims to identify future operating systems design approach and the basic concepts for an efficient Quality of Service (QoS) management using an Object-Oriented (OO) modeling.

1 Introduction

In recent years, a new generation of applications has grown up: multimedia applications. These applications emphasize the limitations of conventional operating systems in offering an efficient framework to support their requirements.

Quality of service became a prevalent approach to manage these applications' demands. Numerous works exist for dealing with the quality of service management paradigm, but future operating systems design requires more transparency and modularity improvement. We maintain that an object-oriented approach can offer a generic and structured framework for quality of service management.

In this paper, we have four goals: (a) define an abstraction, with a dynamic configuration, in order to specify the behavior an application expects from the operating system (b) perform quality of service supervision to detect application misbehavior (c) investigate quality of service control to ensure that applications do not over-consume the negotiated resources, and (d) explore the quality of service adaptation to direct applications so as to adjust their behavior according to a specified quality.

By introducing quality of service at the operating system level, a system will be conceived in terms of active or passive objects. Generic mechanisms will be overlaid on these objects to manage their quality of service and the operations they provide in an object-independent (orthogonal) way. Our experiments carried out in the multimedia area show that the OO basic concepts enhance an operating system capabilities and offer a flexible, transparent and well-structured framework for QoS monitoring.

The remainder of this paper is organized as follows: in Section 2, we present a background on QoS research and we identify the operating mechanisms required for the QoS management. Section 3 describes the design of a QoS generic model and its implementation in Solaris operating system using the C++ language [13]. Section 4 summarizes our experiments in the multimedia area and Section 5 considers some directions for future study.

2 OS Support for QoS

Extensive research [3, 5] has been completed in the quality of service area. We identify the four main mechanisms for an efficient support of the main feature of the multimedia applications: the dynamic aspect [2].

• The **parametrization** mechanism provides the means for applications to specify their quality of service requirements. The QoS is expressed by Vogel et al. [16] as a set of (parameter-value) pairs and each parameter is considered to be a typed variable whose value can range over a given set. Nahrstedt and Smith [11] define Profiles where all QoS parameters are stored. Each parameter is specified in a form consistent with its use. For example, a delay parameter is specified as the range <expected value, worst value>, jitter is specified as the triplet <best processing time, average processing time, worst acceptable processing time>.

• **supervision** and **control** mechanisms. These mechanisms are strongly linked: the first enables detection of application misbehavior and prevents overload situations; while the second one ensures that applications do not over-consume the negotiated resources. Tokuda et al. [14] define a QoS control under the RT-Mach processor reservation capacity that consists in preempting the application whose reservation runs out and scheduling an application with a valid reservation. This timing control is used to ensure the timing protection notion [10]. Tokuda and Kitayama [15] suggest two dynamic QoS control schemes: a self-stabilization scheme and a QoS manager-based scheme. In the first scheme, an application tries to achieve the best QoS level using the current available system resources. In the second, a QoS manager maintains the requested QoS level for sessions as well as dynamically readjusts the QoS level according to the availability of the system resources. In the same context, Nakajima and Tezuka [12] add another control scheme: the user-adjustable QoS scheme. Here, changing the QoS does not depend on system loads but on user preferences.

• **adaptation** mechanism. Most of multimedia applications offer an adaptive feature and tolerate variation on their quality of service. In dynamic environments, this feature allows an application to behave according to changes by increasing/decreasing its QoS. Diot [7] presents various ways of dynamically adjusting an application behavior to the network available resources. The adaptation schemes rely on an observation of the network load and an application adapts its QoS according to this load. Käppner and Wolf [8] enhance the meaning of media scaling technique [6] from communications systems to the end-system level and introduce the service class "scalable QoS". When an overload situation occurs, instead of interrupting the service of that stream, its quality is gracefully degraded to keep it meaningful to the user.

This article is not concerned with the quality of service negotiation mechanism which, we believe, is required for an efficient QoS management. This mechanism is the subject of other studies conducted in the laboratory.

3 Modeling QoS

The purpose of this section is to describe the approach adopted for the design of a QoS model that incorporates the mechanisms presented above and its implementation using C++ language. For the length of this section, a simple example of a buffer is used to illustrate the different mechanisms.

Our design is governed by the following criteria:
   • *Modularity*: by introducing the quality of service to the objects level, we do not modify an object logic. What is modified is its access protocol.
   • *Transparency*: an application keeps the same body and interface. It manipulates a QoS-endowed object as it did with the original object.
   • *Dynamism*: an object QoS and its environment dynamic changes are taken into account at the object level.

While respecting these indispensable features, we use the object-oriented modeling to provide an adequate QoS management support. In our model, the considered basic entity is the *object* and our approach consists in reasoning implicitly on the application by considering its objects.

Given a programmer abstract class `object`, the approach aims at incorporating QoS to that object without altering either its semantics or the body and the interface of applications that manipulate it. The approach consists of subtyping the `object` by a `QoSobject` that embeds its quality of service (cf. section 3.1). The code below summarizes this approach.

```
void Application(object& O)        void Application(QoSobject& O)
{                                  {
 // Application body                 // Same body of the application
}                                  }
```

The inheritance mechanism gives two fundamental properties of transparency and modularity and enables redefinition of the object methods. This mechanism is used in our model for an object behavior evaluation purpose allowing thus the supervision of its quality of service (cf. section 3.3). QoS information is exchanged between the operating system and the applications to let applications react to their misbehavior and adjust their quality of service (cf. section 3.4). To achieve this, system calls and upcalls [4] are used for interfacing the applications and the system entities.

3.1 QoS Expression

In this model, an application quality of service is represented by a set of dials, with each dial representing a QoS parameter. A dial (refer to the code below) is specified by the triplet (interval, indicator, step). The indicator specifies the value of the dial, the interval is the range of values that could be covered by the indicator and the step specifies the step of covering the interval. The parameterization mechanism enables a dynamic configuration of the QoS parameters, thus translating the QoS dynamic aspect. In this article, a "dial value" may be understood to represent the value of its indicator.

```
template <class T> class Interval: public Set<T>
{
  ...
}; // Interval


template <class T> class Dial: public Interval<T>
{
 protected:
  T indicator, step;
 public:
  virtual int Admissible();
  ...
}; // Dial
```

In the QoS model design, an application quality of service is represented at the operating system level by the QoSParameters class (refer to Figure 1). This class specifies the QoS quantitative aspect (set of dials) and the qualitative aspect such as best-effort, guarantee services.

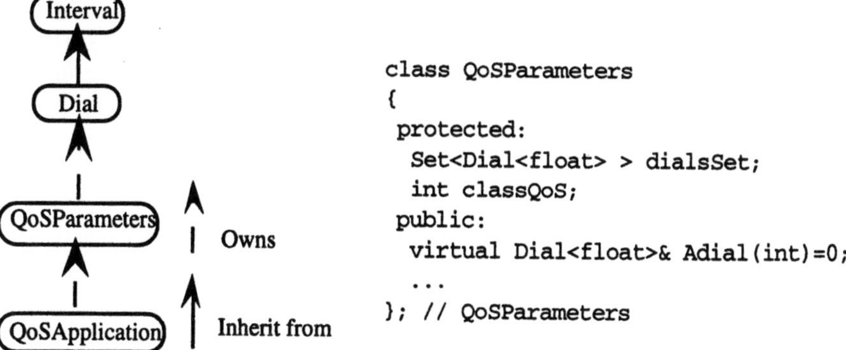

Figure 1. Classes hierarchy

Overall supervision of quality of service relies on supervision of the QoS parameters and therefore on supervision of each dial, called *dial admissibility test* in our model. The `Admissible` method defined for each dial tests if the current value of the dial is valid. We have implemented a default `Admissible` method that tests if the dial value is included in the corresponding range. A user application remains free to redefine its own dials admissibility methods and to give them the required semantics.

The QoS expression is extended in our model to the objects. We define one key class that performs quality of service expression without modifying an object's semantics. Our approach is to conceive a QoS-endowed object as being an `QoSobject`: the `QoSobject` class inherits from the `object` class. Below is the code corresponding to this class:

```
template <class object, class parameter> class QoSobject:
public object
{
 public:
  QoSobject(parameter*);
  virtual QoSParameters& QoSParameter()=0;

  ...
}; // QoSobject
```

All the objects that express quality of service (for instance, a `QoSBuffer` object) inherit from the `QoSobject` class and therefore implicitly from the object to which they associate quality of service (for instance, a `Buffer` object). This introduces a transparency feature which allows the applications to consider the new object as the initial one.

3.2 QoS Control

For dealing with the QoS violation problem and to prevent system overload situations, we use an *avoidance approach* to ensure that an application has a behavior which conforms to that specified through its QoS parameters. In this approach, system resources are managed on the same model as the memory resource in conventional systems. The control is performed at each resource utilization and before using a resource, an application allocates the required quantity.

Two basic control are performed in our model:
   • Control based on *resource-access-methods*: a redefinition of resource allocation methods (`new`, `malloc`) allows to verify the validity of an allocation demand and to reject an application demand if it attempts to use more resources than the negotiated threshold quantity.

   • Control based on *object behavior*: this control forces an execution unit to comply with its execution profile and prevents it from facing over-run situations.

Using the example of periodic threads presented below, we aim to illustrate on the one hand the execution control performed at the threads level, and on the other hand how we solve in this example the static method restriction in C++ programming language. Note that a method declared static cannot access non-static members [13].

The code below presents the Thread class. Upon its creation, the thread object is inserted in a static set. We define a static method Self that returns the thread object via the system call thr_self. thr_self function returns the unique identifier of the calling thread.

```
class Thread
{
 static Set<Thread&> threadSet;
protected:
 virtual int main()= 0;
public:
 static Thread& Self()
 {
  return (threadSet[thr_self()]);
 }
 ...
}; // Thread
```

By using the thread abstraction class, we then focus on the specification of periodic threads behavior. A PeriodicThread class that inherits from the Thread class is defined and its main method describes the thread periodic profile illustrated in Figure 2. The QoS parameters considered in this implementation are the period and the computation time. More complex parameters and a more advanced execution scheme may be specified. The purpose of this study is to illustrate basic concepts using a simple example.

Figure 2. A thread periodic temporal profile

The execution thread control is achieved by suspending the thread processing as soon as its time quantum has ended.

```
int PeriodicThread :: main()
{
 sigset(SIGALRM, PeriodHandler);
 for (;;)
 {
  // Activate an alarm
  Arm(ComputationTime);
```

```
  // Memorization of the processing state
  processingState= STARTED;

  // Execute the thread processing
  Processing();
  processingState= ENDED;

  // Waiting for the end of the computation time notice
  sigpause(SIGALRM);
 }
 return 0;
}
```

Situations in which the processing that has to be done during thread computation time is incomplete are dealt with as timing fault situations. Indeed, a `TimeOut` exception is raised which signifies that the processing has failed to achieve the user timing specification and it needs a longer computation time.

It is important to recall that C++ signal handlers are static members (on the example, `PeriodHandler` method). The reader may observe in the code below that by using the `Self` method, we can access, through the thread object, the non-static members of the class (on the example, `processingState` attribute).

```
static void PeriodicThread :: PeriodHandler(int _signal)
throw(TimeOut)
{
 // If the processing is not ended an exception is thrown
 PeriodicThread& th= (PeriodicThread&)(Self());
 switch (th.processingState)
 {
  case STARTED: throw (TimeOut());
  ...
 }
 // The thread sleeps until the next period
}
```

3.3 QoS Supervision

To effectively ensure QoS guarantees, new operating system architecture support different mechanisms such as resource reservation [1, 14]. But as a commitment cannot always be granted and therefore, in order to prevent overload situations, a QoS supervision is required for detection of QoS violation situations. In our model, supervision is performed at two levels:

• Supervision at *operating system* level is performed as a consequence of the redefinition of system resources methods. A `QoSviolation` exception is raised for valid allocation fails indicating that the operating system cannot fulfill the application's requirements.

• Supervision at *application* level needs a description of the application's quality of service (`QoSParameters`) and an evaluation of its behavior. This evaluation is performed as a result of the redefinition of access methods of the QoS-endowed objects (those inheriting from `QoSobject` class).

Let us consider a `QoSBuffer` object that corresponds to a buffer endowed with quality of service. The redefinition of the `QoSBuffer` `Put` method enables the memorization of the loss events by updating the `Loss` dial. Note that it is performed by giving a new access protocol to the buffer object without altering the semantics of the `Put` operation (refer to the code below). The supervision mechanism on that example will perform a `Loss` dial *admissibility test*.

```
void QoSBuffer<T> :: Put(T in) throw(IsFull)
{
 const int lossIndex= 2;
 try
 {
  Buffer<T> :: Put(in);
 }
 // Application behavior evaluation
 catch (IsFull NotIgnored)
 {
  // Data loss observation
  QoSParameter().Adial(lossIndex)++;
 }
}
```

Situations in which the value of the `Loss` dial is non-admissible, imply that the application needs more memory resources (when the `Loss` dial value is greater than the upper bound of its corresponding interval) or it may, to some degree, reduce memory consumption (when the `Loss` dial value is lesser than the lower bound of its corresponding interval). This information must be transmitted to the objects in order for them to react to dynamic situations.

In our QoS model, the supervision is performed by systematically analyzing the various objects an application manipulates. Through objects, the supervisor can be informed about the application's needs (specification of its QoS parameters) and behavior (redefinition of its object's access methods).

We define a generic `Supervisor` class that possesses a set of abstract objects whose QoS must be supervised and we implement a default supervision scheme that consists of a circular control of objects and tests the *admissibility* of each object dials (refer to the code below). If a dial value is non-admissible, the supervisor, by

294

invoking the object adaptation method, enables the application quality adjustment (cf. section 3.4). Other supervision schemes may be implemented such as supervision based on object priority. The `Adapt` method used in the code below is presented in greater detail in section 3.4.

```
template <class object> class Supervisor
{
 protected:
  Set<object&> theObjects;
 public:
  virtual void Supervise()
  {
    for (int i=0; i<theObjects.Cardinal(); i++)
     for (int j=0; j<theObjects[i].QoSParameter().Cardinal(); j++)
     {
       int adjust=theObjects[i].QoSParameter().Adial(j).Admissible();
       if (adjust) theObjects[i].Adapt(j, adjust);
     }
  }
  ...
}; // Supervisor
```

Conceptually, we distinguish three supervision models:
* *Active* supervision: there is one (or more) supervising process (or thread).
* *Passive* supervision: the QoS-endowed objects perform their own supervision. They possess a supervisor activated whenever the object is manipulated.
* Any combination of the two previous models.

A supervision mechanism does not have to introduce an important supplementary CPU load. It would be interesting to implement a passive supervision scheme or to combine the two schemes.

3.4 QoS Adaptation

The previous section presents the QoS supervision mechanism and outlines the necessity of a QoS adaptation for adjusting object behavior. A quality of service adaptation is due either to (a) an internal cause: the object behavior is not compliant with that specified by its QoS parameters, or (b) side-effects, in this case other applications' behavior can affect the performance of the application in question. This is the case, for example, of an application that resumes its execution and frees the system resources. This may allow for an improvement in other admitted applications quality.

The quality of service adaptation is expressed at the level of a `QoSobject` by the definition of a virtual method `Adapt`. Since QoS adaptation is specific to an application, the `Adapt` method is implemented at the application level. This method is parameterized by the dial identifier whose value is non-admissible and by the nature of the adaptation: QoS reduction or increase. On the buffer example, it corresponds to either a Reduce operation, thus freeing some memory resources or an Append operation for increasing the application memory consumption.

```
template <class object, class parameter> class QoSobject:
public object
{
  public:

    ...

    virtual void Adapt(int, int)=0;
}; // QoSobject
```

4 Experiments in the Multimedia Area

This section presents the instantiation of the mechanisms described above to the multimedia area. We have implemented an experimental image server running on a Solaris 2.5 Sparc 20 workstation and using the XIL Imaging library 1.2.

The server behavior is as follows: at each user demand, it creates a thread to process the user service. The considered object in this instantiation is the *thread* and the considered QoS parameters are the thread period and execution time. All the QoS mechanisms are performed at the *thread object level.*

When applying for a display movie service, the user selects a movie, a display quality (frame per second) and submits its request to the server. On the server side, the user-chosen quality is mapped into a processing period and a computation time for the display thread. As an image source, we have used a sequence of frames generated by a camera or a frame sequence from an MPEG file. The QoS adjustment is achieved as a consequence of the control, supervision and adaptation mechanisms. While supervising the number of displays that cannot be achieved (Loss dial), and the supervisor detects an inability of that thread to perform the required number of computations to achieve the requested service, it invokes the thread adaptation method to allow it to adjust its behavior. By decreasing/increasing its period, the thread dynamically updates its processing frequency and thus the frame rate.

The basic difficulty encountered in this implementation is related to the Xil library that is not MT-save. This has led to modification of our basic design; we handle all the display request in the same periodic thread. We expect the forthcoming version to be MT-save. However, as a simple experiment, this implementation shows that the suggested QoS organization offers a structured and systematic QoS management support.

5 Conclusion

Beyond the performance required at the operating system level, a high degree of transparency and modularity for the integration of the quality of service mechanisms must be achieved. This brings a simple and a more structured QoS support at the operating system level. This study considers the quality of service management problem from a methodological point of view. We focus on the QoS modeling by exploiting the object-oriented paradigm. Through this model, we examine the advantage of transparency and genericity that an object-oriented approach brings to a dynamic QoS management support. We expect to integrate in our model the QoS negotiation mechanism. Other extensions are actually involving an integration of the reflection concept [9]. A meta-object protocol will allow a flexible and simple superposition of the QoS mechanisms to any object.

References

1. Anderson D. P, Tzou S., Wahbe R., Govindan R. and Andrews M. Support for Continuous Media in the DASH System. Proceedings of the Tenth Conference on Distributed Computing Systems 1990
2. Buford J. F. K. Multimedia Systems. Addison Wesley, New York, 1994
3. Campbell A., Coulson G. and Hutchison D. A Quality of Service Architecture, ACM Computer Communication Review vol 24 n° 2 1994
4. Clark D. D. The Structuring of Systems Using Upcalls, Proceedings of the Tenth ACM Symposium on Operating Systems Principles 1985
5. Danthine A., Baguette Y., Leduc G and Leonard L. The OSI 95 Connection-mode Transport Service Enhanced QoS, Fourth IFIP Conference on High Performance Networking 1992
6. Delgrossi L., Halstrick C., Hehmann D., Herrtwich R.G., Krone O., Sandvoss J. and Vogt C. Media Scaling in a Multimedia Communication System, Proceedings of the First ACM Multimedia Conference 1993
7. Diot C. Adaptive Applications and QoS guaranties, Proceedings of the International Conference on Multimedia and Networking 1995
8. Käppner T. and Wolf L.C. Media Scaling in Distributed Multimedia Object Services, Proceedings of the Second International Workshop on Advanced Teleservices and High-Speed Communication Architecture 1994
9. Kiczales G., des Rivières J. and Bobrow D. G. The Art of the Metaobject Protocol, MIT press, Massachusetts, 1991
10. Mercer C., Rajkumar R. and Zelenka J. Temporal Protection in Real-Time Operating Systems, Proceedings of the 11th IEEE Workshop on Real-Time Operating Systems and Software 1994
11. Nahrstedt K. and Smith J. M. The QoS Broker, IEEE Multimedia vol 2 n° 1 1995; 2: 53-67
12. Nakajima T. and Tezuka H. A Continuous Media Application supporting Dynamic QoS Control on Real-Time Mach, Proceedings of the Second ACM International Conference on Multimedia 1994
13. Stroustrup S. The C++ Programming Language, Addison Wesley, USA, 1991
14. Tokuda H., Nakajima T. and Rao P. Real-Time Mach: Towards a Predictable Real-Time System, USENIX Mach Workshop 1990
15. Tokuda H. and Kitayama T. Dynamic QoS Control Based on Real-Time Threads, Proceedings of the Fourth International Workshop on Network and Operating System Support for Digital Audio and Video 1993
16. Vogel A., Kerhervé B., Bochmann G. v. and Gecsei J. Distributed Multimedia and QoS: A survey, IEEE Multimedia vol 2 n° 2 1995

RE-USABILITY II

A Descriptive Language for Information Object Reuse through Virtual Documents

Anne-Marie Vercoustre[1] and François Paradis
CSIRO Mathematical and Information Sciences
723 Swanston Street, Carlton,
3053 Victoria, Australia
{Anne-Marie.Vercoustre, Francois.Paradis}@cmis.csiro.au

Abstract

The importance of reuse is well recognised for electronic document writing. However, it is rarely achieved satisfactorily because of the complexity of the task: integrating different formats, handling updates of information, addressing document author's need for intuitiveness and simplicity, etc. In this paper, we present a language for information reuse that allows users to write *virtual documents*, where *dynamic* information objects can be retrieved from various sources, transformed, and included along with *static* information in SGML documents. The language uses a tree-like structure for the representation of information objects, and allows querying without a complete knowledge of the structure or the types of information. The data structures and the syntax of the language are presented through an example application. A major strength of our approach is to treat the document as a non-monolithic set of reusable information objects.

1 Introduction

Information reuse has a long established intellectual heritage encompassing relational databases, text-mark-up, record management systems and object-oriented thinking. To a great extend, the work of producing new documents involves reusing pieces of previously existing documents [18], modifying them and assembling them in a new way, according to the purpose of the new document.

The widespread adoption of electronic documents should allow for more information reuse. However it is often hard to put in practice, because the documents are not defined at the level of granularity and modularity needed for information reuse. Even with standards such as SGML [10], the inclusion of elements from one document to another can be very difficult, because the elements are strongly typed and there could be incompatibilities between the DTDs (document grammars) [5].

As the Web becomes a major source of information, a lot of interest has arisen, not only for searching for information, but for reusing this information in new pages, or directly from applications. Unfortunately HTML tags do not provide a significant level of structure for identifying and extracting information, since they are mostly used for presentation issues. A solution is to build a model for a set of homogeneous pages using a structuring schema [3,6].

Updating information within documents also requires a lot of effort: it is very costly to create a new version of the full document each time the information has changed or new information has been added. The difficulty is to make these changes consistently throughout an entire documentation. A solution to this problem is to use

---

[1] This author's permanent position is INRIA-Rocquencourt, France.

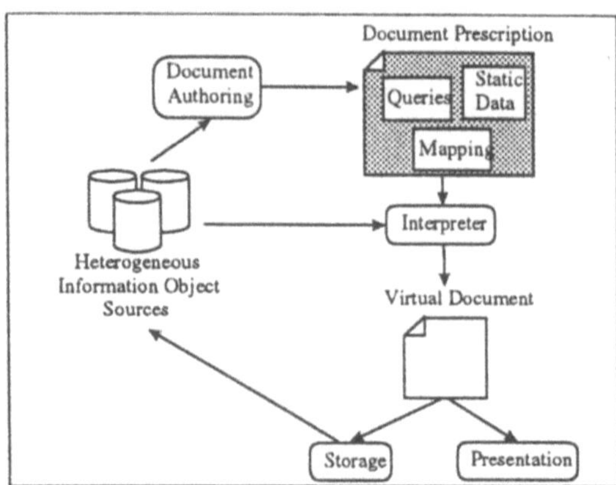

Figure 1: RIO Architecture

virtual documents: that is, documents that are dynamically generated on demand and therefore always reflect the new states of the world. Unfortunately, writing the "instructions" to generate a virtual document is a tedious process that often requires more programming skills than document writing.

This paper introduces a new language for writing virtual documents, which allows the creation of new documents by extracting the relevant information from existing documents, and assembling it into a new document. Three important features of the language are the following:

- *descriptive syntax*. The focus in our language is on the information objects rather than on the procedures as in script or command-based languages.
- *heterogenous information*. The information that can be inserted in a virtual document can come from various sources and in different formats: tables from SQL, objects from OQL, semi-structured data from HTML pages, etc. Our language proposes a tree-like representation of all information objects.
- *mapping*. We propose mapping rules in order to include the "dynamic" information of the document in the appropriate DTD.

We first discuss the context of our work and present an example of its application. We then give a brief overview of the tree-like structures used by the language, before presenting the language itself. We conclude with a comparison with other approaches and further work.

2 The RIO project

The RIO (Reuse of Information Object) project [23] aims to develop techniques which can support information reuse in various contexts. The focus of the project is currently on the reuse of structured information from heterogeneous sources, including OO or relational databases, SGML and HTML documents, and possibly any kind of *semi-structured* data [1].

Our approach is to introduce a *document prescription* of the virtual document to be generated. A document prescription consists of:

- Static data, that is the structure and the text that doesn't change in the document.
- Queries, or the commands needed to generate the dynamic part of the document.

```
<!DOCTYPE  project [
<!ELEMENT project -- (summary, attractiveness, feasibility, priorities, customers,
scope)>
<!ATTLIST project   gate NUMBER "0"
                    idID  #IMPLIED
                    class  (internal, CRC, industrial)              >
<!ELEMENT summary -- (header, description+, outcome+, actions*)  >
<!ELEMENT header oo (title, author, date, portfolio, business)   >
<!ELEMENT description -o (#PCDATA)                                >
<!ELEMENT outcome -o (#PCDATA)                                    >
<!ELEMENT action -o (#PCDATA)                                     >

...

]>
```

Figure 2: DTD for a project document

- Transformation instructions, to convert the reused information objects into new document objects.

The overall architecture of the system is described in Figure 1. In order to produce a virtual document, the interpreter of the document prescription executes the following tasks: send the "native" queries to the database server and get the results back; assemble the results into a generic tree representation; select, join and transform objects in the tree model; and finally, map the selected objects into the document structures of the target virtual document.

In the following section we give an example of a virtual document that we will use along the paper to present our generic data model as well as the prescription language.

3 An example

Our example is a yearly activity report for our EDC (Electronic Document and Commerce) group. The report contains the list of people who belong to the group, a description of the various projects they have been involved in the current year, as well as their collective list of publications. The existing sources of information are:

- an SQL database of persons, with names, title, location, portfolio; this database is primarily used for generating our internal and external Staff Web pages.
- An OO database of SGML documents that contains a short description (2 to 6 pages) of the current projects (research or industrial). These documents conform to the (incomplete) DTD shown in Figure 2. Let's call them *project* documents. The project documents are stored in the OO database using the same kind of mapping between the DTD and the database classes as described in [8].
- A database of bibliographic references to our external publications. This database can only be accessed through the Web, which means that the available source of information is an HTML page of bibliographic references.

The activity report is generated by combining the following information: the EDC employees from the SQL database, project descriptions from excerpts of the project documents, and publications from the HTML pages, using a join with the EDC employees.

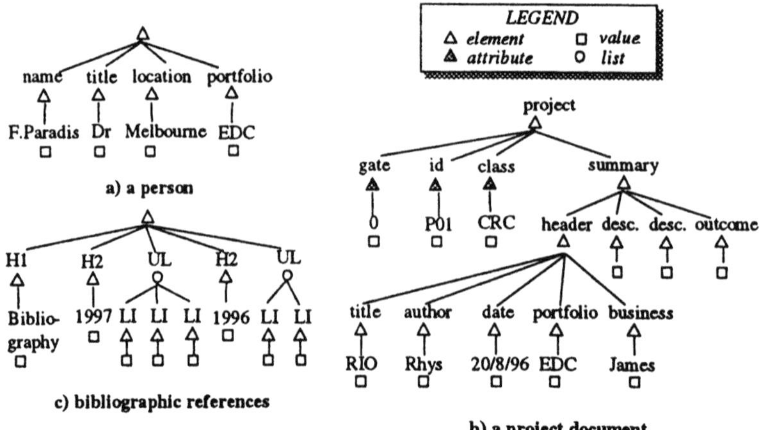

Figure 3: Tree representation examples

Section 4 will present our language with detailed examples for building the parts of the activity report. But before introducing our language, we need to present the tree data model used for integrating the answers from the various databases or other information sources.

4 The tree model

We introduce our integration model which is very similar to those presented in [1,3]. As in these approach we are not using a model that encompasses all the source models. Instead we use a generic and minimalist approach. The data structure we use consists of ordered labeled trees. Each tree node can have one of the following type:

- a node of type "value" has no children. Its label is the appropriate atomic value.
- a node of type "element" has one child (of any of the four types) for each of its component. Its label is the name of the element.
- a node of type "attribute" has one child of type "value" that contains the value of the attribute. Its label is the name of the attribute.
- a node of type "list" has as many children as elements in the list.

Figure 3 shows examples of tree representations for the objects of our example application.

SQL tables are represented with element nodes, with an unlabeled node for each row, which has the columns as children. Of course this mapping is not unique; for an alternative see [3,p.2]. Figure 3a gives an example of a person from our STAFF database. The full table would be represented by a list of persons.

SGML elements are represented by element nodes with a label corresponding to the tag name. These nodes have one child for each element content. SGML attributes are represented by an attribute node under the element node. As lists play a very strong role in documents (in contrast with standard databases) we also retain the information that an element corresponds to a list. Figure 3b gives an example of a project document from our Project database.

HTML elements are represented by a simplified version of their parsing tree, in the same manner than for SGML elements. However a typical HTML tree will be more "flat" than an SGML one, as it lacks the logical structure of the document. Figure 3c gives an example of a our publications database, which is stored as one HTML file, containing several lists of publications organised by year.

Unlike conventional object-oriented techniques, the elements in our trees are untyped. This doesn't have an appreciable impact on global efficiency as most of the retrieval is performed at a lower level by the native queries. Our structures can be considered like parse trees, where several nodes can have the same label.

It must be noted here that objects can form cyclic graphs, so we might need to represent links between nodes using an object identifier. However since our current focus is on SGML documents rather than general object-oriented databases, we only need to consider links between documents or between parts of document. In SGML these links are purely syntactic, so we can keep them in the tree as they are, ie. by their SGML tags.

5 The prescription language

In order to write the document prescriptions and to query the tree structures described above, a *prescription language* was designed. In this section we describe in details the two main components of the language: query and transformation instructions. We then conclude with an example that shows how these are included in a document along with static information.

5.1 Queries

A key issue for the query component of the prescription language is to maintain the diversity and flexibility of the underlying systems, while dealing with information that is quite different in nature. Our approach is to allow queries to be expressed in the native database language, but to supplement them with our own search mechanism to select and combine the results. A typical statement, to retrieve employees from the STAFF SQL database who have authored a project document in the PROJ OQL database, would be as follows:

```
pick $e
from sql(select * from STAFF) as $e,
     oql(select p.summary.header from Proj p) as $h
where $e.name = $h.author
```

The language can be roughly divided into four parts: the selection of information, the construction of new information, the querying commands, and the assignments. We now present those four parts with examples.

5.1.1 Information selection

An important feature of the language is the ability to select any part of a query result. Given our uniform tree-representation of all information, this sums up to selection of nodes in a tree. Our approach is based on the idea of *generalised path expressions* [8], which permit browsing a tree without a complete knowledge of its structure.

The *dot* operator (".") is defined for accessing the direct children of a node using their label, while the *dot-dot* operator ("..") is used to recursively access the direct and indirect children of a node. Assuming for example that $d denotes a project document[2], then the following are valid selection expressions:

1.1) $d.summary   *selects the summary*
1.2) $d.summary.description   *selects all summary descriptions*

---

[2] See section 5.1.4 below for making assignments to identifiers.

1.3) $d..description   *selects all descriptions*

These expressions actually return *all* the matching subtrees - in a list if there is more than one element - unlike other OO approaches where there can only be one possible match (as is the case with OQL for example). As descriptions can only occur directly under summaries, query 1.3 is equivalent to 1.2. Supposing that descriptions could be nested, then query 1.3 would return all descriptions whatever their level. If this is not desirable, a more strict selection can be achieved with the dot operator.

One can also use the node types for selection. For example:

1.4) $d.#ATTR   *all attributes (gate, id, class)*
1.5) $d.id#ATTR.#VALUE or   *id value*
       $d.id.#VALUE

Here #ATTR and #VALUE refer to the attribute and value node types, respectively.

Children can be selected according to their rank using the "[]" operator in OQL fashion. The children are then considered as a list starting at position 0. The #FIRST and #LAST keywords can be used to refer to the first and last elements, respectively. For example:

1.6) $d.summary.[#FIRST]   *selects the summary header*
1.7) $d.#ATTR[0]   *get the first attribute*
1.8) $d..description[#FIRST]   *selects the first description*

The range (":") and union ("&") operators are defined for multiple selections. For example:

1.9) $d.#ATTR[#FIRST:#LAST]   *all attributes; equivalent to 1.4*
1.10) $d.summary&feasability   *the summary and the feasability*
1.11) $d.summary:feasability   *the summary, attractiveness and*
                                  feasability
1.12) $d..header&description[0] *the header and first description*

If no element is found, the selection will return an empty list.

5.1.2 Information construction

It is possible to construct nodes of a given type, using the list, elem and attr functions. For example:

2.1)   list($d..title,$d..author) or   *a list node with title and author*
       ($d..title,$d..author)
2.2)   elem(paragraph,   *element node with label*
          $d..description)   *"paragraph" and with*
                                         descriptions as children
2.3)   attr(version,$d.id.#VALUE)   *attribute node with label*
                                         "version", and document id as
                                         child (value)

In our language, strings are considered as value nodes with the actual characters stored in the label. The str function can be used to construct a string from a tree, concatenating all "content" nodes (ie. value nodes that are not the child of an attribute). When passed several arguments, it also concatenates them. For example:

2.4)	str($d) or str($d..#ELEM.#VALUE)	*content of the whole document*
2.5)	str($d.summary,$d.scope)	*summary and the scope*

The type and label of a node can be accessed with the corresponding functions.

2.6)	type($d.id)	*the string "#ATTR"*
2.7)	label($d.id)	*the string "id"*

Finally, information can be added or removed from a tree with adopt and excluding, respectively. For example:

2.8)	$d **excluding** priorities	*the document without priorities*
2.9)	$d **adopt** attr(version,1.0)	*the document with version*

5.1.3 Querying

Native queries can be expressed with the corresponding function. For example:

3.1)	`sql(select * from STAFF)`	*select all records from STAFF* *SQL database*

Queries on our tree representation follow the syntax "pick...from...where" (the from and where clauses being optional), which is similar in style and semantics to SQL "select...from...where". For example:

3.2)	**pick** $d..description or **pick** description **from** $d	*select all descriptions from $d* *(equivalent to 1.3)*
3.3)	**pick** $p **from** oql(select project from Proj p) **as** $p **where** $p..portfolio = "EDC"	*select project documents that* *belong to the "EDC" portfolio"* *from the Proj OQL database*

Note that selection and construction operations are also interpreted as valid queries; so all examples of the previous sections are also queries.

5.1.4 Assignments

Query results can be saved using an *assignment* expression. An *identifer* is used to refer to them. For example:

4.1)	**define** $e **as** sql(select * from STAFF);	*defines $e as all employees*
	$e.name	*get all employees names*

5.2 Mapping

The purpose of the mapping instructions is to convert elements from the generic tree representing the answers to queries, into elements of the virtual document. In particular, the mapping instructions must permit these various SGML constructions: PCDATA, attributes, aggregates, recursive lists.[3] In addition, often-used constructions, such as tables (a common example of a recursive list), must be easy to express.

Our approach is to keep all the SGML-dependent syntax in the *static* part of the document prescription, and to define the mapping instructions as part of SGML elements in the document. The mapping instructions are written as SGML processing,

---

[3] Choice (ie. alternatives) are not to be considered since we are dealing with documents, not with DTDs.

and always refer implicitly to the tag that includes them (which we call the *including tag*). For example:

```
<title><?processing instruction></title>
```

We now see in details the mapping operations through the various SGML structures that can be built.

5.2.1 *Text*

Query statements are mapped into text. The processing instruction:

```
<?$q>
```

is interpreted as text($q), which is a function similar to str, except that it inserts blanks between elements. Multiple queries are treated as lists. The interpretation of:

```
<?$q1; ...; $qn>
```

is given by text($q1,...,$qn).

5.2.2 *SGML trees*

In many cases, we are not only interested in the textual content of the query results, but also in the actual structure of the tree. The sgml function can be used for generating an SGML fragment of document that maps exactly the tree structure. The straight mapping of a tree into an SGML document involves a pre-order tree traversal, using the element labels as the tags and their value as the content.

The sgml function can be very useful to simplify the mapping language by first building the appropriate tree using the construction language, eventually adding, removing or modifying the elements. It also makes it easy to include part of existing document into a document with the same DTD (eg. HTML/HTML). More complex library functions could be implemented, possibly in DSSSL, for other standard transformations (eg. Article to HTML).

5.2.3 *Lists*

The map instruction is used to create a sequence of SGML elements from the results of a query. An expression like <?map $var in $list><tag>...</tag>, is replaced by the interpreter by as many tag elements as there are elements in $list.[4] Within the tag element, $var can be used to refer to the current element in the list. For example:

```
<?map $name in list('François','John')><LI>my name is <?$name></LI>
```

produces:

```
<LI>my name is François</LI>
<LI>my name is John</LI>
```

Another form of the map allows an *index variable*, to refer to the current element number. For instance to add a counter in the previous list, one could do:

```
<?map $name[$i] in list('François','John')><LI>(<?$i>) My name is <?
$name></LI>
```

5.2.4 *Tables*

Complex structures like tables can be built using map instructions. For example, given the following query, which retrieves the personnel involved in the "EDC" portfolio:

```
<?define $staff as (pick * from
    sql(select * from STAFF where portfolio='EDC')>
```

[4] The syntax <?map $var in $list><?begin>...<?end> is also provided to repeat elements that are not properly enclosed within tags.

then the following prescription would output a table where the rows are those
employees, and the columns their name and title.

```
<TABLE>
    <TR><TD>name</TD><TD>title</TD></TR>
    <?map $s in $staff><TR>
            <TD><?$s.name></TD> <TD><?$s.title></TD></TR>
</TABLE>
```

The above example can be rewritten using nested maps as follows:

```
<TABLE>
    <TR><?map $field in unique
$staff.name&title><TD><?label($field)></TD></TR>
    <?map $s in $staff><TR>
            <?map $ss in unique $s.name&title><TD><?$ss></TD></TR>
</TABLE>
```

This sort of construct can be particularly useful when the structure of the records is not
known. Removing ".name&title" in the example above would produce an employee
table with all their fields.

5.2.5 Attributes

The attributes instruction is used to add dynamic attributes to tags. It takes as an
argument either an attribute node or a list of attribute nodes. For example, the
following:

```
<A><?attributes attr(href,'#sect1')>section 1</A>
```

produces <A href=#sect1>section 1</A>. When attribute values can be taken directly
from trees, the syntax is still more immediate. Suppose for example that $s refers to
some HTML element with attribute name equals to sect1. Then the following:

```
<A><?attributes $s.name>...</A>
```

would produce <A name=sect1>...</A>.

5.2.6 Links

A typical example of the use of internal links is the creation of a table of content at the
beginning of an HTML page, with links to further sections. It can be implemented in
three steps: first the retrieval and construction of the sections, second the construction
of the table of contents, and third the inclusion of the sections in the document.
Assuming $proj refers to a list of projects documents, as defined in section 3, then the
sections can be constructed as follows:

```
<? define $sections as
    (pick $s adopt attr(name,idname(sect))
     from $proj.summary )>
```

As the sections are retrieved, they are added (with the adopt operation) a name
attribute that will be used for referencing them. The function idname is used for
generating label names; it returns a new identifier with its string parameter each time it
is called (here: sect1, sect2, ...).

The table of contents consists of a list of pointers to the sections: it can be built by
mapping every section title into a <LI> element, and adding an href attribute that
points to the corresponding section.

```
<UL>
    <?map $s in $sections><LI>
        <A><?attributes attr(href, str('#', $s.name.#VALUE))>
        <?$s.header.title ></A></LI>
</UL>
```

```
<HTML>
<?define $staff as sql(select * from STAFF where portfolio="EDC")>
<?define $proj as oql(select p from Proj p where p.portfolio="EDC")>
<?define $pub as url(http://www.mel.dit.csiro.au/pubs/pubs.html)>
<H1>Activity report for 1997</H1>
<H2>Participants</H2>
<UL><LI><?map $staff.name></LI></UL>
<H2>Projects</H2>
<UL><?map $p in $proj><LI>
    <H3><?$p.summary.header.title></H3>
    <P><?$p.summary excluding header></P></LI>
</UL>
<H2>Publications</H2>
<P><?pick $onepub from $pub.H2 as $header[$i],
           $pub.[$i+1].LI as $ onepub,
           $ staff.name as $name
   where $header contains "1997", $ onepub contains $name>
</P>
</HTML>
```

Figure 4: The yearly activity report prescription

The str function concatenates the strings like the text function, but without adding extraneous spaces.

Finally the sections can be included in th e document with the following:

```
<?map $s in $sections><A><attributes $ s.name>
    <h2><?$s.header.title></h2>
    <P><?$s.description></P></A>
```

Here each section consists of an anchor element (<A>), with a header (<H2>) and description paragraph (<P>).

External links can be built the same way using the tags provided by the DTD.

5.3 A complete example

Figure 4 shows the prescription for the activity report of the EDC portfolio for year 1997, in HTML format. The document consists of some initialisation statements, which retrieve information from the various databases, followed by three sections: the participants, the projects, and the publications. The first two sections are taken directly from the sql and oql queries: the participants are the list of EDC staff members, and the projects is the list of items containing the projects title and their summary. The publications section is more complicated to construct. We first find the 1997 publications in the "flat" HTML structure, and then only keep those containing a participant name.

The pick statement in the publications section requires a bit more explanation. The expression "$pub.H2 as $header[$i]" matches $header with an H2 element (which is further restricted in the where clause to contain "1997"), and $i with its rank. The expression "$pub.[$i+1]" matches the element immediately following $header, which happens to be a list where every item is a publication ($onepub). Finally, only publications containing a member of the staff are kept.

6 Related work

Other works have looked at querying structured or semi-structured information, either from a database point of view, as with OQL [21], or from a document processing point of view, as with HyQ [13]. We have already mentioned that our syntax is quite similar to OQL. This language, however, is inadequate for "loosely" structured queries. In order to issue query 1.3 in OQL, one would have to define a method to recursively access the `description` fields of the children nodes. HyQ does not provide any primitive for constructing information, furthermore, it tends to be complex and not very intuitive. Consider for example the formulation of query 1.3 in HyQ:

```
<HyQ qdomain=$d>
Select(DOMTREE Eq(Proploc(CAND GI) 'description'))
</HyQ>
```

Our selection of objects is similar to the generalised path expressions found in POQL [2]; however, the interpretation is simplified since our tree structures are untyped rather than being constrained by a database schema. This need to query semi-structured data without strict typing conventions has been recognised in Lorel [4], which use coercion between types to address the problem. An alternative to path expressions is tree patterns, as in SgmlQL [16]. SgmlQL actually goes beyond the querying, with primitives to construct new trees from existing ones, however, as any of these languages, it does not address the problem of conversion to a different DTD.

DTD conversion has been addressed already by a number of approaches: either by general-purpose languages such as DSSSL[14], or within SGML editors for supporting cut-and-paste between incompatible elements [5]. Other languages for restructuring information, like Lorel, focus on the integration of heterogeneous data structures or translation from one world to another, including from/to a document format. These languages, as well as DSSSL, could be used for implementing library *coercion* functions to map complex or frequently used structures, but are beyond the reach of document writers because of their complexity,.

Various languages for querying the Web in a database style have been developed [6,15,19]. They allow searching for specific elements in pages, as well following links, but they do not support querying the full SGML structure.

Languages for building documents from existing sources of information have been less explored.

SGML offers a static way of assembling entities from external files. All the assembled parts must conform to the DTD of the embedding document and there is no language for dynamic transformations. [22] enlightened the need for assembling dynamically generated parts of documents, and suggested using the *process instruction* mechanism. Our language precisely defines a language for building the virtual components, to be embedded in process instructions, then providing an SGML-compliant solution.

For reusing Web pages, Araneous [6] offers a limited model for creating new Web pages after querying existing ones. The constructed pages can only include text, lists and links to other pages, and not the full-range of HTML constructs; from the definition of new pages, a new set of *static* HTML pages are created.

Various ways of including pieces of information within a static HTML page exist, but HTML itself does not offer much more than <IMG> tags, and a server side *include*. Advanced servers, like PHP [17] or w3-msql [11] offer interface for accessing SQL databases from HTML. This works by embedding SQL queries and control instructions in HTML comments that are pre-processed on the server. Their script-based approach have the disadvantage of mixing the commands with the HTML syntax, which makes it difficult to update them or to include them in other documents. They do not allow for merging results from various databases.

MacWeb [20] synthesises documents by dynamically combining fragments of information that are organised in an object-oriented knowledge base. It uses a script language for describing the structure and the semantic content of the virtual document, which makes it difficult to author the document specification.

7 Conclusion

Reusing information contained in documents is becoming a major issue, whether it is proprietary information or information available from the Internet. In this paper we have presented a language for reusing information objects from heterogeneous sources. Our approach is to use a *middleware* format to integrate the results of queries to the various sources and to map its into a new (virtual) document.

The virtual document prescription is document-centred, which allows for authoring virtual document in a more descriptive ways than using a program or a scripting language. The prescription can also be viewed as a configuration specification for the virtual documents (a "makefile" for document), that can be stored as a document.

The language is designed primarily for reusing information objects from databases and structured documents. It works also with HTML documents, but the HTML tags may not be the right granularity for information objects. If XML [7] is adopted, it will provide the explicit structuring schema for Web pages for extracting objects.

Further extensions to the language under considerations include:

- adding parameters to the language. A virtual document prescription would then act as a generic template for a variety of virtual documents.
- partial instantiation of the virtual document prescription for document edition, or for efficiency.
- control instructions: The virtual document construction may depend upon the actual results of queries (eg. no answer or to many answers).

We are also considering extending an SGML editor to support the creation of virtual documents.

References

[1]   S. Abiteboul, "Querying semi-structured data", ICDT (invited talk), 1997.

[2]   S. Abiteboul, S. Cluet, V. Christophides, T. Milo, G.Moerkotte, and J. Simeon, "Querying documents in object databases", *Journal of Digital Libraries*, 1997. To appear. http://www-db.standford.edu.

[3]   S. Abiteboul, S. Cluet, and T. Milo. "Correspondence and translation for heterogeeous data", in *Proc. ICDT 97*.

[4]   S. Abiteboul, D. Quass, J. McHugh, J.Widom, and J. Wiener. "The Lorel query language for semi tructured data", *Journal of Digital Libraries*, 1996. Ftp://db.standford.edu/pub/papers/lorel96.ps

[5]   Akpotsui, V. Quint, C. Roisin, "Type Modeling for Document Transformation in Structured Editor", *Mathematical and Computer Modelling*, 1994.

[6]   P.Atzeni, G. Mecca, P. Merialdo, and E. Tabet, *Structure in the Web*, Technical Report 19-96, Dipartimente di Informatica e Automazione, Universita' di Roma, 1996.

[7] T. Bray, and C.M. Sperberg-McQueen, *Extensible Markup Language (XML)*, W3C Working Draft Nov 96, available from http://www.w3.org/pub/WWW/TR/WD-xml-961114.html

[8] V. Christophides, S. Abiteboul, S. Cluet, and M. Scholl, "From Structured Documents to Novel Query Facilities", in *Proceedings of the ACM SIGMOD Conference on Management of Data*, Minneapolis, Minnesota, pp313-324, 1994.

[9] Steven J. DeRose and David G. Durand, *Making Hypermedia Work: A User's Guide to HyTime*, Kluwer Academic Publishers, 1994.

[10] C.F. Golfarb, *The SGML Handbook*, Clarendon Press, Oxford, 1990.

[11] Hughes Technology, *W3-mSQL & Lite Library*, http://Hughes.com.au/library/lite/

[12] ISO 8879. *Information Processing-Text and office systems-Standad Generalized Markup Language* (SGML), 1986.

[13] ISO 10774. *Information Technolgy- Hypermedia/Time-based Structuring language* (HyTime), 1992.

[14] ISO 10179. *Document Style and specification Language* (DSSSL), 1996.

[15] D. Konopnicki and O.Shmueli, "W3QS: A query System for the World Wide Web", in *VLDB*, 1995.

[16] J.Le Maitre, E. Murisasco, M. Rolbert, "SgmlQL, un langage d'interrogation de documents structurés", *Proceedings of BDA'95*, Nancy August 95 (*in French*). See also *SgmlQL reference manual* (*in English*) at: http://www.lpl.univ-aix.fr/projects/multext/MtSgmlQL/MQL2.html

[17] R. Lerdorf, *PHP/FI Documentation*, http://www.vex.net/php/doc.phtml

[18] D.M. Levy, "Document reuse and Documents systems", *Electronic Publishing*, Vol.6(4) pages 339-348, December 1993.

[19] A. Mendelzohn, G. A. Milhaila, and T. Milo, "Querying the World Wide Web", *PDIS*, 1996, available at ftp: ftp.math.tau.ac.il/pub/milo/websql.ps

[20] J. Nanard, M. Nanard, "Using Types to incorporate Knowledge in Hypertext", *Proceedings of the 3rd ACM Conference On Hypertexts*, ACM Press, San Antonio (Texas), pp. 329-344, December 1991.

[21] ODMG. "Object Query Language", draft version of chapter 7 to appear in *The Object Database Standard: ODMG V2.0*, 1997.

[22] D. Skar, "Gratuating from File-based to Info-based Document Construction", *SGML Asia Pacific Conference*, Sydney, September 1996.

[23] A.M. Vercoustre, J. Dell'Oro, and B. Hills, "Reuse of Information through virtual documents", *Australian Document Computing Symposium, Melbourne*, April 97.

Generic Reusable Business Object Modelling -A Framework and its Application in British Telecommunications plc[1].

Islam Choudhury[1], Yuan Sun[2] and Dilip Patel[3]

[1,3]School of Computing, Information Systems and Maths, South Bank University, 103 Borough Road, London, SE1 0AA, UK
choudhia@sbu.ac.uk / dilip@sbu.ac.uk

[2]Compuware Ltd, 163 Bath Road Slough, Berkshire SL1 4AA, UK.
yuan_sun@compuware.com

ABSTRACT

This paper outlines a framework for building a Generic Reusable Business Object Model (GRBOM) and its application in BT. A GRBOM is a conceptual model which accurately specifies the business knowledge in the form of an object-oriented model. It captures the core business processes and business objects of a particular domain within an industry independent of any application development. A GRBOM can be reused in multiple projects either within the same organisation who built the model or by other organisations within different industrial sectors.

KEY WORDS: Genericity, Reuse, Conceptual Enterprise Modelling, Business Object Modelling, Generic Business Process, Generic Business Object, Role Repository

1. Introduction

It is increasingly being recognised and advocated by many authors (Jacobson 1995, Taylor 1995, Partridge 1996, Graham 1994, Martin 1992) that the success of information systems in organisations lies in the initial overall conceptual and clear understanding of the business, an acceptance that business is in a constant state of flux and that there is a need to shift from an application view to a business view. This recognition has led to the current trend into more research into Information Architecture development (e.g. Sowa and Zachman 1992), which is also referred to as Enterprise Modelling (e.g. Car *et al.* 1994). Niederman *et al.* (1991) have ranked Information Architecture development as first in importance as a key issue in Information Systems Development.

This work tackles issues in Business Object Modelling (BOM) (Arrow *et al.* 1995 and Jacobson *et al.* 1995) which can be usefully utilised in Enterprise Modelling. We suggest that problems existing in information systems are due to the fact that business information systems continue to be developed on the basis of business requirements which are only a snapshot of a business's

---

[1] This research is funded by British Telecommunications plc., (BT).

dynamic life. This type of development, not taking into account the conceptual understanding of the overall business and possible future changes, has resulted in large amounts of waste. Experts agree that an Enterprise Model offers the potential to serve as a basis for building a co-ordinated, responsive, long-lasting set of business applications and can be used in multiple projects over a period of time (Jackson, M. 1994, Nelborn *et al.* 1992). Digre (1995) has highlighted the need for building generic industry models and Rutt and Stringer (1996) of the OMG Vertical Industry Domain Task Force (OMGVIDTF) have emphasised the importance of a Telecommunication Vertical Industry Model. However, we will concentrate our efforts on building a model within the telecommunications industry but one which can be applied to other industries as well. The OMG Business Object Domain Task Force (Arrow *et al* 1995) has developed the concept of Business Objects which can provide a very useful way to model the business. Some of the problems with Enterprise Modelling is the management of the complexity inherent in an enterprise and the responsiveness to change and improvement.

We suggest that to manage the complexity inherent in an enterprise, we should capture the core business objects and business processes of a particular domain within an industry. To manage the responsiveness to change and improvement the object oriented paradigm should be utilised in the form of a Business Object Model. Our approach outlines a framework that one may use to overcome the above problems to some extent. We propose the development of a generic and reusable object oriented model of a business and have named this a Generic Reusable Business Object Model (GRBOM). This approach is different to the current object oriented business object modelling approach which suggests the building of a business model for a specific application at a specific time. Current Enterprise Modelling which deals with the generic nature of different industries is dealt with in Enterprise Integration research (Vernadat 1992). This concentrates on developing a detailed high level Enterprise Model which deals with the interactions of the people, processes, machines and suppliers etc. and the integration of the whole industry for the purpose of improving the business logistics in order to justify budgets and organisational structure of that particular industry, they are too inwardly focused. We strongly suggest that business must work with the understanding of the global environment and focus on how their particular industry fits into that environment. Our intention is to build an object model of a particular domain within an industry which can be the starting point of several application developments either within the organisation which built the model or by organisations of different industrial sectors.

In section 2 we present and explain the GRBOM Framework requirements and its five dimensions: genericity, reuse, change, business object model and patterns. Section 3 shows the application of the GRBOM using Select OMT Case Tool to help build a business object model (BOM) of the Customer Services Domain of BT, utilising Jacobson's Use Case Engineering (Jacobson 1995) and Rumbaugh's Object Modelling Technique (Rumbaugh *et al.* 1991). We extend the approach by adding a higher level layer as the Core Business Model that can be directly mapped onto the BOM. Finally, in section 4 we describe further work that is underway to evaluate the GRBOM.

2. GRBOM Framework

In this section we explain the requirements and structure of the GRBOM Framework. Table 1 summaries in a list, what is required of a Business Object Model in general (Aranguren 1992) and the additional requirements for a GRBOM framework.

	Requirements for Business Object Model in General	Additional Specific Requirements for a GRBOM
1	Better understanding of complexity in business processes and operations	Providing a methodology for capturing the core (common or generic) components of a domain
2	Enabling simulation of alternatives	Discovery process - discover the appropriate business objects and relations for the problems and environments
3	Identification of optimum solution	With support from a CASE tool, (e.g., Select OMT)
4	Use for direct execution to control and monitor business processes and operation	Be context dependent (e.g., within a financial, manufacturing or telecommunication industry domain)
5	Model creation and execution support	Scope dependent (e.g., parts of the customer domain within the above mentioned industry but can broaden)
6	Supporting distributed and heterogeneous environments	Outputs will be generic business objects, generic business processes, patterns, a business modelling process and a Business Object Model.
7	Describing the business informally in terms of functionality and dynamic behaviour	Be generic in the sense that it will be flexible, tailorable, adaptable, can evolve as situations change and is general to various industrial sectors.
8	Work in certain contexts.	Describe the factors of change.

Table 1 - Requirements of a GRBOM

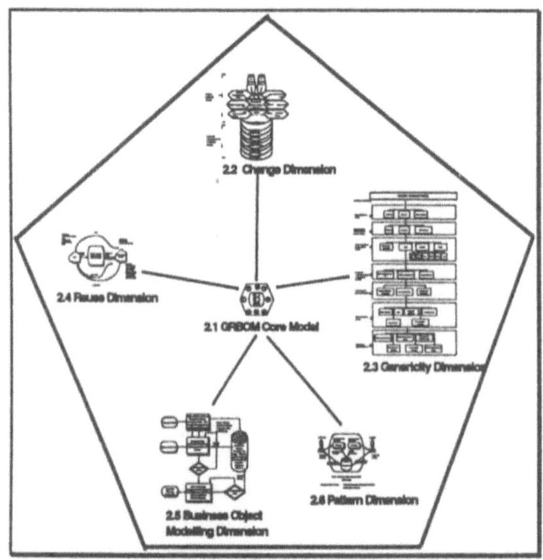

Figure 1. GRBOM Framework

To fulfil the dynamic requirements, the building of a Generic Reusable Business Object Model Framework should develop in five dimensions : change, genericity, reusability, business object model and patterns. At the centre of the GRBOM framework is the Core Business Model. An overview of the GRBOM framework is presented in Figure 1 and each of the dimensions are explained in the relevant sub- sections. These dimensions, working together, provide a complete picture of the GRBOM. The GRBOM is instantiated through its application in a particular domain of a specific industry in the form of an object oriented core business object model.

2.1 The GRBOM -Core Business Model

At the centre of the GRBOM is the Core Business Model. This is built by analysing the existing documentation, systems and operations within the domain of interest of a particular industry. Then the generic business processes, business objects and the interconnections are captured and represented in a GRBOM - Core Business Model (CBM). Figure 2 shows the GRBOM-CBM as applied to the customer services of the telecommunications industry.

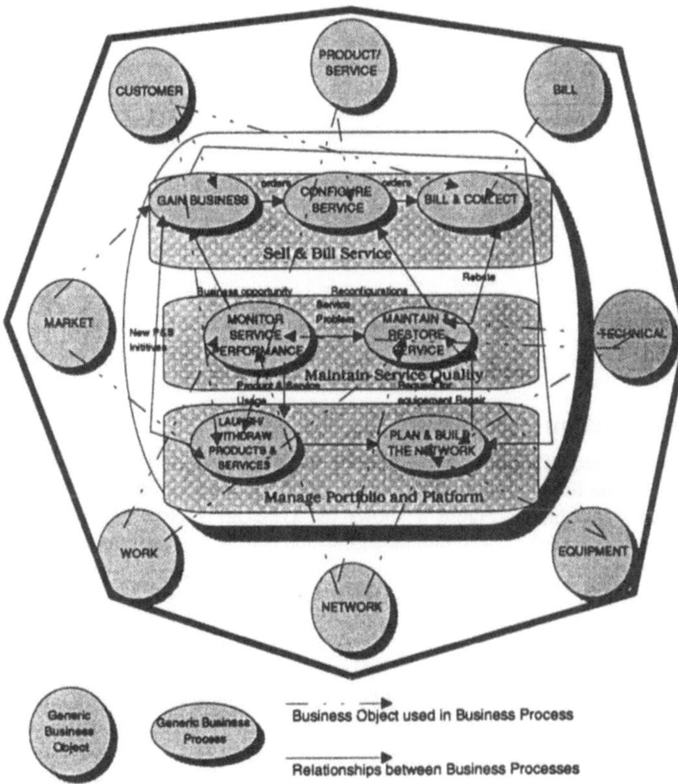

Figure 2. Telecommunication Industry-Customer Services Domain-Core Business Model

316

In order for the model to be generic, reusable and to be applicable to different industrial sectors, the proposed model must be built within the GRBOM framework which considers the five dimensions as mentioned in Figure 1.

2.2 GRBOM - Change Dimension

One of the most important requirements of the GRBOM is adaptability and flexibility. To be capable of this, the CBM must be prepared for possible changes and respond accordingly. We suggest that the change dimension must capture factors that cause change and factors with which to characterise and analyse change. Fig 3. shows the GRBOM - change dimension.

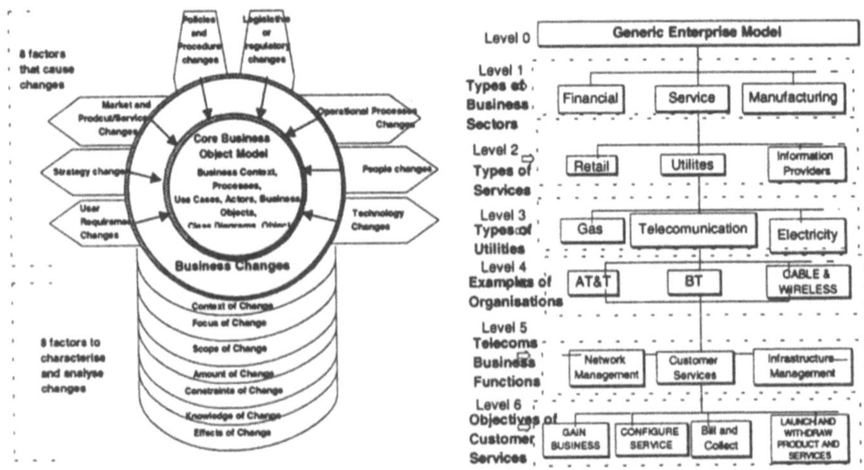

Figure3-GRBOM-Change Dimension   Figure 4. GRBOM - Genericity Dimension-

2.3 Genericity Dimension

Genericity is the staged refined of entire models, it uses stepwise instantiation to go from the general to the specific or from the specific to the general. The GRBOM is a reference model of a particular domain within an industry. Figure 4 shows the GRBOM - Genericity Dimension, showing how customer services of the telecommunications industry fits into the overall scheme of industrial sectors. A CBM can be built for each level of the Genericity Diagram. Different genericity diagrams can be built for different domains and different industries.

2.4 Reuse Dimension

The GRBOM is a reference model that can be reused by systems developers in the development of multiple projects. Figure 5. shows the GRBOM reuse dimension. The diagram shows the positioning of the CBM in relation to business modelling and Information Systems modelling. The CBM is designed for reuse (DfR) and then applications are developed with design with reuse (DwR) in multiple projects.

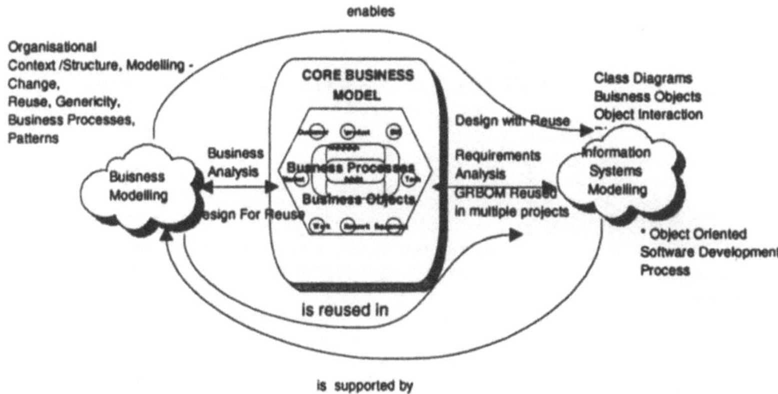

Figure 5. GRBOM Reuse Dimension

2.5 Business Object Modelling Dimension

Jacobson's Use Case Engineering and Rumbough's OMT were used to build an Object-Oriented Model of the CBM (section 2.1, figure.2). Figure 6 shows the overall business object modelling dimension. The Generic Processes in the Core Model were represented as a series of Use Cases containing various Business Objects. Object Management Group Business Object Domain Task Force (OMGBODTF) has defined Business Objects as "a representation of a thing in the business having attributes, behaviour, relationships and constraints" (Arrow *et al.* 1995). Select OMT was used as a CASE tool to support the building of GRBOM models and because it provides a repository to store the Business Objects and Models. Select OMT is a fully functional CASE tool that supports Rumbaugh's Object Modelling Technique, Jacobson's Use Cases and Object Interaction Diagrams. The business processes and business objects of the Core Business Model are mapped to use cases and business objects of the business object model, see figure 7. The business objects are made up of interface objects, control objects and entity objects.

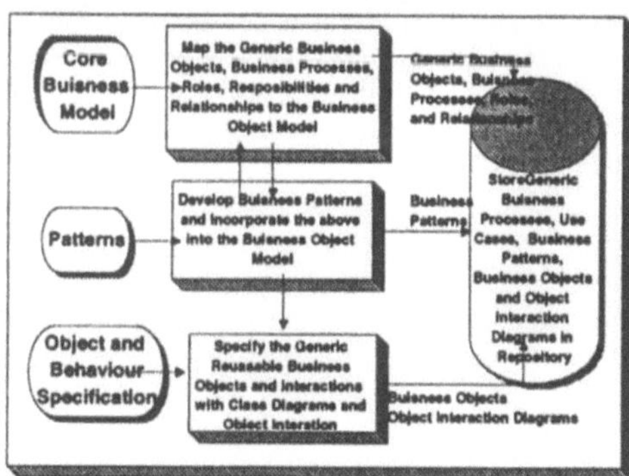

Figure 6. GRBOM - Business Object Modelling Dimension

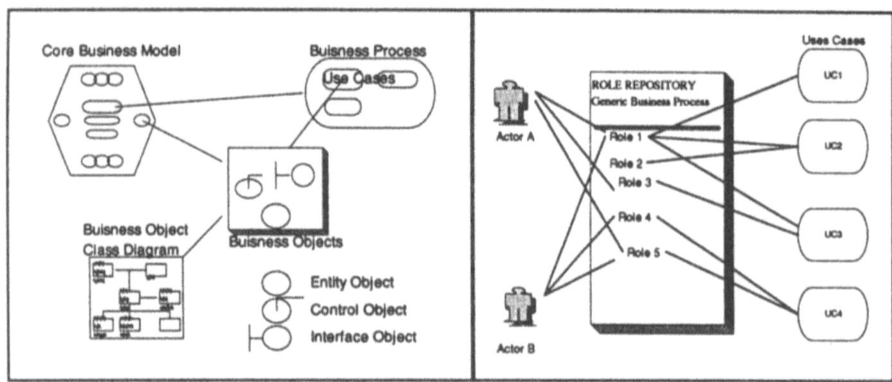

<table>
<tr><td>Figure 7- CBM mapping to BOM</td><td>Figure 8. The Role Repository</td></tr>
</table>

2.5.1 Extension to Jacobson's Use Case Engineering (UCE).

One extra part that Jacobson's UCE and Select OMT does not provide but is added to our GRBOM is a Role Repository (RR). Figure 8 shows the structure of a RR. A RR is useful as opposed to having only an Actor repository. This is because Actors are assigned to a specific Use Case, however the same actor may be capable of carrying out roles in other use cases but this actor is not specified to do so, hence a new actor has to be introduced to model this new role. It is usually the case in real business that one actor may have many roles and the actor role may be different at different times and for different circumstances. Hence it would be useful to model this aspect of the real world. A Role Repository allows any actor with the specific abilities to be assigned to as many roles as required and is capable of performing. Each of these roles are then described by use cases. A RR is built for each of the Generic Business Processes within the Core Business Model.

2.6 Patterns Dimension

During business analysis and during the development of a RR, various patterns are identified and some examples of the structure of these patterns are presented in Figure 9. The basic pattern - Event - Process - Resource (EPR) pattern was developed from the Resource-Event-Agent Pattern (Greets and McCarthy 1995). The EPR pattern is presented with instances of that pattern. These patterns can help in Use Case Analysis and Business Object Model Development. Patterns are captured for each Generic Business Process within the CBM.

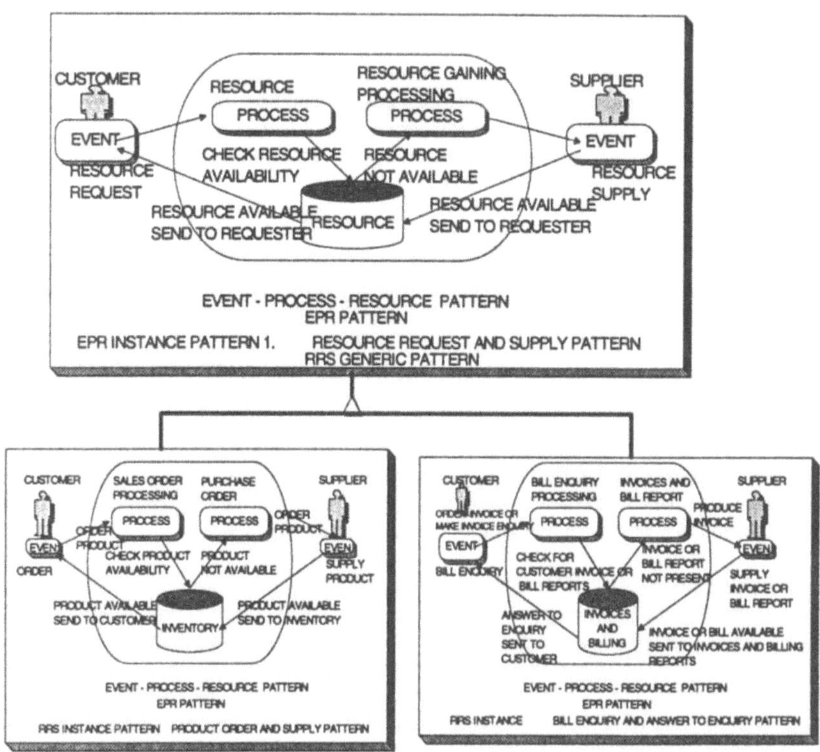

Figure 9- GRBOM- Patterns Dimension

3. Application of the GRBOM in BT

Once the theoretical foundations of a GRBOM were laid down it was important to evaluate it. The first stage of this evaluation was to actually apply the GRBOM in a real organisation. Hence, a case study was carried out at BT Labs in Ipswich, UK. The next sections explain why we chose to study the customer service of a Telecommunication Industry. We, then show how the GRBOM was actually applied to build an object oriented model of the customer service of BT, bearing in mind that this model should be general to the Telecommunication Industry and should be reusable.

3.1 Customer Service

A good quality and efficient customer service information system is one of the most important parts of any service organisation (St Clair 1993). Customer service is a vital part of BT as it has a very large database of 27 million-plus telephone customers with various demands. A fast efficient response is required to meet these demands. The largest growth area for BT is customer services and especially one of its most important business concerns is that of domestic calls which brought in £1.2bn in 1995. The changes that are taking place within the telecommunication industry has increased competitive pressures and Peter Bonfield (Chief Executive of BT) has warned that BT could lose more than half its current customer base of 27 million to foreign and UK rivals over the next five years (Hayward, 1996). This indicates the urgency to build a generic model of the customer services domain within BT so that the required systems that need to be developed to adapt and keep pace of the change can be developed quickly and efficiently. The core customer services business objects and processes within BT were captured using Jacobson's object-oriented business processes reengineering approach, concentrating on BT's Operational Support System for Customer Service.

3.2 The GRBOM Core Business Model

The Customer Services of BT was analysed thoroughly from existing documents and by interviewing staff at BT Labs Ipswich. A CBM was built taking into account the five dimensions. Building of the model is done simultaneously and itteratively. Section 2.1, Figure 2 shows the Telecommunication Industry - Customer Services Core Business Model. 'TI-CSD-CBM L5'

3.3 The Change Dimension

The change dimension (section 2.2, figure 3) was the starting point for analysing factors that cause change and factors with which to characterise and analyse change. The next paragraph summarises the change dimension that was taken into consideration in building the CBM.

The Telecommunication Industry is increasing in complexity and is in a state of instability. New markets, new technology and new ways of doing business are creating new opportunities and new challenges. Even the understanding and definition of what exactly is telecommunications is rapidly changing. Telecommunication is not only the management of an infrastructure of cables, wires, satellites, home telephones and mobile phones. It also has to use state of the art technologies and maintain the highest level of service to its customers. Market forces are changing, government controlled regulatory barriers are disappearing and an increasing number of companies are entering the telecommunication industry intensifying competition. Increasing complexity and constant changes to the structure and running of the business requires information systems that can keep pace. A solution would be to develop a system that captures a sound understanding of the business, preserves existing investments and can be easily adapted as changes take place and new demands are placed on the system. We suggested that a GRBOM can help a telecommunications organisation address some of the above mentioned issues.

3.4 Genericity Dimension

The Genericity Dimension (section 2.2, Figure 4) shows a genericity model of the Customer Services Domain of the Telecommunication Industry. As can be seen in Figure 4 the customer services domain of BT can be generalised to the telecommunication industry. This in turn can be generalised to the utilities industry which in turn can be generalised to the Service Industry Sector. We suggest that the GRBOM that captures the business processes and business objects of customer services domain of BT should have some similar properties to that of other telecommunication industries. Also there should be similar properties in other utility industries and the Service Industry Sector in general. The Generic Enterprise model can be instantiated to a GRBOM Core Business Model (CBM) for each of the lower levels. The scope of this research paper is just to show the GRBOM at the Customer Services Level of the Telecommunication Industry, this is represented as GRBOM-CBM-L5. Further research is currently being carried out by the authors to build a genericity diagram for the customer services of a Credit Insurance company which can be generalised to the Insurance Industry and to the Finance Industry Sector.

3.5 GRBOM-The Reuse Dimension

As mentioned in section 2.4, the GRBOM has to initially be built for reuse. This takes place in the initial development. Once the model is built it can then be reused in multiple project developments. The GRBOM will be used as a starting point of a billing system development and a marketing system development. Also the GRBOM can be reused by different organisations of different industries. Further work is under way to evaluate this by building a GRBOM representing the customer services domain of the Finance Industry. The same GRBOM built for the customer services domain of the telecommunications industry is reused with slight modifications to incorporate specific concepts of the Finance Industry.

3.6 GRBOM - Business Object Model Dimension

An object oriented model of the CBM was developed as in section 2.5, the Business Object Model Dimension. Each Business Object and Business Process Object and links from the CBM were mapped to Class Diagrams (as shown in section 2.5, figure 7) and the final result is a complete 'Telecommunication Industry Customer Services Domain Business Object Model Level 5'; TI-CSD-BOM-L5, part of which is shown in figure 12. Figure 12 shows an example of the Launch and Withdraw Products and Services Generic Business Process Object which shows all the business objects including their attributes, operations and relations. One of the objects that are utilised is the Market Object (see figure 12). As explained in section 2.5.1. a Role Repository is a useful component of the GRBOM. Figure 13 shows an example for part of the Customer Services Domain Generic Business Process Launch and Withdraw Products and Services Role Repository (CSD-GBP-LWPS-RR). This RR helped in the development of the patterns as described in section. 3.6 which follows.

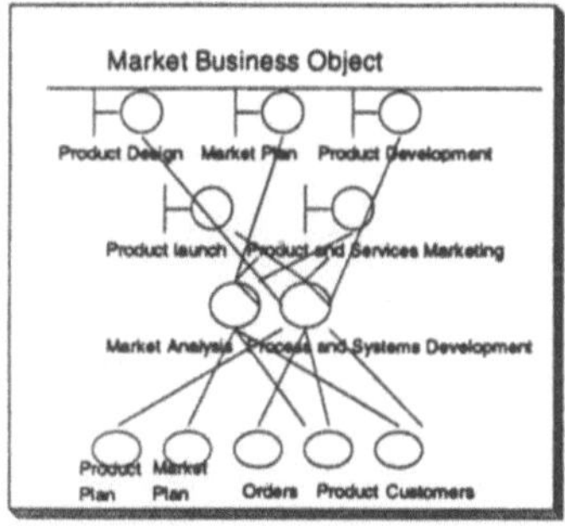

10 Part of a market Business Object

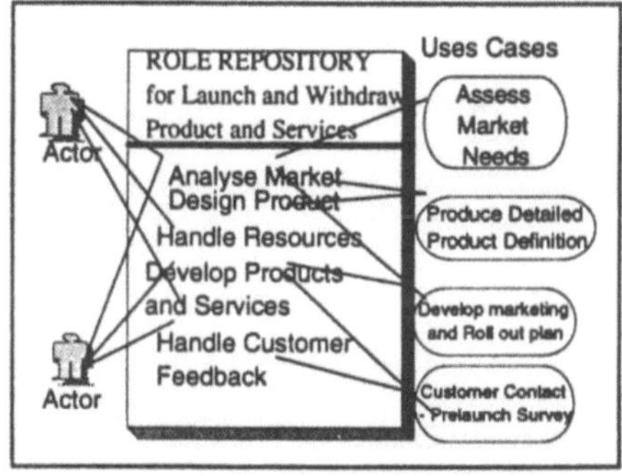

11. Part of the Role Repository for Launch
    and Withdraw Products and Services

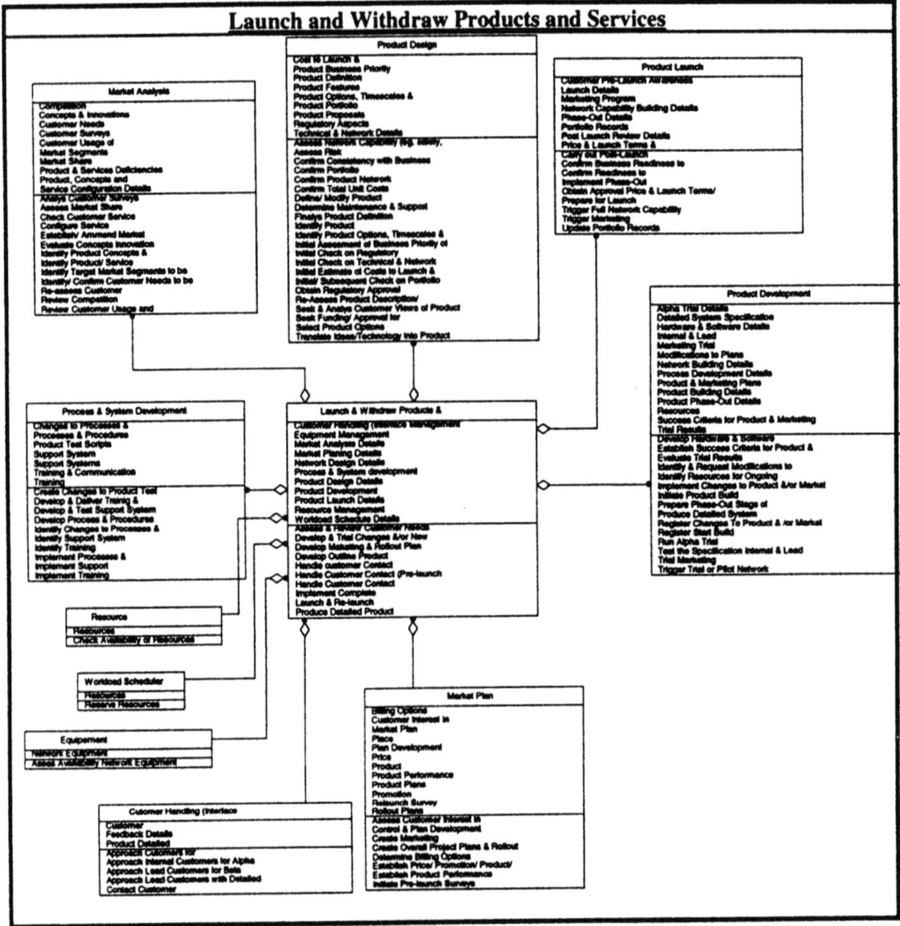

Figure 12 Launch and Withdraw Product and Services - Generic Business Process Object

3.7 GRBOM Patterns Dimension

Whilst analysing the Customer Services Domain Generic Business Process Launch and Withdraw Products and Services (CSD-GBP-LWPS) and during the development of a RR we managed to capture 10 basic patterns at Level1; 20 Level2 patterns and 90 Level 3 patterns. Figure 9 shows an example of a level 1 pattern (product order and supply pattern) within the CSD-GBP-LWPS. These patterns helped us to build the GRBOM.

4. Evaluation and Further Work

The GRBOM will be evaluated against BT's existing object-oriented customer models, which have already been analysed by previous analysts to develop various systems for BT applications, for example customer billing systems, customer enquiry systems, customer marketing systems, etc. The generic nature of the GRBOM will be evaluated by instantiating the model in different domains for example the Finance domain. We are currently carrying out a similar Case Study in the Customer Services domain of a Credit Insurance company which can be generalised to the Insurance Industry which in turn can be generalised to the Finance Industry sector. In order to justify the usefulness of the GRBOM, evaluation criteria are currently being developed and these will be used in subsequent testing and further development of the GRBOM framework.

It is necessary to operationalise the above identified conceptual attributes of genericity, change, reusability, business object modelling, patterns and its business validity to enable empirical investigation. Further research into GRBOM will concentrate on the following aspects:

a) The conceptualisation and visualisation of the terms, genericity, reusability, business object modelling and its business validity.

b) Investigating means of operationalising the identified attributes of GRBOM for the purpose of using the model as a reference model as the starting point of several application developments.

c) Further case studies, including one already started in the Finance Industry, will be carried out to evaluate the generality and usefulness of GRBOM.

5. Conclusion

We have justified the need for a GRBOM so that the essence of an organisation can be captured and represented in an object oriented model which is general, reusable and adaptable. A GRBOM framework was presented which identified the important components of such a model. The components were explained in terms of five dimensions: genericity, change, business object modelling, reuse and patterns. At the heart of the model is the Core Business Model. An investigation into the customer services domain of BT revealed that it is possible to use the GRBOM framework and some results were presented. It must be emphasised that the development of a GRBOM is not a step by step method but a simultaneous and iterative method within the GRBOM framework. The object-oriented paradigm provided very useful modelling constructs. The genericity dimension helped in identifying how a particular domain in an a specific organisation fits into the industrial sectors that exist in our current understanding of the world. This enables us to identify an appropriate level of abstraction to enable reuse across industries. Further work is underway to evaluate the model by way of empirical investigation. The results will be published in a future paper.

6. Acknowledgements

We would like to thank BT for their support in funding this project and for allowing us to carry out a Case Study at their Labs in Ipswich, UK. In particular, we would mention Dr. Ben Whittle, Dr. Paul Spurdens and all the staff at BT SoftLabs, who made this project viable. We would also like to thank the staff at the Center for Information and Office Systems (CIOS) at South Bank University who offered help and advice in the writing of this paper.

324

7.   References

Aranguren, R., Eirich, P., Fox, M., *et al.* The Process of Model Integration. *Proceedings of the First International Conference on Enterprise Integration.* Petrie, C.J. 1992, pp 33-41

Arrow, L., Barnwell, R., Burt, C. and Anderson, M. OMG Business Object Survey. OMG Document 95-6-4. 25 May 1995

Carr, N.C. and Phipps, B. Editors. Enterprise State of the Art Survey. Part 4 Reuse Applied to Enterprise Modelling. September 30, 1994.

Digre, T. Business Application Components in Sutherland, J., Patel, D., Casanave, C., *et al.*(ed) Business Object Design and Implementation, *OOPSLA 95 Workshop Proceedings,*. Springer1997

Graham, I. Migrating to Object Technology, 1994, *Addison Wesley.*

Greets, G.L. and McCarthy, W.E. Modeling Business Enterprises with Resource-Event-Agent Object Templates in Sutherland, J., Patel, D., Casanave, C., *et al.*(ed) Business Object Design and Implementation, *OOPSLA 95 Workshop Proceedings,* Springer1997.

Hayward, D. BT reports a fall in market share *COMPUTING* 21 November 1996. pp 10.

Jacobson, I., Ericson, M. and Jacobson, A. The Object Advantage. Business Process Reengineering with Object Technology. *ACM Press.* 1995.

Jackson, M. The Role of Software Architecture in Requirements Engineering *The 1st International Conference on Requirements Engineering,* IEEE Computer Society Press 1994.

Martin, J. and Odell, J. Object Oriented Analysis and Design 1992, *Prentice Hall.*

Nelborn, C., Bubenko, J. and Gustafsson, M. Enterprise Modelling - Key to Capturing Requirements for Information Systems, *SISU, F3 Project Internal Report,* 1992.

Niederman, F., Brancheau, J.C. and Wetherbe, J.C. Information Systems Management Issues for the 1990s *MIS Quarterly* December 1991

Partridge, C. Business Objects Reengineering for Reuse. Butterworth-Heinmaan 1996

Rumbaugh, J., Blaha, M., Premerlani, W., *et al* Object-Oriented Modelling and Design *Prentice Hall* 1991

Rutt, T., and Stringer, D. The OMG Telecom Domain Task Force *First Class : OMG: Meeting the challenge of Vertical Industries.* August/ September 1996

Sowa, J.F., and Zachman, J.A. Extending and formalising the framework for information systems architecture. *IBM Systems Journal* Vol 31, No 3, 1992

St Clair, G. Customer Service in the Information Environment. *Bowker-Saur* 1993

Taylor, D. A. Business Engineering with Object Technology. *John Wiley and Sons, Inc.* 1995

Vernadat, F.B. 1992. CIMOSA - A European Development for Enterprise Integration. Part2: Enterprise Modelling. ESPIRIT Consortium AMICE. *Proceedings of the First International Conference on Enterprise Integration.* Petrie, C.J. 1992, pp 179-188

Object-Oriented Approaches to Software Reuse

Jan Seruga, Francis Pasinos
Department of Computing and Technology, Australian Catholic University,
Sydney, Australia

Abstract
The study attempted to investigate on the major developments in the Australian (NSW) industry to identify how object-oriented technology has influenced local developers, their current practices and technical approaches in software reuse.

Software Development Process

The continuing growth of software development costs and the complexity of modern information systems have led organisations to realise that to survive in a competitive business environment, they must have a successful software development process. Bieman and Karunanithi (1995, p. 271) demonstrate the importance of implementing an effective software development process within a business stating that "Developing software in a predictable time period with acceptable quality and reliability is a major problem in the computer industry. There is a high demand for software of increasing complexity and need to modify and extend existing software systems".

The concept of software reuse can be defined as the process of implementing or updating software systems using existing software components. Software reuse is similar to a recycling process where rather than building a software system from the outset (the traditional software development practice), reuse capitalises on the similarity of software to build new systems.

According to McGregor and Sykes (1992), to have reuse play a major role in software development, "Program components must have a life independent of the application for which they were originally developed."

Following reuse technology over the years has shown that attempts to make software reuse a reality has not always been successful, but recently developers and businesses have gained a step closer to obtaining the full benefits from software reuse and solving the problems associated with the software crisis. By continually updating the reuse concept and introducing new technologies such as object-oriented technology and associated design methods, it has helped support reuse to change it from a simple idea to an on-going reality.

Many developers and businesses are now embracing object-oriented (OO) methods as they offer many preconditions for reuse such as inheritance and specialisation of generic objects. The results obtained from the industry designed survey indicate the growing interest in utilising OO technology to implement reuse in an organisation.

Businesses have turned to software reuse as the answer to reducing costs and risks associated with software development as well as increase the quality and reliability of software. The introduction of object-oriented technology has enabled business to implement reuse on a large scale thus increasing their chance to be competitive in the business environment.

Software Reuse Development in Australia

Although software reuse is recognised as a great productivity idea, it has had varied success. Many software developers and managers in the US show little interest in explicitly incorporating reusability into their software development methodology because of the time, effort and risk that goes with reuse (McClure, 1995). On the other hand, the Japanese are regarded as world leaders of software reuse as they utilise reuse to a greater extent than any other country and have documented many well-known success stories. Management strategies have been the main responsibility for the Japanese's success. This leads to the question - "What about Australia and its development compared to the rest of the world?". Extensive research into the literature has shown minimal relevant data that relates to Australia's involvement with software reuse. Most of the available literature is limited to certain design and implementation aspects of reusability but does not explore the impact or extent of utilisation, and whether Australian businesses are benefiting from implementing reuse. For this reason an industry survey was constructed to analyse the development of reuse in Australian industry.

This part provides a quantitative analysis of an industry survey that targets software development companies, national and international businesses throughout Sydney, NSW, Australia. In this study an industry survey was distributed to 45 organisations which were randomly selected from a sample listed within a journal "Management of Information Systems" - 1995 & 1996 editions. Throughout the article, the surveyed organisations will be referred to as "Local Australian Businesses". By conducting the survey, the study aims to extend the body of research into local industry experience. Beyond this, the study provides general issues and can be used as a basis for further study in the field.

The following questions provide a focus for the research:

- What technical approaches are being utilised in object-oriented software reuse?
- How does software reuse change the way corporate developers undertake systems development?
- To what extent has the push towards object-oriented technology influenced the interest in reusability?
-

Aims of the Survey

The survey aims to:

- Determine the extent selected Australian businesses are using object-oriented technology to develop software for reuse.
- Outline the major problems organisations are having with reuse.
- Investigate the significance of reuse in software development.

Results of the Survey

Results of the survey indicate that all businesses fall under one of three categories:

	Category of software development	Number of businesses
1.	*Develop and design software* (Software development companies or businesses that design their own or others' software systems)	37
2.	*Consider the design of software* (Businesses that did not design software but had an external agency design for them)	5
3.	*Do not consider development or design of software* (Organisation that does not consider the development or design of software at all)	3
	TOTAL:	**45**

Out of the 45 responses, 37 organisations were involved with the development and design of software, 5 organisations considered the design of software, and 3 organisations did not consider the development of software at all. To gain a more accurate understanding of reuse and its effect on businesses, the analysis will focus on those organisations involved or consider the development and design of software.

The results of the survey indicate that Local Australian Businesses' consideration of software reuse in development is quite profound. 85 per cent of the businesses consider the benefits of reuse and 77 per cent have software development processes designed for reuse.

Object-Oriented Development

Figure 1 clearly illustrates that the majority of businesses have utilised object-oriented technology for 3 years or less. Obviously with this inexperience that local industries possess, it is difficult to report if the full benefits of object-oriented technology and reuse have been achieved. However, the large number of companies that currently consider object-oriented technology (69 per cent of the surveyed businesses) for implementing reuse in software development, shows that the interest in reusability is growing and there is promise for the future.

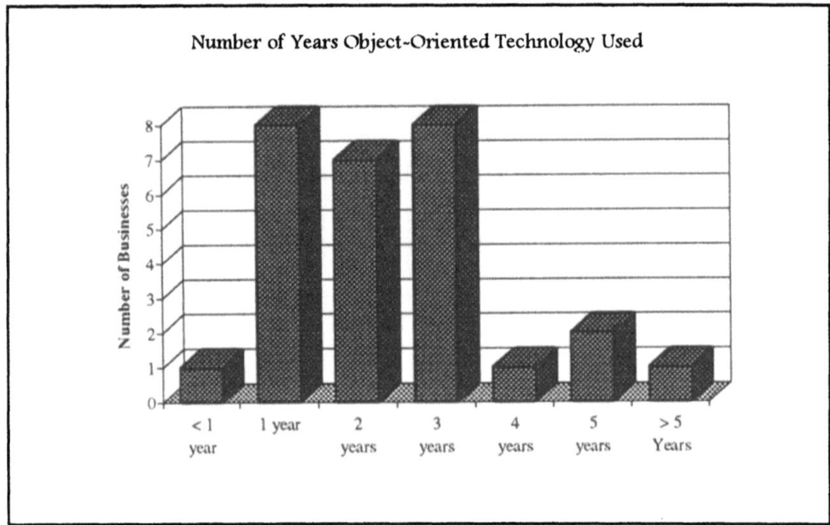

Figure 1. Number of Years Object-Oriented Technology Used

Many organisations have answered that utilising object-oriented technology can enable them to:

- design for reuse,
- allow for easier design and coding, and
- accomplish faster development as shown in Figure 2.

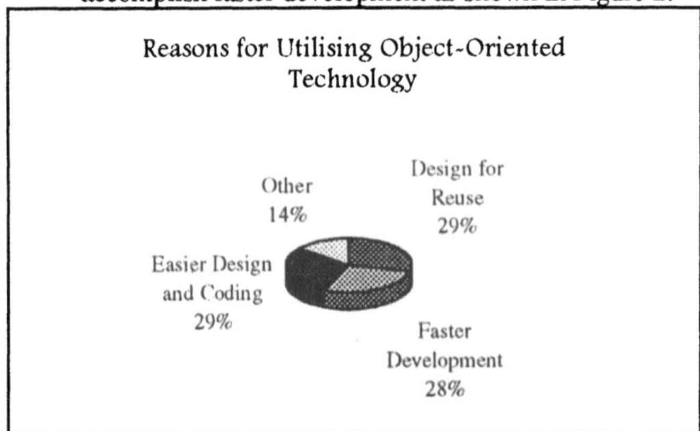

Figure 2. Reasons for Using Object-Oriented Technology

Approaches to Reusability

The three most popular approaches to reusability in surveyed organisations are:

- the use of objects as building blocks,
- software templates, and
- inheritance and specialisation of generic objects (Figure3).

Prior studies (Markis, 1995; Walton & Maiden, 1993) have suggested that the above three approaches are beneficial for software reuse. This is a good indication that businesses are headed to the right direction when approaching reusability.

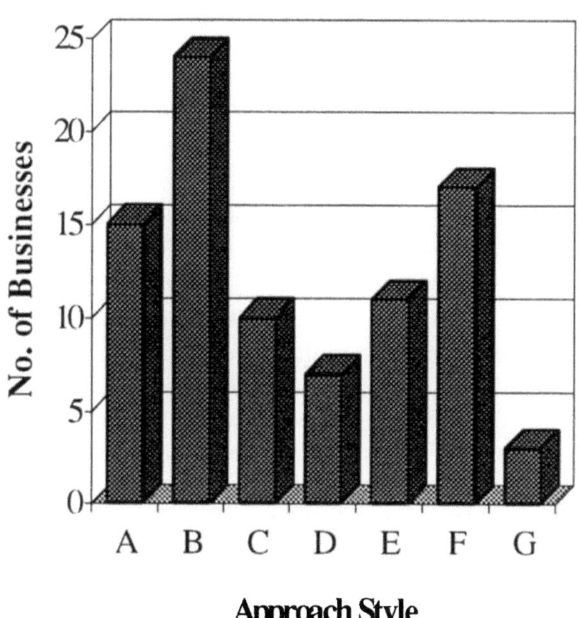

A. Inheritance and/or specialisation of generic objects

B. Use of objects as building blocks

C. Encapsulation

D. Polymorphism

E. Object-oriented analysis and design

F. Use of software templates

G. Other

Figure 3. Approaches to Reuse

Problems with Reusability

Figure 4 demonstrates the number and type of problems that are being faced when designing for reuse.

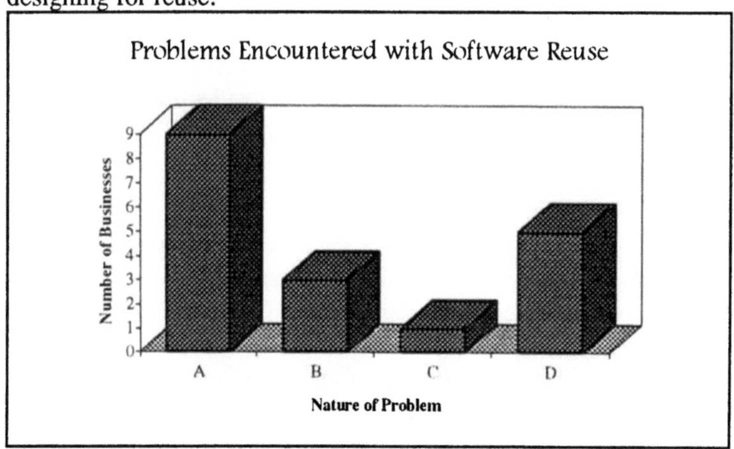

A. Management of reuse components B. Management of human resources

C. Legal   D. Technical

Figure 4. Problems with Software Reuse

Surprisingly, the survey has indicated that only a small number of businesses have claimed to have major problems with reusability. However, with the number that did respond the statistics clearly show that the majority of problems lie with the non-technical aspects of software design particularly with management of both software components and human resources. This coincides with prior studies (Frakes and Isoda, 1994) in the field that it is the non-technical issues that need attention. The most popular problem expressed by businesses relating to management of components was that the growing complexity of code results in redesigning of components. The most popular technical problem was that programming languages did not deliver the proper support to facilitate software reuse because of modest language design and poor implementation.

Significance of Reusability in Software Design

The survey also determines the significance of designing for reuse. One of the questions of the industry survey asked "On a scale of 1-10 (1 is the least and 10 is at most), how does software reuse form as a significant part of your software/program design?" Figure 5. illustrates given answers and concludes that the majority of businesses view reusability as very significant in software design, most being grouped between 6 and 8 on the scale.

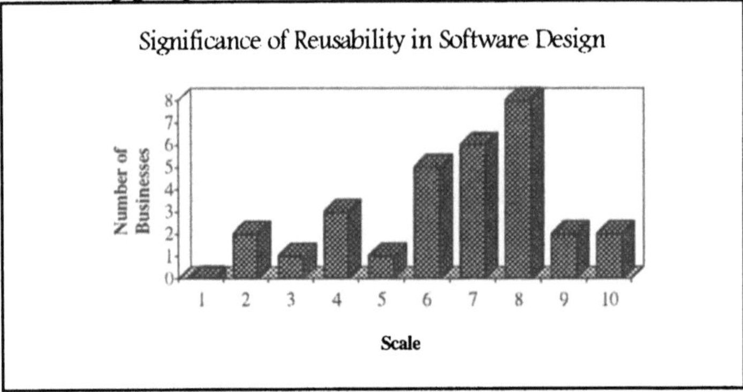

Figure 5. Significance of Reusability in Software Design

85 per cent of the surveyed businesses expressed that reuse presented significant benefits. The most popular benefits include: the reuse of code allows for faster development because of easier modification and maintenance of software, debugging programming code is easier since bugs are readily identified, and testing of particular code was eliminated since code was previously tested in prior projects.

Additional Statistics from the Survey

- Statistics indicate that only 23 per cent of those businesses who design for reuse have some type of programming support system.
- A majority of businesses keep libraries or repositories of components to reuse (33 out of 37).
- 76 per cent of the businesses consider designing *with* reuse.
- The most popular languages being used to facilitate reuse are:
    C++, Visual Basic, C, Delphi, SmallTalk, Object Cobol, Clarion, Access Basic

Conclusion

Software reuse in Local Australian Businesses appears promising in the short-term since little problems have arisen and the majority of businesses are approaching reusability in a reliable technical manner. However, to measure the true success of reusability the long-term effects of its implementation must be considered. The survey results reveal that only a small percentage of businesses have any type of support system. The limited technical and management support suggests that reuse in the long-term may not provide the full benefits of software quality or productivity. For reuse to play an integral role in productivity and quality, it is essential that the surveyed businesses place more emphasis on support systems. McGregor and Sykes (1992) believe that support systems are important in making reuse an ongoing success.

Eliminating the design with reuse is also important as a large percentage of surveyed businesses still gives emphasis to this. Time and resources may be saved if businesses focused on designing for reuse rather than with reuse. Reuse in Local Australian Businesses appears to be fixed and has a growing trend. Many businesses are turning towards reuse as a way of increasing productivity and quality and a way of reducing costs. The majority are also utilising object-oriented design methods as a way of implementing reuse structures.

Local Australian Businesses have viewed the benefits of software reuse, claiming faster development and coding, and simplified debugging and testing of software.

References

Bieman, J.M. and Karunanithi, S. Measurement of language-supported reuse in object-oriented and object-based software. J. Systems Software, 1995; 30: 271-293.

Frakes, W.B. and Isoda, S. Success factors of systematic reuse. IEEE Software, 1994; 28: 15-19.

Markis, V. Final Report. Object-Oriented Approaches in Software Development, 1995; November: 1.

McClure, C.L. Reuse find common ground. Forum & Letters Software Magazine, 1995; June: 6,8.

McGregor, J.D. and Sykes, D.A. Object-oriented software development: engineering software for reuse. Van Nostrand Reinhold New York, NY, 1992.

Walton, P. and Maiden, N. Integrated software reuse: management and techniques. Ashgate Brookfield, Vermont, 1993

ARCHITECTURAL ISSUES

Realizing Object-Relational Databases by Mixing Tables with Objects*

Chengfei Liu† Maria E Orlowska†‡ Hui Li‡
†CRC for Distributed Systems Technology
‡School of Information Technology
The University of Queensland
Brisbane, Qld 4072, Australia
Email: {liu,maria,huili}@dstc.edu.au

Abstract

In this paper, we propose an approach for implementing object-relational DBMSs by using a heterogeneous database system architecture. The paper first discusses the type extensibility of an object-relational DBMS and its query language. Then the architecture is presented for realizing object-relational technology on the top of relational and object-oriented DBMSs. In particular, two main functions – schema transformation and query translation are further studied.

1 Introduction

The converging trend of relational and object-oriented database technologies results in *object-relational DBMSs*, which is advocated by Stonebraker as the next great wave of database technology [10]. Relational database technology is very successful in business processing application areas. It was regarded as a real triumph of academia as the data sublanguage SQL became an industry standard in 1986. However, relational systems do have limitations, e.g., hard to express complex objects, unable to support extended data types, unable to support set-valued attributes, etc. In fact, these limitations were well recognized early in the late 70's. Many *semantic data models* have been proposed to overcome the limitations of relational systems [8]. In particular, NF^2 (*nested*) relations were proposed to handle hierarchically organized data [6]. Various specialized databases, such as engineering, spatial and multimedia DBs, were also studied specifically to meet the needs of advanced database applications, where applications require more complex structures for objects, new data types, and the need to define nonstandard application-specific operations. About a decade ago, the database community began to investigate general methods by means of mixing objects with databases. A number of different ways were explored: extended relational database systems, object-oriented (OO) database systems [3], toolkits for constructing special-purpose database systems, and

---

* The work reported in this paper has been funded in part by the Cooperative Research Centres Program through the Department of the Prime Minister and Cabinet of the Commonwealth Government of Australia.

persistent programming languages. As claimed by Carey [2], the extended relational database systems, as they are called object-relational (OR) database systems now, appear likely to merge as the ultimate winner in terms of providing objects for mainstream enterprise database applications.

An ORDBMS starts with the relational model and its query language, SQL, and builds from there. As such, it has a strong base: conceptual simplicity, open standard query language, powerful transaction management and recovery facilities, efficiency, availability, scalability, rich set of applications, etc. All of these are what an OODBMS lacks. Besides, an ORDBMS also accommodates many object features. Among them are abstract data types(ADTs), row types, references, multivalued attributes and inheritance. *ADTs* are user-defined base types, their role is to enable the set of built-in data types of a DBMS to be extended with new data types such as text, image, polygon, etc. *Row types* are a direct and natural extension of the type system for tuples. In addition to base type attributes, *row objects* are permitted to contain *reference-valued attributes* and *multivalued attributes*. The introduction of reference-valued attribute [5] will not only provide shareability of type instances, but also will enable us to support OO capabilities for rows in existing tables. A multivalued attribute value can be a set, a bag, a list or an array of base type elements. Lastly, *inheritance* is also supported to enable natural variations among row types or ADTs to be captured in the schema.

Currently, different approaches are being taken by vendors to provide OR database products: native implementation such as Informix's Illustra – commercialized version of Postgres [9], Fujitsu's ODB II – commercialized version of Jasmine [4], Omniscience and UniSQL; incremental evolution taken by CA-Ingres, DB2/6000 C/S, Oracle 8, etc.; wrapper approach taken by HP's Odapter. Building an ORDBMS is a complex, time-consuming task, requiring hundreds of man years of effort. It is always psychologically difficult for people to discard investment in old systems. For the purpose of providing new technology without giving up old systems, we put forward a new approach, utilizing a heterogeneous database architecture as a vehicle for ORDBMS implementation. Compared with the wrapper and gateway approaches discussed by Stonebraker [10], our approach is biased towards using existing resources, i.e., existing relational and OO systems. In this paper, we will show how a heterogeneous database architecture can be employed to realize OR databases in a top-down manner.

The rest of the paper is organized as follows. In section 2, we discuss type extensibility of OR database systems and their query language. A heterogeneous database architecture is presented and discussed for implementation of OR systems in section 3. Two key functions of the architecture, the schema transformation and query partition, are further studied in section 4 and section 5, respectively. Section 6 concludes the paper.

2 Object-Relational Databases

The fundamental difference between OR and relational technologies is type extensibility. In the following, we discuss the type extensibility, followed by the discussion of extended query features due to the type extensibility.

2.1 Type Extensibility

As we know, the relational model represents the database as a collection of relations. A relation schema R, denoted by $R(A_1, A_2, \cdots, A_n)$, is made up of a relation name R and a list of attributes $A_1, A_2, \cdots, A_n$. Each attribute A_i is the name of a role played by the domain D_i in the relation schema R. A domain is set of atomic (indivisible) values. In relational databases, these values are described by a limited set of built-in base data types, e.g., integer, string, float number and time. A set of operations are also fixed for each data type. Except aggregating a list of attributes as a relation, there is no other type constructors provided. As such, it is difficult to write database applications for handling complex data. OR database technology copes with this by extending data types in several ways.

base type extension – With the notion of Abstract Data Types(ADTs), an ORDBMS permits users to define their own types. Some important types of complex data such as images, arrays, time series may be implemented by the vendors and be provided as a library(such as *datablades* in Illustra). No matter whether it is provided by the system or is defined by users, an ADT provides an encapsulated view of a type of data, and thus is also regarded as a base type, just like an integer type. The only way to access the value of a base type is to invoke an operation or a method defined on the type. However, unlike the built-in base types, ADTs are allowed to add new methods later on. In addition, inheritance mechanism might be used to build an ADT which can inherit existing base types.

collection type – Relational DBMSs only support single-valued attributes. By defining a collection type on an element type, ORDBMSs allow multi-valued attributes, i.e., an attribute takes as its value a collection of values with same element data type. Several collection types can be defined, e.g., set, multiset, sequence, array, etc. For the briefness of discussion, we only discuss set type in the paper.

reference type – It is also useful to support references as a type constructor. Though it is not included in current draft of SQL3 standard [11], it has already been adopted as SQL3's change proposal [5], and appeared in some pioneer systems such as Illustra.

row type – A row type is natural extension of the notion of relation. It is defined on a sequence of pairs (F_i, T_i), F_i is a field name and T_i can be any data type, not restricted to a built-in base type as in relational systems. This allows the system to support complex objects.

Based on above discussion, we give a definition of data types in OR databases as follows.

Definition 1 *A* data type *in OR databases is recursively defined as*
(a) a built-in data type, *such as integer, string;*
(b) an abstract data type (ADT);
(c) if T is a data type, set(T) is also a data type which is called set type;
(d) if $T_1, T_2, \cdots, T_n$ *are data types,* $(F_1 : T_1, F_2 : T_2, \cdots, F_n : T_n)$ *is also a data type called* row type, *where* F_i *is the name of a field of the row type. If a row type is given a name, it is called a* named row type (NRT), *otherwise, it is called an* unnamed row type;
(e) if T is a NRT, ref(T) is also a data type which is called reference type.

Since OR approach is based on relational approach, the top-most level of an OR database schema is still a collection of extended table (relation) definitions. Like relational system, only these tables (which contain top-level entities) are stored persistently in an OR database. However, unlike relational system, the modeling powers of these tables are much stronger than those in relational system. In OR databases, every table is defined on a row type. As such, the columns in the table may not be restricted to built-in data types. In fact, they can be data types which are as rich as those supported by OO database systems. Based on definition 1, we give a definition of an OR database schema as follows.

Definition 2 *An OR database schema* $\mathcal{S}$ *is defined as* $\mathcal{S} = (\mathcal{TBL}, \mathcal{NRT}, \mathcal{ADT}, f)$ *where*
(a) $\mathcal{TBL}$ *is a set of table definitions;*
(b) $\mathcal{NRT}$ *is a set of definitions for NRTs;*
(c) $\mathcal{ADT}$ *is a set of definition for ADTs;*
(d) f is a mapping $f : \mathcal{TBL} \to \mathcal{NRT}$.

The relationship between $\mathcal{TBL}$ and $\mathcal{NRT}$ is expressed by the mapping f, i.e., tables can only be defined on NRTs. Tables can not be directly defined on ADTs, the definition of an ADT can be used only as the type definition of a NRT field.

Example 1 *In the following we define an OR database schema* S_c *for a hypothetical company:* $S_c = (\{emp, dept\}, \{emp\_t, dept\_t\}, \{point\}, \{emp \mapsto emp\_t, dept \mapsto dept\_t\})$. *All the ADTs, NRTs and tables are defined in a SQL3-like database language. This example database schema will be used throughout the paper.*

```
create ADT point (                 create NRT dept_t (
      x_coordinate float,                dname varchar(30),
      y_coordinate float;                budget float,
      distance(point, point) float);     location point,
create NRT emp_t (                       manager ref(emp_t));
      name varchar(30),            create table emp of emp_t
      salary decimal(9,2),               scope for dept is dept,
      interest set(varchar(40)),         scope for friend is emp;
      location point,              create table dept of dept_t
      dept ref(dept_t),                  scope for manager is emp;
      friend set(ref(emp_t)));
```

It is controversial how an OR system can keep the simplicity of relational systems while taking advantage of the modeling power of OO systems. Current SQL3 draft [11] only supports unnamed row types, ADTs and collection types. In the separate "SQL/Object" part of SQL3 [5], *named row types(NRTs)* are introduced with *polymorphism, identity, no inheritance*, and *no encapsulation*. Reference types are also introduced but only references to row types are allowed. In contrast, an ADT supports *polymorphism,inheritance, encapsulation*, but *no identity*. Beech [1] suggests that a possible future simplification of SQL3 is a combination of ADTs and NRTs. However, this may compromise the simplicity of relational systems. Our viewpoint is to keep both relational flavour and OO modeling power in OR systems. As definition 2 shown, we differentiate NRTs from ADTs. This makes difference between OR and OO schemas. An OO schema is defined by a set of class definitions, each class implies both extension definition (which corresponds to the table definition of an OR schema) and intension definition (which corresponds to the *union* of NRT and ADT definitions of an OR schema). In addition, our SQL3-like language also supports NRTs and reference types, which are not included in current SQL3 draft.

2.2   Extended Query Features

Due to type extensibility, SQL92 is no longer suffcient for querying OR databases. In supporting type extensibility, we extend SQL92 with the following query features which are supported in our SQL3-like language. Compared with the *giant* SQL3 draft, our SQL3-like language is very simplified, with its only focus on type extensibility.

method invocation – Since ADTs may have methods defined, method invocations are allowed to appear in the SELECT and WHERE clauses.

path expressions – Since NRTs and reference types are introduced, path expressions are used to navigate the complex structures of objects and their relationships to other objects via references. A deref() function is used to dereference an object identity to get its object.

set operations – Set operations are also allowed in the WHERE statement.

The followings are examples of OR queries.

Example 2 *find the names of all employees who have interest in ORDB and work for the department which is located in central area (within 2 kilometers from the central point) and has budget more than 1 million dollars.*

```
select e.name
from emp e
where e.deref(dept).budget > 1,000,000 and
      "ORDB" in e.interest and
      distance(e.location, CENTRAL_POINT) < 2;
```

Example 3 *find the names of managers who have friends woking in the same department and their salaries are more than $100,000.*

```
select d.deref(manager).name
```

```
from dept d, emp e
where d = e.deref(dept) and e in d.deref(manager).friend
      and e.salary >= 100,000;
```

Notice in the above example queries, we have used method invocations, set operations and path expressions to represent the queries. All these query features are used to support the type extensibility, therefore, they can not be found in SQL92.

3 HDB Architecture for ORDBMS

In this section, we address how a heterogeneous database (HDB) architecture can be used as a vehicle for realizing OR technology. Given a SQL3-like language, we need an ORDB engine to implement it. The HDB engine shown in Figure 1 can be used for this purpose. In fact, the HDB engine is a virtual ORDB engine, it is built based on local RDB engine and OODB engine. We provide so-called *functional transparency*. In the architecture, we are only interested in how a global ORDB request is functionally transformed into local RDB and OODB subrequests. By functional transparency we mean users need not know such functional transformation. Given a SQL3-like request, the HDB engine interprets the request in terms of supporting RDB and OODB engines. In the following, we describe each component in the architecture.

Interface – It receives users' SQL3-like requests, does syntactical check and hands them to corresponding components for processing. It is also responsible to return the results of the requests back to users.

Schema Transformer – It handles SQL3-like requests for schema definition. The main function of this component is to keep the information of OR schema into the global directory and to transform the schema into schemas of both local RDB and OODB engines. A transformation plan is generated by this component which is delivered to the executor for execution. The schema mapping information is also kept in the global directory. The detail of this component is further discussed in section 4.

Query Partitioner – This component is responsible for translating SQL3-like queries which are issued against global OR schema into local queries on both local RDB and OODB engines. The schema mapping information is used for such transformation. All local queries form a query plan which is handed over to the executor. This component will be discussed in detail in section 5.

Executor – The executor is responsible for coordinating the distributed execution of the execution plan (both transformation and query plan). There is a RDB engine employed at the global level to hold temporary results which may pass between local relational system and OO system, to merge the results. Since users are on the top of an ORDB interface, they may require the result in a form which is more than a flat table. Therefore, some functions are added for this purpose, such as, *nest* for reconstructing set-valued column values, *deref* for obtaining the objects, etc.

RDB-Agent – The RDB-agent is responsible for monitoring the execution

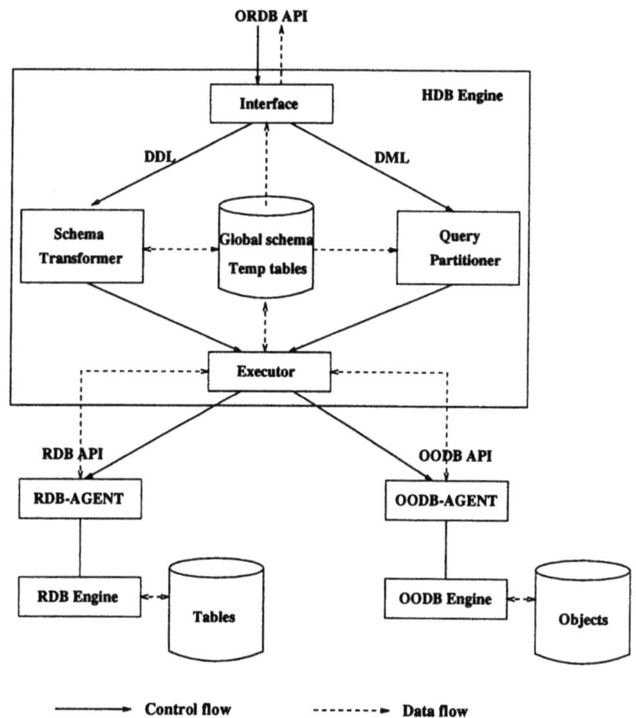

Figure 1: HDB Architecture for Mixing Objects with Tables

of local queries against transformed local relational schema and returning the results.

OODB-Agent – The functions of this agent include: (a) translating SQL3-like queries to ODMG-93 OQL [3] queries which is supposed to be supported by the OODB engine; (b) monitoring the execution of local queries against transformed local OO schema; (c) returning results to the executor.

4   Schema Transformation

C. Yu et al. [12, 7] have studied translations between relational systems and object-oriented systems. In providing relational (OO) frontend to an OO (relational) system, two tasks with opposite directions are necessary: one is the transformation from OO (relational) schema to its relational (OO) equivalent schema, the other is translation of relational (OO) queries to OO (relational) equivalent. Our work is different, we are supporting top-down OR database design, both schema transformation and query translation tasks are one-directional, i.e., from OR to both relational and OO. Besides, in [7], only structural part of OO schema is translated to relational. In this approach we consider both structural and behavioral aspects of an OR system.

In this section, we show how a global OR schema can be transformed into corresponding local relational and OO schemas. Our criteria is to transform the OR schema as much as we can to relational schema as a trivial transformation always exists from OR schema completely to OO local schema.

In the following, we first informally describe the steps of an algorithm for mapping OR schema to its corresponding relational schema and OO schema. Then, we summarize with a correspondence between an OR table and its transformed relational tables and OO classes.

4.1 Transformation Algorithm

Input An OR schema.

Output A relational schema and an associated OO schema.

We use two lists to keep useful intermediate information. $\mathcal{NRT}$ for definitions of NRTs, $\mathcal{TRAN}$ for table structures to be transformed. Initially, they are empty.

Step 1: For every NRT defined in the OR schema, create a structure in $\mathcal{NRT}$ to record the NRT name and its field definitions.

Step 2: For every ADT, output a definition of a class called *deputy class* which is used to implement the ADT. The definition of the deputy class is formed by including definitions of attributes and methods of the ADT definition and the definition of an extra object identity attribute *oid*.

Step 3: For table named ORT defined in the OR schema, create a (frame) structure in $\mathcal{TRAN}$ to record the table name, copy the field definitions of the NRT in $\mathcal{NRT}$ on which it is defined as the field definitions of the table, and if scopes of referenced fields are defined with the table, keep the names of scope tables within the field definition. A table called *frame table* with name ORT_R will be created later in the relational schema based on this frame structure.

Step 4: Loop for each table structure in $\mathcal{TRAN}$ until $\mathcal{TRAN}$ becomes empty.

Step 5: For each table structure in $\mathcal{TRAN}$, let its table name TBL, create a relational table definition with table name TBL_R. For each field definition $F : T$ in TBL, we classify 8 cases for different processing. Remove the structure of TBL after all its field definitions have been processed.

Case 1: If T is a built-in type, output a column definition $F : T$ for TBL_R.

Case 2: If T is an ADT, output a column definition $F : long$ for TBL_R, we use type *long* to represent object identity.

Case 3: If T is a NRT, replace the field definition with all field definitions of the NRT T for processing. The newly added field definitions can be found in $\mathcal{NRT}$, their field names need to be renamed with the prefix $F\_$.

Case 4: If T is a reference type $ref(RNRT)$, there should be a scope clause declaring the table, say $RTBL$, it really references to. Let $RPK : T_{RPK}$ its primary key definition, then output a column definition $F : T_{RPK}$ for TBL_R.

Case 5: If T is a set type $set(ET)$ and ET is a built-in type, output a definition for a table called *auxiliary table* $TBL\_F\_R(PK : T_{PK}, TBL\_F : ET)$, where $PK : T_{PK}$ is the primary key definition for TBL_R.

Case 6: If T is a set type $set(ET)$ and ET is an ADT, output a definition of a class called *auxiliary class* $TBL\_F\_C(oid : long, TBL_F : set(ET))$.

Case 7: If T is a set type $set(ET)$ and ET is a NRT, create an auxiliary structure in $\mathcal{TRAN}$ with TBL_F_R as table name and $(PK : T_{PK}, EF_1 : ET_1, \cdots, EF_m : ET_m)$ as its field definition, where $PK : T_{PK}$ is the primary key definition for TBL_R and $(EF_1 : ET_1, \cdots, EF_m : ET_m)$ is the definition for ET which can be retrieved from $\mathcal{NRT}$.

Case 8: If T is a set type $set(ET)$, ET is a reference type $ref(RNRT)$, there should be a scope clause declaring the table, say $RTBL$, it really references to. Let $PK : T_{PK}$ and $RPK : T_{RPK}$ be primary key definitions of TBL and $RTBL$, respectively, then output a definition of a table called *auxiliary table* $TBL\_F\_R(PK : T_{PK}, F\_RPK : T_{RPK})$.

The above algorithm transforms an OO schema defined in definition 2 into a relational schema and an OO schema, if any. For every table in the OR schema, a frame table definition is always generated in the relational schema, together with definitions of auxiliary tables and classes, if any. A deputy class definition is always generated in the OO schema which implements an ADT in the OR schema. The definitions of NRTs in the OR schema are embedded in the transformed relational and OO schemas. In section 4.2 we will show how the transformed local relational and OO schemas correspond to the global OR schema. An example of schema transformation is given below.

Example 4 *The transformed relational schema and OO schema of the OR schema of Example 1 are given below.*

```
create table emp_R (                create class point (
     name varchar(30),                   oid: long,
     salary decimal(9,2),                x_coordinate: float,
     location long,                      y_coordinate: float;
     dept varchar(30));                  distance(point): float);
create table dept_R (               create table emp_interest_R (
     dname varchar(30),                  name varchar(30),
     budget float,                       emp_interest varchar(40));
     location long,                 create table emp_friend_R (
     manager varchar(30));               name varchar(30),
                                         friend_name varchar(30));
```

4.2 Global and Local Schema Correspondence

As shown in above section, an OR table TBL can be transformed into a frame relational table TBL_R, together with a set of auxiliary relational tables and a set of auxiliary classes. An ADT can be transformed into a deputy class. Suppose TBL is defined on the NRT $NRT_0(F_0 : BT_0, F_1 : BT_1, F_2 : ADT_2, F_3 : NRT_3, F_4 : ref(NRT_4), F_5 : set(BT_5), F_6 : set(ADT_6), F_7 : set(NRT_7), F_8 : set(ref(NRT_8)))$ where definitions of F_i $(1 \leq i \leq 8)$ are in correspondence with 8 cases discussed above. Let DC_2, DC_6 are deputy classes for ADT_2, ADT_6; AC_6 is auxiliary class for $set(ADT_6)$; TBL_5, TBL_7, TBL_8 are auxiliary tables for $set(BT_5), set(NRT_7), set(ref(NRT_8))$; $RTBL_4$ and $RTBL_8$ are scope tables for F_4 and F_8. Suppose NRTs, existing tables and transformed tables have the following definitions: $NRT_3(F_0^3, \cdots, F_r^3), NRT_4(F_0^4, \cdots), NRT_7(RF_0^7, \cdots),$

$$NRT_8(F_0^8, \cdots); RTBL_4(F_0^4, \cdots), RTBL_8(F_0^8, \cdots); TBL_5(F_0, BF_5),$$
$$TBL_7(F_0, RF_0^7, \cdots), TBL_8(F_0, F_0^8); AC_6(oid : long, AF_6 : set(DC_6)).$$

The global table TBL can be represented as

select $TBL\_R.F_1, TBL\_R.deref(F_2), TBL\_R.F_0^3, \cdots, TBL\_R.F_r^3, TBL\_R.F_4,$
$nest(TBL_5.BF_5), TBL\_R.deref(F_6), nest(TBL_7.RF_7), nest(TBL_8.F_0^8)$
from $TBL\_R, TBL_5, TBL_7, TBL_8, DC_2, AC_6, RTBL_4, RTBL_8$
where $TBL\_R.F_2 = DC_2.oid$ and $TBL\_R.F_4 = RTBL_4.F_0^4$ and $TBL\_R.F_0 = TBL_5.F_0$
and $TBL\_R.F_6 = AC_6.oid$ and $TBL\_R.F_0 = TBL_7.F_0$ and $TBL\_R.F_0 = TBL_8.F_0$
and $TBL_8.F_0^8 = RTBL_8.F_0^8$

The predicates used in bridging relational side to OO side are called *bridge constraints*, e.g., $TBL\_R.F_2 = DC_2.oid$ and $TBL\_R.F_6 = AC_6.oid$ in the above *where* clauses are bridge constraints.

Example 5 *The correspondence between OR table* emp *in example 1 and its transformed representations in example 4 is given below.*

select $emp\_R.name, emp\_R.salary, nest(emp\_interest\_R.interest), emp\_R.deref(point.oid),$
$emp\_R.dept, nest(emp\_friend\_R.emp\_friend)$
from $emp\_R, emp\_interest\_R, emp\_friend\_R, point, dept\_R$
where $emp\_R.name = emp\_interest\_R.name$ and $emp\_R.name = emp\_friend\_R.name$
and $emp\_R.location = point.oid$ and $emp\_R.dept = dept\_R.dname$

5 Query Partition

Given a query against global OR schema, it must be translated to local queries against its transformed local relational and OO schemas for execution. We design a query partition algorithm which has two major steps: *substitution* and *decomposition*. Due to space limitation, we only give main ideas of the algorithm with an illustrative example.

(1) substitution of a global OR query with local representation
First we substitute every global table TBL and its tuple variable x in the *from* clause with local frame table TBL_R and tuple variable y. Then for every occurrence in the form $x.F.\cdots$, where F is a field of the table the tuple variable x defined on, we have 8 cases of substitutions which are related to global and local schema correspondence discussed in section 4.2.

After this step, the query of example 2 can be substituted to

```
select e.name
from emp_R e, dept_R d, emp_interest_R i, point p
where e.dept = d.dname and d.budget > 1,000,000 and
      e.name = i.name and i.emp_interest = "ORDB" and
      e.location = p.oid and p.distance(CENTRAL_POINT) < 2;
```

(2) decomposition of the substituted query into a query plan
After substitution step finishes, first find out bridge constraints in the *where* clause. There are two forms of bridge constraints: the first is a binary predicate with a table column and a class attribute as its operands, the second is a method invocation with at least one table column as its parameter. Suppose n bridge

constraints appear in a *where* clause, the *where* clause is then divided into $n + 1$ parts, create a local query for each part, one at relational side and n at OO side. At the global level, create another query which implement all bridge constraints. If a bridge constraint is in first form, the corresponding local OO query can be executed in parallel with the local relational query. Otherwise, the OO local query should be executed after the relational local query because the OO query needs the result of the relational one as input. The parameter column value should be also projected in the relational query.

In the *where* clause of substituted query generated by the above step, there is one bridge constraint *e.location* $=$ *p.oid* and it divides the predicates in the *where* clause into two parts: (a) *e.dept* $=$ *d.dname* and *d.budget* $> 1,000,000$ and *e.name* $=$ *i.name* and *i.emp_interest* $=$ *"ORDB"*; (b) *p.distance(CENTRAL_POINT)* < 2. Therefore, the query can be partitioned into three subqueries, where the local OO subquery (1.b) can be executed in parallel with the local relational subquery (1.a).

```
(1.a) create table temp_R as
          select e.name as name, e.location as location
          from emp_R e, dept_R d, emp_interest_R i
          where e.dept = d.dname and d.budget > 1,000,000 and
                e.name = i.name and i.emp_interest = "ORDB";
(1.b) create table temp_OO as
          select struct(oid: p.oid)
          from p in point
          where p.distance(CENTRAL_POINT) < 2;
(2)   select r.name
      from temp_R r, temp_OO o
      where r.location = o.oid;
```

If there is no bridge constraint, this means the query as a whole can be executed at relational side.

6   Conclusion

Recently, ORDBMSs have gained a great deal of attention in the database community. In this paper, we introduced a new approach, applying heterogeneous database architecture to *simulate* ORDBMSs. Instead of building ORDBMSs from scratch, we can build them on the top of existing relational DBMSs and OODBMSs. The heterogeneous database architecture which is used for this purpose has been described in the paper. In particular, we focused on the discussion of two main components of the architecture: schema transformer and query partitioner. The algorithms for both schema transformation and query partition have been proposed.

Acknowledgements

The authors would like to thank Kathleen Williamson for her careful reading on a draft version of this paper.

References

[1] D. Beech. Can SQL3 be simplified? *Database Programming and Design*, pages 46–50, January 1997.

[2] Michael J. Carey and David J. DeWitt. Of objects and databases: A decade of turmoil. In *Proceedings of the 22nd International conference on VLDB*, pages 3–14, Mumbai (Bombay), India, September 1996. VLDB, Morgan Kaufmann.

[3] R. G. G. Cattell, editor. *The Object Database Standard: ODMG-93*. Morgan Kaufmann Publishers, 1994.

[4] H. Ishikawa, Y. Yamane, Y. Izumida, and N. Kawato. An object-oriented database system Jasmine: Implementation, application, and extension. *IEEE Transactions on Knowledge and Data Engineering*, 8(2):285–304, 1996.

[5] ISO DBL LHR-077 and ANSI X3H2-95-456 R2. *Introducing Reference Types and Cleaning up SQL3's Object Model*, November 1995. by K. Kulkarni, M. Carey, L. DeMichiel, N. Mattos, W. Hong, M. Ubell, A. Nori, V. Krishnamurthy and D. Beech.

[6] A. Makinouchi. A consideration on normal form of not-necessarily-normalized relation in the relational data model. In *Proceedings of the 3rd VLDB Conference*, pages 202–211, Tokyo, October 1977.

[7] W. Meng, C. Yu, W. Kim, G. Wang, T. Pham, and S. Dao. Construction of a relational front-end for object-oriented database systems. In *Proceeding of 9th International Conference on Data Engineering*, pages 476–483, 1993.

[8] Joan Peckham and Fred Maryanski. Semantic data models. *ACM Computing Surveys*, 20(3), September 1988.

[9] M. Stonebraker, L. A. Rowe, and M. Hirohama. The implementation of POSTGRES. *IEEE Transactions on Knowledge and Data Engineering*, 2(1):125–142, February 1990.

[10] Michael Stonebraker. *Object-Relational DBMSs: The Next Great Wave*. Morgan Kaufmann, 1996.

[11] ISO DBL YOW-004 and ANSI X3H2-95-084. *(ISO/ANSI Working Draft) Database Language SQL3*, March 1995. Jim Melton (ed).

[12] C. Yu, Y. Zhang, W. Meng, W. Kim, G. Wang, T. Pham, and S. Dao. Translation of object-oriented queries to relational queries. In *Proceeding of 11th International Conference on Data Engineering*, pages 90–97, 1995.

CORBA and ODBMSs in Viewpoint Development Environment Architectures

Wolfgang Emmerich

Interoperable Systems Research Centre, City University
Northampton Square, London EC1V 0HB, UK

Abstract

Viewpoints are reflections of software systems from multiple perspectives. A number of consistency conditions apply to viewpoints and developers require a tool for each type of viewpoint. These tools need to support consistency management. Inter-viewpoint consistency can only be checked when tools are integrated into a viewpoint development environment. We briefly outline the functionality developers require from these environments. We discuss the suitability of abstract syntax graphs as a common viewpoint representation scheme. The main purpose of the paper is to present an object-oriented architecture for viewpoint-based environments. The architecture benefits from the integration of object database management systems and object request brokers.

1 Introduction

The production process of modern software systems passes many stages, such as requirements analysis, architectural design, detailed design, coding, testing. During these stages, the system is considered from multiple perspectives. Requirements analysis tends to take different end-user perspectives and focus, for instance, on the functionality a system should offer from different users' point of view. Architectural design takes the perspective of an engineer who decides how the system should be constructed. These perspectives highlight the principal system components and their interaction mechanisms. Note, that multiple perspectives may even be required during a single stage. Dardenne et al., for instance, suggest in [4] different requirements engineering perspectives for goals, actions, agents, constraints, entities and relationships. Developers have to materialise those different perspectives for documentation and communication purposes in documents or artifacts, which we refer to as *viewpoints* [14] so as to emphasise that they provide different perspectives on the same system. This viewpoint-oriented perspective on software processes is shared by an increasing number of authors (see [17]).

Viewpoints are defined as a loosely-coupled, locally managed objects encapsulating representation knowledge, development process knowledge and partial specification knowledge about a system. Viewpoints are structured into five slots: The *style* slot describes the representation scheme used by the viewpoint. The *work plan* slot describes development actions together with a strategy for their application to construct the viewpoint. The *domain* slot identifies the viewpoint and sets its context in the overall system under construction. The *specification* slot describes the viewpoint domain in the representation scheme determined by the style slot. The *work record* slot records the history and current state of the viewpoint development.

Viewpoints are defined in a formal language, determined by the viewpoint's style slot. As different viewpoints represent different perspectives on the same system they are not fully independent of each other; there are multiple consistency constraints between the different viewpoints. A viewpoint defining a goal in a requirements specification, for instance, might use an entity definition and this use must match the entity declaration in some other viewpoint. The high number of viewpoints likely in a system definition, together with the various consistency constraints, generate a demand for integrated *tool support*. Tools should, in particular, provide for intra- and inter-viewpoint consistency checks and manage temporary inconsistencies. Intra-viewpoint checks should reveal syntactic and static semantic errors within the viewpoint, while inter-viewpoint consistency checks should reveal inconsistencies between different related viewpoints.

Section 2 is devoted to a discussion of the functionality required from viewpoint-based tools in order to apply viewpoint-based methods effectively. In Section 3, we discuss an architecture for the integration of multiple tools into an environment that enables multiple developers to cooperate while using such methods. We particularly focus on the *a posteriori* integration of autonomously constructed tools. In Section 4, we discuss related work and outline open problems that need further attention in Section 5.

2 Viewpoint-based Environments

To apply a viewpoint-based method effectively, developers need a tool for each viewpoint template. Developers require particular functionality from each such tool. Some functions, however, cannot be provided by a single tool, but require the integration of tools associated with different related viewpoints. We refer to a set of these integrated tools as a *viewpoint-based development environment*.

A single tool enables developers as well as other tools to instantiate a viewpoint template and to complete the contents of the viewpoint, that is the specification slots. Therefore, the tool should offer *editing commands* for all the assembly actions identified in the work plan of the viewpoint template.

Inter-viewpoint consistency constraints imply relationships between different fragments contained in different viewpoints. It is often important for a developer to be able to traverse these relationships efficiently. A requirements engineer who is concerned with requirements traceability, for instance, may want to review the class in an object-oriented design that refines an entity definition. The viewpoint tool for entity definitions should, for example, offer a browsing command that makes a Booch viewpoint tool highlight the class definition refining the entity. The Booch viewpoint tool, in turn, may offer a browsing command to find the C++ interface of the class. Note, that already this simple browsing facility requires viewpoint tools to be integrated.

Support for assembly actions and browsing facilities does not necessarily require that viewpoint-based tools be constructed. They could equally well be supported by generic text/graphic editors and hypertext viewers. The support that distinguishes a viewpoint-based tool from a generic editor is *consistency handling.* With respect to tool support, there are several facets of consistency handling. Consistency checks may be applied in a *lazy* or *eager* way. In a lazy consistency checking approach developers of a viewpoint will decide when to perform a check and what constraints to check for. In an eager approach the viewpoint-based tool checks for consistency while the user modifies a viewpoint and provides immediate consistency feedback. Observed inconsistencies may be *tolerated* or *prohibited.* Tolerated inconsistencies must be managed and different *resolution strategies* may or may not be enforced at some stage of the viewpoint development.

If multiple developers cooperate on the resolution of inconsistencies, it will inevitably be necessary to review the impact of everyone's changes as they occur. With an eager approach towards constraint checking, the visualisation of inconsistencies in one developer's viewpoint should be removed as soon as some other developer has removed the source of the inconsistency. We note that viewpoint-based tools have to be integrated in a way that they can access and update each other's viewpoints in a concurrent way.

It is often not appropriate for a developer to be disturbed by other developers' changes. Developers may want to work in isolation for some period of time, especially when they perform major changes to a viewpoint. Moreover, their changes should only become visible to other developers after they have reached a certain degree of (in-viewpoint) consistency. A way of achieving this is to arrange for viewpoint-based tools that are able to maintain different *versions* of a viewpoint. Version management has so far only gained widespread attention for source code viewpoints that are produced during the implementation stage, but we strongly believe that any viewpoint produced during any stage of a software process deserves the same attention. The concept of viewpoint versions is not only required not only to isolate developers from each other, but also to keep track of viewpoint history while a system is under maintenance. When a system is ported to a new platform, for instance, the versions of viewpoints for the previous platform must be retained. Developers will then need to *freeze* versions of a viewpoint so as to prevent it from being further modified. This will be necessary whenever a viewpoint has reached a state to which it might have to be restored in the future. Developers will then need a mechanism to *derive* a version from another frozen version and *select* a particular version. Then successive changes must only be done in that selected version. If no version is selected, a *default version* of a viewpoint will be used. Further version management support is required for labelling versions, traversing through the version history graph and for merging different alternatives into a common successor version.

3 Environment Architecture

Although viewpoints result from the different perspectives of different agents, it will be essential to have a common conceptual representation for all viewpoints so as to facilitate the definition of inter-viewpoint check actions. Having a common conceptual representation, however, does not imply that all viewpoints are supported in a uniform way and stored centrally.

3.1 Conceptual Viewpoint Representation

The style slots of viewpoints determine formal graphical or textual languages. Even viewpoints that express informal perspectives may have a structure of, for example chapters and sections, that can be expressed in a mark-up language such as SGML [12]. In search of a common conceptual viewpoint representation, we can, therefore, assume that any viewpoint has some form of syntactic structure that can be exploited.

The definitions of inter-viewpoint consistency constraints make reference to syntactic viewpoint fragments [9]. If a consistency condition relates two fragments, it is highly beneficial to materialise this relationship within the viewpoint representation, as opposed to computing it whenever the relationship is needed; the relationship should be materialised as soon as the related fragments are consistent with each other. Change propagations and browsing operations can then be implemented fairly efficiently by traversing the relationship. If one or the other related fragment is changed, relationships can be exploited for incremental reevaluation during check actions. Fragments to be related are often lexemes that match terminal symbols of the underlying grammar rather than more coarse-grained morphemes. Given that lexemes are usually involved in relationships, it will be necessary to model the complete syntactic structure of viewpoints using the common conceptual representation.

To break down the syntactic structure of a viewpoint, the specification slot of each viewpoint can be represented as an abstract syntax tree (AST), whose structure is determined by the grammar in the style slot. Nodes in this AST represent morphemes and lexemes. Nodes that represent morphemes are generated by productions of the viewpoint grammar and are referred to as *non-terminal nodes*. Lexemes are represented as *terminal nodes*, which have been matched with terminal symbols of the viewpoint grammar. Edges in these ASTs represent the syntactic decomposition and are referred to as *syntactic edges*. Nodes may have attributes for storing layout information or semantic data, for example symbol tables or details about inconsistencies to be resolved.

ASTs are generalised to abstract syntax graphs (ASGs) by the introduction of *semantic edges*. Such an edge between two nodes represents a semantic relationships between the two lexemes or morphemes represented by the nodes. Note that these edges lead to nodes contained in ASTs of other viewpoints if they are due to an inter-viewpoint consistency constraint. Therefore, the representation of all viewpoints that are produced in a project can be considered as one *project-wide abstract syntax* graph (see [8, 5]). The distinction between syntactic and semantic edges achieves the identification of those *subgraphs* that model single viewpoints. All nodes that are in the transitive closure of nodes reachable via syntactic edges from a designated root node belong to the viewpoint together with all semantic edges connecting nodes within that set. These edges model semantic relationships due to in-viewpoint consistency constraints.

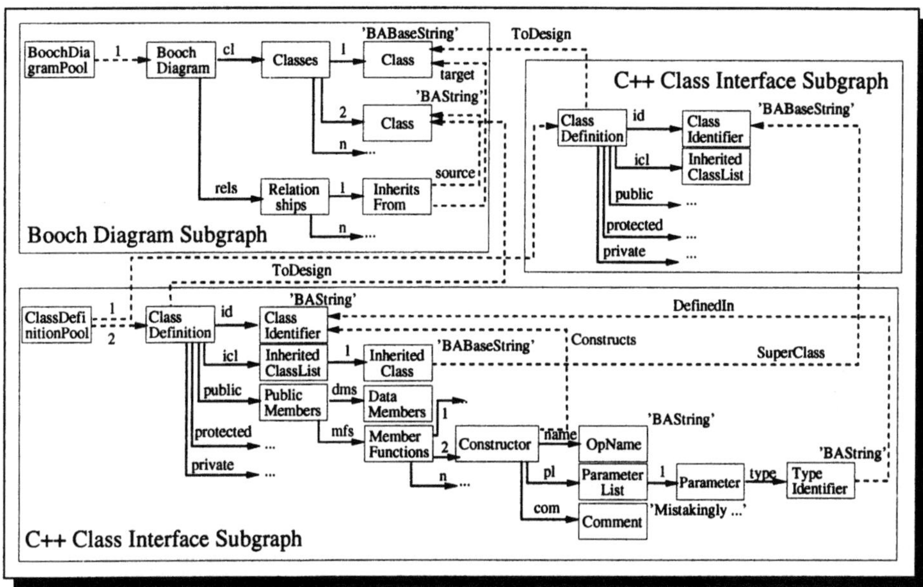

Figure 1: Fragment of a Project-wide Abstract Syntax Graph

As an example, consider Figure 1, which shows three excerpts from viewpoint subgraphs. The subgraph in the upper left corner represents a graphical Booch diagram viewpoint. The subgraph below represents an interface for a C++ class `BAString` that occurs in the Booch diagram and the subgraph in the upper right represents the class interface of `BABaseString`, the super class of `BAString`. Node attributes, given in quotes at the upper right corner of a node representation, store lexemes. Syntactic edges are drawn with solid arrows and semantic edges are displayed as dashed arrows. The edge `ToDesign`, for instance relates the root node of a C++ class interface viewpoint subgraph to the node in the Booch diagram viewpoint subgraph that designs the class. Although edges are directed, they are considered traversable in both directions. The two nodes labelled `BoochDiagramPool` and `ClassDefinitionPool` act as directories for the two viewpoint templates involved and are the starting point for queries that have to look-up a particular viewpoint that has been instantiated from that template.

This representation scheme is particularly appropriate for the efficient implementation of actions identified in a viewpoint template's workplan. Assembly actions are merely replacements of AST subtrees. In- and intra-viewpoint check action can be implemented on the basis of traversals through the project-

352

wide ASGs. Semantic edges considerably reduce search spaces and shorten traversal paths. Checking, for instance, the inter-viewpoint consistency constraint that each inheritance link in a Booch diagram viewpoint should be reflected by a respective declaration in the C++ class interface viewpoint can be implemented in the Booch diagram in the following way: For each `InheritsFrom` node in a Booch diagram viewpoint subgraph, an edge `target` leads to a superclass c_s of a class c identified by the `source` edge. The `ToDesign` edges leading to c_s and c can be traversed in reverse direction to find the root nodes c'_s and c' of the C++ class interface subgraph refining c_s and c. Then the `icl` edge starting from c' is used to find the list of inherited classes. After that the list is traversed and searched for a node whose lexeme attribute equals the lexeme attribute of c_s. Finally, a new semantic edge is created to connect the found `InheritedClass` node with the class identifier node that is reached by traversing edge `id` from c'_s. This edge might then be exploited for change propagations of the class name of c'_s or for efficiently browsing to all subclasses of c'_s.

3.2 Autonomous Viewpoint Implementation

The question arises how abstract syntax graphs can be implemented in an *autonomous* manner. Autonomy is particularly important in order to achieve interoperability of tools, which might not be changeable if they have been bought off-the-shelf. Then the abstract syntax graph structures and operations have to be implemented using the integration capabilities that off-the-shelf tools offer. Two major problems have to be solved to accomplish autonomy: heterogeneity and distribution. Heterogeneity of subgraph implementation occurs since different tools will use different hardware- and operating system platforms. It is also quite likely that different programming languages have been used for implementing tools. As different hardware platforms use different data representation formats and as different programming languages might be incompatible with each other, an integration framework is needed to resolve such heterogeneity. Distribution is required for both the type and instance level implementation of project-wide ASGs. At a type level, viewpoint owners have to define the structure and operations of ASG subgraphs to represent their viewpoint templates. At an instance level, subgraphs have to be distributed so as to meet the performance expectations of developers. A centralised ASG database server might become a performance bottleneck when serving a large numbers of users. Therefore, distributed ASG servers are needed for different viewpoint subgraphs to overcome such a performance bottleneck.

An architecture that has faced the challenge of supporting distributed and heterogeneous computation is OMG's CORBA [16]. To use a CORBA implementation for achieving a distributed and heterogeneous implementation of viewpoints effectively, project-wide ASGs have to be defined using the object-oriented concepts supported in CORBA's interface definition language (IDL). In [6] we have discussed how ASGs can be defined with object-oriented concepts. These considerations also apply to IDL. The main idea is to use classes to define ASG node types. Attributes model both node attributes and edges.

Edges are modelled as a pair of attributes so as to allow for traversals in both directions. Attribute types restrict the type of nodes to which edges may lead. Inheritance is used to model common properties of node types. Heterogeneous edges, i.e. edges that may lead to different types of nodes, are modelled by polymorphism. ASG operations that represent workplan actions are modelled as operations of classes. We suggest the use of IDL modules for restricting the name space of definitions such as node type declarations.

```
module BoochDiagrams {                module ClassInterfaces {
 interface Class;                       interface ClassDefinition;
};                                     };

module ClassInterfaces {              module BoochDiagrams {
 interface ClassDefinition:NonTerminal{ interface Classes : NonTerminal {
  readonly ClassIdentifier id;          readonly sequence<Class> l;
  readonly InheritedClassList icl;      Class addClass();
  readonly Members public;              void deleteClass(in Class cursor);
  readonly Members protected;           ...
  readonly Members private;            };
  readonly
    BoochDiagrams::Class ToDesign;
  ...                                  interface Class : Terminal {
 };                                     readonly CORBA::String value;
 interface ClassIdentifier:Terminal {   readonly InheritsFrom INVtarget;
  readonly CORBA::String value;         readonly ClassInterface::
  readonly InheritedClass INVDefinedIn;         ClassDefinition INVToDesign;
  void ChangeId(in CORBA::String new);  void ChangeId(in CORBA::String new);
  ...                                   ...
 };                                    };
 ...                                   ...
};                                    };
```

Figure 2: ASG definition in IDL

As an example, consider the excerpts from two IDL fragments shown in Figure 2. The definitions on the left-hand side model nodes of the C++ class interface subgraph displayed in Figure 1 and the definitions on the right-hand side model nodes of the Booch class diagram subgraph. Let us now review how the semantic edge ToDesign that leads from the C++ class interface subgraph into the Booch diagram subgraph is modelled. The class interface implementation contains a forward declaration, an import that declares the existence of a module BoochDiagrams with a class Class. This import enables the qualified type BoochDiagrams::Class to be used in the definition of class ClassDefinition as an attribute type for ToDesign. The reverse direction of the edge ToDesign is modelled by attribute INVToDesign in class Class of module BoochDiagrams. Attributes are declared here as read-only, which means that the edges they model can be traversed, but not modified by any other means than the operations defined for the class. The operation ChangeIdent in class Class, for instance, might change the name of a class in a BoochDiagram and then implement a change propagation to the related C++ class interface definition viewpoint that is reached by following the INVToDesign attribute.

It is not necessary to model all node types of a subgraph in IDL, because only those nodes that participate in inter-subgraph semantic edges have to be accessed from heterogeneous and distributed viewpoint-based tools. Therefore, only these have to be exposed in an IDL interface. In-subgraph traversal paths starting from these node types can be implemented in terms of local operations. This considerably increases performance for in-subgraph traversals and modifications, since local rather than remote operation invocations are used.

3.3 ODBMSs for Persistent Viewpoint Storage

Some viewpoint tools may be bought off-the-shelf, others may be constructed anew. In this subsection we sketch how object database management systems can be employed for the construction of new tools.

Given that CORBA is not required for in-subgraph traversals and operations, subgraphs can be stored in an object database management system (ODBMS) in the way suggested in [7]. A review of current database technology that lead to the selection of ODBMSs is provided in [2]. ODBMSs have been standardised by the object database management group [3], a group associated with the OMG. ODBMSs combine object-oriented programming languages with database technology. ODBMSs that comply to this standard offer an object definition language (ODL) for schema definition purposes. ODL is a strict superset of IDL. Database technology is used to transparently manage (1) the mapping of objects to secondary storage media, (2) integrity preservation of objects against system failures, (3) control of concurrent access to these objects and (4) network access from multiple clients to a central object server.

Objects managed by ODBMSs are persistent if they are reachable from a *persistent root*. Persistent roots are designated in the schema. To store subgraphs of a project-wide ASG persistently, we declare a set as a persistent root for each type of root node of each subgraph. As soon as we enter an object that implements a root node into this set the object becomes persistent. As the subgraph is spanned by a tree of syntactic edges, each node in the subgraph is reachable from the root node and therefore it is also persistent.

To meet the requirement of version management, multiple versions of those subgraphs that represent viewpoints have to be managed. Since these subgraphs are implemented by multiple rather than single objects, version management of collections of objects has to be supported. Mechanisms for that have not (yet) been addressed in the ODMG standard, though there are object databases that provide version management facilities for collections of objects.

O_2 [1], an ODMG compliant ODBMS, has been extended with such version management facilities, as discussed in-depth in [6]. The facilities are offered as a pre-defined class o2_version that maintains a collection of objects that are versioned together. The class then provides methods to add or delete objects from this collection and maintains a version history graph for it. It provides operations to traverse through this graph, to derive new version, to compare the differences between versions, to merge versions, to store a default version and to select a version other than the default version. O_2 manages a lazy object duplication strategy, which means that different versions of a version collection share versions of component objects as long as they do not differ. For an evaluation of this duplication technique, see [6].

This versioning facility can be exploited during viewpoint-based tool construction for version management of subgraphs stored in an O_2 ODB. Thus, an instance of class `o2_version` is associated with the root node of each subgraph. New objects implementing new nodes of the graph are inserted into the version collection associated with the root of the graph. Then version management operations for subgraphs can be implemented directly on the basis of methods exported from `o2_version`.

ODBMSs support the concept of ACID transactions that protect the integrity of ASG subgraphs against hardware- or software failures. They also ensure serialisability of concurrent object updates. This will avoid inconsistent analysis and lost update problems that can occur during concurrent ASG updates. Viewpoint-based tools use these transactions to implement single assembly or check actions, rather than complete editing sessions. The duration of these actions tend to be in the order of magnitude of several hundred milliseconds rather than hours or days. The advantage of using commands rather than sessions as the unit of concurrency control is that other developers see the effect of a modification immediately after the action has been completed. As discussed in [6], computer supported cooperative work can be achieved in this way.

3.4 Combining CORBA and ODBMSs

Assuming that viewpoint development environments might contain external tools that do not store viewpoints as objects within an ODBMS, the need arises for those tools to use an object request broker to access ODBMS objects. This means that ODBMS objects have to implement IDL object interfaces. Vice versa, tool operations of ODBMS based tools are implemented within an ODBMS schema. They might have to access viewpoints that are represented as CORBA objects and that are managed outside the scope of the ODBMS. Hence, an integration between ODBMSs and CORBA is required to facilitate integrated viewpoint based environments.

In order to enable an external tool to invoke an operation from an object stored in an ODBMS the operation has to be specified in IDL and its implementation has to invoke the operation of the ODBMS schema. Some ODBMSs, such as O_2 and ObjectStore provide facilities to generate IDL interfaces and their implementation directly from the schema. If these generation facilities are not provided, the IDL interfaces have to be hand-coded. Any ODMG-93 compliant ODBMS has a C, C++ or Smalltalk language binding to implement the methods of the schema. For any of these languages IDL language bindings that determine how IDL operations are implemented are also standardised. Finally, the skeleton and the method implementation have to be registered in the CORBA implementation repository so that they are activated as soon as the external tool issues the operation execution request.

Attributes that implement inter-subgraph semantic edges, i.e. edges that lead to subgraphs that are potentially managed outside the ODBMS, are implemented in the ODBMS schema as attributes that store externalised CORBA object references as character strings. If the ODBMS is ODMG-93 compliant, the schema will be implemented in C, C++ or Smalltalk. Using the respective CORBA IDL binding to C, C++ or Smalltalk, methods of the ODBMS schema can internalise a CORBA object reference and then use the CORBA static or dynamic invocation interface to invoke an operation belonging to a subgraph that is managed by a remote CORBA object server.

An ODBMS transaction can guarantee integrity and serialisability of operations that modify objects managed under control of the ODBMS. ODBMS transactions, however, cannot guarantee integrity and serialisability of accesses to objects managed outside the scope of the ODBMS. This is the case if builders of viewpoint-based tools have decided not to implement subgraphs in an ODBMS schema, or to store them in different databases managed by different servers. Then distributed transactions have to be employed and the different ODBMS transaction managers have to participate. The CORBA transaction service supports these distributed transactions by using a two-phase commit protocol.

Most database systems, be they relational or object-oriented, support the XA transaction protocol defined by the X/Open Group. The XA protocol standardises an application programming interface that is used during two-phase commit. Using the XA interface, the CORBA transaction service can be implemented in a way such that databases participate in distributed transactions. The CORBA transaction service defines interfaces for transactional clients, transactional servers and transaction coordinators. A tool issuing a command that involves more than one abstract syntax graph database server would be a transactional client and request the transaction coordinator to begin a transaction. Any object database participating in that distributed transaction registers itself with the implementation of the transaction coordinator using the XA protocol. When the tool wants to complete the tool command it requests a commit from the coordinator. To implement that commit the coordinator uses (in the first phase) the XA protocol to obtain completion votes from any participating database. If all participating databases express that they are able to commit, the coordinator implementation would use the XA interface to ask all databases to commit (in the second phase). The implementation of transactional servers, which is very complicated in general due to server uncertainty and a necessity of forward recovery, is fully achieved by the participating databases as part of the XA protocol implementation.

3.5 Summary

The architecture that has been developed in this section is summarised in Figure 3. At a conceptual level, different viewpoint representations form one project-wide abstract syntax graph. Edges between nodes of subgraphs representing different viewpoints are used for checking and preserving inter-viewpoint consistency.

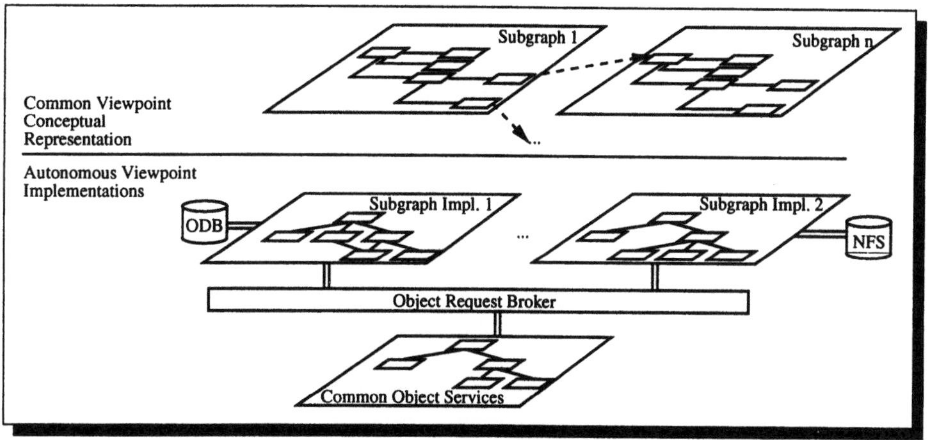

Figure 3: Architecture for Viewpoint-based Environments

The different subgraphs, however, can be implemented in a fairly autonomous manner. Interoperability between the distributed and heterogeneous viewpoint representations is achieved using CORBA. An object request broker may integrate tools, for instance constructed using object databases running on a UNIX platform, with tools that might store viewpoint representations in the file system and operate on a Windows platform. The broker resolves differences in data representations and programming languages. The CORBA transaction service is used to implement transactions that span the boundaries of single database.

4 Related Work

The idea of using syntactic structures for viewpoint representation was developed during the early eighties in a number of projects including Gandalf [11] and the Cornell Synthesizer Generator [15]. Tools generated by these systems are used in programming environments, that means they are intended to support viewpoints in one language only. Therefore, they initially did not address the problem of inter-viewpoint consistency constraints. Garlan suggested the use of different views of the same common representation [10]. As there is only one common conceptual representation this approach, however, removes the possibility of inter-viewpoint consistency constraint violations. Moreover, none of these early tools provide sufficient support for concurrency control; most store viewpoints in a flattened representation in the file system. In the circumstance of concurrent tool execution, this implies that changes done by one tool to a viewpoint are lost as soon as some other tool, which had read the viewpoint before the other has written it, writes its changes to the file system. Version management is also not supported explicitly by any of these tools.

A proof-of-concept prototype for viewpoints was provided in the Viewer environment [14]. This prototype was implemented in Smalltalk. While demonstrating the appropriateness of viewpoint concepts, the Viewer prototype does not address version management, distribution or heterogeneity, as our architecture does. Tools within the viewer run in the same process and concurrent tool execution is not addressed. Persistence is achieved by storing an image of that process and transaction management that is needed for supporting multiple users is not addressed at all.

The IPSEN environment [13] was among the first environments that considered inter-viewpoint consistency. Tools checking these inter-viewpoint consistency constraints are physically executed in one process. Hence, the basic mechanism to achieve inter-viewpoint consistency is implemented by procedure calls and the integration of autonomously constructed tools into the IPSEN environment is not addressed. Cooperative support is not supported since the home grown database system underlying IPSEN has only very limited concurrency control facilities.

5 Summary and Further Work

As our motivation, we have summarised how viewpoints can be used as a conceptual framework for the integration of software development methods and tools. We have discussed project-wide abstract syntax graphs for viewpoint representation and persistent storage of viewpoints. We have then outlined how syntax graphs can be implemented as distributed CORBA objects. For tools that can be constructed anew we have indicated how persistence, version management and transaction support can be achieved using ODMG object databases. Finally, we have sketched how CORBA and ODMG databases can be combined to achieve interoperability of heterogeneous and distributed viewpoint based tools.

The construction of tools on top of object databases has been fully validated and explored [6]. We have preliminary but promising experience with a-priori, CORBA-based integration of tools using different object database servers (of the same type).

The approach outlined in this paper, however, will only achieve its full potential if we can show that it is generally applicable to the integration of off-the-shelf software development tools. In order to make such a general claim, we will have to demonstrate that every off-the-shelf tool can be wrapped with one or more CORBA objects. To support this claim a more detailed survey of the integration mechanisms that are available in current off-the-shelf tools will have to be made.

We believe that our solution to integration of viewpoint development tools is also applicable to other information systems, where information is kept in different autonomous and heterogeneous data stores. We have yet to investigate this possibility.

Acknowledgements

My colleagues Stephen J. Morris and George Spanoudakis provided me with valuable comments on earlier drafts, which allowed me to improve contents and presentation of the paper.

References

[1] F. Bancilhon, C. Delobel, and P. Kanellakis. *Building an Object-Oriented Database System: the Story of O_2*. Morgan Kaufmann, 1992.

[2] N. S. Barghouti, W. Emmerich, W. Schäfer, and A. H. Skarra. Information Management in Process-Centered Software Engineering Enviroments. In A. Fuggetta and A. Wolf, editors, *Software Process*, number 4 in Trends in Software, chapter 3, pages 53–87. Wiley, 1996.

[3] R. Cattell, editor. *The Object Database Standard: ODMG-93*. Morgan Kaufman, 1993.

[4] A. Dardenne, A. van Lamswerde, and S. Fickas. Goal-directed Requirements Acquisition. *Science of Computer Programming*, 20:3–50, 1993.

[5] W. Emmerich. Tool Specification with GTSL. In *Proc. of the 8th Int. Workshop on Software Specification and Design, Schloss Velen, Germany*, pages 26–35. IEEE Computer Society Press, 1996.

[6] W. Emmerich, J. Arlow, J. Madec, and M. Phoenix. Tool Construction for the British Airways SEE with the O_2 ODBMS. *Theory and Practice of Object Systems*, 1997. To appear.

[7] W. Emmerich, P. Kroha, and W. Schäfer. Object-oriented Database Management Systems for Construction of CASE Environments. In V. Mařik, J. Lažanksý, and R. R. Wagner, editors, *Database and Expert Systems Applications — Proc. of the 4th Int. Conf. DEXA '93, Prague, Czech Republic*, volume 720 of *Lecture Notes in Computer Science*, pages 631–642. Springer, 1993.

[8] W. Emmerich, W. Schäfer, and J. Welsh. Databases for Software Engineering Environments — The Goal has not yet been attained. In I. Sommerville and M. Paul, editors, *Software Engineering ESEC '93 — Proc. of the 4th European Software Engineering Conference, Garmisch-Partenkirchen, Germany*, volume 717 of *Lecture Notes in Computer Science*, pages 145–162. Springer, 1993.

[9] A. Finkelstein, D. Gabbay, H. Hunter, J. Kramer, and B. Nuseibeh. Inconsistency Handling in Multi-Perspective Specifications. *IEEE Transactions on Software Engineering*, 20(8):569–578, 1994.

[10] D. Garlan. *Views for Tools in Integrated Environments*. PhD thesis, Carnegie Mellon University, 1987.

[11] A. N. Habermann and D. Notkin. Gandalf: Software Development Environments. *IEEE Transactions on Software Engineering*, 12(12):1117–1127, 1986.

[12] ISO 8879. Information processing – Text and Office Systems – Standardised General Markup Language SGML. Technical report, International Standards Organisation, 1986.

[13] M. Nagl. An Incremental and Integrated Software Development Environment. *Computer Physics Communications*, 38:245–276, 1985.

[14] B. Nuseibeh, J. Kramer, and A. Finkelstein. A Framework for Expressing the Relationships Between Multiple Views in Requirements Specification. *IEEE Transactions on Software Engineering*, 20(10):760–773, 1994.

[15] T. W. Reps and T. Teitelbaum. *The Synthesizer Generator – a system for constructing language based editors*. Springer, 1988.

[16] R. M Soley, editor. Object Management Architecture Guide. Technical report, Object Management Group, 492 Old Connecticut Path, Framingham, MA 01701, USA, 1992.

[17] L. Vidal, A. Finkelstein, G. Spanoudakis, and A. L. Wolf, editors. *Viewpoint '96. In Joint Proc. of the SIGSOFT '96 Workshops*. ACM Press, 1996.

An Agent-Based Coordination Model on Workflow Databases

Takeo Kunishima

Graduate School of Information Science

Nara Institute of Science and Technology

8916-5, Takayama, Ikoma, Nara 630-01, JAPAN

Kazumasa Yokota

Faculty of Computer Science and System Engineering

Okayama Prefectural University

Soja, Okayama 719-11, JAPAN

Abstract

Workflow management, one of the important technologies for supporting collaborative work, requires database technologies like distributed data management or transaction management. However, as workflow management systems have several heterogeneities like heterogeneity about agents, spatial heterogeneity, temporal heterogeneity, etc., collaboration model for workflow management should resolve these heterogeneities. In this paper, we propose a collaboration model for workflow management using a heterogeneous distributed problem solver *Helios*. Agents, environments in which agents coordinate each other, and coordination among agents are modeled by message passing among agents. These modeling give semantics of agents in Workflow Base, previously proposed formal workflow database model based on object-oriented data model, as coordination entities.

1 Introduction

Workflow management is a technology supporting the reengineering of business process [1]. It involves two activities: defining workflows, i.e., flows of the business process to control their execution; and supporting redesign (optimization etc.) of business process. As business process is generally cooperative work in a heterogeneous, autonomous, and distributed environment, *workflow management systems* (WFMS) should manage various resources about business process — workflow definitions, their execution status, products data produced during the process execution, etc. Hence database technologies are indispensable for the infrastructure of WFMSs [2], and researches about workflow management from database point of view have been made in recent years, mainly from transaction management [3–6].

Though transaction management technology in database area is important for workflow automation, it is not enough for workflow management. In general, users as well as programs collaborate each other in business process on WFMSs.

In other words, collaborative entities (agents) on WFMSs may behave in non-procedural way. Moreover, as each agent has multiple different works at the same time, agent must dynamically decide his own strategies for doing works and must negotiate other agents according to the strategies. Therefore the protocols among agents in WFMSs are quite complex.

Considering a big problem such as workflow, we can find many applications which require multiple heterogeneous problem solvers: *modeling heterogeneity* (The complexity of a given problem requires a combination of multiple heterogeneous problem solvers), *spatial heterogeneity* (Spatially distributed problem solvers are required to process a given problem), *temporal heterogeneity* (For a new problem, a new problem solver is not necessarily developed: that is, multiple existing problem solvers must be reused for a new problem), etc. There have been some approaches: an arithmetic calculator in Prolog and a constraint logic programming language with a single constraint solver. Such a restricted approach seems to be neither flexible nor promising for most applications. To make a collaborative work possible on groupware like workflow management systems, related programs and persons should have a common protocol, which resolves each heterogeneity with some protocol.

In this paper, we discuss how to model such environments for workflow management on *Workflow Base*, a formal model of workflow database previously proposed [7].

The remainder of this paper is as follows: the outline of Workflow Base is shown in Section 2. In Section 3, we propose two agent definitions, logic-oriented approach and problem solver approach, and discuss merits and demerits between these two definitions. The way of coordination among agents are shown in Section 4. Lastly, we discuss the relationships between Workflow Base and the agent coordination proposed in this paper in Section 5. Section 6 is a conclusion.

2　Workflow Base

In this section, we show details of Workflow Base. The features of this model and the merits are as follows:

- A workflow is defined as a set of objects (activity objects), by which database management of workflows becomes easier.
- Two kinds of flows are defined. Hierarchical workflows can be described by using these flows.
- Generalization/specialization hierarchy of workflows is introduced. This makes relationships among workflows clearer, and workflows more reusable.
- A rule-based execution model of workflow is defined.
- Integrity constraints over workflows are defined.
- Database operators over workflows are introduced. These operators bring powerful view functions into WFMSs.

Because of space limitations, only the concepts necessary for the below discussions are shown. For more details, see [7].

2.1 Workflow Model

An *activity object*, which corresponds to a unit of work, is recursively defined as follows:

$$a = (I, O, P, S) \text{ where } \begin{array}{l} I = \{i_1, \cdots, i_n\} \; (n \geq 1) \\ O = \{o_1, \cdots, o_m\} \; (m \geq 1) \\ P = \text{string} \\ S = \text{WFT} \end{array}$$

where I is a set of inputs of a, O is a set of outputs of a, P is an agent who is responsible for the execution of a, and S is a WFT (defined in the following) of a, which executes subworks of a. Intuitively, a receives I, P executes its necessary work, and a sends O. During the execution, if necessary, a divides I, dispatches them to S, monitors their execution processes, and composes O from their results.

Strictly speaking, an activity object is defined as a quintet (a, I, O, P, S), whose identifier is a. For simplicity, we denote simply a or $a = (I, O, P, S)$. Further, when I, O, and P are singletons, $\{\}$ is omitted, if there is no misunderstanding.

A *workflow template* (WFT) W is defined as a set, $\{a_1, \cdots, a_n\}$, of activity objects $a_1, \cdots, a_n$ $(n \geq 0)$. Exactly, it is $(W, \{a_1, \cdots, a_n\})$, the identifier of which is W. For simplicity, we denote $W = \{a_1, \cdots, a_n\}$, as in an activity object.

There are two kinds of flows in a WFT as follows:

1. *horizontal flow* "$\Longrightarrow$"

$$a_1 \Longrightarrow a_2 \;\; \overset{def}{=} \;\; (O_1 \supseteq I_2)$$

$$\{a_1, a_2, \cdots, a_n\} \Longrightarrow a \;\; \overset{def}{=} \;\; (\sum_{i=1}^{n} O_i \supseteq I) \wedge \forall j \, \neg(\bigcup_{i=1}^{n} O_i - O_j \supseteq I)$$

The second definition specifies the minimality of inputs.

2. *vertical flow* "$\longrightarrow$"

$$a \longrightarrow a_i \;\; \overset{def}{=} \;\; a_i \in S \text{ where } a = (I, O, P, S)$$

If $a_1 \longrightarrow a_2$, a_2 is called a *child* of a_1 and a_1 is a *parent* of a_2.

An auxiliary flow named *partial horizontal flow*, $a_1 \rightharpoonup a_2$ is defined as follows: $a_1 \rightharpoonup a_2 \overset{def}{=} O_1 \cup I_2 \neq \emptyset$. When a horizontal flow $\{a_1, \cdots, a_n\} \Longrightarrow a$ holds, n partial horizontal flows, $a_1 \rightharpoonup a, \cdots, a_n \rightharpoonup a$, hold. Now we use reverse flow notations for simplicity: $a_1 \Longleftarrow a_2 \overset{def}{=} a_2 \Longrightarrow a_1$, etc.

Workflow is defined as a WFT W satisfying this restriction:

$$\forall \, a_1, a_2 \in W, a_1 \neq a_2. \; a_1 \rightsquigarrow a_2 \vee a_2 \rightsquigarrow a_1.$$

Here, $\rightsquigarrow \overset{def}{=} \{\Longrightarrow \wedge \Longleftarrow \wedge \rightharpoonup \wedge \leftharpoonup \wedge \longrightarrow\}^+$.

This definition is easily extended into a set of workflows. Consider a set, S, of workflows, each of which is connected to another workflow in S: that is,

$$\forall w_1, w_2 \in S, w_1 \neq w_2.\ w_1 \rightsquigarrow w_2 \vee w_2 \rightsquigarrow w_2.$$

Such a set of workflows is also called as a workflow.

On the workflows defined above, several restrictions can be considered: closedness, acyclicity, redundancy, triangle restriction, etc. Though these restrictions are important for workflow management with database technologies, we omit these explanations in this paper. See [7] for more details.

2.2 Execution Model

2.2.1 Execution Model for Activity Objects

Consider a domain $\mathcal{M}$ of message objects consisting of inputs and outputs, and a domain $\mathcal{P}$ of agents. An activity object $a = (I, O, P, S)$ is basically a function from I to O, defined as follows:

1. $I \in 2^{\mathcal{M}}, O \in 2^{\mathcal{M}}$
2. $P \in 2^{\mathcal{P}}$
3. $a \in \mathcal{A}, S \subseteq \mathcal{A}$, where $\mathcal{A}$ is a set of activity objects, defined as follows:

$$\mathcal{A} := 2^{\mathcal{M}} \times 2^{\mathcal{M}} \times 2^{\mathcal{P}} \times 2^{\mathcal{A}}$$

Although P can be defined as a function on $\mathcal{M}$, we take another domain $\mathcal{P}$, because we consider that two activity objects with the same inputs and the same outputs, but the different agents should be defined as different objects.

2.2.2 Execution Model for Workflows

To execute a WFT for a work, we must define its execution model. The execution model of a WFT consists from two models, *P-box* and *C-box*, each of which corresponds to horizontal and vertical flows, respectively.

A horizontal flow defines the following production rules:

$$
\begin{aligned}
\text{If } a_1 \Longrightarrow a_2, &\quad \text{then } a_2 \Leftarrow a_1 \\
\text{If } a_1 \Longrightarrow a_3 \text{ and } a_2 \Longrightarrow a_3, &\quad \text{then } a_3 \Leftarrow a_1, a_2 \\
\text{If } a_1 \Longrightarrow a_2 \text{ and } a_1 \Longrightarrow a_3, &\quad \text{then } a_2 \Leftarrow a_1 \text{ and } a_3 \Leftarrow a_1 \\
\text{If } a_1, &\quad \text{then } a_1 \Leftarrow.
\end{aligned}
$$

The right hand side of $\Leftarrow$ is a set of conditions, while the left hand side is an action. This rule is evaluated forwardly as in ordinary production rules. That is, by receiving all end conditions of the corresponding activity objects, the corresponding activity object to the action is activated. An activity object itself is represented as a fact. A production system, as a set of such production rules, is stored in **P-box** in the WFT.

On the other hand, a vertical flow represents a set of definite clauses as in logic programming such as Prolog. That is, when an activity object a generates children $a_1, a_2, \cdots, a_n$, the execution model is represented as follows:

$$a \leftarrow a_1, a_2, \cdots, a_n$$

Intuitively, constraints and binding information are propagated from a to a_1, $a_2, \cdots, a_n$, and if all children objects end successfully, then a ends its execution successfully. That is, these rules are evaluated backwardly as in Prolog. Such a set of definite clauses is stored in a **C-box** in the WFT. As dynamically generated child objects are also activity objects, they are stored in P-box, not in C-box.

3 Agents on Workflow Base

3.1 Logic-Oriented Agents Definition

In the previous section, we consider a workflow as a set of activity objects by corresponding an activity object to a work. An agent which (or who) is responsible for a work is embedded in its activity object. However, as an agent usually has multiple kinds of works, we consider another definition of an agent:

$$a/[w(I) = O] \Leftarrow S|C$$

where a is an agent identity, w is an work identity, I is a set of inputs, O is a set of outputs, S is a set of sub-agents, which are called by a, and C is a set of constraints which are delivered from a to S. As in deductive object-oriented languages such as F-logic [8], we can correspond the rule to conventional object-orientation concepts: a work identity corresponds to a method identifier, I is a set of input values, O is a set of return values, and $S|C$ is its implementation.

As an agent do many kinds of works, it is defined as follows:

$$a/[w_1(I_1) = O_1] \Leftarrow S_1|C_1$$
$$a/[w_2(I_2) = O_2] \Leftarrow S_2|C_2$$
$$\vdots$$
$$a/[w_n(I_n) = O_n] \Leftarrow S_n|C_n$$

or

$$a/[w_1(I_1) = O_1, w_2(I_2) = O_2, \cdots w_n(I_n) = O_n]$$
$$\Leftarrow S_1 \cup S_2 \cup \cdots \cup S_n | C_1 \cup C_2 \cup \cdots \cup C_n$$

In this definition, we introduce concurrency in a easily because each work does not share variables with other works, however it is very difficult to control it. Further, as each agent is not encapsulated, it is difficult to correspond an agent to a person who is responsible for its work.

3.2   Agents as Problem Solvers

Considering autonomous agents who execute various works, we had better introduce a concept of an *agent*, which can be defined independently from definitions of workflows.

A workflow defines a set of works and their structured flows, where each work may be executed either automatically by a program, or by a person: i.e., simply speaking, the executer of work can be abstracted as a *problem solver* or an *agent*. In this paper, we use a *problem solver* as a general term for a database system, a knowledge-base system, a constraint solver, an expert system, an application program, and a person, and we employ a concept *agent*, proposed by a heterogeneous distributed cooperative problem solver, *Helios* [9,10], as an abstracted problem solver with the same protocol. Each agent can estimate workload and schedule a set of works.

In this subsection, we define an agent in the sense of *Helios* and discuss an agent as a person.

3.2.1   Agents and Environments

A basic concept (in *Helios*) is an *agent*, defined as follows:

$$\text{agent} \quad := \quad \text{(capsule, problem-solver)} \mid$$
$$\text{(capsule, environment, \{agent}_1, \ldots, \text{agent}_n\})$$

where a *capsule* is a module which contains a translator, and each problem-solver is enclosed in a capsule. An encapsulated problem solver is called an *agent*, and a problem-solver is called a *substance*.

A *simple* agent is defined as a pair of a *capsule* and a problem-solver: conceptually, the problem-solver is encapsulated in the capsule.

A *complex* agent is defined as a triple of a capsule, an environment, and a set of agents (agent$_1$,...,agent$_n$), where an environment is a field where agent$_1$,...,agent$_n$ can exist and communicate mutually. Conceptually, a pair of an environment and a set of agents can be considered as a problem-solver; a new agent can be defined by encapsulating them. That is, an agent can be hierarchically organized. Since an encapsulated problem-solver or an environment can be considered as an agent and the outside of an agent is an environment, the user can be considered as an environment.

A common space for agents is called an *environment*. An environment takes care of message-passing between agents in it, and manages global information for those agents. Each agent has its own logical name that is unique in the environment. Figure 1 shows such structures.

A capsule and an environment is defined as follows:

$$\text{capsule} \quad := \quad \text{(agent-name, methods, self-model,}$$
$$\text{translation-rules, negotiation-strategy)}$$
$$\text{environment} \quad := \quad \text{(agent-names, common-type-system,}$$
$$\text{negotiation-protocol, ontology)}$$

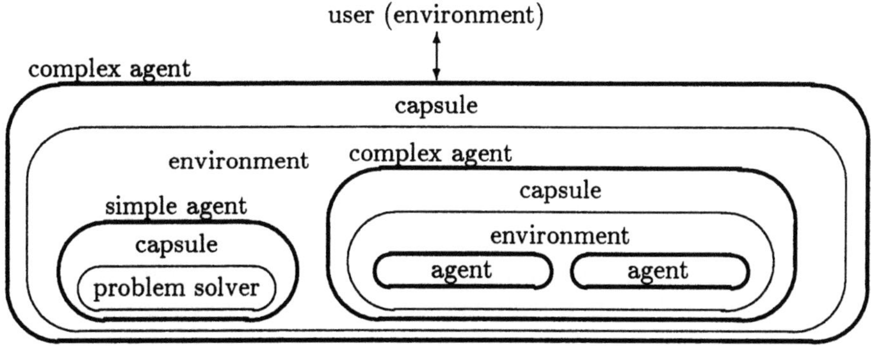

Figure 1: Basic Model of Agent

In a capsule, an *agent-name* is an identifier of the agent. Each agent has its own agent-name that is unique in the environment. A *method* is a definition of *import methods* and *export methods*. An import method defines a method by which the agent is called, and an export method defines a method that the agent can call. An agent with only import methods is called *passive* and an agent with both methods is called *active*: only an agent which sends new messages through export methods can negotiate with other agents. A *self model* defines what the agent can do in terms of the name of functions provided by the agent. An environment extracts the necessary information from self models in agents to dispatch messages between agents. *Translation-rules* define translation between internal representation of the agent and common representation given by its environment in the initialization of the problem solving system.

In an environment, *agent names* state which agents are in the environment. A *common type system* defines a type system used to type all messages in the cnvironment. A *negotiation protocol* defines the protocol used by all agents in the environment. Under a *negotiation protocol* in an environment, each agent defines a *negotiation strategy* to communicate with other agents. An *ontology* defines the transformation of the contents of messages between agents, while a capsule converts the syntax and type of messages between the common type system and the intrinsic type system of the corresponding problem-solver.

To define this information, we introduce a capsule description language *CAPL* (CAPsule description Language), and an environment description language *ENVL* (ENVironment description Language). Programs written in those languages are processed by their corresponding compilers.

Although various information is defined locally in each environment and each agent, a *message* between agents is in the form of a global *communication protocol* consisting of the following:

- Message identifier
  An identifier used for identifying a message. This field is unique within an environment.

- Message type

  As described above, a message is either a method invocation or an answer. The former message is called a *query message*, and the latter message is called a *reply message*. This field is used to distinguish a query message from a reply message.

- Sender agent identifier

  This field contains the agent name of the agent that sends this message.

- Designation of destination agents

  The methods of designating destination agents in a query message are described below. In a reply message, this field contains the agent name of the agent that is the sender of the corresponding query message.

- Transaction identifier

  If the update of the content of a destination problem-solver is attendant on the invocation of a message, then a transaction identifier is required to control it. This field contains a transaction identifier. For nested transactions, a transaction identifier with a nested structure is used.

- Status

  This field contains information on the status of invoked methods for error handling.

- Message content

  In a query message, this field contains a method invocation, and in a reply message, this field contains the answer to the invocation.

In the previous subsection, we consider some difficulties in logic-oriented approach. On the other hand, in this agent-oriented approach, as each agent is autonomous, concurrency control can be done by a capsule or a substance, and correspondence with a person is made possible by wrapping by a capsule.

3.2.2 Users

A user can play three roles in *Helios*: an end user, an outermost environment, and a problem solver if he keep the above same protocol.

For communication between a user and an agent, a user can give his user model, which corresponds to a common type system and data structures defined in an outermost capsule. Given a user model to an agent, its capsule transforms all messages between the user and the agent.

A user is defined as the outermost environment where there is only one (simple or complex) agent. If an internal agent cannot solve a problem, the problem is thrown out in the outer environment. Hence, a user receives unsolvable problems finally. If the user returns the answer to the agent, the agent continues to process the suspended message.

Furthermore, a user may be defined also as an agent, that is, a user can process a message sent by its capsule and return its result to the capsule. This feature helps not only prototyping a system, but also constructing a groupware environment, if multiple users are defined as agents. In this paper, we use such features of an agent as an executer of a work. Such models make prototyping multi-agent programming in our model easier.

4 Coordination among Agents

In *Helios*, messages are dispatched as follows:

- Initialization
  First, during the initialization of agent processes in the environment, the environment constructs a map of a logical agent name and a physical process address (or IP address). Secondly, the environment gathers method information and function information in self models from each agent and constructs two kinds of maps: a method and an agent name; a function name and an agent name. Such maps work for dispatching messages among agents.

- Dispatching:
  As a method or a function does not necessarily corresponds to an agent uniquely, a message is possibly sent to multiple agents. This mechanism is useful for the followings:

  - It is unnecessary to specify an agent name in problem solvers explicitly.
  - It is possible to send simultaneously a message to possible agents.

  An environment decides to send a message sequentially or in parallel to candidates listed by the maps, and processes answers sequentially or by grouping as a set. In the case of set grouping, aggregation functions can be specified in an environment. Such a mode can be selected in a query message.

As already mentioned, differently from *Helios*, an agent P in Workflow Base is responsible for dispatching works (messages) to agents and coordinating their execution. In the sense, P provides the capsule c and includes the functions of an environment e.

A message is analyzed and its corresponding processing plan is constructed as a dependency graph by a parent agent as in a query in conventional distributed databases. Synchronization information between sub-messages is attached to each sub-message and controlled by the capsule of each agent: i.e.,if necessary, child agents can communicate with each other. The coordination protocol between a parent agent and child agents is rather simple:

- success/failure:
  An child agent sends a success or failure message to the parent agent. The parent agent redispatches the work to another child agent or cancels all works dispatched to all child agents related to the work. There might be various reasons of failures: unsatisfaction of time constraints, lack of resources, and so on.

- resource requirements:
  A child agent can request some resources necessary for executing its own work to the parent agent. The parent agent sends additional resources to the child agent if the parent has enough resources. If the parent does

not have necessary resources, it requests them to other child agents. If a child agent has enough ones, it sends them to the parent.

We assume that a person involved in some workflow has an appropriate interface to the capsule of the corresponding agent. As a person can do many works, he is connected to many capsules. In this paper, we do not discuss the topic.

5   Relations between Workflow Base and Agent Definitions

We have two kinds of definitions about a workflow: a workflow definition and a agent definition. As mentioned in Section 2, a workflow base consists of a workflow definition and its execution model.

A workflow definition corresponds to a static aspect of workflow, while an execution model corresponds to its dynamic aspect, where activity objects are dynamically generated and activated in P-box and their relations are defined. in C-box in the form of definite clauses.

In our workflow model, (I, O, P, S), an agent P controls a set, $S = \{a_1, a_2, \cdots, a_m\}$, of activity objects. It can be written as a complex agent as follows: $P = (c, e, \{a_1, a_2, \cdots, a_n\})$. Horizontal flows and vertical flows are corresponding to the messages between agents in the same complex agent and to the messages between agents and their parent complex agent, respectively.

A definite clause, $p \leftarrow q_1, q_2, \cdots, q_n$, is a dispatching plan: that is, from an agent-based definition point of view, they are agents in the same environment and the definite clause is a dispatching plan of p. On the other hand, a production rule $a \Leftarrow a_1, \cdots, a_n$ corresponds to the message passing from $a_1, \cdots, a_n$ to a.

An isolated activity object in P-box corresponds to an individual agent definition, which might be either simple or complex. In the case of complex agents, auxiliary definitions of agents have to be defined in P-box. Therefore, by defining activity objects as in Section 2.2.2 and agents as in Section 3.2 in P-box, we can bridge a gap between workflow and multiagent concepts and could extend coordination strategies for controling workflow management.

6   Conclusion

Considering a big problem such as workflow, we can find many applications which require multiple *heterogeneous* problem solvers. To make a collaborative work possible, related programs and persons should have a common protocol, which resolve each heterogeneity with some protocol.

There have been some approaches: an arithmetic calculator in Prolog and a constraint logic programming language with a single constraint solver. Such a restricted approach seems to be neither flexible nor promising for most applications.

371

From workflow and workflow base points of view, in a unit of workflow definition, all agents should have the same protocol, for which we use an environment concept as in *Helios*. In this paper, we discussed how to define such environments for workflow management. A problem solver, a generic term of database systems, knowledge-base systems, constraint solvers, application programs, persons, and so on, is called an *agent* by wrapped by a common protocol.

We do not discuss in this paper the strategies for agents and how to decide the strategies. This is one of the important future works.

References

[1] D. Georgakopoulos, M. Hornick, and A. Sheth, "An overview of workflow management: From process modeling to workflow automation infrastructure," *Journal of Distributed and Parallel Dataabases*, vol. 3, pp. 119–153, Apr. 1995.

[2] G. Alonso and H.-J. Schek, "Research issues in large workflow management systems," in *Proceedings of NSF Workshop on Workflow and Process Automation in Information Science*, pp. 126–132, May 1996.

[3] M. Rusinkiewicz and A. Sheth, "Transactional workflow management in distributed systems," in *Proceedings of International Workshop on Advances in Databases and Informations Systems*, pp. 18–33, May 1994.

[4] N. Krishnakumar and A. Sheth, "Managing heterogeneous multi-system task to support enterprise-wide operations," *Journal of Distributed and Parallel Databases*, vol. 3, pp. 155–186, Apr. 1995.

[5] G. Alonso, D. Agrawal, A. E. Abbadi, M. Kamath, R. Günthör, and C. Mohan, "Advanced transaction moldels in workflow contexts," in *Proceedings of the 12nd International Conference of Data Engineering*, Feb. 1996.

[6] D. Jean, A. Cichocki, and M. Rusinkiewicz, "A database environment for workflow specification and execution," in *Proceedings of International Symposium on Cooperative Database Systems for Advanced Applications*, vol. 2, (Kyoto), pp. 491–500, Dec. 1996.

[7] T. Kunishima and K. Yokota, "Flexible workflow frameworks for supporting collaborative work," in *Proceedings of International Symposium on Cooperative Database Systems for Advance Applications*, vol. 2, (Kyoto), pp. 501–508, Dec. 1996.

[8] M. Kifer and G. Lausen, "F-Logic — a higher order language for reasoning about objects, inheritance, and schema," in *Proc. ACM SIGMOD Intl. Conf. Management of Data*, (Portland), pp. 134–146, June 1989.

[9] K. Yokota and A. Aiba, "A new framework of very large knowledge bases," in *Knowledge Building and Knowledge Sharing* (K. Fuchi and T. Yokoi, eds.), pp. 192–199, Ohmsha and IOS Press, 1994.

[10] A. Aiba, K. Yokota, and H. Tsuda, "Heterogeneous distributed cooperative problem solving system Helios and its cooperation mechanisms," *International Journal of Cooperative Information Systems*, vol. 4, pp. 369–385, Dec. 1995.

OBJECT ORIENTATION IN SPATIAL STRUCTURES

Inheritance of Multimedia Class Having Temporal-Spatial Structures

Jisook Park and Sukho Lee

Dept. of Computer Engineering, Seoul National University, Korea

Abstract

Many new multimedia applications require capabilities not only for representing and storing temporal-spatial structures of multimedia data but also for reusing them. This paper is an effort to provide an inheritance mechanism for efficiently reusing the previously defined temporal-spatial structures. In this mechanism, temporal-spatial structures are defined within the database schema on the class level and are inherited into all subclasses in a class hierarchy. This paper formally develops an inheritance function which can be applied to all possible combinations of classes having various temporal-spatial structures. The proposed mechanism enables users to incrementally define the complex temporal-spatial structures without schema redefinition overhead.

1 Introduction

Many new requirements for multimedia applications have been identified from the viewpoints of data [7, 11] and database systems [2, 11]. Some of the requirements, such as flexible definition of the schema and media operations, are covered by object-oriented paradigm. For example, ORION and UniSQL [6, 10] support monomedia input/output methods to capture monomedia objects by adding corresponding classes/types for monomedia data. However, they have their limitations in modeling the temporal and spatial characteristics of multimedia data, because they do not provide syntax and semantics to express temporal-spatial aspects directly.

In [4], integration of multimedia objects retrieved from distributed databases is discussed. Their model provides the facilities to *post-process* retrieval results for spatio-temporal composition, thus it cannot be used for information retrieval. [1] presents a model for supporting time-dependent operations in OODBs. But, this model has no consideration on the spatial aspects of multimedia data and cannot provide capability for reusing the temporal relationships.

As a result, most existing models or systems for multimedia applications put focus on how to store and retrieve monomedia data or how to represent the temporal-spatial structures of multimedia data. They do not consider how to *reuse* the previously defined temporal-spatial structures of multimedia data when a new structure is defined.

We focus on how effectively the temporal-spatial structures of multimedia data can be defined and *reused*. The main point of this paper is on the use of inheritance as a reusing mechanism as follows: The temporal-spatial structures are *defined* within the database schema *on the class level* and they are *inherited* into all subclasses in a class hierarchy. In traditional object-oriented databases, a class contains only a set of attributes as the class structure. In this paper, however, the structure of a class includes not only attributes but also the temporal-spatial relations between them. Therefore, a new inheritance mechanism is needed to support the inheritance of the temporal-spatial structure as a whole. This paper formally defines an inheritance function which can be applied to all possible combinations of classes having various temporal-spatial structures. Consequently, users are quite free from schema redefining efforts.

The remainder of this paper is organized as follows. Section 2 introduces the syntax for defining and inheriting the temporal-spatial structures and outlines the proposed inheritance mechanism. Section 3 defines the temporal-spatial priorities between temporal-spatial structures and Sect. 4 explains an inheritance function regarding all combinations of temporal-spatial structures based on the priorities. Finally, conclusions and future research directions are discussed in Sect. 5.

2   Overview of Inheritance Mechanism

This section introduces the syntax of our model, TSM(Temporal-Spatial Model) [9, 5] , and outlines the proposed inheritance mechanism.

2.1   Representation of Temporal-Spatial Structures

Figure 1 shows an essential part of our DDL [9] which supports defining and inheriting temporal-spatial structures. These statements have two major differences in comparison with traditional object oriented data definition statements. First, extended domain types are used to define the integrated temporal-spatial structures of multimedia objects. Second, they allow users to explicitly assign the position of the newly defined structure within the inherited structure using the *order statement*.

```
< create_statement > ::= CREATE CLASS <class_name>
                         <inherit_statement>
                         <object_structure_definition>
                         <object_behavior_definition>
<inherit_statement> ::= SUPER <class_name>
                         <order_statement>
<order_statement> ::=
                    | <present_order> <attribute_name>
<present_order> ::= BEFORE | AFTER
< object_structure_definition > ::= [<dummy_attribute_name> :] <domain_type>
< object_behavior_definition > ::= METHOD < method_list >
```

Figure 1: Syntax of Data Definition and Inheritance

(1) Domain Type

A domain type provides possible value/object/oid range, structure skeleton, and possible operations applied to the domain object. Given the set B={Int, Real, String}, M={Text, Graphic, Image, Audio}, the set of class names C, and the tag set TS={s,sc,t,p}, the domain types for temporal-spatial structures as explained in [5] can be defined as follows:

- spatial composition: $sc[a_1 : d_1, a_2 : d_2, \cdots, a_n : d_n]$, $sc\{d\}$
    - describes relations of component objects within a space
- spatial sequence: $s< a_1 : d_1, a_2 : d_2, \cdots, a_n : d_n >$, $s\{d\}$
    - describes sequential ordering of spaces
- temporal sequence: $t< a_1 : d_1, a_2 : d_2, \cdots, a_n : d_n >$, $t\{d\}$
    - describes sequential ordering of objects in time
- parallel: $p[a_1 : d_1, a_2 : d_2, \cdots, a_n : d_n]$
    - describes parallel occurrence of objects in time

Here, $a_1, a_2, \cdots, a_n$ are attributes and $d_1, d_2, \cdots, d_n$ are domain types. The tag *s* means *spatial*, *sc* means *spatial composition*, *t* means *temporal*, and *p* means *parallel*. Figure 2 shows introductory example classes defined using the statements in Fig. 1 and the extended domain types. The class **Person** has five attributes which are composed spatially and the class **Professor** also two attributes composed in a space. The two attributes of the class **Student** will be shown sequentially in time and the attributes **audioProfile** and **papers** of the class **GraduateStud** will be presented simultaneously. The class **UnderGraduate** has two attributes **activity** and **interests** composed spatially.

```
CREATE CLASS Person SUPER Object
sc[ name: String,
    birthDate: Date,
    addr: String,
    picture: Image,
    family: sc{Person} ]
CREATE CLASS Professor SUPER Person
sc[ supervise: Lab,
    career: t{Paper} ]
CREATE CLASS Student SUPER Person
t< studentProfile: sc[deptName: String,
                      studNumber: Int,
                      friends: sc{Student} ],
    hobby: Video >
CREATE CLASS GraduateStud SUPER Student
p[ audioProfile: Audio,
    papers: t{Paper} ]
CREATE CLASS UnderGraduate SUPER Student
BEFORE hobby
sc[ activity: Image,
    interests: Text ]
```

Figure 2: Example Multimedia Classes

(2) Order Statement

The temporal-spatial structure of a class is directly used for data presentation. Therefore, in the viewpoints of presentations, it is required to provide flexible defining facilities such as inserting a newly defined structure within the previously defined structure. Our DDL as described in Fig. 1 enables users to explicitly specify positions of the newly defined structures within the superclass's structure using 'BEFORE/AFTER' statement. In the class UnderGraduate of Fig. 2, for example, 'BEFORE' statement is used to insert its' structure before hobby of the class Student. As a result, the objects of UnderGraduate will be presented as follows: studentProfile is firstly presented, then the activity and interests are shown, finally the hobby is played. If no *order statement* is specified, the inherited structure precedes the newly defined class structure.

2.2   Semantics of Inheritance

We will now shortly describe our inheritance mechanism. As described in Fig. 2, a class structure includes not only attributes but also temporal-spatial relations between them. Therefore, a class inherits the temporal-spatial structure as a whole from its direct/indirect superclasses. Then, what will be the result of inheritance? For this question, two answers are possible as follows.

At first, if the two structures have the same temporal-spatial relation, then the result structure will be constructed by simply combining the attributes, i.e. inherited attributes *plus* additional attributes, related with the same temporal-spatial relation. For example, given two classes Professor and Person defined in Fig. 2, they have the same temporal-spatial relation 'sc[ ]'. Accordingly, Professor will get 7 attributes related with 'sc[ ]' after inheriting the structure of Person as follows.

```
CLASS Professor
sc[ name:String, birthDate:Date, addr:String, picture:Image, family:sc{Person},
    supervise:Lab, career:t{Papers} ]
```

Second, if their temporal-spatial relations are different from each other, then the result may be a *new* structure which is formed by combining the inherited structure with its' own structure. This paper proposes a solution to effectively generate the *new* structure. We will first assign priorities between all possible combinations of temporal-spatial structures. Then, the *new* structure is generated as follows: *The class structure with higher priority is defined within the class structure with lower priority.* This inheritance mechanism guarantees that the subclass has a meaningful temporal-spatial structure without any conflict in time and space. In the following sections, we will capture these concepts in a more formal way and develop an inheritance function that is consistent with the intuition given in this section.

3   Priority Assignment

In this section, the concepts of temporal cohesion and spatial cohesion are introduced. Then, priorities are assigned between all combinations of temporal-spatial structures using those concepts.

3.1   Temporal Priority

Given objects a and b which are related with temporal-spatial relations R, we use the term $R(a, b)$ to note the temporal-spatial structure of them.

Definition 1 *Duration* of an object o ($o \in O, O$ is the set of objects) will be represented as a pair (t_1, t_2), which denotes the valid interval of o in time axis.

Definition 2 *Temporal coherence operator* denoted by $\cap_t$ is an operator applied between objects. The result of this operation represents an intersection of durations of operand objects. Given objects a and b ($a, b \in O$) , the temporal coherence operator is defined as follows.

$$a \cap_t b = |\, t_2 - t_1 \,|, \quad \text{where } (t_1, t_2) \subset D(a) \text{ and } (t_1, t_2) \subset D(b).$$

Figure 3 shows how the temporal coherence operator can be applied to temporal-spatial structures in TSM. For example, objects a and b in Fig. 3. (a) are presented simultaneously, thus they have an intersection τ.

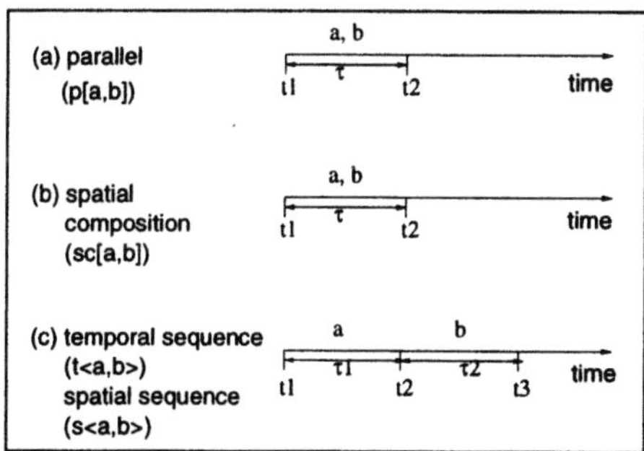

Figure 3: Temporal Cohesion and Temporal Priority

Definition 3 *Temporal cohesion* assesses the tightness with which related objects are 'presented together' in time axis and is determined by the temporal coherence operation. Given $R(a, b)$ and $R'(a', b')$, if $a \cap_t b$ is larger than $a' \cap_t b'$, then the temporal cohesion of $R(a, b)$ is larger than that of $R'(a', b')$.

As described in Fig. 3, the temporal cohesions of parallel relations such as parallel or spatial composition are larger than those of sequential relations such as temporal sequence or spatial sequence.

Definition 4 *Temporal priority* is assigned as follows: the larger the temporal cohesion, the higher the temporal priority level. Given $R(a,b)$ and $R'(a',b')$, the difference and equivalence in temporal priority are represented as follows.

$$R(a,b) \ >_t \ R'(a',b'), \quad R(a,b) \ =_t \ R'(a',b').$$

The temporal priorities between the temporal-spatial structures in TSM are as follows.

$$\text{p[a,b]} \ =_t \ \text{sc[a,b]} \ >_t \ \text{s<a,b>} \ =_t \ \text{t<a,b>}$$

3.2 Spatial Priority

We assume that a space represents a two-dimensional layout plane and it has a valid time period ρ as indicated in Fig. 4. Let P be the set of spaces.

Definition 5 *Region* of an object o will be represented as a pair $(x_1@y_1, x_2@y_2)$, upper-left and lower-right corner of a square representing o in a space $p \in P$.

Definition 6 Given objects a and b $(a,b \in O)$, *spatial coherence operator* denoted by $\cap_s$ is defined as follows.

1. $a \cap_s b = p$,   *if* $\exists p$ such that $R(a) \subset p$ and $R(b) \subset p$, $p \in P$,
2. $a \cap_s b = 0$,   *if* $\not\exists p$ such that $R(a) \subset p$ and $R(b) \subset p$, $p \in P$,
3. $a \cap_s b = \phi$,   *if* $\not\exists R(a)$ or $\not\exists R(b)$.

In Fig. 4, objects a and b in (a) belong to the same space p, $p \in P$ and a and b in (b) are located in different spaces, $p1$ and $p2$, with an interval ρ in time. Therefore, the result of (a) is p where both a and b are placed and the result of (b) is 0. In addition to these cases, the third case indicates the temporal relations such as parallel or temporal sequence in which component objects may not have any region.

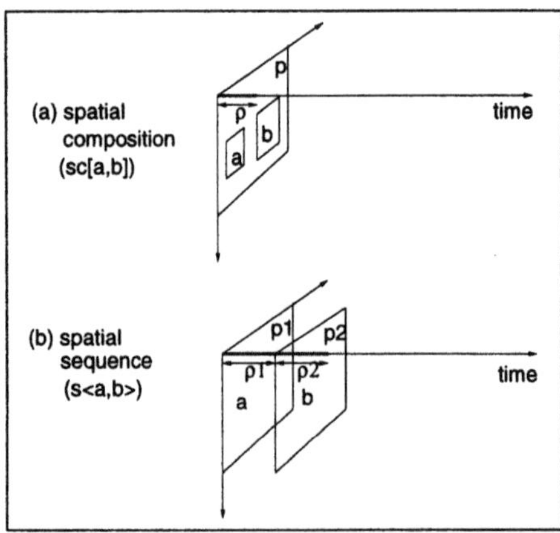

Figure 4: Spatial Cohesion and Spatial Priority

Definition 7 *Spatial cohesion* assesses the tightness with which related objects are 'presented together' in spaces. Given $R(a,b)$ and $R'(a',b')$, the spatial cohesion of $R(a,b)$ is larger than that of $R'(a',b')$ in the following cases: 1) if $a \cap_s b$ is not null (i.e. p or 0) and $a' \cap_s b'$ is null, or 2) if $a \cap_s b$ returns p and $a' \cap_s b'$ returns 0.

Definition 8 *Spatial priority* is assigned as follows: the larger the spatial cohesion, the higher the spatial priority level. Given $R(a,b)$ and $R'(a',b')$, the difference and equivalence in spatial priority are represented as follows.

$$R(a,b) >_s R'(a',b'), \quad R(a,b) =_s R'(a',b').$$

The spatial priorities among the temporal-spatial structures in TSM are as follows.

$$\text{sc[a,b]} >_s \text{s<a,b>} >_s \text{t<a,b>} =_s \text{p[a,b]}$$

3.3 Temporal-Spatial Priority

Temporal-spatial priority is determined by temporal priority and spatial priority in which temporal priority is given much weight. In other words, temporal priority is considered before than spatial priority. Spatial priorities are considered if and only if the temporal priorities are the same.

Definition 9 *Temporal-spatial priority* indicates the relative importance of each temporal-spatial structure against the others. Given $R(a,b)$ and $R'(a',b')$, temporal-spatial priority is defined as follows (here, $>_{ts}$ and $=_{ts}$ are used to denote the difference and equivalence in temporal-spatial priority).

1. $R(a,b) >_{ts} R'(a',b')$,   if $R(a,b) >_t R'(a',b')$,
2. $R(a,b) >_{ts} R'(a',b')$,   if $R(a,b) =_t R'(a',b')$ and $R(a,b) >_s R'(a',b')$,
3. $R'(a',b') >_{ts} R(a,b)$,   otherwise .

Table 1 shows the temporal-spatial priorities between the temporal-spatial structures in TSM.

Table 1: Temporal-Spatial Priorities between Structures in TSM

	t<>	s<>	p[]	sc[]
t<>	$=_{ts}$	$<_{ts}$	$<_{ts}$	$<_{ts}$
s<>	$>_{ts}$	$=_{ts}$	$<_{ts}$	$<_{ts}$
p[]	$>_{ts}$	$>_{ts}$	$=_{ts}$	$<_{ts}$
sc[]	$>_{ts}$	$>_{ts}$	$>_{ts}$	$=_{ts}$

4 Inheritance of Temporal-Spatial Structures

This section defines an inheritance function and a class structure generating function using temporal-spatial priorities.

4.1 Inherited Structure

In this section, we use $TS(c)$ to denote an extended constructor of a class c. It is represented by a temporal-spatial tag with a type constructor. Similarly, we use $A(c)$ to denote the set of attributes of c. For the class Professor in Fig. 2, $TS(\text{Professor})$ and $A(\text{Professor})$ will be represented as follows.

$TS(\text{Professor}) = \text{sc}[\ ]$,
$A(\text{Professor}) = \{\text{supervise: Lab, career: t}\{\text{Paper}\}\}$

Now, we will define the inheritance function and will show the validity of this function.

Definition 10 *Inherited class structure* is the result of the following function ι_m. Given the set of classes C, $DT(C)$ denotes the set of domain types of C.

$$\iota_m \colon DT(C) \times DT(C) \to DT(C)$$

Given any c and $c' (c, c' \in C$, c is a subclass of $c')$, the function ι_m is applied as follows. Here, $name(a)$ denotes the name of an attribute a.

1. $\iota_m(DT(c), DT(c')) = TS(c)(A(c) \cup a)$,
   if $DT(c') >_{ts} DT(c)$, where $name(a) = name(c')$ and $DT(a) = \sigma_m(c')$,
2. $\iota_m(DT(c), DT(c')) = TS(c')(A(c') \cup a)$,
   if $DT(c) >_{ts} DT(c')$, where $name(a) = name(c)$ and $DT(a) = \sigma_m(c)$,
3. $\iota_m(DT(c), DT(c')) = \text{t}< a_1 : DT(c'), a_2 : DT(c) >$, if $TS(c') = TS(c) = \text{p}[]$,
   $\exists a_i \in A(c')$ and $\exists a_j \in A(c)$ such that $DT(a_i) = DT(a_j) = \text{Audio}$,
4. $\iota_m(DT(c), DT(c')) = TS(c)(A(c) \cup A(c'))$, otherwise .

The four conditions of the above function can be categorized into two groups. At first, in the first and second conditions where the temporal-spatial priorities of c and c' are different from each other, the class structure with higher priority is defined as the domain type of a new attribute named that class within the class structure with lower priority. Consider the classes Person and Student defined in Fig. 2. The priority of Person is higher than that of Student, thus the structure of Person is defined as the domain type of a new attribute, named person (beginning with a lower-case letter), of Student as follows.

$\iota_m(\text{DT(Person),DT(Student)})$
$= \text{t}<\text{person:sc[name:String, birthDate:Date, addr:String,}$
$\qquad\qquad \text{picture:Image, family:sc}\{\text{Person}\}] \underline{\text{INHERITED}},$
$\qquad \text{studentProfile: sc[deptName:String, studNumber:Int, friends:sc}\{\text{Student}\}],$
$\qquad \text{hobby: Video} >.$

In the third and fourth conditions of the above function, c and c' have the same temporal-spatial priority. In these cases, the attributes of c and c' are combined into a set and they are related with the temporal-spatial relation of c/c' as previously stated in Sect. 2. However, we should consider an exceptional case in which the result structure has a conflict. Let us consider two classes

c and c', both of which have p[ ] and contain an attribute in Audio. If we combine the attributes of c and c' together with p[ ] as the fourth condition, then the two objects in Audio will be played simultaneously. Consequently the presentation of them won't be meaningful. The third case resolves this conflict as follows: each parallel relations of c and c' will be presented sequentially.

The following theorem shows the validity of the inheritance function ι_m.

Theorem 1 *The function ι_m is closed given the set of class names C and the set of domain types $DT(C)$ in TSM.*

Proof: Given C and $DT(C)$, we can prove the validity of ι_m by showing that $\iota_m(DT(C))$ will be also $DT(C)$. The temporal-spatial structures of classes in TSM can be divided into four types and there exist sixteen combinations for the four types. For all of the sixteen cases, the results of the function $\iota_m(DT(C))$ are also $DT(C)$ as explained in Table 2. For example, given two classes c and c' (one is a subclass of the other), if the structure of c is 't<>' and that of c' is 'p[ ]', then the result of $\iota_m(DT(c), DT(c'))$ will be 't< p[ ] >', which means 'p[ ]' is included in 't<>' as the domain type of an attributes of 't<>' because the priority of 'p[ ]' is higher than that of 't<>'. $\qquad\square$

Table 2: The result of ι_m for temporal-spatial structures in TSM

	t<>	s<>	p[ ]	sc[ ]
t<>	t<>	t< s<> >	t< p[ ] >	t< sc[ ] >
s<>	t< s< > >	s<>	s<p[ ]>	s< sc[ ]>
p[ ]	t< p[ ] >	s< p[ ] >	p[ ] t< p[ ],p[ ] >	p[sc[ ]]
sc[ ]	t< sc[ ] >	s< sc[ ] >	p[sc[ ]]	sc[ ]

4.2   Class Structure With Inheritance

Given a class $c \in C$, the class structure of c can be generated by applying the inheritance function recursively to each superclass from c to the root class.

Definition 11 Given a class hierarchy Θ, the set of class names C, *class structures* of C can be generated by the following function σ_m.

$$\sigma_m : C \to DT(C).$$

Given any two class names c and $c'(c, c' \in C$), the function σ_m is applied as follows.

1. $\sigma_m(c) = DT(c)$, if c is a direct subclass of **Object**,
2. $\sigma_m(c) = \iota_m(DT(c), \sigma_m(c'))$, if c is a subclass of c'.

In the above definition, if c is a direct subclass of **Object**, then the class structure equals to its own domain type. If c has one or more direct/indirect superclasses except **Object**, then the class structure of c can be generated by applying the inheritance function recursively from c to the root class.

4.3   Illustrating Examples

Let us examine how automatically the class structures for example classes in Fig. 2 can be generated by using ι_m and σ_m. At first, the class Person is a direct subclass of Object, thus it has no inherited structure as follows.

σ_m(Person) = DT(Person)
    = sc[name:String, birthDate:Date, addr:String,
        picture:Image BKEY, family:sc{Person}]

The class structure of Student can be generated by combining it with its superclass Person. Since Person has a higher priority than Student, the structure of Person is defined as the domain type of a new attribute named person in the class Student (Refer to Sect. 4.1). Similarly, the class structure of the class GraduateStud is also constructed by combining it with the structure inherited from its superclasses Student and Person. The priority level of GraduateStud is higher than Student. Therefore, the structure of GraduateStud is defined as the domain type of an attribute named graduateStud as follows.

σ_m(GraduateStud) = ι_m(DT(GraduateStud), σ_m(Student))
= ι_m(DT(GraduateStud), ι_m(DT(Student),DT(Person)))
= t< person:sc[name:String, birthDate:Date, addr:String,
            picture:Image, family:sc{Person}] <u>INHERITED</u>,
    studentProfile:sc[deptName:String, studNumber:Int,
            friends:sc{Student}] <u>INHERITED</u>,
    hobby:Video <u>INHERITED</u>,
    graduateStud:p[audioProfile:Audio, papers:t{Paper}] >

Figure 5 graphically shows the presentation sequence of the class Graduat-eStud. The symbol '*' means 'zero or more'.

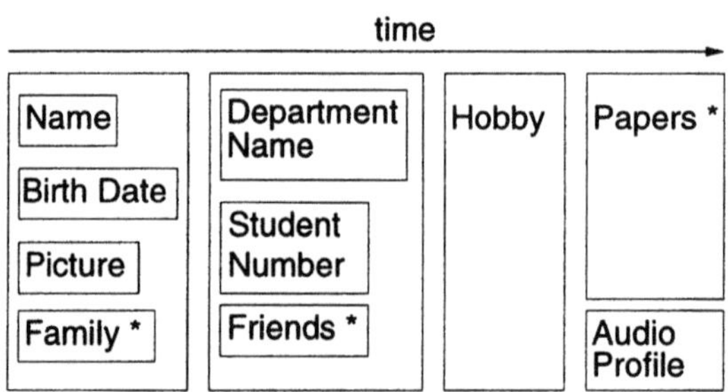

Figure 5: Presentation of GraduateStud

5   Conclusion

We have presented an inheritance mechanism which supports facilities representing and reusing the temporal-spatial structures of multimedia data. In this mechanism, the temporal-spatial structures are defined on the class level and they are inherited into all subclasses in a class hierarchy. We have introduced the concepts of temporal/spatial cohesions to explain the semantics of inheritance and have proposed an inheritance function which can be applied to all combinations of classes having various temporal-spatial structures.

The proposed mechanism allows users to define a new temporal-spatial structure incrementally by reusing the previously defined structures. Moreover, users can explicitly position the additional temporal-spatial structure within the inherited structure using 'BEFORE/AFTER' statement. The system management overhead is also reduced because the data duplication on the schema is minimized.

The inheritance mechanism is developed for the prototype multimedia system ALPHA [3, 8]. We will adapt the proposed mechanism to the stadardized data language such as SQL3 in the next step.

References

[1] Aberer, K. and Klas, W., "Supporting Temporal Multimedia Operations in Object-Oriented Database Systems," IEEE Int. Conf. on Multimedia Computing and Systems, pp.352-361, May, 1994.

[2] Christodoulakis, S., "Multimedia Data Base Management: Applications and Problems - A Position Paper," in Proc. ACM SIGMOD, pp.304-305, 1985.

[3] Lee, S., et. al, "Design and Implementation of the Multimedia DBMS ALPHA," Journal of Korea Information Science Society, Vol.22, No.2, pp.1181-1188, 1994.

[4] Little, T.D.C. and Ghafoor, A., "Spatio-Temporal Composition of Distributed Multimedia Objects for Value-Added Networks," IEEE computer, Vol.24, No.10, pp.42-50, 1991.

[5] Nah, Y., Lee, S., Hwang, S., "Two-level Modeling Schemes for Temporal-Spatial Multimedia Data Representation," in Proc. of DEXA, pp.102-107, 1992.

[6] Kim, W., Modern Database Systems, ACM Press, Addison-Wesley, New York, 1995.

[7] Klas, W., Neuhold, E.j., and Schrefl, M., "Using An Object-Oriented Approach To Model Multimedia Data," Computer Communication, Butterworth, Vol.13, No.4, pp.204-216, 1990.

[8] Park, J., Lee, S., Cha, J., and Nah, Y., "A Presentation Scheduling Scheme for Multimedia Databases," in Proc. of COMSAC'97, 1996.

[9] Park, J., Lee, S., "An Inheritance Mechanism for Reusing Temporal-Spatial Structures in Multimedia Databases," DBTR-17-1, Dept. of Computer Eng., Seoul National Univ., 1997.

[10] Woelk, D. and Kim, W., "Multimedia Information Management in an Object-Oriented Database System," in Proc. of VLDB, pp.319-329, 1987.

[11] Woelk, D., Luther, W., and Kim, W., "Multimedia Applications and Database Requirements," in Proc. of IEEE Computer Society Office Automation Sympo., pp.180-189, 1987.

Design and Implementation of Object-Oriented Spatial Views[*]

Sang-Ho Moon and Bong-Hee Hong

Department of Computer Engineering, Pusan National University
30 Changjeon-Dong, Kumjeong-Ku, Pusan, 609-735, Korea
e-mail: shmoon@hyowon.cc.pusan.ac.kr

Abstract

The objective of this paper is to propose an extension of the object-oriented view concepts for providing a variety of user's perspective views on spatial databases. This paper deals with the issues of design and implementation of materialized spatial views in object-oriented spatial databases. The semantics of object-oriented spatial views and the functionalities for implementing spatial views are proposed. We also present incremental spatial view maintenance by using view derivation relationships.

1 Introduction

Spatial views allow the virtual structures and behaviors of spatial objects to be defined for adapting the spatial objects to different applications. For spatial views, it should be able to view one geometric model for a set of spatial objects with different geometric representation according to different user's perspectives [8]. For example, a traffic management may regard roads as a set of lines, while a road management may see roads as a set of areas.

We define a spatial view as a *virtual class* that is derived by a spatial query on one or more stored base classes which define spatial objects and/or other spatial views. The definition of a stored base class includes a list of spatial attributes, non-spatial attributes, a list of methods, and a list of superclasses. A virtual class in object-oriented databases(OODBs) is a class whose objects are not actually stored.

Many works on the view concepts for OODBs have done in [1, 6, 9, 10, 16], but little work has been done on the support of spatial views in object-oriented spatial databases [12, 14]. Most previous works focus on the semantics of object-oriented views [1, 9, 16], view materialization [6, 9, 10], and view updates [5, 6]. However, the spatial characteristics necessary for the support of spatial views have not been discussed so far. We have identified certain differences between object-oriented views and spatial views. The differences include the semantics of spatial views, materialization of spatial views, and incremental update of materialized spatial views.

In this paper, we discuss the design and implementation of object-oriented spatial

---

[*] This work was supported in part by the Ministry of Science and Technology of Korea under the National GIS project and in part by Research Institute of Computer and Information Communication in Pusan National University.

views built on top of the object-oriented spatial database system Gothic [11]. We present the semantics of spatial views, and then identify the requirements for materializing the instances of a spatial view. Our materialization techniques include incremental view maintenace using view derivation relationships between materialized spatial view objects and their source objects.

This paper is organized into 6 sections. In Section 2, we discuss related works. The formal definition of our spatial view model is presented in Section 3. In Section 4, we briefly describe the implementation of materialized spatial views. Section 5 presents an incremental view maintenance for updating materialized spatial views. We show an example of materialization of spatial views in Section 6. In Section 7, a conclusion and future work are described.

2 Related Works

The first work on the spatial view concept is the proposal of an extension of the relational view [14]. Claramunt points out that the spatial view concepts provide a graphic database view adapted to spatial application requirements. However, our work on the spatial view concept differs from [14] in that we focus on the extension of object-oriented views to spatial data.

Our spatial view modeling scheme is an extension of the object-oriented views [1, 6, 9, 10, 16]. However, there are certain differences between object-oriented views and spatial views. The data type of an attribute in an object-oriented view is the same as that of the corresponding attribute of its source class, or its superclass or subclass [16]. In a spatial view, however, the data type of the view's attribute may be different from that of the source class's attribute. Since view materialization has been proven to improve query execution time, an object-preserving or an object-generating materialized view can be used in OODBs. Our spatial view approach only supports object-generating views. Object-preservation provides the advantage of eliminating duplication of the attribute value of an instance of a source class, but requires a great deal of overhead to produce a new geometry which should be derived from source classes, whenever a query on a spatial view is re-executed.

3 Object-Oriented Spatial View Modeling

3.1 A Basic Spatial Data Model

In this paper, *spatial object* refers to a collection of spatial primitives that represent the spatial characteristics of a geographic feature, and *spatial primitive* refers to elements used in describing the geometric attributes of a geographic feature. Thus, we define point, line, and area classes as the subclasses of a class `Spatial_Primitive`.

Two approaches to modeling spatial objects in spatial databases have been proposed: the *object-centered data model* and the *geometry-centered data model* [13]. In the object-centered data model, any user-defined class can be declared as a subclass of the abstract class `Spatial_Object` which is the root class for spatial objects (Figure1 (a)). In the geometry-centered data model, a user-defined class can be declared as a subclass of the class `Spatial_Primitive`, as shown in Figure1(b).

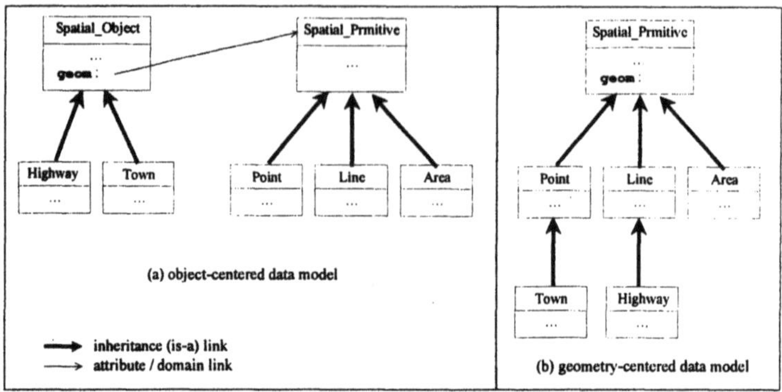

Figure 1. Two Kinds of Spatial Data Models

The object-centered data model gives users flexibility to dynamically define a spatial view adapted to spatial application requirements. SQL3 proposes the *Abstract Data Types* like spatial primitives of the object-centered data model [17]. However, the object-centered data model is not directly supported by Gothic. To implement the spatial view concept based on the object-centered data model, the object-centered representation of spatial objects must be simulated in Gothic as shown in Figure2(b).

Class Highway	**Class** Highway

superclass: Spatial_Object,
     name: string
 	
    ...
   geom: Line
   methods
 	
    ...
end
	superclass: Line,
	     name: string,
	
	    ...
	   geom: set of coordinates
	   methods
	
	    ...
	end

(a) object-centered data model	(b) geometry-centered data model

Figure 2. Inherited Attributes of a Base Class

Let **BC**, **SVC**, and **SPC** denote a set of base classes, a set of spatial view classes, and a set of spatial primitive classes, respectively. In the object-centered data model, the domain of the attribute **geom** of a user-defined class should be one of spatial primitive classes as follows, $dom(BC_i, geom) \in SPC$ *where* $BC_i \in BC$.

3.2 Spatial View Definition

. Spatial_View spatial-view-name (view-attributes, **geom**)   *// schema elements*
   [Methods (methods_list);]
     AS   SELECT Attributes, *GeometryMappingFunction*   *// query description*
         FROM   *SourceClasses*
         [WHERE   *Predicates*]

Figure 3. Syntax for defining spatial views

The definition of a spatial view consists of *schema elements* and a *view-defining query*. The schema elements include a list of view attributes, a derived geometry, and a list of methods. The list of view attributes is a list of non-spatial attributes of a spatial view. The derived geometry is denoted as the attribute **geom** in order to represent its spatial representation. We refer the base classes and/or view classes on which a certain spatial view has been defined to *source classes*. The list of methods may be the methods of source classes, or be newly defined for a spatial view. The view defining query consists of three components: *geometry mapping function, source classes*, and *predicates*. Figure 3 shows the syntax for defining a spatial view

3.3 Semantics of Spatial Views

Given a spatial view class SVC_i, $SourceClasses(SVC_i)$ refers to a set of source classes from which SVC_i is derived. From now on, we make use of the following notation '*derived-from*' to describe a derivation relationship between a view class and its source classes, and the dot notation to refer to the attributes of a class: $C_j.A_i$ denotes the attribute A_i of a class C_j.

Definition 1 A spatial view class SVC_i is *derived from* its underlying source classes SC^j (where j is the index number of source classes) by its *view defining query,* denoted as $query(SVC_i)$.

$$SVC_i \text{ derived-from } SC^j \quad \text{if } SVC_i \in \mathbf{SVC} \text{ and } SC^j \in SourceClasses(SVC_i)$$

We classify the source classes of a spatial view into two types: *geometry-source classes* and *nongeometry-source classes*. A *geometry-source class* is a class that is directly used to derive the spatial view's geometry. A *nongeometry-source class* is a class that is not a geometry-source class of a view.

Definition 2 Given a spatial view class $SVC_i \in \mathbf{SVC}$, its source classes are geometry-source classes, denoted as $Geom\_SourceClasses(SVC_i)$, and/or nongeometry-source classes, denoted as $Nongeom\_SourceClasses(SVC_i)$.

$$SourceClasses(SVC_i) =$$
$$Geom\_SourceClasses(SVC_i) \cup Nongeom\_SourceClasses(SVC_i)$$

Like source classes, a view object may be related to one or more *geometry-* and/or *nongeometry-source objects*. Let $SourceObjects(SVO_j)$ be the set of source objects from which a spatial view object SVO_j is derived. We use the following notation $[C_i]$ to refer to the set of object instances of a class C_i, i.e., the extent of the class.

Definition 3 Given a spatial view object SVO_j, its source objects are geometry-source objects, denoted as $Geom\_SourceObjects(SVO_j)$, and/or nongeometry-source objects, denoted as $Nongeom\_SourceObjects(SVO_j)$.

$$SourceObjects(SVO_j) = Geom\_SourceObjects(SVO_j) \cup$$
$$Nongeom\_SourceObjects(SVO_j) \quad \text{if } SVO_j \in [SVC_i] \text{ and } SVC_i \in \mathbf{SVC},$$
$$\text{where } Geom\_SourceObjects(SVO_j) \in [Geom\_SourceClasses(SVC_i)] \text{ and}$$
$$Nongeom\_SourceObjects(SVO_j) \in [Nongeom\_SourceClasses(SVC_i)]$$

In the following, let **GMF** and **SOP** be a set of geometry mapping functions and a set of spatial operators such as buffer, overlap, and merge which create a new geometry, respectively.

Definition 4 The geometry of a spatial view can be derived without any change of geometry or newly computed from its geometry-source classes according to the geometry mapping functions described in the view-defining query.

$$SVC_i.geom = GMF_j(Geom\_SourceClasses(SVC_i))$$
$$\text{if } GMF_j \in query(SVC_i) \text{ and } GMF_j \in \mathbf{GMF} \text{ and } SVC_i \in \mathbf{SVC}$$

Definition 5 A geometry mapping function may be a non-spatial operator, denoted by Π_{geom}, which projects the attribute **geom** of source classes, and/or a spatial operator which computes a new geometry.

$$\text{GMF} \;=\; \{\Pi_{geom}\} \cup \text{SOP}$$

Let $A(C_j)$ denote the set of attributes of a class C_j. We use a function $dom(A_i, C_j)$, $A_i \in A(C_j)$, which returns the domain of the attribute A_i in the class C_j. Let $value(A_i, O_j)$, where $O_j \in [C_k]$ and $A_i \in A(C_k)$, be a function which returns the value of the attribute A_i in a object O_j.

With respect to the geometry, we classify spatial views into two groups: a *geometry-preserving spatial view* and a *geometry-generating spatial view*. Let GP_SVC and GG_SVC be a set of geometry-preserving spatial view classes and a set of geometry-generating spatial view classes respectively, thus SVC = GP_SVC $\cup$ GG_SVC.

Definition 6 A *geometry-preserving spatial view* is a view whose geometry is identical to that of its geometry-source class. A *geometry-generating spatial view* is a view whose geometry is different from that of its geometry-source class. The **domain** of the attribute **geom** of a spatial view may be identical to or different from the domain of the corresponding geometry-source class, which is determined by the applied geometry mapping function.

1. $SVC_i \in$ GP_SVC   iff $GMF_j = \Pi_{geom}$,   or

   $SVC_i \in$ GG_SVC   iff $GMF_j \in$ SOP,

   where $GMF_j \in query(SVC_i)$ and $GMF_j \in$ GMF

2. if $SVC_i \in$ GP_SVC,   then

   $dom(SVC_i, geom) \in \{dom(SC^k, geom) \mid SC^k \in Geom\_SourceClasses(SVC_i)\}$

3. if $SVC_i \in$ GG_SVC,   then

   $dom(SVC_i, geom) \in \{dom(SC^k, geom) \mid SC^k \in Geom\_SourceClasses(SVC_i)\}$, or

   $dom(SVC_i, geom) \notin \{dom(SC^k, geom) \mid SC^k \in Geom\_SourceClasses(SVC_i)\}$

Definition 7 For a geometry-preserving spatial view, the value of the attribute **geom** in an instance of the corresponding virtual class should be an instance of the spaital primitive class. Moreover, the value of the attribute **geom** of the view object is a spatial primitive object which is referenced by a geometry-source object. Let SPO be a set of spatial primitive objects.

   $value(SVO_j, geom) = SPO_k$ if $SVO_j \in [SVC_i]$ and $SVC_i \in$ GP_SVC and

   $SPO_k = value(Geom\_SourceObjects(SVO_j), geom)$ and $SPO_k \in$ SPO

Definition 8 The value of the **geom** attribute in a geometry-generating spatial view should be a newly generated spatial primitive object. A spatial view's geometry produced by evaluating its view-defining query is stored as an instance of a spatial primitive class.

   $value(SVO_j, geom) = SPO_k$ and $SPO_k \in$ SPO   if $SVO_j \in [SVC_i]$ and $SVC_i \in$ GG_SVC and $GMF_l \in query(SVC_i)$ and $GMF_l \in$ GMF and $SPO_k = GMF_l(Geom\_SourceObjects(SVO_j))$

4 Implementation of Materialized Spatial Views

From the viewpoint of materialization, two kinds of spatial views should be differently materialized. A geometry-preserving spatial view object does not have different geometries from its source objects. To materialize geometry-generating spatial views, we have to create a spatial primitive object for representing a new geometry which is derived from the geometries of source objects. The OID of a newly created spatial primitive object should be stored in the attribute **geom** of a materialized spatial view object.

In order to implement materialized spatial views in our prototype, we design a special class, called **Spatial_View**, which has the functionalities common in all spatial view classes. The abstract superclass **Spatial_View** resembles the class **virtual_object** [10] in implementing the view definition. Once defined, a virtual class definition is compiled, and then stored as a subclass of the abstract class **Spatial_View**. Figure 4 shows the definition of the abstract class **Spatial_View**, where the keyword **class** denotes *class attributes* for representing the definition of a spatial view.

```
Class Spatial_View
      class view_attrib: array      // stores the names of the attributes of a view
      class src_attrib: array        // stores the names of the attributes of the source classes
                                     corresponded to the attributes of a view
      class src_class : array        // stores the source classes of a view
      class geom_src_class: array    // stores the geometry-source classes of a view
      class geom_map_fun: string     // stores the geometry mapping function of a view
      class condition: string        // stores the WHERE clause of the view-defining query
   methods
         make_virtual_class(view_definition: string),
         add_view_attrib(),
         populate_view_extents(),
         is_geom_preserving():boolean,
         ....
   end
```

Figure 4. Definition of the class **Spatial_View**

As mentioned before, Gothic offers a geometry-centered data model to provide fast graphic display, as shown in Figure 1(b). To implement a spatial view on top of Gothic, we have to automatically generate a virtual class which is designated as a subclass of the special class **Spatial_View**. At the same time, the virtual class should be designated as a subclass of the class **Spatial_Primitive**..

The functionalities for the implementation of materialized spatial views are provided by the class **Spatial_View** through its methods. When a spatial view is defined, a virtual class is thus created as a subclass of the class **Spatial_View** by applying the method **make_virtual_class**. The method **add_view_attrib** is used for describing the list of attributes of the virtual class in the class attribute **view_attrib**. The domain of an attribute of an instance of the virtual class may be determined by the corresponding attribute described in the class attribute **src_attrib**.

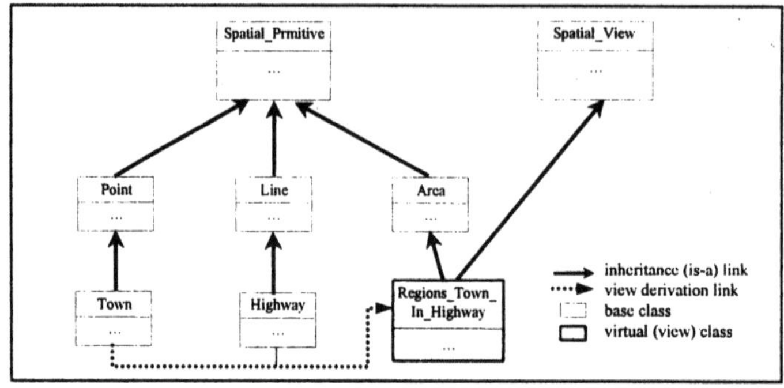

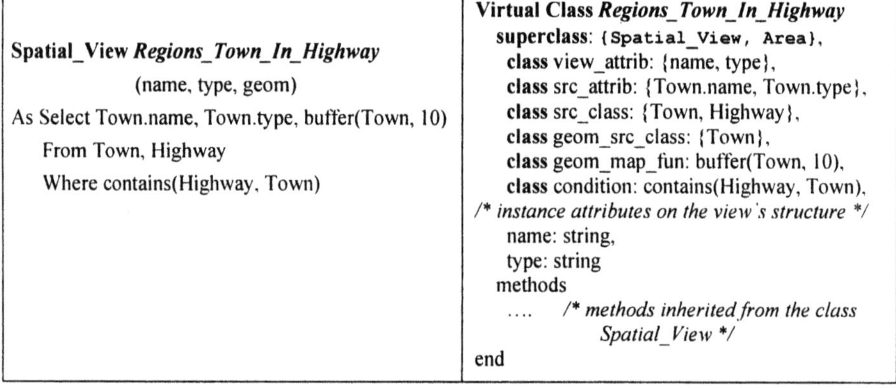

Spatial_View *Regions_Town_In_Highway*

(name, type, geom)

As Select Town.name, Town.type, buffer(Town, 10)

   From Town, Highway

   Where contains(Highway, Town)

Virtual Class *Regions_Town_In_Highway*

  superclass: {`Spatial_View`, `Area`},

    class view_attrib: {name, type},

    class src_attrib: {Town.name, Town.type},

    class src_class: {Town, Highway},

    class geom_src_class: {Town},

    class geom_map_fun: buffer(Town, 10),

    class condition: contains(Highway, Town),

/* *instance attributes on the view's structure* */

  name: string,

  type: string

methods

    ....   /* *methods inherited from the class*

               Spatial_View */

end

Figure 5. An example of a spatial view and its corresponding virtual class

The method `populate_view_extents` allows a virtual class to populate its extents. The method `is_geom_preserving` is invoked to test whether a view is the geometry-preserving spatial view or the geometry-generating spatial view. Figure 5 shows the definition of a geometry-generating spatial view `Regions_Town_In_Highway` and the generated virtual class.

5 Incremental Spatial View Maintenance

5.1 Definition of View Derivation Relationships

To quickly find all of the materialized view objects related to the updated source object, we propose a *view derivation relationship* type between spatial view objects and source objects. Suppose that virtual OIDs are generated for identifying the materialized instances of a spatial view. Object identity of spatial views makes it possible to establish view derivation relationships.

A view derivation relationship type **VDR** is defined as a set of relationship instances $\mathbf{VDR_i}$ between materialized spatial view objects $\mathbf{SVO_m}$ and their source objects $\mathbf{SO_n^j}$, where j represents the index number of source classes. For example, consider a spatial view `Regions_Town_In_Highway` derived from two source classes: `Highway` and `Town`. Let $\mathbf{SVO_m}$ be a spatial view object, and $\mathbf{T_{oidi}}$ and $\mathbf{H_{oidi}}$ be source objects of `Highway` and `Town`, respectively. As shown in Figure 6(a), assume that four spatial view objects are given. In this case, a number of view derivation relationships are generated as in Figure 6(b). Now, we can generate the view derivation relationship as follows.

$$`` VDR_i = <SVO_m, SO_{n1}^1, SO_{n2}^2 > \text{ where } SO_{n1}^1 = \{T_{oidi}\} \text{ and } SO_{n2}^2 = \{H_{oidi}\} ''.$$

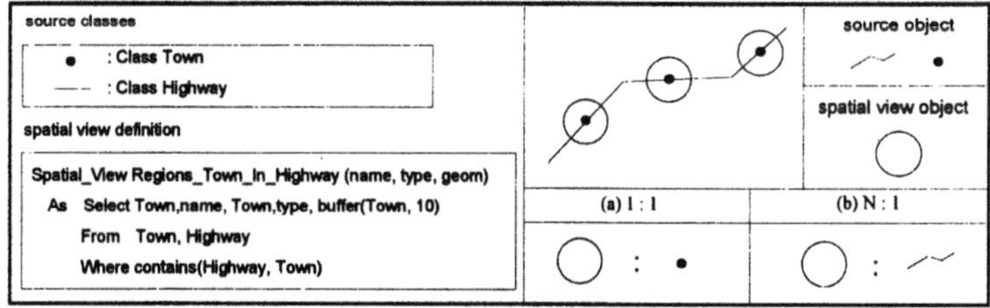

Figure 6. An example of view derivation relationships

5.2 Cardinality Ratios of View Derivation Relationships

Relationship types usually have certain *cardinality constraints* that limit the possible combinations of spatial view objects and source objects. The number of relationship instances between spatial view objects and source objects is defined as *cardinality ratio*. Common cardinality ratios for binary relationships are 1:1, N:1, 1:N, and M:N. It is because the semantics of incrementally updating materialized spatial views differ from each other according to cardinality ratios that we classify view derivation relationships into four kinds of cardinality ratios.

Figure 7(a) shows that the cardinality ratio of the view derivation relationship between **Regions_Town_In_Highways** and **Towns** is 1:1. The binary relationship between **Regions_Town_In_Highways** and **Highways** is of cardinality ratio N:1, as shown in Figure 7(b). This means that each **Highway** can be related to numerous **Regions_Town_In_Highways**, but a **Regions_Town_In_Highway** can be related to only one **Highway**.

Figure 7. An example of a 1:1 and an N:1 relationship

A 1:N relationship indicates that each view object is derived from several source objects, but a source object is only related to one view object. An M:N relationship is the combination of both a 1:N and an N:1 relationship. That is, one spatial view object is derived from several source objects, and vice versa.

5.3 Update Semantics of Materialized Spatial Views

The most important thing to be considered in maintaining materialized spatial views is that the update semantics of materialized spatial view objects are different from each other according to the cardinality constraints of view derivation relationships. After updating the materialized spatial view objects, view derivation relationships will be changed. However, some updates of source objects may result in only updating view derivation relationships without changing materialized spatial view objects themselves.

As shown in Figure 8, the cardinality ratio of the relationships between spatial view objects SVO_m and source objects H_i is N:1. In these relationships, the update of H_i causes both the derived spatial view objects and the related view derivation relationships to be updated.

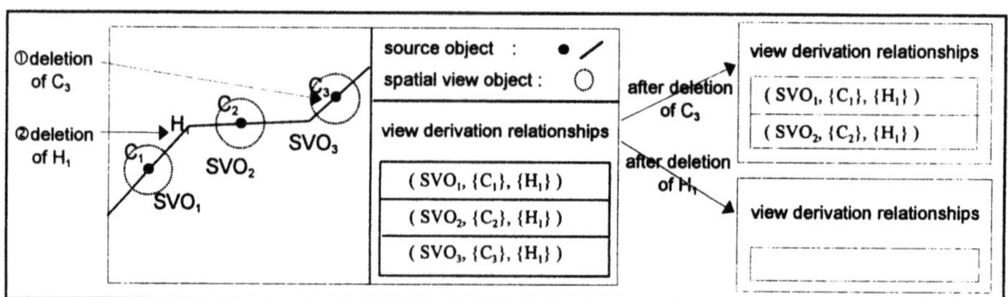

Figure 8. Updating of view derivation relationships in a 1:1 and an N:1

The update semantics of a 1:N relationship are different from those of an N:1 relationship. For 1:N, it is sufficient only to update the view derivation relationships for propagating the update of a source object. We omit to describe the update semantics of a 1:1 and M:N relationship.

A complete set of incremental update algorithms to keep materialized spatial view objects in a consistent state was designed and implemented on top of Gothic which is an object-oriented GIS software [11]. Space limitation, however, prohibits detailed descriptions on the whole implementation.

6 A Spatial View Example

6.1 An Example of Materialized Spatial Views

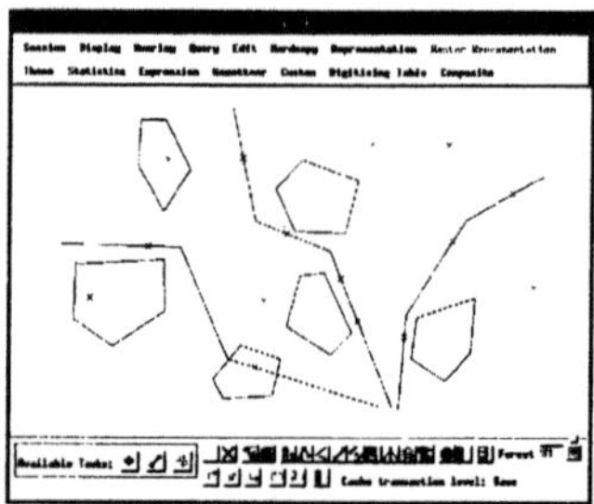

Figure 9. Display of the basic spatial objects

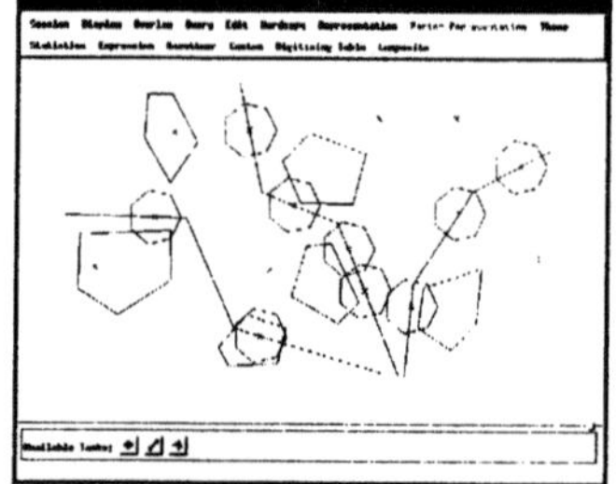

Figure 10. Display of the materialized spatial view **Regions_Town_In_Highway**

Suppose that a sample spatial database contains three base classes: **Highway** with a line geometry, **Town** with a point geometry, and **Forest** with an area geometry. Figure 9 displays the spatial representation of highways, towns, and forests. The spatial view class **Regions_Town_In_Highway** is defined in Figure 5. This spatial view example shows the visualization of buffering towns intersected with any highway in Figure 11. The materialized spatial view corresponds to a geometry-generating spatial view.

6.2 An Example of Incremental Spatial View Maintenance

To the best of our knowledge, little work has been done regarding the implementation and evaluation of incrementally updating algorithms for maintaining materialized spatial views. The update of a source object **highway** having a line geometry in the right upper side is shown in Figure 11. Figure 12 shows the result of updating materialized spatial views, which are affected by the updated source object. After updating the highway, two materialized view objects having an area geometry disappear, and a new materialized view object is inserted.

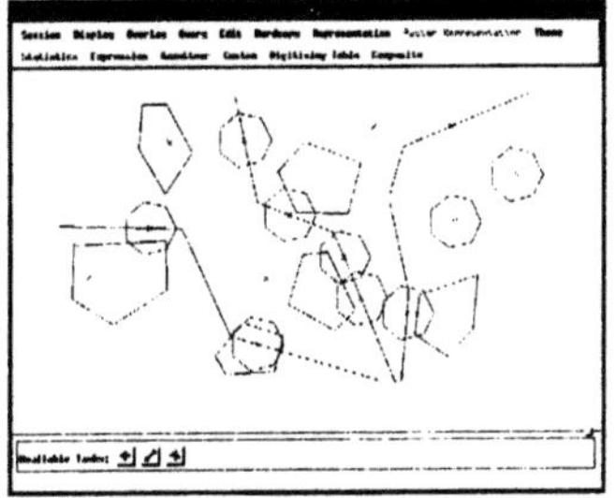

Figure 11. Update of a source object, highway	Figure 12. Update of the materialized spatial views

We evaluate our incremental update algorithms of materialized spatial views. Our experiments demonstrate the benefit of using view derivation relationships. However, our approach has the overhead of creating view derivation relatonships. As shown in Figure 13, the update times of the materialized spatial views affected by the updated source object almost do not increase when our view update algorithms are applied. However, when the other incremental view maintenance using a *registration service* [5] is applied, the update times of materialized view objects increase in proportion to the number of materialized spatial view objects. This is because the existing view maintenance method has to look through all the materialized spatial view objects to find the directly affected objects.

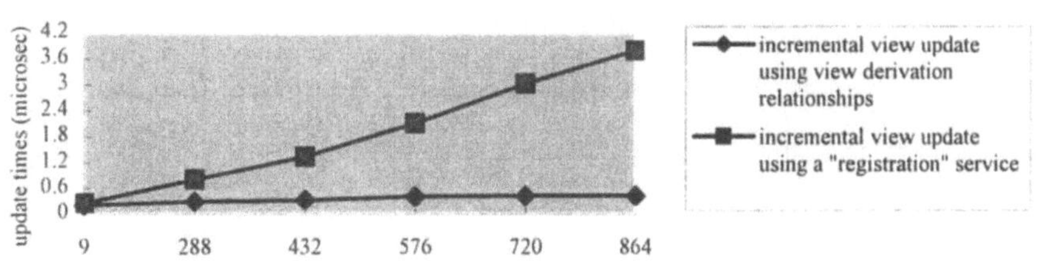

Figure 13. Comparison of two incremental view update schemes

7 Conclusion and Future Work

This paper discusses the semantic issues of object-oriented spatial views. To implement the spatial view concepts on top of Gothic, we propose an abstract superclass `Spaital_View` which defines all the functionalities common in all spatial views. Finally, we presented an incremental spatial view maintenance scheme, which keeps materialized spatial views up to date. Our experiments on incremental view update algorithms demonstrate the benefit of using view derivation relationships.

As future work, we will study updatable spatial views which can update source objects through spatial views, and also spatial schema view which represents virtual schema derived from the underlying base schema.

References

1. Serge Abiteboul and Anthony Bonner, "Objects and Views", Proc. of ACM-SIGMOD Int'l Conf. on Management of Data, pp 238-247, May 1991.
2. Jose A.Blakeley, Per-Ake Larson, and Fank Wm Tompa, "Efficiently Updating Materialized Views", Proc. of ACM-SIGMOD Int'l Conf. on Management of Data, pp 61-71, May 1986
3. Ashish Gupta, Inderpal Singh Mumick, and V. S. Subrahmanian, "Maintaining Views Incrementally", Proc. of ACM-SIGMOD Int'l Conf. on Management of Data, pp 157-166, May 1993
4. Ashish Gupta and Inderpal Singh Mumick, "Maintenance of Materialized Views: Problems, Techniques, and Applications", Proc. of IEEE Int'l Conf. on Data Engineering, pp 3-18, 1995
5. Harumi A. Kuno and Elke A. Rundensteiner, "Using Object-Oriented Principles to Optimize Update Propagation to Materialized Views", Proc. of IEEE Int'l Conf. on Data Engineering '96, 1996.
6. Harumi A. Kuno and Elke A. Rundensteiner, "The MultiView OODB View System: Design and Implementation", Theory and Practice of Object Systems, vol. 2 no. 3, pp 203-225, 1996.
7. Z. Peng and Y. Kambayashi, "Deputy Mechanisms for Object-Oriented Databases", Proc. of IEEE Int'l Conf. on Data Engineering '95, 1995.
8. Robert Laurini and Derek Thompson, "Fundamentals of Spatial Information Systems", Academic Press, 1992.
9. Giovanna Guerrini, Elisa Bertino, Barbara Catania, and Jesus Garcia-Molina, "A Formal Model of Views for Object-Oriented Database Systems", Technical Report, DISI-96-2, 1996.
10. C. Souza dos Santos, "Design and Implementation of Object-Oriented Views", Proc. of Int'l Conf. on DEXA '95, pp 91-102, 1995.
11. Laser-Scan, "Writing and Developing Applications using GOTHIC ADE", Issue 2.0, 1995.
12. Sang-Ho Moon and Bong-Hee Hong, "Incremental Update Algorithms for Materialized Spatial Views by Using View Derivation Relationships", Proc. of Int'l Conf. on DEXA '97, September 1997. *(will be published)*
13. Richard G. Newell, "Practical Experiences of Using Object-Orientation to Implement a GIS", Proc. of GIS/LIS 92, pp 624-629, 1992.
14. Claramunt C. and Mainguenaud M., "Dynamic and Flexible Vision of a Spatial Database", Proc. of Int'l Conf. on DEXA '95, pp 483-493, 1995.
15. X. C. Delannoy, Ana Simonet, and Michel Simonet, "Database Views with Dynamic Assertions", Proc. of Int'l Conf. on OOIS '96, pp 333-339, 1996.
16. Won Kim and W. Kelley, "On View Support in Object-Oriented Database Systems", Modern Database Systems, ACM Press, pp 108-129, 1995.
17. ISO/IEC 13249-3:199x, "SQL Multimedia and Applications Packages – Part 3: Spatial", 1997.

Two Levels of Spatial Data Modeling
for
an Object-Oriented Spatial Database
System

Yang Hee Kim

Department of Computer Science, Suwon Industrial College

Botong-ri, Jungnam-myun, Whasung-gun,

Kyungki-do, 445-960, KOREA

E-mail:yhkim@mail.suwon-ic.ac.kr

TEL:0339-350-2283

FAX:0339-52-6506

Abstract

Data modeling is a critical stage of database design. For modeling the structure of an object-oriented spatial database system appropriately, in this paper, we propose two levels of spatial object-oriented data models: (1) a spatial object model called SAS; (2) an internal description model. SAS supports spatial object types and their polymorphic operations. And the internal description model suppports efficient and appropriate framework to store spatial coordinates and topology between two spatial objects. Our model frame gives the independence between the thematic division of data and cartagraphic presentation. The paper concludes by discussing implementation stage. The commercially available OODB ObjectStore is used as implematation platform.

1 Introduction

Recently there has been much interest in spatial database systems which combine conventional (aspatial) and spatially related data. The main difference between spatial data and aspatial data is their complexity. Spatial objects are described by their associated aspatial and very complex spatial properties. The most important application of the spatial database systems is the Geographic Information System (GIS), so we consider modeling in GIS application. A data model provides a tool for specifying the structural and behavioural properties of a database. The purpose of data modeling is to bring about the design of a database which performs efficiently; contains correct information; whose logical structure is natural enough to be understood by users; and is as easy as possible to maintain and extend.

Geographic information systems are spatial database systems that allow the manipulation, storage, retrieval, and analysis of geographic object as well as the display of data in the form of maps[15]. Some spatial data modelings have been suggested in [1, 16, 17]. M. Scholl's model [16] consists of two stages to represent geometric informations: the *map stage* to represent aspatial data and the *geometric stage* for sptial data. But, the map stage is represented by the relational model meanwhile the geometric stage uses object-oriented concepts. Therefore, this model has shortcoming of requirng two different techniques for one system, namely, techniques for relational model and object-oriented model. B. David's model [1] consists of conceptual and internal stages. The first one abstractly defines properties of geometric data in order to represent geometric information. The second stage is for implementation. This data model represents properly topological relationship, but its hierarchical structure are too complex. Also the representation of aspatial data, and connection between spatial attribute and aspatial attribute were not mentioned. M. F. Worboy's model uses IFO to represent geometric information [17]. The IFO model provides more natural and efficient representation compare with relational model and combine spatial and aspatial attibute using inheritance. But it is lack the hierarchy of aspatial attribute and it does not support spatial operators.

In GIS, the database describes a collection of geographic objects over a two dimensional map. Each geographic object can be classified as belonging to a particular class such as city, road, lake, etc. Most geographical database systems use multiple map layers to organize geographic objects. There exist two different types of map layers: a structure layer and a thematic layer. A structure layer is a set of logically related features which are all based on the same topological data structure and a thematic layer is a set of features that belong to the same theme.

In this paper, we propose the two levels of spatial data models: a *spatial object model* called s̲p̲atial s̲ignature (SAS) for the thematic layer and an *internal description model* for the structure layer. This model frame supports various spatial operators, simple internal primitive object type hierarchy, and object-oriented techniques for the different layer. Figure 1 shows the structure of the two levels of object-oriented spatial data models.

We use the object-oriented approach as a design model, since it allows the representation of complex geographic objects and makes the system extensible and reusable.

This paper is organized as follows. In Section 2 we introduce the spatial object model called SAS. In Section 3 we present an internal description model. Section 4 describes the implementation stage. The conclusions are presented in Section 5.

2   Spatial Object Model

In this section, we give the spatial object model called s̲p̲atial s̲ignature (SAS). SAS describe a formal framework for modeling the structure of spatial objects in space as well as their relationships, properties, and operations. SAS data model is a collection of spatial object types (spatial sorts) and spatial polymorphic operators. It is based on a signature and an extended signature. A signature is a pair (S, Σ) with S is a set (whose elements are called *sorts*) and $\Sigma =$

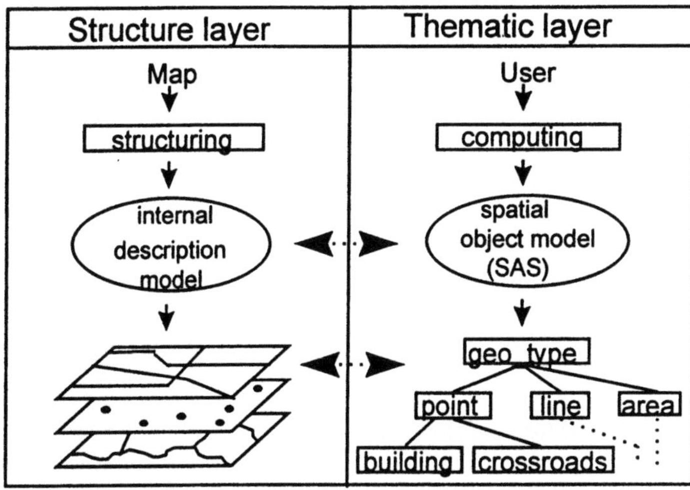

Figure 1: Two levels of data models

$\{\Sigma_{w,s}\}_{w \in S^*, s \in S}$, is a family of sets (whose elements are called *operators*) and an extended signature is to be introduced for list sorts, product sorts, and function sorts[8].

2.1 Spatial Object Type

In SAS, we extend ObjectStore's metatype hierarchy to support spatial object types. Figure 2 depicts the extended type hierarchy for aspatial and spatial objects. The leaf nodes are directly instantiable.

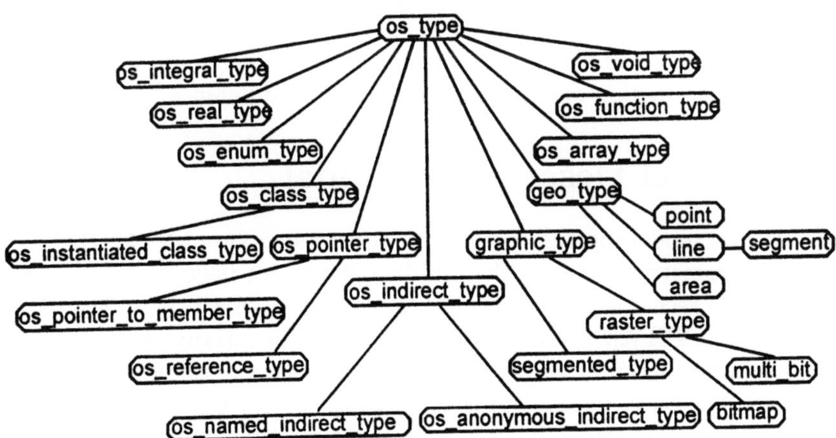

Figure 2: Spatial object type hierarchy

Every object representing a type is an instance of a subtype of the metatype os_type in ObjectStore. To extend metatype hierarchy, we add two new types, geo_type and graphic_type. Graphic_type represents things for graphic display. Geo_type represents various vectorized objects such as points, lines, and various type of areas. A point is the values of n coordinates in n-dimensional vector space. A line is a finite sequence of straight line segments. An area is a polygon and it may have holes.

2.2 Spatial Operator

We give spatial operators on spatial sorts. In [12], operators on the sorts are defined as follows.

- *Location operators* are the most basic operators for the spatial object processing. They search the location value of the spatial object and retrieve the coordinate of the object, or the boundary of the object.

- *Arithmetic operators* perform arithmetical measurements for spatial objects and have os_integral_type as their return type. An example would be the calculation of the distance between two geo_types.

- *Topological relationships* are the most fundamental operators on geo_type[11]. Topological relationships of two spatial objects are DISJOINT, MEETS, EQUALS, INTERSECTS, COVERS, COVEREDBY, INSIDE, and OUTSIDE.

- *Mouse operators* provide the function of selecting an object from the previous query result using the mouse. Examples of the mouse operators are pick(), window(), point(), line(), and circle().

- *Object construction operators* are defined to construct new spatial objects which satisfy certain topological relationships. If the relationships do not hold, the operator returns an empty spatial object. Examples of the object construction operators are split, merge, difference, and intersection.

3 Internal Description Model

The internal model together with internal data structure is important in GIS. Different geometrical and topological data structures have been formalized by the results of recent work on exchange format standardization, such as SDTS[4] and DIGEST-VPF[2]. In this section, we present the internal description model which supports internal vector map structure with various levels of topology. Maps are the basic internal objects in geographical database system. The internal description model is on a basis of the multiple map layers whose type is a multiple-valued vector map structure layer[3]. Using multiple map layers technique for internal structure is nature to organize data and is efficient in terms of object manipulation and storage.

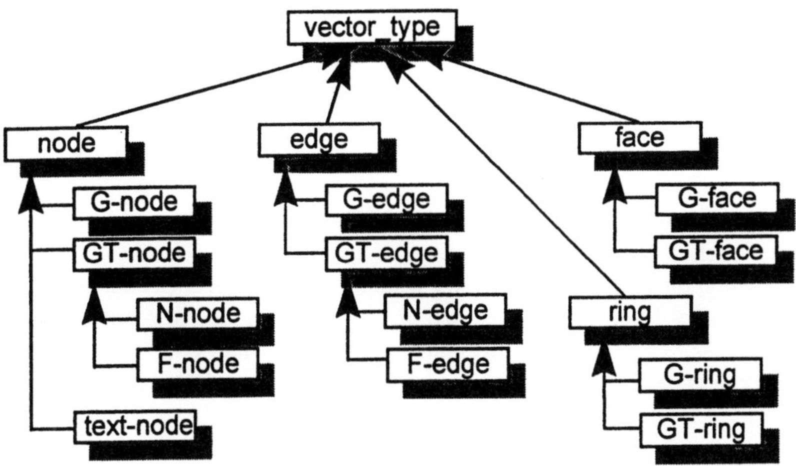

Figure 3: Internal primitive object type hierarchy

3.1 Structure Layer

Multiple map layers with a multiple-valued vector map structure represent several thematic objects which are captured by spatial signature. Each layer consists of the set of modules and maintains the topological integrity. An efficient and appropriate data model to handle geographical locations and spatial relationship between objects are required to manage spatial object. That is very important since a poor internal structure would strongly affect response time to queries. For this reason, we have considered three topological levels (geometry, network topology, and full topology level) that may match the user's need.

Each module consists of the set of internal primitive objects which is the lowest internal object. Figure 3 depicts the type hierarchy for the internal primitive objects. The end nodes of the hierarchy are instantiated with objects.

All of the internal primitive objects shown in Figure 3 are discussed in details. Node type represents a zero dimensional object that specifies geometric location or the topological connectivities of one or more edges. GT-node type represents a point used for identifying the location of point features (or areal features collapsed to a point), such as towers, buildings, places, buoys, etc., and a zero-dimensional object that is a topological junction of two or more links or chains, or an end point of a link or chain. F-node type represents a node which is contained in a single face only. N-node type represents a zero-dimensional object that is a topological junction of two or more lines. Text node type represents a reference point used for displaying map and chart text (e.g., feature names) to assist in feature identification. G-node type represents an internal or extreme point of a line, or not a topological junction of two or more lines.

Edge type represents a connected nonbranching sequence of line segments specified as the ordered sequence of points between those line segments. G-edge type represents a sequence of G-nodes. GT-edge type represents a sequence of one or more N-nodes and zero or more G-nodes. N-edge type is an edge which has N-node as start node and end node. F-edge type is a N-edge which has information about left and right faces.

Ring type is a sequence of nonintersecting edges with closure. A ring represents a closed boundary, but not the interior area inside the closed boundary (for full topology level only). G-ring is a sequence of closed G-nodes. GT-ring is a sequence of closed F-edges.

Face type represents the area which is constituded closed boundaries (for full topology level only). Face has one outer boundary and zero or more inner boundaries. G-face type represents a face which has G-ring boundaries. GT-face type represents a face whose boundaries are made up GT-rings.

3.2   Three Topological Levels

Using the internal description model, we are able to manage concurrently three different levels of topology. So user can match topological levels depend on his necessity. The definition of primitive objects depends on topological levels.

- *Geometry level* describes only geographical location information of each spatial object, but no topological information is explicitly present. Area information may be captured in geometry level by the use of closed lines (G-ring) which circumscribe an area and G-face. Primitive objects are text node, G-node, G-edge, G-ring, and G-face.

- *Network topology level* describes locational information as well as edge to node topological relationships, where every edge must begin and end on a node; however, edges may cross.

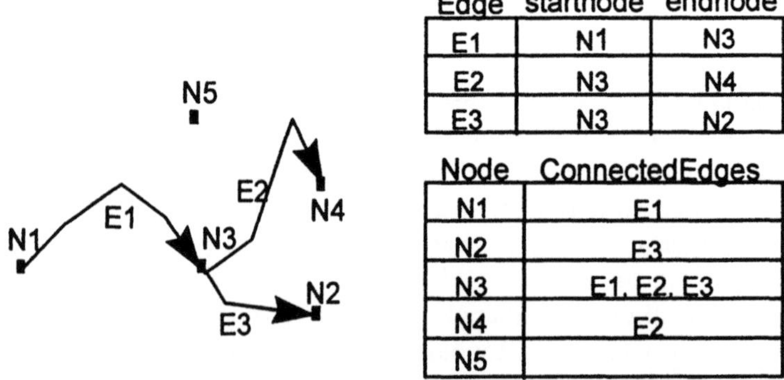

Edge	startnode	endnode
E1	N1	N3
E2	N3	N4
E3	N3	N2

Node	ConnectedEdges
N1	E1
N2	E3
N3	E1, E2, E3
N4	E2
N5	

Figure 4: Example of network topology level

This level of topology is sufficient to describe connectivity. Planar graph introduces the additional mathematical constraint that edges may not cross except at a node. This permits adjacency to be calculated although it is not directly stored in the structure. Primitive objects of network topology level are G-node, text node, N-node, and N-edge. Figure 4 illustrate an example of network topology level and Figure 5 illustrate the topological relationship between N-node and N-edge in the network topology level.

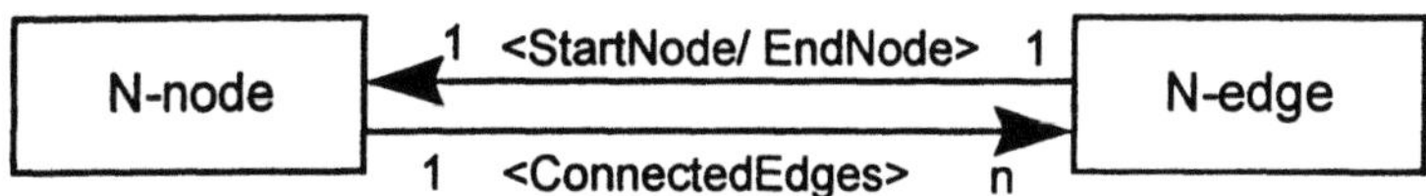

Figure 5: The topological relationship between N-node and N-edge

- *Full topology level* introduces the concept of a face and describes face to edge as well as node to face topological relationships and locational information. Primitive objects of full topology level are N-node, F-node, F-edge, GT-ring, and GT-face. Figure 6 illustrate an example of full topology level and Figure 7 illustrate the topological relationship between primitive objects in the full topology level.

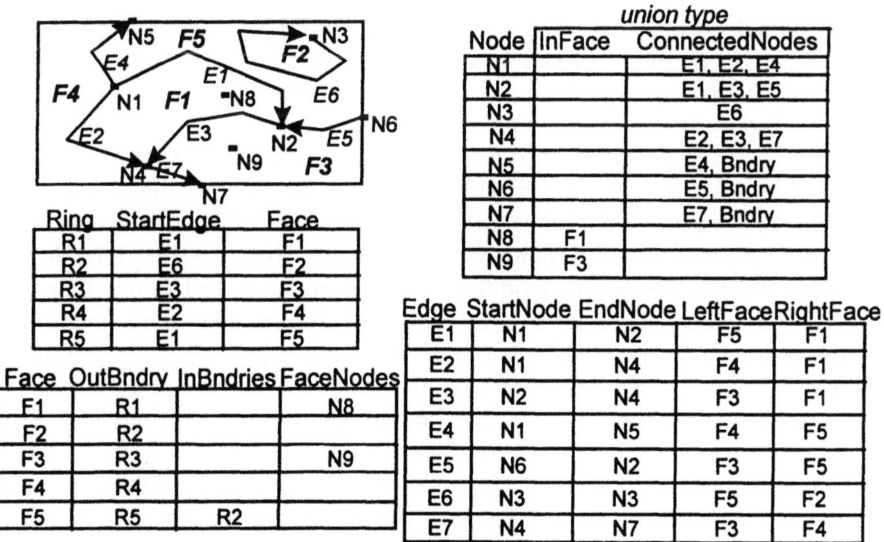

Node	InFace	union type ConnectedNodes
N1		E1, E2, E4
N2		E1, E3, E5
N3		E6
N4		E2, E3, E7
N5		E4, Bndry
N6		E5, Bndry
N7		E7, Bndry
N8	F1	
N9	F3	

Ring	StartEdge	Face
R1	E1	F1
R2	E6	F2
R3	E3	F3
R4	E2	F4
R5	E1	F5

Face	OutBndry	InBndries	FaceNodes
F1	R1		N8
F2	R2		
F3	R3		N9
F4	R4		
F5	R5	R2	

Edge	StartNode	EndNode	LeftFace	RightFace
E1	N1	N2	F5	F1
E2	N1	N4	F4	F1
E3	N2	N4	F3	F1
E4	N1	N5	F4	F5
E5	N6	N2	F3	F5
E6	N3	N3	F5	F2
E7	N4	N7	F3	F4

Figure 6: Example of full topology level

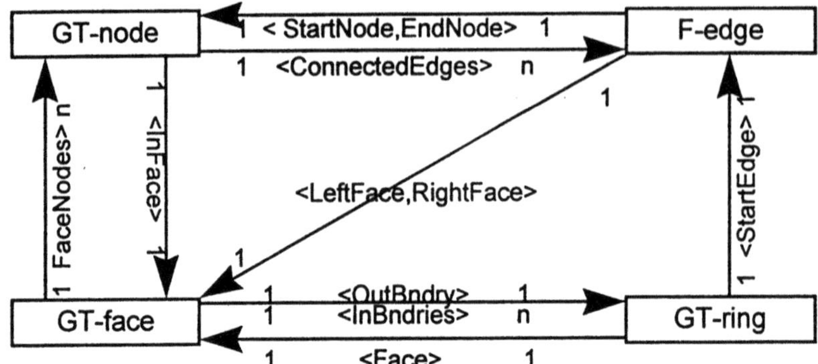

Figure 7: The topological relationship between primitive objects

4   Implementation

The discussion up to this point has forcused upon the two levels of spatial object-oriented data models. When the modeling is complete there follows the implementation stage. A commercial OODB ObjectStore[13] is chosen for implementation platform. Nevertheless, an OODBMS does not directly support spatial object types and spatial operations. That is, ObjectStore does not support efficient spatial object access structure such as R-tree[10] and Grid-file[14], and collection type provided by ObjectStore does not provide spatial operation processing. Also it does not contain relationship between spatial objects which is necessary for spatial operation processing. Therefore, a spatial subsystem is added in OODB ObjectStore to support these functions.

Geo_Collection is the collection class which groups spatial objects together in spatial subsystem. And it has the following subtypes: geo_Set, geo_Array, geo_List, and geo_Bag. Spatial subsystem contains the SAM (spatial access management) module which stores geo_Collection in the form of os_Collection[13] in ObjectStore. The spatial operation processing module takes a spatial operation as an input and returns a geo_Collection as a result of operation processing.

A *schema* is a set of type definitions including their definitions of the structure and the behavior. And it is not fixed once written but evolves over time in order to capture the ever-changing requirements. New types are introduced, old types deleted, operations modified, errors eliminated, and so on. It is also true for the schema of spatial objects. The SEM(Schema Manager) component is tightly linked to a spatial subsystem and build schema hierarchy, import schemata, rename schema components, and check the validity of a schema. In order to implement spatial operations, we use geo_root which provides a way of recording and accessing persistent data. This root's value serves as an *entry point* into a database. Most of the persistent data in that database is then retrieved automatically when referenced, that is, via nevigation from an entry point object.

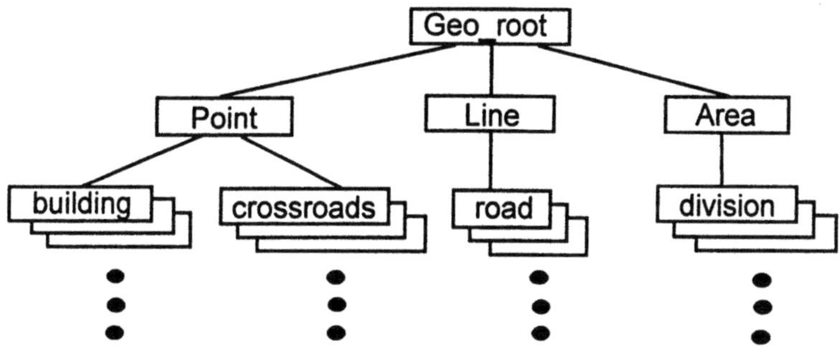

Figure 8: Data management hierarchy for an example

Figure 8 shows the data management hierarchy for an example and a persistent variable 'geo_root' serves as the entry point object of an example. The process of reading persistent data is entirely invisible to the user. Therefore when spatial operation processing, user can search data with entry point and public functions in database root. A storage structure of an example illustrates in Figure 9.

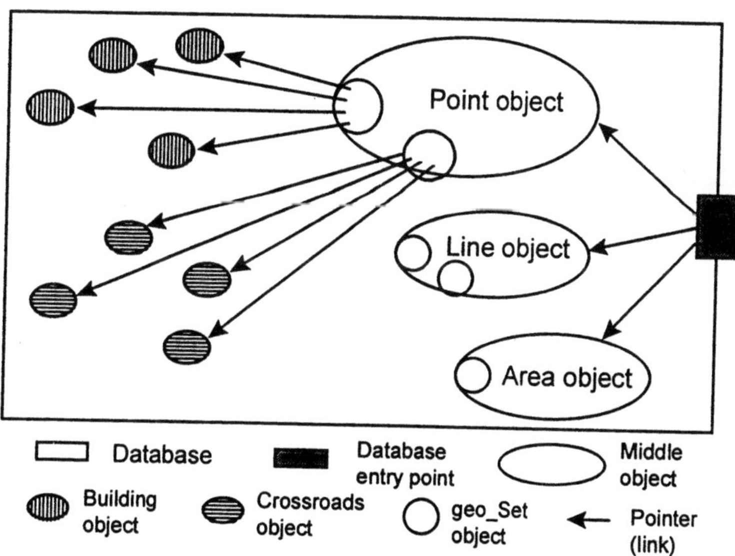

Figure 9: Storage structure of an example

5 Conclusion

In this paper, we have presented the two levels of object-oriented data models: a spatial object model called SAS and an internal description model. SAS supports spatial object types and their polymorphic operations. To make the spatial sorts of the SAS, two new object types, geo_type and graphic_type, have been added in the ObjectStore's metatype hierarchy. Also several polymorphic operations have been defined on spatial sorts such as location operations, arithmetic operations, topological relationships, mouse operations, and object construction operations. Using this model frame, it is possible to define additional types and operators depending on its applications, which makes the system extensible. The internal description model suppports efficient and appropriate framework to store spatial coordinates and topology between two spatial objects. In the internal description model, we considered map as a set of layers. The two levels of an object-oriented data models give the independence between the thematic division of data and cartagraphic presentation.

Finally, we proposed the implementation stage. ObjectStore is used as an implementation platform. Since an OODBMS does not directly support spatial object types, spatial operations, and spatial indexing, we added a spatial subsystem. The spatial subsystem contains the definition of classes and methods that are important for the representation and management of spatial objects. In particualr, SAS data model and internal description model is implemented here and we used R-tree[10] spatial indexing structure.

Spatial operators have been partially implemented. We will add a new spatial indexing structure . Also, we will extend our model to support cartographic time later on.

References

[1] B. David, L. Raynal, G. Schorter and V. Mansart, "GeO2: Why objects in a geographical DBMS ?", in Proc. of the 3rd Internatinal Symposium SSD, pp. 264-276, June 1993.

[2] DGIWG, DIGEST(digital geographic information exchange standard), edition 1.2, Defence Mapping Agency, USA, Digital Geographic Information Working Group, January 1994.

[3] B. Falcidieno, C. Pienovi, and M. Spagnuolo, "Descriptive modeling and prescriptive modeling in spatial data handling", in Proceedings of the Internaltional Conference GIS-From Space to Territory: Theories and Methods of Spatio-Temporal Reasoning Pisa, Italy, Sep. 21-23, LNCS Vol.367, New York:Springer-Verlag, pp.122-135, 1992.

[4] Spatial Data Transfer Standard (SDTS), Fedenal Information Processing Standards Publication, August 1992.

[5] O. Günther and W. Riekert, "The Design of GODOT: An Object-Oriented Geographic Information System", Bulletin of the Technical Committe on Data Engineering, Vol.16, No.3, pp.4-9, Sept., 1993.

[6] R. Güting, "Geo-relational algebra: a model and query language for geometric database systems", in Proc. Int. Conf. Extending Database Technology, Venice, Italy, LNCS Vol. 303. New York: Springer-Verlag, pp. 506-527, 1988.

[7] R. Güting, "Gral: An extensible relational database system for geometric applications ", in Proceedings of the Fifteenth International Conference on VLDB, 1989.

[8] R. Güting, "Second-order signature: A tool for specifying data models, query processing, and optimization", in Proceedings of the ACM SIGMOD Conference, pp.277-286, 1993.

[9] R. Güting, "An Introduction to Spatial Database Systems", VLDB Journal, 3, pp.357-399, 1994.

[10] R. Guttman, "R-trees: A dynamic index structure for spatial searching", in Proc. ACM SIGMOD International Conf. on the Management of Data, pp.47-57, 1984.

[11] Y. H. Kim, et al., "Topological relationships between spatial objects for object-oriented Geographic Information Systems", in Proceeding of the GIS association of Korea fall conference, pp.43-50, 1995.

[12] Y. H. Kim, et al., "The object-oriented design of KROSS: An object-oriented spatial database system", Lecture Notes in Computer Science 1134, pp.603-612, Springer-Verlag, 1996.

[13] C. Lamb, et al., "The ObjectStore database system", Communications of the ACM, Vol.34, No.10, pp.50-63, 1991.

[14] J. Nievergelt, H. Hinterberger, and K. C. Sevcik, "The Grid File: An adaptable, symmetric multikey file structure", ACM Transcations on Database Systems, Vol.9, pp.38-71, 1984.

[15] B. Ooi, Efficient Query Processing in Geographic Information Systems, Lecture Notes in Computer Science 471, Springer-Verlag, 1990.

[16] M. Scholl and A. Voisard, "Thematic map modeling", in Proceedings of the First International Symposium on Large Spatial Databases, pp.167-190, July 1989.

[17] M. F. Worboys, H. M. Hearnshaw, and D. J. Maguire, "Object-oriented data modelling for spatial databases", International Journal of Geographical Information Systems, Vol.4, No.4, pp.369-383, 1990.

DATABASE DESIGN AND VIEWS

Object-Oriented Design of a Database Engine for Multidimensional Discrete Data

P. Furtado[1], R. Ritsch, N. Widmann, P. Zoller, P. Baumann
FORWISS (Bavarian Research Center for Knowledge-Based Systems)
Munich, Germany

Abstract

Multidimensional discrete data (MDD), i.e. arrays of arbitrary size, dimension and base type, occur in a variety of application fields. The object-oriented DBMS RasDaMan[2] provides domain-independent management of MDD. In the design and development of the RasDaMan system, an informed assessment of current solutions to the management of persistent MDD led to the identification of major limitations remaining in object and object relational DBMSs and to the proposal of alternative approaches. In this paper, we present a discussion of those issues and report on the main design decisions taken for the RasDaMan system.

1 Introduction

Raster data has become one of the most often occurring types of data in computer systems. Examples of raster data objects range from common 1-D sound sequences and 2-D images, to domain-specific objects originated from sampling natural phenomena, like a 4-D climate simulation, or from artificial sources such as simulators and business data analyzers, e.g. an 8-D OLAP datacube. Even though these objects differ greatly, they share the same basic properties and requirements. Each raster data object is a multidimensional array of cells of some base type, hence the term Multidimensional Discrete Data or MDD. Although MDD forms a very well-defined category of data structures, for a long time it has received surprisingly little attention among research communities on object-orientation and database issues.

Investigation in MDD application areas such as medical imaging/PACS, geographic information systems, and OLAP/data mining have shown that there is a common need for MDD services, provided this functionality can be decoupled from the legion of application specific data formats in use. Functions such as subcube extraction or projection, and aggregation along specified dimensions play an important role in all these application fields [2]. Even content-based retrieval methods require base MDD operations that only consider pixel level information, with no interpretation of contents.

---

[1]PhD work sponsored by a PRAXIS XXI scholarship.
[2]sponsored by the European Commission in the ESPRIT Domain 4: Long-Term Research under grant no. 20073.

In the RasDaMan system, an object-oriented approach to the modeling, storage, manipulation, and retrieval of MDD in databases is followed which is domain-independent. As described in [2], this approach responds to the particular requirements identified for MDD management. Classical DBMS features available on alphanumeric data such as declarativeness, orthogonality, optimizability, and data independence will be made available on MDD, too. An MDD object is an array, a generic collection category, parametrized with its base type, a C++ type, and spatial domain consisting of the lower and upper bounds for each dimension. Every boundary can be left variable, allowing the MDD to grow and shrink during instance lifetime. A C++ application programming interface, RasLib, is offered which extends the ODMG-93 standard [5] binding with MDD functionality.

The RasDaMan query language, RasQL, is used by applications to query collections of MDD objects stored in the database. It provides a set of high-level primitives for executing advanced operations on MDD. RasQL extends standard SQL with MDD operators which can be roughly categorized as follows. Among operations changing the spatial domain of an MDD there are rectangular cutouts (trimming) and extraction of lower-dimensional subarrays (projection) of MDD. Other operations simultaneously change cells values, leaving MDD geometry unaffected. With "local" operations, for each cell value v a new value `f(v)` is derived; with "global" operations, additionally some neighborhood of a cell is used for computation of the derived cell value (e.g., filtering and warping). Condensers, a general (second-order) concept generalizing the relational aggregation operators, allow to selectively derive summary information. Array traversal sequence is left undefined, thereby opening up space for internal query optimization. MDD expressions can be used in the `select` part of a query and, if the outermost expression result type is scalar, in the `where` part.

The remainder is organized as follows. In Section 2, we discuss the state of the art in MDD database technology. The following sections are dedicated to the main components of the system. Section 5 presents conclusions.

2   Related Work

Current DBMSs do not support MDD directly. In order to store such data, the classical approach is to revert to unstructured BLOBs, Binary Large Objects. In this approach, the DBMS does not know anything about the application semantics, but treats the multidimensional data item as a one-dimensional, encoded byte string. This solution is inadequate both from the point of view of performance as well as from that of the data model and operations supported. In the meanwhile, many relational and object-relational DBMSs enable the implementation of new abstract data types (ADTs). In object DBMSs (ODBMSs) [11] the data model allows implementation of any user defined classes which is done in client code. In object-relational and relational DBMSs [7], definition of new types is done by adding extensions to the core engine.

In ODBMSs, seamless integration of persistent data in the programming language is a major goal [13]. For this reason, the properties and operations of the object models they support are represented in object programming languages such as C++ or Smalltalk. The shortcomings of the programming models are then directly reflected in the object model supported by the DBMS. Regarding MDD, very basic modeling is provided by object-oriented programming languages. An array is a 1-D entity by default. Higher dimensional arrays are modeled as arrays of arrays while their internal representation remains linear. No high-level array operations or specialized storage structures are supported in object-oriented programming languages of today, like Java [8], C++ [19], and Smalltalk [9]. Basically, only primitive operations like access to a cell or to the whole array are possible.

ODBMSs rely on the extensibility of the underlying programming language data model to support more complex data types. Even though, in applications using only transient MDD objects, higher level support for MDD functionality may be implemented with reasonable effort as a class, such a solution is not feasible if persistent MDD objects are to be managed. If MDD functionality is required in an application, it has to be fully implemented by the programmer. Because the application is executed at the client side, it is not possible to optimize operations on persistent MDD or adopt specialized storage structures, which is important to enhance performance when dealing with typically large MDD objects. Without those features, much time is spent on transmission of unnecessary data between client and server.

Recently, several DBMSs have started supporting extensible engines. This approach allows more flexibility in the definition of complex types and execution of operations on those types through extensions to the DBMS engine. Nevertheless, extensible types have to be implemented by very specialized DBMS developers and the amount of implementation effort is enormous, particularly if advanced storage structures are to be used. In addition, in those systems it is not possible to extend the query language with new syntax, since only functions can be called on newly defined data types. One of the most prominent systems in this area is Illustra [18] which supports extensions through so-called DataBlades. There are already individual DataBlade extensions for time-series and temporal data, images, as well as 2-D and 3-D spatial and location data, but up to now no DataBlade has been defined for MDD of arbitrary dimensions. This is a major limitation since operations on multidimensional data often involve operands or results of different dimensionalities (for example, a 3-D object may have to be created from a set of 2-D ones, or an n-D MDD object may result from the projection of an n+1-D object).

Specialized support for OLAP applications is provided by some relational DBMSs [14]. Relations are used to store multidimensional OLAP data consisting of sparsely (e.g., 5%) populated arrays in multidimensional domains. As a consequence, performance and storage utilization in those systems is not acceptable for generic MDD application areas dealing with dense multidimensional arrays. Other application specific DBMSs are dedicated to high-level operations on data for particular application areas. Paradise [15] is an example of a DBMS designed for handling 2-D MDD in GIS applications. 2-D arrays are modeled as ADTs in the object-relational model of SHORE [4]. Efficient storage of the raster ADTs is provided in Paradise by tiling the data into a set of SHORE objects. Paradise does not support MDD of more than two dimensions, nor does it provide a general MDD query language.

3 Storage Management

Storage management in RasDaMan aims at providing efficient access to MDD objects or parts of them and transparent support for various storage devices. Due to the typically large sizes of MDD objects and the type of operations most often performed on them, specialized storage management is required to manage those objects efficiently.

3.1 Storage Structure

An MDD object is stored as a set of multidimensional rectangular subarrays, *tiles*, each one stored in a different object of the base DBMS. The cells of one tile are stored as a linear array of bytes, i.e. a BLOB. The system supports arbitrary tiling in that the tiles belonging to an object can have different sizes and can be unaligned, as illustrated on Figure 1 for a 2-D object. This allows for more flexible choice of the adequate tiling for each object. A more in-depth discussion of tiling of MDD objects in RasDaMan can be found in [3].

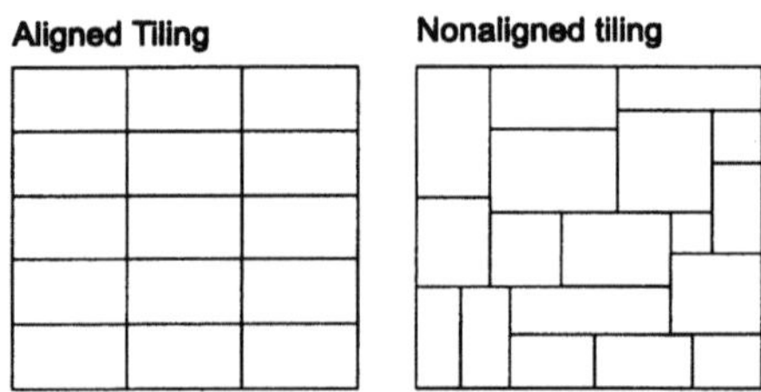

Figure 1: Different MDD Tiling Schemes.

For each object, a spatial index is created which maintains information about the tiles of the object and corresponding spatial information consisting of the coordinates for each tile and the current spatial domain for the object (which may change during the object's lifetime). Different index structures can be created for different objects, for example, a directory structure for a small object with aligned tiles, or an R+-tree [16] for another object with a more complex tiling scheme.

Further metadata, such as a reference to the cell type and the definition spatial domain for the object, also has to be stored. Each persistent MDD object is represented in the base DBMS by an instance of the `DBMDDObject` class which gathers all the information about the object. This instance contains the metadata and a reference to the object's index which, in turn, references the object's tiles.

3.2   Base DBMS Interface

In the design of RasDaMan, an early decision was made for adopting an ODBMS as the storage system. This decision was driven by four main factors:

- an ODBMS allows fast navigational access, which is of prime importance for the implementation of tree-based indexes;

- the DBMS functionality already provided by the ODBMS - for instance, transaction processing and recovery - is already supported and can be used, whereas it would have to be fully implemented if another simple storage system were used;

- the object-oriented MDD functionality can be smoothly integrated in the ODBMS interface;

- using an ODBMS, the RasDaMan system, including the lower level storage management modules, can be designed and implemented in an object-oriented approach, leading to clear design and high quality extensible code.

In order to choose the base ODBMS for RasDaMan, an assessment of several systems, including a small benchmark, was undertaken. The most important choice criteria was the performance of the system when dealing with large sets of tiles which have to be stored as BLOBs. In addition, we considered that it would be positive to have an ODMG conformant system, so that RasLib could be plugged with the ODMG interface of the base system. The commercial ODBMS O_2 [1] was chosen since it proved to be more efficient than the other candidates for the typical MDD data sets tested in the benchmark and it provides an ODMG binding.

Even though the current version was implemented using the O_2 system, care was taken to design the RasDaMan Storage Manager in a way to allow easy portability to another base DBMS or storage system. This is achieved through the Base DBMS Interface layer. The classes in this layer are responsible for all accesses to persistent data. Their interfaces to upper level classes in the system are kept as small and simple as possible. Porting of RasDaMan to another base storage system only requires porting this layer to the new system. The Base DBMS Interface layer provides storage of index structures, tiles, catalog data, and MDD objects and collections of MDD objects, as well as general database functionality.

Implementation of the storage management using the O_2 ODMG C++ binding brought the well-known advantages of seamless integration provided by ODBMSs. The binding allowed ease of implementation of persistent classes according to an adequate object-oriented design. Persistent classes are defined for MDD objects, collections of MDD objects, BLOB tiles, indexes and index nodes. Instances of those classes are directly used in the C++ code with no need for translation between the database and the programming language data models, as it would be needed had another base storage system been adopted. It also facilitated the use of late binding in the support for the same functionality for persistent and transient data. Due to this, many steps in query evaluation are implemented independently of whether the operands are persistent or transient. At the same time, data may be accessed efficiently through direct navigation in the data structure. This is particularly important in the access to tiles through the index structure.

Other aspects in the adoption of the used version of the O_2 binding were not so positive. One major difficulty regarded error handling. The binding provides no means to detect and deal with error conditions. For instance, if an attempt is made to open a non-existent root object, an error is generated and the application is simply aborted. Even though exception handling is assumed in the ODMG standard, it is not implemented in the O_2 system. The solution to this problem was the usage of lower level routines from the O_2 Engine to test for error conditions.

More flexibility or transparency in some features of the O_2 ODMG binding would be useful in the development of the storage manager, for example, locking, memory management and object identifiers. Explicit locks are not supported by O_2, but are convenient for more advanced applications and, in particular, would be useful in the development of RasDaMan.

The second issue concerns automatic memory management. A counter of references to persistent objects in main memory kept by O_2 allows automatic deallocation when an object is no longer referenced. It is difficult for the application programmer to have information about whether memory is still allocated for an object or not. In an application requiring much memory like ours, this makes implementation more difficult.

Finally, object identifiers (OIDs) are hidden from the user in the current version of O_2. A new implementation of OIDs was therefore required in order to uniquely identify MDD objects at the client side. It is our opinion that the support for visible logical OIDs is important to allow some advanced functionality, e.g., for interdatabase references. In fact, such functionality is announced for the new version of O_2, even though not at the ODMG interface level.

3.3   Index Manager

The Index Manager is responsible for providing all information on access to tiles of persistent MDD objects. The functionality supported by the Index Manager includes identification of tiles affected by a spatial access to an MDD object, calculation of tiles access costs, and determining the most efficient access sequence to a set of tiles. Whenever classes responsible for query evaluation require access to part of an object - typically a multidimensional subinterval of the object's spatial domain - they send a message to the `MDDObject` to request the set of tiles intersecting the area of interest. The `MDDObject` then calls the appropriate method from the index member object to identify the tiles affected. Search is performed using navigation in the persistent index structure and the tiles of interest are returned to the caller in a collection.

In order to allow different objects to have different index structures, polymorphism is used. A super class defines the common interface for MDD objects indexes which can then have several implementations as subclasses. The existence of different indexes allows the most appropriate type of index to be adopted for each object when it is first created. This is of interest due to the arbitrary tiling: a complex spatial index may be required for an object stored using nonaligned tiling, whereas the same index structure may lead to bad storage utilization in another object having a simple aligned tiling. Having a common indexing interface allows execution of the operations on MDD objects without having to care about the type of index for each object. In addition, this implementation allows us to easily add new index techniques to the Index Manager.

4 Query Processing

Processing of queries begins with the translation of the textual query statement into an internal tree-based representation. On this data structure, semantic analysis and optimization take place before an evaluation plan is generated, which finally is executed at the tile level. Figure 2 illustrates the different data structures occurring in this process in rounded boxes and operations on them in angular ones. The following subsections account for the object-oriented design chosen for the different structures.

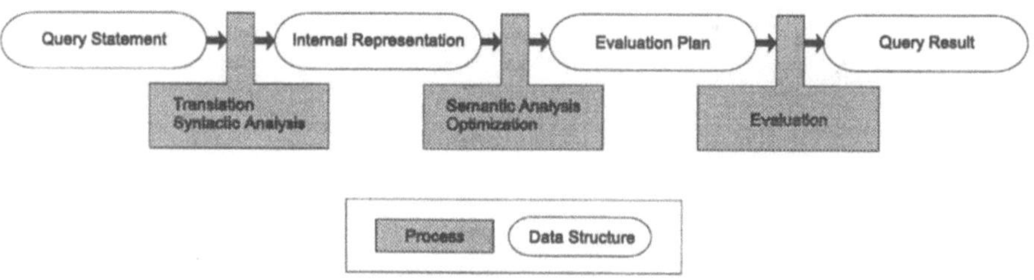

Figure 2: Query Processing Steps.

4.1 Construction and Optimization of the Query Tree

The internal representation is an operator-based query tree which is a procedural description of the query based on operator and dataflow statements. Inner nodes of the tree stand for operators and leaf nodes for data sources which, in our case, are collections of MDD objects. From a data modeling point of view, for each operation, be it a relational one, e.g. selection, or an MDD operation, e.g. projection, a subclass of the node base class exists which inherits functionality like management of descendants or knowing about its parent. Therefore, they all support the same interface and a query tree representing any query statement can be set up using just the methods of the node base class.

Traversal of the tree is described with the type checking process. A pure virtual declaration of the type checking method is declared in the common superclass of all operator classes. This method then is implemented for each specific operator; it takes care that type checking first is propagated to its subtree and then the types of its own operands are verified. At the end, a result is passed to its parent. Usage of a common interface (pure virtual declaration in a type generalization) and encapsulation of operator specific type checks within the operators allow for type checking without knowing about the structure of the operator tree, making extensions of new operators simple and less error-prone.

Query rewrite is a process in which general-purpose heuristics drive semantics preserving transformations. These transformations need to rearrange or exchange operator nodes or even whole subtrees. According to the fact that all operators share the node interface definition, modifications of the tree structure are mostly carried out with the methods of the node base class. Operator specific information is just needed to ensure equivalence and whether the type of a node is to be changed.

The evaluation model abstracts from special operators so that each operation is seen as a processing unit which consumes data from one or more input streams, carries out a specific operation, and produces data sent into exactly one output stream. By combining these processing units in such a way that an output stream from one unit serves as one input stream to the following unit, an evaluation tree is built. The structure is similar to the query tree, so the operator nodes used for internal query representation are also used as elements in the evaluation tree.

The evaluation strategy of the tree is demand driven and based on the ONC protocol [10], according to which each processing unit supports the methods `open()`, `next()` and `close()`. A processing unit (data producer) is first initialized by sending an `open()` message to the object, then data items are received by invoking `next()` as long as no out of data signal is received, and finally the producer is shut by calling `close()`. To evaluate a query, the output stream of the root object is read using the ONC protocol. Invocations of `open()` and `close()` are propagated through the whole tree. If `next()` of a processing unit is called, then it is only passed to those input streams which actually provide data necessary for computation of the next data item.

The protocol is implemented through inheritance of the stream functionality and ad hoc polymorphism. The protocol methods are declared virtual in a common superclass. The methods can provide default implementations which propagate `open()` and `close()` to the descendants and just pass items from the input stream to the output stream within the method `next()`. Each processing unit type can then redefine the implementations according to its specific functionality and late binding takes care of choosing the right implementation.

4.2   Execution Engine

The Execution Engine is responsible for executing basic operations used in the operator nodes of the query plan. The functionality of the Execution Engine is part of the Storage Manager modules where the classes for data sources are defined. The basic data source is a collection of MDD, on which selection operators can be applied to retrieve MDD objects. Finally the basic operations are carried out on tiles, which are retrieved from the MDD objects. In the following, the implementation of the usual arithmetic operations on numeric base types or access to elements of a structured base type will be discussed.

While persistent C++ as supported by the base DBMS O_2 offers the full power of the object-oriented programming paradigm for specifying operations on types, we did not use the C++ type system. One reason for this is that we use the base DBMS only as a storage manager (see Section 3.2); tiles are stored as arrays of C++ `chars`. Another reason is that it should be possible to define new structured base types for cells at runtime without shutting down or even recompiling the RasDaMan server. With a strongly typed and compiled language like C++ new types can be used only after recompilation.

To support base types other than `char`, the RasDaMan DBMS has to provide its own internal type system. We implemented our type system in an object-oriented way, supporting the ODMG-93 primitives like `ULong` or `Bool` and structures. Our type system implementation uses metaclasses as in dynamic object oriented languages like Smalltalk [9] or CLOS [12]. For each base type, a C++ object is created which is an instance of a metaclass. For simple base types, just one instance of the corresponding metaclass exists. For structured base types, one instance of the corresponding metaclass is created for each user defined structured base type, which stores all information needed for the structured type (e.g., name and type of its elements) in member variables.

Each metaclass knows how to carry out operations on cells of its type using a group of `chars` as operands. These operations are returned as function objects if needed. Function objects or functors [6] overload the function call operator `operator()` and can be used to implement higher order functions, i.e. functions returning functions as a result, like provided in LISP [17]. Whenever the executor carries out an operation on a tile, it requests a function object for the operation from the metaclass. This has to be done only once for each tile, the function object is then applied to each cell of the tile.

Given these function objects, the executor calls a method of the tile to carry out an operation on all of its cells or a part specified as a multidimensional interval. It is the responsibility of the executor to break down MDD operations on tiles, specifying, for each tile, the areas which are affected when carrying out an operation involving two MDDs. The schema information, i.e. all instances of metaclasses representing the simple base types supported by the system and the user defined structured base types currently in use, is stored in the RasDaMan DBMS. C++ classes are used to do this which are made persistent with O_2.

5 Conclusions

Compared to existing DBMSs, RasDaMan offers several innovative features regarding MDD management. An MDD object is modeled as an array with specified base type and multidimensional spatial domain. The conceptual MDD model and its ODMG conformant binding provide seamless integration of persistent MDD objects in C++ applications. A query language allows execution of complex, computation intensive operations on the RasDaMan server. A specialized storage structure for large MDD objects is adopted which is composed of multidimensional tiles and spatial indexes on the tiles. Query evaluation is performed at tile-level. Inheritance and ad hoc polymorphism are used to implement the query tree evaluation protocol. Operations on tiles are executed using function objects, which allow support for the RasDaMan provided MDD operations also on MDD objects with user defined cell types.

Although the first version of the system does not fully exploit the optimization potential, initial performance tests showed that both client-server data transmission and storage structure have high impact on the execution performance of MDD operations. A first test case assessed the influence of data transmission on the overall performance. The same MDD operation was performed both on the client and on the server running in two hosts located in a local network, executing a simple trimming operation on the images of a collection. The collection had four 2.5 megabytes (MB) satellite images corresponding to the same geographical area and the trimmed subimages had 750 kilobytes (KB) each. A performance gain higher than two was obtained for this case. A second test case showed the impact of the tiling scheme on the speed of execution of operations on MDD. In this case, a 40 MB 3-D object, consisting of tomogram slices, was stored using two different tiling schemes: cubes (100 KB each) and slices of thickness one along the x-direction. The time required for executing a z-projection on the sliced data was five times that required for the cubed object. Such performance gains can only be achieved if internal support for MDD is provided by the DBMS at the server side.

The implementation of basic storage management using the C++ ODMG binding of O_2 allowed a design of the database engine where the main entities of the system like MDD objects, collections of MDD objects, and tiles, are modeled directly as classes starting from the storage level up to the communication module. The architecture of the system was designed to keep the interface between modules small. This is particularly important in the Base DBMS Interface layer, in order to allow easy porting of the RasDaMan system to another base storage system, and in the communication module. In this later case, the efficacy of the design was already proven when a necessary re-implementation of the communication layer using a different RPC system was done with little effort. In the future, we intend to explore more advanced optimization techniques and support new data types. Implementation of further operations such as affine transformations (e.g., scaling and rotation) is also planned.

References

[1] F. Bancilhon, C. Delobel, P. Kanellakis: **Building an Object-Oriented Database System**. Morgan Kaufmann Publishers, San Mateo-California, 1992.

[2] P. Baumann, P. Furtado, R. Ritsch, N. Widmann: Geo/Environmental and Medical Data Management in the RasDaMan System. **Proceedings of the 23rd VLDB Conference**, Athens-Greece, 1997.

[3] P. Baumann, P. Furtado, R. Ritsch, N. Widmann: The RasDaMan Approach to Multidimensional Database Management. **Proceedings of the 1997 ACM Symposium on Applied Computing**, San Jose-California, February 1997, pp. 166-173.

[4] M. Carey et al.: Shoring up Persistent Objects. **Proceedings of the 1994 ACM-SIGMOD International Conference on Management of Data**, Minneapolis-Minnesota, 1994, pp. 383-394.

[5] R. Cattell: **The Object Database Standard: ODMG-93**. Morgan Kaufmann Publishers, 1996.

[6] J. Coplien: **Advanced C++ Programming Styles and Idioms**. Addison Wesley, 1992.

[7] J. Davis: **INFORMIX-Universal Server: Extending The Relational DBMS To Manage Complex Data**. DataBase Associates International, Informix, 1996.

[8] D. Flanagan: **Java in a Nutshell**. O'Reilly & Associates, Inc., 1996.

[9] A. Goldberg, D. Robson: **Smalltalk-80: the Language**. Addison Wesley, 1989.

[10] G. Graefe: Query Evaluation Techniques for Large Databases. **ACM Computing Surveys**, 1993, vol. 25, no. 2, pp. 73-170.

[11] W. Kim, Ed.: **Modern Database Systems: the Object Model, Interoperability, and Beyond**. ACM Press, New York, 1995.

[12] G. Kiczales, J. des Rivires, D. Bobrow: **The Art of the Metaobject Protocol**. The MIT Press, 1991.

[13] M. Loomis: **Object Databases: The Essentials**. Addison-Wesley, 1995.

[14] Oracle: **Oracle7 Spatial Data Option Overview**. Oracle Corporation, 1996.

[15] J. Patel et al.: Building a Scalable GeoSpatial Database System: Technology, Implementation, and Evaluation. **Proceedings of the 1997 ACM-SIGMOD International Conference on Management of Data**, Tucson-Arizona, 1997.

[16] T. Sellis, N. Roussoupoulos, C. Faloutsos: The R+-tree: A Dynamic Index for Multidimensional Objects. **Proceedings of the 13th VLDB Conference**, Brighton-England, 1987, pp. 507-518.

[17] G. Steele Jr.: **CommonLISP: The Language**. Digital Press, 1984.

[18] M. Stonebreaker, D. Moore: **Object-Relational DBMSs: The Next Great Wave**. Morgan Kaufmann Publishers, 1996.

[19] B. Stroustroup: **The C++ Programming Language**. Addison-Wesley, 1991.

Updating Virtual Complex Objects

Zohra Bellahsene
LIRMM UMR 55060 CNRS - Montpellier II
161 rue ADA 34392 Montpellier Cedex 5, France
e-mail: bella@lirmm.fr

Abstract

In this paper, we identify a class of complex virtual objects which are updatable. Furthermore, we present a method of implementing views focusing on how materialisation technique can be used to provide a solution for maintaining identity for virtual complex objects in order to be unambiguously updated. Our proposition includes a set-oriented language for updating virtual objects enhancing view capabilities in order to be used as a uniform framework for querying and updating a database thereby providing full data independence.

Keywords: object identity, view updating, materialised view, virtual complex object.

1 Introduction

In relational database systems, the difficulty of updating views lies in the propagation of the update operation on base relations. Only virtual relations, including keys, can be updated without ambiguity. In object database systems, when a view is derived from one class, it is not difficult to propagate the update operation if the query language preserves objects' identities (that is the object updated is the same as the base object). In contrast, virtual complex objects are distributed over several underlying base objects. For these objects, a new identifier would have to be created and maintained. Our proposition concerns this kind of virtual objects.

Object-oriented systems associate a unique identifier with each object upon its creation. Accordingly, upon the creation of a virtual object, an identifier (i.e. OID) must be associated with it. When the population of a virtual class is a subset of existing objects, the virtual objects and the corresponding base objects share the same object. The problem of object identification arises for the virtual complex objects because it is difficult to fix the identity of virtual complex objects since the view query is computed and recomputed at each invocation of the view. Let us illustrate the virtual object identification problem through an example. The following example found in [1] gives a complex virtual class named *Family*, expressed in our view definition language as follows:

```
Virtual class Family from Person
query: Select tuple (husband : H, Wife: H->spouse)
       From H in People /* People is a database entry point */
       Where H->sex = 'M';
end;
```

This virtual class is qualified to be complex since its objects are built from two base objects. First, we would like to note that the view specification languages proposed in related work [8, 7] do not allow the expression of a such virtual class.

This view query produces a set of tuples (husband : H, Wife: H->spouse). Each of them is converted to an object and the system must assign a new identifier to each object. Each time this view is invoked, the system generates a set of families objects and assigns an identifier to each one. Then the issue is how can we ensure that each *Family* receives the same identifier every time the query is invoked? To fix the object identity, we need to be able to remember how families are created. This can be done in languages with limited control features. For instance in the F-Logic [2], object identity is a Skolem function of some existing objects. However, our approach can be used in the context of languages with more general control features.

The main contributions of our work are:

- a method based on the OIDs materialisation for identifying virtual complex objects in order to be unambiguously updated,
- a possibility of defining and updating object-relation views,
- a set-oriented update language for virtual objects.

This paper is organised as follows. In section 2, we present the specific terms and concepts that we use in our approach and our view definition language. A method for implementing complex virtual classes is presented in section 3. Section 4 is discussed the view coherence issue. Section 5 describes our update language for virtual complex objects. In section 6, we discuss implementation issues of view updates on top of the O2 database system. Section 7 gives an overview of recent related work on object views. Finally, section 8 contains concluding remarks and future work.

2 A View Definition Language

2.1 Preliminaries

In this section, we introduce the specific concepts that we use to define and implement a view mechanism according our proposition. We assume that object-oriented data model concepts such as object identity, database schema, class, inheritance are familiar to the reader [5]. Our approach is independent from the Database System (DBS). However, the environment of our study is the O2 DBS. Thus, the examples described in this paper are based on the O2 data model [6]. The O2 data model does not provide class extent at the logical level. Extent of a class can be simulated by defining a named collection of objects which is a root of persistency. Names are entry points in the database. From these entry points, other objects can be reached through navigation.

Let us now define the running example throughout this paper, in Figure 1.

```
Class Person                          Class Researcher inherit Person
 type tuple (name: string,            type tuple ( speciality: string,
         surname: string,                     grade: string,
         birth-date: Date,                    salary: string,
         spouse: Person,                      status: string,
         address: string,                     lab: Laboratory,
         sex: character)                      publications: list (Publication))

end;                                  end;


Class Laboratory                      Class   Publication
 type tuple ( name: string,            type tuple(title:string,
         adr: string)                          editor:string,
end;                                           publi_date:Date)

                                       end;


Name The_Researchers: set(Researcher)  /* This is a database entry point*/
Name People: set(person) /* This is another database entry point*/
```

Figure 1. An O2 database schema example.

2.2 Virtual Concepts

Virtual class. A virtual class is defined by specifying an OQL(Object Query Language) [6] query that computes its extent.

Simple virtual class. A simple virtual class is a virtual class that its extent contains only a subset of existing base objects. Updates on simple virtual objects are directly translated to the base objects since they have the same identifiers (i.e. the object identity is preserved).

Complex virtual class. A complex virtual class is built from more than one class. Its extent contains new objects built from several base objects.

A taxonomy of complex virtual classes. We propose a taxonomy of virtual objects in order to define the update semantics according to the virtual class semantics. We distinguish two kinds of complex virtual classes:
(i) *association* virtual classes,
(ii) *composite* virtual classes.
However, only the database administrator can really know the sort of a virtual class since it is application context dependent. Thus, he (she) has to specify the kind of virtual class at its creation.

Association virtual class. An association virtual class is a complex virtual class for that the deletion of its virtual objects must not entail the deletion of the underlying base objects.

Composite virtual class. A composite virtual class is similar to the composite class [5]. A composite virtual object is a part hierarchy of components base objects. The propagation of the delete operation is dependent from the semantics of the reference links that relate the base objects.

2.3 A View Specification Language

In this section, we present in an informally way our view specification language as a basis of the subsequent discussion. The syntax of a virtual class creation is as follows:

[Create] virtual class <virtual class name> [**from** <list of class names>]
Kind of class: (simple/association/composite),
[Inherit <virtual class name>,]
[Extent : <extent name>]
Query : <query expression>;
[Rename Attribute : < (attributes names)>],
[Hide property : <property name> from <source class name>,]
[Add attribute: <attribute specification>,]
[Add method: <method specification>]
end <virtual class name>;

The semantics of this statement is creating a virtual class under the current virtual schema. *Extent* clause gives the virtual class extent. If no extent name is given by the user, the system provides a default name ("The_virtual class name"). The *kind* of the virtual class determines the semantics of its updates. The *query* clause allows to specify the view query that define the class extent and follows OQL syntax.

The *Rename* clause allows a user to rename derived properties. It is also possible to hide some properties from a class by using the *Hide* clause. The clause *Add Attribute* allows to define specific attributes (i.e. non derived attributes). This feature allows to our view language to be used to simulate schema extent operation. Finally, the database administrator can define new methods to take into account specific treatments by using *the Add method* clause.

Example 2.3. This example illustrates a composite virtual class defined on the base schema presented in Figure 1. This virtual class provides a special treatment for invited researchers working in views area.

```
Create virtual schema Research_view;
Virtual class Invited_Researcher from Researcher
Kind of class: composite,
query: Select distinct tuple(name: x->name,
                            specialty: x->speciality,
                            labname: x->lab->name)
      From x in The_Researchers /* is a root of persistency */
      where x->speciality = "object views"
Add attribute original_country: string;
end Invited_Researcher;
```

The virtual class Invited_Researcher is a composite virtual class because it is built from two base classes: the Research class and the Laboratory class. This virtual class contains the following attributes: (name, specialty, namelab and original_country). The last attribute is a specific attribute (which is not derived from existing classes). Let us now define another virtual class from the previous virtual class.

```
Virtual class Foreign_Invited__Researcher From Invited__Researcher
Kind of class: composite,
query: Select x
       From x in The_Invited_Researcher /*the virtual class extent */
       Where x->original_country <> "France";
End Foreign_Invited__Researcher;
```

3 A Materialisation Method for Object Views

In this section, we propose a method to maintain a partial materialisation including the identifier of each virtual object and the identifiers of its root objects that participate in the formation of the virtual complex object. The idea is rather simple: the system assigns an identifier when a new virtual complex object is created by using the "new" operator. And then, we use materialisation technique to store both the identifier of the created object and the identifiers of the relevant root objects (a root object may be either a base object or a virtual object). More precisely, each materialised virtual object is represented by a materialised tuple $(OID, OID_{r1}, OID_{r2}, ..., OID_{rp})$,
where OID is the identifier of the virtual object,
$OID_{r1}, OID_{r2}, ..., OID_{rp}$ are the identifiers of the root objects and p is the number of root objects.

The materialisation provides the immutability of the virtual object identity. We note the materialised information is minimal for providing both the immutability of a virtual object identifier and the direct access to its value through the references of its root objects. Furthermore, the identifier of a complex virtual object becomes independent from its values even when certain updates occur on base objects. Another important advantage provided by our approach is the guaranty of the reference correctness between related virtual objects since their identifiers are immutable. Otherwise, whenever a virtual object may reference another virtual object; if the identifier of the referenced object changes, it can entail dangling references. Furthermore, the view maintenance task is simplified. Only, modifications of value attributes involved in the view query have to be propagated since they may change the virtual class population. However, add and delete object operations have to be propagated. The relevant issue is then to identify which virtual objects are affected by an update operation rather than to rematerialise the whole virtual class. A solution to optimise the update propagation can be found in [7].

Example. Let us now see how our method can cope with the virtual class *Family* defined earlier. First, the view query is executed. It produces a set of tuples (Husband : H, Wife: H->spouse). Each of them is converted to an object and the system assigns a new identifier to each object. The proposed materialisation method consists in describing each *Family* object O_i by a tuple (OID_i, $*O_h$, $*O_f$) where OID_i is the identifier of the object O_i , and $*O_h$, $*O_f$ are respectively the OIDs of *Husband* and *wife* objects. This tuple is then materialised. While the virtual objects values are computed dynamically through the root objects identifiers at the invocation of the view query.

In summary, our solution provides the following features:
- The identifier of a virtual complex object is independent from its value,
- Guarantee the immutability of virtual complex object identifiers,
- Optimises the storage cost since only identifiers are stored,
- The view maintenance task is reduced

4 View Consistency

4.1 View Coherence

We define herein a coherence invariant providing the basis of the specification of the semantics of update propagation.

Coherence Invariant. Let VC_k be a complex virtual class derived directly or indirectly from VC_1, VC_2,..., VC_{k-1} which can be themselves derived classes.

Let P_i be a query predicate associated to the virtual class VC_i for $i = 1..k$. The coherence invariant is enforced by an object O_k of the virtual class VC_k if and only if $(O_k \in$ extent $(VCk) / (P_1(Ok) \wedge P_2(Ok) \wedge... \wedge P_{k-1}(Ok) \wedge P_k (Ok)))=$ true.

4.2 Legal Operation

An update operation is legal if and only if it satisfies the following conditions:
1. It fulfils integrity constraints (provided by the underlying database system),
2. It enforces the coherence invariant according to our definition.

Performing successfully the legal operation test means that the operation is allowed on this view. So, in our approach, only legal operations will be accepted.

5 View Update Primitives

In this section, we present the main update primitives and the related algorithms according to our view implementation method (i.e. materialisation method) presented in section 3. These algorithms are independent from the database system. Update primitives described in this section are inspired from the one proposed for O2query in [4].

5.1 Virtual Object Insertion

The semantics of the insert primitive is to create a new object with specified values and adding it to the specified virtual class. This operation will be propagated to base objects according the virtual class definition. Besides, the identifier of the created virtual object and those of their root objects are stored according our materialisation method. The syntactic form of insert primitive is as follows:

```
Insert into <virtual class name>
```

```
tuple(att₁ = value₁, att₂ = value₂, attₙ = valueₙ )
```

Propagation Rule. A creation of a new virtual object entails the creation of its root base object (s) and objects referenced by this root objects according the virtual class definition.

Algorithm for inserting a virtual complex object. The different steps of the insertion algorithm are :

1. Check that the insertion is legal (according to our definition), if not reject it.
2. Create a new object Ov (however, we just need to keep the identifier of the virtual object, its value will be computed from the base objects).
3. For each virtual root class
   Create recursively a new virtual object and add its identifier to the corresponding materialised tuple.
4. Build a materialised tuple with the identifier of Ov and the identifier of its direct root objects.
5. For each base root class
   Create a new object with the appropriate values that are specified in the insert query;
   Add this object to the corresponding root of base class extent;
   Add its identifier to the corresponding materialised tuple.

Example 5.1. Suppose the user wants to add an Invited_Researcher object.

```
Insert into Invited_Researcher
tuple(name = Dupont, labname = "INRIA", speciality = "Database");
```

Performing this statement the system creates a new virtual object for the *Invited_Researcher class* and assigns a new identifier to it. The propagation of the insert operation consists first in creating a new base object for the *Researcher* class, assigns a new identifier to it and initialises its value with those specified in the tuple clause. A *Laboratory* object (with attribute name equal to "INRIA"), is created if it does not already exist in the database. The *ultimo* but not less important step consists in building a materialised tuple including both the identifier of the inserted object and the identifier of the two base objects namely the corresponding *Researcher* object and the *Laboratory* object.

We have to note that ambiguity problem may arise when the component object are qualified by attribute value (i.e. the attribute is not a key). This is the similar semantic problem as in the relational context when views are defined as join. In this case, a scenario implying the intervention of the user may help to identify precisely the concerned object if more than one object correspond to the specified value.

5.2 Object Modification

A value of an attribute can be an atomic or a reference to another object or a collection of objects (respectively a collection of atomic values). Modifying an object attribute consists in replacing it by an existing object or modifying an attribute value of the referenced object. We do not address the modification of a multi-valued attribute due space limitation, see [3].

The general syntactic form of the modification operation is as follows:

```
Update <virtual class name>
Set <attribute1_name = new_value,...>
Where <predicate>;
```

The semantics of this statement is affecting new values to the specified attributes in the *Set* clause belonging to the objects fulfilling the *Where* predicate.

Algorithm for modifying an attribute value

Modifying_Attribute (VC, $\{A_1, A_2,.., A_k\}$, $\{v_1, v_2,.., v_k\}$, P)
/* affects the value v_i to the attribute $A_{i,}$ for i=1 to k, of objects belonging to the virtual class VC and fulfilling the specified predicate P */
If the operation is not legal according to our definition reject it
Else /* Perform the modification only on the root base objects */
       For each root class RCi until reaching root base objects
           If RCi is base class Then For each o $\in$ extent (RCi)
                  If A $\in$ RCi and P(o) then for i=1..k do o. A_i <- v_i ;
End Modifying_Attribute;

Example 5.2. This example illustrates a case of illegal operation. So, let us imagine that a user wants to modify the value of the *status* attribute value in the virtual class Foreign_Invited_Researcher. Note that the attribute status is inherited from the Researcher class through the derived link. The update query is as follows :

```
Update Foreign_Invited_Researcher
Set status = 'permanent';
```

This update operation will be rejected since it is not a legal operation. More precisely, the new value does not fulfil the coherence invariant according to the query predicate of the Invited_Researcher virtual class which is the derivation root class of Foreign_Invited_Researcher. This example demonstrates that the view coherence has to be checked for the entire derivation graph. In related work [7], [3], the view coherence is checked only according to the virtual class query predicate.

5.3 Deleting Virtual Objects

The semantics of the delete operation is to remove from the virtual class extent all objects fulfilling the *where* clause predicate of the delete query. Its syntactic form is as follows:
```
Delete from <virtual class name> where <predicate>;
```

The deletion operation of objects in a simple virtual class works directly on the related base objects (since the virtual objects have the same identifiers as the base objects). Concerning complex virtual classes, the propagation is performed according the semantics of the virtual class. We distinguish two cases according the kind of the virtual class:
1. If the virtual class is built as an *association* then the deletion of virtual objects must not entail the deletion of the root base objects.

2. Otherwise the propagation is performed according the semantics of the reference links that exist between the component base objects. Furthermore, a reference object may be dependent or independent. A dependent composite reference from X to Y means that the existence of Y depends on the existence of its parent object X. Therefore, the deletion of a parent object entails recursive deletion of all objects referenced by this object through dependent composite references. Thus, If the object to be deleted is composite, then delete its component object if it is not referenced by other composite objects and if the link corresponds to a dependent reference. However, this operation should entail deletion of this object in the superclasses if the DBS provides a class extent and therefore allows to enforce the IS_A constraint.

Algorithm for deleting virtual complex objects
Delete (VC, P) /* Delete the objects belonging to VC and fulfilling the specified
                    predicate P */
If the operation is not legal according to our definition reject it
Else Delete the materialised tuple related to the deleted object (s);
            /* deletion of base objects fulfilling the predicate P */
        For each root class RCi until reaching root base classes do
            If RCi is base class Then If VC is composite Then
                For each o ∈ to a root class extent
                        If P(o) and (o is not referenced by other composite
                        objects and If the link corresponds to a dependent
                        reference) Then delete o;
        /* delete the materialised information concerning the object if it is a
                derivation root */
                If VC is a derivation root class then remove the identifier of the
                deleted object(s) in the related materialised tuple;
End Delete;

Example 5.3.1. This example illustrates a deletion of virtual objects belonging to an *association* virtual class. Suppose, the user wants to delete a *Family* objects with name "Dupont". The syntactic form of the update query is as follows:

```
Delete from Family where husband->name = "Dupont";
```

The effect of this query is to delete all objects of *Family* extent that fulfil the *Where* predicate. However, the underlying base objects (that is husband and wife objects) will not be deleted because the virtual class *Family* is built as an *association*.

6 Implementing View Updates

In this section, we discuss implementation issues related to the object view updates primitives we have implemented on top of the O2 DBS.

6.1 Updatable Virtual Classes

Virtual classes defined according our view definition language follow the OQL syntax. However, we are constrained to impose some restrictions due to the absence of the class extent notion in O2 DBS. Consequently, our view language has been implemented with the restriction stating that the variables appearing in its query definition belongs to the virtual class schema.

Definition. A virtual class is closed if and only if either any variable appearing in the query predicate is included in the target list of the view query or in paths having as starting point a variable included in target list.

Example 6.1. Imagine the DBA wants to define a view representing the invited researcher which are professor. The definition of such view is as follows:
```
Create virtual class Invited_Professor
query: Select R From R in The_Invited_Researcher
       Where grade = "Professor";
end Invited_Professor;
```

This virtual class is not closed since the grade attribute has not been included in the Invited_Resarcher class schema.

6.2 Inserting New Objects

In fact, two cases may occur whenever adding a new complex virtual object:
(i) the object component are entirely new (that is some parts of the object do not already exist in the database). The propagation process consists in inserting the new component objects in the database.
(ii) certain component objects may exist already in the database. In this case, one has to establish links between the corresponding component objects and the virtual object. Due to the absence of class extent, it is not possible to new precisely if a component object exists or not. Consequently, we have to create all new component objects.

6.3 Delete Virtual Objects

O2 DBS does not provide a possibility to express the different semantics of reference links. Consequently, our implemented delete propagation strategy consists in deleting all component base objects.

7 Related Work

In the related work we are aware of [8], view updatability is guaranteed by object preservation (that is the updated virtual object and the base object have the same identifier). This approach described in [8], is based on an object query language having the following properties: object preservation, type/class separation, multiple instantiation and multiple class membership. Thus, this approach does not address virtual complex classes (according to our definition).
A proposition for updating objects in O2Views can be found in [3]. However, update operations are not allowed on virtual complex objects, and the view coherence is checked only according to the virtual class query predicate. In this paper, we propose a solution for updating virtual complex objects.

Concerning the issue of identifying new virtual complex object, a solution based on the core attributes (i.e. target list attributes of the view query) is proposed in [1]. Consequently, when the value of a core attribute changes, the system must assume that it is dealing with a new object. This approach presents the main drawback to make the identifier value-dependent. Thus, the designer has to be worried about implementation aspect such as object identity managing.

8 Conclusion

The first result of the work presented in this paper is providing the immutability of virtual complex objects. This result allows the complex views to be queried and unambiguously updated in most cases. Furthermore, our approach allows to define and to update object-relation views thus providing a relational view on top of an object database.

The update primitives described in this paper bas been implemented on top of O2 DBS. We learnt from this experimentation that the object data model must be extended, to facilitate the implementation of a view system, with the following capabilities:

- providing the extent of a class defined as the set of all objects belonging to this class,
- providing a rich taxonomy of reference links to define a semantics dependant strategy of complex virtual objects updates.

In this paper, the view maintenance issue is partially addressed since only updates on virtual objects are propagated on the underlying derived virtual objects. To complement our study, we are currently develop propagation algorithms for view maintenance including base objects updates.

Acknowledgement

I would like to thank Denis Carniel for its implementation work.

References

1. Abiteboul S., Bonnerr A. ,"Objects and Views", in Proc. ACM SIGMOD, Int. Conference on Management of Data, pp 238-247, Denver, Colorado, May, 1991.
2. Abiteboul S., Hull R, Vianu V, "Foundations of Databases", Addison Wesley, 1995
3. Amer-yahia S, P. Breche P., Souza dos Santos C., "Objects Views and Updates", in Proc. of Journées Bases de Données Avancées BDA'96, Cassis, August, 1996.
4. Cluet S., "Langages et Optimisation de Requêtes pour Systèmes de gestion de Base de Données Orientés-objet", PhD of the university Paris-Sud centre d'Orsay, 1991.
5. Kim W., "Introduction to Object-Oriented Databases", MIT Press, Cambridge, Massachusetts, London, England, 1990.
6. O2Technology, The O2 User Manual, 1994.
7. Ra Y.G., Kuno H., Rundensteiner E. A., "Using Object-Oriented Principles to Optimize Update Propagation to Materialised Views", Electrical Engineering and Computer Science and Engineering Division, University of Michigan, Ann Arbor, Technical Report CSE-TR-252-95.
8. Scholl H. M. and Tresch Mark"Updatable Views in Object-Oriented Databases", in Proc. of Deductive and Object-Oriented Databases, Springer Verlag, Germany, 1991.

Re-engineering Relational Normal Forms in an Object-Oriented Framework

James L. Johnson
Western Washington University
Bellingham, Washington 98225, USA

George Fernandez
Royal Melbourne Institute of Technology
Melbourne, Victoria, Australia

Abstract

In relational database design, the normal forms have long served as a guide to the proper dispersion of application attributes across multiple tables. These canonical formats, ranging from First to Fifth Normal Form, enforce increasingly complex constraints to foreclose more and more subtle opportunities for inconsistency in the application data. Although object-oriented database design disperses application attributes across classes rather than tables, constraint enforcement remains an important concern. In the transition from a relational to an object-oriented environment, the database designer must reconcile normalization processes with newer approaches that identify the core application classes (e.g., Jacobson's Objectory, Rumbaugh's Object Modeling Technique, or Booch's method). In particular, the reengineering of a legacy system may involve the study of a relational design in which normal forms were used to establish the database tables. This paper reviews relational normal forms, interprets them in an object-oriented context, and provide guidelines to port relational normal forms to an object-oriented database.

1   Introduction

Given the relevance of the object-oriented approach in the development of database applications and the preponderance of relational databases in existing systems, the process of converting from a relational schema to an object-oriented model is particularly important. When re-engineering a relational application with an object-oriented database, the designer tries to preserve all the functionality of the original application while restructuring the data to exploit the object-oriented features of the new database. Research in database re-engineering indicates that the mapping process from the relational model to an object-oriented one should include a critical examination of a variety of source documents, including the schema and database extension, data patterns, views, and application code [1, 2, 3]. This analysis elucidates the data and provides a more complete specification of the existing system. Moreover, it is a safer approach because it allows the knowledge acquired in the earlier design phase to be checked for consistency in the re-engineering phase.

As a consequence of the relational model's limited semantic capabilites, the structure of application data is often expressed via a set of constraints to be enforced at all times. Some constraints are taken care of by a careful definition of the database tables, while others require enforcement by the applications that update the data.

In relational databases, normal forms provide a method for the enforcement of some consistency constraints. The violation of a normal form implies that the value of a certain entry in a target row can be anticipated, and therefore database updates must ensure that the predicted entry isn't modified. Intuitively, the prediction comes from a comparison between the target row and another similar row in a table. The normal forms frustrate such prediction by ensuring that no rows exist that are sufficiently similar to the target. In each case, the relational solution decomposes a table with a normal form violation into two or more components [4]. The original table can always be reconstructed as the lossless join of the components.

An object-oriented application is centered around classes and class instances rather than tables. When a cell entry can be predicted in the relational case, a similar comparison between the corresponding class objects provides the same prediction in the object-oriented case and, therefore, opportunities for inconsistency arise in a similar manner. In this paper we show that the relational solution, decomposition, is also applicable in an object-oriented database, and that where the relational solution exports an attribute cluster to a separate table, an object-oriented translation can be provided that encapsulates the same cluster in a distinct class. We discuss how relational normal forms can be expressed in an object-oriented database to ensure that the original constraints are still valid, and for each normal form we suggest a corresponding class structure in the translation that preserves the functionality of the existing relational application.

2 Constraints

In a relational database, the table rows represent instances of some application entity. The upper portion of Figure 1, for example, shows a student table, where each row describes a particular student in a university environment. A student row contains entries under the attribute columns (e.g., name, height, and weight) that pertain to the real student. The studentID attribute, by contrast, is more artificial: it serves as a key, which uniquely identifies a row. By embedding a key attribute in a remote table, where it is known as a foreign key, the database designer can represent a one-to-many relationship between two application entities. In Figure 1, common studentID values associate a given student with his grades, while common courseID values associate the grades with specific courses.

The lower portion of Figure 1, on the left, shows a student object in the

Student			
studentID	name	height	weight
46	James	71.5	184
52	William	68.0	204
69	Shelley	69.5	160
78	Jill	66.5	170

Course			
courseID	number	name	credits
206	CS 401	Automata Theory	3
239	CS 405	Algorithm Analysis	4
248	CS 420	Computer Architecture	4
267	CS 430	Database Theory	3

Grade		
studentID	courseID	mark
46	206	A
46	267	B
52	206	B
52	248	C
69	239	A
69	248	A
69	267	B
78	206	A

Figure 1: Students, courses, and grades in relational and object-oriented databases

equivalent object-oriented database. Just as in its row counterpart, the object contains attribute values: name = James, height = 71.5, and weight = 184. Although it could be convenient to keep the studentID attribute, it isn't strictly necessary from the standpoint of a key because each object possesses a unique object identifier (OID), generated by the system when the object is created. In an object-oriented database, the OID represents the object in other places, just as the key attribute value represents a row in other relational tables.

The student object in Figure 1 contains a *grades* attribute, whose value is somewhat different from the other attribute values. Although name, height, and weight all contain strings or numbers, grades contains a *collection* of grade objects. The expansion to the right reveals the two grade objects associated with this student. Each grade contains a mark, the owning student, and the corresponding course. In an implementation, of course, the grades attribute would contain OIDs, rather than the objects themselves. A user, however, can envision a student's grades as existing within the student, in the same manner as the student's name, height, and weight.

As illustrated in the figure, related objects mutually contain each other. A student contains his grade collection, and each grade contains its owning student. Just as common attributes among tables link related rows in a relational database, this mutual embedding of related objects serves the same purpose in an object-oriented database.

The importance of application constraint enforcement has been widely discussed in the literature, in many different forms [5, 6, 7, 8, 9]. Constraints ensure that the database consistently reflects the application, which is an essential requirement regardless of the relational or object-oriented context of the design. In the database of Figure 1, for instance, the application may require that courses numbered 400 or above must always carry three or more credits. The relational designer must ensure that the course table never contains a row describing a 2-credit, 400-level course, while the object-oriented designer must keep the course class from creating a 2-credit, 400-level course object. In the most general case, the data entry/edit programs must check for constraint violations before all database modifications. This is not only a burdensome job, but very dangerous as well: a failure to check all the possibilities will allow the database to enter an inconsistent state.

But this is not always necessary. For certain types of constraints the very structure of the database dictated by the model prevents constraint violation. In a relational database, the referential integrity constraint forces a foreign key value to be null or to refer to an existing row in the referenced table. In the grades table of Figure 1, for example, the relational database designer must prevent a careless user entering an inappropriate courseID or studentID value. An object-oriented database designer has no such worries. The owning student appears inside the grade, just as the mark itself does. It isn't possible to embed a nonexistent student in the grade object, so the question of referential integrity doesn't arise. In the implementation, of course, the student's OID appears in the grade object, but that doesn't alter the conclusion: the structure of an object-oriented database prevents any referential integrity violation. This example shows how an object-oriented database can enforce certain constraints through the model, rather than through application code, in the sense that if the database design follows the object-oriented model, a referential integrity violation is not possible. There is a transfer of responsibility from the domain of the application programmer to the DBMS, which reduces application costs and improves quality in the use of the data [10].

The relational normal forms, from First Normal Form through Fifth Normal Form, are characterized by increasing attribute dispersion, since the normalization process distributes application attributes across multiple tables. The segregated attribute clusters then guarantee that certain application constraints will always hold, regardless of the tables' content. The degree of attribute segregation correlates roughly with the extent of application constraint enforcement: a greater attribute dispersion across separate tables results in greater application constraint enforcement. When the normalization process breaks a table into two components, the contents of the table can be recreated as the join of the two components. The contents of the join table, however, may differ

Student (unnormalized)					
studentID	name	height	weight	courses	grades
46	James	71.5	184	CS 401, CS 430	A, B
52	William	68.0	204	CS 401, CS 420	B, C
69	Shelley	69.5	160	CS 405, CS 420, CS 430	A, A, B
78	Jill	66.5	170	CS 401	A

Student (1NF)								
studentID	name	height	weight	courseID	number	courseName	credits	mark
46	James	71.5	184	206	CS 401	Automata Theory	3	A
46	James	71.5	184	267	CS 430	Database Theory	3	B
52	William	68.0	204	206	CS 401	Automata Theory	3	B
52	William	68.0	204	248	CS 420	Computer Architecture	4	C
69	Shelley	69.5	160	239	CS 405	Algorithm Analysis	4	A
69	Shelley	69.5	160	248	CS 420	Computer Architecture	4	A
69	Shelley	69.5	160	267	CS 430	Database Theory	3	B
78	Jill	66.5	170	206	CS 401	Automata Theory	3	A

Figure 2: A First Normal Form violation and its resolution

from the contents of the original table. Certain old tuples may be missing, and certain new tuples may appear. These differences are precisely the changes necessary to force constraint satisfaction on the original table. The changes vary from one normal form to the next, and they will be reviewed in subsequent sections. For the present, the point is that further decomposition into three or more components further restricts the contents of the original table when it is rematerialized as a join. The multicomponent join adds or deletes tuples so as to force satisfaction of more complex application constraints.

In subsequent sections we review the constraints associated with each normal form and provide a corresponding object-oriented interpretation. We show that in some cases the object-oriented structure subsumes the constraint associated with the normal form, while in others we provide a natural configuration of classes that provides the same enforcement in the object-oriented context. These insights provide starting points in the transition from a relational environment to an object-oriented one.

3 The first two normal forms

A table is in First Normal Form (1NF) if its cells are constrained to atomic entries. That is, no cell can contain a repeating group. Using a subset of the data, Figure 2 (upper portion) consolidates the student example of Figure 1 into a single table. Because courses and grades contain repeating groups, 1NF violations occur. By spreading the repeating groups across several rows and duplicating the common information, the violation can be removed. The lower table in Figure 2 illustrates the point.

All commercial relational database products constrain tables to 1NF. Their schemas require a type specification (e.g., string, integer, float, date, or currency) for each attribute. Row entries under a given attribute must contain an entry of the corresponding type, making 1NF violations impossible. Object-oriented class definitions also provide options that constrain attribute values in the corresponding objects. Generally, an attribute can contain any value: a simple string or number, an object of another class, or a collection of such objects. An appropriate constraint clause in the class definition, however, can restrict the choice. Choosing a simple string or number or a single object of another class, the designer enforces the equivalent of 1NF in the object-oriented context.

Most of the time, the 1NF constraint—no repeating groups—isn't an application constraint, but rather a restriction forced by the schema rules of relational database products. If, as in the example, a given student actually takes multiple courses, the courses attribute shouldn't be restricted to a single value. When the schema rules force this constraint, you must resort to multiple rows to describe a single student, as shown in the lower portion of Figure 2. Although it could do so, the object-oriented version in the lower portion of Figure 1 imposes no such restriction and therefore models the application more faithfully.

If the application were to restrict each student to a single course, this would represent a true application constraint. In a relational schema, you could enforce the constraint by declaring studentID to be a key. This would preclude multiple rows for the same student, and the lower table structure of Figure 2 would maintain the constraint. This is tantamount to reverting to the upper format of Figure 2, with "courses" and "grades" renamed as "course" and "grade." The schema restriction would then allow a single course value for each student. In either case, the object-oriented equivalent class definition would use a clause to restrict the grades attribute to a single object.

In a relational-to-object-oriented translation, the less restrictive policy that allows collections as attribute values should be exploited to better reflect the application's world. In the case of a true one-to-many association between application entities, such as the student-grade relationship, you establish a grade collection as the value of a student attribute, and also establish the owning student as an attribute within the grade class. The same mechanism also serves in some many-to-many relationships. Each student could contain a collection of courses, and each course could contain a collection of related students. This representation is insufficient here because it provides no place for the mark (grade) associated with each related student-course pair.

Often the relational solution breaks out a separate table solely as a concession to the 1NF schema requirement. Suppose that course contains a multivalued attribute called grading-options, which can be any nonempty subset of {A-F, pass/no-pass, audit}. The 1NF requirement forces the relational database designer to create two new tables: one for the three strings and a second to associate particular courses with specific strings. The object-oriented translation can simply collapse the two extra tables into a single course attribute, grading-option, which contains a string collection.

Moving on to Second Normal Form (2NF), recall that a table attribute is prime if it is part of a key for the table; otherwise it is non-prime. If X and Y are attribute groups, $X \longrightarrow Y$ is the constraint that any two rows agreeing on the X values must also agree on the Y values. A table satisfies 2NF, with respect to the application constraints, if the following condition holds. If X $\longrightarrow$ A is an application constraint, where A is a non-prime attribute and X contains part of a key, then X must contain an entire key. Intuitively, this means that a non-prime attribute can be determined only by a full key; a partial key can never suffice.

Consider again the lower table of Figure 2. Suppose the application allows duplication among student names, weights, and heights, and also among course numbers, names, and credits. However, studentID remains identified with a single student, and courseID associates with a single course. The only key to the table is then the concatenation studentID-courseID. The constraint studentID $\longrightarrow$ height becomes a 2NF violation because height is non-prime and studentID contains a partial key.

The 2NF violation induces several undesirable characteristics in the lower table of Figure 2—repetitive storage of the same information, and therefore opportunities for inconsistency during updates. The normalization process removes the 2NF violation by separating the table into three parts. One part contains the attributes pertaining only to a student; a second part contains the attributes pertaining only to a course. A third part is necessary for those attributes, such as mark, that describe a student-course combination. The new arrangement returns to the original presentation of Figure 1. With this structure, it isn't possible to introduce an inconsistent state by forgetting to update a course's credits in all places, since the course's credits appear in only one place.

Intuitively, 2NF violations occur when two or more application entities are described in a single table. This can also happen in an object-oriented database. For example, it is possible to describe a student-course class that contains the attributes of the lower table in Figure 2. Objects minted from this class represent student-course combinations, which correspond to the table rows in the figure. Similar inconsistency problems arise because the course information is repeated (as numeric and string data) in many student-course objects. A change to a pure course attribute, such as credits, must be propagated to all these objects. The object-oriented solution parallels the 2NF resolution in the relational case: you must separate the class definitions for student from those for course. As shown in the lower part of Figure 1, both student and course objects contain grade collections, which serve to mediate the student-course relationship. A relational-to-object-oriented translation should, therefore, break out separate classes to parallel the tables associated with removing a 2NF violation.

Essentially every object-oriented design text [11, 12, 13, 14, 15] stresses the importance of implementing application entities as separate classes. Following this precept, the designer would arrive at a decomposition in which student, course, and grade appear as separate classes. The question is then: Why follow the normal form decomposition to achieve a class structure that evolves naturally from object-oriented design guidelines?

There are two reasons. First, in a re-engineering context, following the normal form decomposition provides confirmation that the original designer iden-

Course					
courseID	number	name	credits	building	room
206	CS 401	Automata Theory	3	Bond Hall	BH 111
239	CS 405	Algorithm Analysis	4	Arntzen Hall	AH 102
248	CS 420	Computer Architecture	4	Bond Hall	BH 229
267	CS 430	Database Theory	3	Bond Hall	BH 160

Course						Classroom	
courseID	number	name	credits	room		building	room
206	CS 401	Automata Theory	3	BH 111		Bond Hall	BH 111
239	CS 405	Algorithm Analysis	4	AH 102		Bond Hall	BH 229
248	CS 420	Computer Architecture	4	BH 229		Arntzen Hall	AH 102
267	CS 430	Database Theory	3	BH 160		Bond Hall	BH 160

Figure 3: Third Normal Form violation and its resolution

tified the application entities in the same manner. Second, given the current state of the art in object-oriented design, no design method specifies exactly how to identify the application entities. Suggestions such as "get to know the application domain", or "look for the nouns in the requirements specifications" are not precise enough for a designer attempting to handle a complex problem. If the original relational designers have identified constraints that forced a decomposition, the attribute packets in the components will likely represent application entities, particularly with the lower normal forms. A complicated application may challenge a designer's ingenuity in extracting the proper application classes, in which case the classes defined by the decomposed relational tables should be used to help.

4　The third normal form and its Boyce-Codd enhancement

A table is in Third Normal Form (3NF) if the following condition holds. If $X \longrightarrow A$ is an application constraint, where A is a non-prime attribute, then X must contain a key. This is a stronger constraint than 2NF. 2NF allows $X \longrightarrow A$ when X contains no prime attributes at all, but 3NF removes this possibility. Suppose, for example, that the course table of Figure 1 includes the room and building where the course is taught. The new table appears in the upper part of Figure 3, and the remaining tables (i.e., Student and Grade) remain as in Figure 1.

Because a room remains fixed in its building, the constraint room $\longrightarrow$ building must apply. The only key to the course table remains courseID, so this constraint doesn't induce a 2NF violation: the determinant room contains no partial key. However, it does produce a 3NF violation, which opens opportunities for inconsistency in a manner similar to that associated with 2NF violations. In particular, updates to the building and room attributes can't proceed independently. Instead, data entry/edit programs must verify that a specified room-building combination doesn't contradict some other row in the table. To remove this oversight burden, the normalization process decomposes

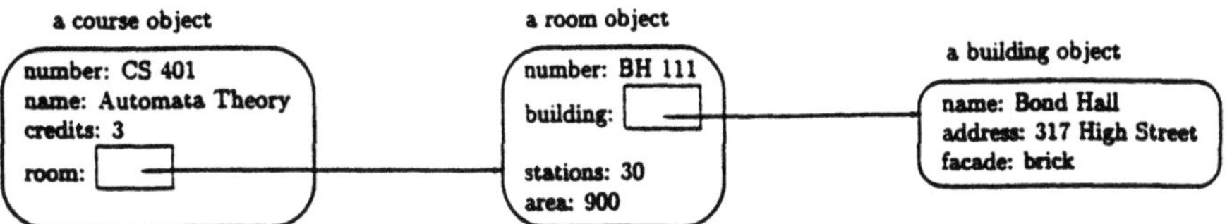

Figure 4: Class arrangement equivalent to third normal form solution

the course table into two components, as shown in the lower half of Figure 3. In the classroom table room is a key, so it isn't possible to place a room in more than one building.

The equivalent object-oriented database is not immune to this problem. If the course class contains independent string-valued attributes for building and room, building-room combinations can appear in the many instances created from the class, and the possibility arises that a room may be associated with one building in one object and with a different building in another. To preclude such inconsistencies, the class definition should be changed along the lines of the 3NF solution of Figure 3. Instead of independent attributes for building and room, a course object should contain a single location attribute, whose value is constrained to an object from the classroom class. The classroom class, therefore, corresponds to the separate classroom table in the 3NF solution. A classroom object contains descriptive attributes for the room and an embedded building object. It isn't possible for distinct course objects to associate the same room with more than one building because the location attribute must be filled with one of the consistent building-room combinations from the classroom class.

Figure 4 shows the object containments that approximate the third normal form decomposition of Figure 3. The important point is that room, together with its dependent building, no longer appear physically within course. Even without reference to the third normal form decomposition, the object-oriented designer would recognize room as a distinct application entity and consequently implement it as a separate class. For this same reason, Figure 4 also implements building as a separate class, even though the corresponding relational solution does not use a distinct table. The relational table arrangement, therefore, does not provide a direct mapping to object-oriented classes. Rather, the object-oriented translation should identify the application classes by using both proper object-oriented methods (e.g., Booch or Jacobson), together with careful analysis of the relational tables and the underlying normalization process.

A constraint $X \longrightarrow A$ can escape being a 3NF violator, even when X contains no key, if A is prime. Boyce-Codd Normal Form (BCNF) removes this possibility. A table is in BCNF if a constraint $X \longrightarrow A$ occurs only when X contains a key. Consider the application whose table shells appear in Figure 5. The relevant entities are student, course, and advisor, and each commands a separate table. The constraints in each case involve only the key (i.e., studentID, courseID, or advisorID) determining the non-prime descriptive attributes of the entity. No 2NF, 3NF, or BCNF violations appear in these

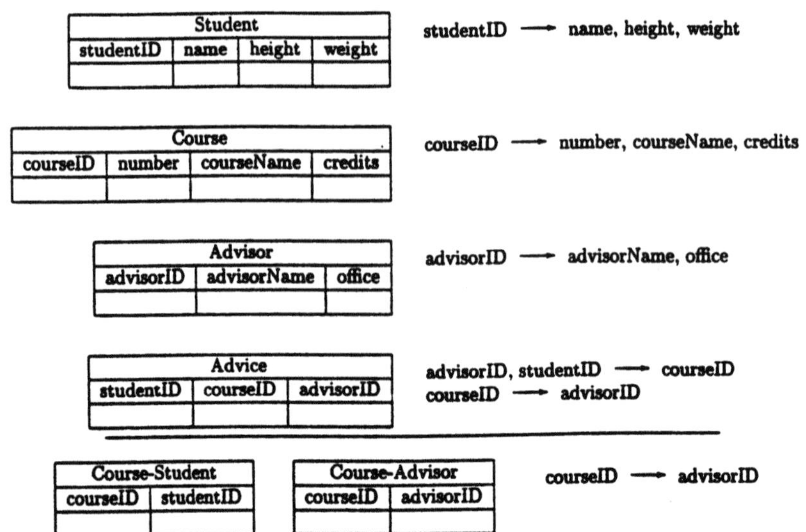

Figure 5: A Boyce-Codd Normal Form violation (top) and its resolution (bottom)

tables because the constraints all involve a complete key on the left side.

The fourth table describes how students, courses, and advisers interact to produce advice sessions. If a student could consult any adviser about any course, the advice table would have no restrictions: any combination of studentID, courseID, and advisorID could occur. The application, however, does have restrictions on advice sessions. In particular, each course has just one advisor, although a given advisor may work (unassisted) with several courses. But once a student approaches an advisor in a particular course, the advisor can't work with that student in a different course—even though the advisor may handle other students in other courses. These complicated rules are summarized by advisorID, studentID $\longrightarrow$ courseID and courseID $\longrightarrow$ advisorID.

This example is isomorphic to the canonical situation that textbooks use to distinguish between 3NF and BCNF. In the advice table, possible keys are the advisorID-studentID combination and the courseID-studentID combination. So all attributes are prime. The first constraint, advisorID, studentID $\longrightarrow$ courseID, induces no 2NF, 3NF, or BCNF violation because a full key appears on its left side. The second constraint, courseID $\longrightarrow$ advisorID, induces no 2NF or 3NF violation because its right side is prime. It does, however, induce a BCNF violation because its left side contains no key.

The BCNF violation provides an opportunity for inconsistency in the table, just as in the 3NF case. The fact that the right side of the violating constraint is prime is just a technicality. A given courseID can appear many times, corresponding to many students seeking advice from the course's advisor. A key constraint is therefore not available to enforce courseID $\longrightarrow$ advisorID, and the burden of checking that two or more rows with the same courseID do not have the same advisorID has to be embedded in the access program's logic.

The solution is to break the table into two components, as shown at the bottom of Figure 5. Because courseID is now a key in the second table, courseID $\longrightarrow$ advisorID induces no BCNF violation. The other constraint (i.e., advisorID, studentID $\longrightarrow$ courseID) doesn't induce a violation either because it doesn't apply to either of the component tables. Unfortunately, it still applies to the join of the two components, so the database faces a potentially more difficult job. Before consumating an update to either component, the database system must join the two tables (new versions) and ensure that the advisorID-studentID pair remains a key.

Because the decomposition causes a constraint to be split across components, the decomposition loses the dependency-preserving property. This is clearly undesirable because certain constraints must now be enforced on table joins, rather than on individual tables. Loss of dependency preservation is a well-known risk of BCNF. As may be implied by the contrived nature of the example, most 3NF decompositions are already in BCNF. A distinction occurs only when a prime attribute determines part of a key, a situation more frequently found in academic textbooks than in actual practice. Nevertheless, when this complication does arise, many designers fall back to 3NF and use other means to prevent inconsistency.

Figure 6 provides a straightforward translation to an object-oriented setting. Advisor and course appear as distinct classes, and the one-to-many relationship from advisor to course must be captured by restricting the advisor attribute, within course, to a single object. The courses attribute, within advisor, can contain a collection of courses. Therefore, the course $\longrightarrow$ advisor constraint is enforced, and the redundancies associated with repeating advisor information across several courses are eliminated.

However, the advisor, student $\longrightarrow$ course constraint remains unspecified, just as in the relational case. As mentioned in discussing the relational solution of Figure 5, the table configuration does not enforce advisorID, studentID $\longrightarrow$ courseID. Instead, user access programs must control the effect of updates on the join of the two tables—a potentially expensive operation. The object-oriented translation of Figure 6 is no worse: user access programs must ensure that the courses associated with a given student specify distinct advisors. In terms of Figure 6, this constraint requires that the course collection of a particular student (the rectangular enclosure) intersect the course collection of a particular advisor (a free-form enclosure) in at most one course. In practice, enforcing this constraint amounts to iterating over the student's course collection and compiling a list of associated advisors. If the list contains more than one entry, then advisor, student $\longrightarrow$ course is violated. This operation is somewhat less expensive than the relational join because it must chase down only the objects associated with a particular student. It is objectionable, nevertheless, because it depends on special code to enforce the constraint.

Special syntax in the class definitions could be provided to capture the advisor, student $\longrightarrow$ course constraint (although no object-oriented database does it at the moment). Currently, class definitions typically allow an attribute

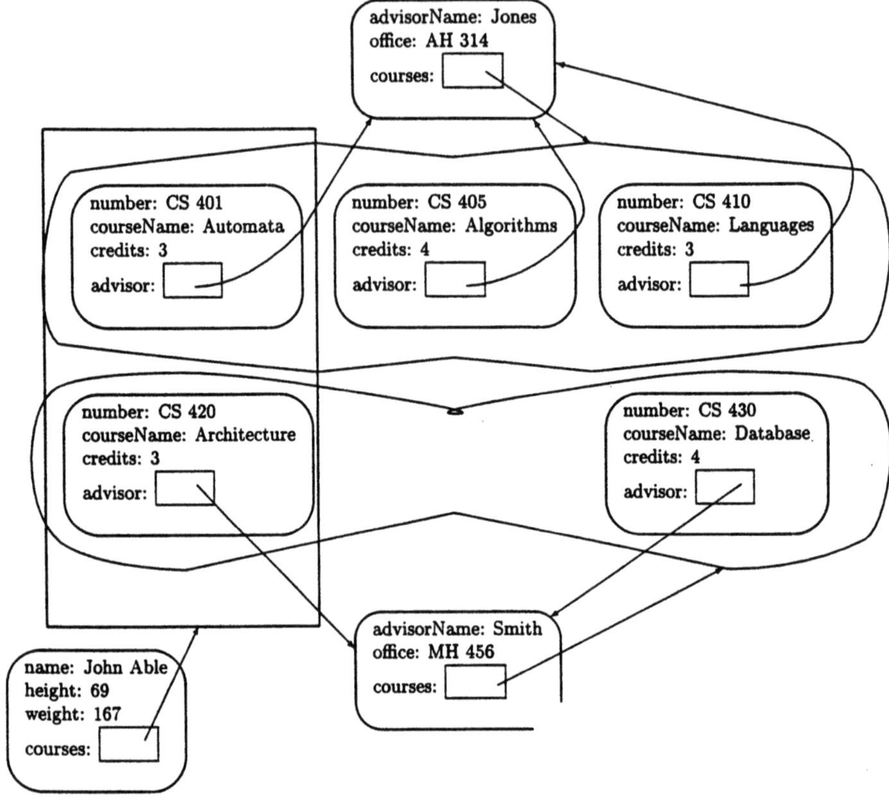

Figure 6: Object-oriented translation of a BCNF decomposition

constraint clause to limit the value to a single object or to a collection of objects from some specified class. Here, the courses attribute within student must be limited not just to a collection of course objects, but to course objects with no duplicated advisors. The clause might appear as follows in the definition of the student class.

class student
        attribute: name constraint: string;
        attribute: height constraint: positiveNumber;
        attribute: weight constraint: positiveNumber;
        attribute: courses constraint: collection (course), unique course.advisor

5 Fourth Normal Form

A multivalued dependency constraint, $X \longrightarrow\!\!\!\rightarrow Y$, is weaker than a functional dependency, $X \longrightarrow Y$. Unlike a functional dependency, which keeps a new row out of a table when it duplicates the X attributes of an existing row but fails to duplicate the Y attributes, a multivalued dependency forces new rows into a table when existing rows agree on the X attributes. Specifically, $X \twoheadrightarrow Y$ imposes the following condition on a table. Let Z be the attributes outside of both X and Y. If two rows agree on X, then two further rows must appear that agree on X and cross-associate the values in Y and Z. Graphically, if the first two rows appear in table R (to the right below), then the second two must also appear.

Note that if $X \longrightarrow Y$, then y_2 must equal y_1 and the cross-association simply regenerates the original two rows. Therefore, $X \longrightarrow Y$ is a stronger condition that implies $X \twoheadrightarrow Y$

If Z is empty, the cross-association condition is trivially satisfied, regardless of the content of the table; this is called a trivial multivalued dependency. A table is in Fourth Normal Form (4NF) if, for every non-trivial $X \twoheadrightarrow Y$ that appears among the constraints, X contains a key. Because $X \longrightarrow Y$ implies $X \twoheadrightarrow Y$, 4NF implies BCNF.

Table R		
X	Y	Z
x	y_1	z_1
x	y_2	z_2
$\vdots$	$\vdots$	$\vdots$
x	y_1	z_2
x	y_2	z_1

Table R_1	
X	Y
x	y_1
x	y_2

Table R_2	
X	Z
x	z_1
x	z_2

A non-4NF table affords opportunities for inconsistency. Referring again to table R, for example, the database designer must worry about data entry/edit operations that install the first two rows but fail to install the second two. If the left side of a multivalued dependency contains a key, no such opportunity for inconsistency exists. If X is a key for table R (i.e., no 4NF violation), then the first two rows must be identical: $y_1 = y_2$ and $z_1 = z_2$. Cross association then regenerates the same row, so no further rows are needed.

When $X \twoheadrightarrow Y$ is a constraint but X doesn't contain a key, a better representation uses two tables, as shown in the decomposition of table R into R_1 and R_2 in the example. Data entry/edit can now enter arbitrary Y and Z values in conjunction with a given X value. The join of the two components will always contain the required rows.

The analysis of the object-oriented translation must contemplate several possibilities:

- A multivalued dependency $X \twoheadrightarrow Y$ appears simply because the corresponding functional dependency, $X \longrightarrow Y$, occurs. The translation can be handled with the techniques of the previous sections.

- A multivalued dependency appears simply to satisfy the relational format— no repeating groups. Suppose, for example, that a given student can have several phone numbers and several e-mail addresses, and that there is no association between particular phone numbers and e-mail addresses. From a given phone, the student can monitor all his e-mail accounts (by remote login perhaps), and he can answer any of his phones from any location (by call forwarding). To model the fact that phones and e-mails

Student					
studentID	name	height	weight	phone	e-mail
46	James	71.5	184	202-123-4567	jamescs.univ.edu
46	James	71.5	184	212-321-7654	jrestsoftcorp.com
46	James	71.5	184	202-123-4567	jrestsoftcorp.com
46	James	71.5	184	212-321-7654	jamescs.univ.edu
⋮	⋮	⋮	⋮	⋮	⋮

Student Base Data			
studentID	name	height	weight
46	James	71.5	184
⋮	⋮	⋮	⋮

Student Phone & E-mail		
studentID	phone	e-mail
46	202-123-4567	jamescs.univ.edu
46	212-321-7654	jrestsoftcorp.com
46	202-123-4567	jrestsoftcorp.com
46	212-321-7654	jamescs.univ.edu
⋮	⋮	⋮

Student Base Data			
studentID	name	height	weight
46	James	71.5	184
⋮	⋮	⋮	⋮

Student Phone	
studentID	phone
46	202-123-4567
46	212-321-7654
⋮	⋮

Student E-mail	
studentID	e-mail
46	jamescs.univ.edu
46	jrestsoftcorp.com
⋮	⋮

Figure 7: Fourth Normal Form violation and its resolution

are not pairwise associated, a student must appear as several rows that elaborate all combinations of the two attributes.

The upper table in Figure 7 illustrates the situation. The row repetition introduces a number of problems. First, studentID is no longer a key, although it does determine name, height, and weight. So the table doesn't even satisfy 2NF. The two-table decomposition in the middle of the figure solves that problem, but it leaves the 4NF violation associated with the multivalued attributes: studentID $\longrightarrow\!\!\!\rightarrow$ phone. The bottom three-table decomposition addresses this final difficulty. A join of the three tables recovers all the required rows.

In this example, the multivalued dependency arises because no significance is attached to a given phone number appearing in the same row with a given e-mail address. Instead, a student can be reached at any of a group of phone numbers or at any of a group of e-mail addresses. If relational databases allowed repeating groups in table cells, you could simply enter all the phone number under a phones attribute, and similarly for the e-mail addresses. The multivalued dependency is necessary only to circumvent the table restriction to atomic entries. In this case the object-oriented translation is particularly straightforward and involves no class decomposition: just use collections to house the multivalued attributes. In the example, the student class would contain name, height, and weight attributes, each restricted to a string, and phone and e-mail attributes, each restricted to a collection of strings.

- A multivalued dependency arises from restricted relationships within the application. Consider again the database of students, courses, and advi-

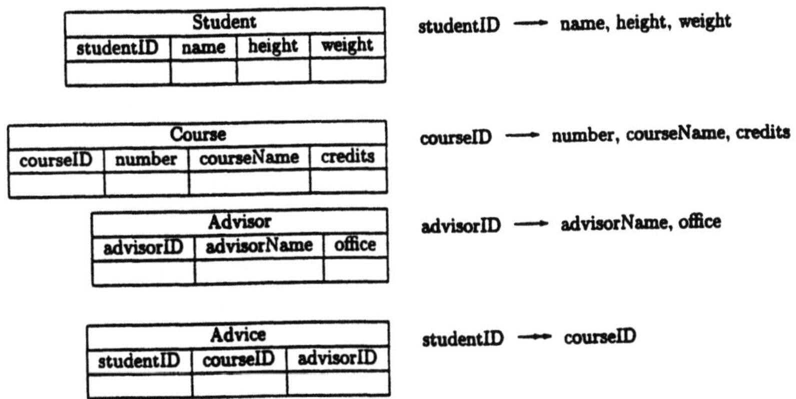

Figure 8: Fourth Normal Form violation arising from an application constraint

sors. The constraints are different now, as shown in Figure 8. In the table that records the relationships among students, courses, and advisors, a multivalued dependency states that students are associated with a *set* of courses and a *set* of advisors. There is no requirement that the student use a particular advisor with a particular course. Rather, the student is free to choose any advisor from the specified advisor set to deal with any course in the specified course set. The multivalued dependency, studentID ⟶⟶ courseID, documents this constraint (or rather, lack of constraint). As it stands, the last table violates 4NF, and it should be decomposed into two components: (studentID, courseID) and (studentID, advisorID).

From the standpoint of an object-oriented translation, this case is the same as the one with multivalued descriptive attributes. Where a student previously held multiple phone numbers and e-mail addresses, he now has multiple courses and advisors. In both cases, the database representation must avoid the impression that a particular (phone, e-mail) or (course, advisor) pair is significant. So, the object-oriented solution is the same: embed the associated course and advisor collections in the student object. Because specific courses and advisors aren't aligned in rows, no significance attaches to a particular course-advisor combination. This free association between courses and advisors (for a given student) is precisely the intent of the multivalued dependency.

Complex interactions among the application's governing functional and multivalued dependencies can make the analysis more difficult than the examples presented here. Although the details are beyond the scope of this paper, there exist algorithms that compute the dependency basis for a given attribute cluster in a relational database [5]. For example, the dependency basis for studentID could include name, height, weight, phone, e-mail, course, advisor, and other groups—not necessarily all singletons. It can then be shown that studentID multidetermines the union of any members from its dependency basis. So you have studentID $\longrightarrow\!\!\!\!\rightarrow$ phone, course among other possibilities. Using separate tables, a 4NF decomposition must isolate studentID with each member of its dependency basis. The corresponding object-oriented translation then follows the rules:

- The student class definition must contain an attribute for each member of the dependency basis.

- If studentID determines a dependency basis member (always a singleton) in the functional dependency sense, the corresponding attribute is restricted to a single object of the appropriate class.

- If studentID multidetermines, but does not determine, a singleton dependency-basis member, the attribute is allowed to hold an object collection of the appropriate class.

- If (final possibility) studentID multidetermines, but does not functionally determine, a non-singleton dependency-basis member, the attributes of the dependency basis member must be packaged as a separate class, and the student class endowed with an attribute that can hold a collection of objects from this new class.

When $X \longrightarrow\!\!\!\!\rightarrow Y$ constrains a table R, R must always equal the join of its projections on XY and XZ, where $Z = R - XY$. Thus, if $y_1, y_2, \ldots, y_n$ and $z_1, z_2, \ldots, z_m$ are the Y and Z attributes, respectively, that are associated with a given X value x, then x must appear repeatedly in R, using a separate row to associate x with each y_i, z_j pair. This display requires nm rows, whereas the 4NF decomposition into XY and XZ needs only $n+m$ shorter rows. Moreover, the 4NF decomposition guarantees that none of the required nm rows will be missing from R when it is reconstructed as the join of XY and XZ.

Although these concepts are important in a relational database design, they are, as illustrated in the previous section, a non-issue in the corresponding object-oriented translation. The class X contains attributes, Y-cousins and Z-cousins, say, each restricted to a collection of Y objects and Z objects, respectively. For an object x of class X, the Y-cousins attribute contains all Y objects related to x (i.e., the $y_1, y_2, \ldots, y_n$) and similarly for Z-cousins. If the application needs to elaborate the y_i, z_j pairs associated with a particular x, it must iterate through the Y-cousins and Z-cousins collections to construct their Cartesian product. This process guarantees that all pairs are listed and thus enforces the $X \longrightarrow\!\!\!\!\rightarrow Y$ constraint. This enforcement follows from the class structure, specifically from the multivalued attributes, and therefore requires no class decomposition. Even if the relational design split R into XY and XZ, the object-oriented translation can instead implement a single class, X, where the constraint cannot be violated.

Except in the trivial case where the multivalued dependency specifies a multivalued descriptive attribute, a 4NF decomposition applies to an intersection table, which manages the relationship between three application entities. That is, $X \longrightarrow YZ$, where X, Y, and Z are keys for three distinct application entities. The interesection table is necessary in the relational schema because the ternary relationship is many-to-many between any two participants. In the object-oriented translation, not only is the 4NF decomposition into XY and XZ unecessary, but the entire table is superfluous. Class structures must exist already for X, Y, and Z, and it is sufficient to embed two collections in X: its Y associates and its Z associates.

6 Fifth Normal Form

The 4NF conclusion differs from our findings in the 3NF and BCNF cases, where the table decomposition suggests a parallel class decomposition in the object-oriented translation. A constraint giving rise to a 4NF decomposition can be handled without auxiliary classes, requiring only embedded collections. The object-oriented translation of a Fifth Normal Form (5NF) is conceptually similar to the 4NF case.

You can view a 4NF decomposition as a response to an application constraint that requires a table to appear as the join of two components. Suppose, for example, that table R consists of attribute packets X, Y, and Z and that an the application requires $X \longrightarrow Y$. Using $*$ to indicate a natural join, this constraint is the same as requiring $R = (XY) * (XZ)$. If this requirement provides opportunity for inconsistency, then a 4NF violation occurs, which necessitates a decomposition into $R_1 = XY$ and $R_2 = XZ$. If X is a key, however, then no opportunity for inconsistency arises; the table remains at all times equal to the join of its XY and XZ projections. In this latter case, the decomposition is not necessary to enforce the constraint.

A generalization of this viewpoint considers application constraints that require a table to appear as the join of three or more components. These are join constraints. A join constraint that forces R to equal the join of its projections on $R_1, R_2, \ldots, R_n$ is written as $JD(R_1, R_2, \ldots, R_n)$. For example, suppose that X, Y, and Z are tables corresponding to application entities. Containing the attributes X-key, Y-key, and Z-key, an intersection table, R, manages the ternary relation among them and is subject to the constraint that it is always equal to the join of its three projections: (X-key, Y-key), (Y-key, Z-key), and (X-key, Z-key). Equivalently, if $(x, y, z'), (x', y, z)$, and (x, y', z) appear in R, then (x, y, z) must also appear. A real-world constraint of this form always seems rather contrived, but it is possible. For instance, suppose that X, Y, and Z are student, course, and advisor in a university setting and that their relationship must conform to the following rule. If student x receives advising services for course y and also consults with advisor z, who is known to provide advice on course y, then student x must receive advice on course y from advisor z. (Probably not the most bizarre rule in a university context.) Table R, then, must satisfy the condition: $JD[(X$-key, Y-key), (Y-key, Z-key), (X-key, Z-key)].

If this condition is a logical consequence of functional dependency con-

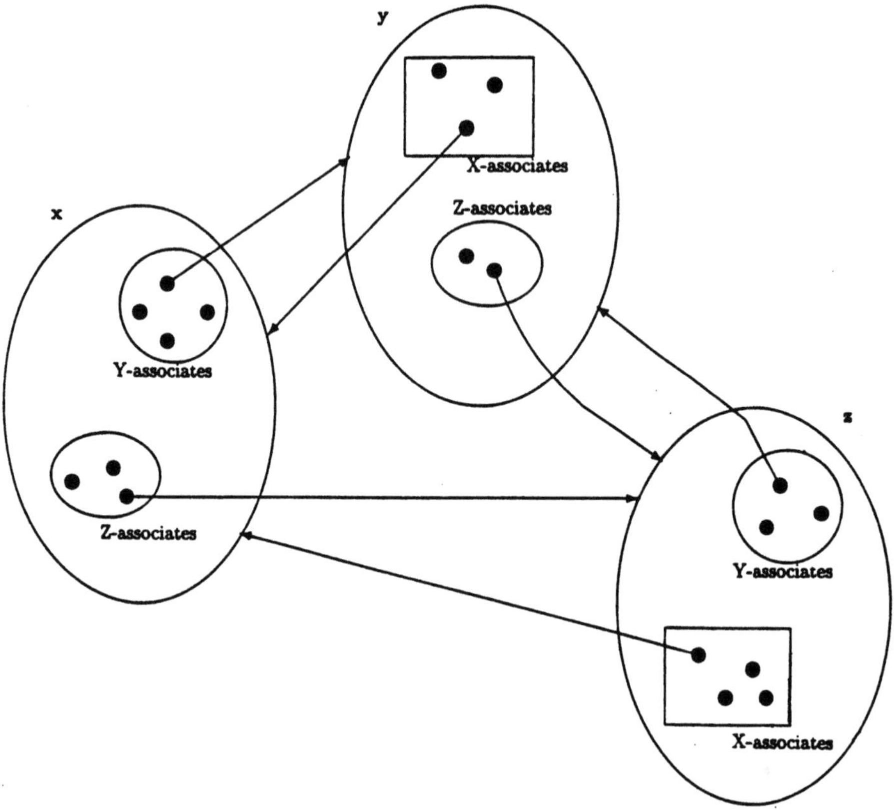

Figure 9: Object embeddings that enforce a 5NF constraint

straints, then it will not afford an opportunity for inconsistency. For example, suppose $X \longrightarrow Y$ is also an application constraint. Then the antecedent tuples $(x, y, z'), (x', y, z)$, and (x, y', z) are actually $(x, y, z'), (x', y, z)$, and (x, y, z). That is, the required conclusion tuple appears automatically. The chase algorithm [16, 17] can be used to determine systematically when a join constraint follows as a logical consequence of existing functional dependency constraints.

If JD$[(X$-key, Y-key$), (Y$-key, Z-key$), (X$-key, Z-key$)]$ is not a logical consequence of functional dependency constraints, the intersection table exhibits a 5NF violation, which can be removed by replacing it with its three projections: XY, YZ, and XZ. This guarantees that (x, y, z) will appear in the join when $(x, y), (y, z)$, and (x, z) appear in the components. In this way, the constraint will always be satisfied. In the object-oriented translation, however, the intersection should not be represented by a class, much less decomposed subclasses. Instead, class X embeds two attribute collections: its Y associates and its Z associates. Classes Y and Z contain similar embeddings. Figure 9 illustrates the point.

The application can now construct a correct list of related (x, y, z) triples by extending each x with all (y, z) pairs from its embeddings, provided that the y and z mutually contain each other. The figure shows the way in which X, Y, and Z objects should be connected. This construction ensures that the pairwise associations, $(x, y), (x, z)$, and (y, z), each represented by mutual inclusions, force the triple (x, y, z) into the list of the ternary relationship.

7   Conclusion

In relational databases, normal forms provide a method for the enforcement of some consistency constraints. A normal form violation implies that a certain entry in a target row can be anticipated, and therefore database updates must ensure that the predicted entry isn't modified.

The analysis here investigated the different kinds of functional and multivalued dependency constraints. In each case, the relational solution decomposes a table with a violation into two or more components. An object-oriented database uses classes instead of tables, but there is a close relationship between the two concepts, and similar opportunity for inconsistencies. Fortunately, the relational solution, decomposition, is also applicable in the object-oriented database. Where the relational solution exports an attribute cluster to a separate table, the object-oriented translation encapsulates the same cluster in a distinct class. An attribute of the original class then embeds an object of the new class or a collection of such objects. The details vary with the particular normal form that is being imitated.

In some cases, the more expressive modeling power of the object-oriented approach actually allows a coalescence of several tables into a single class. These opportunities occur when a 4NF or 5NF decomposition in the relational setting serves only to circumvent the restriction of table entries to non-repeating groups. Because the object-oriented model allows attributes to assume group values, a 4NF and 5NF decomposition can be reassembled into a single class. The application can then, if necessary, reconstruct a list of the properly related triples (or higher-order tuples) with the assurance that these lists will always contain the special tuples that are forced by the corresponding constraints.

The normalization process from relational database design remains useful in its object-oriented counterpart. The tables that result from the increasingly restrictive normal forms provide suggestions for the class structure of the object-oriented translation. Re-engineering operations seeking to preserve the functionality of relational applications while reimplementing them with an object-oriented database will find these insights useful to define the new database classes, and also to check that the newly defined structure agrees with the original design.

References

1 Premerlani W., Blaha, M., "An Approach for Reverse Engineering of Relational Databases," *Communications of the ACM*, 37:4, May, 1994.

[2] Castellanos, M., "Semantic Enrichment of Interoperable Databases," *Interoperability in Multidatabases: Research Issues in Database Engineering*, IEEE-CS Press, 1993.

[3] Chiang R., Barron T., Storey V., "Reverse Engineering of Relational Databases: Extraction of an EER Model from a Relational Database," *Data & Data Engineering*, 10:12, 1994.

[4] Kent, W., "A simple guide to five normal forms in relational database theory," *Communications of the ACM* 26:2, pp. 120–125, 1983.

[5] Johnson, James L. *Database: Models, Languages, Design*, Oxford University Press, 1997.

[6] Bertino, E. and Martino, L. "Object-oriented database management systems: concepts and issues," *IEEE Computer* 24:4, pp. 33–47, 1991.

[7] Date C.J., "A Contribution to the Study of Database Integrity," *Relational Database Writings 1985-1989*, Addison-Wesley 1990.

[8] Blaha, M.R., Premerlani, W.J., and Rumbaugh, J.E., "Relational database design using an object-oriented methodology," *Communications of the ACM*, 31:4, pp. 414–427, 1988.

[9] Stonebraker M., Wong E., "Access Control in a Relational Data Base Management System by Query Modification," Proc. ACM National Conference, 1974.

[10] Nijssen G.M., "Database Semantics," *Infotech State of the Art on Databases*, (M.P. Atkinson, ed), Infotech.

[11] Brown, David, *An Introduction to Object-Oriented Analysis: Objects in Plain English*, John Wiley & Sons, 1997.

[12] Loomis, M.E.S. *Object Databases: The Essentials*, Addison-Wesley, 1995.

[13] Booch, Grady. *Object-oriented Analysis and Design with Applications, Second Edition*, Benjamin/Cummings, 1994.

[14] Jacobson, I. *Object-Oriented Software Engineering*, Addison-Wesley, 1992.

[15] Rumbaugh, J.E.; Blaha, M.; Premerlani, W.; Eddy, F.; Lorensen, W. *Object-Oriented Modeling and Design*, Prentice-Hall, 1991.

[16] Beeri, C., Vardi, M. Y. "A proof procedure for data dependencies," *Journal of the ACM* Vol. 31, No. 4, 1984, pp. 718–741.

[17] Maier, D., Mendelzon, A. O., Sagiv, Y. "Testing implications of data dependencies," *ACM Trans. on Database Systems*, Vol. 4, No. 4, 1979, pp. 455–469.

SOFTWARE ENGINEERING/DEVELOPMENT

A Framework for Component–Oriented Tool Integration

Kai–Uwe Sattler

Department of Computer Science, University of Magdeburg
D–39016 Magdeburg, Germany

Abstract

Tool environments supporting the development of complex products need to be open and flexible. These requirements cannot be fulfilled in an adequate way by predefined coordination structures and interfaces. This paper presents a framework for control integration in open tool environments. The approach is based on a component model which supports the description of tool interconnections in an abstract implementation–independent manner.

1 Introduction

The development of complex technical products requires the use of computer based tools. These tools provide services for users to accomplish their tasks. They support the modelling of the shape of a product, the adjustment of parameters or the simulation of load. For efficient use these tools must be integrated. Tool environments provide the required mechanisms for the integration. In order to describe the different dimensions of the integration, one usually identifies three aspects: data, control and presentation integration [1].

Data integration deals with the management of design data and documents in a consistent way. Moreover, this aspect includes services for all the tools to store and retrieve their data. *Control integration* enables the direct interaction between tools to share their services and to coordinate activities without the intervention of the user. The subject of *presentation integration* is to support a homogeneous user interface to all services of the system. Other classifications identify additional aspects: *platform integration*, which represents services for network and operating system transparency and *process integration*, which refers to the support of the development process [2].

In the last few years, several tool environments and reference models have been developed. Mostly these approaches base on a central repository for data management with a standardized access interface for the tools. A global manager allows the user to control the activities of tools, e.g. to start and stop a tool in order to process data.

Recently it has become clear that openness and flexibility are important characteristics of a tool environment. Openness indicates the ability to integrate newly developed or third–party tools; flexibility means the adaptability of the overall system structure to changing circumstances. An open and flexible tool environment should provide facilities to compose tools as building blocks in a new manner needed by special requirements. Prerequisites for this aim are first plugable tools and second suitable composition mechanisms. Furthermore, for a simple adaptation the user should be able to describe any system configuration at an abstract implementation–independent level and instantiate it at runtime.

This paper presents an approach for control integration in tool environments based on the description and runtime mapping of tool interconnections. The remainder of the paper is structured as follows. In section 2 we propose a model of basic abstractions for tool components and their connections. In section 3 we present a framework as software infrastructure of a component based tool environment. Related work is discussed in section 4. Finally, section 5 concludes the paper and points to further work.

2 Component Model

Within the scope of a tool environment the tools are the building blocks or components. The granularity of these tools ranges from simple objects with a few services up to full featured applications. The component model accomplishes the representation of the environment configuration in the form of interacting tool components. We separate two aspects of a configuration:

- The *computation part* for describing the tool services and their requirements to the environment.

- The *coordination part* for organizing the behaviour of a group of components by managing interdependencies between their activities.

This distinction is supported by the basic abstractions of the model: components and interactors.

A *component* is a software entity with well–defined interfaces. An interface is an abstraction of the component behaviour and encapsulates the internal representation of state and implementation. A component can be implemented in several ways: by a single object, a group of collaborating objects, a function library or an encapsulated execution flow. The interfaces and the implementation of a component are defined by its *component class*. In principle there are two kinds of component interfaces. *Operational interfaces* define a set of operations which can be performed by a component or which a component can invoke at another one. *Event interfaces* define a set of events which can be announced by a component.

An interface can be derived from other interfaces and extend these with new operations or events. However, the derivation is only allowed within the scope of the same kind of interfaces.

A component has to implement at least an operational interface. In addition, it can define a set of event channels and slots. These elements are abstract interaction points: an *event channel* represents the point where the component announces events; a *slot* is the point where the component invokes services from another component. Channels and slots are defined by an identifier plus the provided event interface or the required operational interface. They enable the explicit binding between components.

To illustrate these concepts, a simple scenario shall be considered (Figure 1). A modelling tool for the design of assemblies requires services in order to select parts which should be assembled. These services could be provided by a simple file selection tool or by a more advanced tool based on an engineering database. The interface to the selection tool is represented by a slot. Furthermore, the assembly tool should notify other tools about changes in the assembly structure. For this purpose the assembly tool offers an event channel. In this way a product structure browser is able to update its view. In addition, the assembly tool provides services for other tools, like creating new assemblies.

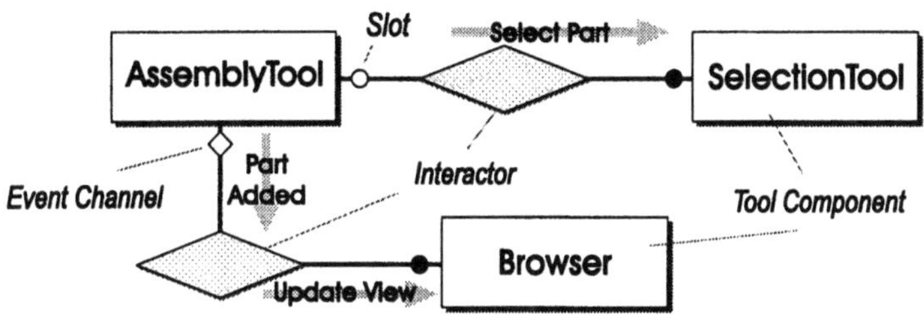

Figure 1: Example Scenario

Tool components can be connected in different ways for various tasks. These interconnections between the components form the coordination part of a configuration. They are represented by the concept of interactors. An *interactor* is an object encapsulating the collaboration of a group of objects in form of interaction relations. Interactors support the definition of interactions in an implementation–independent way and help to reduce the dependencies between components. In addition, they provide a way for describing synchronization aspects, different interaction styles or interface adaptation. The properties of interactors are defined by *interactor templates* consisting of a set of roles, a set of attributes and a set of links between the interaction points of the components.

A *role* is a placeholder for a member of the relationship and specifies the requirements to this represented component. *Links* define the behavioural dependencies between roles by describing the message flow. There are the following kinds of links:

- *Simple links* connect the slot of a component with the service provider. All operation requests are directly delivered to the provider.

- *Event links* are based on the mediator approach [3]. There can be operation invocations or sequences of invocations associated with events of an interactor role. The invocations are performed when the corresponding event ist announced.

- *Operational links* are the most flexible kind. Here the interactor defines how the interface of a requesting role's interaction part is implemented by services of other role objects. An interactor can forward requests, map one request to another one or process parameters via operational links.

The benefits from using interactors are the decoupling of interacting components, the binding of components with incompatible interfaces (concerning interface types and interaction styles) and the representation of n–ary relations. In our scenario inter-actors could be responsible for binding the assembly tool with the selection tool (via simple or operational link) and for the propagation of updates to the structure browser (via event link).

With these concepts a configuration of the environment is defined by a set of components interconnected by interactors. The configuration represents the section necessary for processing a task from the set of tools of the environments.

3   Integration Framework

TiFRAME is an object–oriented framework intended for the control integration layer in tool environments. Based on the model from section 2 the framework supports the composition and coordination of heterogenous tool components. The framework consists of two parts: the configuration language TIL for describing components and their interconnections and the runtime environment for instantiating configurations described in TIL. Special characteristics of TiFRAME are the integration of different communication platforms and the absence of predefined interfaces and protocols. Thereby the use of various implementations and the integration of existing tools is simplified.

3.1   Language Support

In order to adjust the tool environment to specific tasks it should be possible for the user to describe "his" configuration on an abstract, implementation–independent level. Graphical or textual configuration languages are suitable mechanisms for this aim. For the use with the TiFRAME framework we have developed a language called *Tool Interconnection Language (TIL)*.

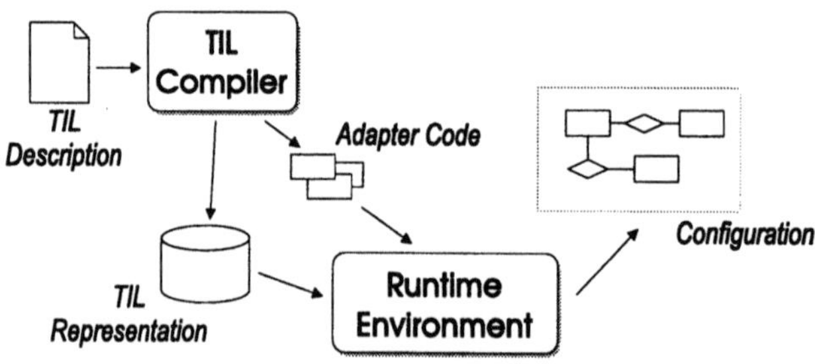

Figure 2: Integration process using TIL

From the TIL specification the compiler generates an internal representation of a configuration readable by the runtime environment and the adapter code required for interconnecting the components (Figure 2). The compiler checks the specified interaction relations for interface compatibility. Based on the configuration description the runtime environment is able to instantiate and connect the components directly or via the generated adapters.

The configuration language provides only elements necessary for specifying component interfaces and interconnections because the components are usually implemented in existing programming languages. According to our component model we distinguish between interfaces as abstract types and component classes as type implementations. In order to simplify the integration of existing tools the description of operational interfaces in TIL is derived from the *Interface Definition Language (IDL)* of the OMG [4].

```
interface AssemblyServices {
    void edit_assembly (in Assembly a);
    Assembly get_active_assembly ();
};
```

In this way it is possible to import existing IDL specifications in TIL without changes and to treat CORBA objects as components in TiFRAME. This opens the framework for future component development, because CORBA has gained widespread acceptance and commercial support. Event interfaces are specified in a modified notation considering the characteristics of event notifications (e.g., no output or return parameters):

```
events AssemblyEvents {
    assembly_updated (Assembly a);
    part_added (Assembly a);
};
```

The definition of a component class at a minimum requires the supported operational interface (supports) and the reference to the implementation. The implementation part defines the framework adapter (bridge) for accessing the native component implementation and the framework for creating a component instance. The optional event interfaces of the component are specified in the announces clause by giving an operation (using) for accessing the interaction point (the event channel). Slots – interaction points where services of other components are required – are specified in a similar way in the requires clause:

```
component AssemblyTool {
    supports AssemblyServices;
    announces AssemblyEvents notifier
            using update_listener;
    requires PartSelection selector
            using attach_selector;
    primitive implementation {
        bridge = "IIOP";
        class = "tiframe.cad.AssemblyTool";
    };
};
```

Apart from component classes implemented by native code, components can also be defined as a composition of other components. In this case the implementation part of the component class describes the subcomponents, their interactions (represented by interactors) and the associations between the interaction points of the composite component and the subcomponents (the using part in the supports clause).

```
component ModellingTool {
    supports AssemblyServices using editor;
    composite implementation {
        AssemblyTool editor = new AssemblyTool;
        SelectionTool selector = new SelectionTool;
        new simple_link<editor, selector>;
    };
};
```

An interactor template is defined by a set of roles representing the participants of the interaction relation and a behavioural part. The roles are characterized by the required type (in terms of the interface or the component class) and an identifier. In addition, a set of attributes can be defined. An interactor template provides a common definition for a set of components related through their interfaces. Similar to parameterized types in languages like C++ or Eiffel a single interactor template might be used to instantiate individual interactors for connecting different components. The roles of the template specify the requirements to the parameters (the components):

```
interactor simple_link<AssemblyTool editor,
        PartSelector pselector> {
    editor.selector → pselector;
};

interactor observation<AssemblyTool editor,
        StructureBrowser browser> {
    editor.notifier → {
        part_added (asm) { browser.update_view_for (asm); }
    };
};
```

The behavioural part of an interactor template specifies a set of links between the role objects in the notation `initiator → responder`. The `initiator` part of a link consists of interaction points initiating the communication represented by a role object. The `responder` part of a link respresents interaction points which implement the interface required by the initiator. In the most simple case, this might be the operational interface of a component represented by a role object (see interactor `simple_link`). For complex interactions, like 1–to–n relations or interface adaptations, it is possible to specify the `responder` part operationally. In this case actions are associated with the operations and events of the initiator interface. The actions will be performed with the corresponding invocation request or notification (see interactor `observation`). An action is a sequence of statements for manipulating arguments, accessing attributes and invoking operations of role objects. Based on these actions the TIL compiler generates the appropriated adapter code for connecting the component instances.

A configuration specified in TIL describes the instantiation of components and their interconnections via interactors. Instances are created by using the *new* operator and can be assigned to variables. The instantiation of an interactor requires component instances or their interaction points as parameters.

```
configuration SimpleConf {
    AssemblyTool editor = new AssemblyTool;
    StructureBrowser browser = new StructureBrowser;
    SelectionTool selector = new SelectionTool;

    new simple_link<editor, selector>;
    new observation<editor, browser>;
};
```

In this sense a TIL configuration specifies the initial structure of the tool environment. During the computation further components might be instantiated – either by component instances already defined or as a part of coordination activities specified in the actions of interactors.

3.2 Runtime Environment

The TIFRAME runtime environment provides mechanisms for the mapping from a component–based configuration to a particular set of interconnected tools. In detail the following functions are implemented: the instantiation of configurations according to a given TIL specification, the mapping from components and their connections to tool implementations or framework objects, and the access to component services in order to support framework–based applications.

The runtime environment of the framework consists of a collection of classes organized in several layers. The *configuration layer* contains services for instantiating configurations and for accessing the various components. The completion of this layer requires the services from the *component layer*. This layer represents the components and interactors independent from their implementation and their communication interfaces. All components are treated in a uniform way by introducing *proxy* objects. A proxy is a local representative for a tool component in a different address space [5]. It hides the different mechanisms required for interacting with the real component. The *bridging layer* provides services for the communication between proxies and real components as well as the mapping of the component properties to the implementation. This layer defines an abstract interface for the communication bus and enables the use of concrete communication solutions by using platform–specific bridges.

In order to support a flexible integration of different component implementation and communication platforms we use a reflective approach [6] for mapping the component model. With this approach the components and interactors form the *base level*. In addition there is a *meta level* containing information about the objects from the base level. This information specifies the structural and behavioural aspects required for relating the base level objects to their implementation. It is encapsulated by *metaobjects*. A metaobject represents the following information about components or interactors:

- structural properties (interfaces, slots, channels, roles or links) and their mapping to the native or composite implementation

- mechanisms required for activating or instantiating the objects

- mechanisms for invoking operations and for registering with event announcements

Usually, metaobjects are initialized by a model specified in TIL, but it is possible to manipulate them at runtime with framework services. The base level objects are directly connected with their metaobjects. Every action (like instantiation, operation invocation or connection) is controlled by the related metaobject. When considering an operation invocation, the metaobject intercepts the request, selects the appropriated communication mechanism, deals with parameter conversation and finally invokes the real operation implementation. The invocation requires an additional request to the meta level, if the component represents a composition of other components.

The interception is carried out by the proxy between the component layer and the bridging layer. For that purpose every proxy contains a reference to the related metaobject and forwards the requests to this. Figure 3 illustrates the message flow resulting from the interaction between base and meta levels.

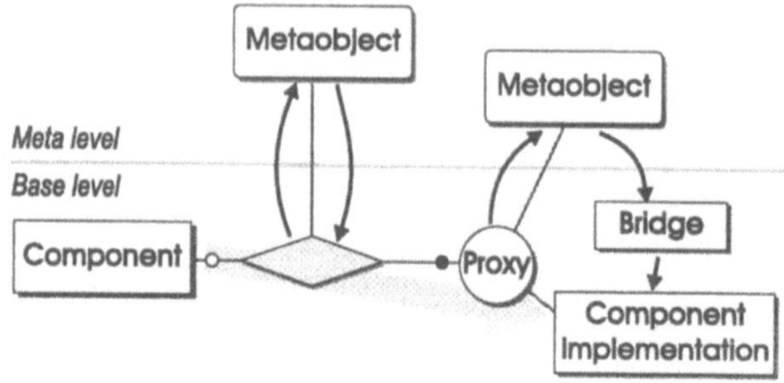

Figure 3: Message flow in an interactor

The use of interactors and metaobjects leads to an increased communication overhead and to performance loss. So if two components do not require any interface adaptation (the case of simple links), they can be directly connected. The communication takes place through component–owned mechanisms without intervention of framework services. The framework is responsible only for instantiating and interconnecting these components.

As a part of a complete tool environment the framework provides the services required for the control integration. The environment has to implement the services for managing the tool data. The activation of the tools and the coordination of their activities is managed by the framework services. Furthermore, the use of the framework enables the implementation of process management and user interface services without consideration of special mechanisms required for tool activation or communication.

4 Related Work

The work presented in this paper is a synthesis of results from various research areas, particularly software composition, coordination and tool integration.

The explicit representation of the interaction and coordination aspect of a software system is the subject of several recent contributions. Approaches like *formal connectors* [7], *synchronizers* [8] or *contracts* [9] introduce special abstractions for decoupling the interaction part from the component implementation. Our concept of interactors was inspired by these ideas.

Darwin [10] is a language for constructing distributed programs from hierarchically structured specifications of a set of component instances and their interconnections. Components are viewed in terms of both the services they provide to components and the services they require to interact with others. Furthermore, components can be composed of several already defined component instances. The *Darwin* language does not interpret service types, these are only used by the system environment. Bindings are allowed only between compatible service types. The semantics of these bindings are predefined as the association of a service required by one component with a service provided by another one in form of a method call.

Olan [11] extends the *Darwin* approach with the notion of connectors. Connectors mediate the interaction between components. They define interaction rules in terms of the required interfaces, the protocols used for communication and a set of constraints. *Olan* provides several predefined connector types, but in the current version the configuration language does not support user–defined connectors. The runtime environment of *Olan* consists of a component–based virtual machine on top of an object request broker. Besides supporting the composition of components and connectors *Olan* provides services for application management. There is no information available on the integration of existing components and therefore on the suitability for tool environments.

The problem of interoperability between components with incompatible interfaces is discussed in [12]. This approach is based on an *Interface Adaption Language (IAL)* for describing the mapping between data types and object interfaces. At runtime the object mapping is carried out by an *object mapper* component, which generates so called "inter–objects" for representing remote servers automatically.

Apart from approaches addressing the composition and configuration of software systems, much work has been done in the area of tool integration and integrated environments. A comprehensive classification of existing CASE technology is presented in [13]. This classification considers production–process, metaprocess and enabling technologies and identifies three categories of CASE products: tools, workbenches and environments.

An important contribution to the area of integrated environments was the ECMA reference model [14]. This model defines a framework for constructing software–engineering environments. Control integration in this framework is based on a central message server, which was first introduced with the *Field* environment [15]. In *Field* tools communicate by sending and receiving messages via the message server. A tool sends a message to the server to announce specific events.Other tools can register with the server to be notified of events announced. With the notification these tools can process the corresponding service. However, the tools need to support interfaces and interaction protocols prescribed by the environment to be integrable. The integration of such tools, that do not support these interfaces, requires special adaptations.

The *ToolBus* architecture [16] is an approach for tool integration based on the separation of coordination and computation. The interactions between tools are described by so called T–scripts containing sequences of communication and control primitives. Tools can communicate solely through the ToolBus. Inside the bus two communication mechanisms are available: first the synchronous message passing between two tools and second the asynchronous sending of notifications (called "notes") to a group of interested tools. Existing tools have to be encapsulated by adapters, which are responsible for data transformation and communication protocol adjustment.

5 Conclusion

Integrated applications demand flexibility and openness of software environments. Standard applications with a fixed set of tools cannot support different development processes, enterprise–specific requirements, or the fast introduction of newest technologies in an adequate and cost–effective way. The request for the development of customized applications by interconnecting prefabricated elements seems to be evident.

In this paper we have presented an approach of a framework for tool integration. Our approach is based on a model which enables the explicit coordination of tool activities by using interactors as semantic relations. The *Tool Interconnection Language (TIL)* provides a way for describing the structural and behavioural properties of these relations as well as their use for the configuration of the tool environment. A compiler generates the "glue" code required for the interface adaptation and the interaction control from a TIL specification. The runtime environment of the framework supports the instantiation and interconnection of the tool components. The mapping from the abstractions of the component model to the tool implementations and the integration of different communication platforms is supported by a reflective approach in conjunction with a bridging layer.

An initial release of the framework is implemented in Java [17]. This implementation is part of a project for developing configurable engineering environments. Tools like CAD modellers, word processors or calculation and management tools are treated as TiFRAME components. These components are implemented as CORBA objects (by "wrapping" existing applications) or Java applications. The control integration relationships of the components can be described completely in TIL.

Further work on the framework includes the development of mechanisms for process integration based on the notion of tasks associated with configurations as well as the support of specification activities by interactive tools.

References

[1] D. Schefström and G. van den Broek. *Tool Integration – Environments and Frameworks*. John Wiley & Sons, 1993.

[2] A.I. Wasserman. Tool Integration in Software Engineering Environments. In F. Long, editor, *Software Engineering Environments: Proc. Int. Workshop on Environments*, LNCS 467, pages 137–149. Springer Verlag, 1990.

[3] K.J. Sullivan. Mediators: Easing the design and evolution of integrated systems. Technical Report 94-08-01, Departement of Computer Science and Engineering, University of Washington, 1994.

[4] Object Management Group. The Common Object Request Broker: Architecture and Specification, Revision 2.0. OMG Document 97–02–25, July 1996.

[5] E. Gamma, R. Helm, R. Johnson, and J. Vlissides. *Design Patterns: Elements of Reusable Object–Oriented Software*. Addison–Wesley, Reading, Mass., 1995.

[6] P. Maes. *Meta–Level Architectures and Reflection*. Elsevier Science Publishers B.V., 1988.

[7] R. Allen and D. Garlan. Formal connectors. Technical Report CMU–CS–94–115, Carnegie Mellon University, Pittsburgh, 1994.

[8] S. Frølund and G. Agha. A Language Framework for Multi–Object Coordination. In O.M. Nierstrasz, editor, *ECOOP'93 – Object–Oriented Programming: 7th European Conference*, LNCS 707, pages 346–360. Springer Verlag, July 1993.

[9] I.M. Holland. Specifying reusable components using Contracts. In O. Lehrmann Madsen, editor, *Proc. of the European Conference of Object Oriented Programming (ECOOP'92)*, LNCS 615, pages 287–308. Springer Verlag, 1992.

[10] J. Magee, N. Dulay, S. Eisenbach, and J. Kramer. Specifying Distributed Software Architectures. In W. Schäfer and P. Botella, editors, *Proc. of the 5th European Software Engineering Conference (ESEC 95)*, LNCS 989, pages 137–153, Sitges, Spain, September 1995.

[11] L. Bellissard, S. Ben Atallah, A. Kerbrat, and M. Riveill. Component–based Programming and Application Management with Olan. In *Proc. of Workshop on Object–Based Parallel and Distributed Computation*, LNCS 1107. Springer Verlag, June 1995.

[12] D. Konstantas. Object Oriented Interoperability. In O.M. Nierstrasz, editor, *ECOOP'93 – Object–Oriented Programming: 7th European Conference*, LNCS 707, pages 80–102. Springer Verlag, July 1993.

[13] A. Fuggetta. A Classification of CASE Technology. *IEEE Computer*, pages 25–38, December 1993.

[14] European Computer Manufacturers Association. Reference Model for Frameworks of Software Engineering Environments. Technical Report ECMA TR/55 (3rd edition), June 1993.

[15] S. Reiss. Connecting tools using message passing in the Field environment. *IEEE Software*, 7(4):57–66, July 1990.

[16] J.A. Bergstra and P. Klint. The ToolBus Coordination Architecture. In P. Ciancarini and C. Hankin, editors, *Coordination Languages and Models*, LNCS 1061, pages 75–88. Springer Verlag, 1996.

[17] K. Arnold and J. Gosling. *The Java Programming Language*. Addison-Wesley, Reading, Mass., 1996.

A Refined Meta-Model Approach to Education for the Transition to Object Technology

Doroshenko, Eugene Eric
Department of Information Systems, University of Tasmania
Launceston, Australia

email: Eugene.Doroshenko@infosys.utas.edu.au

Abstract

This paper presents a refined meta-model approach to classification of software methodologies for training and technology transition. Meta-model concepts, along with recommendations for formation of a meta-model architecture are introduced. Some results of application and are given, along with preliminary assessments by other researchers. Although the approach assists education, automation is still required.

Introduction

Part of the transition to object technology is educating people in a different software methodology, namely the object-oriented methodology. Classification acts as a foundation for communication in biology, geology, and linguistics, and supports knowledge acquisition of a new subject [1]. In particular, the wide application of EBNF [2][3] suggests that classification serves similar purposes in software methodologies, some examples are programming languages [4], specification and design languages [5][6], and object technology standards [7]. Thus, expansion on the role of classification is chosen for education in software methodologies with an emphasis on object technology.

An educator could form their own classification, but this may take considerable time with classification considered a difficult process [8]. However, there are many frameworks and models (FMs) that classify software methodologies for applications, including research surveying [9], technology transfer [10], and software process improvement [11], with some of them automated [10][12][13]. These FMs can provide the necessary features in a classification scheme, reduce time spent in classification formation, and minimise "reinventing the wheel". A difficulty encountered with this approach is that the integration process itself can become unmanageable. Even if integration of features is achieved the classification scheme would be static, and any attempts to enhance the classification using other contributions, expand it for training in post-OO methodologies, or tailer it for teaching preferences and needs would be ad hoc at best. Hence, a classification scheme should expand to integrate new features, in addition to containing features already present in current FMs. To do this, a common thread needs to be identified among FMs, and one common thread is the use of meta-modelling [14][15][16][17][13][18][19][20]. However, meta-modelling appears immature and needs refinement to support classification of software methodologies and extension of the classification scheme.

Therefore, meta-modelling is refined by introducing a number of meta-model concepts along with recommendations for key features in a meta-model architecture. Included in the recommendations is how a meta-model architecture supports extension to a classification scheme. The concepts and recommendations are a guide to use of meta-modelling for classification of software methodologies. An indication of how the meta-model architecture supports classification of software methodologies is given using an example component and meta-model concepts. The example component is used to illustrate some issues in extension of a classification scheme. The same component is used to show how meta-model concepts support education in software methodologies. Some results of applying the classification, along with further requirements for application conclude the paper. The approach did assist structuring of training materials, and mediate communication between educator and student, but automation is required to reduce the problems of classification and further application. Feature integration and extension is not described at great length, as the primary focus is application of a meta-model based classification for education in software methodologies.

Meta-Model Concepts

The concept of meta-modelling rarely extends beyond the following description, "A meta-model is a model that describes models". Steele and Han [19], based on Nissen et al [13], distinguish between models (m0) that describe a particular application (Eg A Warehouse class icon), meta-models (m1) that describe the models used to build particular application models (Eg A class icon that describes class icons including a warehouse class icon), and meta-meta models (m2) that describe meta-models used to build software methodologies (Eg Icon model that describes particular icons including a class icon). This discrimination extends the concept of meta-modelling into multiple levels and provides a good foundation for meta-model instances, but the descriptions given introduce only one new concept into meta-modelling and a modified description of meta-models. The new concept being the meta-model level, the modified description being "a meta-model is a model that describes models, which includes meta-models". To refine meta-modelling, some meta-model concepts for specifying a meta-model architecture are introduced by detailing the links between meta-model levels and enumerating the qualities of meta-models.

A meta-model architecture has a number of components called meta-level components (MLCs). For example, the method process LGS (See below) is an example MLC. A meta-level component is at a given meta-level (MetLn or mn; n is an integer) and has some kind of interpretation or meaning in a model based on the level (IMea). For example, the method process LGS is at MetL2, and its interpretation is the description given under the heading "An Example MLC: the Method Process LGS". An MLC is a type with instances of itself at its own level, which become types or MLCs at the next lower meta-level. For example, at meta-level 2, the method process LGS has instances such as the micro development process in Figure 3. At meta-level 1 the micro development process becomes a MetL1 MLC as part of a software methodology. The sum of MLCs at a given MetLn constitute a n*meta model or mn model. For example, the method process LGS and CASE tool navigation LGS are part of a meta-meta model or m2 model (Figure 1). An MLC's meaning is enhanced if it has one or more definition methods that systematically describe it to some degree (DefM), which are MLCs at one metal-level higher than itself. For example, the method process LGS is defined using the graphic definition language (Figure 1). If there are a number of MLCs at a given MetLn, then an MLC may have a definition location in a meta-model (DefL) that is an MLC one meta-level higher than itself. For example, the definition of the method process LGS is located in the language-graphic component (Figure 1). Thus, the DefM and DefL attributes detail the MetLn of the MLC by counting the DefL or DefM links from lower level MLCs to higher level MLCs. An MLC may describe one or more MLCs at one meta-level lower than itself, the lowest being MetL1 (MLCDesc), this is a reverse of DefL and DefM. MetL1 MLCs describe models of some kind, but not MLCs.

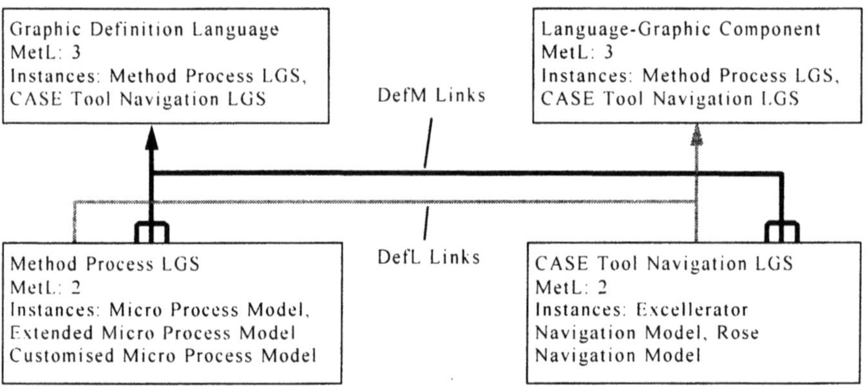

Figure 1 Examples of MLCs

At each meta-level there are relationships or dependencies that link MLCs together (MLCDep). Dependency types include prerequisite or existence dependency (an MLC instance depends on another MLC instance before defining itself), aggregate dependency (An MLC instance is part of or composed of other MLC instances), and classification dependency (One MLC instance is a more specific kind of another MLC instance). The dependencies are similar to the three basic associations in object-oriented modelling, namely Using or Communication, Aggregation, and Inheritance respectively. The MetLn, DefM, DefL and IMea attributes of an MLC are a foundation for establishing and enhancing MLCDep between MLCs at the same meta-level (MetLn) and MLCDesc between MLCs at adjacent meta-levels. MLCDep and IMea qualities are the most flexible and least specific part of a meta-model architecture. For applying meta-model concepts to classification of software methodologies a meta-model architecture should

- have at least three meta-levels to provide a means of model expansion (MetL1 MLCs are classifications of different software methodologies. MetL2 MLCs classify different parts of software methodologies. MetL3 MLCs classify MetL2

MLCs. To support expansion of the classification scheme, new software methodologies are added by adding new MetL1 MLCs, and the architecture expands by adding new MetL2 MLCs defined with the MetL3 MLCs.),

- have some means of expressing MetL2 MLCs graphically and textually to make use of their complimentary advantages (This requires at least two MetL3 MLCs as DefMs. Some approaches to graphic classification are NDL and GOPRR [21][16], and text classification are TDL and EBNF [21][2][3][7].),
- have some means of classifying vocabulary (The model components in Doroshenko [22] used as meta-level 2 MLCs is one approach.), and
- make use of features in seven key sources [9][14][21][13][19][20][22].

An Example MLC: the Method Process LGS

Table 1 summarises contributions to the method process Language Graphic Specification (LGS). The method process LGS models the process of creating and refining software models. Booch (Figure 6-1, p 235) has an informal illustration of a process for developing models, called the micro development process [8]. Bosman, without knowledge of the method process diagram, uses the illustration of Booch to refine the process for testing [23][24]. This is generalised by Doroshenko, where the method process for developing any model (object model, E-R model, etc) is described using a method process diagram method [25][21]. Related approaches to describing the process also exist [9][19][20], but each one lacks certain features or has a different modelling approach.

Table 1: Contributions the Method Process LGS

Source	Location	Activity Types	Iteration	Steps	Phases/ Subphases	Techniques
[8]	229 - 248	Identify, Refine	Yes	Yes	Yes/No	No
[25]	37 - 39	Identify. Refine	Yes	Yes	Yes/No	No
[21]	167 - 168	Identify, Refine, Evaluate	Yes	Yes	Yes/No	Yes
[26]	143 - 145	Identify, Refine	Yes	Yes	Yes/Yes	No
[27]	157 - 158	Identify. Refine	Yes	Yes	Yes/No	No
[9]	37 - 39	Identify, Placement, Specification, Optimisation	No	Yes	Yes/No	No
[19]	685 - 686	Identify, Refine	Yes	Yes	Yes/Yes	No
[20]	596 - 599		Yes	Yes	Yes/Yes	Yes

Table 1 shows variation in activity types. Some approaches use products as representations of all or part of a system model, such as an entity relationship diagram [25][21][19]. In contrast, others have a product (Functional data model) and a technique (Normalisation/ER Diagram), with normalisation as the working practice, and the ER Diagram as the representation practice [20]. The concept of technique is more atomic in Doroshenko [21] where a technique can exist to normalise an entity in a diagram to 2NF, compared to Vlasbolm et al [20] where a technique can refer to normalisation of an entire diagram. Steele and Han refer to a whole product being effected separate from activities [19], compared to Doroshenko who refers to a whole or part of a product being effected as part of activities [21]. This illustrates a typical problem faced in classification of software methodologies using FMs; a large number of features and different perspectives on a common theme. The meta-model architecture assists classification by providing a range of options for classification. For example, features can be included as part of a component, like activities. Features can be instances of a component, like Identify and Refine in <Term>. The common aspects are captured in the structure of MLCs, whereas the differences are captured by manipulating the instances of MLCs, in this case the method process LGS.

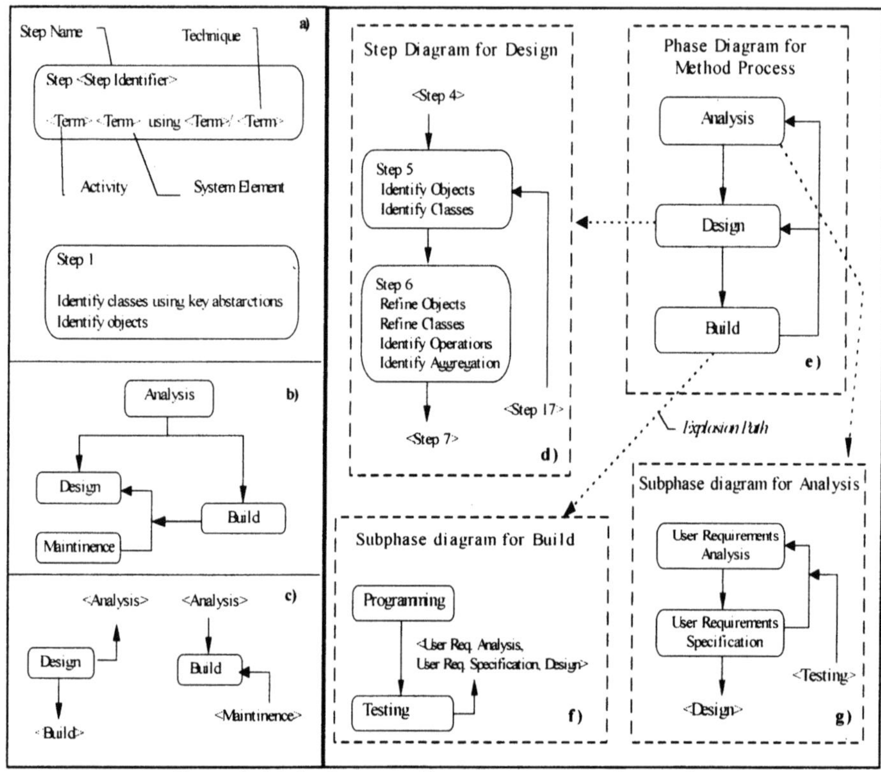

Figure 2 Method process diagram structure and examples

A method process has a number of phases that set some aim or purpose. A Phase is composed of a number of subphases, which set intermediate aims in the method process. A phase or subphase is attributed to one or more steps in the method process. Each step is uniquely identified. Each step has a limited number of steps from which it can proceed, this includes iteration using a previous step. The step order reflects the ordering of the phases and subphases. Each step has one or more activity options, which set atomic aims in the method process. Each activity has an activity type, refers to part of a product representing a system model effected, and may be associated with some technique that fulfils the expected result of the activity. Activity types include identify (Add some new part to a product), refine (Modify a product within the limits of some part), and evaluate (Assess the quality of a product). Some activities may not be classifiable, but are to significant to leave out. Figure 2 illustrates some examples.

Graphic specification of a method process (Method process model diagram) starts with a phase diagram which contains phases represented as rectangles enclosing the phase name (Figure 2e)), and arrows representing phase order and iteration (Figure 2b)). Each phase icon explodes to subphase diagram (Figure 2e) & g)), which is a phase diagram with words enclosed by "<" ">" signs (Figure 2c)), or a step diagram (Figure 2e) & d)) containing step icons, words enclosed by "<" ">" signs, and arrows representing step order and iteration like phase diagrams. In subphase diagrams words enclosed by "<" ">" represent phases that are part of another phase or subphase diagram, in step diagrams these represent steps that are part of another step diagram. Iteration and phase order in phase and subphase diagrams are resolved as step order and iteration in step diagrams based on the explosion path (Figure 2e) & d)). Step icons can show activities for a step (Figure 2a)), and options exist to show steps, activities, and subphases in a phase icon based on the explosion path.

The specification incorporates the work of Doroshenko [25][21], but handling the other approaches requires manipulation of activities appearing in step icons (Figure 2a)). Different activity types in Table 1 can appear as <Term> for the activity. To use the Vlasbolm [20] approach, <Term> for activity can model the activity, <Term> for element can model the product, and <Term> [/<Term>] for technique can model the working practice/representation practice. To use the Steele and Han [19] approach, start by using just <Term> for the activities, then follow with Identify, Refine or Evaluate in <Term> for the activity and the product in <Term> for the element.

Application

Three classification processes that populate the meta-model architecture prior to education are outlined with reference to inhouse training, outsource training and tertiary education. Classification processes, if done by a trainer or educator, assist his or her knowledge acquisition of software methodologies through the act of classification. These processes are method creation, method extension, and method customisation. A fourth process, method acquisition, is then applied to assist education of students.

Method creation is where method knowledge about software development is established and results in creation of vocabulary terms and MetL2 MLC instances that collectively represent knowledge of a method. For example, Figure 3a) illustrates a product of method creation using the method process LGS based on the micro development process [8]. Vocabulary includes attribute, object, and class. For inhouse training, only current method knowledge and required method knowledge are classified. For outsource training, the range of methods currently known about, and the range of methods required are classified based on customer demand and training resources. For tertiary education, the most common aspects of method knowledge are classified as a foundation for core teaching in the subject.

Method extension is where method knowledge is extended to enhance method application and results in addition of vocabulary terms, along with MLC instances that are modified from previous ones. For example, Figure 3b) illustrates a modified micro development process that extends the one in Figure 3a) using refinement of aggregation [28] and testing [23]. Additional vocabulary includes class test case and owns aggregation. For inhouse training, extensions are formed if enhanced knowledge in an area is required. For outsource training, extensions are formed to add training options based on new customer demands and training resources. For tertiary education, extensions are formed based on academic expertise of method knowledge.

Method customisation is where method knowledge is restricted to a subset of total method knowledge prior to method acquisition and results in a subset of vocabulary terms chosen from the ones present in the model, along with simplified MLC instances. For example, Figure 4a) illustrates a simplified micro development process that excludes aggregation refinements from the one in Figure 3b). Excluded vocabulary includes owns aggregation and has aggregation. For inhouse training, this is usually not an option, because in-house training is only concerned with required method knowledge, not method knowledge that might be required. For outsource training, method customisation is done based on particular customer requirements for method knowledge. For tertiary education, method customisation is done if small staff numbers require alternation in education of different aspects of method knowledge.

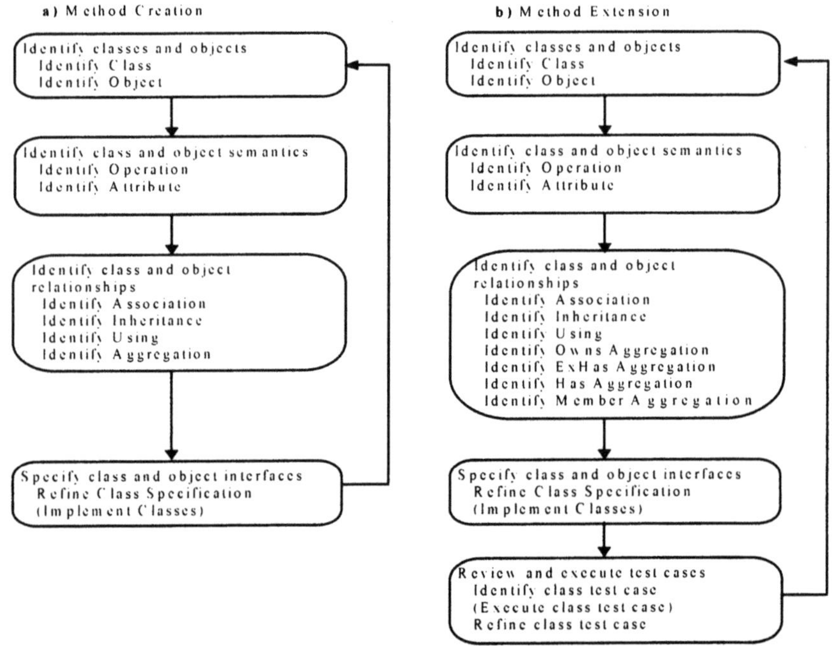

Figure 3 Extracts of Method process diagram instances (MetL2 MLC instances)

Method acquisition is where method knowledge imparted to a student. For example, acquisition about the micro development process with testing extensions in Figure 4a). Inhouse trainers, outsource trainers, and tertiary educators use the same process for method acquisition. There are three basic levels for method acquisition processes.

The meta-level one process is where instances of MetL2 MLCs are used for educating students. The meta-level two process is where students interpret and use MetL2 MLCs. The meta-level three process is where students create and modify MetL2 MLCs. As students operate at higher levels, educators act more like mentors, and less like procedural trainers.

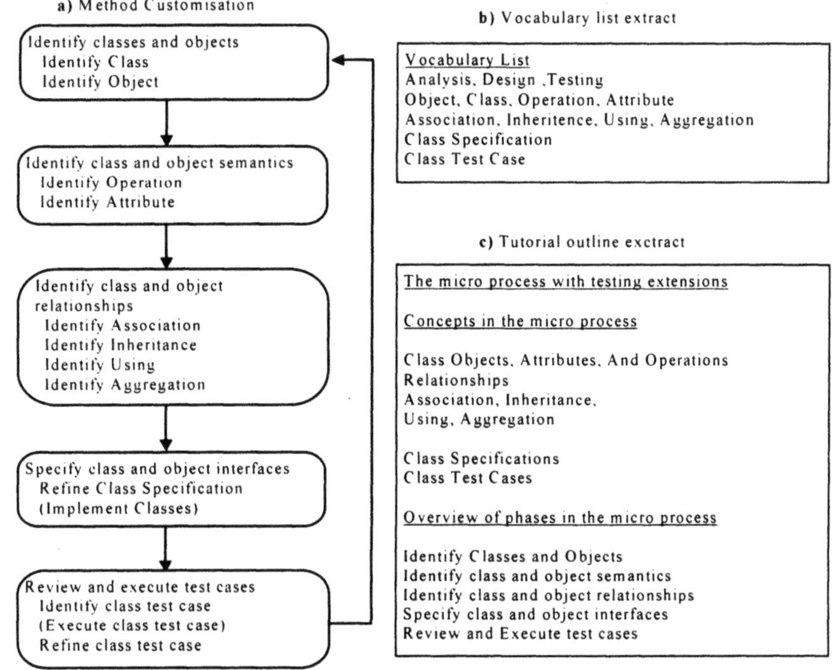

Figure 4 Method Process Classification and Teaching Products

The Meta-Level One Process

At meta-level 1, instances of MetL2 MLCs can assist structuring of training materials and act as illustrative tools for presentations. For example, Figure 4a) is used to illustrate the micro development process and how it is enhanced for object-oriented testing. Two example teaching products derived from Figure 4a) are a vocabulary list (Figure 4b)) and a tutorial outline (Figure 4c)). Lowry and Doroshenko [29] illustrate a more comprehensive example.

The products derived from MLCs were most useful, both in preparation and presentation. However, the specification instances themselves gained mixed reaction. Sometimes the students cannot see the purpose of such a specification. For example, when teaching a methodology with CASE tools, most students were more focused on how to use the tool, rather than the method process for application. Some students referred to some MLCs when inquiring about aspects of a method (Eg Figure 4a)). In this way, the MLCs acted as focal points for communication between student and educator.

The Meta-Level Two Process

At meta-level 2 (2a)), students are educated on what MetL2 MLCs classify for self education purposes, similar to learning about EBNF and applying it to learning the syntax of a new programming language. For example, the description about the method process LGS is imparted to the student for self-education about the enhanced micro development process in Figure 4**a)**.

Although some students were interested in some specifications, such as the CASE tool navigation LGS, most had little motivation to know about the classifications. The students who were interested were among the brightest and exhibited intellectual curiosity in the subject. Time constraints for teaching a subject also limited the assessment of this process.

A second application (meta-level 2b)) is where students are educated on how to classify method knowledge based on MetL2 MLCs. Students from their own MetL2 MLC instances based on literature for some software methodology. For example, formation of method process model diagrams using the method process LGS. In this way students learn about aspects of a software methodology the same way an educator does when using the classification processes described earlier.

This kind of approach is currently restricted to honours and research students, resulting in two honours theses (1st class) and one paper so far [30][25][29]. The method appears successful for the students, and provides a foundation for teaching products, but how it works for professionals or undergraduates is unknown.

The Meta-Level Three Process

At meta-level 3 (3a)), educators form new MetL2 MLCs to enhance application of the classification scheme. For example, a CASE tool navigation LGS illustrates how to navigate models represented in a CASE tool. It is defined using the graphic definition language and defined in the language-graphic component (Figure 1).

This process was used to some effect. For example, the CASE tool navigation LGS was defined in response to student demand for knowledge about using CASE tools. After use of the CASE tool navigation LGS instance, the method process LGS instance became more relevant as students were no longer overwhelmed by the technology but wanted to know what to do with it. The difficulty in forming specifications with modest automation did hamper such efforts, although the potential to create useful classifications was evident.

A second application (meta-level 3b)) is where students form their own MetL2 MLCs for classifying software methodologies. This has not been applied to date.

Conclusion

An attempt is made to explain how meta-model concepts can contribute to technology transition via training and education, with an emphasis on object technology. This is done by using meta-model concepts to form a meta-model architecture that classifies software methodologies. Classification of software methodologies educate the educator, while the classification scheme acts as a communication vehicle and a foundation for teaching materials. Some unresolved issues need consideration.

The work has been informally presented to some trainers and educators in software methodologies. They were interested in the approach, particularly its long term view about training in software methodologies (Post-OO), but had difficulty grasping the subject, and suggested that further research should be centred on automation of the meta-model architecture. A few researchers suggested that classification formation is predominantly the work of academics and researchers. This suggests that undergraduate students and professional practitioners go no further than meta-level 2a), while processes at meta-level 2b) and above are the domain of research students, academics, and researchers. However, tailoring of the personal software process indicates that practitioners should operate at meta-level 2b) [31]. The meta-model concepts and architecture provide some cohesion and guidance. In particular, use of MLCs as DefMs assists the initial stages of classification. Nonetheless, classification is still a labour intensive activity and dependent on the skill of the classifier. Education for Post-OO software methodologies needs consideration, with two candidates being expert systems [32][33], and neural networks [34]. Given that a prototype of the model is applied to three different software methodology paradigms [25][30], use of meta-model concepts for training in post-OO software methodologies is worthy of consideration.

References

1. Kleiser. G. How To Build Metal Power. Funk & Wagnalls Co New York. 1917

2. Backus. J. W. The syntax and semantics of the proposed international algebraic language of the Zurich ACM-GAMM Conference. International Conference on Information Processing. Unesco. 1959; 125 - 132

3. Naur. P. Revised report on the algorithmic language Algol. Communications of the ACM 1963: 6:1-17

4. Sethi. R. Programming Languages: Concepts and Constructs. Addison-Wesley Reading. MA. 1989

5. De Champeaux. D.. Lea. D.. et al. Object-Oriented Systems Development. Addison-Wesley Reading Mass.. 1993

6. Firesmith. D. G. Object-oriented Requirements Analysis and Logical Design. Wiley & Sons New York. 1993

7. OMG The Common Object Request Broker: Architecture and Specification. Revision 2.0. Object Management Group Farimingham. MA. 1995

8. Booch. G. Object-Oriented Analysis and Design with Applications. Benjamin/Cummings Redwood City. 1994

9. Monarchi. D. E.. Puhr. G. I. A Research Typology for Object-Oriented Analysis and Design. Communications of the ACM 1992; 35:35-47

10. Korson. T. D., Vaishnavi. V. K. Managing Emerging Software Technologies: A Technology Transfer Framework. Communications of the ACM 1992; 35:101 - 111

11. Curtis. B.. Kellner. M. I.. et al. Process Modelling. Communications of the ACM 1992; 35:75 - 90

12. Krasner. H.. Terrel. J.. et al. Lessons Learned from a Software Process Modelling System. Communications of the ACM 1992: 35:91-100

13. Nissen. H. W.. Jeusfeld. M. A.. et al. Managing Multiple Requirements Perspectives with Metamodels. IEEE Software 1996; March:37 - 47

14. Beringer. D. Limits of Seamlessness in Object-oriented Software Development. TOOLS Europe. Prentice-Hall. 1994; 1 - 11

15. Freeman. M. J.. Layzell. P. J. A meta-model of information systems to support reverse engineering. Information and Software Technology 1994: 36:283 - 294

16. Kelley. S. A matrix editor for a metaCASE environment. Information and Software Technology 1994: 36:361 - 371

17. Loomis. M.. Odell. J. Object Analysis & Design Facility RFP-1. Object Management Group Farmingham USA, 1996

18. Steele. P. M.. Zaslavsky, A. B. CASE Tool support for Integration of System Modelling Techniques. Australasian Conference on Information Systems. 1993: 521 - 534

19. Steele. P. M.. Han. J. A Layered Architecture for Describing Information Systems Development Methodologies. Australasian Conference on Information Systems. Australian Computer Society. 1996: 2:677-688

20. Vlasbolm. G.. Rijsenbrij. D.. et al. Flexibalization of the methodology of system development. Information and Software Technology 1995: 37:595 - 607

21. Doroshenko. E. E. Toward a language-graphic model for CASE tool construction: helping the corner store OT vendor. Australasian Conference on Information Systems. Australian Computer Society Inc. 1996: 1:161 - 172

22. Doroshenko. E. E. A Model for Research Surveying in Software Methodologies. Australasian Conference on Information Systems. 1997:

23. Bosman. O. Testing and Iterative Development. 13th International Conference and Exposition on Testing Computer Software. USPDI, 1996: 1-10

24. Bosman. O. Tetsing object-oriented software: adopting the Booch process. Object World 1996. Object World. 1996: 2:551-568

25. Doroshenko. E. E. Common Concepts in Object-oriented Methodologies. Applied computing and Mathematics. University of Tasmania. 1994

26. Henderson-Sellers. B.. Edwards. J. M. The Object-Oriented Systems Life Cycle. Communications of the ACM 1990: 33:142-159

27. Iivari. J. Object-orientation as structural. functional and behavioural modelling: a comparison of six methods for object-oriented analysis. Information and Software Technology 1995: 37:155-163 .

28. Maciaszek. L. A.. De Troyer. O. M. F.. et al. Generalization versus Aggregation in Object Application Development - the "AD-HOC" Approach. Australasian Conference on Information Systems. Australian Computer Society Inc. 1996: 2:431 - 442

29. Lowry. G. R.. Doroshenko. E. E. Object-orientation in Software Engineering Education. International Conference on Software Engineering: Education & Practice. IEEE Computer Society Press. 1996: 336 - 343

30. Roper. N. Common Concepts in Structured Process Methodologies. Applied Computing & Mathematics. University of Tasmania. 1995

31. Humphrey. W. S. A Discipline for Software Engineering. Addison-Wesley Reading MA. 1995

32. Guimaraes. T.. Yoon. Y. An Exploratory Assessment of the Use and Benefits of ESDLC in Practice. Information resources management journal 1996: 9:15

33. Terplan. K. Communication Networks Management. PTR Prentice-Hall Englewood Cliffs New Jersey, 1992

34. Shihab. K. I. Learning and Reasoning by Analogy and their Application to Computer Performance Evaluation. International Conference on Data and Knowledge Systems for Manufacturing & Engineering. Chinese University of Hong Kong. 1994: 651 - 657

Version-Based Index Management in an Object Database System to support Software Engineering Applications*

Wiebke Reimer

Dep. of Mathematics and Computer Science, University of Paderborn

D-33095 Paderborn

Abstract

For an object database system in order to provide object versioning, the impact of the version model on the index management must be studied, since both *indexed collections* and *objects in an indexed collection* can be versioned. Based on a version model suitable for software engineering applications, we investigate the operations to be provided by the index management, and how they can be implemented in an efficient way.

1   Introduction

Software engineering environments (SEEs) are one out of many applications for which object database systems (ODBS) have shown to be most appropriate concerning data modeling capabilities and performance characteristics. The requirements that SEE implementations impose on ODBSs have been investigated extensively in [1, 2, 3], for instance. Among other things, SEEs require – as do other ODBS applications – that the ODBS should provide versioning of objects. A distinguishing feature of SEEs, however, is the specific version model they demand. Given a version model required for SEEs, we investigate in this paper its consequences for the implementation of various kinds of indexes to be provided by an ODBS's index management.

There are two possibilities for implementing version-based indexes: Two-dimensional B^+-trees (2D-B^+-trees) with shared index nodes, or One-dimensional B^+-trees (1D-B^+-trees) with multi-version key values in their leaves. In general, the latter implementation is less efficient. We show that:

(A)   indexes on versioned collections cannot be implemented with 2D-B^+-trees, which is due to the identity-oriented data model of ODBSs;

(B)   indexes on collections which contain versioned objects cannot be implemented with 2D-B^+-trees either, which is due to a property of the underlying version model, namely that we allow modifications of objects in *non-leaf* versions of the version history;

---

*This work was partly done while the author visited O_2 Technology, Versailles, France. That stay was partially funded by the Gottlieb Daimler- und Karl Benz-Stiftung, Ladenburg, Germany under Grant 2.93.45.

(C) versioned collections (in contrast to *indexes* on versioned collections) can be implemented with 2D-B$^+$-trees.

Section 2 first sketches how SEEs employ ODBSs, in order to provide a basic understanding of the domain we consider here. It then presents the version and index model. Section 3 and Section 4 deal with case *(A)* and *(B)* respectively. The combination of both, an index on a *versioned* collection with *versioned* objects, is not dealt with separately since it is a straightforward combination of *(A)* and *(B)*. Case *(C)* is dealt with in Section 5. Section 6 provides a short summary and briefly discusses further conditions to be taken into account when extending a pre-existing database system with version-based index management.

2   Version and Index Model

2.1   SEEs as ODBS applications

A tightly integrated SEE is a collection of tools supporting document construction during the various phases of the software production process. Its major characteristic is the support of an incremental and intertwined production and maintenance process. In order to provide this support, an SEE must maintain fine-grained intra- and inter-document dependencies. The appropriate internal data structure to store documents and maintain these dependencies is an abstract syntax graph (ASG) [4]. ASG nodes represent syntactic increments of a document. They are connected by two kinds of (labeled) directed edges: *syntactic* edges indicating son increments of a complex increment, and *non-syntactic* edges representing context-sensitive information. Edges of the latter kind enable efficient consistency checking and change propagation by tools operating on documents. Maintaining fine-grained dependencies also allows for sophisticated version and configuration management, including change control and propagation, automatic configuration, merging on a semantic level, etc. [5]

For maintenance of ASGs, object database systems (ODBS) have shown to be most appropriate concerning data modeling capabilities and performance characteristics [2, 3]. In an ODBS, ASG nodes are implemented as complex objects. In case of a *non-terminal* ASG node, the object's attributes define the node's syntactic and non-syntactic edges. In case of a *terminal* ASG node, they define the node's value and non-syntactic edges. Versioning software documents combined with maintaining fine-grained dependencies as sketched above requires that versions of ASGs be maintained in the database.

Speeding up associative search by employing indexes is crucial for SEEs. For instance, consider a large scale software system comprising thousands of KLOC being developed in an SEE. The SEE might maintain a set containing all procedures in order to enable searching for procedures by name. Indexing the set of procedures accordingly speeds up these queries. Similarly, guaranteeing project-wide uniqueness of module names requires the definition of a unique index on the collection of all modules in the system.

2.2 Version Model

This section introduces the version model required from an ODBS in order to implement the functionality of an SEE. See [1] for details on the rationales and for an implementation which exploits versioning in the described way.

Version unit: The *version unit* (VU) is the entity to which operations such as version derivation, version selection etc. apply. We require that an arbitrary collection of objects might constitute a VU. Operations on the VU do then implicitly apply to its constituents.

This enables an SEE to version entire documents: For each document, a separate VU is created. All objects representing one document in the database, i.e. all objects that implement increments which are reachable from the document's root increment via syntactic edges, are versioned in the same VU.

Generic references: We require that object references be generic instead of version-specific. That is, an "entire" object being versioned, a so-called *multi-version object* (MVO), has an identity, but its versions do not. Any application accessing the database does so within the context of a selected version for each VU. So, whenever a MVO is referenced, the database system is in charge of directing access to the MVO's currently selected version.

Operations: We need the "usual" operations on VUs such as *creation* of an initial version of a VU; *deleting, freezing* and *selecting* a version; *navigation* in the version derivation graph etc. A new version can be *derived* from an arbitrary version of the VU. Some authors call this "full persistence" of data, as compared to "partial persistence" where a version can only be derived from the most recently created one, which leads to a linear version history. Note that in contrast to many other application areas, versioning in engineering applications is not implicit: Modifying a versioned object does not automatically create a new version, but derivation is an operation explicitly called by the user.[1]

Updates in Non-leaf Versions: Additionally, we need functionality which is quite specific to SEEs as database application: Even when a *non-leaf version* of a VU is selected, i.e. a version from which others have already been derived, objects versioned in that VU can be modified. Modifying an object in a non-leaf version has no impact on any of its successor versions. This is an essential difference between our version model and any other we know of. Apart from O_2 [6] (the version management of which was specifically designed for supporting SEEs) there is no ODBS providing this feature [7].

Note that this feature is to be provided by the *ODBS* for versioning *objects*, but not by an *SEE* for versioning *documents*. In SEEs, we follow the obvious approach that a document must be frozen before one can derive a new version from it, and that frozen documents cannot be modified, i.e. they are stable. On the database level this implies that, given an object representing an ASG node within a stable document, attributes which implement the node's *syntactic* edges cannot be modified. But this does not hold for attributes which implement *non-syntactic* edges, i.e. which represent inter-document dependencies:

---

[1] As mentioned earlier, SEEs require a merge operation, too. We may neglect it here, however, since it does not impose additional problems regarding version-based index management.

In order to efficiently provide the mentioned tool functionality, these dependencies are implemented as bidirectional links. Therefore the corresponding attributes may need to be modified even in non-leaf versions, in order to delete or establish relationships to other (non-stable) documents.

2.3 Requirements on Version-Based Index Management

The most common data structure for implementing indexes is the B^+-tree [8]. The operations to be provided by an index in an ODBS are given below. Recall that in the object oriented data model a key value does not necessarily identify an object, as do unique keys in a relational database system.

- *exact_match(kval)* returns the set of objects in the indexed collection that have key *kval*.
- *range_query(kmin, kmax)* returns the set of objects with a key value not larger than *kmax* and not smaller than *kmin*. Due to space restictions, we neglect *range_query* in the sequel. Its implementation is based on an *exact_match(kmin)* in a straightforward manner.
- *insert(kval, oid)* and *delete(kval, oid)* are issued when an object *oid* with key value *kval* is inserted into or deleted from the indexed collection.
- *change_key(old, new, oid)* is issued when the key value *old* of the collection element *oid* is set to *new*. This operation is equivalent to the sequence *delete(old, oid); insert(new, oid)*.

When adapting an ODBS's index management to the version model introduced above we have to consider two cases each of which leads to the definition of a version-based index data structure given hereafter: *(A)* The indexed collection is versioned, and *(B)* the elements in an indexed collection are versioned. How to implement these indexes discussed in Section 3 and 4 respectively.

(A) A M̲ulti-V̲ersion I̲ndex

- $exact\_match^{MVI}(v_{sel}, kval)$ returns the set of objects which have key *kval* and which are contained in version v_{sel} of the indexed collection.
- $derive^{MVI}(v_{sel}, v_{new})$ is issued upon derivation of a collection version v_{new} which is successor of v_{sel}.
- $insert^{MVI}(v_{sel}, kval, oid)$ and $delete^{MVI}(v_{sel}, kval, oid)$ are issued when an object *oid* with key value *kval* is inserted into or deleted from version v_{sel} of the indexed collection.
- $change\_key^{MVI}(old, new, oid)$ is issued when the key value *old* of object *oid* is set to *new*.

Note that $change\_key^{MVI}$ is performed in the course of an operation on a collection *element*, whereas the other index operations are performed in the course of operations on the *collection*. Therefore, all operations except for $change\_key^{MVI}$ are related to a particular collection version v_{sel}. Also, $change\_key^{MVI}$ is not, as in the non-versioned case, equivalent to a sequence of $insert^{MVI}$ and $delete^{MVI}$.

(B) An I̲ndex which supports V̲ersioned E̲lements

Unlike in *(A)*, we need to supply VU identifiers as parameters since the collection elements may be versioned in different VUs.

- *exact_match*[IVE] *({(vu_j, v_{j_i}) | j=1..m}, kval).* Here m is the number of version units, and v_{j_i} is the selected version of version unit vu_j. The operation returns the set of collection elements carrying key *kval* in their respective selected version.

- *derive*[IVE] *(vu, v, v_{new})* is issued upon derivation of a successor v_{new} from version v in VU *vu*.

- *insert*[IVE]*(oid, vu, {(v_i, kval_i) | i=1..n})* and *delete*[IVE]*(oid, vu, {(v_i, kval_i) | i=1..n}))* are issued when *oid*, versioned in *vu*, is inserted into resp. deleted from the indexed collection. n is the number of versions of *vu*. For each version v_i of *vu*, *oid*'s key value in v_i is given in *kval_i*.

- *change_key*[IVE] *(old, new, oid, vu, v)* is issued when *oid*'s key value in version v is changed from *old* to *new*. *vu* is the version unit to which *oid* belongs.

3 Multi-Version Indexes

For Multi-Version Index implementation it is essential that mechanisms be used which maintain different versions of a tree in an efficient way. Instead of duplicating entire trees for each version, common parts of different versions should be shared. This may be inappropriate, however, if versions differ "too much". Section 3.1 presents two ways of implementing versioned B^+-trees. In Section 3.2 we investigate their appropriateness for Multi-Version Indexes.

3.1 Related Work

The problem of granting a linked data structure the capability of remembering its state in different versions has been studied in the field of computational geometry for more than 15 years, initially by [9]. More recently, multi-version access structures for operations on external storage have been investigated for Spatial Databases. Since there, versioning is employed for keeping track of the change over time of spatial data only ("partial persistence"), we cannot employ the various versioned access structures proposed for Spatial Databases.

With "full persistence", there are mainly two ways of maintaining versions of a B^+-tree, described in more detail in Sections 3.1.1 and 3.1.2:

2D-B^+-trees: A graph structure is constructed that incorporates distinct, but partly shared B^+-tree versions. Father-son-relationships between nodes are expressed in relation with versions. Traversal is guided in context with the version selected when accessing the collection. These methods guarantee a tree height determined only by the number of objects contained in the version in which the index is being accessed.

1D-B^+-trees with multi-version key values: A single, standard B^+-tree is built containing all keys present in at least one version of the indexed collection. The leaf nodes contain additional information that allow to determine the "visibility" of a key value in a given version. Here, the costs for accessing the index in a particular version are determined by the total number of keys in all versions.

3.1.1 2D-B$^+$-trees

As an example for a 2D-B$^+$-tree supporting non-linear versioning we describe the "Fat Node Method" [10] which traces back to the work on versions of linked data structures in [11].

The 2D-B$^+$-tree consists of two kinds of nodes: *index nodes* and *version nodes*. Index nodes are similar to nodes in standard B$^+$-trees: They contain a sequence of key records each consisting of a key value together with a reference to a version node or – in case of a leaf node – an object identifier. An index node is preceded by a *version node* which guides access to different index nodes depending on the selected version. A version node thus encapsulates the changes made to an index node's initial version. An index node has exactly one incoming pointer and is at least half-full. Pointers in different (inner) index nodes may indicate the same version node, thereby allowing for sharing subtrees. (To be precise, the data structure is no longer a tree but a graph.) An additional data structure associates a root version node to each version of the indexed collection.

The number of nodes accessed and/or modified for lookup and updates in a particular version depends on the number of elements in that version only. In particular, the path length to any leaf node reachable in that version is the same – as is the case in standard B$^+$-trees. Storage space may be as high as $\theta(n_v)$, where n_v is the number of versions in the VU. [2]

Below we briefly sketch the implementation of version-based index operations. For details, see [10]. Fig. 1 gives an example.

- $exact\_match^{\mathrm{MVI}}(v_{sel}, kval)$:
  During traversal, we alternately encounter index and version nodes. When accessing a version node V, the "youngest" predecessor version of v_{sel} among all versions listed in V is determined: $v_{pred}:=youngest\_pred(V, v_{sel})$. Traversal continues at the index node $I:=idx\_node(V, v_{pred})$ associated with v_{pred}. Searching a key value $kval$ in an index node I is performed as usual. Either I is a leaf node, which terminates the search, or search continues at a version node V'.
  We say that I's "incoming version" is v_{pred} (denoted $version(I) := v_{pred}$) and I's "incoming version node" is V ($vnode(I) := V$).
- $derive^{\mathrm{MVI}}(v_{sel}, v_{new})$ requires no modification of the 2D-B$^+$-tree.
- $insert^{\mathrm{MVI}}(v_{sel}, kval, oid)$ (where v$_{sel}$ is a leaf version):
  An $exact\_match^{\mathrm{MVI}}(v_{sel}, kval)$ leads to the index node I into which to insert the key record *(kval, oid)*. If $version(I)=v_{sel}$, the key record is inserted into I. If $version(I)\neq v_{sel}$, this means that I is relevant for versions other than v_{sel}. I is then copied to a new node I' and the key record *(kval, oid)* is inserted into I'. *vnode(I)* is extended with a field indicating that $idx\_node(V, v_{sel}) = I'$.
  If an insertion in an index node I results in I being over-full, the data is

---

[2] We note that [10] contains an improvement of the Fat Node Method, the Fat Field Method, with a better storage space efficiency. We do not consider it here, however, since it is much more complicated than the Fat Node Method, without differing in the basic concepts discussed in this paper.

spread over I and a new node I'. A new version node V' is created and filled such that $youngest\_pred(V',v_{sel})=v_{sel}$ and $idx\_node(V',v_{sel})=I'$. Let J be the index node through which $vnode(I)$ was reached during the initial $exact\_match^{MVI}$. A new key record (k_0, V') where k_0 is the leftmost key value in I' is inserted into J. This can, recursively, require to split the root node.

- $delete^{MVI}(v_{sel}, kval, oid)$ (where v_{sel} is a leaf version): analogously
- $change\_key^{MVI}(old, new, oid)$: This operation is not supported.

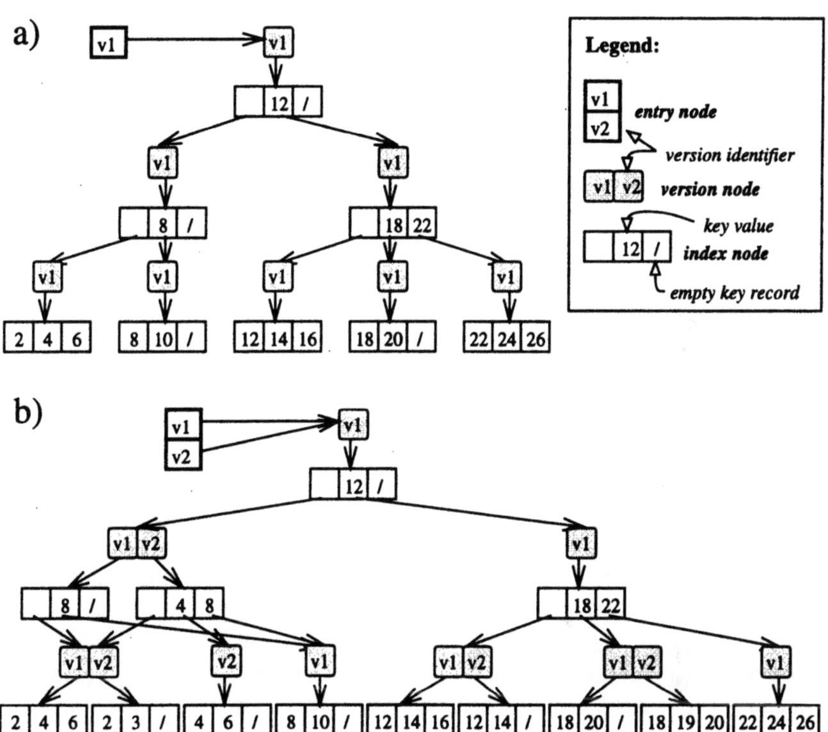

Figure 1: Example of the Fat Node Method for B$^+$-trees.
Fig. 1 a) shows a B$^+$-tree (of low order, for simplicity's sake) existing in one version v_1. The key values are the even numbers from 2 to 26. Fig. 1 b) shows the graph structure after deriving version v_2 from v_1, where key value 3 is inserted (causing a split), value 19 is inserted, and value 16 is deleted. (Each non-empty key record in a leaf node contains an object identifier that has been omitted in the figure.)

3.1.2 1D-B$^+$-trees with multi-version key values

Here, a B$^+$-tree is constructed like in the non-versioned case. All key values are contained in that B$^+$-tree regardless of in *what* collection versions the corresponding object is contained. Only in leaf nodes, a key record *(kval, oid)* is extended with data that allow to determine the collection versions which contain *oid*: For each *oid*, there is an "in-field" with the version in which *oid* was inserted into the collection, and an "out-field" containing the set of versions in which *oid* was deleted from the collection. The key record structure is therefore *(kval, ⟨oid, in, out⟩)* where *in* is a version identifier and *out* a set of version identifiers.

The implementation of version-based operations is based on standard B$^+$-tree operations. Fig. 2 gives an example using the scenario from Fig. 1.

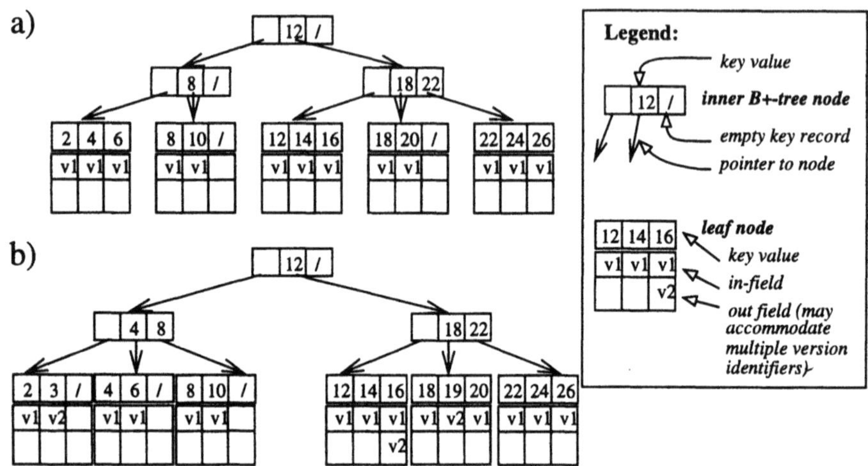

Figure 2: Example of the Late Resolution Method for B$^+$-trees.
(The object identifier in each non-empty key record in a leaf node has again been omitted.)

- *exact_match*^{MVI} *(v_{sel}, kval)*: Perform *exact_match(kval)*. For a retrieved tuple ⟨*oid, v, {v_1 ... v_k}*⟩: If v_{sel} is a successor of v and there is no $i \in \{1..k\}$ such that v_{sel} is a successor of v_i, then *oid* is returned.
- *derive*^{MVI} *(v_{sel}, v_{new})* requires no modification of the B$^+$-tree.
- *insert*^{MVI} *(v_{sel}, kval, oid)* (where v_{sel} is a leaf version): *insert(kval,⟨oid,v_{sel},{}⟩)*
- *delete*^{MVI} *(v_{sel}, kval, oid)* (where v_{sel} is a leaf version): *kval* can only be removed from the B$^+$-tree if there is no other collection version containing an element with key value *kval*. If this is the case, perform *delete*^{MVI} analogously to *insert*^{MVI}.
- *change_key*^{MVI} *(old, new, oid)*: is not supported.

In contrast to 2D-B$^+$-trees, the cost for accessing the index in a given version v depends on the *total* number of keys in the B$^+$-tree, i.e. on data being contained in versions other than v. Given a VU with n versions $v_1 ... v_n$, let $keys(v_i)$ be the number of distinct key values in collection version v_i, $i \in \{1..n\}$. The more the total number of keys, $\sum_{i=1}^{n} keys(v_i)$, exceeds $(keys(v_{sel}))^2$, the less time efficient is index access in v_{sel}, as compared to 2D-B$^+$-trees.

3.2 Implementation of Multi-Version Indexes

Both data structures presented above do not fully comply with the requirements for Multi-Version Indexes: *(1)* insert^{MVI} and delete^{MVI} must be applicable in non-leaf versions, and *(2)* change_key^{MVI} must be supported. Below we investigate how to extend the presented 1D- and 2D-B$^+$-trees for these requirements.

3.2.1 2D-B$^+$-trees

(1) insert^{MVI}/delete^{MVI} in non-leaf versions

How could updates in non-leaf collection versions be implemented in 2D-B$^+$-trees? Let us give an an example: Consider an indexed collection with initial version v_1 and three versions v_2, v_3 and v_4 derived from v_1. Assume an object is added to collection version v_1, and I_1 is the leaf index node into which to insert the corresponding key record. In none of v_1's successor versions the inserted key record must be seen. Any other key record in I_1, however, is still valid for v_2, v_3 and v_4. It is therefore at least necessary to copy I_1 to a new index node I_1' before inserting the new key record in I_1. Even worse, for each successor version a separate copy is needed: v_2, v_3 and v_4 cannot share the index node I_1' since this would require that they have a common predecessor version which is successor of v_1 at the same time. Therefore three index nodes I_2, I_3, I_4 must be created, and three fields added to V such that $I_i = idx\_node(v_i)$, for $i \in \{2,3,4\}$.

The above example illustrates the problem in employing 2D-B$^+$-trees to our version model: A collection update in a non-leaf version inherently requires to break up a shared node into multiple nodes shared by fewer versions. This can very soon lead to a multi-version B$^+$-tree which is degenerated regarding its purpose of sharing subtrees among versions. Therefore it undermines the overall purpose of 2D-B$^+$-trees, which is to share an index node among a version and its successors.

However, instead of adopting 2D-B$^+$-trees we can adopt our version model such that updates occur only in leaf versions. The idea is to consider each versioned collection as having its own version history, instead of complying with the VU's version history. That collection-specific history is expressed in a *collection-specific version tree* which is constructed as follows:

For each version v_i of the VU, the collection-specific version tree contains several versions $w_i^1, \ldots, w_i^{n_i}$ corresponding to v_i, only the last of which corresponds to the most recent state of the collection in v_i. The others correspond to intermediate states of the collection in version v_i. When creating v_i in the VU, version w_i^1 is also created. Each time a version v_j is derived from v_i in the VU, two versions are derived from $w_i^{n_i}$ in the collection-specific version tree: w_j^1 representing the initial state of the collection in v_j, plus $w_i^{n_i+1}$ as the "new" most recent version which corresponds to v_i. Then n_i is incremented.

By basing the 2D-B$^+$-trees on that collection-specific version tree, we comply with the requirement to modify the collection only in leaf versions. The disadvantage, however, is that the number of versions – and in consequence the space costs – grow.

(2) change_key^{MVI}

As mentioned before, *change_key^{MVI}* does not relate to a particular collection version but affects all collection versions containing the modified object.

Firstly, a problem with 2D-B$^+$-trees is to determine *which* collection versions contain the modified object, in order to delete the "old" key record for all these versions. Obviously, it is not feasible to access the index once in each version to check whether that version contains the modified object, since there may be many paths, each one related to a particular version, that need to be followed until all leaf nodes containing the modified object's key value were located. It is just as infeasible to record for each object not only in what collection it takes part in, but also in what *versions* of a collection.

Secondly, even if the problem of determining the set of versions to be modified were solved satisfactorily, we would need to insert key records with the object's new key value for each collection version that contains the object. Then, updates may be required in *many* different leaves of the versioned graph structure, which means an unacceptable overhead for update operations on objects.

3.2.2 1D-B$^+$-trees with multi-version key values

(1) insert^{MVI}/delete^{MVI} in non-leaf versions

Insertion and deletion in a non-leaf version can easily be incorporated into this method. Inserting an object in a non-leaf version v can be treated as adding it in v with deleting it in any successor of v immediately afterwards. That is, we simply insert a key record $(kval, \langle oid, v, \{v_{succ_1}, \ldots, v_{succ_k}\}\rangle)$ where $\{v_{succ_1}, \ldots, v_{succ_k}\}$ are the successors of v. Deletion is performed similarly.

(2) change_key^{MVI}

Here, we have the advantage of finding all data representing the object in question by following *one* path in the B$^+$-tree leading to *one* leaf node. Deletion is carried out there, and just one further node with the new key value must be retrieved for insertion of the tuple $\langle oid, in, out \rangle$ that was deleted in the old key value's record.

3.2.3 Conclusion

Although in general being the more efficient solution, 2D-B$^+$-trees cannot implement Multi-Version Indexes because they cannot implement operation *change_key^{MVI}* with an acceptable run-time performance. 1D-B$^+$-trees are therefore most suitable for the implementation of Multi-Version Indexes.

Note that in the original Fat Node Method, *change_key^{MVI}* is not required since the underlying data model is a relational one: A data item's identity is its key value, which in turn means that a key value cannot be modified.

4 Indexes which support Versioned Elements

While Section 3 discussed indexes on a versioned collection, this section deals with an index on a collection which contains versioned objects, i.e. MVOs. Let us point out the basic problem of having MVOs in an indexed collection. Why, actually, do we need to record version information in the B$^+$-tree; why can't we just store a simple key-to-object mapping for every distinct key value an MVO carries in its various versions?

Consider an MVO *mvoId* existing in four versions v_1 up to v_4. Its key value in v_1, v_2 and v_3 is $kval_1$, and in v_4 it is $kval_2$. We would then have two key records for *mvoId* in the B^+-tree: $(kval_1,\ mvoId)$ and $(kval_2,\ mvoId)$. Both index lookup ($exact\_match^{\text{IVE}}$) and key value updates ($change\_key^{\text{IVE}}$) impose problems: Lookup requires that we determine if a key value in a key record, for instance $kval2$, is visible in the selected version of the corresponding object ($mvoId$). Only in this case, the object identifier can be returned. An update of *mvoId*'s key value in version v_i requires that we determine if *mvoId* carries the same key value in another version $v_j \neq v_i$, since it cannot be deleted then (for instance when changing $kval1$ in v_3).

An observation we can make is that a collection can contain MVOs which belong to *different* VUs. An example of the SEE domain: The SEEs maintains the collection of C++-procedures contained in all modules of a project, in order to enable project-wide searching for procedure names. Then, procedures defined in the *same* module are versioned in one VU, since each module is implemented as a single VU. Procedures defined in *different* modules are therefore versioned in different VUs.

Looking for an implementation of an Index which supports Versioned Elements, we first consider the special – and probably easier – case in which all MVOs in the indexed collection belong to the *same* VU.

The special case - all elements belong to the same VU

One could suggest that if all collection elements are versioned in the same VU vu, this could be treated like a collection which is versioned in vu and contains non-versioned elements. That is, an operation op^{IVE} could be implemented by Multi-Version Index operations $op_1^{\text{MVI}}, \ldots, op_k^{\text{MVI}}$ as shown below. Note that $change\_key^{\text{MVI}}$ is not required, which would enable to employ a 2D-B^+-tree.

- $exact\_match^{\text{IVE}}(\{vu,\ v\},\ kval) = \text{exact\_match}^{\text{MVI}}(\text{v, kval})$.
- $derive^{\text{IVE}}(vu,\ v,\ v_{new}) = \text{derive}^{\text{MVI}}(\text{v, v}_{new})$.
- $insert^{\text{IVE}}(oid,\ vu,\ \{(v_i,\ kval_i)\ |\ i{=}1..n\}) = \text{insert}^{\text{MVI}}(\text{v}_1,\ \text{kval}_1,\ \text{oid})\ ;\ \ldots\ ;$ $\text{insert}^{\text{MVI}}(\text{v}_n,\ \text{kval}_n,\ \text{oid})$.
- $delete^{\text{IVE}}(oid,\ vu,\ \{(v_i,\ kval_i)\ |\ i{=}1..n\}))$ (analogously)
- $change\_key^{\text{IVE}}(old, new, oid, vu, v) = \text{delete}^{\text{MVI}}(\text{v,old,oid})\ ;\ \text{insert}^{\text{MVI}}(\text{v,new,oid})$.

The analogy drawn above between

– a collection of versioned objects belonging to a single VU, and

– a versioned collection of non-versioned objects

is appropriate on the conceptual level when regarding what key-to-object mappings are visible in which version of the VU. Yet we need to review updates in non-leaf versions: In Section 3.2.1 *(A)* we have argued that 2D-B^+-trees must be based on a collection-specific version tree instead of the VU's version graph. But what applied to the versioned collection there holds for the versioned elements here: Each MVO must be seen as having its own history of derivations, and the 2D-B^+-tree cannot, of course, be based on more than one version history. (Let alone the fact that it is not feasible to maintain a separate version tree for each MVO.)

The general case - elements belonging to multiple VUs

Application of 2D-B$^+$-trees is disabled in the special case, so this holds all the more for the general case where we have collection elements versioned in different VUs. As was the case for the implementation of Multi-Version Indexes, we must postpone resolution of version information to the lowest level possible, i.e. we maintain a kind of 1D-B$^+$-tree similar to the one presented in Section 3.1.2. Key records in leaf nodes are again extended with version data. Here, that data relate to the version history of the MVO's VU and allow to determine, for a given tuple *(kval, oid)*, if the currently selected version of *oid* carries key value *kval*.

5   B+-trees implementing Large Collections

B$^+$-trees are not only employed for implementing an index on a collection, but also for implementing a (large) collection itself. While in the former case, the B$^+$-tree is a redundant structure, in the latter case the B$^+$-tree is the collection.

Two kinds of collection implementations can be distinguished: **(a) Sets:** A B$^+$-tree is constructed with element identifiers as key values. In leaf nodes, the second part of a key record is omitted. **(b) Insertable Lists:** The data structure commonly used here is an ordered tree [12]. Inner nodes have as key values the *numbers* of keys stored in the corresponding subtree of that node. Leaf node records do not contain key values but only element identifiers (that is, in leaf nodes the first part of key records is omitted).

Versioning a set or list which is implemented by a B$^+$-tree imposes requirements that differ slightly from those defined for Multi-Version Indexes. This leads to definition *(C)* of an Index which implements a Large Collection:

- *exact_match^{ILC} (v_{sel}, kval)*
  set: *kval* is an object identifier. Returns true if object *kval* is contained in version v_{sel} of the set.
  list: *kval* is an integer. Returns the element at position *kval* in list version v_{sel}.
- *derive^{ILC}(v_{sel}, v_{new})* is issued upon derivation of a successor v_{new} from v_{sel}.
- *insert^{ILC}(v_{sel}, kval, oid)*, *delete^{ILC}(v_{sel}, kval, oid)*:
  set: *kval* is an object identifier; parameter *oid* is not supplied. The method is issued upon insertion resp. deletion of object *kval* in version v_{sel} of the set.
  list: *kval* is a integer. The method is issued upon insertion resp. deletion of *oid* at position *kval* of version v_{sel} of the list.

The important difference as compared to a Multi-Version Index is that an operation *change_key* is not required: For sets, the key values are object identifiers, and these cannot be modified. For lists, the key values are list positions in a particular version of the list, instead of (modifiable) properties of list elements, and cannot be changed therefore. As a consequence, we can implement large versioned collections with 2D-B$^+$-trees.

Whereas a less efficient implementation of versioned sets with 1D-B$^+$-trees is possible, this does not hold for versioned lists: Key values in ordered trees are not given by absolute values, but each key value is a relative position which depends on other key values in the tree. Resolving version data in leaf nodes, as done in 1D-B$^+$-trees, is impossible, since there, one has already reached an absolute list position.

6 Conclusion

We have introduced a version model required from an ODBS which enables the construction of an SEE on top. The requirements imposed on the ODBS's index management by that version model lead to the definition of two version-based data structures: *(A)* Multi-Version Indexes and *(B)* Indexes which support Versioned Elements. Although versions of B$^+$-trees in general can be kept efficiently with 2D-B$^+$-trees, both *(A)* and *(B)* must be implemented with a 1D-B$^+$-tree where version information is stored in leaf nodes. 2D-B$^+$-trees can only be applied in the third case, *(C)*, the implementation of a versioned collection.

So far we have assumed that applications employing versioning make extensive use of *all* the provided features, in particular of modifying objects in non-leaf versions. Here experience is needed about how versioning is really employed, in order to come to a sound judgement of the pro's and con's of the various implementation alternatives.

An ODBS's architecture usually contains a core storage management module providing fundamental database functionality, based on record-structured sequential files and some kind of B$^+$-trees. That storage system is a very critical part because it determines runtime performance and space requirements of database applications. Unfortunately, as far as we know, all existing ODBSs have been built without such an, admittedly special purpose, application in mind as we have described in this paper. Thus they do not provide data structures such as 2D-B$^+$-trees. Most often, the core storage system does not have the notion of versions, since the version management is a layer built on top. We have therefore also investigated possibilities of implementing version-based indexes on top of a basically "standard" B$^+$-tree management. We used the O_2 system which is the only ODBS complying with our requirements on the version model. See [13] for a detailed discussion of that implementation.

Acknowledgements

I thank Wilhelm Schäfer who read earlier drafts of this paper and offered many constructive comments. Many thanks to Wolfgang Emmerich and Joëlle Madec for their assistance and feedback on my work, and to Claude Delobel and François Bancilhon for having enabled my stay at O_2 Technology.

References

[1] W. Emmerich, Tool Construction for Process-Centered Software Development Environments based on Object Database Systems, Dissertation, University of Paderborn, Germany, 1995

[2] W. Emmerich, W. Schäfer and J. Welsh", Databases for Software Engineering Environments — The Goal has not yet been attained, p. 145–62, I. Sommerville and M. Paul, Proc. of the 4th ESEC, Garmisch-Partenkirchen, Germany, 1993, LNCS 717, Springer

[3] N.S. Barghouti, W. Emmerich, W. Schäfer and A. Skarra, Information Management in Process-Centred Software Engineering Environments, Trends in Software, Special Issue on the Software Process, Oct. 1995, p. 1–33

[4] G. Engels, C. Lewerentz, M. Nagl, W. Schäfer and A. Schürr, Building Integrated Software Development Environments — Part 1: Tool Specification, ACM Transactions on Software Engineering and Methodology, Vol. 1, No. 2, p. 135–67

[5] S. Sachweh and W. Schäfer, Version Management for tightly integrated Software Engineering Environments, p. 21–31, M. S. Verrall, Proceedings of the 7th International Conference on Software Engineering Environments, Leiden, The Netherlands, 1995, IEEE Computer Society Press

[6] F. Bancilhon, C. Delobel and P. Kanellakis, Building an Object-Oriented Database System: the Story of O_2, Morgan Kaufmann, 1992

[7] O_2 Version Management Reference Manual *version 4.6 – temporary documentation*, O2 Technology, 1995

[8] D. Comer, The Ubiquitous B-Tree, ACM Computing Surveys, 1979, Vol. 11, No. 2, p. 121–37

[9] D.P. Dobkin and J.I. Munro, Efficient uses of the past, Proc. 21st Annual IEEE Symposium on Foundations of Computer Science, 1980, p. 200-6

[10] S. Lanka and E. Mays, Fully persistent B^+-trees, SIGMOD Record, Vol. 20, No. 2, 1991, p. 426–35

[11] J.R. Driscoll, N. Sarnak, D.D. Sleator and R.E. Tarjan, Making Data Structures Persistent, Journal of Computer and System Sciences, 1989, No. 38, p. 86–124

[12] M.R. Stonebraker, Document Processing in a Relational Database System, p. 143–158, ACM Transactions on Office Information Systems, Vol. 1, No. 2, 1983

[13] W. Reimer, Versions of B^+-trees and B^+-trees of versioned objects in the O_2 Database Management System, Master's Thesis, University of Dortmund, Germany 1994

LARGE SCALE ENVIRONMENTS

Disseminating Object-Oriented Applications in Large Scale Environments[*]

Arnd G. Grosse, Dietmar A. Kottmann, Jörn Hartroth

Institute of Telematics, University of Karlsruhe

76128 Karlsruhe, Germany

Abstract

As a result of new programming languages for the internet like Java, the paradigm of disseminating applications over the net has recently become popular. The process of dissemination is straightforward, as long as it is only done in local networks. But emerging applications in entertainment, electronic commerce or even embedded computing need to be disseminated on a country-wide or global scale. On this scale, dissemination can cause considerable costs. How this cost can be minimized for object-oriented applications is the topic of this paper.

1 Introduction

One of the most rapidly emerging ideas is to use the internet as a platform for deploying and maintaining applications. The basic enabling technology for this idea are frameworks like Java [14] or ActiveX [7] that allow the dynamic installation of code over the net. Besides the simple idea to reduce the total cost of ownership for computers through replacing PCs with NCs (Network Computers; cf. e.g. [11]), the technology is up to cause a major breakthrough for problems associated with application deployment like distribution, installation, maintenance, version control, and updates. The latter is already supported by new commercial products like Java-based Castanet [6]. Such solutions promise a massive cost reduction for the process of deploying applications to a large number of customers. Besides often cited examples in the entertainment or electronic commerce sector, this is also an important feature for several embedded applications. Just consider an embedded least-cost telephone-routing system that is installed in your home and chooses the cheapest provider for your next telephone call. When providers change their telephone rates, new parameters have to be downloaded. When a provider introduces a newly structured rate, not only parameters but also the code to compare this new rate with existing ones has to be downloaded. The same happens when a new provider enters the market. Hence, it is necessary to update your embedded system dynamically. This has to done cost-efficiently for a very large number of widely distributed embedded systems. Similar examples can be found in other embedded applications that contribute to the vision of pervasive computing [3]. Currently available system support, i.e. middleware, is insufficient for the deployment of applications in such scenarios. Especially the problem of disseminating updates cost-efficiently is most often only treated

[*]This work is partially supported by the grant SFB346-A6 of the German Research Council (Deutsche Forschungsgemeinschaft – DFG)

in an ad-hoc fashion. In this paper we present a framework that tackles exactly this problem for object-oriented applications. After introducing the basic framework in chapter 2, we show in chapter 3 how the dissemination process can be optimized for large scale environments through automatically combining different dissemination policies. Then we refine the basic framework in chapter 4 to an object-oriented model which forms the basis of our current Java-based prototype. Finally, chapter 5 concludes the paper.

2   Dissemination in Large Scale Environment

Applications are created and managed by one institution that we call the *source* and used by a (large) number of other institutions that we call *sinks*. The best dissemination strategy for an object trivially depends on how often it is updated by the source and the usage frequencies of the sinks. As they vary on a granularity finer than objects, we break an object into its three essential *parts*: its (static or configuration) state, its class code, and its interface. In the least-cost telephone routing example, each time a provider (the source) changes one of his telephone rates, he changes the parameters – i.e. the state – while leaving the structure of the rate – i.e. the class – untouched. The same happens in electronic product catalogues when an electronic shop (the source) changes the pricing for the offered articles. Classes are only updated when the application itself migrates to a new version. In our examples this is the case when newly structured telephone rates are introduced or when the electronic product catalogue should feature a special presentation for a bargain offer. Like in conventional distributed systems, interfaces are used independently of classes and state to allow a user to find new applications in the net. This is the task normally performed by nameservers (cf. [15]) or traders (cf. [2]). As the information about offered applications, i.e. interfaces, has to be disseminated over the net, they also have to be treated in an unified framework. Mention, that the proposed mechanism applies to the dissemination of updated parts at the source and not to changes at the sink when using the part inside an application. Also the dissemination of dynamic state back from the sink towards the source and a kind of notification event towards the sink by the system when a part has changed is beyond of the scope of this paper though it is for further research.

3   On Choosing the Best Dissemination Policy

As we consider the distribution of applications, we can safely assume that the regarded states are part of the application's configuration and are thus only updated by the source. So we can neglect synchronization problems that arise when multiple users concurrently modify a common object. Hence, it is only important that updates are properly distributed to sinks. A problem common to all three parts of an object. Under these assumptions, the dissemination problem can be modelled in one unified framework that we call SOFT (**S**caleable **O**bject **F**low **T**ree). A SOFT is responsible for one part and consists of one source, several sinks, and a number of system-level-entities that forward updates from the source towards the sinks.

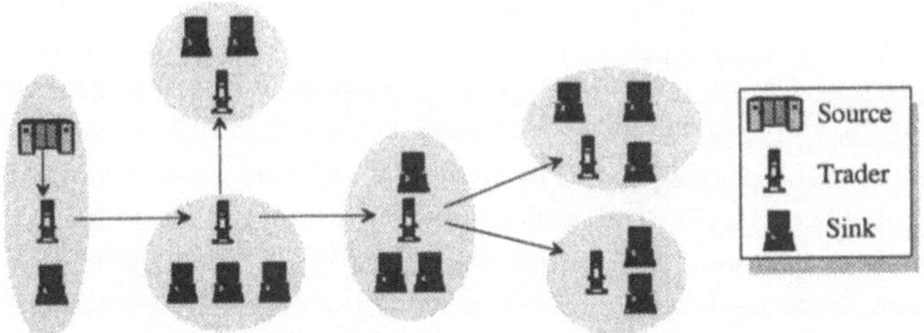

Figure 1: An Example SOFT.

The system level entities can be considered as entities analogous to traders in ODP-based distributed systems (cf. [2] for ODP or [10] for the inclusion of traders as an object service in CORBA-based systems) or Harvest-servers that form a hierarchical cache for WWW-based information [4]. We also use the term trader to name the system-level entities of a SOFT, although they unify the functions of conventional traders, Harvest's caches, and Castanet repeaters. As in these systems, traders are manually linked according to administrative requirements. Hence, each SOFT is structured as a tree, as shown in figure 1. Note that each part of an object has its own SOFT to keep the presentation of the optimization considerations in the next chapter simple. However, it is natural to model the structurally equivalent SOFTs for all parts of all objects of an application in one framework as later on presented in chapter 4.

Objects can be propagated in SOFTs along several different policies. The choice of a dissemination policy for a given SOFT structure under given usage frequencies has a substantial impact on the overall cost of disseminating. We start our discussion of usage policies with the most simple SOFT structure that consists of only two traders. We use this structure to give insight into the trade-offs between the different policies and to introduce our analytical model for comparing them. After that we extend the model to general SOFT structures and show how to find the optimal policies for arbitrary structures under given usage frequencies automatically.

3.1 Dissemination Policies for the Basic 2 Trader Model

When we apply the SOFT concept to a two trader infrastructure, one of the two traders receives all updates, while reads are directed to both traders. We refer to the former trader as the *root*. As the database of the root is always up to date, all reads can be satisfied locally. Hence, they are considered to be free of charge, as only reads to the second trader, which we term the *leaf*, need additional communication. There are two well known policies for disseminating information between 2 traders:

Under the **pull-policy** only the root stores all information. Each time the leaf receives a read request, it inquires the information from the root. The study of this trading-policy was pioneered by ODP [2]. Under the **push-policy** both traders store all information. Hence, each read request can be satisfied locally, while the root has to propagate each update immediately to the leaf. This trading-policy was first treated in ANSA [1] and validated in Rhodos [8].

As an extension to those two policies we introduce a third one that can be considered as lying somewhere in between the original policies. Under the **lazy-push-policy** the root stores all information while the information stored at the leaf varies dynamically. The first time the root receives an update, it stores it in its local database. When the leaf receives a read request, it inquires the information from the root and caches it in its local database. Additionally, the root sets a flag that the information has been forwarded. When the root receives the next update, it updates its database. To preserve consistency, it signals the leaf that the cache is invalid when the flag is set. Under the lazy-push-policy, the first read to the leaf after an update is more expensive as under the push-policy, while updates are cheaper, because in the worst case only a small signal message has to be sent to the leaf instead of transmitting a full-fledged object. Compared to the push-policy, updates are more expensive, while reads are cheaper, as only the first read after an update needs remote communication.

To compare the three policies we use an analytical model. We assume that updates to the source are Poisson distributed with parameter λ_1, and reads to the sink are independently Poisson distributed with parameter λ_2. Be aware of the potentially high independence between the source and the sink in a large scale environment for which Poisson distribution has to be assumed. Note that we can ignore the reads to the root. Let Θ be $\lambda_1/(\lambda_1 + \lambda_2)$. Observe that, since the Poisson distribution is memoryless, at any point in time Θ is the probability that the next request is a write, and $1 - \Theta = \lambda_2/(\lambda_1 + \lambda_2)$ is the probability that the next request is a read. Further, let ω denote the cost for transmitting a signal message between the root T_1 and the leaf T_2, and let $k \geq 1$ be the factor by which transmitting the part is more expensive than transmitting the signal; i.e. the cost for transmitting the part is $k\omega$. The resulting model is depicted in figure 2.

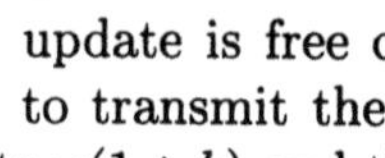

Figure 2: The Analytical Model for 2 Traders.

Now we are looking for the *expected cost* $EX_P(\Theta)$ for the different dissemination policies P. They are computed as follows:

Under the **pull-policy**, an update is free of charge. To perform a read, the leaf has to signal the root to transmit the part, and the part has to be transmitted. Hence, a read costs $\omega(1 + k)$ and the expected cost is $EX_L(\Theta) = (1 - \Theta)(1 + k)\omega$.

Under the **push-policy**, each read is free of charge, while an update has to be propagated to the leaf. Hence, an update costs $k\omega$ and the expected cost is $EX_S(\Theta) = \Theta k\omega$.

Under the **lazy-push-policy**, one has to distinguish the state S_2 that the leaf has the part in its cache from the state S_1 that the part is only stored at the root. In S_1, an update is free of charge, while a read costs $(1 + k)\omega$ and transfers the system in state S_2. In S_2, an update costs ω, and puts the system in state S_1, while a read is free of charge. This state transition diagram is depicted in figure 3. Let $P(S_1)$ and $P(S_2)$ denote the steady state probability of the system being in state S_1 and S_2. They can be computed under usage of the boundary condition $P(S_1) + P(S_2) = 1$ using standard techniques (cf. [16]), which leads to the probabilities $P(S_1) = \Theta$, and $P(S_2) = 1 - \Theta$. Hence, we have $EX_Z(\Theta) = (1 - \Theta)[(1 + k)\omega\Theta + 0(1 - \Theta)] + \Theta[0\Theta + \omega(1 - \Theta)] = \Theta(1 - \Theta)\omega[2 + k]$.

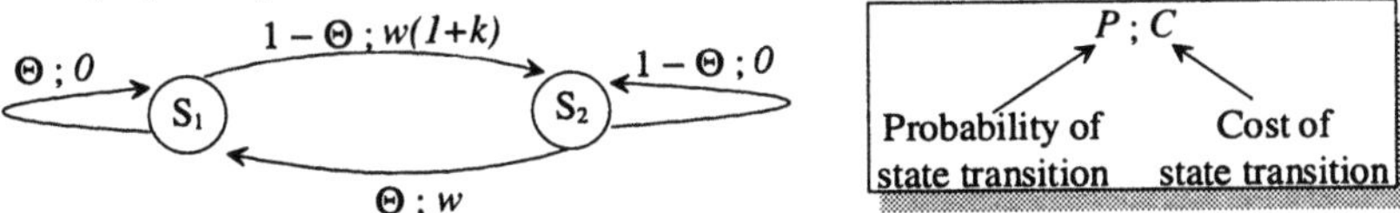

Figure 3: Assessing the Lazy-Push-Model.

A straightforward computation shows that $EX_S(\Theta) \leq EX_L(\Theta)$ if and only if $\Theta \leq (1 + k)/(1 + 2k)$, $EX_S(\Theta) \leq EX_Z(\Theta)$ if and only if $\Theta \leq 2/(2 + k)$, and $EX_L(\Theta) \leq EX_Z(\Theta)$ if and only if $(1 + k)/(2 + k) \leq \Theta$. As we have $0 < 2/(2 + k) < (1 + k)/(1 + 2k) < (1 + k)/(2 + k) < 1$ for $k \geq 1$, the three policies can be compared as shown in table 1.

Interval	Preference	Best Policy
$0 \leq \Theta \leq \frac{2}{2+k}$	$EX_S(\Theta) \prec EX_Z(\Theta) \prec EX_L(\Theta)$	**Push**
$\frac{2}{2+k} \leq \Theta \leq \frac{1+k}{1+2k}$	$EX_Z(\Theta) \prec EX_S(\Theta) \prec EX_L(\Theta)$	**Lazy-Push**
$\frac{1+k}{1+2k} \leq \Theta \leq \frac{1+k}{2+k}$	$EX_Z(\Theta) \prec EX_L(\Theta) \prec EX_S(\Theta)$	**Lazy-Push**
$\frac{1+k}{2+k} \leq \Theta \leq 1$	$EX_L(\Theta) \prec EX_Z(\Theta) \prec EX_S(\Theta)$	**Pull**

Table 1: Comparing the Policies for the 2 Trader Scenario.

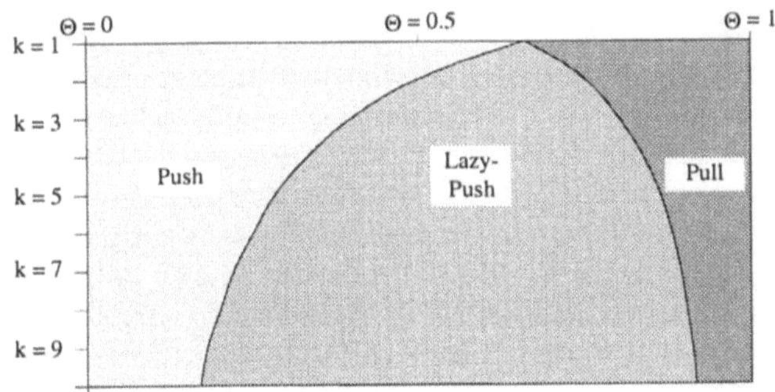

Figure 4: The Best Policy for Differing Object Sizes and Update Probabilities.

The best policies for different update probabilities Θ and part sizes k are shown in figure 4. When Θ and k are known it is straightforward to choose the best dissemination policy with table 1 and figure 4. As can be seen from figure 4, the push-policy performs best when updates are rare (i.e. $\Theta \approx 0$), the pull policy performs best when updates are frequent (i.e. $\Theta \approx 1$, and the lazy-push-policy performs best, as long as no extreme situation is reached. Further, the interval for Θ, in which the lazy-push-policy outperforms the other policies increases with the part size k. If we assume that a signal message needs 10 Byte and a part 10000 Byte, then k is 1000, and the lazy-push-policy is best for all update probabilities between 0.2% and 99.9%. This might be the reason, why the trader community so far did not consider an equivalent of the lazy-push-policy. As traders in distinction to SOFTs trade only small interfaces, there is nothing but a short interval of update probabilities in which the lazy-push-policy is the best choice.

3.2 Best Policy for Large Dissemination Structures

The analytical model for general SOFT structures assumes that updates are Poisson distributed with parameter λ_1 at trader T_1 and that reads are independently Poisson distributed with parameter λ_i at trader T_i for $i \geq 1$. We assume that $\lambda_1 > 0$, as otherwise an unlimited push is trivially the best policy for all traders. Furthermore, there are different communication costs ω_{ij} between different traders. The resulting model for the example SOFT from figure 1 is shown in figure 5. Once again we can neglect read requests at trader T_1. Now we have to compute the best dissemination policy for each trader. We only sketch the derivation, as its details are beyond the scope of this paper. An extensive treatment of the problem can be found in [5].

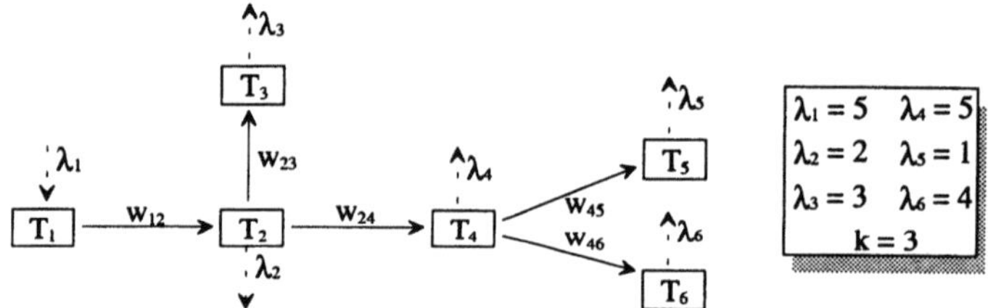

Figure 5: The Analytical Model for a General SOFT.

It is shown in [5] that no policy assignment can be optimal in which a trader that uses a push-policy has a trader that uses a pull- or lazy-push-policy as an ancestor in the dissemination tree. Hence, the optimal policy assignment has to be structured as depicted in figure 6(a). To compute the optimal policy assignment we first compute the optimal choice between pull- and lazy-push-policies for each subtree of the SOFT. As will be shown below, this choice can be made independently of the policies assigned to the ancestors of the subtree. Hence, we start a first computation round that begins with the traders at the leaves of the SOFT and ends with the trader at the root. Afterwards, we begin a second round starting with the root and decide whether it is better to replace the pull- or lazy-push-policy with the push-policy at the trader in consideration. Note that the pull- and lazy-push-policies assigned to the untouched subtrees remain optimal, as their optimality is independent of the policies assigned to their ancestors.

The two rounds of the assignment algorithm are depicted in figure 6(a). Figure 6(b) shows how the computation in the first round proceeds through the subtrees of the SOFT structure from figure 5. Note that it is unnecessary to perform a computation for the root, as this trader always stores all parts. Finally, the second round proceeds through the reverse steps of the first round.

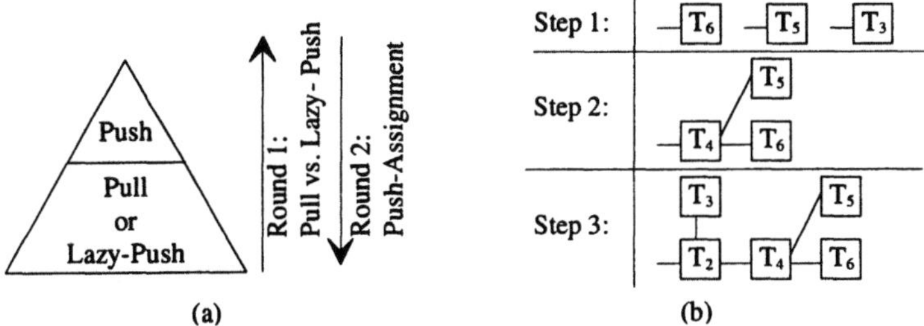

Figure 6: Computations of the Optimization Algorithm.

First round: The first computation round begins at the leaves. Let us consider under which circumstances it is better to use a pull-policy than a lazy-push-policy for a leaf trader T_x. The cost of an update at T_1 or an read at T_x are equivalent, as long, as T_x has an empty cache. When the part is cached by T_x, the pull policy saves P for an update and has additional expenses of $(1 + k)P$ for a read, when P denotes the cost for reaching the next ancestor that stores the part. Hence, for a leaf T_x pull is better than lazy-push if and only if $(\lambda_x)/(\lambda_1) \leq (1)/(1 + k)$.

For an inner node T_x, there is once again no difference, as long as T_x has an empty cache. When the part is cached, the pull-policy saves P for an update, as long, as no descendent of T_x has also cached the object. On the other hand, the pull-policy has additional expenses of $(1 + k)P$ for reads to trader T_x and all descendants T_z of T_x that have no trader T_y with lazy-push-policy on the path between T_x and T_z. For the latter traders there is only once an additional expense for the whole subtree that starts with the first lazy-push-trader beyond T_x, as afterwards T_y also caches the object. The relative savings of using the lazy-push-policy can now be computed via a state transition diagram. The diagram for trader T_4 of figure 5 is shown in figure 7.

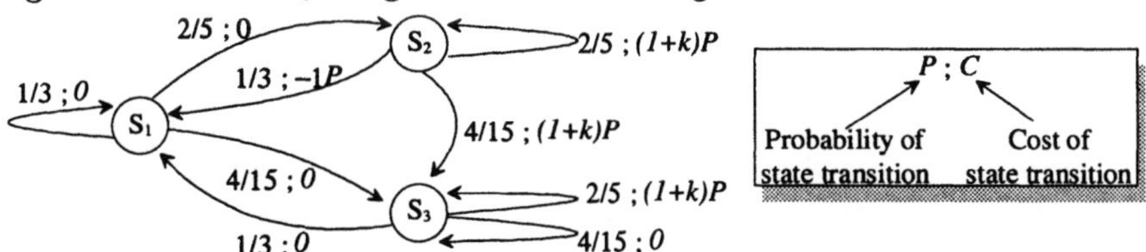

Figure 7: State Transition Diagram for Cost Advantage of using Lazy-Push for Trader T_4.

Second Round: At the beginning of the second round, we know the optimal assignment of pull- and lazy-push-policies for all subtrees. Proceeding in the reverse direction we have to decide whether it is cheaper to use a mixed pull-/lazy-push-policy for the subtree or to change the policy of the root of the subtree to a push-policy. To ease this computation, we can distinguish the four cases that the root uses pull or lazy-push and that there are additional nodes in the subtree that use lazy-push or not. For a pull root with no lazy-push nodes in the subtree, the computation is as straightforward as the decision between the pull- and lazy-push-policy for leaves. For a lazy-push root, we need a two state state-transition model, as the one used in chapter 3.1 to asses the lazy-push-policy for the 2-trader SOFT. Only for the rare case of a pull root and at least one lazy-push-node in the subtree, we have to use a full fledged state-transition model as the one used in the first round for inner nodes. All those derivations are explained in detail in [5]. The resulting optimal dissemination structure for our example from figure 5 is shown in figure 8.

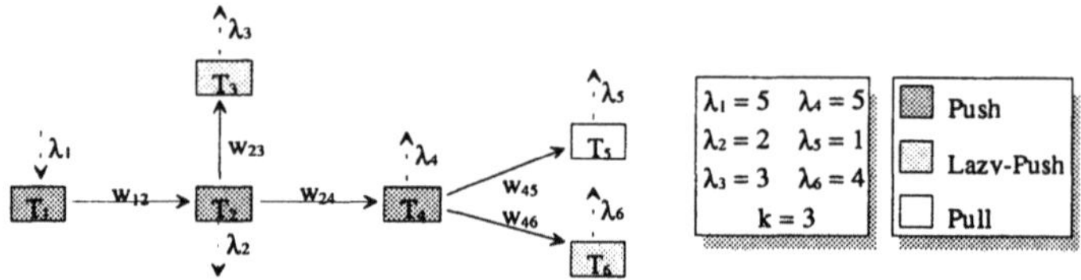

Figure 8: Optimal Policy-Assignment for the Example Structure.

So far we have presented how to assign the optimal dissemination policies to the traders in a SOFT. Before we proceed with further aspects of SOFTs, let us point out three important facts. Firstly, the algorithm of chapter 3.2 allows the automatic optimization of policies given the SOFT structure, the size of the object to trade, and the usage frequencies. It does not need the communication cost between traders. Although we introduced them, they are no part of the optimization equations. Secondly, the algorithm can be further optimized to allow the efficient inclusion or removal of traders or the efficient change of usage frequencies. The latter comes in handy to correct an initially guessed usage frequency through monitoring. Thirdly, the SOFTs of one application have a common SOFT topology, but differ in the usage frequency for interfaces, classes, and states. Hence, their optimal policy assignments might differ. Generally, the read frequency is highest for the interfaces, then comes the classes, and finally the states. This order is reversed for the update frequency.

4 Modelling of Dissemination Structures

The previous chapter has shown the benefits of a scaleable object dissemination structures system based on traders. But one important question has not been answered yet. It is the question how SOFTs can be modelled and integrated into a running system. We decided to use the Unified Modelling Language (UML) developed by Rational Inc.[12] for the object-oriented modelling of a SOFT. Our object-oriented model of SOFTs is based on the Version 1.0 of UML which was the answer of Rational to OMG's request for proposals for a standard modelling technique to be included into their Object Management Architecture [9].

4.1 Reconsidering SOFTs

Applications might comprise several thousand objects. In most cases there are multiple instances of the same class. So there exist multiple objects that share a common interface and a common class code. Sticking to our basic concept that each part of an object is associated with its own SOFT, a plenitude of structurally equivalent SOFTs would result. Hence, we generalize the term "part" such that it is no longer directly associated with a single object. Parts still denote interfaces, class code, or state. Naturally, a state part belongs to a single object, but interface or class code parts can be shared by multiple objects. Thus, a SOFT comprises a part, one source, several sinks, and a number of traders, and update or usage frequencies, that generally result from aggregating the respective frequencies of all objects that share the part.

4.2 Object-Oriented Model of SOFTs

Our object-oriented model of SOFT in UML syntax is shown in figure 9. A SOFT is an aggregation of exactly one SOFT-Root and at least one federation tree. Note that neither an empty nor an one-node-tree is a valid SOFT. It can be derived that a SOFT consists of minimum two federated traders in which the one called the offering trader is associated to the source and the other called the using trader is associated to sinks. Note that there is no necessity to represent sources and sinks in our model, as the optimization of dissemination structures only concerns the involved traders. The SOFT-Root is an aggregation of the offering trader and the offered part. The 1:1-association between offering trader and part has an associated class denoted by a dashed line and called change rate to describe the update frequency of the part.

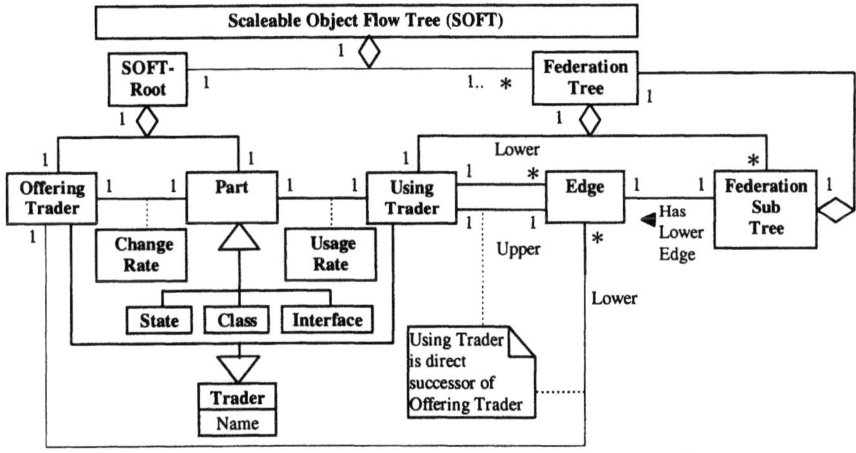

Figure 9: UML-Model of SOFT.

A federation tree itself describes a non-empty subtree of a SOFT having exactly one using trader as the root of the tree. This trader is also associated to the part. The association also has an association class called "usage rate" to denote usage frequency at this trader. Note that an usage rate of zero indicates a trader that is only forwarding the part. For simplicity it should not be a leaf of the SOFT though it could be. Besides the root trader in the federation tree many federation sub trees are part of the federation tree.

The root trader is connected to each of these subtrees with an edge. Besides the edges to its federation sub trees, a using trader can have an edge to the offering trader if and only if the latter is its direct successor. This is modelled by a symbol describing the constraint which itself is associated by two dashed lines to the two associations determining the edge. Each federation subtree itself is an aggregation of a federation tree. By this recursive modelling any possible federation tree of any depth can be described. The recursion ends if the federation tree has an using trader but no aggregated federation sub tree. Additionally, the trader class at the bottom of the model indicates that both using and offering trader are subclasses from a trader.

4.3 Functional Model of the Dissemination Mechanism

Each time a part changes it has to be transmitted to the traders along the graph of the SOFT. Note that this forwarding only spawns push-traders. The functional model of this dissemination mechanism is shown in figure 10. It is modelled by an extension to the functional model of OMT [13]. This extension is called OMKfm (Object-oriented Modelling technique Karlsruhe - functional method). Ovals describe functions, and rectangles describe actors which are participators to functions. This role is denoted by two parallel lines between actor and function. Actors and function can further be refined up to non-dividable actors and functions, the so called subjects and processes.

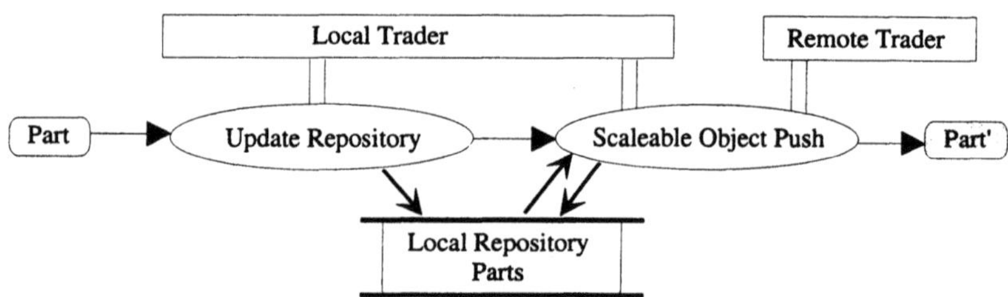

Figure 10: OMKfm-Model of Scaleable Information Pushing.

The function *update repository* is called when an event occurs. A line with a filled arrowhead indicates the event. It is a special kind of an information flow described by non-filled arrowheads. Like normal information flows events can carry an object. This object, i.e. the part, is shown by the associated rounded rectangle. The update function replaces the old part by the new one in the local repository. The repository as an instance of a data store is modelled by two limiting lines linked with two vertical lines. After updating the repository, the update function indicates with an event to the core function of the model, the scaleable object pusher, that a part has changed. This function uses the dissemination policies as discussed in chapter 3. The participation of the remote trader to the function is also shown in figure 10.

5 Conclusion And Outlook

In this paper we described an approach to disseminate object-oriented applications in a large scale environment to a large user population. Our approach, called SOFT, unifies the functionality which is today provided by different system-level services like traders and caches. We showed that different dissemination policies have to be combined to get the cheapest overall dissemination cost. Furthermore, we presented an algorithm that derives the best combination of dissemination policies given initial guesses about update and usage frequencies. This combination can further be optimised at runtime via monitoring actual usage patterns. Our ongoing research currently focuses on the automatic optimisation of SOFT structures and on developing a monitoring framework to fine-tune SOFTs at runtime.

References

[1] ANSA. ANSAware 3.0 Implementation Manual, ANSA document RM.097.01, February 1991.

[2] M.Y. Bearman. ODP-Trader, 2nd IFIP International Conference on Open Distributed Processing (ODP'93), North Holland, 1994.

[3] J. Birnbaum. Pervasive Information Systems, Communications of the ACM, Vol. 40, No.2, February 1997, pp. 40-42.

[4] C.M. Bowman, P.B. Danzig, M.F. Schwartz, U. Manber. Scaleable Internet Resource Discovery: Research Problems and Approaches, Communications of the ACM, Vol. 37, No.8, August 1994, pp. 98-107.

[5] D.A. Kottmann, A.G. Grosse. Optimale Kooperationsstrategien für verteilte Trader-Netze (in german), Technical Report 8/97, Department of Computer Science, University of Karlsruhe, 1997.

[6] Marimba Inc. Castanet, http://www.marimba.com/datasheets/castanet-ds.html, 1997.

[7] Microsoft Corporation. Activation the Internet with ActiveX, Microsoft Corporation White Paper, http://www.microsoft.com/activex/actx-gen/vision.ZIP, July 1996.

[8] Y. Ni, A. Goscinski A., Trader Cooperation to enable Object Sharing among Users of Homogeneous Distributed Systems, Computer Communications, Vol. 17, No. 3, March 1994, pp. 218–229.

[9] Object Management Group. Object Management Architecture, OMG TC Document 92.11.1, September 1992.

[10] Object Management Group. OMG RFP5 Submission – Trading Object Service, OMG-Document orbos/96-07-08, July 1996.

[11] Oracle Corporation. The Network Computer, Oracle Corporation White Paper, http://nswt.tuwien.ac.at:8000/nc/papers/oracle_wp.html, April 1996.

[12] Rational Software Corp et al. Microsoft, Hewlett-Packard, Oracle, Texas Instruments, MCI Systemhouse, Unisys, ICON Computing. Proposal to the Object Management Group's Analysis and Design Task Force in Response to OADTF-RFP1, OMG-Documents ad/97-01-01 to ad/97-01-14, January 1997.

[13] J. Rumbaugh, M. Blaha, W. Premerlani, F. Eddy, W. Lorensen. Object-Oriented Modeling and Design, Prentice-Hall International, Inc., 1991.

[14] Sun Microsystems Inc. Java Language Overview, Sun Microsystems White Paper, ftp://ftp.javasoft.com/docs/java-overview.ps, 1996.

[15] A.S. Tanenbaum. Distributed Operating Systems, Prentice-Hall, Englewood Cliffs, 1995.

[16] K.S. Trivedi. Probability & Statistics with Reliability, Queuing and Computer Science Applications, Prentice Hall, Englewood Cliffs, New Jersey, 1982.

CJava: Introducing Concurrent Objects in Java

Gianpaolo Cugola and Carlo Ghezzi

`[cugola,ghezzi]@elet.polimi.it`
Dipartimento di Elettronica e Informazione
Politecnico di Milano
P.za Leonardo da Vinci 32
20133 Milano (Italy)

Abstract

Java is rapidly becoming one of the most popular object-oriented languages. It is portable and architecture neutral, it is easy to use, it is designed to support the development of highly reliable and robust applications, it is dynamic. But it is not truly concurrent. Indeed, Java supports a limited form of concurrency through a class `Thread`, provided as part of the Java standard library. Concurrency features, however, do not integrate nicely with the object-oriented paradigm. Java programmers are required to take care of many details to develop concurrent applications. In this paper, we describe the language CJava, an extension of Java featuring concurrent objects. We also discuss how CJava can be mapped into Java.

1 Introduction

Released by Sun at the end of 1994, Java [1, 2] is rapidly becoming one of the most popular object-oriented (OO) languages. Thanks to its innovative approach to translation and execution, it supports the development of platform independent applications that are able to evolve at run-time by linking new modules from several sources (e.g., by downloading them through the net) to fulfill the users' requirements.

Despite all these interesting features, Java has weakness in its support to concurrent programming. Class `Thread`, provided as part of the Java standard library, supports only a limited form of large grain concurrent programming that is not integrated nicely with the object-oriented paradigm. Java programmers are required to take care of many details in the development of concurrent applications. If they need the concurrent execution of segments of code, they have to (1) create new subclasses of class `Thread` explicitly, (2) instantiate these subclasses to create new thread objects, and (3) explicitly program the synchronization constraints needed to avoid conflicts that may result from concurrent accesses to resources.

Conversely, concurrent object-oriented languages (COOLs) [3,4,5] provide fine grain concurrency, transparent to the programmer and better integrated with the object-oriented paradigm. In *COOLs*, each concurrent object receives messages and answers them by executing its methods asynchronously. When a concurrent object receives a message, a new thread of control is automatically started to execute the corresponding method.

This approach matches the standard view of objects as active entities that are capable of receiving both synchronous and asynchronous messages and answer these messages by executing their methods [6].

This paper describes CJava, a concurrent extension to Java featuring concurrent objects. It focuses on the description of the language and its characteristics. A detailed description of the language, with particular attention to the problem of the inheritance anomaly [7], may be found in [8].

The paper is organized as follows: Section 2 describes the features provided by Java to support concurrent programming. This will help the reader appreciate how CJava differs from Java and how an implementation of CJava may be provided by means of a preprocessor that translates CJava into Java. Section 3 describes details of the CJava language. Section 4 describes the current implementation of the language. Finally, Section 5 briefly compares CJava with other COOLs, draws some conclusions, and describes future work.

2 Concurrency support in Java

Java supports concurrency by means of class `Thread`, which provides a rich collection of methods to start a thread, stop a thread, and check a thread's status. To control the access to data shared by different threads, the Java run-time system provides monitor and condition lock primitives (see [9] for a detailed description of concurrency support in Java).

To create a new thread, the Java programmer creates a subclass of class `Thread`, redefining its method `run`. Such a new subclass is then instantiated to create a thread object that may be started by calling its method `start`. After being started, a thread object executes its method `run` in parallel with the thread that called the `start`[1].

Threads communicate among themselves by means of *condition variables*. Condition variables are passive objects defined by a class exporting one or more `synchronized` methods. Methods within a class that are declared `synchronized` run under control of *monitors* to ensure that the object's internal state remains consistent. A monitor associated with a specific condition variable works as a lock on that variable. When a thread holds the monitor for some condition variable other threads are locked out and cannot inspect or modify its contents.

In Java, every class and instantiated object has its own monitor that comes into play if required. To execute a synchronized method on an object O, a thread has to acquire the monitor associated with O. The monitor is automatically released when the synchronized method returns.

Java provides also methods `notify`, `notifyAll` and `wait` that can be invoked from within a synchronized method to coordinate the activities of multiple threads that need to use the same resources. Method `wait` causes the current thread to release the monitor it holds and to wait (possibly forever) until another thread notifies that some condition has changed (by calling methods `notify` or

---

[1] Java provides also a different approach to create new threads without the need of subclassing the class `Thread`, but it also requires the identification of a particular method (the method `run`) which is the only method that runs concurrently after thread creation.

```
class Printer {
  protected boolean onLine=false;
  public void online()
    {onLine=true;}
  public void offline()
    {onLine=false;}
  public void print(Document d) {
    if(online) {
      ... // print the document
    } else return;
  }
}
```

a) the class `Printer`

```
class ConcurrentPrinter {
  protected boolean onLine=false;
  public void online()
    {onLine=true;}
  public void offline()
    {onLine=false;}
  public void print(Document d) {
    PrintThread pt=new PrintThread(this,d);
    pt.start();
  }
  public synchronized void _print(Document d){
    if(online) {
      ... // print the document
    } else return;
  }
}

class PrintThread extends Thread {
  private Document doc;
  private ConcurrentPrinter printer;
  public PrintThread(ConcurrentPrinter p,
                     Document d)
    {printer=p; doc=d;}
  public void run() {printer._print(doc);}
}
```

b) the class `ConcurrentPrinter`

Figure 1: A concurrent printer in Java

`notifyAll`).

An example will give an idea of how a multi-threaded program can be implemented in Java. Suppose we need to develop a concurrent version of class `Printer` described in Figure 1a that starts a new thread each time the method `print` is called, in order to print the document in parallel with the caller. The new thread has to wait the other printing jobs to complete before printing the document to avoid conflicts while accessing the printer driver. Figure 1b shows the Java implementation of such concurrent printer.

The example suggests that programming concurrent applications in Java is not a trivial task. Ad-hoc thread classes (e.g., class `PrintThread`) have to be created, threads have to be explicitly instantiated and started, and the code to guarantee that shared resources are accessed in mutual exclusion has to be added (e.g., the statement `synchronized` in method `_print`). The matters become increasingly complex when more than one method is allowed to run concurrently into the same object. In such cases, synchronization between the different threads has to be carefully programmed by using methods `wait` and `notify` (this feature is not present in our simple example). Conversely, COOLs like CJava make concurrency transparent to the programmer. CJava programmers are not required to take care of the details of concurrency related issues and may concentrate on application programming.

3 The CJava language

CJava is a concurrent extension of Java. It supports both inter and intra objects concurrency. An OO language supports *inter-object concurrency* if it allows different objects to run in parallel; it supports *intra-object concurrency* if each object is allowed to process its incoming messages in parallel. In the former case concurrency is limited to messages sent to different objects; in the latter case it also regards the messages sent to the same object.

CJava extends Java by providing three main constructs: *concurrent classes, method preconditions,* and *futures.*

3.1 Concurrent classes

Concurrent classes are classes whose objects are concurrent, i.e., they are able to answer asynchronously the messages they receive by invoking new threads of execution which run in parallel with the thread of the caller. Conceptually, when a *concurrent object* (that is, an object that belongs to a concurrent class) receives a message, a new thread is started to execute the corresponding method. Thereafter, the caller and the callee run in parallel.

A concurrent class is defined in CJava by prefixing the class definition with the keyword `concurrent`. Concurrent objects may be instantiated from concurrent classes by using the standard Java statement `new`. Messages are sent to concurrent objects by using the standard dot notation (e.g., a message `M()` is sent to a concurrent object `CO` by using the notation `CO.M()`).

As mentioned above, CJava supports both inter and intra object concurrency. As a consequence, after sending a message `M()` to a concurrent object `CO`, the sender may continue executing, possibly sending other messages to other objects or even to the same object, without having to wait for the completion of the currently active instance of `CO.M()`. Since the methods of concurrent classes may be executed concurrently, they are called *concurrent methods.*

Concurrent classes may inherit from other classes by using the standard Java statement `extends`. Like Java, CJava supports single inheritance only. The exact semantics of class inheritance in presence of concurrency will be detailed later, after describing method preconditions. By now, it is enough to say that a concurrent class inherits all of the attributes and methods of its superclass obeying to the standard visibility rules defined in Java. By default, a concurrent class that does not extend any other class is considered to extend the concurrent class `ConcurrentObject` that is part of the CJava run-time system.

To avoid any interference between concurrent (i.e., asynchronous) and synchronous methods within the same class, concurrent classes cannot be subclasses of non-concurrent classes and vice versa.

Concurrent methods are specified as standard Java methods with three modifications:
1.   they may require preconditions (see next subsection);
2.   they cannot be synchronized in the Java sense (i.e., via synchronized methods, and `wait` and `notify` primitives). Synchronization constraints have to be expressed using method preconditions only. If a concurrent method were allowed to be synchronized in the Java sense, the synchronization constraints stated by the method's precondition could conflict with those resulting from the use of the Java synchronization primitives;
3.   they cannot throw exceptions. In fact, the standard behavior of exception handling cannot be naturally integrated with the asynchronous semantics of concurrent method calls. In languages supporting exception handling like Java

and C++, when an exception is thrown the runtime stack in unwound by following the dynamic chain of allocated frames until a unit providing a suitable exception handler is found; or, if none is found, the program is terminated [10]. The implicit assumption is that unit activation is synchronous. This assumption is invalid in COOLs. If a concurrent method could throw an exception it would be unclear if and how the exception should be propagated to the unit that generated the asynchronous call. Thus, for simplicity, at this stage we decided to forbid exception throwing by concurrent methods.

As a final assumption, the local method calls issued by concurrent methods (i.e., calls to the same object) are executed synchronously. No precondition evaluation is performed. This reduces the chance of deadlock and makes the design of concurrent classes simpler and more natural.

3.2 Method preconditions

One of the primary concerns of COOLs is the synchronization of concurrent objects. When an object is in a certain state, it can accept only a subset of the messages corresponding to its exported methods in order to maintain its internal integrity. This is achieved through the object's synchronization constraints.

To implement objects' synchronization constraints, COOLs need ad hoc synchronization primitives. Several approaches have been described in the literature to provide synchronization primitives [5]. Some of them are imperative, others are declarative, and others mix declarations with imperative code. The *synchronization schema* (i.e., the approach taken by a COOL to implement the synchronization constraints via the synchronization primitives it provides) is a fundamental semantic concept that can be used to distinguish among COOLs

CJava's synchronization schema is based on *method preconditions*. Each method of a concurrent class may provide its own precondition, expressed as a boolean expression placed after the keyword `precondition` attached to the method's signature.

When a message M is sent to a concurrent object CO, M is added to CO's *list of pending messages (LPM)*. Then, a new thread is created which evaluates the precondition associated with the method corresponding to the message M. If the precondition is true, the thread removes the message M from CO's LPM, adds the corresponding method to CO's *list of running methods (LRM)*, and executes the method's body. If it is false, the thread waits until the precondition becomes true. The policy chosen to handle resumption of pending messages can be specified by the programmer, as stated below. When the execution of the body ends, the method is removed from LRM.

This implementation scheme (asynchronous invocation of methods with preconditions used to enforce synchronization constraints) is adopted for messages received from other objects only. Local calls are executed synchronously (i.e., using standard procedure calls) and the preconditions of the called methods (if any) are ignored.

The operation that adds a message to the list of pending messages is executed synchronously with message passing. This means that the order of the pending messages in LPM reflects the order of the calls. Additionally, we assume an atomic execution of the procedure that (1) evaluates the precondition of a method whose message is pending, (2) deletes the corresponding message from LPM and (3) adds the method to LRM [8].

In traditional OO languages, if a synchronous invocation `x.op1` is followed by an invocation `y.op2`, the execution of `op1` precedes the execution of `op2`. *This is not guaranteed in CJava if* `x` *and* `y` *are concurrent objects. It is not guaranteed also if methods* `op1` *and* `op2` *are invoked on the same object* `x`. The CJava run-time system does not guarantee that the execution order of called methods reflects the order of the corresponding incoming calls. The CJava programmer is free of specifying the ordering he/she prefers in answering messages. In particular, the programmer can implement synchronization constraints based on the order of received messages by using the CJava predicates `pending`, `pendingBefore` and `running`.

- Predicate `pending("method name")` is used to evaluate if a certain message is pending (i.e., it belongs to LPM). The predicate returns true if a call to the method whose name is "method name" has been issued but the corresponding method body did not start running yet.
- Predicate `pendingBefore("method name")` returns an integer representing the number of messages corresponding to the method whose name is "method name" which precede the message that is being processed in the list of pending messages. As an example, suppose to have the following fragment of CJava code:

```
p.print(doc1);
p.print(doc2);
p.offline();
p.print(doc3);
```

  where p is an object belonging to class `ConcurrentPrinter` described in Figure 2. Suppose that all these messages are saved into p's LPM as they are issued because the corresponding preconditions are found to be false. When the first call to method `print` is issued, let us assume that `pendingBefore("print")` evaluates to 0 (this means that no other pending `print` messages precede the `print` message resulting from the first call in LPM). When the second call is issued, `pendingBefore("print")` evaluates to 1. When the third call is issued, `pendingBefore("print")` evaluates to 2. Similarly, `pendingBefore("offline")` for the third call to `print` evaluates to 1. Suppose now that the second call starts running. The corresponding message is removed from the LPM and therefore `pendingBefore("print")` for the third call evaluates to 1.
- Predicate `running("method name")` returns true or false depending whether the mentioned method belongs to LRM or not[2].

Figure 2 gives an example of how to use method preconditions in CJava. It shows the CJava implementation of concurrent class `ConcurrentPrinter` introduced in Section 2. Methods `online` and `offline` are specified to run in mutual

---

[2] The predicate `running` may be used to implement the synchronization constraints based on conflict sets described in [9].

```
concurrent class ConcurrentPrinter {
  protected boolean onLine=false;
  public void online() {
    precondition !running("online") && !running("offline"){
    onLine=true;
  }
  public void offline()
    precondition !running("offline") && !running("online"){
    onLine=false;
  }
  public void print(Document d)
    precondition onLine && !running("print") && pendingBefore("print")==0 {
    ... // print the document
  }
}
```

Figure 2: A concurrent printer in CJava

exclusion. As in the previous case of Figure 1, method `print` may run in parallel with both `online` and `offline`. Moreover, only a single call to method `print` may be accepted and running at any time. The class definition uses the predicate `pendingBefore` to guarantee that the `print` messages sent to a `ConcurrentPrinter` object are processed in the same order in which they are received. The predicate `running` is used to implement the consistency constraints for class `Printer`. It guarantees that methods `online` and `offline` run in mutual exclusion and that only a single instance of method `print` can be running at any time.

Like C++, Java allows method overloading. The same class may provide two or more methods with the same name if they have different signatures. On the other hand, using the statements `pending` or `running`, the CJava programmer cannot distinguish between two different methods having the same name. This is not an undesired side effect, but rather a deliberate design choice made to enforce a good programming style. Expert programmers know that two methods with the same name should have the same "meaning" (i.e., they should perform the same task). It should not be relevant which of the two methods is running with respect to synchronization constraints. This is why we decided not to allow CJava programmers to distinguish among methods having the same name but different signatures in method preconditions.

As mentioned before, CJava supports single inheritance. A concurrent class `ConcSon` may inherit from another concurrent class `ConcParent`. As a result, `ConcSon` inherits all the methods (both preconditions and bodies) and attributes of `ConcParent` obeying to the standard visibility rules defined in Java.

The methods inherited from `ConcParent` may be redefined in `ConcSon`. One of the main features of CJava is that method preconditions and method bodies may be redefined separately within subclasses. The precondition of a method M of `ConcSon` may refer to the precondition of a method having the same name and defined in superclass `ConcParent` of `ConcSon` by using the statement `super(arg_1,...,arg_n)` where `arg1,...,argn` are values whose type matches the signature of M. The precondition of a method M of `ConcSon` may also refer to the precondition of a method defined in the same class and having the same name but different signature by using the statement `this(arg_1,...,arg_n)`. In

```
concurrent class EnhancedPrinter extends ConcurrentPrinter {
  protected boolean tonerLow=false;
  public void print(Document d, boolean letterQuality)
    precondition this(d) {
    ...
  }
  public changeToner {
    tonerLow=false;
  }
  public void print(Document d)
    precondition super(d) && !tonerLow {
    super.print(d);
  }
}
```

Figure 3: Class EnhancedPrinter in CJava

this way, CJava programmers may reuse the same precondition for a set of methods that differ only in their signature but perform the same task, obeying to the same synchronization constraints. It is also possible to reuse a parent's method body in a subclass by invoking the method as "super.method_name".

The example given in Figure 3 shows how the statements super and this, together with the pseudo-variable super, may be used to allow method bodies and preconditions to be redefined separately. Figure 3 shows the CJava implementation of a class EnhancedPrinter that extends class Printer by adding a method print with two parameters to print a document specifying if letter quality is needed. An enhanced printer is also able to know whether the toner is low or not and provides a method to change the toner. The two methods print (the new one and the one inherited from the superclass Printer) share the same precondition. In particular they may be called only if the constraints of the superclass method print are satisfied and if the toner is not low. In class EnhancedPrinter, method print(Document) was redefined to add the !tonerLow expression to the precondition defined in the superclass and method print(Document,boolean) was added, with the same precondition as the redefined method print(Document). In the example, the body of method print(Document) coincides with the one defined in the superclass (that is, the new body simply calls the superclass' method body).

The example shows how the CJava ability of reusing superclass' method preconditions and bodies separately, enhances the possibility of incrementally building on existing code, thus allowing CJava programmers to develop collections of concurrent classes belonging to the same inheritance hierarchy.

3.3 Futures

Concurrent execution of methods is not confined to procedures (i.e., methods that not return any result back to the caller). The invocation of a function (i.e., a method returning a non void value) is also asynchronous; it delivers a *future*. Futures are analogous to bills of exchange. They are not the results the callers need but they may be used as proxies for those results. Futures' management is completely transparent to the programmer.

Through futures, the caller and the called objects are synchronized using an approach similar to the *wait-by-necessity* approach, first described in [11]. In particular, the caller thread is synchronized with the callee (i.e., it has to wait) only when it attempts to use the result of a method that did not complete yet. As an example, consider the following CJava program fragment:

```
i=cq.top();
System.out.println("I got a value from cq");
System.out.println("The integer I got is: "+i);
```

where i is an integer variable and cq is a reference to an object belonging to a class ConcurrentQueue implementing a concurrent queue of integers that provides a method top to inspect the top of the queue. The first call to println may be executed without the need of waiting for top to complete. Conversely, before executing the second call to println, the caller needs to wait the execution of top to complete (the statement println, in fact, needs to use the result of the call to top). Variable i is what we called a "future".

4 CJava implementation

The current implementation of CJava is based on a preprocessor that translates CJava programs to Java. The preprocessor translates each CJava concurrent method into a set of Java methods which:

- add the message corresponding to the called method to LPM,
- evaluate the method precondition,
- instantiate a new thread to execute the method body,
- perform the operations described in the method body.

Different strategies can be followed to perform the translation. In particular, one needs to decide who is responsible for evaluating method preconditions and who is responsible for instantiating the threads that execute the called methods. The main alternatives are:

1. The caller evaluates the preconditions of the called method, waits for the precondition to become true and then instantiates a new thread to execute the called method's body. This means that the caller and the callee synchronize at call time. This approach is similar to the one adopted by Ada's rendezvous [10].

2. The caller instantiates a new thread that is responsible for waiting for the precondition to become true and executing the called method body when its precondition becomes true.

3. The caller simply appends the message corresponding to the called method to the object's LPM. A separate thread (which is part of the run-time system) evaluates method preconditions and instantiates new threads to execute the method bodies of the called methods whose preconditions are true.

4. As before, the caller simply appends the message corresponding to the called method to the LPM. A separate thread (which is part of the run-time system) instantiates a new thread for each received message. These new threads have the responsibility of waiting for method preconditions to become true and executing method bodies when their precondition becomes true.

If one of the last two strategies is chosen, one must decide if the separate thread that is described as part of the run-time system exists in a single instance system-wide, or there exist one instance for each concurrent object.

Alternative 1, which was adopted by B. Meyer in his description of the concurrent extension to Eiffel [12], was rejected because it reduces the level of concurrency. Moreover, from a theoretical point of view, it should not be the caller's responsibility to wait for preconditions to become true. Conversely, the alternative 2 increases the overall system concurrency. This is why it was adopted in the first version of our preprocessor.

The preliminary experimental evaluation of our preprocessor has shown that thread creation in Java is a time consuming operation. The caller spends time to instantiate the new threads that evaluate preconditions and execute bodies. To minimize the "message passing" time (i.e., the time spent by the caller to simply execute the call, independently from the time needed to accomplish the call) we abandoned alternative 2 in favor of alternatives 3 and 4. Alternative 4 was finally selected in order to increase the level of concurrency, as we discussed above.

We decided also to have one thread for each concurrent object that periodically examines the received messages queue and instantiates a new thread for each message. This new thread, as mentioned before, has the responsibility of waiting for the method precondition to become true and of executing the method body.

5 Conclusions and future work

The paper describes the design and implementation of the language CJava, a concurrent extension to Java. CJava overcomes the Java limitations in supporting fine-grained concurrent programming by featuring concurrent classes. It provides a declarative approach based on method preconditions to describe the synchronization constraints that concurrent objects have to fulfill in order to avoid the occurrence of race conditions and to keep their internal state consistent even in the presence of parallel executing methods.

Two main features distinguish CJava from other COOLs: its ability of concurrently answering messages having the same object as target and its ability of separately reusing the methods' implementation code and the synchronization code that each class inherits from its superclass.

Most of existing COOLs allow concurrency among different objects only (inter-objects concurrency). Examples of such languages are CEIFFEL [13], POOL-I [14,15], Eiffel// [16], μC++ [17], ConcurrentSmalltalk-90 [18], Hybrid [19], and ABCL [20]. Conversely, CJava exploits concurrency even within a single object (intra-object concurrency). Each CJava concurrent object may answer to several messages in parallel. This greatly increases parallelism in CJava applications.

The ability of separately reusing a method's implementation and the synchronization code inherited by subclasses is fundamental to allow extensive code reuse [8]. Most of the existing COOLs force synchronization code to be inherited together with method implementations. This reduces the ability of reusing code because, in most cases, the synchronization code needs to be rewritten in subclasses even if the method bodies would not [7].

The current implementation of CJava is based on a preprocessor that translates CJava programs in Java, together with a small number of classes that implement the CJava run-time system. Some of these classes are based on native implementations (i.e., they include native code). As a consequence, the current implementation of the CJava run-time system is not platform independent. Future work will take benefit of the new Reflection API provided with the version 1.1 of the Java environment to obtain a pure Java version of the CJava run-time system, thus providing full platform independence for CJava programs.

References

1.   J. Gosling, B. Joy, and G. Steele, The Java Language Specification. Addison-Wesley Inc., 1996.
2.   P. Niemeyer and J. Peck, Exploring Java. M. Loukides and P. Ferguson editors, O'Reilly & Associates Inc., 1996.
3.   Object-Oriented Concurrent Programming. A. Yonezawa and M. Tokoro editors. MIT Press, 1987.
4.   Research Directions in Concurrent Object-Oriented Programming. G. Agha, P. Wegner and A. Yonezawa editors. MIT Press, 1993.
5.   G. Agha, Concurrent Object-Oriented Programming. Communications of the ACM, Vol. 33, No. 9, September 1990.
6.   G. Booch, Object-Oriented Analysis and Design with Applications, Second Edition, Benjamin/Cummings, 1993.
7.   S. Matsuoka and A. Yonezawa, Analysis of inheritance anomaly in object-oriented concurrent programming languages. Research directions in Concurrent Object-Oriented Programming, G. Agha, A. Yonezawa, and P. Wegner editors, the MIT Press, 1993.
8.   G. Cugola. CJava: a Proposal to Circumvent the Inheritance Anomaly in True Concurrent Object-Oriented Languages. Internal report n. 97.42, Politecnico di Milano, Dipartimento di Elettronica e Informazione, June 1997.
9.   D. Lea, Concurrent Programming in Java: Design Principles and Patterns.Addison-Wesley, 1997
10.   C. Ghezzi and M. Jazayeri, Programming Language Concepts, 3rd Edition, J. Wiley & Sons, 1997.
11.   D. Caromel, Service, asynchrony and wait-by-necessity. Journal of OO programming, Vol. 2, No. 4, November 1989.
12.   B. Meyer, Systematic concurrent object-oriented programming. Communications of the ACM, Vol. 36, No. 9, September 1993, pp. 56-80.
13.   K.P. Löhr, Concurrency Annotations for Reusable Software. Communications of the ACM, Vol. 36, No. 9, September 1993, pp. 81-89
14.   P. America, Inheritance and Subtyping in a Parallel Object-Oriented Language. Proceedings of the ECOOP '87 conference, Paris, Springer LNCS 276 (1997), pp. 234-242
15.   P. America, A Parallel Object-Oriented Language with Inheritance and Subtyping. Proceedings of the ECOOP/OPSLA '90 conference. SIGPLAN Notices, Vol. 25, No. 10, October 1990, pp. 161-168
16.   D. Caromel, Toward a Method of Object-Oriented Concurrent Programming. Communications of the ACM, Vol. 36, No. 9, September 1993, pp. 90-102
17.   P. A. Buhr, G. Ditchfield, R. A. Stroobosscher, B. M. Younger, and C. R. Zarnke, μC++: Concurrency in the Object-Oriented Language C++. Software Practice and Experience, Vol. 20, No. 2, February 1992.
18.   H. Okamura and M. Tokoro, ConcurrentSmalltalk-90. Proceedings of TOOLS Pacific'90, Dec. 1990.
19.   O. M. Nierstrasz, Active Objects in Hybrid. Proceedings of the OOPSLA'87 conference. SIGPLAN Notices, Vol. 22, No. 12, December 1987, pp. 243-253
20.   A. Yonezawa, ABCL: an Object-Oriented Concurrent System. MIT Press., 1990.

If you have any concerns about our products,
you can contact us on
ProductSafety@springernature.com

In case Publisher is established outside the EU,
the EU authorized representative is:
Springer Nature Customer Service Center GmbH
Europaplatz 3, 69115 Heidelberg, Germany

Printed by Libri Plureos GmbH
in Hamburg, Germany